DATE DUE

GAYLORD   #3523PI   Printed in USA

About Island Press

Island Press is the only nonprofit organization in the United States whose principal purpose is the publication of books on environmental issues and natural resource management. We provide solutions-oriented information to professionals, public officials, business and community leaders, and concerned citizens who are shaping responses to environmental problems.

In 1998, Island Press celebrates its fourteenth anniversary as the leading provider of timely and practical books that take a multidisciplinary approach to critical environmental concerns. Our growing list of titles reflects our commitment to bringing the best of an expanding body of literature to the environmental community throughout North America and the world.

Support for Island Press is provided by The Jenifer Altman Foundation, The Bullitt Foundation, The Mary Flagler Cary Charitable Trust, The Nathan Cummings Foundation, The Geraldine R. Dodge Foundation, The Ford Foundation, The Vira I. Heinz Endowment, The W. Alton Jones Foundation, The John D. and Catherine T. MacArthur Foundation, The Andrew W. Mellon Foundation, The Charles Stewart Mott Foundation, The Curtis and Edith Munson Foundation, The National Fish and Wildlife Foundation, The National Science Foundation, The New-Land Foundation, The David and Lucile Packard Foundation, The Surdna Foundation, The Winslow Foundation, The Pew Charitable Trusts, and individual donors.

Restoring Streams in Cities

This book is dedicated to Luna B. Leopold and David Lyon, who got me started on Buffalo Creek.

Restoring Streams in Cities

A Guide for Planners, Policy Makers, and Citizens

Ann L. Riley

Island Press

Washington, D.C. • Covelo, California

Book cover: Baxter Creek was restored from an underground culvert below a grassed median in the middle of Poincett Street in El Cerrito, California. The top photo shows conditions before the project. The middle photo shows the creek restoration immediately after completion. The bottom photo shows the creek one year later. Sponsors of the project included the city of El Cerrito, the Urban Creeks Council of California, and the California Department of Water Resources. The creek channel restoration was designed and implemented by the Waterways Restoration Institute, Berkeley, California.

Copyright © 1998 Ann L. Riley

ISLAND PRESS is a trademark of The Center for Resource Economics.
Illustrations by Ann L. Riley, Stefen, and Dennis O'Connor
All photographs are by the author unless otherwise noted.

The author gratefully acknowledges permission to reprint the following illustrations: Figure 4.5 from "The Importance of Fluvial Geomorphology in Hydraulic Engineering," by E. W. Lane, in *Proceedings of ASCE,* July 1955, with permission of the American Society of Civil Engineers. Figure 4.9 from "River Channel Change with Time, An Example," by Luna B. Leopold, in *The Bulletin of the Geological Society of America,* vol. 48, with permission of the Geological Society of America, Boulder, Colorado. Copyright © 1973. Figures 4.14 and 4.15 from *Fluvial Processes in Geomorphology,* by Luna B. Leopold, M. Gordon Wolman, and John P. Miller. Copyright © 1964 by W. H. Freeman and Company. Figures 4.12 and 4.13 from *Water in Environmental Planning,* by Thomas Dunne and Luna B. Leopold. Copyright © 1978 by W. H. Freeman and Company. Figure 4.16 from "A Classification of Natural Rivers," by David L. Rosgen, in *Catena,* vol. 22 (1994). Used with kind permission of Elsevier Science, The Netherlands.

Library of Congress Catalog-in-Publication Data
Riley, Ann L. (Ann Lawrence), 1950–
     Restoring streams in cities: a guide for planners, policymakers,
  and citizens / Ann L. Riley; illustrations by A.L. Riley, Stefen,
  and Dennis O'Connor.
        p.   cm.
     Includes bibliographical references and index.
     ISBN 1-55963-043-4 (cloth). —ISBN 1-55963-042-6 (paper)
       1. Stream conservation—Planning.   2. Stream conservation—
  Government policy.   3. Stream conservation—Citizen partcipation.
  I. Title.
  QH75.R535   1998   97-42715
  333.91'6216—dc21   CIP

Printed on recycled, acid-free paper ∞ ♻
Manufactured in the United States of America
10 9 8 7 6 5 4 3 2

Contents

List of Figures and Tables

Acknowledgments

The research, writing, and preparation of this manuscript were made possible by the Urban Creeks Council of California.

Sponsors
The David and Lucille Packard Foundation
The Dean Witter Foundation
The Compton Foundation
Natural Resources Conservation Service
U.S. Bureau of Reclamation
U.S. Environmental Protection Agency
San Francisco Estuary Project
U.S. National Park Service
California Department of Water Resources
Association of State Wetland Managers
Association of State Floodplain Managers

The diversity of interest groups involved in urban stream restoration is reflected in the broad array of contributors that made this book possible, as listed above. Individuals to whom I'm particularly indebted for supporting this book include Pearlie S. Reed, assistant chief of the Natural Resources Conservation Service, and Dan Beard, past commissioner of the U.S. Bureau of Reclamation.

The many people who contributed to the content of this book include a multitude of dedicated citizens working in the area of urban stream restoration who are too numerous to list. I am particularly indebted to the following people, who contributed content and reviewed the manuscript: Peter Goodwin of Philip Williams Associates; Dave Dawdy, consulting hydrologist; Luna Leopold, professor emeritus of geology and landscape architecture at the University of California at Berkeley; Gilbert White of the Natural Hazards Research and Applications Information Center; Jon Kusler of the Association of State Wetland Managers; Tom Munsey of the U.S. Army Corps of Engineers; Doug Shields, Jr., of the U.S. Department of Agriculture, Mid-South Area National Sedimentation Laboratory; and Don Roseboom of the Illinois Water Survey. Dennis O'Connor and Stefen transformed my indecipherable scribbles into coherent graphics, and Nancy Northern must take full credit for manuscript preparation. Zack Stewart provided an important writing retreat at

Canesa Park, North Beach, San Francisco, as did Diana Jacobs and Rick Elefant at
the Mattole River. Frank Free of the San Francisco Bay Writer's Union provided
valuable support. The content of this book and foundation of my urban stream
restoration practice must be credited to the work of Luna Leopold, Phil Williams,
Dave Rosgen, Robbin Sotir, and Don Roseboom—all of whom are pioneering practitioners of river restoration.

About the Urban Creeks Council of California

The Urban Creeks Council of California is a statewide organization in California
composed of five regional chapters and approximately forty local affiliate organizations. It was formed to encourage the preservation, protection, restoration, and
management of natural streams in urban (or human-made) environments.

The council's goal is to educate the general public on the aesthetic, recreational,
and ecological values of natural streams located near our homes and places of employment and in commercial and industrial sections of towns and cities.

The Urban Creeks Council holds meetings, develops educational materials, and
hosts workshops and field outings to increase public and engineering and planning
professionals' awareness of the values of natural streams.

The council encourages alternative flood-control project design, streambank stabilization methods, and land-use planning measures to decrease potential property
damage from streams. Urban Creeks Council members help organize clubs, citizen
groups, and neighborhoods who wish to carry out stream cleanups and restoration
projects. Of all its activities, its greatest emphasis is on the successful accomplishment of physical stream restoration projects, which serve as models to perpetuate
the practice of restoration.

About the Coalition to Restore Urban Waters

The Coalition to Restore Urban Waters is a national network of diverse grassroots
groups that protect and restore urban watersheds, waterways, and wetlands. The
coalition includes all peoples and groups, including ethnically diverse and disenfranchised interests, local and state conservation corps and service corps, educational institutions, nonprofit creeks councils, conservation groups, and citizens
committed to restoration of urban waters.

The coalition works with local communities to address the unique values, opportunities, and issues of urban waterways. Urban waterways are an important link between the environment, the economy, recreation, and neighborhood identity in the
community. While the coalition focuses on urban ecosystems, it recognizes the connection among urban environments and rural, suburban, and wildlands watersheds.

This coalition was established to provide its partners with networking and information sharing; technical assistance and successful restoration models; promotion

of economic opportunities through restoration of urban waters; assistance with funding opportunities; a forum for collaboration among traditionally defined environmental groups and low-income, unemployed, or otherwise disenfranchised urban populations; opportunities for environmental education, curricula, community awareness, and environmental stewardship; a forum for partnerships among grassroots groups and national environmental groups, fisheries groups, government agencies, peace corps, service and conservation corps, business interests, tribal organizations, and minority organizations.

The views expressed in this book may not necessarily be those of the agencies and organizations that are listed here.

Introduction

The Complicated Business Called Stream Restoration

Last fall Sam Miller organized a few buddies from his Rotary Club, collected some neighbors and his daughter (and a few of her Girl Scout friends) to clean the junk out of Hang Man's Creek in nearby Civic Park. Miller hadn't felt so good about something he'd done in a long time. The mayor even shook his hand at church the next Sunday. The group of Civic Park volunteers then decided that it would be a fine thing—even their civic duty—to plant some trees along Hang Man's Creek.

The tree-planting project was a grand affair, with donations of plants and planting stakes by local businesses, and the city councilman showed up to help. When fall came around again, Miller got a phone call from a Rotary Club friend. The trees and the nice shrubs along Hang Man's Creek had been dutifully mowed down by county maintenance crews who were carefully carrying out their routine four-year stream channel maintenance. The Civic Park volunteers were enraged, the mayor was mad, the county public works director got mad at the mayor, and the county commissioner didn't know what to do. There was a juicy piece in the local newspaper about the whole spat, and then various state agencies took different sides on the issue of what should be done about Hang Man's Creek. A multi-agency, multilevel task force was eventually formed to try to work out the conflicting views of how to manage Hang Man's Creek.

This story is as common as shopping carts in a creek. How could something so simple as fixing up your local creek become so complicated? This book is written for the Sam Millers, the neighbors, the mayors, the county commissioners, the flood-control engineers, and all the other people who are caught in these very common conflicts.

The engineering traditions of culverting, channelizing (straightening), riprapping (rocking), and clearing vegetation from streams and rivers ran into vocal protests in the 1960s, precipitating a congressional investigation and the issuance of reports. The old conflicts are still with us in the 1990s. The engineering solutions for controlling flood damage and erosion used since the late 1930s to accommodate new development for our growing population continue to be in direct conflict with our needs for environmental education and all the other values we assign the natural environment. What is different in the 1990s is that the protestors are better organized and better placed to change the engineering traditions. Also, what is significantly different is the presence of many engineers and managers who want to see the old practices for stream management changed and who want to experiment with new management assumptions, better hydraulic models for designing projects, and more efficient and environmentally sensitive stream "maintenance" strategies. This book aims to inform the lay person about the use of restoration methods for repairing ecological damage created by conventional engineering works. One of the book's most important goals, however, is to expand our collective thinking about restoration methods, to include them as alternatives to the use of traditional engineering practices in the first place.

To accomplish anything these days, you almost have to be an expert in six different fields at once. Stream management and restoration are particularly this way. A civil engineer needs to know more than just the latest Army Corps of Engineers Hydrologic Engineering Center hydraulic models to design a flood-control project. A civil engineer must also know hydrology, geomorphology, environmental regulations, citizen participation methods, and even ecology. The citizens and public officials trying to figure out how to restore their community stream as an aesthetic amenity, bring the fish back, and address flooding problems need to know something about the traditions and practices of federal, state, and local water agencies, where funds come from for stream projects, what the engineering options are, and how successful stream restoration projects have been planned. For this reason, this book cannot do its job without exposing the reader to some history, hydrology, hydraulics, government agencies and programs, citizen participation methods, and examples of stream restoration techniques. All of these components determine the outcome of a stream restoration project. Only a divine entity could claim to be an expert in all these areas, so it is necessary for all of us to put together teams with people who have aptitudes or experience in the different areas. It is actually a more rewarding experience to do things that way.

Urban stream restoration is an unusually visible and popular component of the restoration movement because the idea of integrating nature back into cities captures people's imaginations. Citizen movements are developing in all parts of the country to try to prevent the loss of remaining urban streams; to respond to development pressures and flood-control projects; to bring back fish and aquatic life in urban streams; to feature rivers and streams as important aesthetic contributions to the economic life of commercial city centers; to use streams as "outdoor classrooms" for school projects; and even to recover streams buried in culverts. Riparian, or streamside, woodland areas and adjacent wetlands are now recognized to be some of the most important wildlife habitat and sanctuaries in the country. An important objective for stream restoration and protection is simply to keep from losing a basic component of our national heritage—the diversity of our natural resources—and a sense of geographic place.

While this book discusses all these important objectives of stream restoration, it has an overriding theme, which is the use of restoration as an alternative to traditional, environmentally destructive, and expensive public works projects. Restoration is widely thought of as a means of attempting to bring back the environmental values of an ecosystem after the damage has been done. Instead, we should regard restoration as a way to avoid those damages to begin with. Restoration methods can be a means of modifying the environment to meet engineering objectives in an ecologically sensitive way in contrast to the conventional environmental mitigation project, which attempts to compensate for or disguise the ecological damages of a conventional public works project.

Most people who hear the words "stream restoration" assume they refer to cleaning up water pollution. While the water quality of urban streams is important, in many situations we are first faced with the need to bring back the "physical" attributes of a stream that is underground in a pipe, encased in concrete, or devoid of meanders and vegetation. This book is most concerned with the restoration of the creek's shape, its banks, meanders, pools, riffles, and streamside vegetation. Once these attributes of streams are returned, the improved quality of the water follows.

Stream-channel restoration projects combined with some watershed management activities (such as fencing, erosion control, and tree-planting projects) and land-use planning and regulations can turn a stream from a public nuisance to a public amenity. Stream restoration methods can anticipate and respond to the problems of flood and erosion damage caused by urbanization and provide design concepts to be used in lieu of the most common destroyers of the urban stream environment: rock or concrete rubble (riprap) bank stabilization projects, channelization or stream straightening and vegetation removal projects, and culverting or piping of streams underground. In densely built-up cities, for example, badly damaged streams can be repaired and redeemed as aesthetic resources with some ecological integrity.

This book describes more options for the treatment of the urban stream than are usually considered by conventional engineering projects. Both the general public and the professional engineer can benefit by being aware of these options. The variety of approaches described can help even seasoned professionals be more competitive in the changing marketplace of public attitudes, environmental regulations, and increasingly scarce government dollars. The Natural Resources Conservation Service, the Tennessee Valley Authority, and increasing numbers of state agencies and local water conservation and flood-control districts now have policy directives to avoid channelization and design environmentally sensitive stream management projects and plans.

Citizens interested in stream restoration should be aware that it is citizens who are responsible for the government taking on restoration as a new mission. In the 1980s, a grassroots movement was responsible for starting interesting state-level stream restoration programs in Florida, Illinois, Missouri, Wisconsin, Washington, Oregon, and California, among others. Innovative local restoration projects are now being carried out in every region of the country and have attracted the attention and response of the federal government. Administrators in the Army Corps of Engineers, the U.S. Bureau of Reclamation, and the Natural Resources Conservation Service are revamping the missions of their agencies to put a greater emphasis on environmental quality and restoration.

Because public awareness and activism are largely responsible for the development of the urban stream restoration phenomenon, this book is designed to provide citizens with the broad background that will make them a powerful influence in determining what happens to the streams they are interested in.

What Will Be Discussed

The principal threat to the integration of the stream into urban environments is inappropriate development, which creates the problem of property damages from flooding and erosion. A report written for the Council on Environmental Quality in 1972 estimated that approximately 235,000 miles of streams and rivers had already been channelized or were slated at that time to be channelized in the United States to respond to property damage from floods. (That is enough channel to circle the globe almost ten times.) That 1972 report was the last time government officials formally made an attempt to quantify the miles of channelization projects being constructed or planned. "Channelization," or stream straightening, and stream-lining, using rock or concrete, have been the standard methods used in the attempt to control streams in urban environments. "Controlling" streams through the use of such expensive public works projects has been a notoriously expensive undertaking with frustrating results. (See figure I-1.)

Geographers, hydrologists, and hydraulics experts have noted that such projects have encouraged unsafe development in flood-hazard and stream-erosion zones and that there have been unanticipated performance problems with the traditional engineering techniques. The stream restoration measures described here would replace the losing proposition of trying to control streams with an interdisciplinary approach of managing the stream as a feature in the urban environment. This book will provide a logical sequence of land-use planning, site design, watershed restoration measures, stream-channel modifications, and flood proofing of structures that should be used in lieu of stream channelization projects. Examples of effective and environmentally sensitive bank stabilization and flood-damage-reduction projects are described to replace the now dated conventional practices.

Any book on urban stream restoration must first address the basic conflicts between the urban dweller and the potential erosion and flood risks to structures, roads, utilities, and drainage systems. A community can choose the option of consigning an urban stream to an open or closed storm sewer, or it can decide to manage the stream as a community amenity. It is possible to address urban public works needs without sacrificing the option to develop a stream as a recreational resource with trails, paths, and an urban sport fishery. A stream can be used as a dynamic economic feature to draw shoppers and tourists to a business district. Some communities use their streams as educational laboratories in classrooms from kindergartens to university graduate schools. This book will describe the planning processes used by communities to develop stream restoration projects as well as what those projects look like.

FIGURE I.1. EXAMPLES OF CONVENTIONAL ENGINEERING OF STREAMS.
(a) Channelization and bank stabilization using concrete mattresses and sacks and metal sheet piling, Boneyard Creek, flowing through the engineering school at the University of Illinois, Urbana. (b) Channelization and riprap, Galindo Creek, Concord, California. (c) Channelization, and chain-link fence, concrete lining, Los Angeles River, California. (d) Riprap bank stabilization, San Joaquin River, Fresno, California. (e) Culvert and downstream bank stabilization, Sausal Creek, Oakland, California.

Whether you are a citizen or a public official tackling an urban stream restoration project, you are first going to have to build community support for restoring a stream, acquiring a greenbelt or trails along it, or designing nontraditional or innovative solutions to erosion and flooding. The next need you are going to have is to sort out what professional help you will need to carry out your community goals. You'll want to know what professionals such as planners, hydraulic engineers, fluvial geomorphologists, and biologists generally do or don't do. In many cases, you will need to know about the National Flood Insurance Program. If a federal flood-control project is being planned for your area, the complexity of your planning, project design, and funding will be increased, and you are going to need to ask the right questions of the public officials and agencies involved. The first chapters (1–5) of this book give you the background you need to make intelligent choices, ask the necessary questions, and hire the right kind of help.

A chapter on history follows the information on the above basics because too much of what we do occurs in a historical vacuum. It is useful to know that we are not involved in a new field experimenting with untried ideas and technology, but that we are carrying on an American tradition when we restore streams. Some historical background also goes a long way in helping to understand some of the government agencies many of you will necessarily be working with.

Recent developments influencing stream restoration include a waning in federal water-project budgets, a greater emphasis on state and local involvement in streams and rivers, the necessity to be creative in fund-raising, and a significant escalation in public initiatives including locally placed watershed councils and citizen-sponsored restoration projects. Some agencies have adapted to new ways of thinking about streams better than others, but most traditional water engineering agencies are, at minimum, aware of the public pressure to change to more environmentally sensitive practices. Use chapters 2 and 7 to help identify the federal programs, technical assistance, and funding opportunities that will help your project. However, because technical assistance and funding opportunities may be more available at the state level at this time in history, and it is too difficult to cover all the state resources in this book, you should turn to a conservation organization in your state for guidance on state, regional, and local programs that may be useful.

While this book intends to describe the urban stream restoration movement, it also intends to get you involved—and hopes to get your hands dirty. Chapters 8 and 9 tell you how to do this, whether it is collecting watershed and stream-channel data, installing revegetation projects, or protecting buildings from overbank stream flows.

Finally, new coalitions are forming among unlikely bedfellows, including state and local conservation corps, inner-city neighborhoods, sport and commercial fishermen, rural and urban economically depressed areas, business organizations, and traditional conservation and environmental organizations to press for national support of stream restoration programs. When you pick up this book, the bandwagon may be rolling through your town. Jump on it—or create your own.

CHAPTER ONE

The Basics

Basics on Streams

Streams are a resource generally taken for granted or completely ignored, but we all live in a watershed. To begin learning about your local streams, become familiar with the watershed they run through and the history that comes with them.

What Is a Creek?

It has been very much a surprise to me that the most common question phoned into my office has been "What is the difference between a creek and a stream?"—or "How do I tell the difference between a stream, a brook, and a river?" No one has quantified the differences between brooks, creeks, gulches, washes, and rivers, and these mostly loosely defined terms represent cultural and regional customs more than they define or "standardize" a geographic feature.

Look at a U.S. Geological Survey map of your area and pick out the names of the drainages. If you are living in the northeastern part of the United States, you can see a number of "brooks" on your topographic map. In the Adirondacks, I hiked along Johns Brook, Wolf Jaws Brook, Calamity Brook, Black Brook, and Deer Brook. In the Boston vicinity (eastern Massachusetts and New Hampshire), you may live near Lubbur Brook, Meadow Brook, Bachelder Brook, Bull Brook, Muddy Run, or Frost Fish Brook. In Virginia in the suburbs of Washington, D.C., you may walk along South Run, or you may live along Stony Run, Roland Run, or Whitemash Run in the suburbs of Baltimore. In Washington, D.C., along the Potomac River, you can walk along Rock Creek or the Chesapeake and Ohio Canal. A map of the Carolinas shows widespread use of the word "creek." You may live along Buffalo Creek in Greensboro, Bolin Creek in Chapel Hill, Jefferson Creek or Crabtree Creek in Raleigh. Creek also appears to be the preferred nomenclature for waterways in Iowa and Wisconsin. In Duluth, you may live along Dutchman or Bluff creek. North and South Dakotas' maps also show a preponderous use of creeks for the waterways.

A Wyoming map shows common usage of creek but also shows the use of the term "fork," as in Hams Fork, Blacks Fork, and Henry's Fork, tributaries to the Green River. Different branches of the same creek are also sometimes called fork, such as the North and South forks of Owl Creek near Thermopolis. Draws and gulches appear on topographic maps near Pinedale, Wyoming, with names like Millie Draw,

Clarke Draw, Nutting Draw, and Horse Draw and Coyote Gulch, tributaries to the Hoback River. North Hay Gulch, Big Draw, and Brodie Draw are tributaries to the Green River. Deadman Wash, Table Wash, Alkali Wash, and Pine Creek Wash flow near Rock Springs, Wyoming. In New Mexico near Roswell, Rio Penasco, Rio Bonito, and Rio Hondo flow into the Pecos River. Arroyos and washes abound in Arizona and New Mexico, including the well-known Indian Bend Wash flowing through the middle of Scottsdale, Arizona. Dreamy Draw Wash flows through Paradise Valley.

What someone in Wyoming calls a draw, or in New Hampshire a creek, someone in Florida, Alabama, or Louisiana may call a rigolet or bayou. Bayous are also known as backwaters off main channels of rivers or streams. Alaska maps show similar backwaters as arms. "Slough" is another synonym for creek, such as Dead Horse Slough, a tributary to Big Chico Creek in Chico, California, and Mercer Slough, which is located in Bellevue, Washington, as a creek and backwater of Lake Washington.

Creek is a generic term for a small stream and originated in New England, where it retains its original meaning as a tidal inlet. In the rest of the country, creek has evolved to mean a flowing stream smaller than a river.[1] When a creek or a stream becomes a river is anyone's call. We can probably find some relative correlation between greater flows and drainages named rivers, but there are also creeks on topographic maps that contain greater flows than so-called rivers.

Brook, another word for creek or stream, also has its origins in English culture and dominates New England. *Arroyo* is Spanish for "brook," but in the southwest landscape, where we find the use of this word, we see it being used to describe not constantly flowing perennial drainages, but channels that are often dry and have occasional, seasonal, or intermittent flows. *Gulch, gully, ravine,* and *draw,* terms used commonly in the western United States, seem to be relatively interchangeable. *Rigolet,* derived from the French *rigole,* or "ditch," is used occasionally in areas of American-French influence. *Fork* generally designates a branch or tributary of a stream.[2]

What this definition problem tells us really is that creeks, brooks, streams, rivers, and the rest are important components of our landscape history. There can be much colorful folklore associated with drainages—large and small—and the researcher of a local history can start with the names of drainages to learn about an area. An example of a folk name associated with creeks is Troublesome Creek, a name given by the general population in an area because of historical local events. Descriptive names such as Stinking Spring, Roaring Run, Rushing Water Creek; incident names such as Murder Creek, Earthquake Creek, Stray Horse Gulch; and exclamation names such as Helpmejack Creek and Goshhelpme Creek all have stories behind the names. Of course, some local drainages are named for the native people who once lived along them or for the early settlers who displaced the native people.[3]

The question of what a creek or stream is in a geographical or geologic sense must be answered in the context of what a watershed is.

Watersheds and the Hydrologic Cycle

Everyone lives in a watershed. The hydrologic cycle of water falling to the earth in the form of rain, snow, sleet, and hail, then running off the land into creeks, rivers, ponds, lakes, marshes, storm sewers, and human-made channels and ultimately into oceans happens everywhere. Some of the water that falls is caught by tree leaves, some soaks into the ground, some runs off pavement, rooftops, and lawns, and some is collected into small rills on the hillsides that collect more water into gullies and channels as creeks, rivers, and desert arroyos. Some of the water from streams, rivers, ponds, lakes, reservoirs, and oceans evaporates and then falls to the earth again in some form of precipitation.

A watershed is the land area drained by a particular stream or river. We can think of a watershed or water basin on the scale of the Mississippi River, which drains with the help of many tributary rivers and streams about 1,250,000 square miles— or we can work on the scale of a creek that drains a watershed area of 1 square mile that contributes stream flow to a larger downstream drainage. A good way to classify your stream to avoid the inherent ambiguity of the words *creek, stream, river,* and *gulch* is to designate its order. Small streams join to form larger streams in a branching pattern that forms a drainage network.[4] Therefore, larger watersheds are made up of a joining of smaller watersheds. Figure 1.1 illustrates this watershed within a watershed by showing the Fremont Creek watershed as a part of the Clear River watershed. The different channels draining these watersheds can be designated by how many tributaries they have, or by order. A first-order stream channel has no tributaries; when two first-order streams join, they create a second-order stream. When two second-order streams join, they create a third-order stream, and so on. If you designate your stream by its order, therefore, others can immediately get a concept of the size of the drainage area you are concerned with.

The total length of rivers in the United States, including all the minor creeks and draws, has been estimated to be about 3 million miles. There are also estimates of the average lengths of the different order streams and their mean drainage areas based on a national average and mean. The average length for a first-order stream is 1 mile, with a mean drainage area of 1 square mile. The average length of a second-order stream is 2.3 miles, with a mean drainage area of 4.7 square miles, and the average length of a third-order stream is about 5.3 miles in a drainage area of about 23 square miles. The average fourth-order stream is an average of 12 miles long in a mean watershed size of 109 square miles. The largest rivers of the world are ten-order drainages. A river the size of the Allegheny River in the eastern United States represents a seventh-order river, the average length of which is 147 miles and the mean drainage area 11,700 square miles.[5]

In Figure 1.1, Fremont Creek is a third-order stream, and upper Fremont Creek above the hypothetical town of Fremont is a second-order stream. For the purposes of planning, you can draw in the watershed above any point in the drainage system. In the same figure, we have drawn the watershed boundaries that affect the town of

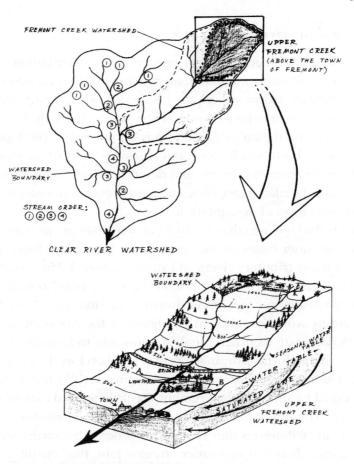

FIGURE 1.1. WATERSHEDS AND STREAM ORDERS.

Fremont for addressing future floodplain-planning problems that will be discussed in chapter 7.

Stream drainages follow the lowest topography and form valleys and become separated from each other by ridges or divides. Streams on one side of a ridge drain the water into one stream system, while the streams on the other side drain a separate valley. Topographic maps use contour lines to designate divides, valleys, and drainage patterns and to connect points of the same elevation. If the lines are evenly spaced and far apart, they represent a gently sloping landscape. Closely spaced and jagged lines indicate a steep and rough landscape. A topographic map gives you a three-dimensional picture of your watershed; the boundaries of the watershed are indicated by the hills and ridges for your drainage. You can measure the drainage area and understand how your stream and its watershed relate to other watersheds. Find out what stream, river, or other body of water your stream flows into. This other body of water may have a great deal of influence on the behavior of your stream.

The water cycle is the other basic concept that helps define the function of your stream. The basic source of most atmospheric water is the ocean, which evaporates and provides the moisture for the precipitation that returns to the earth. The continental United States receives an average of 30 inches of precipitation a year, and evapotranspiration and transpiration from plants return approximately 21 inches to the atmosphere. The balance of 9 inches contributes to the flow of streams and rivers.[6, 7] In the words of Luna Leopold, a well-known river scientist:

> Rivers are both the means and the routes by which the products of continental weathering are carried to the oceans of the world. Except in the most arid areas more water falls as precipitation than is lost by evaporation and transpiration from the land surface to the atmosphere. Thus there is an excess of flow which must flow to the ocean. Rivers then are the routes by which this excess water flows to the ultimate base level. The excess of precipitation over evaporation and transpiration provides the flow of rivers and springs, recharges groundwater storage, and is the supply from which man draws water for his needs.[8]

No matter how big or small your stream is, or what you call it, the same principles govern its behavior. The concepts explained in this book about river dynamics apply to stream orders one through ten. Most of the solutions—or at least the principles behind the solutions—apply to all creeks, streams, rigolets, arroyos, and rivers (although the experience of the author is limited to sixth-order rivers and below). Sometimes this book refers to creeks and sometimes to streams and rivers. Don't be put off by the interchangeable use of these terms. Whether you live by the Missouri River or Old Man's Creek, the content in this book will be helpful to you.

The Value of Streams and Restoration

Streams and rivers are industrial transportation corridors, industrial water supplies, and domestic and agricultural supplies. Their waters produce fish for sportfishing and provide for a recreational industry of white-water rafting, kayaking, and canoeing. They inspire trails, greenbelts, and parks and can enhance the values of commercial areas and downtowns of cities by attracting people to them. They can even be tourist attractions. Riparian (streamside) vegetation along streams has important value for aesthetics, shade, and wildlife habitat.

The industrial, agricultural, and land development values that produce large cash returns from rivers and streams tend to be the values that dominate the uses and management of streams and rivers. There is a modest body of literature developing that assigns monetary values to recreational, aesthetic, wildlife and riparian, and community uses of streams. You may need to rely on some of this literature to help convince political bodies of the importance of the environmental values of streams and rivers and their fisheries.

Resource economists are engaged in describing and quantifying the value of streams using five types of strategies: One is a traditional economic evaluation of natural resources values used by recreation-oriented studies to identify user expenditures associated with a river site. Costs of gear and travel to recreate at the stream are quantified to provide a tangible dollar figure showing how much river users are willing to spend to enjoy the resource. A second method quantifies the changes in real estate and business location values that can be associated with the ability of a waterway to create a higher quality of life for the area in which it is located. A related method quantifies how a stream or river project, such as a flood-control or hydroelectric project, may redistribute the benefits of a river or the costs associated with modifying the river. A fourth innovation in economic analysis quantifies the inherent values that the public places on just knowing the resource is there, for ecological values, regional identity, or other broad concepts.[9] A fifth area of economic evaluation that is in the pioneer stages of being developed is evaluation of the relative benefits of environmental restoration projects that form a part of or substitute for conventional public works, storm-water management, erosion and flood-control projects.[10–12]

A publication available from the National Park Service, *Economic Impacts of Protecting Rivers, Trails and Greenway Corridors,* is an easy-to-understand resource book for computing the economic value of open space, trails, river corridors, and other features of the natural environment to a community's property values and tax base. The report presents quantifiable evidence that these "greenways" increase nearby property values, help support recreation-oriented businesses, attract tourists, attract government expenditures, attract corporation relocations, and reduce local costs for services such as roads, sewers, and flood control. A study in Boulder, Colorado, for example, shows that the aggregate property value for one neighborhood was approximately $5.4 million greater with a greenbelt than without it. The presence of the greenbelt produced about $500,000 additional property tax revenue. The purchase price of the greenbelt was $1.5 million, and the property tax increase alone could recover that cost in just three years.[13]

Another National Park Service study, from 1982, uses economic measures to quantify how the public places value on the intrinsic benefits of fish and wildlife and riparian resources. The methods used to quantify these values include direct inquiry as to the public's willingness to pay for the enhancement of fish and wildlife values and an indirect observation of recreators' activities and expenditures related to the resources. For example, a survey in the city of Sacramento showed that residents assigned a fair value to compensate a landowner for the loss of 1 acre of healthy riparian habitat along the Sacramento River at about $24,000.[14]

A report written for the Department of the Interior by the University of Kentucky specifically addressed the issue of evaluating the aesthetic and recreational potential of small streams located in or near cities. The study focused on two streams near Lexington, Kentucky, which were evaluated for their values for camping, picnicking, trails, aesthetic enjoyment, and scenic and historical resources. Case studies were used to estimate numbers of visits to sites, future demand for greenway use by an urban population plus the proportion of that demand that would be served by each creek site, and the economic benefits that would accrue if the sites were developed as educational preserves or recreational areas. This report was done in the context of a rapidly urbanizing county. While only 40 percent of the population lived in urban areas in 1900, in 1960 the number had grown to 68 percent. It is estimated that nearly 85 percent of the population will be concentrated in urban areas by the year 2000. What this suggests is that the economic values of natural environments in urban areas are going to continually increase because of the increased demand for them.[15]

An interesting, but not surprising, study done in the 1970s indicated that the use and values assigned by the public to urban streams were greater if the water quality was good. Proximity to the stream was directly related to the amount of use and enjoyment the public attributed to the creek. The study was done with surveys of neighborhoods near creeks, and the general level of use of the streams was quite high; 94 percent of the respondents in one sample indicated that they engaged in at least one activity at the stream, and the average number of activities was four. This research also established that property values can be significantly affected by proximity to a park. Properties immediately adjacent to an urban park could assign 40 percent of their value to that location.[16]

A study of particular relevance to this book, published in 1985, compared the tax values of homes located along two streams with nearly identical physical characteristics in the same county in Ohio, except that one stream had been channelized and was subject to regular maintenance dredging, and the other was in its natural form. Equivalent 11.6-kilometer lengths of the streams, with similar human population densities, were compared for the values of the homes. The market values were taken from the 1985 tax rolls and showed that the values of homes on the natural channel were assessed at 331 percent more than the homes adjacent to the channelized stream. The research suggests that restoration of channelized streams is a practical way to increase the community tax base.[17]

Recent research by the Water Resources Institute for the Army Corps of Engineers is developing methods to assess the cost-effectiveness of stream restoration projects and to include the value of environmental features and "outputs" in public works projects.[18,19] Similar research is evaluating the value of urban stream restoration projects funded through a state program in California. One of the findings from this latter study is that urban stream restoration projects seem to provide the added benefit of contributing to long-term community-based organizations and activities that perpetuate urban watershed and community stewardship. The study estimates environmental amenities associated with urban stream restoration projects to be 15 percent of the mean value of residential properties, or in the cases studied approximately $20,000 to $22,000. It estimates the value of the combination of flood and erosion damage reduction at just under $20,000 or 11 percent of the mean value of a residence.[20]

While this book is dedicated to the concepts and methods of restoring streams in cities, it does not mean to imply that there is not equal value in restoring the environmental and social attributes of a broad range of waterways in cities. A unique contribution of the urban waterway movement is the broad range of objectives it brings to the field of environmental restoration. No drainage ditch, culvert, irrigation or barge canal, trapezoidal flood channel, concrete waterway, pond, lake, wetland, or degraded creek goes unvalued. The greatest value of restoration projects, however, may be the restoration of a sense of community pride and participation.

The natural bible for the urban waterway restoration movement is Robert Pyle's *The Thunder Tree: Lessons from an Urban Wildland*, in which he describes the critical part an irrigation canal, the Highline Canal in Colorado, played in his personal development.[21] Notwithstanding the purpose of the canal, to divert the Platte River to promote settlement of the Denver area, the canal provided a lifeline of rich, natural experiences for city-bound youth. Because urban areas are increasingly devoid of any kind of natural environment, much of the country's youth grows up with little sense of geographic place and suffer from a deprivation that Pyle describes as "the extinction of experience." This includes the widespread loss of intimacy with the living world and the state of personal alienation from nature in which many people live. The loss of neighborhood plants, animals, trees, and birds endangers our nation's population from losing the experience of nature. The concepts of ecology and even environmental education become too abstract because they don't relate to the home, the immediate environment, and everyday experiences. Pyle illustrates how this extinction of experience in urban areas has contributed to the loss of the nation's biodiversity.

It is a good idea to remind your allies and your antagonists alike of the emotional role of creeks and streams in their lives. Remind them of the creek in their childhood and the education and joy their children can get from creeks and streams. In a wonderful article that first appeared in *Audubon* magazine, Peter Steinhart reminds us that nearly every one of us has a creek gurgling through our memories:

> Nothing historic ever happens in these recollected creeks. But their persistence in memory suggests that creeks are bigger than they seem, more a part of our hearts and minds than lofty mountains or mighty rivers.
>
> Creektime is measured in strange lives, in sand-flecked caddisworms under the rocks, sudden gossamer clouds of mayflies in the afternoon, a salamander wriggling back to winter water, or minnows darting like slivers of inspiration into the dimness of creek fate. Mysteries float in creeks' riffles, crawl over their pebbled bottoms and slink under the roots of trees. Thoreau declared, "The shallowest water is unfathomed; wherever a boat can float there is more than Atlantic depth and no danger of fancy or imagination running aground."[22]

Identify What Your Stream Needs

Many of us take for granted or just ignore the stream that goes by our backyard or winds through downtown under bridges and through underground culverts. Ironically, what often develops our latent appreciation of streams is some threat to losing them. Local officials may begin removing vegetation and rocking—or riprapping—the stream banks. You may hear of plans to put the stream in large culverts underground or to straighten it to make new land available for development or to reduce flood damages. There may be plans to build a big apartment building up to the edge of the bank, threatening its stability and putting the building and its occupants in a flood-hazard area. The creek may be forgotten and unsightly, used only as a cheap midnight dumping ground, and therefore a perceived neighborhood nuisance.

Perhaps there is no imminent threat to your stream, but it has occurred to you or members of your community that if you were to respond to some of its physical problems and turn it into a community feature with open space, trails, promenades, and pedestrian footbridges, for example, it could put your town on the map for tourists and provide it with a whole new positive character. It may occur to you as a member of the PTA or a local school district board that the stream running by the junior high school has potential as an outdoor science laboratory.

Whatever the initial reasons for your interest, the first thing you will need to do before you begin protecting, enhancing, or restoring your stream is to familiarize yourself with your stream's physical problems, needs, and status in the local political and regulatory scene.

There are five major areas of concern for those whose goal is to have a healthy stream that enhances their neighborhood or town. One of your first concerns should be to save existing healthy streams from the impacts of new urban development by putting land-use regulations in place. A common destroyer of streams is the placement of structures too close to stream banks, creating erosion and flood hazards—an expense that is usually borne by the community taxpayer. If you are in the common situation where you must reconcile conflicts between a stream and existing structures, your second concern will be to use the most environmentally and aesthetically sensitive technology available to protect both the stream and the structures. A third need you may have is negotiating for environmentally sensitive stream-channel maintenance practices by engineering officials. You may also find that in order to restore a stream, you need to remove culverts and concrete linings. Finally, you may need to address water pollution through conventional treatment facilities and restoration methods and address the need for an adequate water supply for life in the stream.

All five of these concerns will require that you interact with professionals from a number of disciplines, all of which have their own language, traditions, and even cultures and values. The chapters that follow will introduce you to the different perspectives and practices of planners, hydrologists, biologists, and hydraulic engineers, all of whom you will no doubt have contact with if you are interested in helping a stream. First, however, you need to identify what problems your stream has or may face in the near future and your objectives in managing or avoiding those problems. Does your stream need protection from land-use changes, or is it already badly impacted by urbanization and you need to control bank erosion? You may need to consider one or more of the following as your management objectives:

Plan and Regulate Stream Corridors

Land-use planning and site design can protect a natural waterway from the classic degradation caused by thoughtless urban development. Land-use planning locates developments away from hazard zones such as floodplains and river meander zones. Plans can designate hazard areas as neighborhood open space, parks, recreational areas, trails, hiking and bicycle paths, and transportation corridors. Site-design standards and regulations provide guidelines for how to design a development once the development is properly located in the community by the land-use plan. Site-design measures can call for protection of stream-corridor buffer zones, minimal impervious surfaces and impacts to native vegetation, and sound storm-water management. Buffer zones of natural streamside vegetation and the use of natural swales and storm-water detention areas instead of sewer pipes greatly reduce the impacts of development on streams by reducing creek storm flows and runoff pollution. Setback requirements that site structures away from creeks lower the risk of future property damages from overbank flows and changing stream meanders. Adequate land-use planning and site-design measures create cost savings for a community by avoiding problems to begin with. A second cousin to basic land-use planning is trail planning. It is easy to integrate recreational assets such as trails for walkers, joggers, and hikers along streams if an undeveloped zone follows along the stream. Planning to add a trail later without an existing undeveloped public right-of-way is much more difficult but is being done as part of the greenways movement to make urban and suburban centers more liveable.

Use Environmentally Sensitive Flood, Erosion, and Channel-Instability Solutions

Many areas do not have adequate setback requirements. If you inherit a situation where structures are in a flood-hazard area or are vulnerable to damage from meandering and eroding stream banks, you will want to seek out the most environmentally sensitive technology available to protect both the stream and the structures. Often, restoration alternatives can substitute for conventional engineering practices to reduce flood and erosion damages.

Streams in urban settings are typically out of balance so that there is excessive erosion or excessive deposition. Excessive erosion can be caused by increased runoff from paved surfaces, such as roads, driveways, and parking lots. Excessive deposition is frequently caused by upstream construction, grazing, or logging. Streams typically undergo two main cycles of adjustments to urbanization. They first tend to fill with sediment from construction sites. The channels later become enlarged in order to carry the increased runoff from the paved surfaces of the built-up city. River and lake waterfronts often have erosion problems because the natural vegetation once prolific along those waterways has been removed. The most appropriate remedy for most of these problems is to revegetate the waterway. Sometimes reshaping the waterway is also required.

If downtown business districts or residential areas are already developed in floodplains, sometimes the most practical—and underused—solution is to protect the buildings so the floodwaters do not come inside when the river crests. There are simple and inexpensive "flood-proofing" projects that can spare the damage and heartache caused by floodwaters. Temporary dams can be inserted in doorways and over windows before the streams crest into town. Small, aesthetically pleasing rock walls or landscaped berms can be added to developments to help avoid floodwater damage to housing developments or business districts. Structures can also be elevated onto higher foundations.

Use Environmentally Sensitive Maintenance Strategies

If you have a channelized stream that has been straightened and has had its natural tree and shrub species removed to increase space in the channel for flood flows, you will want to search for ways to return some of its environmental and aesthetic values. If your stream is now categorized by officials as a flood-control channel, you will have to work within the context of federal and local channel maintenance standards, which are generally designed to minimize the growth of native vegetation. As a flood-control channel, the primary purpose assigned to your stream is to be a conveyance for floodwaters. The old-style, conventional flood-control projects do not include aesthetics or ecological values among their objectives. This means you will have to propose a substitute stream-channel maintenance system, which allows you to integrate environmental objectives with the flood-control objectives. Vegetation management can be carried out using the guidelines in chapter 8. Instead of routinely removing most of the channel's vegetation every few years to increase channel capacity, it is more environmentally beneficial to allow 15–25 percent of the vegetation to remain and maintain it at that level over time. This can provide some environmental value while maintaining conveyance of flood flows. In addition, removal of garbage, debris, furniture, refrigerators, old boots, shopping carts, and other items not only improves the aesthetics of streams but also can remedy erosion problems and increase channel capacities for flood flows. Such cleanup projects are an obvious way to get restoration started.

Replace Culverts and Concrete-Lined Channels
with More Natural Environments

In many urban areas, only remnants of the former riparian environment remain. Streams are often relegated to culverts and buried underground to act as storm sewers. If not buried, they are contained in sterile concrete channels and locked behind chain-link fences. Many cities regret the loss of their streams and rivers as historical, aesthetic, and environmental assets and are trying to undo some of the damage. The city of Milwaukee, Wisconsin, is making plans to remove the concrete from Lincoln Creek in the center of town. Providence, Rhode Island, removed slabs of concrete bridging a river in order to restore the city's waterfront. The cities of Napa, Arcata, El Cerrito, and Berkeley, California; Salt Lake City, Utah; and San Antonio, Texas, and Providence, Rhode Island, have dug up once buried streams and rivers and restored natural channels. Bellevue, Washington; St. Paul, Minnesota; Portland, Oregon; and Denver, Colorado, are among those cities that have plans to "daylight" creeks and jackhammer out concrete.

Improve the Water Quality, Water Supply, and Habitat for Stream Life

To date, most efforts to restore stream environments have focused on water quality and fish habitat improvement. In the past decade, stream restoration programs involving stream bank repair and revegetation have become part of state and local efforts to comply with the nonpoint-source pollution control requirements of the 1987 amendments to the Clean Water Act. There is an extensive body of literature on monitoring and improving water quality and fish habitat restoration available through such groups as the Izaak Walton League in Washington, D.C., the Adopt-a-Stream network in the Northwest, and the River Watch Network in the Northeast. The problems associated with securing adequate water supplies for instream life may involve a complicated system of water rights, with laws varying from state to state. This topic alone requires a book.

What's the Hook for Community Interest?

You have discovered this jewel of a creek in your area. Perhaps it is full of trash, needs "a few" plants in some slumping, eroding sections, and has some suspicious-looking goo floating in the water, it's still, in your eyes, a great creek. You want to bring it back to its potential—which perhaps *you* see, but your friends don't. They think you don't have both oars in the water. You can't restore this creek to community prominence alone. How do you build community support for your idea?

Control Erosion and Reduce Flood Damage

The "hook" may be obvious. The creek regularly floods or the banks are eroding, endangering nearby structures. You are going to suggest some remedies for those problems. That hook sounds like it's based on the negative aspects of the creek, but you can turn it around by offering to provide low-cost, environmentally sensitive erosion control and flood-damage reduction measures. Chapter 9 provides examples of positive, enhancing alternatives for addressing such problems.

The Urban Creeks Council in California began as a small group representing a few neighborhoods on the east side of the San Francisco Bay that found each other because they were trying to stop or alter environmentally damaging flood-control projects on their streams. By 1995, the council had thirty-five affiliates and five chapters across the state. It was successful in getting legislation that started a new state-funded and -administered Urban Streams Restoration Program located in the California Department of Water Resources.[23] The purpose of the program is to provide grants and technical assistance to those local governments and community groups that want to implement less costly and more environmentally sensitive responses to erosion and flooding problems. Between 1985, when the program began, and 1995, the program funded 160 alternative restoration projects, including: innovative bank-stabilization projects using live and dead plant materials; innovative channel design to increase flood capacities; culvert removal and stream daylighting to correct storm-water management problems; and land acquisition solutions to reduce flood damages. The projects require citizen support and frequently use conservation corps labor, and, as a result, they attract community attention and resources.

In Milwaukee, Wisconsin, an extensive greenbelt system follows all the rivers and tributaries located in the metropolitan area because the Milwaukee County Park Commission had the unusual foresight in the 1930s to adopt a plan proposed by Frederick Law Olmsted to put in a river parkway system. A compelling reason for putting the parkway system in place was to protect the growing city of Milwaukee from floods of the Milwaukee, Menomonee, and Kinnickinnic rivers and their tributaries. Because of that objective, some of the river parkways are several miles wide.

Enhance the Neighborhood and Re-create a Sense of Community

If the hook is not so obvious, you can knock on neighbors' doors and get some ideas from them. Don't assume that people will not be interested in or will have negative feelings about the creek. An easy mistake to make is to assume that economically depressed, low-income neighborhoods, communities, and business districts have more pressing concerns. As a manager of the State of California's Stream Restoration Program, I saw some of the most innovative restoration projects occur in economically disadvantaged areas. These projects were not unique and isolated events but statistically significant. Such communities were using the cleanup and restoration of their inner-city creeks to improve their property values, attract businesses into the area, and strengthen older, centrally located business districts that had been on the decline. One densely urbanized area in Oakland wanted to restore Glen Echo Creek and then fence it off in order to have a native California wildlife refuge in the middle of their neighborhood near the business district.

Another inner-city neighborhood in Oakland perceived the value of its creek as a visual and noise buffer for a nearby busy traffic corridor. This neighborhood (Brookdale) also wanted an area where younger children could play out of the way of the older kids at the basketball courts across the busy street.

The Los Angeles River became 48 miles of concrete as a quintessential channelization project of the U.S. Army Corps of Engineers. It was one of the first channelization projects made possible by the 1936 congressional act authorizing Army Corps activities in flood control projects. The huge concrete ditch that ranges from 45 to 300 feet wide has been used to film Hollywood car chases and train Los Angeles police in the art of high-speed driving. Many are unaware that this expanse of concrete is actually a river channel.

The Friends of the Los Angeles River formed in 1988 with the vision of returning some of the river's past ecological values. A selling point for restoration of this river, which has received wide support, has been the idea that the river joins numerous disparate neighborhoods and has the potential for creating a unifying regional identity for the area. Planning for the restoration project is proceeding on the basis of bringing together the various interests along the river that represent different cities, neighborhoods, and cultures.

The Friends of the Chicago River, which adopted the industrial waterway running behind buildings in downtown Chicago, has similar community objectives. A great cultural and economic diversity of neighborhoods lines the Chicago River, and the Friends are working to create neighborhood identity through appreciation and care for the river. The programs of both organizations are characterized by creative efforts to bring the public to the rivers, such as art-adorned floating parades down the Chicago River and high school parades along the Los Angeles River.

Attract Tourism and Revitalize the Downtown Economy

Restoration of streams and rivers has been done by a number of small towns and large cities interested in attracting or enhancing a tourist economy. The restoration of the San Antonio River in San Antonio, Texas, and the now nationally known San Antonio River Walk has put that city on the tourist map. The river was turned into a feature of the downtown with a continuous promenade following both sides of the river and shops, restaurants, and hotels facing the river. A survey done in 1973 of the citizenry of San Antonio obtained a strong positive response to the project, which was later expanded as a result to include more riverfront restoration. The survey response indicated that 96.6 percent of the population felt that the river restoration had created a tourist attraction, and over 80 percent felt that the project was an economic benefit to the city.[24]

The River Walk originated as a flood prevention project after a flood disaster in 1921. The original plan was to put the river in a large underground culvert and pave the area into a street. A woman's conservation group defeated that plan. The plan that was adopted used a bypass channel to circumvent a downtown horseshoe bend in the river so that the area would not flood. Beautification of the bend was originally accomplished by the Works Progress Administration (WPA) in 1939.[25]

The city of San Luis Obispo on the California coast has received almost as much attention as San Antonio, Texas, for its successful downtown stream restoration project. This project is located in a relatively small town on a small creek, but the effect of the restoration has been no less important. The project was funded and sponsored by the downtown merchants' association with the purpose of improving business in the 1960s. The basic design idea was to revegetate and feature the aesthetics of the stream, to draw the public to it via walkways along it and public spaces. Store fronts and restaurants that had their back ends to the creek now face it. Downtown pedestrian traffic moves along creekside sidewalks. Because of the success of the concept, the city is continuing the restoration downstream.

Inspired by the San Antonio example, another small town, Hopkinsville, Kentucky (with a population of 25,000), designed the Little River Walk. Like the San Antonio River Walk, the walk runs along the stream below the street level, establishing a public intimacy with the stream. The project was also conceived as a downtown business district improvement project and helped integrate a new library, a public plaza, and the needs of inner-city children and nearby senior citizen housing. The results of the project are an increase in downtown public visits, measured in part by an increase of 400 percent in library use and an increase in public events downtown. This was an innovative project including the assistance of the Soil Conservation Service and the Tennessee Valley Authority.[26]

Another small town, Napa, located in the Napa Valley of Sonoma County, California, became one of the first towns in the country to restore or daylight a creek that had been buried underground. This is another example of a project in which the main objective was to redevelop a downtown area. Napa also wanted to increase its ability to compete with others in the Napa Valley wine country for tourists. The redevelopment project tore down dilapidated housing in the middle of the downtown area under which the creek ran. The ground was excavated, and the stream channel reappeared as it was years before, contained in a channel with WPA-style rock walls. The creek links park space, parking lots, pedestrian access, and commercial space, including a large department store. This downtown redevelopment project occurred between 1969 and 1974 at the initiative of the city council. In the opinion of local planners it has been an unquestionable success in improving the aesthetic and business environment of the downtown.[27]

Indianapolis' White River Park is directly adjacent to downtown Indianapolis and uses the river and a historic canal as the main pedestrian thoroughfare. The river park was developed because the state legislature wanted to respond to the suburban population flight that occurred after World War II and left the downtown a derelict and dangerous urban waterfront. The legislature also wanted to attract tourism. Another important component of this project is history. A river greenbelt connects historical features such as an old papermill, pumphouse, military park, and cattle bridge. The park design along the river features native woodland plantings and the native Indiana limestone. The further expansion of the White River Park has floundered because of the inability of the state White River Park Commission to act in implementing its river park development plans. A task force of the commission interested in stressing the recreational values of the river such as biking, hiking, canoeing, and multi-use parks reorganized itself as a citizens' group, Friends of the White River. The planning for the river shifted as a result of the Friends and is emphasizing recreational opportunities, environmental education, and volunteer-based restoration projects.[28]

Preserve History and Cultures

The significance of history as a hook for community interest should not be underrated. In the east San Francisco Bay area local historical societies for the cities of Berkeley and Oakland include creeks as part of their architectural tours, generating interest in stewardship of the creeks. Recently, the city of Portland, Oregon, formed the Johnson Creek Council to attract public interest to that creek by emphasizing its historic values, its wetlands, and 14 miles of 1930s Works Progress Administration rock work, fish ladders, and waterfalls. Many creeks will have projects integrated into them that originate from Civilian Conservation Corps or Works Progress Administration projects in the thirties. Usually, those projects were done with sensitivity to the environment and are valued features of the community. Chapter 6, on the history of stream restoration, will provide more background on this subject. The Los Angeles River restoration project previously mentioned has the active support of the local Pomo Indian tribe, which views the restoration of the river as akin to the restoration of their tribal heritage as the Native Americans who used to live along the banks of the natural Los Angeles River.

The city of Naperville, the oldest settlement in DuPage County in the Chicago area, celebrated its 150th birthday in 1981 with the development of a river walk along the west branch of the DuPage River. Local pride over its historic significance as an early settlement helped galvanize public participation in the historical reconstruction of its business district and the restoration of its blighted riverfront. Old buildings slated for demolition were restored, and residents donated their time, money, and materials to turn the riverfront into a linear park following the new historic district. Commemorative markers recognizing donors to the river-walk effort include the Farmer's Monument containing the names of Naperville's old farm families.

Increase Fishing Opportunities

Fish may be another important hook for attracting interest to a stream. Certainly, sport and commercial fishermen have been the traditional interest groups concerned with the well-being of streams and rivers. In the northwestern region of the country, the anadromous salmon and steelhead trout have been described by some as a regional icon. The anadromous fishes are those whose adults migrate from marine or ocean waters into freshwaters for spawning. The Pacific Coast is part of the original range of Pacific salmon and steelhead populations, many of which now return from the ocean to rivers and streams that are near or pass through highly developed urban areas. Because of their different habitat requirements during their migratory lives, anadromous fish need more management attention than most resident fish. The Willamette River in Portland, Oregon; Lake Washington in Seattle; and streams in the surrounding area attract urban sportfishing enthusiasts.[29] As a result of their interest, the region conducts habitat enhancement and artificial propagation projects in the metropolitan areas to mitigate the impacts of urban development on the habitat. The very effective nonprofit Adopt-a-Stream Foundation founded by Tom Murdock organizes volunteer stream restoration projects and attracts support from those committed to restoring native fisheries. The foundation has published a useful book geared toward the northwestern stream restoration movement.[30]

Other areas of the country are seeing a revival of interest in urban fishing, and the American Fisheries Society held a symposium on the basis of that interest in 1983.[31] Atlantic salmon are said to be making a comeback in New England rivers. The transplanting of Pacific Salmon, chinook, and coho to the Great Lakes started a sportfishing boom in some towns on and upstream from the lakes. Crowds of fishermen trying to reach streams located in small cities clogged streets with traffic and overwhelmed sewage systems and parking arrangements. The cities were not prepared for the flood of anglers after the first returns of the salmon, but they quickly adjusted to their new status and, as a result, found themselves with a new economy. The Tennessee Valley Authority (TVA) found that 40 percent of the households in its region participate in sportfishing, and as a result it helped establish urban fishing facilities, which it turned over to local governments and private groups. Interest in fishing also is increasing on the Potomac River in the Washington, D.C., area as a result of water-quality improvements.[32]

Programs in the eastern states such as Maryland's Save Our Streams Program, with its roots in the Izaak Walton League, and North Carolina's Stream Watch Program stress the importance of saving fish and instream life as the motivating force behind their successful citizen volunteer stream-monitoring and restoration projects. The Northeast is very much a part of the river-quality monitoring movement via the River Watch Network led by Jack Byrne out of Vermont. That network is currently monitoring nineteen rivers in ten northeastern states and has expanded to other parts of the country.

Create Jobs, Job Training, and Educational Opportunities

In 1984, Snohomish County, Washington, where the city of Everett is located north of Seattle, used HUD block grants to hire four biologists as temporary stream rehabilitation crew supervisors out of public concern for a salmon stream restoration program. It also hired low- and moderate-income youth in the Washington State Youth Conservation Corps to assist and in the first year finished over fifty projects, ranging from debris and blockage removal to the construction of sophisticated fish ladders and innovative bank restoration measures. Another important hook to political and public interest in these restoration projects is the employment, job training, and youth counseling opportunities they provide. The four biologists, called the Stream Team, are now permanent county employees and are responsible for a wide range of watershed inventory management and restoration activities. A joint county and Adopt-a-Stream Foundation project developed the Lively Environmental Education Center for the Everett School District, which includes a salmon-spawning stream channel and viewing trails, is used by about 6,500 students each year.[33, 34] Education can be an extremely exciting and important hook for community interest.

Youth, service, and conservation corps provide a well-suited labor base for urban stream restoration. In 1995, there were more than twenty-six thousand participants in 120 youth corps operating in 38 states and the District of Columbia, coordinated since 1985 through the nonprofit National Association of Service and Conservation Corps. The field of restoration has a need for the type of labor-intensive work these corps can provide. Environmental restoration projects can provide practical field training and experience combined with an exposure to biological and physical sciences. Low-income and so-called at-risk youth can receive training in basic job skills and be put on meaningful career tracks in environmental management and restoration. One of the best features of urban restoration projects and programs is the way in which they can engage inner-city youth in jobs contributing to their own neighborhoods.

Create Trails and Greenways

The physical fitness and jogging craze of the past two decades provides another persuasive argument for preserving streams as urban greenbelts and restoring their aesthetic values. It has become an increasingly popular idea to plan trails along streams. Well-known examples of important creekside trail systems include Rock Creek Park running through Washington, D.C., and the Boston streamside park system. The Platte River in Colorado has become one of the nation's most extensive urban greenway systems, where thousands of people walk or bicycle along a 60-mile riparian trail connecting nine cities. The draw of the public to that river has resulted in a recent public effort to revegetate a stretch of the river that had been modified by a flood-control project. The resulting Ten Thousand Trees project brought out fourteen hundred volunteers to a well-organized and maintained tree-planting project along the banks of the Platte between the cities of Denver and Chatfield. Both the trail and the revegetation were done with the cooperation and assistance of the Army Corps of Engineers and the Denver Urban Drainage and Flood Control District.[35] An excellent book on greenways and how they can be designed and funded as an enhancement to streams is *Greenways: A Guide to Planning, Design, and Development.*[36]

Mitigate for Land-Use Changes

Some restoration projects occur as a result of land development plans. Land development typically affects streams in negative ways, the most serious impacts involving loss of the resource due to culverting, channel filling, or channelization. Insensitive site design that relegates streams to spaces behind buildings encourages general neglect of the streams, sometimes turning them into dumping grounds. Runoff from impervious paved surfaces and vegetation removal can turn them into eroding storm drains. Federal, state, and local regulations—and occasionaly the enlightened views of developers—sometimes result in stream restoration projects as mitigation for impacts caused by development. These are the most controversial examples of restoration projects, and we must all ask ourselves if we are sure that the stream system we are gaining by the restoration project is a worthy replacement for whatever is being lost.

A good example of a positive gain is the Koll Company North Creek restoration project in Bothell, Washington. North Creek, a major tributary to Lake Washington and the Sammamish River in the Seattle area, once had a rich fish population. A farmer who owned the land relocated the creek, thereby turning it from a creek into a straight, bare, agricultural drainage ditch. Koll Company purchased the land to commercially develop the 140 acres. A combination of pressures, from antidevelopment sentiments; from the city of Bothell, which had a requirement that new development could not exceed 27 percent impervious surface; and from other local, state, and federal regulations, plus an enlightened company president produced a stream restoration project as part of the development plan. The irrigation ditch was essentially removed and a stream channel was relocated and modeled after the configurations of the original North Creek. Meanders, pools, riffles, and revegetation were restored, with a goal of reestablishing the salmon run and spawning areas. State Department of Game and Department of Fisheries biologists oversaw the project. Other objectives of the plan were to provide open space for flooding, for which the creation of a wetlands played an important role, and to provide an educational and park facility as an appealing environment for the new tenants the development company wanted to attract. Whether the project has been successful in the long-term attainment of these objectives is still under evaluation.[37,38]

Reclaim Ecological Values

An ambitious and enormously popular restoration project has been carried out on Boulder Creek, running through the center of Boulder, Colorado (see figure 1.2). The city of Boulder was founded on the creek banks, and the creek flows through busy commercial areas and urban parks. A 3.5-mile restoration project was initiated on that creek in 1984, and the plan released by the city featured the idea of ecological restoration. The interest in the creek was ecological, its aesthetic values and its stream-related recreation, including kayaking, inner tubing, and streamside rambling and bicycle trails.[39–41]

Another university town, Berkeley, California, also conducted stream restoration projects "for restoration's sake" to bring back the environmental values of Strawberry Creek, which runs through the university campus and the center of the town into San Francisco Bay. The university established a high-level Strawberry Creek Task Force including administrators, professors, and campus facilities staff. Mysterious discharge pipes running into the creek were traced to their sources and removed; stream banks were stabilized with planted cribwalls and revegetation projects. The restoration work inspired the university staff to reintroduce native stickleback fish to the creek.

Probably the ultimate restoration project is one that reverses the damages that have been caused by engineering projects. The most dramatic example of this is the Kissimmee River, Florida, restoration project. In its original state, the Kissimmee River meandered through 98 miles of central Florida before emptying into Lake Okeechobee, the nation's second largest freshwater lake. The river has been described as the heart that pumped the blood of the Everglades. It meandered through a virgin wilderness and was famous for its prolific large-mouth bass, wild turkey,

FIGURE 1.2. VALUES OF STREAM RESTORATION.
(a) Ketchikan Creek, Ketchikan, Alaska: Provides tourism, historical, and fisheries values. (b) San Luis Obispo Creek, California: Stream restoration as a foundation for downtown economic revival. (c) Boulder Creek: Provides recreation, ecological benefits, fisheries, and flood-damage reduction. (d) Community Youth Council for Leadership and Education: An example of jobs and training for youth in urban stream restoration.

panther, wild boar, shore birds, and waterfowl. Between 1966 and 1971 this meandering river was channelized by the Army Corps of Engineers into a 50-mile ditch and renamed Canal 38. The canal was built to drain wetlands and provide flood control to assist land speculation and development in central Florida. The undesirable impacts of the project were apparent before the project was finished and included the significant degradation of Lake Okeechobee, to the point that it has been referred to as a dead lake. The average floodplain area was reduced by 60 percent; 40,000 acres of wetlands were lost, with a 75 percent loss of wetland habitat; bald eagle nesting declined by 74 percent; waterfowl populations plummeted by 90 percent; and six species of freshwater fish were lost.[42-44] The combination of threats to water quality and the Florida Everglades and the huge impact to hunters and fishermen resulted in a coalition of rural sportsmen and urban environmentalists who insisted on the reversal of these unacceptable project impacts.[45]

The State of Florida Kissimmee River Restoration Act of 1976 was passed as a result of public pressure, and by 1984 the South Florida Water Management District recommended a river restoration plan based on returning the flows from the ditch through to the original meandering channel, oxbows, and marshes. In the first experimental stages of restoration, flows were diverted from the ditch with sheet-pile weirs placed downstream of the entrance to the oxbows to back the flows up into the oxbows. Water stages were manipulated to more closely correspond to the wet and dry cycles typical of the natural system. With only 12 miles of the restoration work accomplished, bird populations returned to the restored areas.[46] Later research showed that ultimately the best way to restore the river was to fill the channelized canal with soil and allow the river flow to return to its old meanders.[47] The first portion of Canal 38 was filled with soil by the Army Corps of Engineers and the South Florida Water Management District on April 23, 1994. The plan calls for backfilling 22 continuous miles of the canal to restore about 26,500 acres of wetlands and 40 square miles of historic river floodplain. Total cost is expected to be $372 million for a 15-year project.[48]

Restore Water Quality

The specter of the internationally renowned waters of Lake Tahoe turning brown eventually led to the creation of the state agency the Tahoe Conservancy. The conservancy is engaged in both riparian and wetland restoration projects, particularly in the urbanizing portions of the basin, as part of its efforts to protect the water quality of the famous lake. The restoration of riparian corridors and creation of pockets of riparian vegetation in cities around the lake are catching runoff from parking lots and streets to filter nutrients and sediment from urban runoff before they enter the lake.

In 1988, the state of Virginia passed the Chesapeake Bay Preservation Act, which requires local governments within the Tidewater Region to regulate land use to protect the water quality of that important estuary. One requirement of the state regulations is the use of minimum buffer areas to protect stream corridors in sensitive lands that have high potential for contributing to water-quality problems of Chesapeake Bay. A 100-foot buffer is assumed to reduce 40 percent of the nutrients and 75 percent of sediments from entering the sensitive areas. Any tree removal must be followed by planting vegetation that is equally effective in protecting water quality. The water-quality benefits of urban stream restoration can include entrapment of nitrogen and phosphorus, sediment, and the pollutants in them as well as moderation of water temperatures.[49]

Summary of Incentives for Urban Stream Restoration Projects

Many restoration projects come about as a result of a combination of incentives that draw attention to the resource. The Poudre River in Fort Collins, Colorado, is a good example of coalition building among different interests. The Poudre attracted local interest because of its potential to attract tourism and because there was a constituency interested in urban wildlife and fisheries. There was also an interest in flood control, water supply, storm-water management, erosion, and other nitty-gritty urban issues. The Poudre River Trust, made up of citizens, developed a land-use plan for the river corridor, while Trout Unlimited, a sportfishing group, developed a five-year plan to enhance the fishery. In the meantime, the local university started water-quality studies.

Some of the examples of stream or river projects just described may not fit the definition of an ecological restoration project. Some are revegetation projects or trail-building or land-use planning projects. However, their importance lies in what they tell us about the reasons cities, rural towns, and neighborhoods have been motivated to enhance their local streams. The following list of incentives for stream restoration is taken from these cases and should be a useful tool in helping you arrive at what hook you will use to develop community interest for your stream:

- Reduce flood damages.
- Reduce damages from stream bank erosion.
- Preserve or restore a historic or cultural resource.
- Encourage the return of birds and wildlife in urban refuges.
- Develop pedestrian and bicycle trails.
- Upgrade the quality of life in urban and neighborhood environments.
- Restore a regional or local identity.
- Provide greenbelts, open spaces, and parks.
- Create boating and other instream recreation opportunities.
- Create interesting educational opportunities for schools.
- Return or improve recreational and commercial fishing.
- Revive a decaying downtown and a depressed commercial economy.
- Create meaningful jobs and provide job training.
- Increase property values.
- Correct the performance problems and reverse the damages of large or small engineering projects.
- Provide a safe food source for family fishers.
- Return public life and commerce to urban waterfronts.

Strategies to Develop Political Support

The first part of developing political support for your plans is to gain an understanding of the community interest in the stream, river, or waterway. You are then ready for the next step, which is to make that interest a community priority for action. Community activists and organizers often get particularly creative at this stage. If your plan of action for this part of the task isn't fun, you may be using the wrong approach.

The goal should be to make your restoration ideas and plans visible to the public and to put your local political representatives in a situation where they will gain in the public image if they support your plans. Sometimes what political support consists of is the personal commitment of a politically influential person for your ideas. Other times, building political support may mean developing a rapport with city council or county council members or with agency representatives. The strategies you use to build political support can be similar whether you're a citizen, an elected official, or a civil servant.

In Boulder, Colorado, a city planner developed political support for the restoration of Boulder Creek by organizing well-publicized public creekside events. The events came complete with people dressed as mermaids who were helping restock the stream with native trout to capture the attention and imagination of the public (figure 1.3). Frequent creekside ceremonies were held with ribbon cuttings and press coverage to reward city officials for completion of different stages of the restoration plans. Underground stream observatories were built along the creek that include fish feeders. The feeders provide fish food for a fee, and that clever fund-raiser has made significant amounts of money for additional restoration projects.[50]

Streaminders, a citizens' group in Chico, California, went into the classrooms of the local elementary school and taught the children about creeks and the life in them. They used the schoolchildren to do a stream cleanup project and, of course, invited the press. The parents learned about their community creek through their children, and this motivated the local off-road vehicle club to help with the cleanup. The Streaminders also involved the local flyfishing club, the Moose Lodge, and Boy Scout and Girl Scout troops in volunteer projects ranging from the construction of experimental erosion-control projects to the planting of acorns along Lindo River. Their worst problem became finding enough to do for all the people who wanted to volunteer. A particularly interesting project to prevent dumping in the creek involved the painting and erection of murals along the creekside by the schoolchildren, which asked the public not to use the stream as a dump (figure 1.3).[51]

In Grand Junction, Colorado, a group of citizens wanted to change the "grand junkyard" image of the waterfront on the Colorado River. The city had been affected by the oil shale bust of the early 1980s, and the river suffered from the pollution and visual blight of milled uranium tailings and junk cars. To draw attention to the potential positive values of the river, a U.S. senator and key local people were given a raft trip down the river and provided with a perspective on the merits of river restoration. A river commission was formed as a result. Fund-raising strategies included getting pledges from local organizations such as the Lions Club, which pledged its annual carnival proceeds toward the purchase and restoration of an island. As a result of community support, the city purchased three major salvage yards on the river, and the Department of Energy has been cleaning up the tailings piles. There are now 7–8 miles of trail along the river, and a state park is planned for an old downtown mining site.[52]

The city of Bellevue, Washington, which may have the most aggressive and comprehensive urban-watershed management program in the country, takes very seriously the integration of the public and volunteers in its programs. The city holds workshops on good landscape design and maintenance practices to reduce urban runoff pollution; on the life cycle and biology of the native fish; and on riparian revegetation techniques. The city calls this their Stream Team Program, which includes volunteers from both the residential and the commercial segments of the city. Stream teams are coordinated with the help of a volunteer captain, similar to

FIGURE 1.3. METHODS OF COMMUNITY INVOLVEMENT.
(a) Icons representing the city's underground creeks on flags in downtown Berkeley, California. (b) A mermaid assists with the planting of native trout in Boulder Creek, downtown Boulder, Colorado. *Photo credit*: Gary Lacy. (c) The Huron River Watershed Council paints stencils of creeks on storm drains, Ann Arbor, Michigan. (d) Students paint creekside billboards to stop dumping in Little Chico Creek, Chico, California.

the crime-watch block-captain approach. Volunteers learn how to observe and sample water-quality conditions and record daily and storm flows using gauges. The program provides a free newsletter, "News Splash," to the public. The high level of public involvement helps keep up support for the city's stream restoration projects, which include nonpoint-pollution control, salmon habitat restoration, and even the restoration of streams from culverts.[53]

The East Bay Citizens for Creek Restoration and Urban Ecology in the San Francisco Bay area were faced with the situation that most of the native streams had been relegated to underground culverts. To call attention to this hidden resource the citizens received permission from the city of Berkeley to paint the city sidewalks and curbs with stencils that identified the path of the undergrounded creeks. Each creek was identified with a different symbol, such as a water scooter, a quail, a salamander, and so on. Later, flags matching those icons were made and flown in the downtown business district (figure 1.3). As a result, the local groups have built support for the unseen creeks to become daylighted from culverts as above-ground features in the downtown business district and other commercial sections of town.

The Friends of the Chicago River have been particularly creative about drawing attention to an unloved, industrialized, and impacted river flowing through the center of Chicago. Using newspaper ads, they invited people to meet in order to explore the river. The people who showed up were given cameras and film and were invited to take photos of their favorite features of the river. The participants were encouraged to turn those photos into public slide shows and publicity for river-walking tours. The river walking progressed into published river-tour maps distributed around the city.[54] This quickly built a membership base of four thousand. The Friends of the Los Angeles River also first drew attention to that river using art; a large, concrete sculpture of a sycamore tree was prominently displayed in the wasteland of the huge concrete channel.[55]

The strategies found in different communities for developing support for restoration projects typically share the following features: schools or universities are involved; volunteer tree planting or cleanup projects are organized; workshops or conferences are held; celebrations are held; politicians are invited and involved; and, of course, the press is called.

A valuable lesson I learned from community organizing experts is that fewer than five citizens should not arrange a meeting with local officials to talk about project plans. The first reason for this "gang of five" rule is that you should seek out diverse support for your plans before you begin. Consider the business community, environmental groups, the League of Women Voters, and other civic organizations and clubs as your allies. The second reason to present the plans as a group is that you will create a very different dynamic with the local official with five people than you will with one or two. Your plans and requests will become a higher and more urgent priority. Finally, it is critically important to involve your congressman and his or her staff as early as possible in any citizen plans to work with federal water agencies such as the Army Corps of Engineers. The congressional representative has great influence over whether a project in her or his district should receive federal assistance. If you want to use creative planning processes or project designs, your representative can help communicate that effectively to the federal participants.

If you are trying to stop, redesign, or adopt alternatives to a channelization project, find out who is going to benefit from the proposed channelization project and who is going to be asked to pay for it and let your community and its representatives decide if the project is equitable based on that information. Inform your community about the inherent ongoing maintenance costs and potential performance problems of the project. Help people understand what the project will look like. A

neighborhood group in Oakland, California, on Sausal Creek put together an educational slide show of engineering design documents that illustrated attractive
flood-control projects and then showed photos of what similar projects actually
looked like when completed. The contrast helped convince people to look for alternatives to building a traditional box culvert. Arrange to have informed speakers
make presentations on stream management options to your city council, county
council, or relevant committees of those bodies. Most citizens, elected representatives, and many agency employees will need your help in acquiring an education on
flood- and erosion-damage reduction options.

After you have established your stream restoration project as an action item for
your community and local representatives, the hard part begins, which is to set up
an acceptable planning and design process. Some plans will have to contend with a
complexity of problems and a wide variety of "players," or participants. Some plans
will be easier to make because they will focus on one need. The planning process
you use needs to be well thought out because the process generally has a great deal
to do with the product. The next chapter will give you some useful planning models
and strategies. It is a good idea to continue the kinds of high-profile activities mentioned here during the project-planning process. The fact that some kind of action
like a simple erosion-control project, cleanup project, trail building, or tree planting
is occurring lends credibility to your more complex plans. Then, as one local official
advises, "Plan to build, don't plan to plan."[56]

Friends of Trashed Rivers

The Friends of Trashed Rivers found each other on a September day in 1993 at Fort
Mason, San Francisco. Most of the people involved with the waterway restoration
and protection projects described in this chapter joined a crowd of three hundred
people from over twenty states who have also adopted ruined rivers, ditches, canals,
urban waterfronts, and culverted creeks. As a result of that conference, a national
network was formed so that citizen groups, small and large, would have a community of like-oriented people to turn to for moral, technical, and political support.
The Friends of Trashed Rivers annual conference officially spawned a new network,
the Coalition to Restore Urban Waters, which by 1995 had over 375 member organizations and agencies that share information and collaborate on joint projects.

The Coalition to Restore Urban Waters is typical of the urban waterways movement in that its cooperating organizations are a union of what some observers
would term strange bedfellows. The network represents inner-city and minority
neighborhoods, the business community, locally based environmental groups, the
local and state youth conservation corps, land trusts, watershed councils, minority
and tribal organizations. It has formed specifically to address the problems and opportunities associated with urban waterways, but it includes rural organizations
and seeks relationships with its rural community counterparts. Some of its organizations, for example, have working relationships with soil and water conservation
districts and resource conservation districts. Those districts traditionally are of

rural origin, but many of them are becoming suburban or urban as cities encroach on agricultural areas.

The organizations that make up this network are engaged in the wide array of urban waterway restoration and protection projects described in this book, including volunteer water-quality monitoring, physical restoration projects, innovative and "nonstructural" flood-damage reduction alternatives, fisheries habitat restoration, creation of urban greenways, waterfront restoration, jobs training, and environmental education.

What Is Restoration?

The Society for Ecological Restoration defines ecological restoration as "the process of intentionally altering a site to establish a defined indigenous, historical ecosystem. The goal of this process is to emulate the structure, function, diversity, and dynamics of the specified ecosystem." An interesting definition that adds more of a human and social component is "the process of intentionally compensating for damage by humans to the biodiversity and dynamics of indigenous ecosystems by working with and sustaining natural regenerative processes in ways which lead to the re-establishment of sustainable and healthy relationships between nature and culture."[57]

Using these definitions, the first problem the restorationist needs to address is what historical and indigenous (native to the location) conditions to restore to. In some circumstances it may be most practical to restore a waterway to its condition during a particular period of history, such as when it became formally integrated into the urban landscape as a 1930s WPA city park. The restoration project could include, for example, restoration of a creek's native vegetation and historical WPA rock work if the rock does not harm the waterway. Perhaps the history of a waterway from the late 1800s to the present has been as a degraded, polluted industrial channel. You may want to use records or maps from before this era to determine restoration goals. It may be institutionally or ecologically impossible to restore a waterway to a landscape representing conditions before European settlers transformed the landscape to something else. For example, when we select objectives to restore the Chicago River, we cannot return it to a shallow, far-spreading prairie wetland as it was before its lowlands were dredged by humans for use as a shipping channel. Our options at this point are to use a riverine model to guide restoration attempts for the channel and to encourage, to the extent possible, the return of some of the pre-European-settlement prairie wetland species. Restoration, particularly in urban settings, can require complicated compromises and trade-offs in establishing objectives based on the natural and human-built history that has shaped current land uses and ecological systems. A good practice is to refer to local experts who know the regional landscape well to see if any remnant natural rivers, streams, waterways, or wetlands can provide a restoration model for your degraded waterway.

Both ecological and human settlement needs will be met if you strive to create a landscape that is more self-sustaining than existing conditions. This means that the waterway is changed so that it is in greater balance. For a river or stream, this balanced condition usually means that it is not *excessively* eroding or depositing sediment. (Erosion and deposition are natural to streams; we intervene only when we establish that excessive conditions exist.) It also means that it has biologically diverse aquatic life and does not experience extremes in temperature, nutrients, algae growth, or other chemical parameters. If the natural physical features of the waterway are returned, it will not need as much intervention to correct for erosion, sedimentation, or pollution problems.

The physical features of rivers and streams include the streamside trees and shrubs, the channel and its width and depth, pools, riffles, and meanders. The river also includes its floodplain and may feature terraces, which are old, abandoned floodplains located above the current ones. These physical "structures" perform functions in the river ecosystem (figure 1.4), including the transport of water and of sediment, the storage and conveyance of floodwaters, and the creation of terrestrial plant communities and wildlife habitat and aquatic habitat. Finally, stream dynamics include the transport of sediment; conveyance of water; formation of channels, floodplains, and terraces; and the interrelationships among these features and the land uses and vegetation in the watershed. Restoration attempts to return these structures, functions, and dynamics to the extent that it is possible given the constraints of our modern developed landscape.

Sometimes it helps to define what restoration is *not* as a way to clarify its objectives. Fisheries restoration is *not* a fish hatchery, where fish are raised at great expense in captivity and released or sometimes driven to rivers, streams, or lakes for release. Most rivers or lakes with stocked fish cannot support the life cycle of those fish. Consequently, the fish must continually be restocked. Fisheries restoration is reintroducing to a river, creek, or lake wild genetic stock that can maintain a self-sustaining population of fish that are genetically adapted to surviving in natural conditions. Restoration in that case means re-creating spawning and rearing habitats; removing barriers to migration; and restoring shelter, favorable temperatures, and water quality for the species that evolved in those conditions and therefore will survive in them on their own.

Restoration is *not* landscaping. Landscaping at its best has been a means to create new environments that provide sanctuary, adventure, symbolism, recreation, entertainment, and perhaps sustenance. Landscaping is also done to mitigate for a land-use change such as the building of a freeway; the construction of offices, parking lots, and housing developments; and the construction of water projects. Landscape professionals often use planting designs to screen structures, compensating for noise or lost shade or to cover up what we do not want to see. While those are all legitimate undertakings, they are not restoration. Stream restoration is also not the creation of a "native garden" with water running through it.

Planting trees and shrubs along a stream channelization project is *not* restoration—*even* if native species of plants are used. Planting that is done as an add-on to

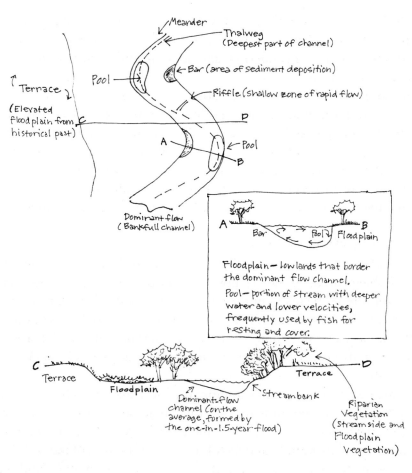

FIGURE 1.4. PHYSICAL COMPONENTS OF A STREAM.

a flood-control channel, or to try to mitigate some of the lost values of the original river for wildlife or aesthetics, but does not function as a part of a natural riparian system, is landscaping. In such cases, we have not restored; we have only tried to mitigate or compensate for the project's environmental damages. However, if the vegetation functions as a component of a stream environment—if it helps slow the velocity of the water, strengthen stream banks, create vortexes to scour pools, shade the channel to prevent invasion of choking rushes and reeds, or re-create habitat for the species of birds, fish, and mammals that once used the site—then it is restoration.

Restoration of a stream is not what the engineering profession calls a channel improvement project, in which a stream's bank vegetation is removed and its channel widened and straightened to carry more flood flows. Stream restoration is, however, the modification of a stream's width, depth, or meander to help restore balance between the sediment load the stream must move and the flow velocities needed to move that load through the system. Stream restoration is the construction of small structures in the upper watershed gullies to control headward erosion and unstable watersheds. Stream restoration is the revegetation of stream banks so that they do not collapse under high-velocity flows but continue to perform as a component in a dynamic system in which meandering, aggradation, and degradation of the stream channel occur in balance.

Stream restoration is not the construction of small or large dams in creek channels. It is not the riprapping or armoring of stream banks to lock them in place so that only the banks up and downstream and across from the armoring are subject to the changing dynamics of the stream. Bank armoring is a classic example of an intervention that requires a never ending series of adjustments by humans to respond to the new problems it causes—in this case the ultimate solution to which is to armor the banks of more of the river until the entire river is riprapped.

Watershed Perspective Required

Environmental professionals typically react to an eroding stream bank by examining the problem area, assessing how serious the erosion is, and considering whether action should be taken immediately or can wait. Most plans to stop excessive erosion involve a localized remedy such as placing rubble or rock against the bank at the point of erosion. Many of these remedies do not stop the erosion as expected, however, usually because not enough time was spent considering why the bank was eroding.

Holistic medicine looks for what combination of stresses may be acting on a body to make it break down and aims to treat the whole person rather than the symptoms. Stream restoration requires the same model. We must go beyond treating a symptom of channel instability and look for the combination of factors causing the problem. It is relatively easy to thumb through a restoration guide and pick out a few bank stabilization designs and try them out. The challenge is to seek the causes of the instability and design the restoration so that it corrects the imbalances in the entire system.

The restoration professional needs to ask a series of questions about the nearby watershed. For example, in a stream with sedimentation problems, it is important to ask where the sediment load is coming from. The source of the sediment may be a culvert put in at the wrong gradient just a few feet away, or it may be a new housing development located miles upstream.

If a permanent change in the watershed, such as a badly designed storm-water system or development project, will continue to contribute large amounts of sediment to the stream channel, you cannot band-aid the symptoms. Your restoration project must address the larger problem. The restoration remedies for a sediment load imbalance could include upstream catchment basins, gully check dams that control upper hillside erosion, and revegetation projects as described in chapter 9. Part of the solution could be to redesign culverts or remove them entirely and replace them with bridges or simple fords (at-stream-grade crossings). Although land stabilization practices, such as revegetation, do not occur near the streambed, they can be directly tied to the stability of the stream. In fact, they may have more long-term influence on the stream channel than projects located in the channel.

Neighborhood Perspective Required

Restoration in cities and towns must include community restoration among its objectives. The greatest value of a restoration project may be the new sense of community identity or neighborhood pride created for the participants in the project. Restoration planning and even project implementation should include all citizens who may have a stake in the project. At worst, public opposition could stop a restoration project because key people felt left out of the decision making or because of misunderstandings about what the project will do. At best, the failure to obtain public participation is a lost opportunity for minimizing vandalism and assuming long-term maintenance and vigilance for the project.

When to Do Restoration

Restoration can be knowing when not to act. Nature is resilient and often adjusts to changes in the watershed. A critical part of a restorationist's role is to know when to allow nature to make adjustments on its own. A variety of human changes might destabilize a stream, including the building of a dam, regulation of stream flows, diversion of water, urban development, fires or timber harvest, culverting, and channel relocation. Natural disasters, such as floods, tornadoes, earthquakes, and hurricanes, may also destabilize the stream's equilibrium. The stream will react to those changes, and its natural adjustments may or may not have unwanted consequences. A restorationist can give local residents insight into the merits and costs of intervention. In many situations, a stream will find a new equilibrium without intervention. In other situations, a stream will defy attempts to manipulate it by blowing out, eroding, or bypassing carefully designed bank protection projects. Sometimes native plant species will return naturally, coming back more quickly and vigorously as volunteers than we can replant them. The uncertainty of these natural changes underscores the importance of consulting with local geomorphologists, hydrologists, and other professionals knowledgeable about local stream dynamics. There is a significant history of misdirected and make-work projects on streams that may do more harm than good to the correction of imbalances in channels and watersheds.

An Alternative to Conventional Engineering Practices

Conventional stream and river engineering practices have resulted in significant social and environmental impacts by creating community blight where natural resources once existed. Reports abound on the environmental impacts of conventional channelization and riprapping projects. The objective of many stream restoration projects is to avoid or minimize those environmental impacts. Restoration can replace environmentally damaging projects with solutions that reduce flood and erosion damages while restoring environmental values. In other cases, a restoration effort can return some of the ecological and aesthetic values to an environment degraded by an older, conventional project.

We are entering a new era of government engineering programs in which public works projects are going to be designed to accommodate a wider range of values and objectives. The concept of multi-objective floodplain management has gained wide acceptance in the past decade in the river engineering and management professions. This concept states that it is of greatest community benefit to manage river floodplains and flood-prone areas for a range of objectives including flood-damage reduction, protection of wildlife habitat, protection or improvement of water quality, ecological restoration, erosion control, provision of recreation, etc. This contrasts with the many older, single-objective public works projects for flood or erosion control.

The concerns restoration professionals have regarding conventional flood-control and bank stabilization projects are the environmental impacts they have caused and the unexpected performance and maintenance problems that are now making the projects controversial. Concrete linings have cracked or collapsed. Flood-control channels have filled with sediment; levees have been breached. Expected storm-flow velocities have not been attained in channels, and as a result flood stages have been higher than planned.

Innovations are now being tried in the design of flood-control projects to avoid environmental impacts and performance and maintenance problems. River meanders are being kept, and floodplains are being restored to both better store and better convey larger volumes of water. Revegetation systems, some of which are described in this book, are replacing concrete, riprap, and sheet piling on stream banks, waterfronts, and lakesides. Restoration methods are providing an exciting alternative to old methods because they can often solve the important engineering problems of lowering property damages *and* provide environmental benefits. They attempt to return to the stream its structure (riparian forests, meanders, pools, riffles, and other physical features), its functions (instream habitat, flood storage, environmental balance, wildlife habitat), and its dynamics (which determine its shape, dimensions, and meander). By doing this, restoration can reduce excessive erosion, return fish habitat, help the stream recover from pollution, and even reduce flood damages. It becomes a win-win solution.

Most objectives for conventional river projects involve draining and reclaiming wetlands, providing flood control by increasing the capacity of stream channels, aiding navigation by increasing the depth of larger rivers, and controlling erosion by substituting artificial channels for eroding natural channels. Channelization projects for flood control usually include removing a stream's native vegetation, straightening it, and then lining it with rock or concrete. Conventional bank stabilization armors stream banks with rock, concrete, sheet metal, sandbags, or grouted rock to prevent erosion.

As early as 1971, the U.S. Congress held hearings in response to growing public disenchantment with these conventional projects. The hearings made a record of the impacts of channelization projects and the need for greater citizen participation and environmental concerns in the planning of projects. The Government Operations Committee issued a report that concluded that the conventional channel projects had been overused with inadequate or no consideration of the environmental impacts. The impacts listed in the report include destruction of wetlands and the associated reduction in wildlife dependent on them; destruction of riparian environments and exposure of the aquatic environment to high temperatures; destruction of bottomland hardwoods; an increase in nutrients and sediment concentrations in waterways; cutoff of oxbows and meanders, which increased the rate of flow and destabilized channel slopes; increased erosion and sedimentation; reduced feeding and breeding grounds for aquatic life; and changes in water table, which can decrease stream discharges for instream life, harm riparian vegetation, and lower well-water supplies. The severe impact to aesthetic values was also frequently mentioned.

The physical alterations common to stream "modification" or channelization projects impact streams by affecting their "structures," such as changing the shape of the stream channel, removing or altering floodplains, and removing the riparian forests. The "functions" of these features are lost when the structures of the ecosystem are modified. For example, when a riparian forest is lost, the shade is lost, the roots holding the stream bank and soil are gone, and the pool providing resting places for fish is lost. When the ecosystem structure and function are lost, a related casualty is the reduction of biological diversity. Without cool water, deep pools, and leaf fall from the trees, which serve as part of the food cycle, fish will likely not be able to survive. When a floodplain is cut off from a river by a channelization or levee project, its function to store sediment and flood flows is lost. The loss of the riparian forest can lead to widespread channel and meander instabilities.

Information Contacts

Urban Fishing Educational Materials

AFTMA Sport Fishing Educational Foundation
2625 Clearbrook River
Arlington Heights, Illinois 60005

American Fisheries Society
5410 Grosvenor Lane
Bethesda, Maryland 20814

Adopt-a-Stream Foundation
Box 5558
Everett, Washington 98204

Kissimmee River Restoration Project
South Florida Water Management District
3301 Gun Club Road
P.O. Box 24680
West Palm Beach, Florida 33416–4680

Fishin' Buddies
9946 South Halsted
Chicago, Illinois 60628

Richard Coleman
Sierra Club
203 Lake Pansy
Winter Haven, Florida 33881

Urban River Restoration Projects

Bill Way
North Creek, Koll Company Project
The Watershed Company
1029 Market Street, Suite B
Kirkland, Washington 98033

Friends of the Los Angeles River
Box 292134
Los Angeles, California 90029

Friends of the Chicago River
407 South Dearborn, Suite 1580
Chicago, Illinois 60605

Friends of the White River
1635 East 77th Street
Indianapolis, Indiana 46290

Stream Team Program Manager
Storm and Surface Water Utility
P.O. Box 90012
Bellevue, Washington 98009

Gary Lacy
Recreation, Engineering and Planning
485 Arapahoe Avenue
Boulder, Colorado 80302

Kathy Portner
Riverfront Project
250 North 5th Street
Grand Junction, Colorado 81501

Streaminders, c/o Jim Ost
1255 East Lindo Avenue
Chico, California 95928

Earle Cummings and Sarah Denzler
Program Manager, Urban Streams Restoration Program
California Department of Water Resources
1025 P Street
Sacramento, California 95814

Milwaukee Area Greenbelt
Department of Natural Resources
2300 North Dr. Martin Luther King, Jr. Drive
Box 12436
Milwaukee, Wisconsin 53212

Roger Krempel
Poudre River
629 Stover
Fort Collins, Colorado 80524

Robert Searns
Platte River Greenway
Urban Edges, Inc.
1624 Humbolt
Denver, Colorado 80202

Urban Creeks Council of California
Strawberry Creek Park Center, #107
1250 Addison Street
Berkeley, California 94702

John Barnett
Greenways Coordinator
City of Boulder Planning Department
P.O. Box 791
Boulder, Colorado 80306

Paul Lange Rentschler
Huron River Watershed Council
415 West Washington Street
Ann Arbor, Michigan 48103

Riverwalk Fund
City of Naperville
P.O. Box 3020
Naperville, Illinois 60566

Urban Waterfront Center
1536 44th Street, N.W.
Washington, D.C. 20007

Urban Committee
National Association of Conservation Districts
P.O. Box 320
Leeds, Massachusetts 01053

Coalition to Restore Urban Waters
c/o Izaak Walton League of America
707 Conservation Lane
Gaithersburg, Maryland 20878

Federal Agencies

Urban Resources Partnership
Natural Resources Conservation Service
P.O. Box 2890
Washington, D.C. 20013
(202) 720–1847

Office of Policy, Planning and Evaluation
Environmental Protection Agency
401 M Street, SW
Washington, D.C. 20460
(202) 260–3848

Commissioner, Bureau of Reclamation
Department of Interior
1849 C Street, NW
Washington, D.C. 20240
(202) 208–4157

Rivers, Trails and Conservation Assistance Program
National Park Service
11th and L Street, NW
Washington, D.C. 20013
(202) 343–3775

Floodplain Management Services
U.S. Army Corps of Engineers
20 Massachusetts Avenue, NW
Washington, D.C. 20314
(202) 272–0169

Floodplain Management
Federal Emergency Management Agency
500 C Street, SW
Washington, D.C. 20472

U.S. Fish and Wildlife Service
National Headquarters
1849 C Street, NW
Washington, D.C. 20240
(202) 208–5634

Tennessee Valley Authority
Knoxville, Tennessee 37902
(615) 632–4792

U.S. Geological Survey
12201 Sunrise Valley Drive
Reston, Virginia 22092
(703) 648–6831

NOTES

1. George R. Stewart, *American Place-Names* (New York: Oxford Press, 1970).

2. Stewart, *American Place-Names.*

3. Stewart, *American Place-Names.*

4. Luna B. Leopold, *Water, A Primer* (San Francisco: W.H. Freeman, 1974).

5. Luna B. Leopold, "Rivers," *American Scientist* 50 (December 1962), p. 511.

6. J. H. Feth, "Water Facts and Figures for Planners and Managers," *U.S. Geological Survey Circular 601–1* (Washington, D.C.: Department of the Interior, 1973).

7. Leopold, "Rivers."

8. Leopold, "Rivers."

9. Kari Dolan and Patrick Field, *Fishing for Values: A Primer for River Protection Activists in the Use of Contingent Valuation as an Economic Tool for Measuring Anadromous Sport Fisheries* (Montpelier, Vermont: National Wildlife Federation; Washington, D.C.: River Watch Network, 1995).

10. Kenneth D. Orth, *Cost Effectiveness Analysis for Environmental Planning: Nine Easy Steps,* IWR Report 94–PS–2 (Alexandria, Virginia: Institute for Water Resources Support Center, U.S. Army Corps of Engineers, 1994).

11. Leonard Shabman, *Environmental Activities in Corps of Engineers Water Resource Programs: Charting a New Direction,* IWR Report 93–PS–1 (Alexandria, Virginia: Institute for Water Resources, Water Resources Support Center, 1993).

12. Carol Streiner and John Loomis, "Estimating the Benefits of the Urban Streams Restoration Program," for the California Department of Water Resources, Sacramento, California: June 1995.

13. National Park Service, *Economic Impacts of Protecting Rivers, Trails and Greenway Corridors: A Resource Book,* 4th edition revised (Washington, D.C.: Rivers and Trails Conservation Assistance, National Park Service, 1995).

14. Phil Meyer, "Economic Evaluation of River Projects, Values for Fish, Wildlife and Riparian Resources, vol. 3 (Davis, California: Meyer Resources, written for the National Park Service, December 1982).

15. John A. Dearinger, *Aesthetic and Recreational Potential of Small Naturalistic Streams near Urban Areas,* Research Report No. 13 (Lexington, Kentucky: University of Kentucky Water Resources Institute, 1968).

16. Robert E. Coughlin and T. R. Hammer, "Estimating the Benefits of Stream Valley and Open Space Preservation Projects," in Lowell C. Harris, ed., *Government Spending and Land Values* (Madison: University of Wisconsin Press, 1973).

17. Karl Schurr, R. Shurr, and D. Barker, "How a Natural River Can Increase the Community's Tax Base," *American Rivers* (December 1985).

18. Orth, *Cost Effectiveness Analysis for Environmental Planning.*

19. Shabman, *Environmental Activities in Corps of Engineers Water Resource Programs.*

20. Sunny Williams and John Loomis, *A Survey of California Department of Water Resources Funded and Non-Funded Urban Stream Organizations* (Boulder: University of Colorado, May 1995).

21. Robert Michael Pyle, *The Thunder Tree: Lessons from an Urban Wildland* (Boston: Houghton Mifflin, 1993).

22. Peter Steinhart, "The Meaning of Creeks," *Audubon* (May 1989), p. 22–23.

23. California Department of Water Resources, *Urban Stream Restoration Program* (Sacramento: Resources Agency, State of California, 1988).

24. Clare A. Gunn, "River Walk Generates Strong Positive Response," *Landscape Architecture* (American Society of Landscape Architects, Louisville, Kentucky) 63, no. 3 (April 1973).

25. Robert Weldon Baird, "Soil Conservation and Urban Design: A New Downtown Concept," in Clay Grady, ed,. *Water and the Landscape* (New York: McGraw-Hill, 1979).

26. Baird, "Soil Conservation."

27. Charles Woods, principal planner, City of Napa, California, personal communication, May 1986.

28. Christopher Findley, "Indianapolis White River Park," *Landscape Architecture* (July-August 1986); John Meade and Brandt Cowser, board of directors of Friends of the White River, personal communications, spring 1990 and fall 1993.

29. Richard B. Thompson, "Efforts to Provide Urban Fisheries for Anadromous Species," in Lockie Jo Allen, ed., *Urban Fishing Symposium Proceedings* (Bethesda, Maryland: American Fisheries Society, 1984).

30. Steven Yates, *Adopting a Stream: A Northwest Handbook* (Seattle: University of Washington Press, 1988).

31. Lockie Jo Allen, ed., *Urban Fishing Symposium Proceedings* (Bethesda, Maryland: American Fisheries Society, 1984).

32. Thompson, "Efforts to Provide Urban Fisheries."

33. Bob Fuerstenberg, hydrologist, and Ruth Schaefer, ecologist, River and Water Resources Section Department of Public Works, King County, Washington, personal communication, November 10, 1989.

34. "Five Years of Stream Rehab," *Streamlines* (newspaper of the Adopt-a-Stream Foundation) 1, no. 3 (Spring–Summer 1989).

35. Robert M. Searns, *Building a Greenway: Denver's Platte River System* (Denver, Colorado: Urban Edges, 1990).

36. Charles A. Flink and Robert M. Searns, *Greenways: A Guide to Planning, Design and Development* (Washington, D.C.: Island Press, 1993).

37. Steve Elliot and P. K. Mason, "Salmon River," *Landscape Architecture* 75, no. 3 (May–June 1985).

38. "Project Features Unique Stream Channel," *Landscape and Irrigation* (March 1985).

39. Gary Lacy and David W. Crumpacker, "The Boulder Creek Corridor Projects: Riparian Ecosystem Management in an Urban Setting," at conference entitled "Riparian Ecosystems and Their Management: Reconciling Conflicting Uses," Tucson, Arizona, April 16–18, 1985.

40. John L. Barnett, greenways coordinator, City of Boulder, Colorado, personal communication, May 1990.

41. "A Plan for Boulder Creek," City of Boulder, Department of Planning and Community Development, 1984.

42. Martin Heuvelmans, *The River Killers* (Harrisburg, Pennsylvania: Stackpole Books, 1974).

43. Stephen Glass, "Rebirth of a River," *Restoration and Management Notes* 5, no. 1 (Summer 1987).

44. South Florida Water Management District, "High Discharge Test on the Kissimmee River," West Palm Beach, Florida, February 1988.

45. Richard Coleman, Sierra Club member and leader in the Kissimmee River restoration effort, Winter Haven, Florida, personal communication, April 1989.

46. South Florida Water Management District, "High Discharge Test"; Richard Coleman, personal communication, 1989.

47. Hsieh Wen Shen, professor of civil engineering, University of California, Berkeley, personal communication, 1989.

48. Margaret Barletto, "Test-Fill Launches Kissimmee Restoration Project," *Everglades Connection* (South Florida Water Management District) 3, no. 3 (Fall 1994).

49. Charles A. Flink et al., *A National Inventory of Stream Corridor Planning Programs,* prepared by Ogden Environmental and Energy Services and Greenways Incorporated for the Louisville and Jefferson County Metropolitan Sewer District, Kentucky, March 1993.

50. Gary Lacy, Boulder Creek project coordinator, presentation at California Creeks Conference, Urban Creeks Council, May 6, 1989.

51. Mary Meyer and Richard Roth, Streaminders, Chico, California, personal communications, 1988.

52. Kathy Portner, City of Grand Junction, Colorado, River Front Project, presentation at Urban Stream Corridor and Stormwater Management Conference, Colorado Springs, Colorado, March 14–16, 1989.

53. Sarah Hubbard-Gray, Stream Team program manager, City of Bellevue, Washington, personal communications, November 1989.

54. David W. Jones, Friends of the Chicago River, Chicago, Illinois, personal communication, April 1991.

55. Lewis MacAdams, Friends of the Los Angeles River, board of directors, presentation at Friends of Trashed Rivers Conference, San Francisco, September 1993.

56. Gary Lacy, Boulder Creek Colorado Project, Urban Streams Restoration Conference, Berkeley, California, 1989.

57. "Definitions," *Society for Ecological Restoration News* (Society for Ecological Restoration; Fall 1994).

58. Committee on Government Operations, U.S. Congress, House Report 93–530, "Stream Channelization: What Federally Financed Draglines and Bulldozers Do to Our Nation's Streams," September 27, 1973.

CHAPTER TWO

The Urban River Planners

Whoever wades into the world of urban stream restoration and management will be presented with a rich cast of characters who represent different professional cultures and divergent perspectives on urban streams. Like Alice in Wonderland, the novice entering this unique world may feel bewildered at first and need an introduction to the characters and their language, culture, and points of view in order to make sense of the surroundings. It's best to approach this adventure as if you were an anthropologist learning about a foreign and exotic culture. To help you negotiate this new field of urban stream restoration, the next four chapters of this book are dedicated to describing the major professional players you will necessarily come in contact with if you want to restore a stream. The major players are: watershed planners, including floodplain and greenway planners; fish, wildlife, and plant biologists and landscape architects, representing the environmental disciplines; and hydrologists, fluvial geomorphologists, and hydraulic engineers, who work with the physical environment and can be involved in stream modification and engineering projects. In the last two decades there has been an increasing appreciation by these professional groups of the advantages of working in interdisciplinary teams. The professions originate from different traditions and histories, define watershed problems from different perspectives, and, of course, value their own professional language. If you are not already in one of these professional categories, or even if you are a member of one of them, it is easy to feel estranged from any of the professions you do not have training in. Whether you are a professional or a layperson, it is necessary to learn about these related fields if you aspire to be involved in stream restoration.

We'll start our adventure of exploring the major four "cultures"—planning, biology, hydrology, and hydraulic engineering—by first understanding the planners. Planners tend to have the broadest perspective on managing rivers and watersheds. The field of "environmental planning" grew out of the acknowledged need to produce professionals who could synthesize and apply technical information from a diversity of fields. Planning done in order to manage rivers and their floodplains is one of the oldest and most accepted forms of planning our environment. Planners of watersheds generally group themselves into three fields: river corridor planning, focused on developing local or regional multi-use parkways or greenways along rivers; floodplain managers, who identify, regulate, and manage flood-hazard areas; and comprehensive watershed managers, who make and attempt to implement plans that address water-quality, water supply, flood-control, and environmental needs in a coordinated way for a region.

The concept of watershed- or water-basin–based planning has cycled back into vogue from earlier national attempts at realizing this concept. Because this concept is going to be a dominant force behind the next wave of water management efforts, it's important to have a historical view of what planners have tried to accomplish under this framework in the past. History seems to show that the use of different schools of planning—including categories of comprehensive and incremental planning using a variety of methods such as rational, visioning, advocacy, and consensus planning—have to be correctly matched with the political conditions present in the state and locality where the planning takes place. Without this proper matching of planning methods with political conditions, our watershed planning efforts will be doomed just as many have failed in the past.

River Corridor Planners and Multi-Objective River Corridor Management

"River corridor" refers to the concept that streams and rivers are more than the channel that you see carrying water most of the time. Included as part of a stream or river is its floodplain, which carries the higher flows. Also included are the riparian trees and plants that grow in the high groundwater tables and moist soils along the drainage way. The word "corridor" then is used by planners to acknowledge that the stream-related environment that must be managed as a whole includes the stream valley and the floodplain that lies adjacent to the channel.

In 1989 Congressmen Joseph McDade of Pennsylvania and Morris Udall of Arizona conducted workshops around the country with the assistance of the National Park Service on "multiple-objective river corridor management and planning."[1] For the uninitiated into the mysteries of government, this mouthful is really bureaucratese for saying that there are many benefits and uses of rivers to be managed and planned for in addition to those associated with industry and transport. Rivers and streams have tended to be dominated by industrial uses such as transport, supplying water for cooling towers, factory operations, and discharging wastes. Rivers are commonly dammed to create hydroelectric power and provide domestic water supplies; large quantities of water are diverted and stored for agricultural uses. Multi-objective river or stream use includes the values of rivers not directly related to these forms of commerce.

After public input from all over the country in these workshops, the congressmen's staffs put together a report that contained a twelve-page laundry list of the public uses and values of rivers—both quantifiable and hard to quantify. The list was divided into aesthetic resources, cultural and historical values, economic uses, natural resources, and recreational uses. The range of uses included wildlife reserves; open-space flood zones to contain floodwaters out of the way of urban development; commercial and sport fisheries; boating recreation; wilderness experiences; and more.

The report on multi-objective river corridor planning and management written under Congressmen McDade and Udall made a policy recommendation to Congress that contains the most comprehensive definition of "multi-objective" planning I have ever seen. Although a bit long-winded, it is a good definition because it describes what the ultimate goal of any water-related plan or project should be: ". . . to encourage comprehensive and cooperative planning among all individuals and institutions concerned with rivers and their adjacent lands, to facilitate decisions regarding such use which reflect a high degree of consensus at all stages of decision making, which maximize public and private benefits with the least adverse impacts on significant river resources values. Such a policy is intended to achieve an appropriate balance among economic, natural, cultural, recreational, tourist, scenic, historic and other similar values associated with rivers and their corridors."[2]

Depending on the orientation of the planner and the purposes for which the river corridor is being managed, it may be referred to as a floodplain, flood zone, flood fringe, floodway, buffer zone, parkway, or greenway. If the planners are calling it a floodway, flood zone, or flood fringe, they are basing their land-use planning, regulations, and land acquisition and management practices on the need to provide room for the stream to flood without causing damage. If the planners are calling the corridor a buffer zone, they are probably basing management on the need to preserve the native vegetation and environment so as to absorb urban or agricultural runoff and pollutants before they enter the stream, to provide a sanctuary for wildlife, and to protect nearby areas from floods and the erosive forces of streams. Planners who call the river corridor a greenway or a parkway are managing the area with the idea that it is providing needed open space and park lands and recreation for an urbanized environment. Planners and landscape architects in the National Park Service and in state and local parks departments typically use these terms. Of course, any river corridor managed as a natural environment provides for all these uses or benefits. What is important to remember though is that the politically savvy planner, citizens' group, or governing council will use the terminology that will most effectively strike a chord with the public who will be affected by the desired policies, regulations, or projects.

The idea of multi-objective stream management has its roots with the geographers, hydrologists, and planners who became concerned with the issue of multi-objective floodplain management, and it is important to understand the history behind that concept.

Floodplain Managers

The government's first involvement in the waterways of our country was to assure that its rivers were navigable; debris was removed, and channels were dredged. In the 1930s the federal government's role was greatly expanded to include draining or "reclaiming" wetlands, building reservoirs for water supplies, and building reservoirs and channelizing streams to control floods. A water project built for one purpose was referred to by water planners as a *single-purpose* project. An example is building a reservoir to provide a domestic water supply. Water planners later found, however, that it could be better policy to construct a project for more than one purpose, because presumably the benefits would be greater for each dollar spent. Thus, a reservoir could be a *multipurpose* one—for example, providing domestic water supplies, storage behind a dam to contain floodwaters, and a lakelike environment for recreational boats. Hoover Dam, on the lower Colorado, is the prototype multipurpose project; it was built to store water for irrigation, produce hydroelectric power, control floods, and augment urban water supplies.

The second significant concept, of planning for entire drainage basins, was popularized through the controversy over how to handle flooding problems on the lower Mississippi River. The U.S. Army Corps of Engineers was authorized in 1928 to make a series of basin-wide studies, one of the first of what are referred to as the "308" reports.

The third concept was championed by the Tennessee Valley Authority, which saw its function as designing multiple-purpose projects in an entire drainage basin with the clear intent to promote social change. The TVA was the first to contemplate such change throughout a watershed—to consciously plan for shifts in income levels and modes of life.[3]

By the forties, after a great proliferation of projects, some water managers found the concept of multipurpose planning to be too simplistic, and they called for *multi-objective* planning. At the same time, they warned that if we relied on structural water projects to meet all our water management needs, we were headed for trouble. We needed to consider more *nonstructural* solutions to flood problems. What did the experts mean by all this?

In 1942 a now widely known and respected geographer by the name of Gilbert White noted that, despite a huge financial commitment to building flood-control projects, the nation's mean annual property loss due to floods was at or over $95 million.[4] In Hoyt and Langbein's *Floods!*, written a decade later in 1955, the two hydrologists found that the national expenditure for flood-control projects had accumulated to about $3.3 billion (in 1950s dollars), while estimates of flood damages had escalated to between $200 and $500 million a year, on the national average.[5] Those early experts in floodplain management were revealing to the public and to decision makers that not only was our dependency on flood-control works costing large sums of money, but the projects inherently had a limit on the degree of protection they could provide, as well.

James Goddard, an engineer with the Tennessee Valley Authority since 1933, turned conventional wisdom upside down by suggesting that it was possible to reduce flood damages without structural projects but that it was not possible to achieve results with structural projects without also using nonstructural or land-use planning measures.[6] It is not humanly possible, he pointed out, to control every flood with a structure. As a matter of fact, the term *flood control* is a misnomer because all we can really do is attempt to *reduce* the damages from floods. Hence the term *flood-damage reduction* became favored by the professional floodplain manager. The structural approaches not only had physical limitations for controlling floods, but because of those limitations, they also created a false sense of security for the population moving into a floodplain who perceived that there was no hazard because a project was in place. The combination of the lack of land-use planning, the dependency on project building as a response to flood problems, and the false sense of security the projects instilled became responsible for increased development in hazardous areas and added to the geometrically increasing national flood-damage costs.

The planning concept of *multiple means* introduced the idea that a single goal, such as flood control, could be sought through a variety of engineering and management means. The concept calls for maintaining flexibility for the future and foreclosing as few choices as practicable. It requires identifying all available alternatives for coping with water problems and improving methods for recognizing the social as well as the physical consequences of water management when weighing alternatives. Hoyt and Langbein's classic 1955 work on floods articulated this concept by recommending an integrated federal policy for dealing with flood losses that would include regulating floodplain use, flood proofing and elevating structures, planning flood-hazard zones as greenways, and relocating structures from hazard areas.

It was as a result of those realizations then that experts began to recommend nonstructural and multi-objective approaches to floodplain management. Both the multipurpose reservoirs and the single-purpose levee and channelization projects were excluding other possible uses for streams and floodplains, such as preservation of riparian woodlands, creation of greenways for urban parks, conservation of anadromous fishery river habitat, and storage of floodwaters in the floodplains. The nonstructural adjustments that could reduce flood damages and preserve more options for how our rivers could be used and managed included zoning and relocating structures away from hazard areas, constructing buildings above the height of the floodwaters, providing flood warning and evacuation systems, flood proofing structures, and even providing flood insurance programs. Although it is no longer the case, in the 1970s federal directives required this type of multiple-means planning for multiple objectives in federal flood project plans.[7]

Another component of multi-objective planning was introduced by early floodplain management experts who argued that too often a project built with public monies benefited only a few private property owners or land speculators. The method the federal government still uses more than fifty years later to determine the benefits of a water project emphasizes that the greatest dollar benefits of a flood-control project are the values assigned to property "protected" from floods. The argument that projects funded with public monies should have broad public benefits—for the regional economy, for the social welfare of the general population, and for environmental quality—is as relevant now as when it was made in the 1940s.[8–10] Recently, progress has been made on these economic evaluation issues.

For example, environmental restoration is now recognized as a purpose of Army Corps projects, and it is now possible for environmental benefits to be considered as equal to the costs of attaining them when a cost-benefit analysis is prepared for a conventional project.

The other important concept that has evolved in part from the floodplain management profession is that coordination among different government agencies is necessary before rational land-use planning can be implemented in floodplains. A report entitled "A Unified National Program for Floodplain Management" found that federal programs dealing with floodplain management were diffused among 28 agencies and 9 programs. Data show that 797 projects involving $795 million were implemented by 11 agencies operating under 44 different legislative authorities.[11] Coordination at the federal level will continue to be a long-term challenge even as efforts are made to streamline federal agencies and more responsibility is assumed by states and regional entities for floodplain management. Coordination among federal agencies and different levels of government will always define the challenges of floodplain management. *Intergovernmental* management and planning refers to the approach of managing floodplains with the cooperation of different levels of government, i.e., the federal, regional, state, and local governments, and requires that communities that are situated next to each other in the same watershed work together toward the same objectives.[12,13]

In a 1991 "Issue Brief," the Metropolitan Planning Council for the Chicago area describes the equally daunting challenges of coordinating intergovernmental policies and actions at the regional level. Planning in the Chicago metropolitan area involves 6 counties, over 260 municipalities, about 1,200 units of local government, and over 7 million people.[14]

The floodplain management issues that must be coordinated among the various authorities that have a role in the fate of your watershed may involve:

- whether floodplain management measures should be adopted;
- whether structural or nonstructural approaches should be used for managing flood damages;
- what level of flood risk the community can cope with and what risk reduction it is willing to pay for;
- how to coordinate the acquisition of land or relocation of structures for floodways, parks, trails, etc.;
- how to establish, if desirable, a regional or local coordinating body with authority over the floodplain;
- what land uses and activities the community wants to promote in the floodplain.[15]

A number of recent innovations in planning concepts and methods have either originated with or been adopted by floodplain managers. The concept of flood-damage reduction has evolved into the more complex and realistic concept of *flood-*

risk management. Risk assessment and management have been used previously in evaluating alternative responses to air and water pollution and regulation of hazardous wastes and pesticides, among other environmental problems. Traditional approaches to reducing flood damages have focused on trying to provide high "levels of protection" from very large, and therefore low-probability or infrequent, storms and floods. Planning on the basis of risk reduction, however, adds an economic and even a social component to the calculation of flooding probabilities. Flood-risk management decisions weigh the avoided damages from an action against the risks of no action. The costs include the loss of options for using the floodplain, the monetary costs of the projects, and unanticipated environmental damages.

Conventional project planning for a level of protection has been based on hydrologic data that estimate the chance of a large flood happening in a single year. For example, a public works agency may tell the community that a project will provide a "one–hundred year level of protection." What the agency means is that based on the hydrologic record and models of the watersheds where the project is located, that project is designed so as to prevent damages from a flood that has a one in one-hundred chance of occurring in any one year. The problem with this planning concept is that people think that magnitude of flood may occur only once in one-hundred years, when in fact it may occur a number of times within one-hundred years. Another problem with planning on this basis is that as we accrue records over a longer period of time, we may discover that a flood occurs more (or less) frequently than expected when we designed and built a project.

Finally, the planning concepts of *risk* and *uncertainty* are just now being introduced to floodplain planning. Risk is now thought of as more than just the hydrologic probability that a certain size flood will occur in a year. Risk must also take into account that physical structures such as dams and levees have limitations and that things can go wrong or fail under pressure. Construction problems, gate failures, erosion of spillways, operator errors, levee overtopping, embankment leakage, and piping of soils, as well as earthquakes, need to be considered as part of the risk picture. Uncertainty refers to the possibility of errors in collection or interpretation of hydrologic data or the use of inadequate models to identify flood discharges and frequencies, flood stages, and floodplain areas in the performance of projects.[16–18]

While considering risks and uncertainty in floodplain planning certainly complicates planning, it is better to be as realistic as possible about what we are investing our tax dollars in. These planning concepts are still in the development stage and the bugs still need to be worked out, but many of you who will be involved in floodplain management will encounter them in the near future. The hope is that this type of planning will provide a community with more realistic information on the benefits of different project alternatives and more choices on the sizes and types of projects.

A second innovation in floodplain planning, which we can anticipate as a result of the newly evolving waterway restoration and watershed management move-ments, is the concept of *adaptive management*.[19] Professionals involved in ecological, land, and resource management are familiar with the idea that envi-ronmental management requires trial and error over time to learn how environ-ments respond to our efforts. This includes monitoring our restoration projects and changing our project designs or management plans to better achieve our ob-jectives. Floodplain management plans and projects should start to take on the characteristic of being dynamic over time, so that a project doesn't end on the date a levee is built, a bank is repaired, or a floodplain is acquired, but the measures used continue to be evaluated and even modified over time to respond to changing environmental conditions or unexpected problems.

Finally, the definition of multi-objective floodplain management is undergoing an evolution that has been influenced by discussions in water resources development and protection agencies in the 1990s on watershed-based programs and the "eco-logical sustainability" of projects. While the focus may remain on solving the prob-lems particular to floodplains, the floodplain is coming to be viewed in a broader context as part of a watershed. A floodplain plan therefore needs to consider the nat-ural and human influences acting on the floodplain from outside its boundaries. Likewise, a floodplain plan should evolve from locally placed organizations such as a watershed council that convenes the broad array of government and private stake-holders who have an interest in what happens to the watershed. While flood-damage reduction or risk management may be an important consideration or need, it should be part of a broader mission to manage for ecological sustainability. The basic idea behind sustainability is that our actions and environmental adjustments should be done with the objective of maximizing the balance between water pro-jects and the dynamics found in nature. By minimizing conflicts between our pro-jects and nature, we will be minimizing the need for maintaining, repairing, and rebuilding our projects. This should minimize impacts to our environment, and it should minimize future costs to our pocketbooks through lowering government costs.

This new, improved definition of multi-objective floodplain management does not change its emphasis on combining broad objectives and developing plans through coordinated and intergovernmental efforts. It does, however, call for a change in the relationship among the players, or stakeholders. The conventional model of floodplain management is usually initiated by a federal program for flood-risk reduction or sometimes by a state program. The dynamics of the federal or state programs and regulations drive the local approach. The new model calls for a locally organized watershed council to take the lead in planning, with state and fed-eral agencies acting as coequal participants to help serve the council.[20]

Comprehensive Watershed Planning

In 1993, the Environmental Protection Agency announced that it was going to take a watershed perspective in addressing water-quality improvement and wetland protection. Part of the agency's incentive to adopt this new perspective was related to its expanding regulatory role over "nonpoint" or runoff sources of pollution and its supporting role with the Army Corps of Engineers to protect the nation's wetlands from fill. A 1987 amendment to the 1972 Clean Water Act added regulations for runoff pollution, which went into effect in 1994 to complement existing regulations to control site-specific, or "point," industrial, commercial, and sewage discharges. (Polluted runoff, or nonpoint pollution, is runoff from streets, parking lots, hillsides, agricultural lots, and logged and grazed areas.) This means that the quality of storm-water runoff has become a concern of the EPA, and therefore the influence of land management and land uses on water quality has become more relevant. Likewise, controversies over the best methods to restore and protect wetlands under Section 404 of the Clean Water Act require a broad perspective of land and resources management.[21]

In the meantime, the Soil Conservation Service, which historically has exercised a broad view of water resources management because it has worked with landowners on watershed conservation plans and projects, renewed its commitment to watershed-based planning. As a way of confirming its broad mission, it was renamed through an act of Congress the Natural Resources Conservation Service.[22] The service has been restructuring its Small Watershed Program (P.L. 566) so that it can better deliver broad ecosystem benefits, including habitat quality, recreation opportunities, and water and soil quality.[23] At the same time, the Bureau of Reclamation established that water conservation and management could not be separated from its traditional mission as a water supply agency. It saw its traditional water-supply development role as outdated and embraced a new water resources management mission.[24] The U.S. Army Corps of Engineers held internal workshops that concluded that the agency needs to focus on ecologically sustainable projects. The first multi-agency annual conferences named "Watershed" were held in 1993, and the administration released "The President's Clean Water Initiative," which calls for the restructuring of federal water resource programs for water pollution prevention and wetland protection based on state-managed watershed management planning.[25]

What Is Watershed-Based Planning?

Clearly, watershed planning is going to enjoy a popular revival into the next century—but what *is* watershed planning? There appear to be as many definitions of watershed-based planning as there are people who are interested in the concept.

A common theme of the definitions is that a watershed is a unit of planning whose physical features may include upstream and downstream portions, highlands, ridge lands, plateaus, valleys, floodplains, stream and river channels, riparian environments, and other wetlands. The interdependency of those geomorphological and ecological features is evaluated in order to arrive at land-use and resources management plans. Watershed plans may have different problem-solving purposes and focuses such as pollution control, flood-risk reduction, erosion control, storm-water management, ecological restoration, fish and wildlife habitat enhancement and protection, increasing recreation opportunities, water-supply development and conservation, navigation improvement, groundwater protection and recharge, and agricultural productivity, but the interrelationship among those purposes is recognized and reflected in the plan's recommended actions.

The United States has an interesting and almost bizarre history of watershed planning. When the country began to address watershed concerns in the 1930s, the government programs evolved so that one agency took on soil conservation, one managed forests, one dealt with hydroelectric concerns, and another took on water quality. Flooding in upper watersheds was located in a different agency from flooding in downstream areas. This division of watershed concerns among agencies has formed the basis of our issues over watershed management.[26]

The philosophical underpinnings of watershed planning have been evolving along with its planning conventions. Watershed plans have at times emphasized the treating of symptoms as opposed to understanding and correcting the cause of imbalances. We have spent too much time treating gullies rather than correcting the sources of gullies. We have spent too many resources adding fish habitat structures when we should have been restoring the structure of the rivers and floodplains. The contemporary view is that watershed management must be viewed more as process than as a discrete product.[27]

The concept of sustainability, which originated in the 1930s, is undergoing a renaissance. The National Academy of Sciences defines sustainability using process-oriented terms. The objective of sustainability, the academy states, is to preserve the productive integrity of natural and human resources that form the base on which stable economic conditions depend. The framework for dealing with the sustainable resources of watersheds includes identifying natural resource problems and concerns; identifying stakeholders; defining the relevant scale of the problems; specifying trade-offs among economic, social, and environmental considerations; exploring the values of stakeholders in deciding among the trade-offs; and identifying the best actions in achieving the desired balance among competing interests.[28]

Schools of Planning

Watershed-based planning has been influenced historically by a number of schools or concepts of planning that have been used with varying degrees of success—or lack of success. The major categories of planning concepts include comprehensive, urban comprehensive, integrated, incremental, integrated-incremental, and community advocacy. Plans can be sponsored by a federal agency, state agency, regional government, or a local agency or district. Often a particular government program structures the planning process, depending on whether the plan is oriented toward water pollution, flood-risk reduction, or a river greenway. A recent innovation in planning practice is to establish a team of agency representatives from all levels of government with equal responsibility for developing and implementing plans. The practices used to develop plans might include the rational method, in which goals and objectives are set; social, environmental, and economic inventories are made; alternative actions are evaluated; actions are selected; and citizen advisory committees are used. Other planning methods could include consensus planning, advocacy planning, and conflict resolution. The three components of planning—the type of plan, the level of government sponsoring the plan, and the planning method used—can be critical to determining the outcomes of any planning process.

The comprehensive school. A comprehensive watershed plan is generally regarded as an example of "rational planning," in which objectives are determined for a number of integrated and related management needs within a watershed planning unit. It is what most people have in mind when describing a watershed-based plan. A comprehensive watershed plan could consider siting residential, commercial, or industrial structures in a way that minimizes erosion and rain runoff from hard or impervious surfaces, encourages groundwater recharge, and protects waterways and wetlands from urban encroachment and pollutants. Steep or unstable slopes, valuable natural areas, natural and historical features, and wildlife habitat can be identified. Special zones can be designated based on unique and valuable resources or constraints. Land-use management and planning objectives can be designated for special areas, and policies, regulations, and design standards can then be adopted to implement the objectives. This process describes the field of environmental planning, which recognizes the need not only to include health and safety factors in our land-use plans, but also to integrate environmental quality and diversity into our planning efforts. Comprehensive planning can also include the social and economic needs of a community. Ian McHarg, a landscape architect, was one of the pioneers in this concept of environmental planning, and his book *Design with Nature* is considered a classic in this field.[29]

The basic steps of developing a comprehensive plan include inventorying the existing land uses in a watershed and mapping its natural features and resources. The landscape inventory distinguishes areas that are subject to natural hazards such as landslides, erosion, floods, and earthquakes, as well as natural amenities. Computerized overlay maps developed through Geographic Information Systems (GIS), of natural factors, hazard zones, special features, and social and economic factors, have helped popularize the use of comprehensive plans.

Ian McHarg provides an example of comprehensive watershed planning in the Potomac River Basin in Maryland. He inventoried the basin's geology, physiography, hydrology, soils, plant associations, wildlife, water problems, cultural resources, mineral resources, water resources, and land uses. He analyzed the way in which the resources helped determine—or constrain—different land uses, the compatibility of different land and resource uses, and the consequences of land uses on resources. In his plan, water management "competes" with other resources requiring management and is not the plan's central focus.

Another well-known comprehensive watershed-management plan is the one developed for the Brandywine watershed in Pennsylvania in the late 1960s. The plan came complete with an inventory of hydrologic conditions, water quality, history, land use, population projections, real estate and land-value studies, and attitudinal surveys of residents. It contained a statement of principles or objectives common to city planning processes, as well as hydrologic, social, economic, legal, and government-related objectives. The implementation plan was developed to meet hydrologic and social needs along with the constraints of the legal, governmental, and economic realities.[30]

Floodplain management is considered a subcategory of watershed-management planning and has remained a narrowly focused field for the most part, but at times it has been the central objective on which comprehensive plans have been developed. The New England River Basins Commission plan for the Connecticut River is cited as an example of a flood management plan that has the perspective of a comprehensive plan in that it balances regional environmental quality, fish and wildlife, recreational needs, and other general social values in the planning of flood-control alternatives.[31]

Be aware that "comprehensive" means different things to different agencies, divisions and offices within an agency, and individuals. An inspection of annotated literature searches on watershed-planning studies and reports reveals a significant number of "comprehensive" studies and plans by all different levels of governments, some of which analyze broad resource and social needs and some of which focus on the rationalization of specific projects. One federal agency's plan to construct a multipurpose dam for water supply, flood control, and recreational benefits was called comprehensive but did not contain watershed-management objectives; provisions for historical preservation, transportation, or the needs of adjacent communities; or community growth objectives—all important issues for the local population.[32]

Comprehensive planning can recognize the potential relationship between water-management planning and the comprehensive city-planning process that is concerned with population growth, business districts, transportation, utilities, etc. Water-resources management can be included in the general plans that help establish local zoning for future growth patterns based on water-supply availability, water quality, and flood hazards.

Water planners have participated in the urban comprehensive planning processes, but the literature does not seem to include much discussion by the water planners about such experiences. This, no doubt, is a function of the rarity with which it occurs. Planners who prepare community general plans tend to leave substantive water-supply and floodplain management and watershed management issues to water districts and flood-control districts. There are some examples of watershed management and water-supply needs being integrated into local planning processes. One such example is the North Marin County Water Management District in Novato, California, which is required to review all development plans sent to the county planning department to determine if they conform to county planning development controls and design standards related to water-supply and management needs.

The incremental school. The school of incremental planning is represented by its chief proponent, Charles Lindbloom, who describes this form of planning as "the science of muddling through."[33] While comprehensive planning may be referred to as a form of rational planning because it entails systematically setting goals and identifying and evaluating alternatives, incremental planning is based on the idea that plans are better realized through decentralized "bargaining" processes. Plans are constructed through a mixture of intuition, experience, and a series of consultations and are tailored to solve a particular need or react to a particular social or environtmental context. Incremental planners tend to be critical of comprehensive planning in part because the mathematical, economic, or scientific model used to weigh alternatives may create the illusion of a scientific and objective plan and the process often entails a top-down planning processes. The relevance of incremental planning is greatly influenced by the fact that decision makers use their knowledge of the incremental steps taken to the present in order to map intelligently the next steps to take.[34]

The school of incremental planning contains a variety of practitioners and proponents who advocate the value of "reflection in action," by which practitioners reflect on what they are doing and make adjustments to future actions and plans. Implementation requires continual interaction with the clients of plans, and project design solutions are proposed to focus on what is needed rather than what is wrong. Every solution contains the seed of its own change and improvement.[35, 36]

Despite the attraction of comprehensive planning as a natural fit for the accomplishment of watershed-based planning, scholars who have observed water planning over the years have leaned toward incremental planning as the most practical approach to actually accomplishing watershed management. Abe Wolman, a professor at Johns Hopkins University and a respected expert in water-resources management practices, reviewed fifty years of river basin management and planning and concluded that it is not a rational science but an art. He observes that piecemeal plans have had more success in being implemented, especially for water pollution control. Evaluations or adequate "post-audits" of comprehensive planning of regional river basins are not done enough, but implementation rates appear low. His conclusion is that watershed or basin planning must be approached on an individual basis because no two rivers are alike with respect to their social, economic, and political environments.[37] The use of "optimizing" strategies common to comprehensive plans, in which plan outcomes are compared to stated goals, are found to be too simplistic for many planning scholars. Those reviewers suggest replacing that method with open-ended evaluations. They argue that planning should simultaneously aim to reduce risks, as in floodplain planning, and increase public learning. Solutions should be tried on a small scale rather than the large scale of comprehensive plans. Decentralization can reduce risks and encourage the adoption of solutions on a case-by-case basis organized around flexible planning methods rather than rigid channels of tasks and authority.[38] Gilbert White, another respected academic and observer of watershed and floodplain planning efforts, is an advocate for what he calls an "integrated but incremental" planning approach. He also recognizes the need to view the planning problem as one in which we borrow from different situations.[39]

White provides a vision of a water management process that borrows from various planning techniques within both the comprehensive and the incremental schools. His philosophical approach is that the aims of a water management plan should be multiple and should consciously recognize evolving public preferences. The means of obtaining objectives should be multiple and should take into account a full range of alternatives, including scientific research. The planning should encourage decentralization of choice among individuals and local agencies. The system should be alert to distinctive hydrologic units or drainage basins but should not attempt to conform the social process of choice to the physical boundaries of the watershed.

White uses the Northeastern Illinois Metropolitan Area Planning Commission Water Resource Plan, prepared in the late 1960s, as an example to illustrate this analytical process.[40] Instead of using a single projection of future water use to be compared with available supply, that water plan used a series of projections or forecasts based on different assumptions about changes in technology, water conservation, demand patterns, floodwater storage, floodplain regulations, recharge of groundwater, and so on. This system of planning began with a definition of goals for metropolitan development, such as identifying alternative patterns of land use, managing floods within a land-use context, and providing recreation. A practical range of management measures were identified, descriptive and quantitative social evaluations of the measures were provided, and land and water management were recognized to be interdependent in the making of land-use plans. The plan was not a single plan for water development; rather it offered a broad strategy in which the principal criteria for selection of projects rejected a "straight-line" strategy of analysis. Heavy emphasis was placed on keeping as many alternatives open in the future as possible.

Although this planning concept has the flexibility that should have worked toward successful results, in that particular case it produced mixed results and did not bring about the coordinated regional response the planners had hoped for. Scattered cities in the planning area took part in an uneven adoption of the different features of the plan. A critical constraint for success in that particular planning case, which is common to all the planning methods discussed here, is the lack of training in the engineering professions in complex planning processes. Nonetheless, in my view as a practitioner in watershed restoration, White's vision of the future for planning strategies is now taking shape in these hybridized forms.

One of the benefits that has surfaced from grassroots urban waterway groups forming a national network is a sharing of experiences with planning schools and methods. The experiences coming out of conferences and workshops of the member organizations of the Coalition to Restore Urban Waters (CRUW) give low ratings to the tradition of comprehensive and rational planning methods and a decided pref-

erence for incremental planning approaches. Those organizations have not completely ruled out comprehensive planning, but of the nonprofit groups in CRUW
workshops involved in water basin planning, only one has made a long-term commitment to and retained a positive attitude toward a regional comprehensive planning effort. That one case is described later in this chapter and entails a unique
political context.

The commonly stated difficulties with rational and comprehensive water basin
planning include the long unpaid time commitments required of citizen groups,
which are often followed by the plans not being implemented. A frequent criticism
includes the large sums of money that can be committed to large-scale inventories
when inventories could be made more simple and locally specific and could thereby
free personnel to do more evaluations of projects and actions.

Organizations that practice incremental planning and tend to be more project focused than watershed-planning focused are criticized for not acting within a coordinated water basin context. In practice, however, incremental planners are usually
acting with a thorough knowledge of water basin stakeholders, resource management conflicts, and public priorities for their watersheds of interest. These groups
are inventing hybrids of planning methods, which will be described in greater detail
toward the end of this chapter under "Action Planning School."

Community-based planning. The community-based schools of planning are characterized by the use of methods such as advocacy planning, consensus planning,
and conflict resolution. These methods have their origins in 1960s urban planning
strategies, but they appeared in water resources and environmental planning in the
1970s. Initially, citizen organizations that were in conflict with federal or state water
projects, forestry, land management, or local development schemes revived these
methods to change the outcome of proposed government projects. The methods
have since been increasingly prescribed by state legislatures and local governments
and agencies to reach political consensus on resource management and project
plans. It is interesting to note that some early planning literature refers to these
methods as components of the "radical" planning school, but they are now seen as
pragmatic, mainstream techniques to reduce political conflicts and build the political base required to take action, as well as a critical aspect of plan implementation.
In fact, these planning methods are no longer associated with their origins in community-based planning but are now being applied by all levels of government. These
methods are used in rational-comprehensive as well as incremental plans.

Advocacy planning uses the strategy of providing local people who have a strong
stake in the outcome of a plan or proposed project (one group of stakeholders) with
their own preferred plan. This preferred plan is presented to other publics (other
stakeholders) including agencies that will influence adoption of the plan or will integrate important parts of the plan into one that gets adopted. Advocacy planning is
usually initiated by disaffected stakeholders who feel unrepresented in a planning
process. Citizen organizations or local districts or governments typically hire

experts to help them develop and represent their own plans. Advocacy planning does not have to be tied to situations involving disaffected stakeholders, however. In some situations, enlightened agencies have helped fund citizens' chosen experts to help guide the development of both planning processes and plan options. (Examples of these are described in the section that follows.) The agencies do this to break impasses over plans and encourage consensus.

Consensus planning is best characterized as equalizing the relationships among different levels of government agencies and between those agencies and non-governmental organizations. It assumes that even though a sponsor for the planning effort may be a federal agency, for example, the other stakeholders will equally influence the nature of the plan, thereby allowing for a genuine consensus to form around what the plan is. Consensus planning is usually sought when it is important to policy makers to arrive at an implementable plan. Agencies accustomed to the control inherent in traditional comprehensive planning are sometimes afraid that they will lose that control in consensus planning. Other fears are that the process will take forever and be expensive, and that even a consensus may not result in implementation. If consensus planning is structured correctly within given time limits, and stakeholders have the expertise they need to become effective, legitimate players in the planning process, this method should produce implementable plans in less time than traditional rational planning.

Conflict resolution can be thought of as a category of consensus planning in that it offers a proven technique for resolving differences and arriving at consensus.

The sections that follow describe examples of all these planning schools and planning methods as they have been practiced by different levels of government. Certain types of plans and planning methods have a tendency to be associated with certain levels of government. However, we are entering an era in which those conventions will probably break down as new schools and planning methods evolve.

Federally Sponsored River Basin Planning

Historical lessons. In regard to this latest embrace of watershed-based planning, federal agencies may be coming full circle to where they were during the 1930s through the 1970s. As early as the 1920s the Army Corps of Engineers was requested by Congress to make general plans for river basins, known as 308 Reports after House Document 308 published in 1927. The reports brought together water experts from all over the nation to exchange technical information, and the benefits of studying river basins gained scientific credibility. The period of 1933–43 was characterized by a flurry of activity in water resources planning, including creation of the National Planning Board (1933–34), the National Resources Board (1934–35), the National Resources Committee (1935–39), and the National Resources Planning Board (1939–43). These organizations were involved with the analysis of river basin problems and the development of multipurpose river basin plans. Between 1939 and 1954, the Federal Interagency River Basin Committee coordinated the planning activities of the federal agencies involved in water resources and provided for the

cooperative preparation of river basin surveys. From 1945 to 1950 regional interagency committees were established for the Columbia River system, the Pacific
Southwest, the Arkansas-White-Red river basins, and the New York–New England
basins to provide integrated river basin plans.

In 1950, after a decade and a half of aggressive flood-control works committing
large federal expenditures and involving interagency turf battles, the Hoover Commission recommended forming a Water Development and Use Service in the Department of the Interior to consolidate the federal agencies involved in water
resources. The president's Water Resources Policy Commission in 1950 recommended a system of national water planning in which all levels of government
would participate. An independent board created by Congress would review the
plans and insure that water projects were economically feasible.

In the 1950s, the division of missions between upper watershed-management
programs in the Soil Conservation Service and lower basin flood-control projects in
the Army Corps exacerbated the fragmentation of water basin planning. The Eisen-
hower Advisory Commission on Water Resources Policy recommended in 1956 that
river basin regions be established as the planning units for water resources programs and that national water policy be coordinated from an executive office. In
1956 the Senate Public Works Committee gave the Army Corps complete authority
to undertake a detailed, comprehensive survey of the Delaware River basin. The
Corps initiated interagency coordination by inviting the participation of other federal agencies and state and local governments and in 1960 published a basin-wide
water resources plan including flood control, urban water supply, recreation, and
pollution control.

Despite this historical concern for water basin–based planning, water resources
historians describe an ongoing congressional opposition to merging and coordinating the functions of federal water agencies. (In 1965 the seventh attempt to do so
since World War I failed.) Executive water policy and coordinating boards were
short lived and the ability of the voluntary Interagency River Basin Committee
(abolished in 1954) to coordinate agency programs was limited by lack of authority,
its chiefly advisory role, and lukewarm congressional support. The regional interagency river basin committees were not staffed, relations with state and local governments were informal, and their limited authority made it difficult for them to
resolve water issues.[41-43] Also, the narrowly construed engineering cultures of the
water agencies were not conducive to the development of integrated, comprehensive plans.

With the arrival of the 1960s came the heyday of comprehensive water basin
planning. After more than half a century of efforts to obtain national water planning
legislation, the Water Resources Planning Act of 1965 became law. The act provided
for a national Water Resources Council to derive water policy, organize regionally
based river basin commissions, and provide financial assistance to the states to support state-level water planning.

National basin commissions were to be developed on a voluntary basis to coordinate the chief players in water resources management, including the local water supply administration, sewage and flood-control districts, state water resource agencies, and the Army Corps, Bureau of Reclamation, Soil Conservation Service, and Environmental Protection Agency. Other key players were the Office of Management and Budget, which prepares the president's budget, and the Senate and House publics works committees. The membership of the river basin commissions was designated as interested federal agencies, states in the region, and any appropriate interstate or international agencies in the region, with a chairman of each commission to be appointed by the president. The commissions were directed to serve as the principal agency for the coordination of federal, state, interstate, local, and nongovernmental organizations for the development of water and related land resources in the basin area. They were to prepare and keep updated coordinated plans and evaluations of alternative plans for water and related resources development. They were to undertake studies and data collection needed to support plans.

This "revolution" in watershed-based planning directives was later complemented by the Clean Water Act of 1972, which initiated a nationwide program of "area-wide" or regional water-quality management plans under its Section 208. Section 209 of the same act required preparation of river basin plans (referred to as Level B plans) for all twenty-one river basins of the United States. At the same time, the Coastal Zone Management Act passed in 1972 encouraged comprehensive planning for coastal areas in the United States. The Army Corps reentered the comprehensive planning arena with its urban studies program, also in 1972. The studies were once again broad-scoped water resource management efforts in which the Corps played a lead role in coordinating committees of agencies and entities with an interest in urban water issues. By 1977, forty-five urban studies had been initiated.[44]

This golden age of federally sponsored, comprehensive, integrated river basin and watershed-based planning had expired by the early 1980s. The General Accounting Office and consultants prepared evaluations on these federal efforts for Congress and the Water Resources Council. They made recommendations that should be heeded by any future efforts to formally reestablish federally sponsored comprehensive watershed planning.[45]

The value of the river basin commission planning was that the commissions provided forums for networking and coordination among key players in water resources. The evaluators concluded, however, that they did not achieve their legislative objective to serve as the principal coordinators, comprehensive planners, policy makers, and priority setters.

Only six regional basin commissions were formed in the northern portion of the country; less than half of the country opted to try to establish commissions. The commissions were not found to produce meaningful, implementable plans, and the priorities and schedules of those plans represented an unusable, confused listing of studies and projects.[46] What went wrong?

The perspective of the states on the coordinating river basin commissions was that they were a place they could network with other agencies and benefit from technical information, but in their view, the states themselves are the real center of water planning. The states set their own water resource management priorities, and then they ask their state congressional delegation for the federal funding they need. They certainly don't need other states telling them what their priorities or needs are. State authorities had serious disagreements with the presidential appointees who headed the commissions over what the powers of the commissions were. As one observer put it, "Why go through the Level B [river basin commission] process or the Water Resources Council if you can get things done by going directly to Congress?"[47]

One of the key players, the Army Corps, held the view that it was spending about $78 million annually (1981 figure) on water project planning and had its own criteria for evaluating water projects and project priorities. A network of water planners sounded fine, but it believed that the Army Corps was the actual national water planner. The Environmental Protection Agency's view was that priorities for water quality–related projects were established internally after proposals were forwarded to it from the states; it considered that basin commissions and their plans had little to do with the EPA. Many agencies didn't bother to send staffs or sent low to midlevel personnel who didn't have much authority to represent the agencies.[48, 49]

The view of Congress was that the priorities of various federal agencies couldn't be compared with each other within a river basin commission because, after all, the different agencies' priorities were actually established in separate policy and appropriations committees. Congress was less than thrilled by the use of the Water Resources Council (WRC) to promote an aggressive executive role in determining national water policy, epitomized by President Carter's "water project hit list" in 1971. That list designated the water projects the WRC found lacking in regional or national benefits.

The Office of Management and Budget (OMB) reported to the General Accounting Office (GAO) that it did not use river basin plans or studies for establishing national water budget priorities because it establishes its own priorities. From the outset the OMB saw the Water Resources Council as an intruder on its turf. Historians report that when OMB could not prevent the WRC from coming into being, it acted to preserve its role as the national water policy maker to delegate to the council the responsibility—but not the authority—to develop federal standards and policies. The council ended up with the capacity to influence water policy but no power to review individual water projects or fix the criteria used for evaluations by federal agencies.[50, 51]

Several recommendations were made to Congress by the General Accounting Office to help offset some of the institutional problems. The GAO recommended that monetary incentives should be used to assure meaningful state participation in the commissions. Grants to states for water programs should be conditioned on state membership in commissions. More important, the GAO noted that the commissions could not be effective without requiring that the project and program priorities they established be integrated into the federal budget process. They further specified that comparisons of the relative priority of each project with other projects within a regional commission should be integrated into the budget review process and that the review should be a requirement of congressional project authorization.

In the meantime, in spite of Section 209 of the 1972 Clean Water Act's explicit recognition of the relationship area-wide water-quality planning should have with the river basin planning efforts, research conducted for the EPA in the 1970s showed that generally the programs had little to do with each other. What have become known as 208 watershed plans have acquired notoriety for being "shelf plans" with low implementation rates. These regionally coordinated plans designed to address polluted runoff or nonpoint sources of pollution were intended to coordinate the many local water districts and agencies through regional governments. These regional institutions or "governments" were often an unwelcome intrusion on local water districts' turfs. Both limited funding for the implementation stages and limited federal authority to compel local governments and districts to adopt land use and management measures to reduce runoff contributed to the low success rates of the Section 208 plans.[52, 53]

The phasing out of the 1970s model cities and other urban-oriented federal programs and disagreements between the EPA and the Army Corps on how to manage water-quality problems contributed to ending the Army Corps' short foray into urban water problems begun with its urban studies program in 1972. This dead-end experiment was an honest effort at a planning innovation in which the urban studies program required an intergovernmental planning process with multi-objective goal setting. A researcher who observed the efforts of the Army Corps to carry out this program noted that once a federal agency works with local interests, it begins to realize how pluralistic the public is. An agency must have a high level of sophistication with multi-objective planning problems in order to produce a pluralistic plan—and the Army Corps did not have the kind of staff expertise to achieve something like that.[54]

Successful federally directed watershed-based plans, given the historical record, are anomalies. Among them is the Tennessee Valley Authority established by Congress in 1933, the most ambitious action ever taken by the federal government to manage water resources on a river basin basis and one that has never been duplicated. The TVA was established as a government corporation with broad powers to plan, construct, and operate projects for all purposes including power, water supply, water quality, flood control, and recreation. While the agency certainly built its share of conventional water structures, it eventually became a national leader in replacing a structural flood-control program with a floodplain management program. Engineers and geographers worked side by side to innovate community-based floodplain management and regulation. Multi-objective floodplain management and watershed management can trace their early origins to this agency. Ironically, some water resource analysts tie the lack of similar integrated basin approaches to the success of the TVA experiment. They describe instances of other federal water resources agencies collaborating to prevent any other regionally based competitive agencies from further intruding on their turf.[55]

A type of federally established river basin agency with marginal success is the interstate compact commissions started on the Delaware River in 1961 and on the Susquehanna River in 1970. These compacts granted far-reaching powers, the authority to finance, construct, and maintain projects and the authority to allocate water among participating states. Establishment of such compact commissions requires approval of both the Congress and the member states, and no new ones have been established since the Susquehanna. Evaluations of these compact commissions have shown that despite their substantial legal authority, the political feasibility of using that authority has been a different matter, with the commissions only cautiously asserting their powers.[56]

Recent developments. The most recent experience we have with regional comprehensive-rational water planning is the EPA-administered National Estuary Program established in 1987 as part of the Clean Water Act. It appears that the intention of the program designers may have been to avoid the vulnerabilities of past comprehensive water-quality planning programs, but their efforts failed to address the necessary issues. As of 1995, twenty-one regionally based National Estuary Programs (NEPs) had been established for coastal bays, sounds, and lagoons. Each NEP is directed by representatives of affected local agencies, business leaders, and citizen organizations. Formal approval of a plan is required by public participants, the regional Environmental Protection Agency, the governor of the state, and the U.S. Environmental Protection Agency. Committees are established to implement the plans.

The jury is still out on the effectiveness of this planning model. From the perspectives of some key public participants in the NEPs, the program has had value because of the credibility and visibility federal involvement lends to the importance of estuary management problems. On the other hand, the planning process is described as cumbersome and difficult for citizen participants because of the many committees and meetings and planning times as long as to five years. The onerous and bureaucratic processes and report preparation greatly dampened public enthusiasm and support for the process because of the significant amount of unpaid time required of public participants.

The program suffered serious setbacks when congressional program budget cuts began at the implementation phases for a number of the NEPs. The most popular features of the program for public participants were the small public education, public involvement, and environmental restoration project grants provided to build public awareness and participation in the estuaries.

Interviews with participating nonprofit organizations revealed that some of those organizations are engaging in their own site-specific planning for estuaries because the NEPs are too broad to be useful for determining implementation strategies. Some fault the plans for being too general because the documents need to be nonthreatening in a broad political arena. Some NEPs are viewed as "status quo" documents.

While the planning processes used were designed with an effort to use a "bottom-to-top" approach for determining policies and priorities, the process was ultimately controlled by the staff of a large federal agency, who ran the committees, issued the reports, and directed the planning process.

What is different about the 1990s revival of federal interest in watershed-based planning that will distinguish it from this less than encouraging history? The river basin commissions and executive directives called for integrating water quality, wildlife habitat, water supply, flood control, navigation, etc., into "comprehensive" plans, just as we are calling for now. Citizen participation was substantial in many of the commissions. In many respects the country's philosophical inclination in the 1960s and 1970s toward an activist government, government planning, substantial program budgets, and solving urban and environmental problems provided an ideal climate—a political advantage not present in the 1990s.

Recommendations and models for the future. Generally, the institutional memory of past federally sponsored watershed planning efforts appearfs to be weak among a number of sectors of the "water community." The challenge of the future will be to evaluate that history as a part of the future design of new watershed programs at all levels of government.

The advent of the 1993 Mississippi River floods forced reevaluations of the directions of federal flood-damage reduction programs. A widely respected report issued for the White House on needed institutional responses for that catastrophe and national floodplain management in general recommended reactivating the Water Resources Council, reestablishing basin commissions (which were all phased out in 1981), and designing federal programs around multiple-objective planning. The report offers a notable contrast to the instances of institutional memory loss within the Washington, D.C., beltway. It acknowledges both the need to reestablish federal coordination of water planning efforts and the need for watershed-based planning while acknowledging past experiences associated with those efforts. It clearly states, "Deficiencies inherent in the original WRC which established a command-and-control, top-down approach to achieve consistency in federal water resources activities should not be repeated."[57]

That White House task-force report, *Sharing the Challenge,* proposes establishing basin commissions administered by state and federal cochairs, in which the role of federal agencies would be to support state initiatives, funding would be shared by state and federal governments, and the focus would be "results oriented" and "collaborative," not on oversight. The report also recommends that incentives programs should be provided to encourage state involvement in floodplain management and that primary responsibility for floodplain management should be assigned to the states, with the federal government offering guidance and technical and financial assistance.

The revival of interest in watershed-based programs, the national floods of 1993, the White House task-force report, and the redefinition of government missions bring national water programs to a critical juncture at the end of the 1990s. The task-force report reminds us that we threw the baby out with the bath water when the country suspended national coordination of federal water programs through the Water Resources Council and abandoned water basin planning. Federal agencies continue to fail to carry out common sense executive orders not to fund or locate projects in flood hazardous areas. There is no coordinated or central direction for federal agencies, some of which have conflicting missions, each one striking out on its own to carve out what it hopes will be the turf it needs to survive through austere budgets. Critical hydrologic and water-quality data needed for plans and prospects are in danger of being lost in unwise budget cutting. Perennial recommendations made by federal interagency task forces to improve government response to flooding remain unacted upon and without authority to guide action.[58] The national response to wetland protection and clean water needs continues to be in great flux.

While the evaluations of the Water Resources Council and the river basin commissions identified needed reforms in their structures and the nature of their functions, the basic need for multidisciplinary, coordinated, collaborative actions on a watershed basis by cooperating levels of government has not been at issue among the water professionals doing the evaluations. In the field of environmental restoration we hold central to the development of successful restoration methods the need to experiment in the field and record our failures. The more mistakes we make, the better our practice evolves. Given this view, we cannot afford to ignore the benefits to our experience of past errors in planning methods. These errors certainly do not signal to us the abandonment of watershed planning.

There are successful models of federally sponsored planning initiatives that can provide guidance for the future. Federal agencies have different planning traditions and cultures. The Army Corps of Engineers, the Bureau of Reclamation, and the Environmental Protection Agency have historically tended to manage top-down programs. Their organizational structures of many district and field offices notwithstanding, their planning and regulatory programs come from a tradition of national standards for determining plans and programs and a perspective of state and local entities as funding and implementation partners of federal projects or programs. The Soil Conservation Service, U.S. Fish and Wildlife Service, Tennessee Valley Authority, and National Park Service have generally practiced a more bottom-to-top form of planning and program management, by which projects are initiated at local levels and decision making is generally located there. Important technical expertise and policy guidance are provided by the federal agencies. The 1990s federal programs have begun making a movement in that direction.

There have been instances in which federal agencies with a top-to-bottom model for planning have suspended normal planning practices and designed an approach to serve the particular problem or case at hand based on local initiatives. The Charles River nonstructural floodplain management plan is an often cited example of the Army Corps' ability to work within a watershed context and follow local initiative to use a land-use planning approach for flood-damage reduction.

The Charles River Watershed Plan, encompassing twenty-seven cities and towns along eighty miles of river in the Boston metropolitan area, is a well-known case of coordinating great numbers of local, state, and federal agencies under the leadership of the U.S. Army Corps of Engineers to manage flood problems. It is a rare and celebrated case in which federal leadership was instrumental in using land acquisition and local land regulations to provide natural valley storage of floodwaters in the floodplains. The federal government was authorized by Congress to purchase lands, and management is shared with state and private entities. A Citizens Advisory Committee is composed of representatives from municipal, industrial, educational, recreational, and real estate interests as part of the coordinating committee of federal and state agencies that drew up the plan. The Citizens Advisory Committee initiated and reviewed project plans, made recommendations, and organized local informational meetings. An already existing citizens' group, the Charles River Watershed Association, which was formed as a nonprofit organization in 1965 for the protection of the natural resources of the river, became an active advocate of the plan. Under contract with the Corps, the association circulated tabloids explaining the plan to the public.[59, 60]

The Soil Conservation Service has a tradition of bottom-to-top planning, and a number of its projects can be studied as planning models for other federal agencies. In one case, the SCS took on a regional, intergovernmental planning role to head the Salt Creek project in northeast Illinois. Following a devastating 1972 flood, the state made plans for structural flood-control structures. DuPage County, however, objected to the structural approach, which violated its natural resources protection and management policies, and it was joined by six communities that endorsed the need for a different approach. The SCS helped the county form a Salt Creek project task force, which included the state of Illinois, the Metropolitan Sanitary District of Greater Chicago, the Cook County Forest Preserve District, four villages, four park districts, and a soil and water conservation district. The task force resulted in the implementation of floodplain zoning, land acquisition, relocations from hazard areas, and development of new recreational facilities. A local floodplain ordinance prohibited any further building or rebuilding on the floodplain and required residential developers in other areas to provide complete water retention and storage for the one-in-100-year storm.[61, 62]

A seemingly low-profile effort that has nonetheless received high marks for its implementation success for watershed-management has been Coordinated Resource Management Plans or CRMPs, as they are referred to. These were started in the 1980s to provide a new cooperative vehicle for federal agencies in particular to provide technical and financial assistance to local entities. The CRMPs may be initiated by a private organization such as a cattlemen's association, a land trust, a resource conservation or soil and water conservation district, a state agency, or even a federal agency. The CRMP process is a collaborative one, in which a team is formed to solve a particular problem—for example, to protect riparian buffer zones from grazing, reduce bank erosion from development, modify watershed hydrology through land practices, or set aside ecological reserves. The CRMP is an ongoing model of private and public planning that should be practiced on a wider scale. The federal agency perceives its role in the CRMP process not as a lead agency pursuing a regulation or project, but as a coequal collaborator to assist a team of agency and private interests to collectively reach a result. The CRMP process also receives high marks from private land interests that are traditional antagonists to federal resource management programs, such as cattle ranchers, because the collaborative process builds on common needs and objectives.[60]

The CRMP process has tended to attract federal agencies such as the Natural Resources Conservation Service, the Bureau of Land Management, and the Forest Service, whose planning and cultural traditions involve interaction with landowners. To encourage all the water-related federal agencies to develop experience and skills working in teams on multi-objective projects, the Tennessee Valley Authority, with the support of the Association of State Floodplain Managers initiated federal multi-objective management workshops beginning in the late 1980s. The workshop organizers selected locales with a combination of water management problems, and they literally bused in representatives from a full array of government agencies to collaborate on teams with local officials to solve the problems.

The positive nature of this form of team planning with local entities has not been lost on the federal agencies. A great deal of ground has been covered during the past ten years to build acceptance of team and interdisciplinary approaches to planning. The concept of multi-objective management and planning has gained wide coverage and acceptance within the federal agencies. A list of federal programs designed to provide technical and financial assistance for locally initiated watershed projects and plans includes: the U.S. Fish and Wildlife Service's Fisher Across America program, Partners in Wildlife program, Lands Habitat Assistance and Restoration program, and riparian-wetland initiative for the 1990s; the Forest Service and Bureau of Land Management's Bring Back the Natives fisheries restoration program; the Department of Agriculture's Wetland Reserve Program, Farms for the Future program, Forestry Incentives Program, and other technical assistance programs conducted with resource and conservation districts; the National Park Service's Rivers, Trails and Conservation Assistance Program; the Army Corps' Floodplain Management Services program; and the Environmental Protection Agency's Near Coastal Waters grant program and support of volunteer monitoring and watershed adoption programs. Regional programs include the Department of the Interior and the Office of Surface Mining's Appalachian Clean Streams Initiative and the TVA, Office of Surface Mining, Army Corps, National Biological Service, National Park Service, U.S. Geological Survey, and Natural Resources Conservation Service's collaboration with the Restore Our Southern Rivers program.[64] The Americorps National Service program attracted substantial involvement from the National Resources Conservation Service and the EPA to form partnerships with nonprofit organizations to accomplish watershed restoration projects in 1995 and 1996.

Two particularly notable recent developments are the Urban Resources Partnership. This partnership is specifically designed to encourage collaborations among federal agencies and to provide a bottom-up approach for conservation assistance to communities. Funding and staffs are combined from the Environmental Protection Agency; the USDA Cooperative State Research, Education, and Extension Service, the Forest Service, and the Natural Resources Conservation Service of USDA; the Department of the Interior Fish and Wildlife Service and National Park Service; and the U.S. Department of Housing and Urban Development. Staffs representing the agencies are located in one office and are now established in ten cities in the country. Local organizations are defining the partnerships and projects for these federal assistance centers. The offices help local NGOs (nongovernmental organizations) and agencies locate a number of federal programs with "one-stop shopping," and scarce federal dollars are expected to go further because they will be combined with local dollars. One of the goals of federal administrators with this program is to reduce traditional competitions among the federal agencies and produce an environment that fosters cross-agency cooperation.

These federal initiatives are still new, and the record they develop in respect to watershed management is still forming. The country's most substantive experience with orienting federal programs to community-based programs occurred with the Office of Economic Opportunity programs of the latter 1960s and early 1970s. I am not aware of policy makers reviewing the successes and failures of those programs or how our knowledge of them could help us structure federal involvement in watershed-based programs in the late 1990s and into the next century. While policy makers may not draw connections between the 1990s watershed planning and restoration movement and the social and economic poverty programs of the 1960s and 1970s, the current movement and those programs share a common objective of better empowering local communities to address problems. I was surprised to learn, after researching the few innovative cases in which federally supported, nonstructural, flood-damage reduction programs replaced conventional structural projects, that a common factor helping determine the outcome of these unusual cases was the influence of individuals and community groups who were part of the Community Employment Training Act (CETA), Community Action, and VISTA programs.[65]

The challenge for these federal programs, many of which are only a few years old, will be to evolve beyond the scope of local grant programs that may emphasize small parcel restoration efforts to programs that at the same time support watershed-based planning efforts that help locals articulate watershed priorities. Another challenge is to draw states into supporting local projects, supporting local and regional inventories, establishing priorities for resource management, and increasing use of multilevel government teams. As partnerships extend, larger, contiguous, and longer-term restoration efforts can result in greater ecological protection. Likewise, the cultivation of more stable, longer-term commitments among partners can perhaps support a secure local restoration jobs base. Finally, the Army Corps of Engineers needs to join the Bureau of Reclamation, the Natural Resources Conservation Service, the EPA, and the National Park Service in redefining its conventional civil works program in a way that makes it easier for its engineers and planners to be team players in watershed management.

State, Regional, and Local Watershed Planning

In response to the disastrous 1993 Mississippi River floods, the White House task-force report written to guide federal reactions stated: "The State should be the entity best able to coordinate the overall watershed and floodplain management activities occurring within its borders." The report recommends a shift toward a state role from what is now primarily a federal-local relationship. It describes a situation in which state involvement in floodplain management is highly variable, with, for example, only sixteen of the states regulating floodplain levees, while twenty-six have watershed-management standards that go beyond minimum federal requirements established under the National Flood Insurance Act. The report finds that "active involvement of the states is necessary to develop flood-reduction projects consistent with multiple floodplain and watershed-management goals as well as other state natural resource and economic goals."[66]

The watershed management planning literature and studies of the recent past—whether the perennial federal interagency floodplain-management task-force reports, the 1994 President's Report on Clean Water Initiatives, or investigations by academics—advocate the importance of strong state watershed-management leadership. They advance the state level of government as the level where incentives and sanctions need to be developed to provide the political climate necessary for local and regional entities to act as effective partners in watershed programs.

While watershed-planning literature concerns itself with different themes, the experts observing watershed-management needs generally support the ideas that watershed-management issues—i.e., sewage treatment, storm-water management, public works projects such as bridges and culverts, encroachment onto floodplains and into stream channels, erosion control, etc.—are local ones. Better intrajurisdictional coordination is needed across local government lines to integrate and implement management programs. The states, which are generally better at avoiding the special local interests and representing broader public interests, and which have unique constitutional powers, are the best level to establish guiding policies through incentives, regulations, and sanctions. The role of regional agencies to coordinate across state lines is seen as desirable but, as described in the previous section, has a limited record of success. Even regional agencies working within state boundaries have great political vulnerability because they are faced with compromising with (and potentially threatening the turfs of) a number of local governments, as well as state entities.[67-73]

Casebooks and conference proceedings on innovations in watershed, floodplain, and river corridor management proliferated in the late 1980s and early 1990s.[74-79] Evaluating those reports for what planning processes appear to be the most successful under different conditions provides some interesting insights on what is going to work best in the future. Strong state statutes seem to bring the most substantive results for watershed-management efforts and offer the option of effective regional planning efforts. Locally based efforts that use nonprofit organizations as the intergovernmental coordinators and as negotiators between landowners and public agencies seem to be able to succeed even under weak federal, state, or regional government influence—as well as to benefit from strong influence from those levels.

State-Sponsored Plans

While it is not practical to review all the examples of substantive state watershed-management programs in those casebooks, it is helpful to review a range of examples for the purpose of describing what appear to be some trends. Successful water-quality protection, wetland and river restoration, floodplain management, greenway protection, and land acquisition programs can be attributed to state efforts through the South Florida Water Management District; the Tahoe Regional Planning Agency and the California State Water Resources Control Board; local governments under the Wisconsin stream and lake shoreline protection program, the Atlanta Regional Commission for the Chattahoochee River, and the West Eugene, Oregon, wetland protection programs. It is fair to conclude that these cases, which can show success in quantifiable terms of lands and resources protected, acquired, or restored, would most likely not have occurred without strong state enabling statutes.

The plan described in chapter 1 to restore the Kissimmee River and its wetlands on a grand scale after the consequences of channelizing were discovered was initiated by the state of Florida. The 1976 Kissimmee River Restoration Act, the state-established Kissimmee River Resource Management and Planning Committee, and aggressive leadership by Governor Bob Graham resulted in funding, research, and project implementation through partnerships with the federal government. The state's initiatives were met initially with an unwilling-to-tepid federal response, but eventually the state's agenda prevailed, and the state-formed South Florida Water Management District now has a successful partnership with all levels of government and NGOs to implement a restoration plan for water-quality improvement, river and wetland restoration, and flood management.

The Lake Tahoe Plan adopted by the Tahoe Regional Planning Agency (TRPA) in 1972 was a result of the concern of the states of California and Nevada that the treasured, pristine quality of Lake Tahoe was being degraded and that some form of basin-wide protections were needed to protect a unique national resource. The states asked for and received congressional authority in 1969 to form an interstate regional planning agency to develop and implement a Tahoe basin management plan. The plan is a classic comprehensive-rational environmental plan that uses a water-basin boundary as its planning unit; is organized around regional economic, social, and environmental-quality objectives; has an extensive inventory of basin natural factors; and institutes land-use regulations based on a balance of environmental-quality and economic objectives. A combination of water-quality regulations administered by the California Regional Water Board and TRPA land-use regulations have significantly modified land-use impacts on Lake Tahoe water quality. The comprehensive plan works in this case because the federal and state enabling acts provide the substantive regulatory and institutional framework needed to carry out the plan.

Another case of a successful comprehensive plan, which is now being implemented by the city of Eugene with the assistance of the regional Lane Council of Governments in southwestern Oregon, occurs within the framework of the state of Oregon's uniquely strong 1973 Land Use Planning Act and a 1989 State Wetlands Act to strengthen the protection of wetlands.

The state of Wisconsin's equally unusual Watershed Planning Program enacted in 1966 established mandatory standards for floodplain regulations to be adopted by local governments. Evaluations of the program showed that by the early 1970s all the counties in Wisconsin had complied with the state standards in local zoning, sanitary, subdivision, and land-use regulations. The state program began with two people in 1966, and by 1980 it had grown to one state position, and seventeen part-time positions in six district offices, a good indicator of its public acceptance.

The Chattahoochee River provides yet a different kind of case in which a regional entity, the Atlanta Regional Commission, was able to attract the support of the Georgia State General Assembly with a Chattahoochee Corridor study. This led to the passage in 1972 of the Metropolitan River Protection Act. The law established a locally enforced two thousand-foot river corridor protection zone, which by the late 1970s has been designated as a National Recreation Area; land-acquisition projects in the corridor have continued through the 1990s. The plan was motivated by concerns for water quality, flood-damage reduction, and recreation, among others. Local development affecting the corridor must be consistent with the regional plan, and the Atlanta Regional Commission determines that consistency. Any action found to be inconsistent must seek approval from the state's Environmental Protection Division.

The common thread among the programs just described is that they are unusual; with the exception of one program, they originated with legislative authority passed in the late 1960s or early 1970s. They can boast significant accomplishments, but of course none of them is flawless, and critics can point to lost opportunities for environmental protection under them. Nonetheless, the desirability of strong state water and resource programs is clear. The momentum in the last two decades has been for states to take on more active roles in water management issues, but the strength of future state leadership in watershed management is still uncertain.

Four cases illustrating different approaches to watershed management are described in the following sections to provide us with some useful lessons for operating in the presence or absence of strong state involvement or leadership. Two of the cases, Brandywine River, Pennsylvania, and Butterfield Creek, Illinois, illustrate planning methods well adapted to areas with weak state or regional planning and regulatory frameworks. The other two cases illustrate what is possible in a framework of strong state laws: the Portland, Oregon, Metropolitan Area 2040 Growth Concept Plan and the West Eugene Wetlands Plan.

Regional Planning under Weak State Involvement

One of the first contemporary and well-documented cases for advancing a watershed-basin and comprehensive planning approach to watershed management was the Brandywine Watershed Plan conceived for a rural but urbanizing area outside of Philadelphia, Pennsylvania, developed between 1965 and 1971. This brave experiment in comprehensive watershed planning may by today's standards represent naive planning methods, but the case, through its failure, provided important lessons for planning attempts that followed it.

The Brandywine Watershed Plan was a comprehensive resource management plan developed by an interdisciplinary team, including physical and biological scientists, economists, attorneys, sociologists, etc. The plan used some of the nation's most prominent experts and is a model of scientifically based, comprehensive-rational planning. All land management recommendations were carefully rationalized on the basis of good science. Nothing was spared to develop a quality plan.

The central feature of the plan was to have the county acquire streamside conservation easements from landowners in order to control degradation to the watershed by the anticipated increase in development. The plan was promoted on the basis of the public benefits it would provide, including improved water quality and supply and the preservation of the countryside aesthetics. It was also promoted on its ability to help reduce flood damages.[80, 81]

Despite the concerted efforts of scientists and planners to convince local authorities to adopt the plan, the effort ended in dismal failure. Ann Strong's account of this case, *Private Property and the Public Interest*, evaluates the reasons. Strong, both a participant and an observer of the planning process, believes that the major obstacles to the adoption of the plan were that the people who opposed it saw themselves as "continual losers at the hands of government" and that to the individual landowner the private costs of the plan seemed to outweigh the public and private benefits. The unacceptable costs to the landowner were: sharing ownership of the land with the government, forgoing the chance to speculate in the land market, and forgoing the chance to seek rezoning of the land for more lucrative uses.

Strong clearly identifies the ways she thinks the plan proponents erred in the process they used to get the plan adopted. The first mistake she identifies is that the plan never recovered from the image that it was being imposed by "outsiders." Further, the area to be affected by the plan was too large, making adoption that much more complicated politically. The plan gave too much weight to the quality of the environment, and the proponents paid too little attention to the necessity of lining up strong leadership for plan support. She says that planners overinvested in the quality of the plan rather than employing adequate field staff to develop public participation and support for the plan. Planners also should have identified opponents of the plan in the early stages and solicited their involvement. Finally, although the planners had identified alternatives for implementing the plan, they hadn't made the choices clear to the public.

Other mistakes included the inadvertent exclusion of some community leaders from the advisory committees and bad timing in the release of promotional literature to the public. Much of the information was packaged in a way that was too complex for the public and the media. The plan proponents had a difficult time simplifying their message, as opposed to the plan's opponents, whose messages were simple and unchanging. Some of the public felt they were being told what was to happen, rather than being asked for their involvement.

On the basis of that experience, Strong concludes that planning for a smaller watershed and reducing the social-political variables are more conducive to land-planning implementation. She also thinks land regulation such as in the previously mentioned Wisconsin approach had a better chance of succeeding than the Brandywine approach because strong state laws provide a better environment for enactment of effective local regulations.[80]

Pennsylvania has not yet achieved strong state watershed or planning laws like Wisconsin, but thirty years later the Brandywine watershed management efforts can be described as a success. Members of a nonprofit organization, the Brandywine Conservancy, walked into the ruins of the Brandywine Watershed Plan experiment and sat in people's kitchens over coffee to commiserate and discuss what should happen in the watershed. Misunderstandings about the attempted planning efforts and a mistrust of government agencies were rampant. The Brandywine Conservancy staff found reason for optimism, however, in the fact that there was a positive tradition of government-private partnerships between the Soil Conservation Service Small Watershed Program (P.L. 566) and the Brandywine Valley Association. The SCS program has always been characterized by federal involvement in response to local conservation district and associations' land management initiatives and site-based planning and projects.

The conservancy staff found it effective to start with a government program the landowners trusted and take part in cooperative projects to establish trust and working relationships. They also began working to bring groups of landowners together in their homes to discuss how they could cooperatively enhance each other's properties. Eventually, the conservancy found it effective to produce maps that conveyed information about environmentally sensitive areas such as floodplains and steep hillsides but without designating actions or "plans" for those areas. The conservancy was able to return the landowners to a discussion about the value of stream buffer zones (a central feature of the old Brandywine plan) by drawing clear distinctions between the self interests of the property owners and the buffer zone benefits of erosion control, flood-damage reduction, and water quality.[82]

The conservancy staff made themselves familiar with the lessons of Brandywine. They needed to work with smaller watershed units and fewer landowners at a time, and they needed to reduce the complicated social-political variables present in the whole-basin, comprehensive plan. They found that an effective strategy for landowner involvement—and buy-in for watershed restoration and protection—was to offer funds for developing conservation plans. The conservancy eventually found that it increased landowner commitment to these plans to cost-share them. Because of the conservancy's nonprofit status, it was able to put creative funding packages together with corporate donations, government funds, and landowner contributions to fund plans, restoration projects, and land-acquisition projects. They found neighbor-neighbor communications and peer pressure to be most effective for preventing farmland sales to subdividers and for protection of open spaces. By the early 1990s the conservancy had succeeded in putting twenty thousand acres into conservation easements.[83]

The Northeastern Illinois Planning Commission (NIPC) provides another practical model as an effective regional agency within a framework of average but unexceptional state programs and no regulatory or policy powers of its own. Its involvement in the Butterfield Creek Watershed plan located in a twenty-six square-mile area about thirty miles south of Chicago illustrates an effective planning and implementation strategy for a regional agency working within limited government authorities.[84]

The NIPC was formed by the Illinois General Assembly in 1957 in response to a decade of rapid urbanization in the Chicago area. The commission was given advisory powers only, to provide technical planning assistance to the six-county greater Chicago region. The NIPC has advocated strengthening the authority of the Illinois departments of conservation, and transportation (where the Division of Water Resources is located) and of the state Environmental Protection Agency over watersheds, streams, and wetlands, but the commission generally provides an advisory or coordinating role within unaggressive and even ambiguous state regulatory authorities. Within this context the commission provides excellent technical assistance to counties and local governments on water quality, storm-water management, and stream protection and restoration options.

The Butterfield Creek watershed is composed of seven communities; 60 percent of the area is in typical suburban development, and 23 percent remains in agriculture. The seven communities and Cook County were motivated to organize a Butterfield Creek Steering Committee with the NIPC in the early 1980s to solicit state and federal assistance for flood control. A 1987 Soil Conservation Service study done for the committee showed that it was not possible to economically justify a structural response to the floods. The NIPC acted as staffing for the committee and helped pull in a full array of technical assistance from the Army Corps, EPA, Fish and Wildlife Service, and Federal Emergency Management Agency, as well as the Soil Conservation Service, to plan how to proceed with solving the flooding problems. The problem solving—or planning that ensued—tied other related objectives, such as storm-water management, water quality, and open-space opportunities, to the flood-damage reduction objective.

The major strategy to emerge from the committee was the drafting of a model storm-water and floodplain management ordinance for application in the communities located in the basin. A village engineer for one of the communities volunteered to write the ordinance with technical assistance from the NIPC staff. The ordinance addresses protecting natural floodplains and wetlands, or natural storage areas, by providing stream buffer zones and requiring site permits for all development. The ordinance exceeded state and federal minimum requirements for floodplain regulations. Five of the seven communities adopted the model code; the others are still considering adoption.[85–87]

Specific natural storage area acquisition projects were identified, and the Butterfield Creek Steering Committee and NIPC have been raising funds for both acquisition and design of storm-water and flood-storage wetlands and relocations of buildings and other structures.[88]

A "plan for action" has given the Butterfield Creek plan credibility. The actions have been immediate and on the ground, using visible demonstration projects to illustrate what is practical and possible. The demonstration projects include designing and developing "natural" wetland areas to treat storm water to improve water quality and detain the flow for storm-water management. Low-cost streambank restoration projects have been installed to educate property owners about effective and natural options. The committee also solicited the help of the State Division of Water Resources to organize educational "open houses," which involve living-room meetings on how to flood-proof homes. Homewood, a Butterfield Creek Steering Committee community, has initiated a pilot program by elevating eight flood prone homes and hopes to extend the pilot to twenty-four more eligible homes.[89]

Regional Planning with Strong State Involvement

Several states have enacted planning laws that provide for substantial state influence on local land-use decisions. The states with such laws include Hawaii, Vermont, Florida, North Carolina, New Jersey, Maine, Georgia, Washington, Wisconsin, and Oregon. Oregon has one of the strongest state land-use laws and that has allowed for some exceptional local and regional comprehensive plans to protect waterways and their watersheds.[90]

The 1973 Oregon Land Use Planning Act is considered an exceptional state directive requiring regional and local responses to control growth, enact land-use plans, and set enforcement measures in place. The act appears to have established the unique political environment needed for comprehensive planning and regional planning governments to be effective. It called for the Oregon Land Conservation and Development Commission to adopt statewide planning goals and guidelines, which became standards for local planning. Each city and county must develop a comprehensive plan that meets the state standards and is approved by the Oregon Land Conservation and Development Commission. Each city must also determine an urban growth boundary within which development is confined and beyond which city services cannot be extended. Once the local plans are approved, the plans and their implementing ordinances—including maps, policies, zoning, land division ordinances and regulations—have the effect of local law. With few exceptions local and state land-use activities must be consistent with the local comprehensive plans. In effect, 36 county plans and 241 city plans comprise a cumulative land-use plan for all private lands in Oregon.[91, 92]

In the Portland metropolitan area, the State Land Use Plan and a state enabling act created Metro, a regional land-use agency. Metro has created a context as close to ideal as you can find in the country in which to carry out classical comprehensive-rational environmental planning. The plan is organized on the basis of watershed units, and plan objectives and policies are organized around the special needs of stream and river corridors. A feature of the plan is its recognition of streams, rivers, and wetlands as part of the infrastructure of the region, worthy of equal consideration with roads and utilities.

The Portland-area Metro is the only regional governing entity in the country with an elected council. The council is composed of seven members representing districts within the region, which includes more than 1.2 million residents in three counties and twenty-four cities. Metro is charged with producing for the region a comprehensive plan (Region 2040 Growth Concept Plan) and an implementation plan (Regional Framework Plan) and determining its urban growth boundary.[93, 94]

Currently, the Metro water resources plan integrates floodplain-management, water-supply, water-quality, and open-space needs. An extensive GIS inventory and mapping system is used. Steep slopes, wetlands, one-in-100-year floodplains, and stream corridors are considered inappropriate for development. The planning process involves many committees composed of planning professionals, citizens, and the local entities that must ultimately implement the plan. The State Land Use Law requires significant citizen participation in the plan formulation. Local governments actively participate and vote in planning committees—in meetings that have been described as "uncharacteristically cooperative, given that realistically local governments are generally loath to accept outside directions."[95] The plan was adopted by Metro in the fall of 1995, and implementation by local governments is projected to be good. It is a case readers should follow. It is the Brandywine dream plan, and it has a good chance of coming true because of the one-of-a-kind Oregon land-use law.

The West Eugene Wetlands Plan, adopted by the Eugene City Council and the Lane County Board of Commissioners in August 1992, is a refinement to the Eugene-Springfield Metropolitan Area General Plan approved under the Oregon Land Use Law. This is an unusual plan, which creates wetland reserves and restores riparian and associated wetlands, as well as directing development to areas where environmental damage to wetlands can be minimized. The planning process was initiated by the city of Eugene and assisted by the Lane Council of Governments, the regional planning agency for the cities of Eugene and Springfield and Lane County. The reason for this plan was the discovery of extensive wetlands in the west Eugene area that had been designated for development toward which Eugene had already made a $12 million investment in roads, water, and sewer systems. Without reasonable development, much of that investment would be lost and services would have to be extended elsewhere at greater costs.[96]

A comprehensive-rational plan was developed during 1988–93 using funding from city general funds and sewer user fees. The plan was adopted and has already seen measures implemented, including land acquisition, development of local ordinances, habitat restoration, and extensions of greenways.[97] The structure of the planning process is interesting because the plan is sponsored by a city but entails a great deal of federal involvement including a federal planner from the Bureau of Land Management who had a central role in its development. The U.S. EPA, Fish and Wildlife Service, and Army Corps of Engineers have been active participants, providing funding, developing restoration plans, and designing permit programs. They were joined by the Oregon Division of State Lands and Department of Environmental Quality to form a technical advisory committee. It is a case in which the city defined the plan, as influenced under strong state laws, and then the city and the regional planning agency aggressively lobbied for federal involvement to provide technical expertise and help implement the plan. Nonprofits, most notably the Nature Conservancy, were made an integral part of the plan formulation. They were seen as critical players because of their fund-raising abilities, influence in attracting the support of government programs, and ability to interact with property owners on land easement and acquisition projects.

The evaluations of the plan and the planning process by those involved provide some good insights. Working within the context of a strong state law was considered an important component of success. Lane Council of Governments staff felt that the citizenry was oriented not to fight over whether there should be such a plan but to concentrate on what the plan should be. A particularly strong staff with sophisticated planning knowledge and skills was also viewed as significant to the plan's success. Collaborative planning and equal and cooperative relationships among agency personnel and citizens were also cited as important.[98] A mistake in the planning process was the issuance of a wetlands restoration conceptual map to the public before landowners were involved more fully in that concept. Elected officials ultimately removed one rural area from the map and stressed reliance on voluntary participation of sellers for participation in the restoration program.[99]

Action Planning School

In describing the planning method she uses to direct the priorities and programs of the Friends of the Chicago River, Executive Director Laurene Von Klan says she ascribes to the "go-for-the-light"school of planning. The go-for-the-light school grew out of a frustration with the traditional, greenway, master-planning approach that is most often prescribed by landscape architects and planners in federal or local technical assistance programs for river corridor planning.[100]

The go-for-the-light school is a form of integrated-incremental planning in which key interest groups (which can include members of the general public) articulate their "vision" or objectives for the watershed. From there the process diverts substantially from conventional comprehensive river corridor planning. Nonprofit organizations—which typically have strong community ties—venture into localities where they sense public interest, surmise that public interest is easily organized, or know of existing organized interest. The NGO meets with people in their homes, in neighborhood-style meetings, to identify the nature of their interest. As in the Brandywine case, the planning is done in small, manageable units, i.e., the neighborhood. The NGO planners proceed on the basis of where this public interest takes them. Certainly, there is cross-pollination in this process, for the NGO also conveys to the interested people what the possibilities can be for actions based on objectives that have already been articulated for the watershed.

The NGOs then take on the easy watershed projects first and in that way develop visibility and credibility around the fact that something is happening. These initial watershed projects may entail starting environmental schoolyards, tree-planting projects, stream-bank repair projects, acquisition of small easements that suggest the start of a trail system, or neighborhood- or school-led tours of a river. From there, the planning proceeds to fill in the gaps or expand around the activities, whether it be to expand the land-acquisition projects, continue larger-scale restoration efforts, or develop more extensive storm-water and water-quality management projects.

An identifying feature of the go-for-the-light school of planning is that, while plans with objectives are made, and initial inventories done, credibility comes from the simultaneously occurring actions. Actions are not an *outcome* of planning; they are a critical *component* of the planning. Gary Lacy, an accomplished restorationist on Boulder Creek, Boulder, Colorado, describes this as "not planning to plan but planning to act." The action planning (or go-for-the-light) school has the same ends in mind as the comprehensive-rational planner in that they aim to end up with an integrated watershed approach made cohesive by public sentiment for common objectives for protection priorities; regional inventories; and acquisition, management, and restoration projects. The only difference is the means, which entails starting with small pieces and building up to the big picture. This has the marked advantages of not overwhelming or threatening people with the big picture and avoiding the inevitable plan-implementation skepticism that now runs rampant in the public realm.

Critics of this planning school charge it with abandoning the big-picture issues. An example of such an issue is the concern of many conservationists that the substantial public subsidy of the navigation industry on the Mississippe River has relegated extensive portions of that large basin to an industrial purpose at the expense of the river's natural environment. Rather than developing a national campaign to stop the navigation industry on the river, the action planning school would address that issue by organizing at the local level, in towns along the river, to build support for alternative freight transportation such as trains and for local and regional river and floodplain restoration projects.

The action planning school is particularly useful in areas where water management controversies have festered for years. The Johnson Creek, Oregon, flood-control planning case is a good example, in which a dismal history was turned into a process that has revived public participation and credibility through results-oriented planning.

The Johnson Creek case resembles the Brandywine case in that traditional federal flood-control planning on the creek failed to develop the local support and funding necessary to implement a master plan of channelization and storm-water projects. Johnson Creek is located in Multnomah and Clackamas counties in the Portland, Oregon, region, an area that served as the older bedroom communities of Portland. The Urban Streams Council, a local nonprofit, responded to the city of Portland's offer to assist community-based initiatives to resolve a thirty-year impasse on flooding issues. The council sent local citizens and its own chosen experts to people's living rooms in the most serious problem areas of the watersheds. Neighborhood barbecues were held to attract people. Public weariness with failed government planning efforts was overcome by using fellow citizens as the initiators of new attempts. The Urban Streams Council had to develop credibility immediately, or it would not be able to create a new flicker of public interest. Credibility was established by organizing small neighborhood action projects such as removing creek logjams and improving stream conveyance through constricted areas near bridges. Demonstration storm-water wetland-detention projects were created in parking lots. Those actions helped draw community leaders back to the planning table, where a city of Portland–financed Johnson Creek Watershed Council was formed to develop watershed plans for objectives ranging from fish habitat restoration to flood-damage reduction. Technically sophisticated and comprehensive plans have been generated by the council, which includes three cities, two counties, neighborhood associations, NGOs, and federal and state agencies. The watershed council not only carries out comprehensive planning, but also concurrently directs a community stewardship grant program, which provides citizens and neighborhood organizations with small (up to $5,000) grants to carry out education, community involvement, monitoring, and restoration projects. A new patience for implementation has evolved whereby both public and government participants realize the wisdom of implementing pieces of the plan as funding and political opportunities best dictate. The citizen and agency members of the council managed to endure a complicated planning process together for five years to produce the Johnson Creek Management Plan, which was formally adopted by the city of Portland. The council also integrated floodplain management policies into the environmental zoning plan of the 2040 Regional Plan and started land-acquisition projects in the floodplain.

A lesson of the action planning school is that the barbecue organizing method appears to have appeal in a diversity of settings involving different cultures and incomes. (One organizer states that she now has a comprehensive regional cuisine preference inventory for the region she works in.)

The consensus planning approach used on Johnson Creek seems similar in many respects to the approach used to resolve flood-control issues on Wildcat–San Pablo Creeks in Richmond, California, though the latter seemed to be better focused and to more profoundly hold community attention and instill more active involvement. There are dramatic differences between the dynamics of the Wildcat–San Pablo Creeks organization and the Johnson Creek organization in that the former originated from bitter and fractured relationships between citizen groups and local government agencies and the latter was nurtured, funded, and in all respects supported and advocated by city officials. Intuition would lead one to put one's money on the success of the Johnson Creek Council over the Wildcat–San Pablo Creeks organization. However, the evaluation of some citizens involved with the Johnson Creek Council indicated that although the city-sponsored council and the facilitators hired to direct it were well intended, they were almost to the point of being patronizing or too paternal. In contrast, the citizen-advocacy quality of the Wildcat–San Pablo Creeks organization kept it a working, dynamic body for a significant period of time before it evolved into a broader-based collaboration between citizen groups and government agencies engaged in ongoing cooperative studies and projects.

An active and respected citizen leader in the Johnson Creek Watershed Council observed what he referred to as the absence of a "committee soul." The citizen members, he felt, became a review committee for the agencies and their consultants—a situation not necessarily intended by the sponsor of the council, the city of Portland. He believes that the planning time to produce a watershed-management plan—five years, in contrast to the one-year Wildcat plan—was much too long. The enhancement projects, the involvement of neighborhoods and schools, and the start of a regional trail through the area were what kept people going to council meetings to "stick it out." The development of a crisis in 1994, when the city of Portland proposed removing funding and support for the then-named Johnson Creek Corridor Committee, changed the committee dynamic. Citizens mobilized to save the committee from city funding cuts. This exercise of citizen influence changed the nature of the committee. It was renamed the Watershed Council to denote a broad, ongoing concern group, and citizens established themselves as rotating chairs of the council. The crisis also helped establish a bond between citizen and agency members who realized that the loss of the organization would mean the loss of a collaborative investment that they collectively valued.

The council is less agency dominated now, but some of the citizen members consider the loss of their "advocacy" group, the Friends of Johnson Creek, which became absorbed by the council, as an unfortunate side effect. In hindsight, they report that it is probably better to retain a healthy independent "friends of watershed" group as one of the many interests of the council.[101]

Recent Trends and Recommendations

Not only have environmental programs oriented toward watershed restoration and management programs begun to reappear at the federal level, but states have been leaders in developing models for new watershed restoration programs, as well. The aforementioned Kississimee River restoration program in Florida is a notable example. Another example is the proliferation of state conservancies in California that are organized on a regional basis to carry out objectives as diverse as providing public coastal access, trail construction, wetland and river restoration, green belt acquisition, protection of farmlands, river corridor management, and restoration of water quality and ecological habitats.

The California conservancies are state agencies located in the regions they serve, and their programs establish partnerships with the private sector, local governments, nonprofit organizations, and federal programs. There are now four state conservancies in California: the Coastal Conservancy, Lake Tahoe Conservancy, Santa Monica Mountains Conservancy, and San Joaquin River Conservancy. They use a wide variety of land easements and acquisition methods first developed to sophisticated levels by such nonprofit organizations as the Nature Conservancy and Ducks Unlimited. They manage grant programs and cost-share projects with all levels of government including local assessment districts. They also engage in some comprehensive planning, but their popularity and productivity are associated with their visible restoration and acquisition projects. The state Coastal Conservancy created in 1976 helped take some of the heat off the more controversial California Coastal Commission established in 1972. The commission has strong land-use regulatory powers granted through a citizen-initiated state proposition and became associated in the public's perception with contentious land-use controversies. The state conservancy concept was to provide a complementary, regionally based agency whose role was to resolve resource conflicts through incentives, grant programs, consensus projects, and partnerships to implement projects.

The bioregional council is another planning concept initiated by the state of California, one that may continue to evolve in various forms, particularly in the Northwest, where it enjoys popularity. The state secretary of resources divided the state into ten bioregions representing common landscapes, biological communities, and logical geographic boundaries. The organizing concept was that integrated and cooperative regional planning, setting resource management priorities, and coordinating cooperative ventures with local entities would take place through the councils. The councils were to help solve conflicts between resource development and conservation issues. The hope was that regional biodiversity would be protected through cooperative state, federal, local, and NGO participation in consensus planning organized at the regional level, rather than being imposed by state or federal laws or programs.

When they were started in 1991, the bioregional councils engendered much enthusiasm and hope for a different way of coordinating resource management programs and resolving conflicts. The state particularly focused its attention on the Sierra Bioregional Council, whose mandate was to resolve Sierra foothill development pressures with water-supply and other natural resource limits; the South Coast Council, which was formed to resolve conflicts between coastal residential development schemes and endangered species habitat; and the Klamath-North Coast Council, which was formed to resolve conflicts between timber extraction industries and fisheries and watershed-quality concerns. However, within only a few years, enthusiasm had significantly waned, and the bioregional councils were no longer viewed as the exciting new pinnacle of resource management strategies.

Evaluations by agency and citizen participants raise similar criticisms of the councils and find general agreement on their shortcomings.

Lacking from this particular structure were incentives for many of the competing local governments, industries, or NGOs to participate. "Formal agreements are only as good as the people willing to make them work. The major challenge in making bioregional planning work is to gain the support of regional administrators, such as forest supervisors or county supervisors," one state agency representative observed.[102] One high-level state official observed that part of the reason for the failure of one bioregional council was the opposition of that region's development community to the council. Hope was expressed among a number of interests for more state-designed incentives for participation.

Another critical component contributing to the decline of the bioregional concept appears to be the politicalization of the bioregional councils by state authorities who hoped to use the councils as a means to "streamline" regulations and to substitute more flexible state habitat-conservation planning methods for the established practices under the federal Endangered Species Act. This state agenda was intended help solve difficult resource conflicts but resulted in undermining the credibility of the councils as forums where bottom-to-top decision making could evolve from a local consensus. The councils began to develop a reputation as tools of Sacramento, the state capital. Agency staff questioned whether good science or politics was driving discussions and decisions.

The bioregional council that most observers agree holds the most hope for long-term tangible successes is the Klamath–North Coast Council, the origins of which predate the state-led bioregional initiative. The participants in that council had already developed working relationships and their own ground rules, and their autonomy from Sacramento influences is viewed as the reason for the council's credibility.[103, 104]

Locally placed organizations were impressed by California's efforts to set bioregional councils in motion and establish credibility for the concept. They perceived, however, that the ultimate failure of the councils was due to the inherent conflict of a state government diluting its influence by assigning more decision making to a local level and diffusing or sharing its influence with other levels of government. The culture of government agencies to preserve their powers, their authority, and themselves made them incapable of following through on the bioregional concept and accepting its consequences.[105] The bioregional council or watershed council concept has enormous possibilities if government agencies can perceive the paradox that they can gain power and influence by sharing them.

Another significant trend is the use of consensus planning processes involving all the stakeholders to resolve difficult water issues. In California, conventional flood-control planning is now characterized by a new formula. When a federal team of planners finds that a structural dam, levee, or channelization project meets federal National Economic Development criteria but the community or significant stakeholders do not consider the federally selected plan suitable, community groups work through their congressional representatives to require a modified planning process involving the development of alternatives not considered by the federal agency. The local government or citizen groups then raise funds to hire their own consultants to develop project alternatives and use their own plans to draw the sponsoring federal agency into a consensus planning process involving more agencies, interests, and alternatives. The originally proposed federal project is either abandoned or significantly redesigned. Approximately thirteen flood-control planning projects followed this model in California between 1986 and 1995.[106]

According to a federal report, in the last thirty years the number of private land trusts has increased from fifty to seven hundred organizations.[107] The Coalition to Restore Urban Waters acquired four hundred partner organizations between 1993 and 1996, and the Izaak Walton League Save Our Streams Program contains a database of approximately four thousand citizen stream groups nationally. It is clear that a significant aspect of the future of watershed-based planning will be the growing influence of locally based, grassroots organizations. Citizen practitioners of urban waterway restoration approach the planning method dilemma with some fresh experiences and perspectives that can help make planning more functional at all levels of government. Urban practioners have borrowed and adopted some planning methods from our rural counterparts and adapted them to specific situations in cities.

It should be possible to develop basic models for federal, state, regional, and local watershed plans that can reduce planning failures and increase implementation rates. From the cases and experiences described in this chapter, I offer the following recommendations—which, of course, will have to be continually reconsidered and adjusted as a result of future experiences:

- It is not productive for federal or state agencies to sponsor comprehensive planning efforts such as interstate or regional watershed plans unless they use a combination of sanctions and incentives to obtain results. Comprehensive planning should be resticted to situations where strong state laws, regulations, enforcement capacity and political climate support that approach.
- Federally assisted greenway and trails planning should diversify its strategies to better match local political conditions and add incremental planning strategies to its methods.
- Federal flood-damage-reduction planning should be restructured using interdisciplinary teams from all levels of government and citizen organizations. Economic evaluations need to be restructured for civil works programs so that community-preferred project options are not eliminated from consideration. Planning needs to include all agency and private stakeholders from the beginning.
- Federal environmental grants and technical assistance programs should focus on supporting the economic stability of locally based watershed councils and conscientiously invite state involvement into the administration of these pro-

grams. Nongovernment organizations are not a panacea for the tremendously difficult institutional challenges facing watershed management, and they can suffer from financial and administrative instabilities. Stronger locally placed councils will most likely result in stronger long-term implementation of plans. Locally placed councils and nonprofit organizations, in general, are currently in an impossible conflict in which expectations for their greatly increased role and influence are not supported with financial and staffing resources—a condition parallel to that of government agencies in the 1990s.

- To increase the effectiveness of state programs, states should develop strong regulatory frameworks and complement them with project grants and incentives programs.

- In most political and regulatory contexts, the locally based watershed council should be the unit of plan development and implementation. Councils should be directed and chaired by citizen representatives who act as liaisons to watershed inhabitants to maximize public involvement and cooperation with watershed management efforts. Citizen organizations should be the "lead agencies" in implementation phases, with government agencies acting as support teams to the citizen organizations and the councils.

- Watershed councils should take care to involve all the interested stakeholder groups in the watershed. "Stakeholders" should be defined not only as those who can profit from an action in the watershed but also as those who have a stake in the quality of life in the communities located in the watershed.

- Government agencies should develop internal cultures that encourage their employees to consider themselves members of the communities they are serving.

- Actions should be organized and funded during the planning process to begin the implementation of widely accepted goals in order to develop credibility for the planning process, and the plans it produces.

- In situations where weak governing powers handicap watershed management, restoration, and protection, incremental plans and actions should be used to advance a more complex "master vision" or plan.

- In the urban waterway movement in particular, biodiversity may not be the first organizing incentive for a watershed council or neighborhood organization. Exposure of inner-city youth to the environment may be an organizing principle, or reducing troublesome water pollution, or environmental jobs training, or recreation. In urban situations, biodiversity may necessarily end up being an incentive for action that evolves on the basis of exposure of the community members to watershed management concepts and needs.

- Plans should be conducted on a scale that can produce site specific management, restoration, and public education projects and programs.

- Plans should be focused on outcomes rather than on tools of watershed analysis such as extensive inventories collected with GIS and computer simulation modeling. These tools should not be confused with the real products of plans.[108]

NOTES

1. Congressmen Joseph M. McDade and Morris K. Udall, "Multi-Objective River Corridor Planning Workshops, Final Report" (Washington, D.C.: National Park Service, March 1989).

2. McDade and Udall, "Multi-Objective River Corridor Planning Workshops."

3. Gilbert White, *Strategies of American Water Management* (Ann Arbor: University of Michigan Press, 1969).

4. Gilbert White, *Human Adjustment to Floods: A Geographical Approach to the Flood Problem in the United States,* University of Chicago Research Paper, No. 29 (Chicago, 1945).

5. William G. Hoyt and Walter Langbein, *Floods!* (Princeton, New Jersey: Princeton University Press, 1955).

6. Jamie W. Moore and Dorothy P. Moore, *The Army Corps of Engineers and the Evolution of Federal Floodplain Management Policy*, Special Publication 20 (Boulder, Colorado: Institute of Behavioral Science, Natural Hazards Research and Applications Information Center, 1989).

7. *Floodplain Management in the United States: An Assessment Report,* vol. 2: "Full Report,"prepared by L. R. Johnston Associates for the Federal Interagency Floodplain Management Task Force, FEMA, FIA-18, Washington, D.C., June 1992.

8. Water Resources Committee of the National Resources Planning Board, under the Office of the President of the U.S., as cited by Beatrice H. Holmes, *A History of Federal Water Resources Programs 1800–1960* (Washington, D.C.: U.S. Department of Agriculture Economic Research Service, June 1972).

9. Otto Eckstein, *Water Resources Development: The Economics of Project Evaluation* (Cambridge: Harvard University Press, 1961).

10. Arthur Maass et al., *Design of Water Resources Systems* (Cambridge: Harvard University Press, 1962).

11. Water Resources Council, *A Unified National Program for Flood Plain Management* (Washington, D.C., September 1979).

12. Rutherford Platt et al., *Intergovernmental Management of Flood Plains* (Boulder: Boulder Institute of Behavioral Science, University of Colorado, 1980).

13. Rutherford Platt, *Options to Improve Federal Nonstructural Response to Floods* (Washington, D.C.: Water Resources Council December 1979).

14. Metropolitan Planning Council, "Issue Brief" (Chicago, 1991).

15. Platt, "Federal Nonstructural Response to Floods."

16. National Research Council, *Flood Risk Management and the American River Basin: An Evaluation* (Washington, D.C.: Water Science and Technology Board, National Academy Press, 1995).

17. U.S. Army Corps of Engineers, "Risk-Based Analysis for Evaluation of Hydrology, Hydraulics and Economics in Flood Damage Reduction Studies," Engineering Circular No. 1105–2–205, Washington, D.C., December 31, 1994.

18. Leonard Shabman, *Environmental Activities in Corps of Engineers Water Resources Programs: Charting a New Direction,* IWR Report 93–PS–1 (Fort Belvoir, Virginia: U.S. Army Institute for Water Resources, November 1993).

19. Shabman, *Environmental Activities in Corps of Engineers Water Resources Programs.*

20. Association of State Floodplain Managers, "Multi-Objective Management Kitchen Cabinet," memorandum from annual meeting, Portland, Maine, May 26, 1995.

21. David G. Davis, deputy director for Office of Wetlands, Oceans and Watershed for the U.S. Environmental Protection Agency, "Watersheds and Wetlands: The View from Inside the Beltway," Wetlands and Watershed Symposium, Association of State Wetland Managers, Sparks, Nevada, May 10–12, 1993.

22. Federal Crop Insurance Reform and Department of Agriculture Reorganization Act of 1994.

23. Natural Resources Conservation Service, *Conservation Technical Assistance and Watersheds Evaluation, Preliminary Report,* Washington, D.C., April 1994.

24. Daniel P. Beard, *Blueprint for Reform: The Commissioner's Plan for Reinventing Reclamation* (Washington, D.C.: U.S. Bureau of Reclamation, November 1, 1993).

25. *President Clinton's Clean Water Initiative* (Washington, D.C.: White House, January 31, 1994).

26. Gilbert F. White, "Watersheds and Streams of Thought," draft for the *Journal of Soil and Water Conservation*, notes from the 50th anniversary of the SCS, Des Moines, Iowa, 1995.

27. "Concepts and Issues in Watershed-management," Working Paper WP–2195 (Washington, D.C.: Evolution Office of the Inter-American Development Bank, September 1995).

28. Water Science and Technology Board, *Criteria for Watershed Sustainability: Proceedings of a Workshop* (Washington, D.C.: National Research Council, National Academy of Sciences, December 6–7, 1994).

29. Ian L. McHarg, *Design with Nature* (New York: Doubleday, 1971).

30. *The Plan and Program for the Brandywine* (Philadelphia: Institute for Environmental Studies, University of Pennsylvania, October 1968).

31. New England River Basins Commission, *The River's Reach: A Unified Program for Flood Plain Management in the Connecticut River Basin* (Boston: New England River Basins Commission, 1976).

32. Ian L. McHarg and Michael G. Clarke, "Skippack Watershed and the Evansburg Project: A Case Study for Water Resources Planning," *Environmental Quality and Water Development* (San Francisco: W. H. Freeman, 1973).

33. Charles E. Lindbloom, "The Science of Muddling Through," *Public Administration Review* (Spring 1959).

34. John Friedman and Barclay Hudson, "Knowledge and Action: A Guide to Planning Theory," *AIP Journal* (January 1974).

35. Donald Schon, *The Reflective Practitioner: How Professionals Think in Action* (New York: Basic Books, 1983).

36. Gerald Nadler, *The Planning and Design Approach* (New York: John Wiley, 1981).

37. A. Wolman, *Some Reflections on River Basin Management* (Baltimore, Maryland: Johns Hopkins University, 1981).

38. Judith I. deNeufville and Karen Christensen, "Is Optimizing Best?" *Policy Studies Journal* 8, no. 3 (1980).

39. White, *Strategies of American Water Management.*

40. John Sheaffer, *The Water Resources in Northeastern Illinois: Planning Its Use* (Chicago: Northeastern Illinois Planning Commission, 1966).

41. Moore and Moore, *The Army Corps of Engineers.*

42. U. S. Comptroller General, *River Basin Commissions Have Been Helpful, But Changes Are Needed*, Report to the Congress of the United States, CED–81–69 (Washington, D.C.: General Accounting Office, May 28, 1981).

43. U.S. Water Resources Council, *Regional Water Resource Management Planning: A Review of Level B Study Impacts,* prepared by Ralph M. Field Associates (Washington, D.C., November 1979).

44. U.S. Water Resources Council, *Regional Water Resources Management Planning.*

45. U.S. General Accounting Office, *Problems Affecting Usefulness of the National Water Assessment* CED–77–50 (Washington, D.C.: Water Resources Council, March 23, 1977).

46. U.S. General Accounting Office, *Problems Affecting Usefulness of the National Water Assessment.*

47. U.S. General Accounting Office, *Problems Affecting Usefulness of the National Water Assessment.*

48. Moore and Moore, *The Army Corps of Engineers.*

49. U.S. Water Resources Council, *Regional Water Resources Management Planning.*

50. Moore and Moore, *The Army Corps of Engineers.*

51. U.S. General Accounting Office, *Problems Affecting Usefulness of the National Water Assessment.*

52. U.S. Environmental Protection Agency, Water Planning Division, *Relationship of Level B Planning Process and Plans to Water Quality Management Planning* (Washington, D.C., November 1976).

53. William K. Ferry, W. O. Maddaus, D. Hurley, and W. Miller, *Case Study Analysis of 208 Program Effectiveness in Improving Regional Water Resources Management*, OWRT 14–34–0001–0483, prepared by Brown and Caldwell (Pasadena, California: Office of Water Research and Technology, U.S. Department of Interior, April 1982).

54. Terry Edgmon, "A Systems Resources Approach to Citizen Participation: The Case of the Corps of Engineers," *Water Resources Bulletin* 15, no. 5 (October 1979): p. 1341.

55. Frank Munger and Anne Houghton, "Politics and Organization in Water Resources Administration: A Comparative Study of Decisions," *Water Resources Research* 1, no. 3 (1965).

56. Platt et al., *Intergovernmental Management of Floodplains.*

57. Interagency Floodplain Management Review Committee, *Sharing the Challenge: Floodplain Management into the 21st Century*, for the Administration Floodplain Management Task Force (Washington, D.C., June 1994).

58. Federal Interagency Floodplain Management Task Force, *Floodplain Management in the United States.*

59. National Park Service, Association of State Wetland Managers, and Association of State Floodplain Managers, *A Casebook in Managing Rivers for Multiple Uses* (Washington, D.C., October 1991).

60. Jon Kusler, *Innovation in Local Floodplain Management, A Summary of Community Experience* (Boulder, Colorado: Natural Hazards Research and Applications Information Center, Institute of Behavioral Science, University of Colorado, 1982).

61. Rutherford H. Platt, ed., *Intergovernmental Management of Floodplains*, Institute of Behavioral Science, Monograph #30 (Boulder, Colorado: University of Colorado, 1980).

62. Andrew M. Spieker, *Water in Urban Planning, Salt Creek Basin, Illinois,* prepared in cooperation with the Northeastern Illinois Planning Commission, U.S. Geological Survey, Water Supply Paper 2002, (Washington, D.C.: U.S. Government Printing Office, 1970).

63. John W. Ross and Sheila L. Massey, "Riparian Area Management, Principles, Politics and Practices," *Proceedings of the California Riparian Systems Conference: Protection, Management and Restoration for the 1990s,* September 22–24, 1988, at Davis, California, General Technical Report PSW–110 (USDA, Pacific Southwest Forest and Range Experiment Station, Berkeley, California, June 1989).

64. Water Policy Branch, Office of Policy Analysis, Office of Planning and Evaluation, U.S. Environmental Protection Agency, *Review of Federal Agency, Nonprofit Organization Partnerships for Stream Restoration* (Washington, D.C., May 1995).

65. A. L. Riley, *Floodplain Use and Misuse* (Berkeley: University of California 1987).

66. Interagency Floodplain Management Review Committee, *Sharing the Challenge.*

67. Patricia Bloomgren, *Strengthening State Floodplain Management,* U.S. Water Resources Council, Association of State Floodplain Managers, Special Publication 3 (Boulder: National Hazards Research and Applications Information Center, University of Colorado, 1982).

68. Alan Hahn and Cynthia Dybolla, "State Environmental Planning and Local Influence: A Comparison of Three Regional Natural Resource Management Agencies," *American Planning Association Journal* 47, no. 3 (July 1981).

69. Elizabeth Haskell, "New Directions in State Environmental Planning," *Journal of the American Institute of Planners,* no. 4 (July 1971).

70. Kusler, *Innovation in Local Floodplain Management.*

71. Platt, *Intergovernmental Management of Floodplains.*

72. Environmental Protection Agency, *Watershed 1993: A National Conference on Watershed Management* (Cincinnati, Ohio: National Center for Environmental Publications, 1993).

73. Environmental Protection Agency, *The Watershed Protection Approach: An Overview,* Office of Water (WH–556F), E.P.A./503/9–92/002 (Washington D. C., December 1991).

74. Jon Kusler, "Multi-objective River Corridor Management: An Introduction to Issues: Recommendations for Implementing Programs," *Wetlands and River Corridor Management: Proceedings of the International Wetlands Symposium* (Berne, New York: Association of State Wetland Managers, 1989).

75. Eve Gruntfest, ed., *Multi-Objective Corridor Planning,* proceedings of the Urban Stream Corridor and Storm-water Management Workshop, Colorado Springs, Colorado, March 14–16, 1989; and the Multi-Objective Management of River Corridors and Their Restoration Workshop, Knoxville, Tennessee, March 21–23, 1989 (Madison, Wisconsin: Association of State Floodplain Managers, May 1991).

76. Charles E. Little, *Greenways for America* (Baltimore, Maryland: Johns Hopkins University Press, 1990).

77. National Park Service, Association of State Wetland Managers, and Association of State Floodplain Managers, *A Casebook in Managing Rivers for Multiple Uses* (Washington, D.C., October 1991).

78. Rolf Diamant, J. Glenn Eugster, and Chris J. Duerksen, *A Citizen's Guide to River Conservation* (Washington, D.C.: Conservation Foundation, 1984).

79. David Bolling, *How to Save a River* (Washington, D.C.: Island Press, 1994).

80. Ann L. Strong, *Private Property and the Public Interest: The Brandywine Experience* (Baltimore, Maryland: Johns Hopkins University Press, 1975).

81. Institute for Environmental Studies, *The Plan and Program for the Brandywine* (Philadelphia: University of Pennsylvania, Regional Science Research Institute, U.S. Geological Survey, et al., October 1968).

82. Bill Sellers, executive director, Environmental Center of the Brandywine Conservancy, Chadds Ford, Pennsylvania, interview, April 1993.

83. Bill Sellers, interview, April 1993.

84. Dennis Dreher, Richard Mariner, and Constance Hunt, *Technical Report: Stream and Wetland Protection: A Natural Resource Management Priority in Northeastern Illinois* (Chicago: Northeastern Illinois Planning Commission, September 1988).

85. Peggy Glassford, "Teaming Up to Save a Stream," *Environment and Development* (Chicago: American Planning Association, August 1993).

86. Thomas H. Price and Dennis Dreher, *Butterfield Creek Flood Hazard Mitigation Plan* (Chicago: Northeastern Illinois Planning Commission, August 1991).

87. Dennis Dreher, Theodore Gray, and Holly Hudson, *Demonstration of an Urban Nonpoint Source Planning Methodology for Butterfield Creek* (Chicago: Northeastern Illinois Planning Commission, May 1992).

88. Richard Mariner, manager of land resources, Northeastern Illinois Planning Commission, Chicago, Illinois, personal communication, September 1995.

89. Glassford, *Teaming Up to Save a Stream.*

90. World Wildlife Fund, *Statewide Wetlands Strategies: A Guide to Protecting and Managing the Resource* (Washington, D.C.: Island Press, 1992).

91. Rush Abrams, Steven Gordon, and Pam Lott, *West Eugene Wetlands, From Crisis to Opportunity: A Case Study* (Eugene, Oregon: Lane Council of Governments, September 1993).

92. Mike Houck, urban naturalist, Audubon Society, Portland, Oregon, interview, July 1995.

93. Metro, *2040 Framework,* Regional Framework Plan, Portland, Oregon, Spring/Summer 1995.

94. Future Vision Commission, *Future Vision Report* (Portland, Oregon: Metro, March 1995).

95. Mike Houck, interview, July 1995.

96. Abrams, Gordon, and Lott, *West Eugene Wetlands.*

97. Lane Council of Governments, *West Eugene Wetlands 1994 Annual Report* (Eugene, Oregon, February 1995).

98. Steve Gordon, Lane Council of Governments, Eugene, Oregon, interview, August 1995.

99. Abrams, Gordon, and Lott, *West Eugene Wetlands.*

100. Laurene Von Klan, executive director, Friends of the Chicago River, Chicago, Illinois, interview, May 1995.

101. Steve Johnson, citizen coordinator of the Johnson Creek Coordinating Committee and Johnson Creek Watershed Council, Portland, Oregon, interview, September 1995.

102. Marc Hoshousky, "Developing Partnerships in Conserving California's Biological Diversity," *Fremontia* (California Native Plant Society) 20, no. 1 (1991).

103. Dan Silver, coordinator for the Endangered Habitats League, Los Angeles, California, personal communication, 1992.

104. Diana Jacobs, ecologist, California State Lands Commission, Sacramento, California, interview, June 1995.

105. Freeman House, Mattole River Restoration Council, Petrolia, California, interview, May 1994 and September 1995.

106. National Research Council, *Flood Risk Management and the American River Basin: An*

Evaluation (Washington, D.C.: Water Science and Technology Board, National Academy Press, 1995).

107. Federal Interagency Floodplain Management Task Force, *Floodplain Management in the United States*.

108. Thomas R. Schueler, "Crafting Better Urban Watershed Protection Plans," *Watershed Protection Techniques* 2, no. 2 (Spring 1996, Silver Spring, Maryland).

CHAPTER THREE

The Environmental Professionals

Environmental scientists face monumental challenges in protecting and restoring the country's rivers and wetlands and associated plant communities, fish, and wildlife, given the current state of those resources. These professionals serve on the front lines of environmental protection, recording the decline of riparian environments, administering regulatory programs, which by their nature are controversial, and working in office environments in which their roles often compete with the project development mission of the organization. Their roles are further challenged by the increasing awareness of the critical significance of riparian ecosystems to the country's biodiversity and wildlife populations as well as the new connections being discovered between ecological diversity, stream environments, floodplain management, and social issues and needs.

Status of Riparian Ecosystems

There is no comprehensive inventory of riparian ecosystems in the United States, but a conservative estimate by a U.S. Fish and Wildlife Service in 1981 indicated that about 23 million acres of riparian areas remained in a natural or seminatural forested condition at that time. The agency estimated that approximately 70 percent of the original floodplain forests had been converted to urban and cultivated agricultural land uses.[1]

Conditions of riparian environments vary from region to region. Losses have been estimated as high as 95 percent for the lower Mississippi River, Colorado River, Sacramento River, and Missouri River. About 60 percent of the major stream segments in the country have been judged unsuitable for inclusion in the National Wild and Scenic Rivers system because of water resource development projects or other developments within the riparian corridors.[2] Wetlands, as a broad category of environments including rivers, have suffered catastrophic losses in this country. A 1990 report written for Congress establishes that the forty-eight-state mainland has lost, on the average, 53 percent of its wetlands, with some states, including California and Ohio, having lost 90 percent or more. The average wetland loss on the mainland amounts to a loss of 60 acres for every hour between the 1780s and the 1980s.[3]

A U.S. Fish and Wildlife Service survey of 666,000 miles of perennial (always flowing) streams, published in 1984, found that 560,000 of those miles, or 85 percent, had been significantly impacted by siltation (40 percent), bank erosion (23 percent), or channel modifications (22 percent). Only 5 percent of the nation's rivers and streams were rated as being able to support a high-value sports fishery; 36 percent had minimal to no value, and 57 percent had low to moderate value for supporting sport fish.[4]

Anadromous fisheries, which depend on freshwater rivers and streams for part of their life cycle, have been declining at alarming rates in the 1990s, a trend that began several decades ago. In September 1993, the spring, summer, and fall chinook salmon runs of the Snake River in the Pacific Northwest were formally listed as endangered. In March 1994, the winter run of California's Sacramento River chinook salmon was reclassified from threatened to endangered. In April of 1994, the Pacific Fishery Management Council of the U.S. Commerce Department banned salmon fishing off the coast of Washington and imposed strict catch limits for Oregon and California waters. That year also saw the filing of petitions by fishing organizations in an effort to obtain endangered species status for the Atlantic salmon, sockeye salmon, and five stocks of Pacific coho salmon, as well as the designation of critical habitat and water-quality standards for the Sacramento River delta smelt.[5, 6]

Although the Clean Water Act has dramatically improved water quality since 1972, and we no longer have burning rivers like the Cuyahoga River in Cleveland, federal data show that 740 million pounds of toxic chemicals still pour into waterways and municipal sewers each year. Approximately 1,300 bodies of water have been so degraded by pesticides, organic chemicals, and metals that state authorities have had to restrict public consumption of the fish in them. Over 1,000 waterways have contaminated bottom sediments. States reported in 1992 that over 258,000 miles of streams and rivers, nearly 8 million acres of lakes and over 9,000 miles of estuaries fail to meet their designated water-quality standards.[7]

Into this sobering picture come the plant biologists, landscape architects, environmental planners, fishery biologists, wildlife biologists, limnologists, archaeologists, and even sociologists. These professions have endured second-class citizenship when it comes to affecting the design of stream-channel modification projects that are meant to accommodate or respond to urbanization. Because of advancements in environmental regulatory law, including the National Environmental Protection Act, the Water Quality Acts, and the Endangered Species Act, the influence of the environmental professional to protect rivers took a great leap forward in the 1970s. However, the ability of those professionals to affect policies and project designs waxes and wanes with the changing political climates and commitments to the environment. The environmental disciplines have inventoried the stream resources of the country, recorded their critical importance to aquatic and terrestrial wildlife, and produced excellent government reports on the impacts of urbanization and conventional river engineering on stream environments. Too often, their role has been to witness the loss of the nation's biodiversity instead of directing its recovery.

The Role of the Environmental Professional

Since the 1960s biologists have been integrated into land management and water project proposal planning and involved in regulation to a degree they were not previously. Traditional water engineering agencies such as the Bureau of Reclamation, the Army Corps of Engineers, and the Soil Conservation Service now have well-established environmental units staffed with planners, landscape architects, and biologists.

The Fish and Wildlife Coordination Act (1958) requires that federal and state wildlife agencies be consulted to determine what measures are necessary to mitigate or compensate for loss of wildlife in watershed modification projects. Environmental disciplines are also brought in to help prepare the required environmental impact statements mandated by the National Environmental Policy Act (1969) to describe project or management alternatives and impacts. That act helped to increase the weight of recommendations made under the Fish and Wildlife Coordination Act. Biologists also play an active role in enforcing federal regulations that are meant to protect natural bodies of water and wetlands from pollution and fill.

The Federal Water Pollution Control Act (1972), which has been amended a number of times, establishes water-quality standards and a permit system for wastewater discharges, and issues grants and loans for construction of waste treatment facilities. The act is administered by the Environmental Protection Agency. Section 405 of the Water Quality Act of 1987 gives the Environmental Protection Agency broad authority to regulate nonpoint storm-water or polluted runoff discharges. Section 404 of the Clean Water Act, jointly administered by the Environmental Protection Agency and the U.S. Army Corps of Engineers, regulates the dumping or placing of dredged or fill material into streams, rivers, and wetlands. The Endangered Species Act (1973) provides for the protection and restoration of threatened or endangered species and their critical habitats. This is one of the strongest programs biologists have, because federal agencies cannot undertake or assist projects that adversely affect a species listed as endangered. Refer to table 3.1, which summarizes the federal environmental legislation that can influence the management or protection of streams. State legislation tends to parallel the federal legislation but can vary greatly from state to state.

The fact that there is a formal, institutionalized system for integrating biologists into government planning is an important advancement that most of us now take for granted. However, normal practice is to tack environmental concerns onto the end of water project or land development plans. Most of the work of environmental professionals is reactive. They receive a plan already prepared, and their assignment is to do "damage control" for the environment. Neither environmental nor social factors are formally and directly addressed.

Researchers in the 1970s evaluated the changes that the traditional engineering agencies were going through as a result of changing public attitudes regarding environmental protection and the new environmental legislation such as the National Environmental Policy Act. Investigations found that government staff in the newly formed agency environmental units felt there was too much compartmentalization

Table 3.1. Federal Legislation Affecting Stream Environmental Resources

Legislation	Agency	Purpose or Scope
Pittman-Robertson Act, 1938 (Public Law 74–415)	Department of Interior U.S. Fish & Wildlife Service	Wildlife propagation and protection by purchase of wildlife areas.
Dingell-Johnson Act, 1950 (Public Law 81–681)	Department of Interior U.S. Fish & Wildlife Service	Protection of game fish in designated areas.
Fish & Wildlife Coordination Act, 1958 (Public Law 85–624) and 1965 (Public Law 89–72)	Department of Interior U.S. Fish & Wildlife Service National Marine Fisheries Service	Agencies must consult with FWS and NMFS and full consideration be given to recommendations for conserving fish and wildlife resources.
Migratory Bird Conservation Act, 1961 (Public Law 94–215)	Department of Interior U.S. Fish & Wildlife Service	Construction and maintenance of designated waterfowl areas—extension of Migratory Bird Hunting Stamp Act of 1937.
Land and Water Conservation Fund, Act 1964 (Public Law 88–578)	Any federal, state, or local agencies	Has provided a major source of funding for open-space acquisition.
Wild & Scenic Rivers Act, 1968 (Public Law 95–625), as amended in 1978 (Public Law 95–625)	Department of Interior and affected states	Protection of rivers and surrounding environment of designated reaches.
National Environmental Policy Act, 1969 (Public Law 91–190), as amended in 1975 (Public Law 94–83)	Council on Environmental Quality (CEQ)	A systematic multidisciplinary approach to environmental impacts of federally permitted or assisted actions and identification of alternative actions.
Federal Water Pollution Control Act, 1972 (Public Law 92–500), as amended by Section 404, "The Clean Water Act," 1977	Environmental Protection Agency Army Corps of Engineers	Permits required for dredging and spoil disposal in wetlands.
Endangered Species Act, 1973 (Public Laws 93–205 and 93–205), as amended in 1979 (Public Law 96–159)	Department of Interior U.S. Fish & Wildlife Service	Protection of endangered and threatened species.
Anadromous Fish Conservation Act, 1974 (Public Law 93–362)	Department of Interior U.S. Fish & Wildlife Service	Protection of reaches of stream and spawning habitat.
National Resources Planning Act, 1974 (Public Law 93–378)	Department of Interior U.S. Forest Service	Integrates activity of Forest Service to increase fish and wildlife resources and increase productivity of soil and waters.
National Forest Management Act, 1976 (Public Law 94–588)	Department of Interior U.S. Forest Service	Streams, stream banks, shorelines, lakes, wetlands, and other water bodies must be protected.
Federal Land Policy and Management Act, 1976 (Public Law 94–579)	Department of Interior	Federal lands to be retained in Federal ownership, where appropriate lands and waters are to be protected in natural conditions to promote recreation and fish and wildlife conservation.
Compliance with NEPA by SCS, 1977; General Guidelines and Procedures, revised in 1979	Department of Agriculture Soil Conservation Service	Rules and specific guidance for applying the NEPA process and CEQ guidelines to channel modifications and guidance for environmental assessment.
Executive Order 11990—Protection of Wetlands, 1977	Executive Office of the President	Minimization of destruction of wetlands.
Executive Order 11988—Floodplain Management, 1977, as amended in 1979	Executive Office of the President	Floodplain management in accordance with NEPA to minimize flood losses.

Act	Agency	Description
Fish and Wildlife Conservation Act, 1980 (Public Law 96–366)	Department of Interior, U.S. Fish & Wildlife Service	Extends protection of fish and wildlife to nongame and nonthreatened species, their food resources and habitat.
Food Security Act of 1985, "Swampbuster" Act	Soil Conservation Service	Stops subsidies to farmers who convert wetlands to crops.
Emergency Wetlands Resources Act, 1986	U.S. Fish & Wildlife Service	Requires state comprehensive outdoor recreation plans to address the importance of wetlands, continues support for National Wetlands Inventory Program started in 1974.
Water Quality Act of 1987 (Public Law 100–4), Section 405	Environmental Protection Agency	Act gives EPA broad authorities to regulate storm-water discharges. Requires permits similar to current wastewater discharge permit program for nonpoint sources.
Water Quality Act of 1987, Section 317, National Estuary Program (Public Law 100–4)	Environmental Protection Agency	Over a period of five years, comprehensive conservation and management plans were developed to establish regional plans to protect the environment of nationally significant estuaries.
Coastal Zone Management Act of 1972 (Public Law 92–583), reauthorized in 1986 and 1990	National Oceanic & Atmospheric Administration	Authorizes grants to states to manage coastal zones to minimize natural hazards and protect the environment.
Water Resources Development Act of 1986 (Public Law 99–62), Section 1135	U.S. Army Corps of Engineers	Authorized a demonstration program for the Army Corps to improve the environmental quality of past Army Corps projects.
Water Resources Development Act of 1990, Sections 306, 307	U.S. Army Corps of Engineers	Upgraded Section 1135 to a Restoration Program with an annual appropriation. Directs the secretary of the army to adopt a new environmental mission and to adopt a no-net-loss wetland action plan.
Water Resources Development Act of 1992	U.S. Army Corps of Engineers	Authorizes the Corps to integrate restoration into dredging projects.
Hazard Mitigation and Relocation Assistance Act of 1993	Federal Emergency Management Agency	Requires FEMA to spend 15% of disaster relief funds on mitigation projects to avoid future flood damages and provide 75:25% cost sharing for flood-damage-avoidance hazard mitigation grants.
1994 Federal Corps Insurance Reform and Department of Agriculture Reorganization Act	Natural Resources Conservation Service	The Soil Conservation Service became the Natural Resources Conservation Service and had a number of resource management programs transferred to it, including the Wetland Reserve Program, Forestry Incentive Program, and Great Plains Conservation Program.
National Flood Insurance Reform Act of 1994 (Public Law 103–325), also known as Reigle Community Development and Regulatory Improvement Act	Federal Emergency Management Agency	Reforms payment of insurance benefits to floodplain dwellers. Creates a new source of funds for floodplain acquisition.
Water Resources Development Act of 1996 (Public Law 104–303), Sections 206, 503	U.S. Army Corps of Engineers	Authorizes aquatic ecosystem restoration and protection projects and a watershed management, restoration and development, technical assistance program.
Federal Agriculture Improvement and Reform Act of 1996 (known as 1996 Farm Bill)	Natural Resources Conservation Service	Adds authority to NRCS purchase floodplain easements under the emergency watershed protection program.

and isolation of functions, that lack of early involvement in project planning was a problem, and that interdisciplinary planning was a difficult concept for the agencies to accept. Members of government environmental units saw themselves as overworked and their units as understaffed and believed that most nonengineering positions were essentially dead-end careers with major planning responsibilities delegated to engineers. They also felt that their units were placed in a devil's advocate role for the agency they worked for, that they were regarded as necessary but were frequently seen as performing a negative function.[8]

What has now evolved within engineering and public works agencies at every level of government is a working environment of two separate cultures. An official in a federal water agency describes those two cultures in table 3.2.

The prevailing culture in public works agencies remains an engineering one, in which the nonengineering professionals are integrated on the basis of a *multi*disciplinary approach as opposed to an *inter*disciplinary approach. This distinction is important. For example, in a multidisciplinary approach the various disciplines contribute whatever technical input is required but do not effectively participate in the decisive alternatives formulation process; in an interdisciplinary approach all the key disciplines are involved equally in the formulation of implementable alternatives.[9] A wiser use of environmental professionals, such as environmental planners, who receive training to prepare them to coordinate interdisciplinary teams, would be to have them direct and participate in interdisciplinary groups composed of the needed mix of professionals to address the particular technical requirements for a project. Instead of environmental concerns being tacked on to a plan on an irregular basis dependent on publicly generated political pressures, those concerns could be integrated into the early planning stages on a systematic basis.

Another common feature of the workplace culture affecting biologists is the view held by many water project professionals that as a project's economic evaluation gets better, the environmental components necessarily suffer, and vice versa. The idea that economic efficiency and environmental quality do not have to be conflicting objectives is only in its infancy, coming to light in discussions on "sustainability." A survey of personnel in a federal water planning agency showed that the prevailing view was that compliance with environmental legislation was the component most responsible for the excessive planning times for flood-control projects.[10]

The whole planning process suffers when the only way objectives outside of "economic efficiency" make their way into plans is during an unwieldy project evaluation rather than during project formulation stages. A system of project planning in which the physical, biological, and social factors are integrated from the start will produce better-designed plans and more timely ones.[11] In the early 1990s federal water agencies began to take a new view of their missions and to emphasize water management as opposed to water project development. The Natural Resources Conservation Service (NRCS) and the National Park Service (NPS) enjoy a certain advantage in cultivating an interdisciplinary approach because of their histories of

Table 3.2. The Two "Cultures" of Multi-Objective Planning

Engineers		Environmental Professionals	
Self-Perception	Environmental Professionals' Perception	Self-Perception	Engineers' Perception
Managers	Narrow	Scientific	Birds & bees
Practical	Shallow	Committed	Fur & feathers
"Can-do"	Traditionalists	Imaginative	Impractical
Decisive	Diggers	Progressive	Academic
Pragmatic	Dammers	Quality oriented	Out of touch
Time sensitive	Dredgers	Nontraditional	Confused
Tough minded	Dumpers	Holistic	Unaware
Inventive	Mud suckers	Enlightened	Utopian
Sensible	Short sighted	Rational	Reactionary
Builders	Spoilers	Conservationists	Elitists
No-nonsense	Arbitrary	Contemporary	Sentimentalists

Note: Column-to-column, not row-to-row comparisons are intended.
Perceptions by Bill Donovan, past chief of the Flood Plain Management Services and Coastal
  Resources Branch, U.S. Army Corps of Engineers.

planning with interdisciplinary teams. Nonetheless, all the agencies, including NRCS and NPS, need to consciously structure project design planning to create egalitarian relationships among engineering and nonengineering staffs.

The Significance of Riparian Environments

The use of the word "riparian" was a short time ago restricted mainly to academic biological research circles, but as the importance of streamside plant communities has been increasingly recognized and appreciated, the word has entered mainstream use. It is derived from the Latin *ripa,* which means the bank of a stream. A recent attempt to clarify what's meant by riparian states that it "pertains to the banks and other adjacent terrestrial (as opposed to aquatic) environs of freshwater bodies, watercourses, estuaries and surface-emergent aquifers (spring, seeps, oases) whose transported freshwaters provide soil moisture sufficiently in excess of that otherwise available through local precipitation to potentially support the growth of mesic vegetation."[12] Biologists then make references to and distinctions between riparian areas, floodplain wetlands, and aquatic systems, which can be confusing to the uninitiated. Aquatic environments refer to the waters in which plant and animal organisms grow and live. "Wetland" is used as a more general, all-encompassing term. A wetland may have both aquatic and riparian components and may include zones that are periodically, seasonally, or continuously submerged in water or that merely have high soil moisture.[13]

The Fish and Wildlife Service categorizes riparian areas as one of five ecological systems that fall in the wetlands category (see figure 3.1); the others are marine,

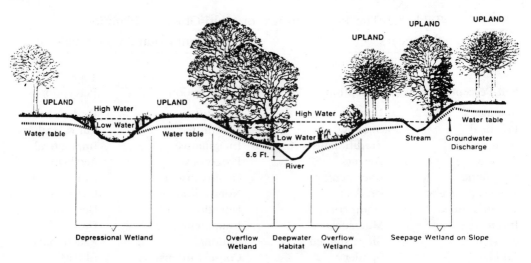

FIGURE 3.1. RIPARIAN AREAS—A CATEGORY OF WETLANDS.
The variety of wetland ecosystems, which includes riparian areas, is a function of hydrology
and topographic location.

lake, estuary, and isolated inland bog and marsh (palustrine) wetland systems.[14]
Section 404 of the 1972 Clean Water Act, which regulates wetlands, includes
riparian areas in its wetland definition, so you may hear the use of the term "wetland" to describe the corridor of water-dependent trees, shrubs, and other vegetation growing along your stream. As a matter of fact, in the last decade or so agencies
have used different definitions of wetlands, and political battles have been fought
over those definitions by entities trying to avoid the jurisdiction of federal or state
regulations or programs that govern wetlands. Some programs emphasize the need
to save or restore *acreage* of wetlands, and others emphasize saving or restoring the
functions of wetlands.

Because of the abundance of water and vegetation along streams, floodplains and
the associated riparian and wetland areas provide habitat for a large and diverse
fish and wildlife species. An interagency government report on floodplains states,
"No other ecosystem is considered more important to the survival of the nation's
fish and wildlife resources."[15] Inland, midwestern floodplains and wetlands are
most noted for waterfowl production and as habitat for migrating birds. The Mississippi River floodplains are major duck and goose resting and feeding grounds
during fall and spring migrations. The bottomland forests of the southern rivers are
primary wintering grounds for North American waterfowl and important breeding
areas for many species. Forested river bottoms in the eastern United States are also
important to birds and mammals. In the more arid West, riparian communities are
particularly valuable, providing habitat for up to 80 percent of western wildlife
species and an essential environment for other wildlife populations in the region.[16]

It is estimated that about 50 percent of the endangered species in the United
States require a wetland habitat at some point in their life cycle.[17] The reason that

such a large number of birds, mammals, and other vertebrates depend on riparian systems has to do with the diversity of conditions in riparian environments. Riparian areas have flowing water, moist and nutrient-rich soils, relatively high plant productivity, and corridors for migration and travel. Such structural complexity adds to the landscape diversity of the region. There is also an important spatial and temporal dimension to the interactions between land and water. Habitat features change dramatically with only small topographic differences such as the gradient from an open-water stream channel to a dense streamside forest; the duration and timing of flooding can be critical to species types and densities. Such changing dynamic conditions must be allowed to affect these plant and animal communities, or we will lose them.[18] An important effect on the biological productivity of rivers and floodplains has been termed the flood pulse. Not only are floodplains, as a physical feature of a river, important to biological diversity, but also the timing and frequency of seasonal overbank flows and floodplain inundations can profoundly affect ecological systems.[19] When such natural pulsations of water have been changed by channelization, drainage, dams, or other influences, plant communities have been found to shift to different species compositions.[20]

Biologists use primary productivity as an indicator of the vitality of an ecosystem. Primary productivity initiates organic energy flow for food webs and maintains the structural integrity of an ecosystem. Riverine environments transport a disproportionate amount of organic matter compared to upland ecosystems. They deliver energy and structural carbon to downstream valleys and estuaries. Studies done on floodplain forests in general and of the southwest United States in particular show that they are among the most productive ecosystems in the world.[21]

Although the riparian areas running through urban environments are increasingly important as refuges for wildlife, native vegetation, and fisheries as national riparian resources decline, it is difficult to find studies that document their habitat values. When urban ecologists check environmental impact documents prepared for streams that are slated for channelization, they are frequently surprised by the diversity of the species inventoried for the report. Government libraries of federal- or state-required environmental impact documents can be used to assemble some information on regional or local urban stream wildlife values. Simple but valuable environmental inventories of local streams are sometimes taken by schools and colleges, and annual Audubon Society bird counts also provide valuable information. One option is to solicit grants to help support local or regional biological inventories. It is important, however, that these inventories be sponsored and/or implemented by those groups actively engaged in the management of the watershed in order to assure their relevance and their use in decision making. The more you can document the fish and wildlife values, in particular, the more public and agency interest you can generate.

Common Causes of Damaged Streams

Objectives for most conventional river projects in the past have included drainage for the reclamation of wetlands, flood control by increasing the capacity of stream channels, improvement of navigation by increasing the depth of larger rivers, and erosion control by substituting artificial channels for eroding natural channels.

Studies on the quality of our nation's waterways indicate that the most wide-spread physical impacts to them are caused by siltation, bank erosion, and channel modifications. Those physical impacts are responsible for a significant portion of our water-quality problems. This would suggest that our restoration efforts focus on controlling hillslope erosion and excessive runoff and on the restoration of the riparian corridor to correct excessive stream-channel erosion.

Water projects emphasizing the construction of reservoirs represent an era that is mostly behind us. Some restoration projects are oriented toward trying to compensate for the watershed imbalances associated with reservoirs. At this time in history, the most geographically widespread and prevalent projects impacting the physical environments of streams are channel modification, or channelization, projects. These are sometimes conducted as "informal" landowner projects with grading equipment and rubble dumped on banks. Sometimes they are planned as full-scale, federally financed, flood-control projects.

Streams impacted by the influences of urbanization, a topic that is covered in the following chapter, have imbalances and problems similar to those of channelized streams. Levee projects are the next concern of the urban stream protection advocate because of their restricting impacts on the natural functions of floodplains.

Channelization projects, which continue to be widely advocated, designed, and constructed through federal, state, and local programs, represent one of the most unnecessary threats to the quality of watersheds because restoration alternatives exist that can be used in their place. Such restoration alternatives can successfully address the flood-risk and erosion-reduction objectives the channelization and riprap projects purport to address, while bringing more effective long-term stability to the watershed. Because channelization projects are so closely associated with profound disruptions of watersheds, it is important for the reader to be familiar with the literature in this area.

Channelization: A History of Public Concern

In 1971, the Conservation and Natural Resources Subcommittee of the House Government Operations Committee responded to growing public disenchantment with channelization projects. The committee's hearing process put on record the impacts of channelization projects and the failure of federal agencies to implement statutory provisions for including citizen participation and environmental concerns in the planning of the projects.[22] A coalition of environmental groups initiated litigation against the Soil Conservation Service in 1971 to prevent channelization of sixty-six miles of Chico Creek in North Carolina, and in March 1972, a draft report by Arthur Little, Inc., contracted for by the Council on Environmental Quality on the effects of channelization, was released.[23] The Government Operations Committee followed that with another report, after holding another series of hearings in 1973, and summarized some of the information from the Little report and the 1971 hearings.

The reports concluded that channelization had been overused with inadequate or no consideration of the environmental impacts. The impacts listed by the reports include: destruction of wetlands and reduction or elimination of wildlife depending on them; destruction of riparian environments and exposure of the aquatic environment to high temperatures; destruction of bottomland hardwoods, which resulted in loss of scarce habitats and an increase of nutrients and sediment concentrations in waterways; cutoff of oxbows and meanders, thereby increasing the rate of flow and decreasing critical backwater habitats; increased erosion and siltation, which removes feeding and breeding grounds for aquatic life; lowering of water tables, which can decrease stream discharge and flows that support instream life and riparian vegetation; and the altering or loss of adjacent or downstream wetlands. The findings concluded that channelization projects are also associated with the loss of aquatic habitat, loss of terrestrial and wetland habitat, channel instability, reduction of water quality, and changes in hydrologic conditions such as water table, drainage, discharge, or flow.

The severe impact to aesthetic values is a frequently mentioned consequence of such projects. The bank "protection" work accompanying channelization often requires a concrete channel or rocked and herbicided slopes and an environment devoid of any significant vegetation. It usually results in an unsightly riprapped environment replacing a riparian forest.

As a result of public attention to the environmental impacts of channelization, the U.S. Fish and Wildlife Service began its own investigation as early as 1971 and issued a policy statement saying that the service would cooperate with environmentally sound stream projects but would oppose all others, and that compensation would be required for unavoidable damages.[24] By the early 1980s more government reports by both the U.S. Fish and Wildlife Service and the U.S. Army Corps of Engineers documented the environmental impacts of channelization projects.[25, 26] Numerous university researchers and practicing professionals wrote publications on the topic through the 1970s. Andrew Brookes's book *Channelized Rivers* is a thorough summary of the research on this subject.[27]

Loss of the Physical Environment and the Biological System

The functions of the physical components of streams and their relationships to the biological components are often left out of the formula for evaluating the impacts of stream channelization. Table 3.3 and the series of drawings in figure 3.2 summarize and illustrate the connections between the loss of biological functions and the loss of physical functions of streams resulting from channel straightening and vegetation removal.

In most stream and river systems, meanders, pools, riffles, and point bars are present in the channel and are responsible for the basic form of the channel. Pools are topographically low areas caused by scouring or convergent flow, and riffles are higher areas or shallows produced by deposition. Point bars are depositional forms located on the inside of meander bends. These forms play significant roles in the

Table 3.3. Potential Impacts of Channelization

Channelization Activities	Consequences		Possible Impacts
	Loss of specific substrate	Fish and Benthos	Habitat niches
			Foods and feeding
	Removal of snags, root masses, etc.		Circulation & respiration
			Excretion, osmoregulation, & ionic regulation
Clearing and snagging	Loss of instream vegetation		Reproduction
			Development & growth
Riprapping	Loss of streamside vegetation		Behavior
			Tolerance to stress
Widening			Density
	Disruption of run-riffle-pool sequence		Distribution
Deepening			Productivity
			Diversity, richness, & redundancy
Realignment	Loss of overall stream length and sinuosity		Biomass
Lining			Energy & materials transfer
	Increase of gradient and velocity	Vegetation	Diversity
			Density
	Dewatering of adjacent lands		Dieback, sunscald, erosion, & competition
			Nutrient cycling
	Physical and chemical changes		Land-use changes
		Wildlife	Wetlands & riparian habitat
	Decreased detritus from riparian vegetation		Cover (reproductive, escape)
			Food
			Diversity
			Density
			Reproduction
			Behavior
			Mobility, migration

Adapted from: U.S. Fish and Wildlife Service, *Manual of Stream Channelization Impacts on Fish and Wildlife*, Washington, D.C., 1982.

biological riverine environment. At low flows, pools are characterized by slow, deep waters, while riffles are characterized by fast, shallow waters. This hydrologic diversity provides the feeding, breeding, and cover requirements for a wide variety of stream organisms. At high flows, boulders in riffles sort stream gravels so that finer gravels are found in pools and coarser materials in riffles. This allows a diversity of fish and aquatic insects to use the bottom of the stream channel for breeding, resting, and feeding. The natural sorting of bed-load materials on riffles and point bars also promotes a diversity of bank vegetation. A certain amount of trees, brush, and other vegetation is needed to provide cover and food for fish and to moderate water temperatures for instream life.[28, 29]

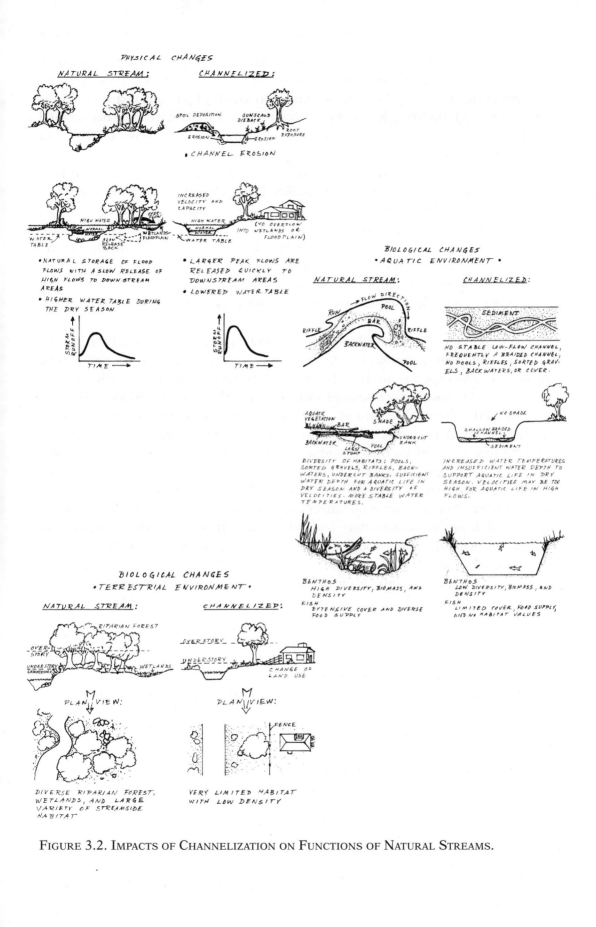

FIGURE 3.2. IMPACTS OF CHANNELIZATION ON FUNCTIONS OF NATURAL STREAMS.

Vegetation has a great influence on the behavior of alluvial stream channels. It exerts a constant pressure on the size and shape of the channel; it enhances the resistance of the stream banks to erosion and increases the hydraulic resistance of the channel to high discharges. Vegetated channels tend to be narrower, deeper, and have steeper banks than unvegetated channels transporting the same discharge of water and sediment.

Hydraulic engineers and hydrologists attest to the value of vegetation in contributing to channel equilibrium and stability. Channel modifications that eliminate or reduce vegetative bank resistance release energy that results in accelerated channel erosion and a wider channel, which is particularly vulnerable to encroachment by thick rushes, reeds, and grasses that clog the channel. Eventually, mature canopy plants evolve through succession and reestablish the channel equilibrium.[30] It is now being argued that it is easier to manage for this more stable climax ecosystem than for the less stable lower succession stages, as will be explained further in chapter 7.[31]

The importance of woody channel debris and logjams as a physical component of rivers and as an important functional feature for instream life is receiving more recognition. An expert from the U.S. Fish and Wildlife Service Forest Sciences Lab in Corvallis, Oregon, has collected historical data on the Columbia River system and concluded that rivers have naturally had great logjams. Logjams used to be an integral part of the riverscape, contributing to the formation of meanders, oxbows, and sloughs that provided for the Columbia's large and diverse anadromous fish populations. The systematic "snagging and clearing" or removal of vegetation and woody debris from large rivers and small streams has changed stream dynamics so that in some cases a river channel is no longer diverted into backwaters and becomes disconnected from its alluvial flats and floodplains, thereby greatly reducing fish habitat. In general, greater species diversity can be found in stream channels with natural banks and debris.[32]

Riparian vegetation performs a long list of important functions in the creation and maintenance of fish habitat. In summary, those functions are as follows:[33]

- Tree roots, shrub species, vines, and other growth bind the stream bank soil and provide resistance to the erosive forces of the water. This produces deeper channels with banks that are undercut but held together with exposed root systems. These undercut banks, complete with overhanging vegetation, provide important escape cover for fish.
- Riparian vegetation moderates water temperatures, making the stream habitable for fish.
- Most of the stream's biological energy and the base of the food chain for stream life come from the leaves, fruit, cones, and other plant detritus from the riparian vegetation.
- Woody debris that falls into the stream forms pools for fish, creates habitat by causing backwater pools, and provides storage areas for sediment that otherwise might be released into spawning areas.

- Riparian vegetation can slow flood velocities and help deposit and store sediment on the floodplains as opposed to the stream channel downstream. During high flows the vegetation lies against the banks and protects them from accelerated erosion.

- A well-vegetated channel helps store water along the stream corridor during the rainy season for slow release to the stream in drier seasons, which helps maintain the base flows of water for the fish.

The aquatic habitats of streams and the fisheries they should support are greatly impacted by channelization projects, but the impacts of channelization go beyond the channels themselves to the floodplains, riparian forests, and adjacent wetlands. Profound and widespread changes in plant and wildlife habitats occur as a result. The consequences of clearing, dredging, and spoil deposition on riparian vegetation includes: lower plant species diversity; lower structural diversity of the riparian woodland, with its different layers of trees and shrubs; dieback of native species from exposure and sunscald; loss of wood productivity and mass; increased erosion; changes in nutrient cycles; plant succession changes in which there is usually a species shift toward more xeric or drier-environment species; invasion of exotic plants and more competition from other water-tolerant or dependent species; and reduction in wetlands, bottomlands, and hardwoods.

The impacts on vegetation determine the effects on wildlife, which can include a full range of amphibians and reptiles, nongame and game birds, small mammals, fur bearers, and large mammals. These animals lose reproductive habitat and food sources, cover from predators, and mobility, as well as nesting, perching, and roosting sites.[34]

There has been a shift in thinking by many professionals to the conclusion that the natural features of streams such as riparian vegetation, pools, riffles, meanders, and floodplains contribute positively to the stability of channels and that those features should, at minimum, be contained in stream modification projects because of the important functions they perform.[34 37]

The Water Quality Connection to Riparian Woodlands

Inland and coastal marshes have received a lot of attention as the wetland systems with the capacity to absorb and act as natural treatment "plants" for polluted, nutrient-laden waters from urban runoff and runoff from agricultural areas. In the late 1970s researchers began to explore the potential of riparian systems to contribute to water quality—and to determine whether impacted riparian systems contribute to the degrading of water quality.

Researchers found that riparian areas are environments that trap sediment. From there they discovered that large amounts of phosphorus (greater than 85 percent) and nitrogen (greater than 70 percent) in surface runoff measured from agricultural areas is attached to sediment.[38] Wendall Gilliam of North Carolina State University and other researchers concluded that a riparian system is the best ecological system for removing sediment—and therefore for removing pollution-causing nutrients from water. They found that 80 percent of the sediment produced by an agricultural watershed was dropped in a stream's riparian zone and that the finer sediments ended up downstream in the swamps and wetlands. They also found that riparian areas are better at reducing phosphorus, while swamps and other nonriparian wetlands are typically high in phosphorus and have the ability to actually contribute it to the environment as opposed to using or absorbing it. They concluded that riparian vegetation is just as effective a filter in urban areas as in agricultural areas and that riparian buffer areas as narrow as 20 feet are valuable in contributing to water quality.[39–41] Research has not only corroborated those findings in other locations in the country but has also determined that trees and shrubs are more effective in removing nutrients—in particular, nitrates—than grassed waterways.[42]

Those who have attempted to measure the decline in water quality that comes from the removal of vegetation with modifications of stream channels find that water temperatures tend to rise and that sediment deposition, turbidity, and nutrient levels tend to increase.[43–45] The development and clearing of riparian areas not only represent a loss of the water treatment capabilities of those areas but may turn such damaged environments into sources of nonpoint pollution. Because those areas have served as sinks for sediment and nutrients, they can export the sediment that has been deposited over many years through disturbance and erosion back into the watershed.[46]

The Social Connection to Environmental Quality

Well-established government agencies and programs are charged with enforcing water-quality standards, regulating the fill of wetlands, and addressing the environmental impacts of proposed changes to the landscape. However, with the exception of federal laws that address the potential archaeological values of project sites, until recently there have been no government programs assigned to directly address the social issues associated with the environmental quality of urban waterways. The community is usually left to its own devices to define what is important to its welfare and to identify how the citizenry will be incorporated into planning processes or decision making.

The advent of a highly visible "social justice" movement in the 1990s brought to wider public attention the information that polluted waters, degraded environments, toxic disposal sites, dumps, and landfills are usually located in low-income communities, which are often communities with large minority populations.[47] In addition to those injustices, it was discovered that many floodplains and wetlands are inhabited by low-income people, either by societal design (in which people of color are segregated into areas where others do not want to live), or because such environments are more affordable. Government programs meant to assist communities with flood problems have been discovered to serve low-income areas only as rare exceptions because the federal economic analysis to qualify communities for projects contains a bias for serving well-off communities with high property values.[48]

The Environmental Protection Agency and the Natural Resources Conservation Service are to be commended for establishing new "social justice" programs within their agencies to address these socially related environmental concerns. In 1990 the Forest Service established a pilot program called Commencement 2000 to recruit low-income and minority youth into environmental sciences. Special training, summer educational opportunities, and environmental curricula developed for inner-city school programs are being provided to draw into college careers youth who may not otherwise have considered such a track. Urban waterway restoration and urban forestry are featured in these programs.[49] The government resource agencies hope they will have a more diverse hiring pool for integrating a more representative cross-section of the public into government programs.

Certainly, the urban waterway movement reflects the influence of the social justice movement. The values of urban stream restoration described in the first chapter that center on neighborhood restoration, job creation, and youth corps opportunities and training are a result of that influence. Citizen-based toxics and water-quality monitoring programs have expanded from their middle-class centers to the inner cities and to many of the most seriously impacted low-income communities.[50]

The 1990s represented the beginning of efforts to make environmental programs and projects more socially equitable. As government agencies and nongovernmental organizations become more active in such efforts, more areas of concern will likely be uncovered.

The public safety issues associated with different options for flood-damage reduction are an example of one such concern, which many in the urban waterway movement believe is not being adequately addressed by government programs. The issues that need to be publicly acknowledged and debated include the potential failure of dams, levees, and channelization projects and how seismic hazards and other natural events may bear on those potential failures. The consequences of such failures need to be better known—such as What communities or parts of a community might be affected? How might they be affected? What are the chances of being affected by a failure? And how can this information help local decision making on the selection of flood-damage-reduction options?

An issue that receives little or no mention in water-planning literature and project-planning documents is the public safety hazard of high-velocity-flow channelization projects, designed to pass large volumes of water through a channel quickly. That type of channel design usually involves large concrete conduits, energy dissipaters in the form of large concrete blocks or boulders, and chain-link fences intended to keep people out. Children and adults get swept into the channels or go thrill riding in them on rafts or boats only to become casualties by smashing into energy dissipaters, being submerged in culverts, or succumbing to the turbulent waters of the channel that they can't escape.

In 1985, because of concerns expressed by a community I was working with about the safety of constructing a high-velocity-flow box culvert near an elementary school, I made a phone survey of various water districts in the country on the safety of different channel designs. Engineers at the Davis, California, and Vicksburg, Mississippi, Research Centers of the U.S. Army Corps of Engineers were helpful in referring me to some of the major water districts in the country that they thought would have the most experience with this issue. I asked an open-ended question regarding the relative safety of closed box culverts, open concrete channels, and open gabion-lined or dirt-lined channels.

The city of Albuquerque and the state of New Mexico appeared to be the only public entities in the country to routinely develop and make available statistics on the safety of irrigation ditches and flood-control channels at that time.

According to the Albuquerque Metropolitan Arroyo Authority, Albuquerque County had one drowning approximately every two to three years.[51] The Authority was responsible for approximately fifty miles of concrete-lined channel and one hundred miles of what it calls "soft-lined" channels, which include open dirt-, gabion-, or riprap-lined channels. Despite a greater number of miles of soft-lined channels, the Authority found that a higher portion of the drownings were in the concrete-lined channels.

The Authority also had statistics for hazards by age group. The group with the highest rate of deaths was that of children three years old or younger, for whom agricultural irrigation ditches near homes provide the greatest hazard. The Authority said that the "siphons" (which are enclosed and go underground and resurface) associated with those irrigation ditches were the worst hazard. For the four- to ten-year-age bracket, the highest number of drownings were in flood-control channels. In those facilities, the Authority attributed the higher death rates to concrete-lined culverts in comparison to the "soft-lined" channels, to the higher velocities, and to the inability of children (or adults) to get out of the concrete channels and boxes. It specifically identified parks and recreational areas and schools as the highest-risk sites for such structures. The Authority used grates and fences to block entrances and access to box culverts and concrete channels, and casualties occurred nonetheless. Children and adults gained entrance by climbing or cutting the fences.

Albuquerque County conducted an extensive rescue and education program. It had installed hand-hold devices in the open concrete channels, and the fire department was trained to rescue open-channel victims—an option it didn't have with boxed culverts. A fifteen-minute film regarding the dangers of flood-control facilities was required for all children in Albuquerque County schools. A safety study conducted by the mayor of Albuquerque emphasized the advantage of open channels for rescue efforts and the dangers of colliding with the debris that frequently collects inside box culverts.[52]

The Boulder, Colorado, Metropolitan Drainage District reported two deaths in 1985 in drop-structures used where the elevation changed in concrete-lined channels.[53] The district preferred not to use closed conduits because they require trash racks and "people protectors" and large inlets to handle the flows. It reported problems with box culverts getting clogged with debris. It also said that boxes offer less protection in large floods because there is less freeboard, or extra space available, to handle discharges greater than the design flood. This had resulted in flood flows over and around the box culverts.

The Boulder District reported that it was no longer fencing flood-control channels because it had concluded that fencing not only does not keep people out, it sometimes traps them in a dangerous situation. Boulder had no lawsuits resulting from that policy.

The Claims Section of the Washington Suburban Sanitary Commission reported no recalled deaths associated with concrete channels and box culverts.[54] The commission had fenced the entire periphery of all projects at a very high cost, to minimize entry. As in Albuquerque and Boulder, however, it found that anyone who wants to gain entry can do so. The safety problem it had seen is that box culverts provide a haven for thieves who escape into them for cover and for drug users and dealers.

An attorney for the Los Angeles Public Works Department provided me with records of drownings in that area for which claims had been filed during the first six months of 1985.[55] Two drownings occurred in natural channels because there were deep pools that provided summer swimming holes. Two drownings occurred in high-velocity flows in the concrete-lined Los Angeles River. In addition, one child was killed in a flashboard and one was killed in a box culvert. Engineers thought that the highest-risk areas were closed and open channels designed to carry high-velocity flows. The supercritical flow channel, in which there was perhaps only 1 foot depth of flow moving at high velocities, was considered the most dangerous because anyone caught in that flow would be subjected to tumbling and tossing in the concrete channel.

This is only a cursory discussion of an issue that is not found in environmental impact statements or other project evaluations. It needs to be dealt with more openly and should have carefully collected and evaluated statistics so that we know what situations produce the most hazards and how to most effectively minimize those hazards.

NOTES

1. Mark M. Brinson, B. L. Swift, R. C. Plantico, and J. S. Barclay, *Riparian Ecosystems: Their Ecology and Status*, FWS/OBS–81/17, prepared for the U.S. Fish and Wildlife Service (Kearneysville, W. Virginia: National Water Resources Analysis Group, August 1981).

2. Ralph W. Tiner, *Wetlands of the United States, Current Status and Recent Trends* (Washington, D.C.: Fish and Wildlife Service, Habitat Resources, March 1984).

3. T. E. Dahl, U.S. Fish and Wildlife Service, U.S. Department of Interior, *Wetlands Losses in the United States, 1780's to 1980's*, A Report to Congress, 1990.

4. R. D. Judy, Jr., P. N. Seeley, and T. M. Murray, *1982 National Fisheries Survey*, vol. 1, "Technical Report: Initial Findings" (Washington, D.C.: U.S. Department of Interior, 1984).

5. Institute for Fisheries Resources, East Coast Federation and Pacific Coast Federation of Fishermen's Associations, "Marine Fishery Habitat Protection: A Report to the United States Congress and Secretary of Commerce," March 1, 1994.

6. "The Tragedy of the Fisheries," *Land Letter,* Special Report, April 20, 1994.

7. *President Clinton's Clean Water Initiative* (Washington, D.C.: White House, January 31, 1994).

8. Daniel A. Mazmanian and Jeanne Nienaber, *Can Organizations Change?* (Washington, D.C.: The Brookings Institution, 1979).

9. William J. Donovan, "Eq Planning: A Reflective Perspective," paper presented at the U.S. Army Corps of Engineers' Environmental Quality Planning Training Course, Springfield; Virginia, May 17–21 and June 7–11, 1982.

10. Gerald E. Galloway, *Impediments in the Process for Development of Federal Water Resources Projects* (Washington, D.C.: U.S. Water Resources Council, September 1981).

11. Galloway, *Impediments in the Process.*

12. Richard E. Warner and Kathleen M. Hendrix, *California Riparian Systems* (Berkeley: University of California Press, 1984).

13. Warner and Hendrix, *California Riparian Systems.*

14. Tiner, *Wetlands of the United States.*

15. Interagency Task Force on Floodplain Management, *A Status Report on the Nation's Floodplain Management Activity,* prepared by L. R. Johnston Associates, April 1989.

16. Interagency Task Force on Floodplain Management, *A Status Report.*

17. Interagency Task Force on Floodplain Management, *A Status Report.*

18. Brinson, et al., *Riparian Ecosystems.*

19. Wolfgang J. Junk, Peter Bayley, and Richard Sparks, "The Flood Pulse Concept in River-Floodplain Systems," in D. P. Dodge, ed., *Proceedings of the International Large Rivers Symposium,* Canadian Special Publication of Fisheries and Aquatic Science, No. 106 (1986).

20. Leigh H. Fredrickson, *Floral and Faunal Changes in Lowland Hardwood Forests in Missouri Resulting from Channelization, Drainage and Impoundment,* FWS/OBS–78/91, (Washington, D.C.: U.S. Fish and Wildlife Service, January 1979).

21. Brinson, et al. *Riparian Ecosystems.*

22. Committee on Government Operations, U.S. Congress House Report 93–530, "Stream Channelization: What Federally Financed Draglines and Bulldozers Do to Our Nation's Streams," September 27, 1973.

23. Arthur D. Little, "Channel Modification, an Environmental, Economic and Financial Assessment," Report to the Council on Environmental Quality, Executive Office of the President, Washington, D.C., 1973.

24. Andrew Brookes, *Channelized Rivers, Perspectives for Environmental Management* (New York: John Wiley, 1988).

25. P. W. Simpson, *Manual of Channelization Impacts on Fish and Wildlife* (Washington, D.C.: Office of Biological Services, U.S. Fish and Wildlife Services, 1982).

26. Edward Thackston and Robert Sneed, *Review of Environmental Consequences of Waterway Design and Construction Practices as of 1979,* Technical Report E–82–4, prepared for the Office of the Chief of Engineers, U.S. Army Corps of Engineers Washington, D.C.

27. Brookes, *Channelized Rivers.*

28. Edward A. Keller, "Channelization: Environmental, Geomorphic and Engineering As-

pects," in D. R. Coates, ed., *Proceedings of Geomorphology and Engineering* (London: George Allen and Unwin, 1976).

29. Phyllis Faber, Ed Keller, Anne Sands, and Barbara Massey, *The Ecology of Riparian Habitats of the Southern California Coastal Region: A Community Profile,* prepared for the U.S. Fish and Wildlife Service Biological Report 85(7–27) (Washington, D.C., September 1989).

30. Thomas Maddock, Jr., "Hydrologic Behavior of Stream Channels," *Transactions of the Thirty-Seventh North American Wildlife and Natural Resources Conference* (Washington, D.C.: Wildlife Management Institute, 1972).

31. Philip Williams, consulting hydraulic engineer, Philip Williams Associates, San Francisco, California, personal communication, 1990.

32. James R. Sedell, Peter A. Bisson, Frederick J. Swanson, and Stanley V. Gregory, "What We Know about Large Trees That Fall into Streams and Rivers," in *From the Forest to the Sea, A Story of Fallen Trees,* Technical Report PNW–G–229 (Corvallis, Oregon: U.S. Forest Service, Pacific Northwest Research Station, 1988).

33. Christopher J. Hunter, *Better Trout Habitat: A Guide to Stream Restoration and Management* (Washington, D.C.: Island Press, 1991).

34. Edward A. Keller, "Channelization: A Search for a Better Way," *Geology* 3 (1976): p. 246–248.

35. E. A. Keller and E. K. Hoffman, "Urban Streams: Sensual Blight or Amenity," *Journal of Soil and Water Conservation* 32 (1977): p. 237–242.

36. Nelson R. Nunnally and Edward A. Keller, *Use of Fluvial Processes to Minimize Adverse Effects of Stream Channelization,* Report No. 144, Water Resources Research Institute (Raleigh: University of North Carolina, July 1979).

37. Nelson R. Nunnally and F. Douglas Shields, *Incorporation of Environmental Features in Flood Control Channel Projects* Technical Report E–85–3 (Vicksburg, Mississippi: U.S. Army Corps of Engineers Waterways Experiment Station, May 1985).

38. James R. Karr and I. J. Schlosser, *Impact of Nearstream Vegetation and Stream Morphology on Water Quality and Stream Biota* (Athens, Georgia: Environmental Research Laboratory, U.S. Environmental Protection Agency, 1977).

39. J. Wendall Gilliam, J. R. Cooper, and T.C. Jacobs, "Riparian Areas As a Control of Nonpoint Pollutants," David L. Correll, ed., in *Watershed Research Perspectives* (Washington, D.C.: Smithsonian Institution Press, 1986).

40. J. R. Cooper and J. W. Gilliam, "Phosphorus Redistribution from Cultivated Fields into Riparian Areas," *Soil Science Society of America Journal* 51, no. 6 (November–December 1987).

41. J. W. Gilliam and R. W. Skaggs, "Nutrient and Sediment Removal in Wetland Buffers," *Proceedings: National Wetland Symposium* (Chicago, Illinois: Association of State Wetland Managers, 1987).

42. Gordon Stuart and John Greis, *Role of Forests in Water Quality in Agricultural Watersheds* (Denver, Colorado: American Water Resources Association, November 1990).

43. Karr and Schlosser, *Impact of Nearstream Vegetation.*

44. F. Douglas Shields, Jr., and Thomas Sanders, "Water Quality Effects of Excavation and Diversion," *Journal of Environmental Engineering* 112, no. 2 (April 1986).

45. Douglas M. Green and J. Boone Kauffman, "Nutrient Recycling at the Land-Water Interface: The Importance of the Riparian Zone," in Robert E. Greenwell, ed., *Practical*

Approaches to Riparian Resource Management: An Educational Workshop (Billings, Montana: Bureau of Land Management, 1989).

46. Gilliam, Cooper, and Jacob, "Riparian Areas As a Control of Nonpoint Pollutants."

47. Robert D. Bullard, *Confronting Environmental Racism: Voices from the Grassroots,* (Boston: South End Press 1993).

48. A. L. Riley, "Overcoming Federal Water Policies," *Environment* 31, no. 10 (December 1989).

49. Amahra Hicks, "Commencement 2000, Strategies for Change," *International Conference on Environental Education 2000, Alliance for Environmental Education* (San Francisco: USDA Forest Service, Pacific Southwest Region, June 1993).

50. Environmental Protection Agency, "Environmental Protection, Has It Been Fair?" EPA *Journal* 18, no. 1 (March–April 1993).

51. Larry Blair, Albuquerque Metropolitan Arroyo Authority, Albuquerque, New Mexico, personal communication, August 1985.

52. Kathy Lionbecker, Office of the Mayor, Albuquerque, New Mexico, personal communication, August 1985.

53. Scott Tucker, Boulder Metropolitan Drainage District, Boulder, Colorado, personal communication, August 1985.

54. Ed Nicewarner, Claims and Insurance Section, Washington Suburban Sanitary Commission, Montgomery County, Maryland, personal communication, August 1985.

55. David Kelsey, attorney, Los Angeles Public Works Department, County of Los Angeles, California, personal communication, August 1985.

CHAPTER FOUR

River Scientists ·

If we are to restore streams in cities, the streams need to be thought of as complex systems with many interacting variables. One of the greatest influences on those variables is humankind's impact on the watershed through urbanization. This chapter addresses how those human influences affect the components of the natural environment, including the land forms, geology, climate, stream discharges, and sediment loads.

Restoration involves identification of the symptoms of stream imbalance or disequilibrium, discovery of the causes of the imbalances, and then attempts to correct, or at the very least, compensate for the causes. A conventional assumption is that restoration of streams in cities is almost an impossibility because it is not possible to achieve a stream dynamic that is not out of balance because of the influences of urbanization. Because of this conviction, well-intended professionals prescribe controlling urban streams in concrete or pipe as the most practical way to make land available for urban uses, stop erosion, and reduce flooding. The restoration of urban streams assumes that even in the worst cases, where streams have little room to meander, erode, deposit, and adjust their slopes, "channel stabilization" projects can be designed in a way that maximizes the environmental values of the resource. Urban stream restoration often involves the opportunity, however, to apply the same principles that one would use to restore a stream in a more rural or natural environment. Urban streams can and do evolve to new equilibriums with larger channel dimensions. Excessive erosion, excessive deposition, and frequency of flood damages can be moderated or brought in balance by reshaping and revegetating urban streams.

Hydrologists and Hydraulic Engineers

There is considerable confusion among the public as to the difference between a hydrologist and a hydraulic engineer. Adding to the confusion, "hydrologist" is almost an old-fashioned term in professional circles and has been replaced by the more complicated "fluvial geomorphologist," a much more precise and contemporary title. Unfortunately, I have seen the eyes of the lay person glaze over when confronted with it and related professional titles.

Hydrologists have traditionally measured the amount of flow in streams and have frequently been concerned with estimating the depth of a stream's flow for a given discharge, which is necessary information for developing floodplain maps. The Federal Council for Science and Technology formulated a useful definition of hydrology in the 1960s: "Hydrology is the science that treats the waters of the earth, their occurrence, circulation and distribution, their chemical and physical properties and their reaction with their environment including their relation to living things. The domain of hydrology emphasizes the full life history of water on earth."[1] A professional hydrologist usually has a background in statistics, the physical sciences, and/or civil engineering.

The term fluvial geomorphologist was first used by Luna Leopold (one of the sons of the early ecologist Aldo Leopold) to demonstrate that he was studying more than the discharges of rivers. A civil engineer and geologist by training, Leopold was the first to use an interdisciplinary approach for understanding flow conditions and how a natural stream channel may evolve over time. Much of his formative early work is only now being recognized by the engineering community as the limitations of traditional flood-control engineering methods are recognized.

Morphology can be defined as "the science of structure or form," and *fluvial* can be defined as "produced by the action of flowing water," so that a definition of fluvial geomorphology is the science of earth forms produced by the action of flowing water. Geomorphology has also been called physiography.[2] As geology is concerned with the history of earth through billions of years, the geomorphologist views the fluvial landscape in a historical perspective and provides information about and insight into the long-term adjustments rivers make to altered hydrologic and hydraulic conditions.[3]

Fluvial geomorphology is concerned specifically with the influences of water and rivers on the erosional cycle of land deposition and degradation over time. The distinction between a hydrologist and a geomorphologist may be hard for the lay person to make, but it could be argued that a hydrologist concentrates on the description, measurement, and analysis of precipitation and the flow of water on the earth's surface and underground, while the fluvial geomorphologist concentrates on understanding the processes that govern the influence of water on the landscape over time. (Some basic references on hydrology and fluvial geomorphology are listed at the end of the references for this chapter.)

A hydraulic engineer is a professional who designs projects to control the variability of natural water flows in order to manage irrigation and urban water supplies and reduce flood damages. Hydraulic engineers are mostly concerned with using computers to model the behavior of flows under conditions where the variables are controlled. Their professional origins involve studying water in laboratory flumes, for example. They deal in the natural world in that their problem may be to transfer water from point A, where there is more precipitation and runoff, to point B, where there is less water. They are often changing the transport of water in a natural channel to transport in a human-built channel. Hydraulic engineers are usually good at predicting flow conditions for specified channel shapes, and they have developed quantitative approaches for understanding sediment transport processes. However, the business of the hydraulic engineer traditionally has not been the understanding or study of the complex interactions of the variables influencing water in nature. The hydraulic engineer's objective is to design projects that move water efficiently and control the natural processes. A standard dictionary definition of hydraulics is that it is the branch of science that deals with the practical implications of the transmission of energy or the effects of the flow of water or other liquid in motion. Our society owes its agricultural and urban water supplies and our stormwater and sewage systems to this important branch of science.

What is unfortunate is that there is not more integration between these branches of water science. It is possible for both the hydrologist and hydraulic engineer to acquire a college degree with a minimum of information about the other related disciplines. The hydrologist or fluvial geomorphologist may have specialized in natural watershed management and the relationship between forestry practices and erosion and runoff, for example, and have only a vague working knowledge of hydraulic models concerned with estimating design flows. The hydraulic engineer may have specialized in the formulation of a new computer program to model the transport of water but may have spent almost no time in the field observing what occurs in nature and had no opportunity to test a model against observed stream flows.[4]

Where does this leave the citizen or public official who would like to arrive at some environmentally sensitive alternatives for managing an urban stream with erosion or flooding problems? If you bring in a hydraulic engineer, the normal predisposition of that professional will be to transform your stream into something more readily understood and manageable, i.e., a canal, culvert, or piped conduit. If you bring in a geomorphologist, you will normally be in better hands for gaining an understanding of alternative actions that work with the environment, as opposed to transforming the environment into something else. The geomorphologist, however, would benefit by knowing about the hydraulic models that could assist with evaluation of particular alternative flood-damage-reduction solutions. A geomorphologist combined with some experts on native plants and revegetation, bank stabilization, and possibly fish biology may be all that you need to devise a sound plan to reduce flood and erosion damages and restore the environmental values of a stream. If you are in a position of wanting to redesign a traditional flood-control channel, it is advisable to seek the help of a hydraulic engineer who is sympathetic to your goals. Such a person can help you interact with the civil works engineers to develop acceptable solutions.

Another way of cutting up the water-professional pie is to classify the professions according to two schools of stream-channel studies. Hydrologists, geomorphologists, and civil engineers study the relationships among the variables that interact with and govern the behavior of streams: stream discharge (or flow), velocity, width, depth, slope, sediment load and size, and channel roughness. These scientists describe and measure the relationships between the channel shapes and sizes, called channel geometry, and hydraulic factors such as stream flows, velocities, roughness of channel, and slope. The relationships among these variables at a given point on a stream channel or as they change downstream are similar even for streams in very different settings and are described by the term "hydraulic geometry."[5] These professionals are interested in noticing, recording, and anticipating "stream dynamics," or the adjustments the different variables make in relationship to each other because of land-use changes, channel modifications, land management actions, and natural phenomena. In other words, their understanding of the stream channel is based on field observations or empirical data. Those who use this empirical information to determine the probable frequency of floods and the probable adjustments a stream will make to changes in the system's variables are in the empirical school.

The professionals who model stream dynamics based on the theoretical properties of energy and general physical principles that have been developed and improved with sophisticated, controlled laboratory experiments with flumes make up the fundamental or theoretical school of stream behavior studies.[6] Both schools have made valuable contributions to the study of streams, and the information from one can be cross-checked with the other.[7]

Empirical approaches have had an important role in determining the nature of the field of channel hydraulics. The first empirical approach to designing channels dates to 1879 and used a concept of maximum velocity in which a large number of channels with different geology and soils and topography and different degrees of stability and instability were observed. This produced data that identified the threshold values for velocities at which channel erosion would begin.

In the late 1800s and early 1900s in India and Pakistan, practitioners who were designing and digging stable irrigation canals developed a series of equations to relate hydraulic and geometric characteristics of streams. These canals were described as "stable" canals or channels in "regimes," and these regime equations, as developed by Lacey, Lindley, and others, are the basis for many channel designs today.[8, 9] In recent times, the equations have been greatly improved using results from flume studies and sediment transport theory. A major limitation for the practitioner who uses the regime equations is that they must be applied to environments similar to the environments from which they were derived. No one has succeeded in developing a general set of equations that apply to natural streams under a wide variety of conditions.[10–12]

While the regime equations do have their basis in empirical data, the assumption that the best channel design is one without meanders and with a minimum of deposition and erosion has been questioned by those who suggest that nature's channel in "dynamic equilibrium" is a better model. Those professionals—considered a part of the empirical school—advocate minimizing the conflict of designs with the natural behavior of stream channels.

The approach to stream channel management and design advocated by this book actually integrates three elements: the relationships between channel geometry and fluvial processes; empirical information on the dynamics in natural streams reacting to watershed changes; and dynamic equilibrium as the basis for channel design as opposed to the concept of an unmoving, straight, "stable" channel in regime.

It is simplistic to refer to those who practice this system of watershed management as members of the empirical school. It may be better to classify them as members of the "restoration school." In summary, stream restoration, can be defined as the adjustment of watersheds and stream channels that employs: the concepts of dynamic equilibrium; the relationships common to all stream systems between channel geometry and fluvial processes; and the use of empirical functional relationships among the variables that interact in the watershed and the stream channel to anticipate stream responses to conditions and changes in the watershed and channel. This recommended approach does not preclude the use of sophisticated computer models, but the use of these three elements can enhance the relevance and accuracy of the modeling results. Hydraulic engineers, hydrologists, and fluvial geomorphologists should all be cooperating members of the restoration school.

Types of Stream Channels

An outgrowth of the newly evolving field of stream restoration is the classification of stream channels to help guide the design of restoration strategies. This section introduces some of the most basic distinctions among stream types to help prepare you for a more detailed description of stream classification in chapter 9. The restoration professional benefits from knowledge of stream types whether she is attempting to restore a stream severely impacted by urbanization or one that has retained a more natural form.

The most obvious factors that can distinquish different stream types are the geology or soils making up the streambed, the gradient or steepness of the stream slope, and the degree to which a stream meanders or is straight. Figure 4.1 illustrates four distinct types of channels: an alluvial, meandering channel; a straight bedrock channel; a channel armored with rocks and cobbles; and a braided channel. These types will be described here as a way of introducing some common terms used to describe rivers. Additional factors that distinquish stream types include the ratio of the widths and depths of bankfull channels; whether streams have wide floodplains or are confined within narrow floodplains; and the widths of the meander belt, or the boundaries of the stream meander pattern. Ultimately, if restoration professionals can determine the stream type a damaged stream should be returned to, they would have significant guidance on how to reshape the channel and its meanders.

All too frequently the type of stream channels found in urban areas are no longer natural channels but have become artificial channels. Artificial linings made from concrete, gunite (a special mix of concrete sprayed from a hose), or rock and built in an attempt to make the channel stationary, prevent the migration of the channel and can also harden the bed to create what is referred to as a fixed-boundary channel.

Some natural channels are bedrock channels, in which the streambed is rock and its size and shape are controlled by the hard bedrock surface. These channels are

FIGURE 4.1. SOME BASIC TYPES OF STREAM CHANNELS.
(a) Alluvial meandering channel (at bankfull flow; refer to diagram in figure 4.4). (b) Straight bedrock channel. (c) Channel bottom "armored" with rocks and cobbles. (d) Braided channel.

generally found in the steeper, higher elevations of watersheds, and the erosive power of the water often creates relatively straight channels and features such as waterfalls, rapids, and gorges. Generally, these are recognized to be stable channels. Natural "armored" channels are channels with beds of cobbles and rocks that resist the downward erosion of the bed. The term "armored" among river management professionals refers to a situation in which smaller particles such as sands, silts, clay, and gravels are transported downstream, leaving in place larger materials such as rocks and cobbles that may inhibit the lowering or movement of the streambed. Armoring can also refer to the placement by human beings of large rocks and cobbles in the streambed and on the banks to prevent channel degradation or meandering. Sometimes armoring is used as a synonym for riprap.

The above channel types are referred to as nonalluvial channels (with the exception of naturally armored channels, considered alluvial since stream flows will eventually move the armor layer), whereas the channels this book is most concerned with are the more common alluvial channels. Alluvium is defined as silt, sand, and gravel deposited by running water. Alluvial streams flow through beds and banks of unconsolidated alluvium. Because that material can be eroded, transported, and deposited, the alluvial river is a dynamic system, its shape, slope, and meander pattern adjusting to the flow of water and the sediment load.

Another way to classify channel types is by how straight they are or how much they meander—what the channel pattern is. Channel patterns vary from straight to meandering to braided. The more a stream meanders within a given distance, the more "sinuous" it is. Sinuosity is a critical factor that must be taken into account in the design of restoration projects.

A braided stream channel is typically wide and shallow and contains a number of separated channels that flow in and around mid-channel sediment bars and islands. Braided channels usually indicate that a stream is supplied with more sediment than it can carry. Other conditions that can lead to braiding are steep slopes, coarse materials with low erosion resistance, sediments deposited at grade changes, and aggradation that allows the channel to shift course.

The type of channel you have to work with is central to the design of a restoration project. It is one of the first things that needs to be determined. Modifications for fish habitat or other restoration work can generally be done with much greater ease on the more inherently stable, upstream, bedrock or rock and cobble channels than the more complicated downstream, alluvial reaches. A braided stream is unstable, changes its alignment rapidly, carries large amounts of sediment, is wide and shallow even at flood flows, and is in general unpredictable.[13] Natural nonalluvial channels generally have fewer stability problems than alluvial channels, and it can be easier to make adjustments to those channels to encourage equilibrium conditions. For that reason, a larger portion of restoration work is directed at alluvial channels. There are exceptions to this, of course. Upper watershed bedrock channels may be impacted by landslides, logging debris, development, or other disturbances and require restoration as a response.

Watershed Influences

The stream channel, of course, is part of a larger system—namely, the watershed. The watershed is of interest to the stream restorationist for three main reasons. The first is that we cannot diagnose a stream's problems and prescribe an antidote without understanding what parts of the whole watershed are contributing to the problems. Chapter 8 recommends a watershed inventory that can be used to evaluate the impacts of land uses, storm-water and flood-control systems, natural areas, and land management practices on stream channels. The second interest we have in the watershed is that its land forms, geology, soils, and climate, along with land use, determine the rates and amount of runoff and transport of sediment, boulders, and debris to stream channels. These variables are commonly used in models to estimate storm-water runoff rates, and the models become the basis for designing urban storm-water and flood-control facilities. The third practical interest the urban stream restorationist has in the watershed is that our knowledge of nearby streams that appear relatively balanced and that drain similarly sized watersheds can help us in the restoration design process.

Watershed processes control the amount and rates of water, sediment, and dissolved materials supplied to the drainages. Streams are a product of the type, amount, and time-spatial distribution of precipitation; the rates of infiltration and evapotranspiration; and the geology, soils, topography, vegetation, and land use.[14] A number of models have been developed to predict the watershed processes of erosion and runoff, in particular. The streamflow simulation techniques vary considerably in data requirements, desired outputs, geographic relevancy, costs, and the required expertise to use them. Regression equations used to simulate drainage responses in which the relationships among geomorphic, climatic, land-use, and discharge variables are mathematically defined can be easy tools for estimating peak discharges on the smaller, ungauged watersheds. Some of these models, such as the U.S. Army Corps of Engineers Streamflow Synthesis (SSARR) and the Stanford Watershed Model Series, are technically very sophisticated. At the other end of the range is the simple "rational method."[15]

The following is a useful summary of the major watershed parameters and processes from a U.S. Army Corps of Engineers report:[16]

Major Watershed Parameters	Major Processes	Major Storages and Outputs
Precipitation	Interception	Soil moisture
Solar radiation	Evapotranspiration	Groundwater
Temperature	Infiltration	Water discharge
Vegetation and land use	Throughflow	Sediment
Discharge	Overland flow	
Soils	Soil erosion	
Geology		
Topography		

Watershed models will estimate values for the parameters, which are a part of the equations used to represent the processes, which when solved give estimated values for the outputs.

The methods used to estimate storm-water runoff and flood frequency range from the widely used and very simple rational method to the more sophisticated probability analysis, unit hydrograph methods, and flood routing. The rational method can be used to predict peak runoff rates from a simple formula that uses data on average rainfall intensity and drainage basin characteristics for the water-shed your stream is located in. The formula is so simple that the layperson can use it to get an idea of the discharges a watershed will generate for the one-in-2-, 5-, 10-, 25-, and 50-year floods. The rational method is commonly applied to areas as large as 5 square miles but preferably should be used for drainages under a half square mile. Different regions and even different cities within the same region will use different variables and values for variables in the equation. You can check with your local public works department to find out what the local practice is. There is often a local engineering handbook that will take you through the steps to solve the equation.

The equation used in the rational method is:

$$Q = CiA$$

where Q is the peak runoff expressed in cubic feet per second; C represents water-shed basin characteristics such as infiltration, slopes, soil-water moisture, shape of the basin, ground cover, etc.; i is the average precipitation intensity in inches per hour; and A the drainage area in acres.

⌒

The rational method has been very useful to estimate peak flows on the smaller ungauged urban streams where I typically do many of my restoration projects. Note that for projects involving difficult or complicated flood management issues, this method should be supplemented by or replaced with the more sophisticated methods.

Land Forms and Drainage Areas

Topographic maps and aerial photographs are essential tools for urban stream restoration projects. Historical topographic maps and photos, and old sketch maps, can provide important information on how the watershed and stream appeared before the impacts of urbanization. These historical maps can show, for example, that what is now a stream was actually a low-lying undrained wetland at one time, a particularly frequent situation in the midwest states. The maps may show old channel meander patterns suggesting the extent of historic floodplains. They can provide evidence of what the streamside vegetation looked like. Even though the maps represent a past era whose streams cannot usually be reproduced in urban settings of the present, they can provide us with some guidelines and restoration objectives.

When we are daylighting a stream that has been underground for a number of years, we can turn to historic maps to gain an understanding of how long and sinuous the channel used to be and what the meander shapes were for the gradients and soils we are working with. When we re-create the new channel, we can use the old channel's sinuosity as the starting point for our design. We can also try to re-create the basic topographic features of floodplains and terraces, providing wider floodplains when possible, to give the streams more room to adjust their shapes and meanders. If we are dealing with a watershed that has undergone considerable land-use changes since the date of the historic map, the discharges will be greater and therefore the urban channel should be designed to be wider. Meander wavelengths can be designed so that they are in proportion to the channel widths.

Up-to-date topographic maps and aerial photos can be used to help you figure the percentage of the watershed that has been urbanized, the area that has been put in storm sewers, watershed drainage areas, and slopes, and can provide information that can be used in watershed models to determine storm runoff rates. One of the most important things you can learn from a topographic map is the size of the drainage area affecting the site you hope to restore. Despite considerable differences in climate and especially mean annual precipitation, channel sizes are similar for the same size drainage areas. By knowing your drainage area size, you can find out if the field measurements for the width and depth of your stream are significantly different from the average values for width and depth of other streams in your region.[17] This information can help you determine if your channel is significantly different from other channels in the same region and how its shape may be out of equilibrium. Notable differences from the regional averages may be a sign of stream adjustments being made to urbanization or other land-use impacts. This may give you clues as to whether your stream is responding to the urbanization cycle that is described in the section "Changes to Stream Channels." This drainage area–channel dimension relationship can also help guide you in the field to locate the active, bankfull channel and estimate the channel-forming discharges. This is information critical for use in designing stream channel restoration projects.

Using a Topographic Map

Topographic maps can be acquired from the U.S. Geological Survey, the agency that prepares them for use in the United States. Other federal and state agencies may make them available as well, and you may be able to purchase them in local university, college, or independent book or map stores.

Use figure 4.2 to develop the concept of how a flat map conveys information about a three-dimensional topography. The maps will indicate the difference in elevation between contours. In the figure, each contour represents a change in elevation of 20 feet. The scale for distance is typically shown on the bottom of the map. For example, on the topographic map that figure 4.2 was taken from, the 1:24000 scale means that 1⅝ inches is equal to a mile. When a contour closes into a small loop, it designates a hilltop. By connecting the tops of the hills surrounding your drainage, you are drawing in the watershed at or near your restoration site. If you have a planimeter, you can set it at the correct map scale and trace the perimeter of the watershed and find out how many square miles it includes. If you do not have a planimeter, simply trace your watershed onto graph paper. Note the number of boxes on the graph paper that form a linear mile for the scale on the map, and then figure the number of boxes that make up a square mile. Count the number of boxes that fall within the watershed boundary to calculate the square miles of the drainage area.

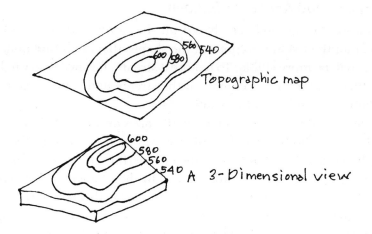

Topographic map

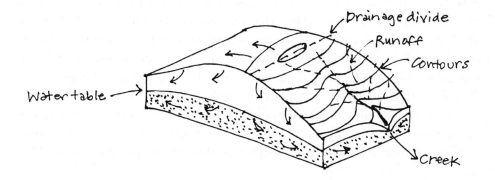

600
580
560
540 A 3-Dimensional view

Drainage divide
Runoff
Contours

Water table

Creek

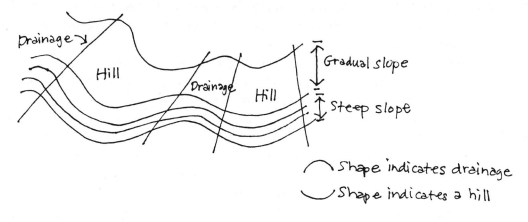

Drainage

Hill

Drainage
Hill

Gradual slope

Steep slope

Shape indicates drainage
Shape indicates a hill

FIGURE 4.2. INTERPRETING A TOPOGRAPHIC MAP.

Floodplains, Terraces, and Bankfull Channels

Stream-channel restoration methods are based on the premise that if we repair stream channels so that their shapes represent the shapes that are found in nature, the stream channels will be more stable. To restore a stream, it is necessary to know the different components and measurements of the stream and watershed, in particular, the floodplains, bankfull channels, and terraces.

A geologist will tend to define a floodplain as the area of a river valley covered with material deposited by floods. The hydrologist will tend to say that the floodplain is that area of a river valley that is periodically overflowed by water in excess of the stream channel.[18] The results are the same, but their viewpoints determine their definitions. Floodplains tend not to be present in the headwaters of tributaries presumably because the stream is mostly down-cutting in the steeper topographies as opposed to meandering laterally. The elevation of the floodplain can change. The land may be rising over time from tectonic mountain-building forces in the earth. A change in climate or changes caused by urbanization can also affect the elevation of a streambed. As a result of sequences of channel erosion and degradation followed by channel deposition and rising channel bed elevation or aggradation, abandoned floodplains, or *terraces*, are formed. If stream-channel degradation and aggradation occur repeatedly, there may be a number of terraces. Many landscapes typically contain terraces, but not all stream valleys have them. The important distinction is that the floodplain is actively related to the current movements of the stream, while a terrace is an abandoned surface no longer related to the present stream.[19, 20] (figure 4.3)

Most streams have a meandering pattern. Material is eroded off one bank of a channel and deposited onto the opposite bank, and that erosion and deposition usually results in the lateral migration of the stream across the valley. Each sideward motion of the stream leaves a nearly level deposit bordering the channel, which is the floodplain. In addition, material may be deposited by floods on top of the floodplain. Stream channels characteristically maintain a constant shape and size as they meander across their floodplains.[21]

A flow over the bank of a channel is by definition a flood. Channels flow at a shallow depth most of the time and fill to the top of their banks with surprisingly uniform frequency among streams in diverse settings and of widely different sizes and orders. The channel will be filled to a bankfull stage or height on the average of every one to two years. Thus, the stream channel is large enough to accommodate the runoff from the watershed in the most frequent storms. The area bordering most channels must flood to some extent on the average of every other year. The bankfull discharge is the flow of water that fills the channel and just begins to overtop the streambank into the floodplain. These bankfull discharges will not occur like clockwork every one and a half years, but rather over a long period of record they occur on the *average* of every 1.5 years. Bankfull discharges form the channel shape because they have enough stream power to erode, transport, and deposit the materials that form the stream banks.

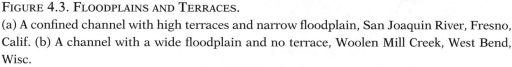

FIGURE 4.3. FLOODPLAINS AND TERRACES.
(a) A confined channel with high terraces and narrow floodplain, San Joaquin River, Fresno, Calif. (b) A channel with a wide floodplain and no terrace, Woolen Mill Creek, West Bend, Wisc.

The relationship between the active, or bankfull, channel and the 1.5-year-recurrence-interval discharge has been supported by a preponderance of data collected from field observations and stream-gauging stations around the country. It is interesting to note, however, that scientists have not been able to draw any relationship between any constant-sized flow and the height or formation of river terraces. The commonly occurring relationship between the 1.5-year discharges measured in the United States and the depth of the active channel was arrived at by making field surveys of many active channels and then checking the field-derived elevation of the active channels against the depths of discharges and flood-frequency data available from gauging stations. The discharges measured at the stations for the active-channel elevations corresponded closely on the average to the discharges in the flood-frequency data for the 1-in-1.5-year discharge.[22–25]

The stream channel that carries the most frequent flows from the commonly recurring smaller storms is referred to as the dominant, active, or bankfull channel by professionals involved in stream restoration. The bankfull stage is attained when a channel is filled, which often occurs, as just discussed, on the *average* of every 1.5 years in the annual flood series. The bankfull width and depth refer to the dimensions of the active, or bankfull, channel (see figures 4.1 and 4.4). This bankfull channel and the bankfull measurements of width and depth are the basic features on which any stream restoration design should be based.

Geomorphologists have developed the important concept that the landscape is formed primarily by events of intermediate frequency and *not* by rare or catastrophic events.[25] A catastrophic flood may greatly alter a stream channel, for

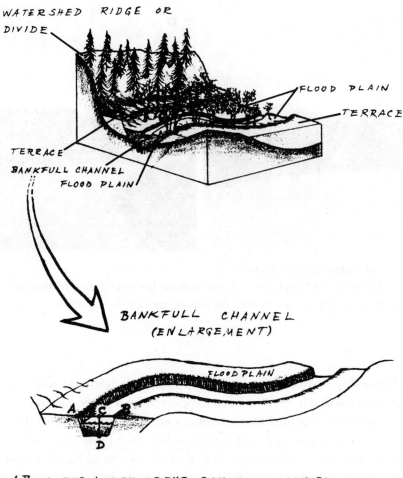

FIGURE 4.4. THE BANKFULL CHANNEL AND ITS WIDTH-DEPTH RATIO.

example, but the frequently occurring flows that follow will tend to return the channel to its previous condition. The dynamic, meandering, active channel maintains a stable shape while it changes its location on the floodplain by continually re-creating its channel geometry. The person who wants to restore a stream, therefore, tries to re-create the bankfull channel dimensions that represent that dynamic equilibrium, including its width, depth, and meader pattern.

It makes good sense to restore equilibrium to the "channel-forming" or "dominant" discharge carried by the bankfull channel rather than to focus scarce time and resources on trying to anticipate the reactions of the stream system to the rare catastrophic flows. (The dominant discharge can be calculated by determining the *effective* discharge, which is defined as a range of flows that over a long period of time transports the most sediment.) After restoring equilibrium to the bankfull channel, our efforts should go toward protecting the stream's adjacent floodplain to absorb the impacts of high flows. Any modification of a stream channel for flood-damage reduction, therefore, needs to accommodate a properly sized bankfull channel and an adjacent floodplain or an adjacent "high-flow channel."

A question we must ask of all channelization projects is do we want to expend significant resources for a long period of time maintaining a channel for stability in a situation that rarely occurs, i.e., a large flood, or should we better use our resources for stabilizing the situation that is present most of the time, i.e., low and moderate stream flows? The rationale for many channelization designs is that natural landscape forms such as bankfull channels and floodplains take up too much room that can better be used for development. As our natural environment is disappearing, however, our society has begun to place higher value on the natural landscape and the benefits it brings to cities. In undeveloped areas we clearly have the option to integrate floodplains and their active channels into urbanization plans. Even in already highly urbanized environments we usually have the opportunity to restore the dimensions of a bankfull channel within a narrow project width or right-of-way, even if we can't restore the historical floodplain.

Concept of Stream Equilibrium

So far we have established that streams and rivers are dynamic systems that are adjusting to natural or human-imposed changes in watersheds. This natural dynamic of eroding, depositing, and changing slopes and meanders over time (stream-channel processes) conflicts with the engineered stable-system concept. This conflict can create significant maintenance for conventionally engineered streams at best—and waterway project failures at worst. Restoration projects differ from conventional engineering projects in that they recognize the changing dynamics of streams and work with them. In this section we are going to further define equilibrium, introduce the closely related concept of graded streams, and describe the relationships between discharges and sediment transport as they affect equilibrium.

As early as the 1940s and 1950s, fluvial geomorphologists began describing both rivers and landscapes as ecological systems with many interacting variables.[26, 27] Interrelated river system variables include the size of the watershed; the amount and size of sediment transported in the river channel; the channel shape, size, slope, and roughness (trees, bushes, rocks, streambed forms, stream-bank surface, floodplain obstructions, channel bends, etc.); and the amount and frequency of flow discharges. A stream in equilibrium is a stream in which these variables are in balance with each other and is sometimes described as being a graded stream. A condition of equilibrium does not mean a steady state or condition at any one particular stream flow because the variables change among stream reaches and over time; the dynamic equilibrium of a channel represents the average condition of a river during its relatively recent history.

Under conditions of dynamic equilibrium, the stream's energy is such that the sediment loads entering a stream reach are equal to those leaving it. Over its long-term evolution, a river or stream will attempt to transport the sediment delivered to it with the available runoff. A graded stream refers to one in which over a period of years, slope and channel characteristics are delicately adjusted to provide with available discharge just the velocity required for the transportation of the sediment load supplied from the drainage basin. If we consider a long geologic time scale, the evolution of a stream is governed by the geology and climate influencing the region. Viewed against a shorter time scale, in days, weeks, or months, streams seldom achieve a steady state because of the continuous small and large changes in water, sediment discharges, vegetation, streambed forms, and other factors.[28–31]

The meandering river demonstrates the balance of erosion and deposition, forming depositional point bars and erosional bends and pools. If discharges in relation to sediment loads are reduced by a geologic or human-made change (e.g., diversions for water supply, landslides, increased sedimentation from urbanization), large amounts of debris may be dropped rapidly in the channel. The deposited material may deflect the current into different channels as the river searches for an easier course. The result can be a braided stream, a channel that is made up of several diverging channels separated by sandbars or islands, which we briefly introduced earlier. Natural levees can be another depositional feature, formed by the overflow of sediment-laden water that deposits its load close to the river. Floodplains themselves are depositional features formed by a constantly shifting, meandering channel that, during flood periods, spreads fine silt, sand, and clay across its valley. Deltas are formed when a stream flows into another body of water and its velocity and transporting power are quickly stopped, causing the sediment load to be dropped.

At this point, the stream restorationist needs to be familiar with the concepts of stream competence, or the ability of a stream to pick up certain sizes of sediment (known as sediment entrainment), and sediment transport, or the capacity of a stream to move a volume of sediment. A stream may be inherently competent to move the types or sizes of sediment in its channel, but its capacity to transport it may be overwhelmed if the volume of the sediment is excessive. This could be caused by watershed disturbances such as construction activities or logging. A stream may be "starved" of sediment sizes and supplies because, for example, a dam has trapped almost all its coarse sediment. The clear water released from dams is sometimes called hungry water because it lacks its usual suspended sediment. In such a case, during high flows the stream will have excess stream power and will entrain and transport (pick up and carry) coarse materials from the riverbanks and cause considerable erosion.

Competence and transport capacity can often be related to changes in velocity. Decline of velocity can be associated with an increase in channel area, width-to-depth ratio, and/or channel bed roughness and a decrease in channel gradient. A restoration project with the objective of increasing or decreasing sediment transport will need to adjust these variables accordingly.

The base level of a stream is also a key concept in the explanation of stream behavior and equilibrium. The base level of a stream is a controlling downstream elevation, such as a lake or ocean. There are often local and, geologically speaking, temporary elevations to which streams tend to cut their beds. For example, the bed of a large river usually forms the base level for its tributaries. If the base level of the river is lowered or raised by natural or artificial means—such as a reservoir, channelization project, or even bridge abutments or culverts—the river will adjust over time to re-create approximately the slope it had before. This means the slopes of the tributaries will also be changing to conform with the slope fluctuations occurring in the river. In general, a stream adjusts to a rise in base level by building up its channel through sedimentation; it adjusts to a fall in base level by eroding its channel. When a streambed is elevated by sedimentation, the stream must then erode its way through that material to reach its base level, and in so doing, it eventually steepens or increases the slope. When a streambed degrades in relationship to its base level, it flattens or decreases its slope.[32]

A stream that exhibits *excessive* erosion or *excessive* deposition over a short period of time is not in equilibrium. Restoration can sometimes help a river system to regain balance faster than it would on its own.

The complexity of the stream's processes, the difficulty of predicting the time required for stream-channel adjustments, and the difficulty of obtaining adequate information on the variables that affect the watershed system are typical problems for any watershed manager or stream restorationist. It is easier in many respects to design a stable channel with rigid beds and banks and straight land forms than to design a restoration project with the objective of attaining dynamic equilibrium. It is possible to design with that objective, however, and your river project will be more sustainable over time if you do.

In 1955, E. W. Lane described an equation of equilibrium that is nicely illustrated by this graphic of Lane's balance in figure 4.5. The equation is

> The quantity of sediment × sediment size is proportional to
> the slope of the stream × the stream's discharge.

Lane's balance illustrates that a change in any of these four variables indicates the need for a corresponding change in one or more of the other variables to restore equilibrium. For example, if a stream is capable of carrying more sediment than it has entering it, it will erode and transport material from its bed and lower its elevation. That will lower the base level for its tributary streams, which will erode in turn, producing a greater sediment load to the main stream. As the eroding channels flatten their grades, their ability to carry away sediment is diminished. As the amount of material carried down the streams increases and the streams' ability to transport the sediment decreases, the streams begin to reach a state of equilibrium. The quantity of sediment, assuming the sediment size and water discharges remained the same, directly influences the slope.

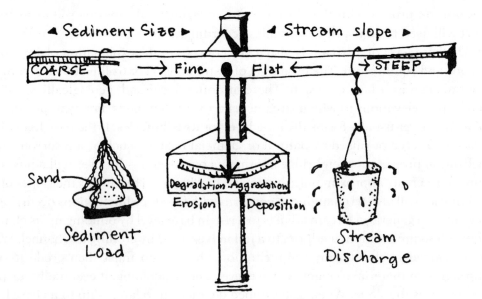

Sediment load x sediment size is proportional to
the slope of the stream x stream discharge

FIGURE 4.5. FACTORS INFLUENCING STREAM EROSION AND SEDIMENTATION.
Source: E. W. Lane, "The Importance of Fluvial Morphology in Hydraulic Engineering," *Proceedings of the American Society of Civil Engineers,* volume 81, no. 745, 1955.

A number of scientists have investigated channel responses to changes in those parameters and their studies support some general relationships among them:[33]

- The depth of flow in a stream channel is proportional to the discharge. Depths increase with increasing discharges but not as much as widths.
- The channel width is proportional to both water discharge and sediment discharge. Widening in response to increased flood discharges can generally be expected. Channel narrowing can usually be expected if discharges are reduced.
- Channel shape, expressed as a width to depth ratio, is directly related to sediment discharge.
- The channel gradient decreases (flattens) with an increase in discharge and increases (steepens) with a decrease in discharge.
- The channel slope is proportional to both sediment discharge and sediment grain size.
- Sinuosity or degree of meandering is proportional to valley slope.
- Meander wavelengths tend to maintain a constant relationship with channel width. Increased discharges tend to increase meander wavelength and channel width.

- Bank erosion, channel width, planform stability, and rates of channel migration across a floodplain are moderated by bank materials and streamside woody vegetation.

How Urbanization Can Change Watersheds and Streams

Watershed Changes

A stream is only as healthy as the watershed where it is located. Scientists who have surveyed urban watersheds describe a common syndrome of loss of native vegetation and wildlife habitat and channel migration; loss of connections among landscape features, such as tributaries to main channels and channels from floodplains; reduction in water quality; and a change of watershed hydrology whereby flows are "flashier," or reach high stages quickly, total runoff is increased, dry-season base flows are reduced, and channel instability is common (table 4.1).[34–36]

Physical Modifications

In urban areas the concept of watershed becomes more complex because the natural topography has been disturbed; the water may be drained through storm drains and in some cases may be diverted by drains into other basins. An area that contributes runoff either naturally or by storm drains to a particular point in a drainage is considered to be a part of that watershed. As an urban dweller in a flat part of town, I waited for it to rain and watched which way the water flowed to the storm sewers to identify what creek my storm drain flows to. That way I could figure out which watershed my house is in.

An urban stream at its worst may be muddy from sediments; have destabilized, sloughing banks and sparse vegetation; carry oils, gasoline, and urban waste from storm sewers; and be the dumping grounds for residential garbage and yard debris including furniture, mattresses, and car batteries. The lack of canopy from large trees may expose the stream channel to more sunlight than normal, encouraging the growth of unwanted rushes, reeds, and algae. These can "choke" the channel, causing stagnant water and braiding. Shopping carts inhabit the urban stream with such predictability that the Urban Creeks Council of California has classified the shopping cart as the "indicator organism" of the urban creek. The council consequently has designated its highest award as the Golden Shopping Cart Award.

The worst physical modification of urban watersheds is the relegation of stream channels and tributaries to underground culverts. Riparian zones are eliminated or separated from the stream channels. Removal of streamside vegetation results in the loss of nutrients to the aquatic organisms, loss of shade, increased bank erosion, lateral movement of the stream channel, increased sedimentation, and decreased pool depths. Floodplains become separated from the stream channels because the channels have become incised or deepened, or the previous land-use practices have added large layers of fill to floodplains, or both of these things have happened.

Table 4.1. Potential Impacts of Urbanization on a Watershed

Change in Land or Water Use	Possible Hydrologic Effect
Transition from pre-urban to early-urban state: Removal of trees or vegetation, construction of scattered city-type houses & limited water & sewage facilities.	Decrease in transpiration & increase in storm flow. Increased sedimentation of streams.
Drilling of wells.	Some lowering of water table.
Construction of septic tanks & sanitary drains.	Some increase in soil moisture & perhaps a rise in water table. Perhaps some waterlogging of land & contamination of nearby wells or streams from overloaded sanitary drain systems.
Transition from early-urban to middle-urban stage: Bulldozing of land for mass housing; some topsoil removal; farm ponds filled in.	Accelerated land erosion and stream sedimentation and aggradation. Elimination of smallest streams by filling or culverting.
Mass construction of houses; paving of streets; building of culverts.	Decreased infiltration resulting in increased storm water and flood flows & lowered ground-water levels. Flooding at channel constrictions (culverts) on remaining small streams. Occasional overtopping or undermining of banks of artificial and natural channels.
Discontinued use and abandonment of some shallow wells.	Rise in water table.
Diversion of nearby streams for public water supply.	Decrease in flow between points of diversion & disposal. Fish and other aquatic life decline or are extinguished. Riparian areas degrade or disappear.
Untreated or inadequately treated sewage discharged into streams or disposal wells.	Pollution of streams or wells. Death of fish & other aquatic life. Inferior quality of water available for supply & recreation at downstream populated areas.
Transition from middle- to late-urban stage: Urbanization of area completed by addition of more houses & streets, & of public, commercial, & industrial buildings	Reduced infiltration & lowered water table. Streets & gutters act as storm drains, creating flashy and higher flood peaks & lower base flow of local streets.

Larger quantities of untreated waste discharged into local streams.	Increased pollution of streams & concurrent increased loss of aquatic life. Additional degradation of water available to downstream users.
Abandonment of remaining shallow wells because of pollution.	Rise in water table.
Increase in population requires establishment of new water supply & distribution systems, construction of distant reservoirs, diverting water from upstream sources within or outside basin.	Increase in local stream flow if supply is from outside basin. Decrease in local stream flow if supply includes local sources also. Wide-scale loss of river systems for fish, wildlife, and recreation.
Channels of streams put in artificial channels & culverts.	Increased flood damage if culverts are undersized, and increased backup flows. Increased downstream flood flows if channelized or culverted. Changes in channel geometry & sediment load. Aggradation and/or degradation up- and downstream of project or structure. Stream-channel stability problems and loss of floodplain storage.
Construction of sanitary drainage system & treatment plant for sewage and improvement of storm drainage system to move water to rivers, bays, lakes, etc.	Removal of additional water from area, further reducing infiltration recharge of aquifer. Degradation of stream channels used as storm-water conveyance systems.
Drilling of deeper, large-capacity industrial wells.	Lowered ground-water level, decreasing pressure of artesian aquifer: perhaps some local overdrafts & land subsidence. Overdraft of aquifer may result in salt water encroachment in coastal area and in pollution or contamination by inferior or brackish waters.
Increased use of water for air conditioning.	Overloading of sewers & other drainage facilities. Possibly some recharge to water table, owing to leakage of disposal lines.
Drilling of recharge wells.	Raising of ground-water (level) surface.
Wastewater reclamation and utilization.	Recharge to ground-water aquifers. More efficient use of water resources.

Adapted from: U.S. Geological Survey Circular 601–1, "Water Facts and Figures for Planners and Managers," J. H. Feth, 1973.

Structural barriers such as levees and flood walls and channelization can be added causes of this separation. Floodplains can be one of the most biologically productive parts of the watershed system as well as a storage and conveyance area for floodwater, but they are often impacted by urbanization.[37, 38]

Runoff and Sediment

Of all the land-use changes that can impact a watershed and its hydrology, urbanization is by far the most significant. Such development increases impervious surfaces, such as asphalt and cement, producing greater volumes of runoff from storms, which "run off" the land quicker than if a natural watershed was absorbing rainfall. Urbanization tends to increase the volume and peak of stream flows. The delivery of runoff to streams after the beginning of rainfall becomes flashier, reducing the lag time between the rainfall and the peak of a stream's flood stage. Figure 4.6 illustrates that for a one-square-mile basin the difference between an unsewered area with 0 percent impervious surfaces and a completely developed and sewered area with 100 percent impervious area is an increase of mean annual discharges on the average of about eight times. Areas 100 percent sewered but 60 percent impervious will increase mean annual discharges on the average of about four times.[39–41]

While urbanized watersheds can be expected to create long-term increases in runoff and stream flows, they cause more complex cycles in contributing sediment to their streams and valleys. One study estimated that the tonnage of sediment per acre derived from urban construction activities may exceed the tonnage eroded from farms by 20,000–40,000 times. While the sediment eroding off a watershed undergoing development can be extremely high in the construction phase (2–200 times the natural yield), the yield is often markedly reduced when the development is completed and may produce less sediment than natural areas.[42–44]

Increased sediment yields in urban areas are a function not only of runoff from construction sites but also of changes in channel shapes. Using figure 4.6, you can estimate that a change in urbanization might cause the annual mean flood to increase in volume by 2.7 times. These increased flows could, for example, increase the width of a stream by two times and the depth by 50 percent. Computations from a Pennsylvania study show that if that type of urban-induced channel erosion occurred for a one-fourth-mile stretch of urban stream in a one-square-mile drainage basin, the amount of sediment produced would be 50,000 cubic feet—or 2,500 tons. This channel erosion alone would produce as much sediment as five years' worth of usual production from an un-urbanized area of the same size.[45]

Urban Watershed Management

Watershed management and restoration programs can address the impacts of urbanization and reduce increases in runoff, erosion, and sedimentation. On-site detention of storm water using site design measures such as natural drainages instead of storm pipes and culverts, detention wetlands, reforestation, rainwater cisterns, and buffer zones can delay the timing and reduce the volume and peaks of runoff and filter the water before it enters stream and river channels. Riparian restoration

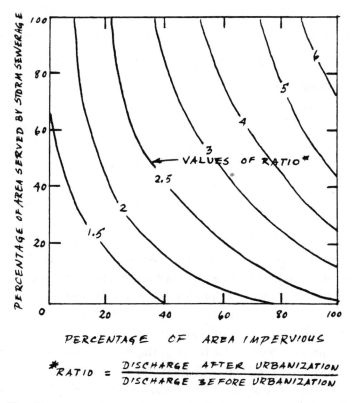

FIGURE 4.6. THE EFFECT OF URBANIZATION ON STORM RUNOFF (FOR A ONE-SQUARE-MILE BASIN).
Source: U.S. Geological Survey Circular 554.

projects can help add stability to stream channels adjusting to greater urban flows. Buffer zones and greenways along waterways can prevent damages to structures from waterways that are adjusting and enlarging under the influence of urbanization. Native woodlands and vegetation can be returned to watershed slopes.

Probably the most confusing issue to the public in the area of urban watershed management and restoration is what impact these land management measures can have on reducing the incidence of flooding. It is widely accepted that extreme floods occur when watershed lands are completely saturated and therefore essentially impervious, so that all rainfall becomes runoff. Research supports the concept that watershed land management measures can reduce runoff rates and flood stages for the frequent low- and moderate-magnitude floods, but extreme events, which by their very definition exceed the ability of even a natural landscape to absorb water, cannot be modified by restoration. For example, one study shows that smaller frequent floods increase by up to ten times after 20 percent urbanization in a watershed, while the extreme events were barely increased at all. Unfortunately, good land management cannot stop a natural cycle of flooding streams.[46, 47] Floodplain management experts say that the most desirable approach for flood management from a watershed perspective is to use land zoning, relocations of structures, and floodproofing and elevation of structures in flood-hazard areas to reduce damages from the large, rare events and to put more resources into the kinds of watershed management practices that will reduce our most common, recurring storm-water and flood problems.

Monitoring the Changes

The U.S. Geological Survey study on the Pickering and East Brandywine Creek basins provides a model for the citizen who is interested in developing a record of the changes that urbanization can bring to a watershed system. The basic data required to observe the changes over time include drainage area and discharge relationships, the discharges and the changes in the shape of the channel, suspended sediment and discharge relationships, and changes in channel meanders and floodplains and terraces. When discharges increase, incised meanders may occur, and, as the stream migrates across the valley floor, a new valley is formed. There are many stream systems in which tremendous property losses have occurred because of the shifting meander of the stream. Water-quality parameters that are recommended for observation include nitrates, phosphates, dissolved oxygen, biochemical oxygen demand, pH, alkalinity, chlorides, total dissolved solids, turbidity, and biochemical oxygen demand, as well as the stream fauna.[48]

A watershed monitoring tool at the heart of the hydrologist's practice is the unit hydrograph shown in figure 4.7. Hydrologists use the unit hydrograph to analyze peak flow rates and the timing of storm runoff and to calculate the amount of storm runoff. A simple hydrograph is a plot of stream-flow discharge in cubic feet per second as a function of time and is illustrated in figure 4.7 along with a unit hydrograph.

The shaded bars on the left of figure 4.7 labeled "rainfall in inches" represent a rainfall hyetograph. Each bar represents the volume of rain that occurred for a specified period of time. Time may be shown in minutes, hours, days, or other units. The total volume of rain in these bars is the volume of rain for that particular storm.[49]

The bell-curved hydrograph shows the volume of storm runoff that enters the stream. The stream may or may not have flow at the beginning of the storm. If it does, that is referred to as the base flow. The area under the hydrograph is equal to the volume of the runoff. The runoff is always less than the volume of rainfall because of rainfall losses to infiltration in the ground or retention on the surface. The time from when the stream flow starts to rise from the rainfall to the peak flow is referred to as the "time to peak," and the time from the center of the mass of rainfall to the center of the mass of the runoff is called the lag time.[50]

A hydrograph is a plot of discharge as a function of time at some gauging station, while in contrast, a *unit* hydrograph relates the rainfall of a basin to the basin's runoff (figure 4.7). The unit hydrograph shows the time distribution of surface runoff resulting from a storm that produces 1 inch of rainfall "excess" over the watershed in some selected interval of time. The runoff volume associated with a unit hydrograph therefore is 1 inch. Hydrologists define the unit hydrograph in this way: "The unit hydrograph of a basin is the hydrograph of one inch of storm run-off generated by a rainstorm of fairly uniform intensity occurring within a specific period

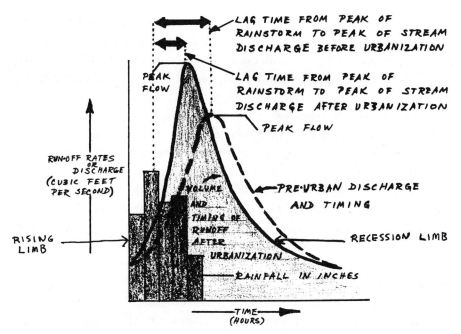

FIGURE 4.7. A UNIT HYDROGRAPH RELATING RAINFALL TO RUNOFF; AND THE EFFECTS OF URBANIZATION ON THE TIMING AND VOLUME OF RUNOFF.

of time."[51] The time interval to attain 1 inch of runoff varies with the drainage area of the basin and with the time response of runoff to rainfall due to basin shape, slope, geology, etc. The principal characteristic that distinguishes one unit hydrograph from another is the lag time between the peak rainfall and peak runoff. A stream that is characterized by a short time between the peak rainfall and the peak runoff can be described as "flashy." With larger streams and rivers for which there may be more time between peak rainfall and peak flood flows, there may be an opportunity to set up a flood warning system and help downstream communities prepare for the coming floodwaters.

The unit hydrograph for a gauged watershed can be easily constructed by recording the rainfall amount during a storm, or by using the record from a recording rain gauge in the basin. Hydrologists will sometimes derive synthetic unit hydrographs for use in ungauged watersheds based on the characteristics of the unit hydrographs for several gauged watersheds in a region.

Synthetic hydrographs will use the unit hydrographs for the gauged streams in an area to relate the lag, peak, and duration of these hydrographs to the geomorphic conditions of the basin such as drainage area and channel gradient. Once correlations have been made between geomorphic variables and characteristics of the unit hydrograph, an estimate of the unit hydrograph can be made for ungauged basins from a few physical measurements of the basin. If the correlations include variables related to human activity, then the synthetic unit hydrograph technique can also be used to predict the hydrologic consequences of development.

One of the most important parameters that must be estimated for a synthetic unit hydrograph is the lag time between the center of mass for the rainstorm and the peak of the hydrograph. Estimating these may be difficult because we may not know what processes dominate the watershed we are concerned with. In some regions stream-flow records may be numerous, but climatic conditions may vary greatly over short distances. The choice among gauging stations to use to develop hydrographs may be difficult. Gauging stations often apply to drainage areas larger than the one the planner is working in. However, a direct measurement of stream-flow and rain gauge readings during one storm can be sufficient to obtain usable results for determining the lag to peak of the unit hydrograph.[52] Anyone who has field measurements can put him or herself at an advantage over a public works department that relies solely on equations to estimate the lag time. Because of the significance of this kind of data, chapter 8 goes into greater detail on how citizens can develop hydrographs for their streams.

Changes to Stream Channels

The common cycle of changes that happen to stream channels between when urban construction begins and when land development ends forms the critical framework for the urban stream restorationist. Without an awareness of this cycle and where you are in it, you will be approaching an urban stream restoration project blind. (Refer to figures 4.8 and 4.9, which illustrate the changes that can happen to urban stream-channel shapes from aggradation, degradation, widening, and meandering.)

Typically, as a watershed is urbanized, construction activities generate more sediment than a natural condition generates. The first response of the channel is to fill, and the channel shape can become deeper and narrower while the channel bed aggrades. As urbanization progresses and new construction sites are replaced with pavement and structures, sediment loads to the creeks diminish and discharges from the area increase above their original levels because of the increase in storm sewers and impervious surfaces. This starts the second stage of stream-channel adjustment, in which channels increase their widths and depths with accelerated bank erosion. Limited research on this cycle estimates that the first part of the cycle occurs within about a decade, with another five to ten years or more for the second cycle of channel enlargement to adjust to a new equilibrium (figure 4.8).[53–55] The delayed response to channel enlargement may be tied to a critical stage required in urban growth in which at least 25 percent of the basin needs to be more than 5 percent impervious.[56]

Scientists also give us a perspective on how much enlargement we may expect from a stream channel acquiring a new shape to accommodate urban conditions. Ratios of enlarged urban channel sizes compared to natural sizes are computed. Ratios of 1.4–3+ seem common, and they go as high as 6.79.[57–59] It would not be unusual then for a channel of a fifty-square-foot cross-sectional area to increase to seventy-five square feet or more due to urbanization.

Stream channels react to urbanization not only by adjusting their widths and depths but also by changing their gradients and meanders. Figure 4.9 illustrates the movements and adjustments of an urbanizing creek in Maryland over a fourteen-

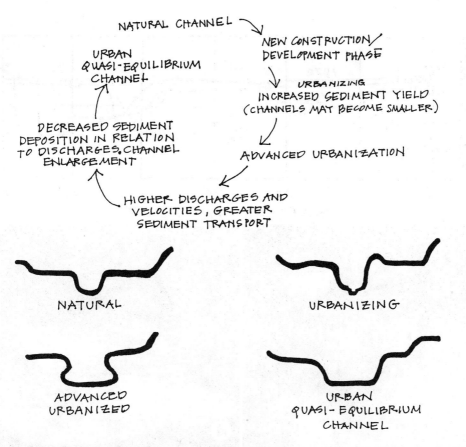

FIGURE 4.8. A TYPICAL CYCLE OF STREAM CHANNEL ADJUSTMENTS TO URBANIZATION.

year period.[60] As illustrated in figure 4.8, the first part of the urbanizing stream cycle is characterized by channel filling, or aggradation. In response to the filling the gradient will increase, or become steeper, because increased energy (gradient) is required for transport of the increased bed load, or channel choking will occur.

If land conservation measures that reduce the sediment load are used at this stage, energy is freed, and as a result the stream flows will pick up and carry material from the channel. Degradation occurs, and the gradient is decreased, or becomes less steep. Once the decreased gradient is in equilibrium with the decreased bed load, the degradation stops.

In the second stage, as the channel responds to the increase in discharges, accelerated bank erosion increases its width and depth. This accelerated erosion can start an increase in lateral bank cutting. If the eroding streambed material is replenished by stream-bank material, then meander formation occurs. The meander formation lengthens the stream, and that decreases the gradient until a new equilibrium is reached. Generally, if the discharge increases in a stream, this results in wider and deeper channels, an increase in meander wave length (and fewer numbers of meanders per unit of distance), and a decrease in the gradient.

Channels undergoing enlargement in steep topographies with weak soils or a

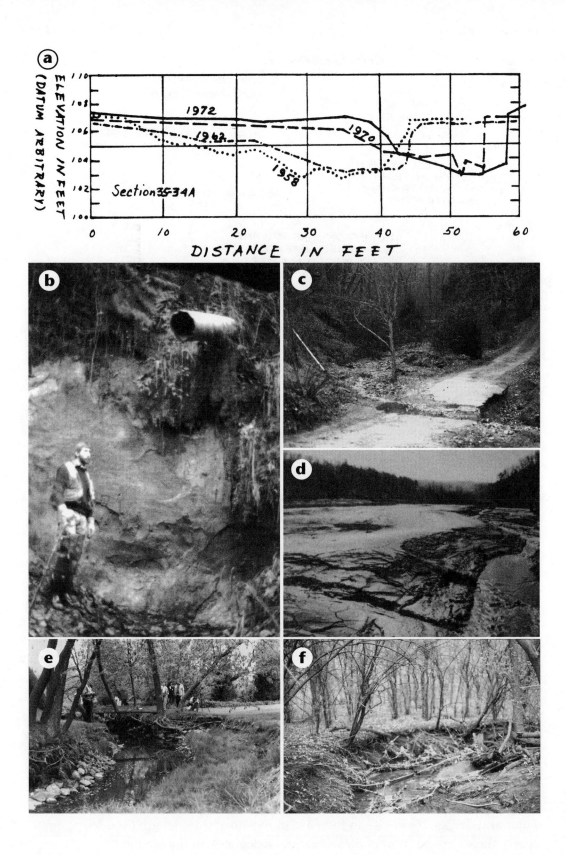

Section 3534A

weak geologic base may not acquire a new equilibrium but instead may rapidly deepen out of proportion to the discharges. The bankfull channel described previously not only becomes larger but also becomes entrenched in its streambed and no longer sends frequent flows to its floodplain. The entrenched channel becomes confined by its banks and continues to erode vertically. Entrenched channels can be equilibrium channels; however, it is common for their banks to become vulnerable to collapse and erosion. Incised channels usually refer to those that are eroding vertically and horizontally at an accelerated and excessive rate and represent unstable situations. The confined flood flows of entrenched and incised channels can be dramatically erosive so that an incised channel can be the most difficult to restore. The most effective method of stabilizing an incised channel is revegetation. Time can also help find a new balance as the depth of degradation decreases downstream, leading to a gentler gradient that will allow a new equilibrium between sediment load and flow energy to evolve.

The second stage of urban channel adjustments can be moderated with land-use planning and site design measures. Buffer zones along waterways, protection of upstream natural areas, reforestation or revegetation projects, and land management strategies such as fencing grazed areas can reduce impervious surfaces and runoff. Land-use planning measures in urban areas such as multi-use greenways along waterways can locate structures out of the boundaries of flood-hazard areas and stream meander zones. Rain runoff can be collected from downspouts from roofs and reused for landscape irrigation during dry periods. Natural draws can be designed to slow the movement of storm water instead of concentrating flows in culverts. Riparian or wetland environments can be restored or created in low catchment areas to detain as well as biologically treat the runoff. Runoff from parking lots can be drained into landscaped detention areas. Many of these restoration, management, and storm-water detention measures can be implemented with the help of conservation crews working with local public works departments, nonprofit citizen organizations, or the business community.

Given the relationships among the variables influencing stream dynamics, you can anticipate some of the reactions streams may make to modifications that may

FIGURE 4.9 (*facing page*). CHANNELS CHANGING THEIR MEANDER AND SHAPE IN RESPONSE TO URBANIZATION.

(a) Changing cross-sections of Watts Branch, Rockville, Maryland, in response to urbanization. *Source:* Luna B. Leopold, "River Change with Time—An Example," *Bulletin of Geological Society of America* 84 (1972). (b) Degrading, or incised, stream. A tributary to Joe's Creek, Puget Sound watershed, Washington. This creek eroded vertically 10 feet in three years because of increased urban storm runoff. The culvert used to be at the bottom of the creek. *Photo credit:* Bob Fuerstenberg. (c) Aggrading stream. A tributary to Issaquah Creek, Washington. The culvert located under the bridge is rendered unfunctional because it is buried in sediment. *Photo credit:* Bob Fuerstenberg. (d) Aggrading river. *Photo credit:* Soil Conservation Service. (e) Widening creek due to urbanization (note slumping of right bank), DuPage County, Illinois. (f) Widening and deepening of the once stable creek at Indigo Savannah, Cook County Forest Preserve, Illinois, due to storm-water culvert additions upstream.

be in the planning. For example, a channel-widening project to increase the channel flood-flow capacity will decrease the flow depths, as well as velocities for frequent low and moderate flows, and probably result in increased channel sedimentation. This, in turn, could lead to channel aggradation, an increase in gradient at the downstream end of the project, and these changes in channel slopes can result in the stream attacking its banks and causing erosion problems. The sedimentation ultimately conflicts with the need to increase channel capacities for flood flows.

If you are interested in cutting out a meander in a stream because it may be in the way of a development project, you are going to be shortening the length of the stream. By shortening the channel length, you will increase the slope of the channel because the stream does not travel as far to drop a given amount of elevation. This, in turn, will increase the velocities of the flow. You are essentially flirting with a serious erosion problem as a result. The stream often responds by attacking banks and developing new meanders in an attempt to regain its original length.

Urban dwellers frequently want to control the movement of a stream meander because the meander is close to a structure, road, utility, etc., sited too near the stream. If it is necessary to control the movement of a meander, it should be anticipated that the channel may adjust vertically by degradation. If you stabilize a single meander with rock, for example, the stream will simply take out the bank in the next downstream bend and erode the opposite bank. In this way, the whole stream system can be destabilized by the random placement of oil drums, rocks, rubble, and other objects people put in creeks to protect their backyards from a changing meander.

Channel revegetation helps moderate most of the problems associated with channel adjustments that occur because of urbanization. The only conflict between stream vegetation and urban stream-management needs may be where stream flood-flow capacities are of greater concern than erosion control or channel stability and vegetation needs to be cleared or thinned to reduce channel roughness or resistance to flows. If this is a concern, refer to chapter 9 on stream-channel management. The use of the bank revegetation systems described in chapter 9 can moderate channel shifting, bank erosion, and widening. While bank widening and meandering may be reduced, it can be expected that the stream will deepen some. This is why we stress that most bank restoration systems should be started below the existing grades of stream channels. If removal of streamside vegetation is proposed, expect the opposite channel responses, i.e., an increase in stream widening, meander shifts, and channel migration across the floodplain.

Overly wide and laterally unstable channels can be restored to an equilibrium condition by returning the channel to a lower width:depth ratio (in which the channel is narrower and/or deeper). A corrected width:depth ratio can help produce the stream energy needed to transport the stream's sediment load. Sometimes spurs or booms (berms protruding into the channel) are installed at angles into the over-widened channel to collect sediment and narrow the channel. Rootwads (tree stumps), brush piles, or tree revetments can help narrow channels while restoring banks. In urban situations streams can adjust naturally by increasing their widths and their width:depth ratios, and that is a process that probably needs to be allowed to continue on its course to a new "quasi equilibrium." In the event that you need to address a particularly over-widened and destabilized reach of creek that is a localized problem, you should find the nearest reach of more stable creek to use as a model for restoration. It is not unusual to find some reaches of urban stream that appear to be relatively stable or have reached a balance. These reaches would be neither excessively eroding nor excessively depositing sediment, and the stream banks would support good vegetative growth. If such reaches of stream are nearby, or have a similar gradient and similar bank materials and drain a similar area, they can be used as a model to re-create their widths and depths for a more destabilized section. We refer to this as a stream reaching its urban equilibrium. Remember, vegetating banks can help slow widening and encourage deepening the channel.

When you are planning a stream restoration project, it is going to be important for you not only to be aware of where your stream is in the urban adjustment cycle, but also to anticipate how site differences in geology and soils along the stream will moderate some of the possible adjustments. Ask local residents about historical and recent land-use changes and changes in stream shape or meander. If a long section of stream needs to start adjusting to increasing watershed discharges, you may find it advantageous to allow some space for stream widening and setback replanting projects. Stream-bank restoration projects can help moderate channel movement at this stage but will be much more vulnerable to washouts at the earlier adjustment stages than at later stages when more equilibrium has been attained. Certainly local building permits and structure setback ordinances need to anticipate such second-stage changes. Remember that a stream will deepen with increased discharges but generally not as much as the width will expand. Channels in erosion-resistant materials will tend to be narrower and deeper than channels composed of more erodible soils (which will tend to be wider and shallower). Vegetation encroaching on a channel will tend to reduce bank erosion but encourage bed erosion, so vegetated channels tend to be deeper and more narrow than unvegetated channels. A stream confined by hard sidewalls in a narrow valley may not be able to form bars or meanders and may be able to adjust only by degradation.

Flood-Control Channel Flows

The usual state of flows in a natural stream channel is that the water flows fairly slowly with eddies near banks, logs, and rocks but without a lot of visible surface disturbance, shooting flows, or standing waves. These relatively tranquil flows usually encountered in nature are referred to as *subcritical* flows. Human impacts to a channel such as obstructing the channel with structures or culverts can concentrate the energy of the water so that a *supercritical* flow of very high velocity and turbulence results. Artificial channels with very steep and smooth slopes can also exhibit supercritical flows. It is not uncommon for the engineers of channelization projects to design them with the objective of creating a supercritical condition to move more water through a smaller channel. By concentrating the flows this way in a narrow channel, the engineer can free up more developable property.

The transitions between subcritical and supercritical flows can be seen in nature on white-water rivers. An abrupt change in the gradient of a river can cause rapids. The low-gradient, relatively quiet water above the rapids represents subcritical conditions, but at the sudden grade drop, water can sheet very quickly into a super-critical condition. Where this rapid water reaches a flattened slope at the end of the rapids, the transition from the supercritical condition back to a subcritical condition creates a hydraulic jump, or a wave that jumps backwards. This wave creates a dangerous hole under its arch, sometimes responsible for sucking in boats and capsizing them.

Because supercritical flows have high velocities and turbulence and can cause standing waves, they are undesirable from a safety standpoint because someone could get caught and submerged in a channel during storm flows. This flow condition is also undesirable due to the amount of potential erosive power it produces in the channel. As a general rule, stream reaches with these unstable, undulating or pulsating supercritical flows should be avoided in the design of channel modification projects.[61]

Hydrologists and hydraulic engineers use a *Froude number*, a term you may come in contact with, particularly if you are reviewing the design of a traditional flood-control channelization project. This number can indicate if a channel is going to have these supercritical flows. The Froude number represents the ratio of inertial forces to gravitational forces. A quantitative measure is given by the equation below. *V* in this equation is the average velocity in the cross-section of the channel being measured, *g* is the acceleration due to gravity, and *D* is the average water depth.

$$Fr = \frac{V}{\sqrt{gD}}$$

At low Froude numbers (much less than 1), the gravitational forces dominate and act to "hold down" any surface disturbances, so the flow has the appearance of a relatively smooth surface. At high Froude numbers (much higher than 1), inertial forces dominate, which means that surface waves can be created. The Froude number will indicate whether the flow is subcritical (Fr $\leq$ 1), supercritical (Fr $\geq$ 1), or critical (Fr = 1). The quantity $\sqrt{gD}$ is the speed of a small surface disturbance or wave in shallow water, as occurs in most riverine flows. When Fr exceeds unity, it means the flow velocity has become faster than a downstream influence can move. At supercritical flows, the downstream flow conditions have no effect on the flow conditions farther upstream. At the transition from a supercritical flow to a subcritical flow, the standing wave called a hydraulic jump occurs (figures 4.10 and 4.11).

This phenomenon has important implications in flood-control engineering design. If the stream is flowing at the more usual subcritical flows, its water surface is controlled by the downstream surface elevations. Thus, influences such as flows spilling onto floodplains or wetlands or being backed up by bridges will affect the depths of flooding upstream. If the flows are supercritical, depths and velocity

FIGURE 4.10. PHOTOS OF SUPERCRITICAL STREAM-CHANNEL FLOWS.
(a) Ballona Creek, Los Angeles County, 1934 flood. *Photo credit:* Los Angeles County drainage area, California, U.S. Army Corps of Engineers. (b) Example of a river flow with all surface disturbances swept downstream. *Photo credit:* Peter Goodwin.

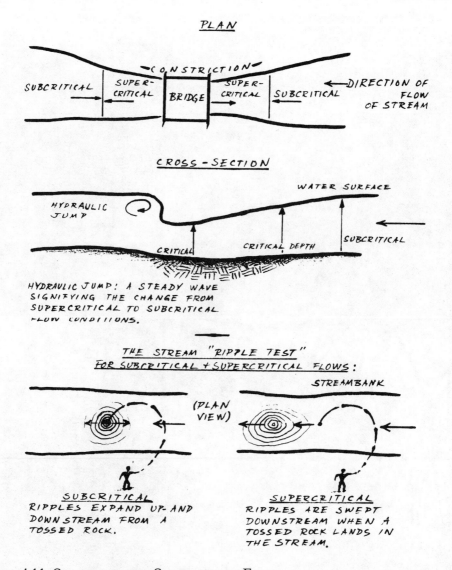

FIGURE 4.11. SUBCRITICAL AND SUPERCRITICAL FLOWS.

depend only on the upstream flow conditions and are independent of downstream influences until the hydraulic jump is reached. The location of the hydraulic jump depends on the balance of upstream and downstream forces and will be in different positions at different discharges.[62]

Of particular concern to the citizenry and public officials who are reviewing the design of these projects should be the safety issues and the potential project performance problems associated with supercritical flow designs. There are cases of drownings in these supercritical sections even where the water has been as shallow as 2–3 feet because of the combination of high velocities, slippery surfaces, and the recirculation of water in hydraulic jumps, which can hold people beneath the surface. At some types of structures it may not be possible to detect these hydraulic jumps from the surface because they may be submerged.[63]

One of the most important problems recently being acknowledged by engineers is that flood-control project designs based on the need to attain supercritical flows in channels may fail to provide the flood protection they are designed for because the supercritical flows are not actually achieved. The supercritical flows may fail to occur because of some unanticipated downstream influence, causing the hydraulic jump to migrate upstream, or sediment or flood debris may increase the roughness of the channel, slowing the flood velocities.[64] The Corte Madera Creek case discussed in the following chapter is an example of such a design failure.

If you are interested in determining whether a reach of stream channel has subcritical or supercritical flows, you can do a simple stream-ripple test. Throw a pebble into the stream and watch the ripples form around where the pebble strikes. If the entire ripple is swept downstream, the flow is supercritical ($V \leq \sqrt{gD}$). If the ripple is able to move upstream (as well as downstream), then the flow is subcritical flow (figure 4.11).

Drainage Areas and Channel Shapes, Sizes, and Discharges

Uniformity among Streams in Diverse Settings

River scientists have learned that rivers the world over operate under the same natural "laws" and that the most important aspects of the river channel are that it is self-formed and self-maintained.[65] As described earlier, these scientists treat a river as a hydraulic system, in which the channel shapes and sizes, or channel geometry, are related to a river's hydraulic factors (stream-flow amounts, flow frequencies, velocities, etc.). This is referred to as the stream's hydraulic geometry.[66] Hydraulic and geomorphic laws apply at all scales of comparable land-form evolution. The Mississippi River, for example, is the largest and most impressive river of the United States, and because of its dimensions, it is frequently considered unique, but it is not. The Mississippi may be thought of as a model for still larger rivers or as a prototype for many smaller rivers.[67] The relative predictability of the dimensions and responses of streams and rivers to a natural environment provides us with guiding principles for restoring streams in more natural or rural environments. It also provides the guiding principles we use for restoring even very damaged urban streams.

One example of the uniformity shown among stream channels is the common branching pattern that forms the drainage network and different stream orders, described in the first chapter (figure 1.1). Another aspect of the uniformity among rivers already discussed is the frequency of the bankfull-flow condition among rivers in diverse settings. In addition, an extremely useful phenomenon for the restorationist is the situation in which the ratios of the widths to the depths of the "bankfull channels" for streams of comparable size have great consistency. Increases in the channel width and depth and velocity of flows occur at similar rates as the stream increases in size downstream. The discharge (or flows) of a stream is a product of the area of the stream channel or its width times its depth and the velocity.

$$\text{Stream discharge } (Q) = \text{width} \times \text{depth} \times \text{velocity}$$
$$\text{or}$$
$$Q = WDV$$

It is interesting and useful to know that the increase in the width, depth, and velocities as the discharges increase is almost always divided among these parameters in the same way. The width increases downstream faster than the depth increases, and the depth increases faster than the velocities. The velocities usually increase some or may remain constant going downstream. (The water in a "swift" mountain creek just looks like it's flowing more quickly. Velocities tend to be greater downstream than they are upstream because of the higher discharges downstream and less energy dissipation.) The relationships among these parameters are so predictable that if, for example, you know some of the parameters of your stream site, such as its channel width and depth or its drainage area, you can estimate its other parameters, such as bankfull discharges and velocities.

In a hydrologically homogeneous region, a pattern is displayed by the curves on a graph when the width, depth, and velocity are plotted against the stream's discharge. Figure 4.12 (A) is an example of a graph showing the relationship between the width, depth, and velocity with discharge at one site on a river. "B" in Figure 4.12 shows that a comparison can be made among locations along the river channel for a particular chosen discharge such as the bankfull discharge. You could use a similar graph representing the streams in your region to estimate the expected bankfull discharge by taking field measurements of your stream's bankfull width and depth. Using these concepts of hydraulic geometry, it is possible to equate depths, widths, and velocities with discharges for similar stream types.[68]

The average channel dimensions and the bankfull discharges are also similar for streams of a given drainage area for similar geographic regions. If you have graphs for your region, such as in Figure 4.13, and can measure your stream basin drainage area on a map, as instructed earlier, you can then estimate the channel dimensions and bankfull discharges for your stream.[69] Runoff is proportional to watershed drainage areas for most watersheds all over the country. Luna Leopold attributes the difference in the slopes of the lines for the various regions shown in the graph in figure 4.13 to the climatic differences between the more rainy coastal states and the more arid inland areas, which are affected more by localized storms.

Another consistent behavior is that the scouring of the stream channel by flows tends to be balanced by fill on the average. Thus, a streambed may erode during a flood, but as the flood recedes, the bed will tend to return to its original elevation after an approximately equal amount of sediment has been redeposited. It is only when the stream erodes laterally into terraces or hillsides higher than the floodplain that the volume of sediment eroded from a watershed exceeds the volume deposited. Only in that case can stream-bank protection works be expected to reduce the total sediment yield from a drainage basin.[70]

Part of the dynamic equilibrium between erosion and deposition has to do with the maximum sediment concentration that a stream can transport under given hydraulic conditions. If the stream is transporting the maximum load of sediment,

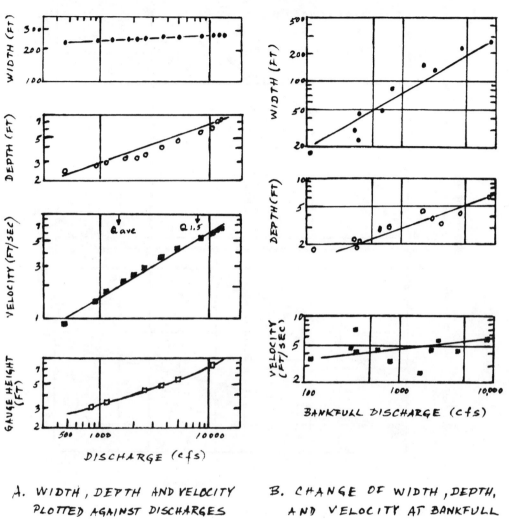

A. WIDTH, DEPTH AND VELOCITY PLOTTED AGAINST DISCHARGES FOR ONE CROSS-SECTION LOCATED ON THE GREEN RIVER, WYOMING.

B. CHANGE OF WIDTH, DEPTH, AND VELOCITY AT BANKFULL DISCHARGE AS THE CROSS-SECTIONS MOVE DOWN-STREAM ON THE GREEN RIVER, WYOMING.

FIGURE 4.12. HYDRAULIC GEOMETRY OF STREAM CHANNELS. *Source:* Tom Dunne and Luna Leopold, *Water in Environmental Planning* (San Francisco: W.H. Freeman, 1978).

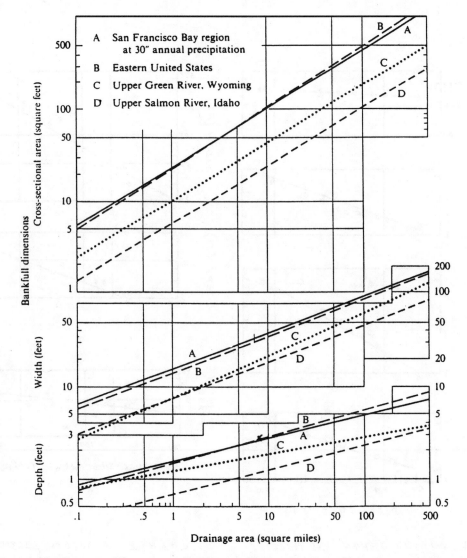

FIGURE 4.13. AVERAGE VALUES OF BANKFULL DIMENSIONS AS FUNCTIONS OF DRAINAGE AREA. *Source:* Tom Dunne and Luna Leopold, *Water in Environmental Planning* (San Francisco: W. H. Freeman, 1978).

the bed will not show erosion, since the amount of sediment picked up will balance the deposited material. Thus, there is a finite amount of sediment a stream can erode and transport at a given time. Because forces within water are altered by the transport of sediment, hydraulic relations developed for clear flowing water could not be applied to water carrying a debris load.[71]

Finally, streams uniformly meander. Natural channels are rarely straight for a distance greater than ten channel widths. The size of the curves of a meander has a constant relationship to the channel in that small channels wind in small curves and large channels wind in large curves. There is also a constant relationship between channel width and the radius of the meander and between channel width and the length of the meander (see figures 4.14 and 4.15). The tendency for a constant ratio of radius to width makes streams of various sizes look similar on maps and is why you have to look at a map scale to determine whether a stream is large or small. On the basis of a large number of field observations, geomorphologists have quantified the relationships among meander length, radius of curvature, amplitude of the meander, and channel width:[72, 73]

- The meander length averages about 11 times the channel width and is nearly always between 10 and 14 channel widths.
- The radius of curvature of the central portion of a channel bend averages about 1/5 of the meander length.
- The radius of curvature is commonly 2–3 times the channel width.
- The meander amplitude is commonly in the range of 0.5–1.5 times the meander wavelength.
- Pools and riffles are spaced at repeating distances at about 5–7 channel widths measured along the channel.

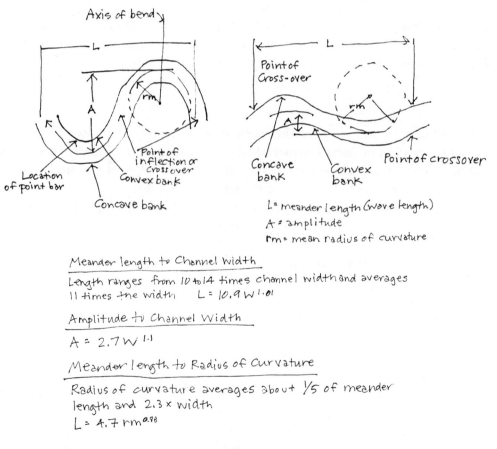

FIGURE 4.14. GEOMETRY OF A MEANDER. *Source:* Regression equations from L. B. Leopold and M. G. Wolman, "River Meanders." *Geological Society of America Bulletin* 71 (1964).

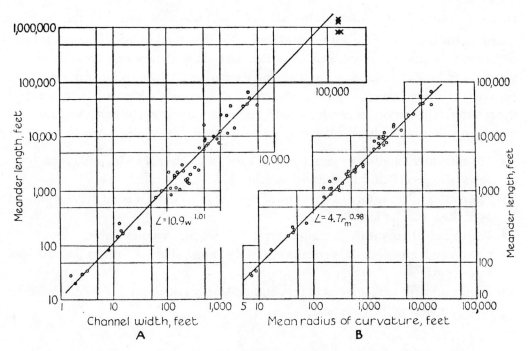

FIGURE 4.15. RELATIONSHIP OF MEANDER LENGTH TO CHANNEL WIDTH AND TO RADIUS OF CURVATURE. *Source:* Luna B. Leopold, M. Gordon Wolman, and John P. Miller, *Fluvial Processes in Geomorphology* (San Francisco: W.H. Freeman, 1964).

The use of a stream classification system developed by Dave Rosgen to guide channel restoration projects has increased the sophistication of stream restoration projects.[74] The stream classification system groups reaches of stream by similar slope, entrenchment of the channel in the stream valley, sinuosity (degree of meandering), bankfull width-depth ratio, and type of soils and geology influencing the channel. Restorationists can record, for example, the slope, bed material, and entrenchment of the stream channel they want to restore and determine what type of stream they are working on (figure 4.16). The stream type can lead you to the average values for channel shape (width:depth ratio) and meander for an equilibrium channel for your stream type or the type that historically represents a more equilibrium condition for the region.

Significance of the Uniformity of Streams

We have established that the objective of stream restoration is to restore the dynamic equilibrium of a channel, and that the equilibrium is a function of the stable relationship natural channels have between their widths, depths, meanders, slopes, sediment loads, and discharges. Because streams behave with such unity, we can use the measurable relationships among these parameters to help reshape damaged stream

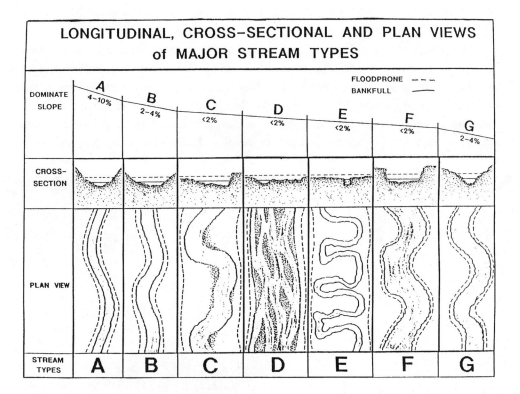

GENERALIZED VISUAL DELINEATION of MAJOR STREAM TYPES

DOMINATE BED MATERIAL	A	B	C	D	E	F	G
1 BEDROCK							
2 BOULDER							
3 COBBLE							
4 GRAVEL							
5 SAND							
6 SILT							
SLOPE	.04 – .099	.02 – .039	< .01	.01 – .019	< .02	< .02	.02 – .039
W/D RATIO	< 12	> 12	> 12	> 50	< 12	> 12	< 12
CF RATIO	1 – 1.4	1.41 – 2.2	2.2 +	2.2 +	2.2 +	1 – 1.4	1 – 1.4

LONGITUDINAL, CROSS-SECTIONAL AND PLAN VIEWS of MAJOR STREAM TYPES

FLOODPRONE – – –
BANKFULL ———

DOMINATE SLOPE	A 4–10%	B 2–4%	C <2%	D <2%	E <2%	F <2%	G 2–4%
CROSS-SECTION							
PLAN VIEW							
STREAM TYPES	A	B	C	D	E	F	G

FIGURE 4.16. A CLASSIFICATION OF RIVERS BY STREAM TYPE FOR APPLICATION IN RESTORATION PROJECTS. *Source:* Dave Rosgen, "A Classification of Rivers," *Catena* 22 (1994).

channels and return them to a more "stable" state of dynamic equilibrium. This strategy will minimize maintenance requirements for a stream channel and, of course, is much less disruptive to the ecosystem. A summary of the important principles to apply to restoration projects based on the material just covered on the nature of rivers is as follows:

1. The bankfull channel is defined by the bankfull discharges (the dominant channel-forming flow), which occur on the average of every 1.5–2 years. Restoration should be most concerned with making adjustments in the watershed so as to "stabilize" or return to equilibrium that feature of the stream system.

2. The consistent flooding frequency of the bankfull channel makes the bankfull discharge a useful value for comparing different stream sites. Such comparisons can provide important information on what your stream channel should be shaped like in order to be in equilibrium. Sometimes engineers design a "trickle" channel or notch into an artificial flood-control channel in an attempt to concentrate flows to, in theory, help fish move through or prevent algae buildup. This is *not* to be confused with what this book refers to as a bankfull channel. The trickle channels, even in dirt-lined project channels, are typically not designed or sized to re-create a dynamic equilibrium and do not perform the functions of a natural bankfull channel (figure 4.17).

3. It is important to be able to distinguish what is a floodplain and what landscape features are terraces. If a stream reaches bankfull flow at a regular frequency, it follows that the floodplain is also flooded at a regular frequency. Terraces, however, may be at varying levels above the floodplains, and there is no consistency among streams in the frequency with which terraces may be flooded. Stream-channel widening projects should widen floodplains by removing sections of

FIGURE 4.17. A "TRICKLE CHANNEL" IS NOT A BANKFULL CHANNEL.

terraces or levees, as opposed to widening and thereby destabilizing the bank-full channels.

4. It is important to identify the floodplain because that is the active area for stream flooding and meandering and therefore the active hazard zone. It is the zone where restoration of riparian vegetation has the greatest restorative value—particularly where it connects with the bankfull channel.

5. It is important to be able to distinguish between a stream that has high terraces and one with low terraces or no terraces at all. Terraces may or may not be in a flood-hazard area. Some terraces may be very close to the bankfull channel but are so high—or the bankfull channel is so incised—that the terrace cannot be reached by floods. You may be lucky to live near a stream with high terraces that will rarely or never be overflowed. A common mistake in that situation is over-complacency about the potential problems of building too close to the edge of the terrace. The bankfull channels may be in a state in which they are degrading and/or changing their meanders. In that case, the foot of the terrace can be un-dercut by the eroding action of the bankfull channel, and the terrace can slump and break away into the channel below. Erosion, as opposed to flooding, is the potential management problem in that situation.

6. Some streams in the United States have stream gauging stations that measure their velocities and flows and keep cross-sectional measurements of their depths and widths. Most streams do not have those measurements, and such stations are particularly rare among small streams. It is useful to know then that streams in similar geographic areas with similar climates have similar shapes and discharges based on how large an area they drain. You can compare your stream to others in your region that have data collected on them.

   Using data from hydrologically similar regions in which the channel widths, depths, and velocities have been plotted against discharges and/or drainage areas, you can immediately estimate the channel dimensions for a given discharge, estimate the discharges for a given channel dimension, and es-timate the channel dimensions or discharges for a certain size drainage area. If you live in an area where those data have not been pulled together, it is not hard to put the information together from data published in the U.S. Geological Survey *Water Supply Papers* or by taking some simple field measurements. (Chapter 8 provides additional information and directions.)

7. You can use this regional information in a field visit to your stream to help you pick out the likely bankfull channel, the floodplain, and the terrace. If, for example, your stream's bankfull channel appears to be much wider than the regional average for the same drainage area, you have an important indicator that some influence is upsetting the width:depth ratio and destabilizing your stream.

8. Stream meanders and pool and riffle sequences have consistent relationships to the geometry of your stream, and so if the stream width is known, you can use

those relationships to guide the reshaping of a straightened stream that will aid in returning its equilibrium.

Field observations for indications of bankfull depths don't always produce definitive results—particularly in channels degraded by the influences of urbanization. Always inspect significant lengths of channel at various locations to try to arrive at an average depth. If field indications seem ambiguous or nonexistent, don't force an inaccurate conclusion. Use regional estimates of the 1.5-year-recurrence-interval discharges and the mean annual discharges and their relationships to channel shapes to estimate bankfull measurements. Urban channel shapes may be widely divergent from regional averages if they are significantly degraded. For example, streams undergoing incision that are deeply entrenched will be cut off from their floodplains, but a newly forming bankfull channel may be distinguishable in the entrenched area. Some streams naturally have almost imperceptible floodplains and therefore the bankfull channel is very difficult to pick out in the field.

The Challenges of Urban Stream Restoration

An inevitable question follows the preceding description of restoration principles: Can the same principles that apply to anticipating the shapes of natural stream systems be applied to restoration problems for urban streams, which by their very nature are disrupted and lack equilibrium?

The challenge of urban stream restoration is to develop a knowledge of stream dynamics, use what has been studied about both natural and urban streams, and then apply that information the best you can.

A highly degraded stream will probably arrive at a wider and deeper equilibrium channel than the regional averages. A challenge added to that can be the human-made structures frequently placed too close to stream banks. For example, an urban stream may need to adjust its slope through forming a wider meander, but such a meander adjustment isn't possible because a concrete wall is in the way. We can start solving that problem by understanding the meander pattern the stream "wants" to take. We restore that meander to the extent possible, and where it can't be restored, we use as unintrusive bank stabilization methods as possible, so as to not make the situation worse. We can design drops in the channel grade to dissipate some of the energy of the shortened channel. The give and take between natural-system dynamics and conflicts with those dynamics created by urbanization is unique to each situation. Unfortunately, those situations may require us to make judgments without all the information we would like. It is particularly important to keep records on our actions and learn from our mistakes and successes and practice adaptive management just as we do in impacted rural areas.

The three problems we focus on solving are (1) selecting a bankfull channel width and depth that will represent urban equilibrium dimensions that won't excessively erode or deposit; (2) designing a proper channel length and sinuosity to match the channel and valley slopes; and (3) providing a floodplain to absorb flashy velocities, overbank flows, and channel adjustments that may occur because of future land use adjustments. The most common mistake is to assume that tight urban spaces cannot accommodate the proper meanders. First, draw a calculated meander based on the relationships of radius of curvature, amplitude, and channel length to channel width to attain a value for the proper sinuosity. The restoration meander need not look exactly like the drawing produced by these calculations. Meanders in nature are very irregular and so are my restored urban stream meanders, which I squeeze around existing trees, parking spaces, and fire hydrants. Making the channel sinuous enough or long enough will take it a long way toward being more stable. I use the existing information on regional values for drainage area and bankfull channel dimensions (figure 4.13) but then refine the data by selecting gauge stations that reflect the conditions of the subregion in which I'm working, including degree of urbanization, stream type, and climate difference. I draw new lines to represent these adjusted values for bankfull dimensions based on these selected stations.

A good way to organize your thinking about an urban stream restoration project is to first try to determine if your stream is at the beginning, middle, or end of its cycle of major adjustments to urbanization. Somewhat ironically, it can be easier to design a project in an old urban area that has been fully urbanized—if there is reasonable stream corridor width to work in. Much of my stream restoration practice occurs in the San Francisco Bay area. I have found that the slope developed to represent the regional averages of bankfull channel width and depth as they relate to drainage area for the graph in figure 4.13 is useful for representing a larger urban channel cross-section equilibrium. The bay area stream gauge data used to develop these drainage area-channel dimensions were collected in the mid-1970s from streams located in a fully urbanized region for several decades. These data make my urban restoration design work much easier because the regional relationships shown in this graph have given me a very good idea of *urban* equilibrium conditions. If you are going to encourage the practice of restoration in a particular urban area, it is a good idea to develop a graph that plots bankfull dimensions against urban equilibrium drainage areas for the region. This can be done by selecting gauging stations (that you visit in the field) that are recording data on streams in urbanized areas that appear to be in relatively healthy urban equilibrium condition.

In trying to shape meanders for urban streams in the San Francisco Bay area, I first look for aerial photos that were taken in the 1940s, which show many more miles of uncovered, unculverted, and unstraightened creeks than exist in the 1990s. Such photos are probably old enough to represent something close to urban equilibrium condition in the older urban areas in the bay area, which were largely settled by the 1920s—and they are early enough to show creeks when they were still above ground. They are mostly useful for helping re-create meander patterns. If I don't have old maps or photos, I try to locate nearby reaches of streams in similar soils and gradient and the same drainage area that appear to be in equilibrium (without excessive erosion or deposition) and use those as a model for sizing widths, depths, and meanders. This is not difficult where I live because there are many small coastal streams draining similar watersheds into San Francisco Bay. I have also found it easy enough to locate "model" or "reference" urban streams or watersheds in other parts of the country where I have practiced on which to base stream restoration efforts. I also refer to the Rosgen stream classification system to get a sense of what the meanders should look like for a particular channel type (based on slopes, soils, geology, and entrenchment). If I have a channel width that I think is a good approximation of an equilibrium width, I use the equations in figure 4.14 to also give me guidance on meander design. If I'm lucky, I can cross-reference old photos, the stream classification system, data from similarly situated urban equilibrium streams, and the equations to arrive at a restoration meander design. Chapter 9 describes the steps used to apply these methods to design a restoration project.

If we review the development history of the watershed and find we are at the beginning of a new urban development phase, then our greatest efforts need to be to protect the resource and our options for the future of the landscape. Our efforts should focus on protecting floodplains as greenways, setting development back from waterways, and integrating the stream as a valued feature in the landscape, with trails, parks, and access. Ordinances for managing erosion, sediment yields, and storm water should be put into effect.

The middle of the urbanization cycle presents the greatest challenges. The first challenge is to decide where the watershed is in this midportion of the cycle, i.e., is the urban channel widening in its beginning stages or in its latter stages? Will bank stabilization projects be doomed because inevitable near future channel adjustments will just take them out? It is usually streams in this urban midlife crisis that create the pressures for channel straightening, concrete boxes, and culverts. To prevent such responses, it is best to put together a program that integrates saving as much land around creeks as possible, influencing the additional development patterns and site designs, and doing very selective creek channel restoration projects. The channel bank restoration projects should use environmentally and aesthetically sensitive methods for localized areas to solve the most volatile conflicts between property, structures, roads, utilities, etc., and the stream. Regrading the stream banks is usually critical in these situations. Allowing the problems to fester without offering some kind of viable solution only builds momentum for controlling the resource in pipes. The bank restoration projects in the most difficult constrained areas may need to employ the more urban-oriented designs in chapter 9, including WPA-style walls and rock work. The inherent hazard, of course, is to use too many hard surfaces and create continuing destabilization as a result. When in doubt, always use vegetation in stream-bank stabilization projects because, except in the most severe cases, it will help moderate the situation.

Urban stream restoration is not for the fainthearted. Localized conditions change. A shopping mall replaces a neighborhood shopping district, trees get cut down, new storm-water systems are added. We are constantly confronted by the need to react to such changes. Stretches of urban stream in relative equilibrium will have reaches thrown out of balance by these localized impacts. In visiting an upper reach of the Chicago River, I assumed we would have an adjusted, balanced, urban channel shape in an older, long-developed area flowing through a protected forest preserve. In fact, the channel had been stable for decades, but brand-new "storm-water improvements" just constructed upstream had created immediate and dramatically accelerated bank erosion and caving. In the Atlanta, Georgia, area, the streams first adjusted to agricultural land-use impacts and developed a new equilibrium based on the urbanization boom from the 1930s to 1960s. Unfortunately, the new urban equilibrium channel does not provide a model for restoration projects because a new wave of urban development in the nineties is changing what the urban equilibrium channel is going to be in the near future. Thus, it is much more difficult to design an urban stream restoration project in the Atlanta area than for the older developed-out cities ringing the San Francisco Bay. There's never a dull moment in urban stream restoration, and you need to consider the surprises and uncertainties a part of the landscape.

NOTES

1. Federal Council for Science and Technology Ad Hoc Panel on Hydrology, "Scientific Hydrology" (Washington, D.C., 1962), as cited by C. T. Haan, Agricultural Engineering Department, University of Kentucky, in "Overview of Rainfall-Runoff Process in Urban Areas," proceedings of *National Symposium on Urban Rainfall and Runoff and Sediment Control* (Lexington: University of Kentucky, July 29–31, 1974).
2. Emory W. Lane, "The Importance of Fluvial Morphology in Hydraulic Engineering," *Proceedings of the American Society of Civil Engineers*, vol. 81, no. 745 (New York: Hydraulics Division, July 1955).
3. Daryl B. Simons and Fuat Senturk, *Sediment Transport Technology* (Fort Collins, Colorado: Water Resources Publications, 1977).
4. Ray K. Linsley, "Flood Estimates: How Good Are They?" *Water Resources Research* 22, no. 9 (August 1986).
5. Luna B. Leopold and Thomas Maddock, Jr., "The Hydraulic Geometry of Stream Channels and Some Physiographic Implications," U.S. Geological Survey Professional Paper 252 (Washington, D.C., 1953).
6. J. R. L. Allen, "Changeable Rivers: Some Aspects of Their Mechanics and Sedimentation," in K. J. Gregory, ed. *River Channel Changes* (New York: John Wiley, 1977).
7. Luna B. Leopold, M. Gordon Wolman, and John P. Miller, *Fluvial Process in Geomorphology* (San Francisco: W. H. Freeman, 1964).
8. G. Lacey, "Stable Channels in Alluvium," *Proceedings of the Institute of Civil Engineers*, vol. 229, 1930, p. 259–292.
9. E. S. Lindley, "Regime Channels," *Proceedings of the Punjab Engineering Congress* 7 (1919), p. 63–74.
10. Simons and Senturk, *Sediment Transport Technology*.
11. Andrew Brookes, *Channelized Rivers, Perspectives for Environmental Management* (New York: John Wiley, 1988).
12. Nelson R. Nunnally and Edward A. Keller, *Use of Fluvial Processes to Minimize Adverse Effects of Stream Channelization*, Report No. 144, Water Resources Research Institute (Raleigh: University of North Carolina, July 1979).
13. Simons and Senturk, *Sediment Transport Technology*.
14. Luna Leopold, *Water, A Primer* (San Francisco: W. H. Freeman, 1974).
15. Nelson R. Nunnally, *A Rapid, Low-Cost Technique for Estimating Peak Flow for Selected Flood Events* (Raleigh: University of North Carolina: Water Resources Research Institute, May 1982).

16. Nelson R. Nunnally and F. Douglas Shields, *Incorporation of Environmental Features in Flood Control Channel Projects*, Technical Report E–85-3 (Vicksburg, Mississippi: U.S. Army Corps of Engineers Waterways Experiment Station, May 1985).

17. Thomas Dunne and Luna B. Leopold, *Water in Environmental Planning* (San Francisco: W. H. Freeman, 1978).

18. Burchard H. Heede, "Stream Dynamics: An Overview for Land Managers," General Technical Report RM–72, Rocky Mt. Forest and Range Experiment Station, April 1980.

19. Thomas Maddock, "A Primer on Floodplain Dynamics," *Journal of Soil and Water Conservation* (March–April 1976), p. 44–47.

20. Leopold, *Water, A Primer*.

21. M. Gordon Wolman and Luna B. Leopold, "River Floodplains: Some Observations on Their Formations," U.S. Geological Survey Professional Paper 282–C (Washington, D.C., 1957).

22. M. Gordon Wolman and J. P. Miller, "Magnitude and Frequency of Forces in Geomorphic Processes," *Journal of Geology* 68, no. 1 (1960).

23. Leopold, Wolman, and Miller, *Fluvial Processes in Geomorphology*.

24. Dunne and Leopold, *Water in Environmental Planning*.

25. Luna B. Leopold, *A View of the River* (Cambridge: Harvard University Press, 1994).

26. J. H. Mackin, "Concept of the Graded River," *Geological Society of America Bulletin* 59 (1948), p. 463–512.

27. Lane, "The Importance of Fluvial Morphology in Hydraulic Engineering."

28. G. H. Dury, "The Concept of Grade" in G. H. Dury, ed., *Essays in Geomorphology* (London: Heinemann, 1966).

29. Garrett Hardin, "The Cybernetics of Competition: A Biologist's View of Society," *Perspectives in Biology and Medicine* 7, no. 1 (1963), p. 58–84.

30. Luna B. Leopold and W. B. Lanbein, "The Concept of Entropy in Landscape Evolution," U.S. Geological Survey Professional Paper 500–A (Washington, D.C., 1962).

31. Luna B. Leopold and Thomas Maddock, Jr., "The Hydraulic Geometry of Stream Channels and Some Physiographic Implications," U.S. Geological Survey Professional Paper 252 (Washington, D.C., 1953).

32. Burchard H. Heede, "Designing for Equilibrium in Streams" in W. L. Jackson, ed., *Engineering Considerations in Small Stream Management*, reprinted from *Water Resources Bulletin* (American Water Resources Association) 22, no. 3 (1986).

33. Leopold and Maddock, 1953; E. W. Lane, 1955; S. A. Schumm, "Fluvial Geomorphology—The Historical Perspective," in H. W. Shen, ed., *River Mechanics*, vol. 1 (Fort Collins, Colorado: Water Resources Publications, 1971); J. Santos-Cayudo and D. B. Simons, "River Response" in H. W. Shen, ed., *Environmental Impacts on Rivers* (Fort Collins, Colorado: Water Resources Publications, 1972); and T. Maddock, "Hydrologic Behavior of Stream Channels," *Transactions of the Thirty-Seventh North American Wildlife and Natural Resources Conference* (Washington, D.C.: Wildlife Management Institute, March 1972).

34. Luna B. Leopold, "Hydrology for Urban Land Planning—A Guidebook on the Hydrologic Effects of Urban Land Use," U.S. Geological Survey Circular 554 (Washington D.C., 1968).

35. R. D. Klein, "Urbanization and Stream Quality Impairment," *Water Resources Bulletin* 15 (1979), p. 948–963.

36. C. C. Park, "Man, River Systems and Environmental Impacts," *Progress in Physical Geography* 5 (1981).

37. R. J. Steedman, *Comparative Analysis of Stream Degradation and Rehabilitation in the Toronto Area* (Toronto, Canada: University of Toronto, 1987).

38. C. B. Stalnaker, R. T. Milhouse, and K. D. Bovee, "Hydrology and Hydraulics Applied to Fishery Management in Large Rivers" in D. P. Dodge, ed., *Proceedings of the International Large Rivers Symposium,* Canadian Special Publication of Fisheries and Aquatic Science, No. 106 (1989).

39. Leopold, "Hydrology for Urban Land Planning."

40. G. E. Hollis, "The Effect of Urbanization on Floods of Different Recurrence in Harlow Essex" in K. J. Gregory and D. E. Walling, eds., *Fluvial Processes in Instrumental Watersheds,* Special Publication No. 6 (London: Institute of British Geographers, 1974).

41. G. E. Hollis, "The Effect of Urbanization on Floods of Different Recurrence Intervals," *Water Resources Research* 11 (1975), p. 431–435.

42. M. G. Wolman, "Problems Posed by Sediment Derived from Construction Activities in Maryland," Report to the Maryland Water Pollution Control Commission (Annapolis, Maryland, 1964).

43. M. G. Wolman, "A Cycle of Sedimentation and Erosion in Urban River Channels," *Geografiska Annaler* 49A (1967), p. 385–395.

44. F. J. Keller, "Effect of Urban Growth on Sediment Discharge, Northwest Branch Anacostia River Basin, Maryland," U.S. Geological Survey Professional Paper 450C (Washington, D.C., 1962).

45. Leopold, "Hydrology for Urban Land Planning."

46. Hollis, "The Effect of Urbanization on Floods of Different Recurrence Intervals."

47. Luna B. Leopold and Thomas Maddock, Jr., *The Flood Control Controversy* (New York: Ronald Press, 1954).

48. Adam Miller, John Troxell, and Luna Leopold, "Hydrology of Two Small River Basins in Pennsylvania Before Urbanization," U.S. Geological Survey Professional Paper 701-A (Washington, D.C., 1971).

49. Leopold, *Water, A Primer.*

50. Leopold, *Water, A Primer.*

51. Dunne and Leopold, *Water in Environmental Planning.*

52. Dunne and Leopold, *Water in Environmental Planning.*

53. M. G. Wolman and A. P. Schick, "Effects of Construction on Fluvial Sediment: Urban and Suburban Areas of Maryland," *Water Resources Research* 3 (1967), p. 451–462.

54. A. M. Robinson, "The Effects of Urbanization on Stream Channel Morphology," *Proceedings of the National Symposium on Urban Hydrology, Hydraulics and Sediment Control* (Lexington: University of Kentucky, 1976).

55. L. B. Leopold, "River Change with Time, An Example," *Bulletin of the Geological Society of America* 84 (1973), p. 1845–1860.

56. M. Morisawa and E. La Flure, "Hydraulic Geometry Stream Equilibrium and Urbanization" in D. D. Rhodes and G. P. Williams, eds., *Adjustments of the Fluvial System* (Dubuque, Iowa: Kendall-Hunt, 1979).

57. C. Knight, "Urbanization and Natural Stream Channel Morphology: The Case of Two English New Towns" in G. E. Hollis, ed., *Man's Impact on the Hydrologic Cycle of the United Kingdom* (Norwich, England: Geobooks, 1979).

58. T. R. Hammer, "Stream Channel Enlargement Due to Urbanization," *Water Resources Research* 8 (1972), 1530–1540.

59. C. C. Park, "Man-Induced Changes in Stream Channel Capacity" in K. J. Gregory, ed., *River Channel Changes* (Chichester: John Wiley, 1977).

60. Leopold, "River Change with Time."

61. H. J. Koloseus, "Rigid Boundary Hydraulics for Steady Flow" in Hsieh Wen Shen, ed., *River Mechanics I* (Fort Collins, Colorado: 1971).

62. Peter Goodwin, hydraulic engineer, principal, Philip Williams Associates, San Francisco, California; professor at University of Bradford, England, until 1989; cofounder of Computational Hydraulics and Environmental Modeling Research Group; associate professor of civil engineering at University of Idaho, Boise, personal communication, June 1995, San Francisco, California.

63. Peter Goodwin, personal communication, June 1995, San Francisco, California.

64. Philip B. Williams, "Rethinking Flood-Control Channel Design," *Civil Engineering* (American Society of Civil Engineers) 60, no. 1 (January 1990).

65. Luna B. Leopold, "Rivers," *American Scientist* 50 (December 1962).

66. Leopold and Maddock, "Hydraulic Geometry of Stream Channels and Some Physiographic Implications," U.S. Geological Survey Professional Paper 252 (Washington, D.C., 1953).

67. Simons and Senturk, *Sediment Transport Technology.*

68. David L. Rosgen, "A Classification of Natural Rivers," *CATENA* 22 (1994), p. 169–199.

69. Leopold and Dunne, *Water in Environmental Planning.*

70. Wolman and Leopold, "River Floodplains: Some Observations on Their Formations."

71. Leopold, "Rivers."

72. Luna Leopold and Gordon Wolman, "River Meanders," *Geological Society of America Bulletin* 71 (1960), p. 769–793.

73. Leopold, Wolman, and Miller, *Fluvial Processes in Geomorphology.*

74. Rosgen, "A Classification of Natural Rivers"; and Dave Rosgen, *Applied River Morphology* (Pagosa Springs, Colorado: Wildland Hydrology, 1996).

CLASSIC REFERENCES

E. M. Wilson, *Engineering Hydrology* (New York: Macmillan Press, 1977).

R. K. Linsley, Jr., M. A. Kohler, and H. L. H. Paulhus, *Applied Hydrology* (New York: McGraw-Hill, 1949).

V. T. Chow, D. R. Maidment, and L. W. Mays, *Applied Hydrology* (New York: McGraw-Hill, 1988).

W. Viessman, J. W. Knapp, G. L. Lewis, and T. E. Harbaugh, *Introduction to Hydrology* (New York: Harper and Row, 1977).

Luna B. Leopold, M. Gordon Wolman, and John P. Miller, *Fluvial Processes in Geomorphology* (San Francisco: W. H. Freeman & Company, 1964).

CHAPTER FIVE

Hydraulic Engineers

Hydraulic engineering has developed into an advanced science, with American engineers in the forefront of developing sophisticated models to predict the responses of water flowing through channels. One of the themes common to all the sections of this book involves the need to integrate the remarkable advances made in all the fields of hydraulic engineering, hydrology, and biology. This integration of the fields will ultimately advance the sophistication of all these disciplines. The conventional engineering practiced since the 1930s has concentrated its efforts on reducing the number of variables to be considered in the design of stream modification projects. Experience is teaching us that we now need to apply the expertise of hydraulic engineers to a new technical frontier, which involves the modeling of environmental systems characterized by a complexity of interacting variables. Past channel project design assumptions have resulted in unanticipated project performance problems because the variables that nature inevitably introduces were not accommodated by the design. The future of hydraulic engineering lies in assisting the designs of more complicated stream-channel systems in which the objective is a more self-sustaining dynamic equilibrium as opposed to a "stable" channel.

Conventional Flood-Control Engineering

The hydraulic engineer has the technological knowledge to design channels for the transport of water and levees to contain floods that require the purchase of a minimum of land right-of-way and result in a minimum of disruption to development in a floodplain. The engineer has also attained a remarkable technical sophistication in developing multiple-purpose reservoirs. Hydraulic engineering in the design of flood-control channels has enjoyed the advancements of computerized mathematical models that quickly analyze data to estimate the magnitude and frequency of floods and the water-surface elevations of storm flows through a channel. The computer models relieve the hydraulic engineer of arduous hand calculations to arrive at an estimate of the probable performance of a flood-control channel and the probability of a storm flow for which the channel is designed.

Flood-control channel design has been based on the objective of constructing a channel for a selected volume of storm flows (hydraulic capacity) for a minimum cost of construction and maintenance. Typically, in rural areas this results in the construction of a trapezoidal channel, while in cities with high land costs a rectangular channel is often considered the least costly. The three most common shapes of channels, on which there may be some variations, are: a box culvert, in which a stream is completely contained in an underground concrete box; a rectangular channel made of reinforced concrete or mass concrete, steel sheet pile, or trench sheeting; and a trapezoidal channel with a flat bottom and sloping sides. Not infrequently the trapezoidal channel is lined with large rock, referred to as riprap. The theoretical basis for the design of these channels is that they should have a cross-sectional area that provides the maximum efficiency in carrying flows with a minimum excavation. Channels with unlined or bare earth banks are often designed with trapezoidal shapes to provide stability for side slopes.[1,2] Many smaller streams in central urban areas are relocated in underground concrete pipes or culverts.

The design philosophy behind a traditional flood-control project is to enlarge a natural stream channel by widening and/or deepening it and to smooth the stream-channel banks and straighten the course of the stream. Essentially, this process transforms a natural landscape feature with all its associated life into a engineered canal with the purpose of increasing the velocity of a large storm flow. The canal contains the storm flows that once would have spread onto a floodplain so that greater volumes of water pass through the canal at lower elevations. These channels are not designed to be modified stream environments; they are designed to replace a stream environment with an engineering facility to convey unusually high-volume flows.

The factors a hydraulic engineer must take into account when designing a "flood-control channel" are the magnitude of the flow of water and sediment, the steepness of the slope, and the characteristics of the ground and surfaces the water flows over. The velocity of the water is directly related to the channel slope—or water-surface slope, if the flows are uniform—and the cross-sectional area of flow. Channel resistance or "roughness" refers to channel bed materials, bends, bars, boulders, vegetation, pools, riffles, and bedrock outcrops. A higher channel resistance ultimately retards flows and creates turbulence. Transport of sediment also requires additional energy. The flood-control channel, then, is designed to increase the volume of flows, the slope, and the cross-sectional area and decrease the channel resistance.

The most common flood-control channel cross-section is a trapezoid. The design parameters are the bottom elevation, referred to as the "invert" in engineering drawings, the channel depth and width, and the slope of the sidewalls. Side slopes designed for maximum hydraulic efficiency would have a 2:1 slope. The slopes in engineering drawings can be shown as that ratio or expressed as: 2H:1V, or 2 feet horizontal distance for every 1 foot vertical distance. The slopes may be designed less steep because of the erodability of different bank materials. Land costs, as mentioned, may be the major factor driving project design, however. A trapezoidal channel with 3:1 slopes, with the same conveyance capacity as a rectangular channel, will be wider than a rectangular channel. Therefore, rectangular channels are prescribed for minimizing the project right-of-way. The anticipated water velocities will also determine the design of slope and type of channel lining. Concrete-lined, as opposed to dirt-lined, channels are more expensive to construct. In some cases, where a high hydraulic gradient is available, the flow can be fed into a completely enclosed cylindrical pressure conduit, and the water flows under pressure much like a water-supply distribution system.[3] Plan and cross-sectional views of channelization projects with trapezoidal and rectangular shapes are shown in figures 5.1 and 5.2. The channel is divided into reaches, and the downstream end of the project is identified as station 00+00. Engineers use this form of numbering to indicate the distance from the downstream end of the project. Station 10+50 means that that point is 1,050 feet upstream from the start of the project.

The calculation of the capacity of a human-made or natural stream channel is based on the relationship already described between the stream discharge, channel width and depth, and velocity of flows.

The discharge of the stream is equal to the cross-sectional area of the channel times the velocity of the flows:

$$Q = AV \quad \text{or} \quad Q = WDV$$

where Q is the discharge in cubic feet per second, A the area in square feet, V the velocity in feet per second, W the width in feet, and D the average depth in feet.

The velocity depends on the depth of the flows, the slope of the flows or the water-surface gradient, and the resistance of the surfaces or boundaries of the channel that tend to retard the flow of the water. Velocity can be described by the well-known Chezy formula as:

$$V = CRS$$

In this equation C is a resistance factor for channel boundaries (Chezy coefficient); R is the hydraulic radius, which is the ratio of the cross-sectional area of flowing

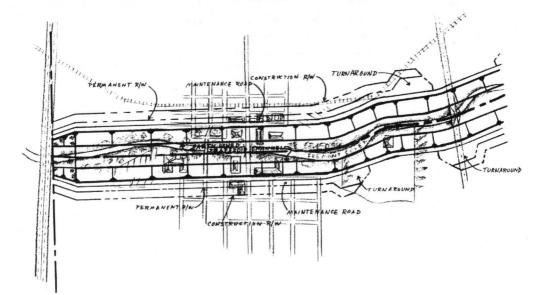

FIGURE 5.1. A TYPICAL CHANNELIZATION PROJECT.

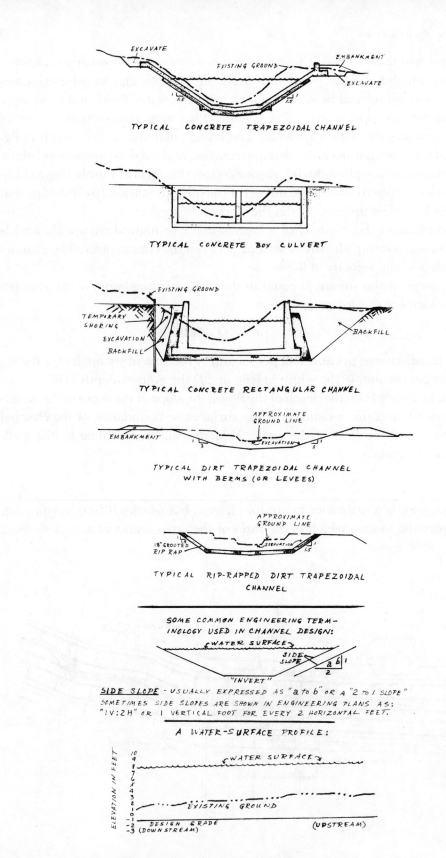

FIGURE 5.2. COMMON FLOOD-CONTROL CHANNEL DESIGNS.

water over the wetted perimeter (i.e., that part of the channel cross-section sub-merged under the water of a given flow—about equal to the mean depth of the flow in wide channels); and S is the energy gradient, or the slope of the water surface.

The comparable formula to this that is widely used by hydraulic engineers to design flood-control channels to the correct channel capacity is the Manning equation:

$$V = \frac{1.49R^{2/3}S^{1/2}}{n}$$

In this formula the channel resistance coefficient is represented by n and is frequently referred to as the Manning n or the roughness coefficient by hydraulic engineers.

Natural mountain streams with rocky beds, boulders, and trees offer a high resistance to flows and therefore have a higher n value (0.040–0.050 or higher). A stream in which the vegetation has been removed and its slopes turned into smooth concrete sides would have a low n value such as 0.012.[4] The U.S. Geological Survey publishes a book with photographs of different stream channels that represent the different Manning n values.[5] Another flow equation occasionally in use is referred to as the Darcy-Weisbach equation.

The Manning equation was developed to represent conditions of a uniform flow of water parallel to the streambed and a constant hydraulic radius and depth. For lack of a better solution, it is assumed that this equation is valid for nonuniform reaches invariably found in natural channels.

Hydraulic models used in floodplain and stream management are mostly concerned with predicting the water-surface elevation of flood flows or channel capacities to carry flows. A simple computation can be made for a single point on a stream using the Manning equation. This equation will give good results if there are no obstructions downstream that could cause a backwater effect. Although the equation represents only the conditions found at a single cross-section, it can frequently provide the restorationist with a good sense of the capacity of a channel restoration project to convey different-sized flows. If there are backwater effects from bridges, culverts, or other obstructions into the channel, then it may be necessary to use a backwater model to determine the elevations or stages of flood flows. The most commonly used model for calculating river hydraulics is referred to as the step-backwater analysis. The method uses channel cross-sections and other hydraulic parameters to maintain a continuity of mass and energy from one river cross-section to the next and provides a water-surface elevation profile for a reach of stream. This analysis is usually computerized and can include separate analyses for conditions involving bridges, weir flow, channel modification, and other special circumstances.

The Army Corps of Engineers, which is an influential trendsetter in the hydraulic engineering field, developed a computerized mathematical multi-transect backwater model called HEC-2 to calculate the elevation that a certain storm flow would be expected to reach in a flood-control channel based on the relationships in the Manning equation. The Manning equation can be used to calculate the friction losses of the flowing water between two different points or cross-sections on the channel, while what is referred to as the "standard step" method applies Bernoulli's theorem, which is used to calculate the total energy in each different reach of the channel. By calculating the changes in hydraulic energy between two cross-sections, the elevation of the flow is estimated. The HEC-2 can evaluate the hydraulic effects of levees, floodways, bridges, culverts, and weirs, as well as channel projects, and is used for calculating the profiles (the up and down river views of a channel and the floodwater elevations) for various frequency floods for both natural and modified conditions. HEC stands for the Corps' Hydrologic Engineering Center in Davis, California, where this model was developed in 1968. The Soil Conservation Service uses its own program, the WSP-2, and the U.S. Geological Survey uses WSPRO, but the HEC-2 program is a popular computer model widely used by local water districts, states, and consulting firms and has become a standardized method for designing channelization projects.[6-9]

The HEC-2 model is the most used hydraulic model and for this reason is probably the most abused as well. Its assets include that it is widely available and easy to use. Its liabilities are that the model does not take into account the complex factors that can govern river flows and floods, as some of the river projects described later in this chapter illustrate, and the data going into the models can be woefully inadequate. Little actual field data may be used to calibrate an HEC-2 model. The model requires dividing the channel into homogenous reaches; measuring the length of the reaches; measuring the cross-sections; and assigning n or roughness values to represent each reach. The depth or elevation of a storm discharge is determined for the mouth of the stream or some downstream station. The accuracy of this value for the elevation of the "starting" discharge can be important because the program uses this basic data to calculate the upstream water-surface elevations (for subcritical flows). The estimation of the discharges carried by the stream frequently does not involve any field measurements of stages or velocities. Enough carefully surveyed cross-sections of channels and floodplains may not be entered into the model to represent the conditions for the existing or modified channel. The selection of the value for the Manning n roughness coefficient is known to be a subjective process, and it is possible to get a wide range of values selected for the same conditions—leading some engineers to refer to it as the "fudge factor."

It's important for political representatives, public administrators, and the interested public—as well as practicing civil engineers—to know the basics about these models that are used to design traditional flood-control projects, and to understand their usefulness and their limitations. The literature that evaluates the traditional flood-control project so far has been mainly concerned with the now well-known environmental impacts of these projects. After a fifty-year record of these projects, a new focus of project evaluations is on their performance problems in meeting the flood-control or channel stabilization objectives they were designed for. Evaluations of the design objectives and the strengths and weaknesses of the hydraulic models are now being undertaken by the engineering profession.

Because the design philosophy behind these projects is to reduce a dynamic and complex stream system to a simplified, stable canal system, the environmental values of a stream are inherently in conflict with the flood-control project objectives. Channel capacity must be increased; therefore, the natural channel geometry must go. Velocities must be increased; therefore, vegetation must be removed and the channel boundaries must be cleared with herbicides on a regular basis. Large channels with fast-flowing water offer no easy escape if someone falls in, and if a channel contains dangerous energy dissipaters, they can impact and trap a victim. Therefore, for safety reasons, such conduits must be enclosed with high chain-link or barbed-wire fences.

There is a long history of public objection to the use of these design assumptions by the engineering profession. The public has implored engineers to design something more compatible with their city centers and neighborhoods. Rather than change their project design assumptions, however, engineers reluctantly compromise their designs when public pressure is great enough. They will add some trees or shrubs, preferably placed carefully away from the project high-water mark and sparsely grouped, so as to minimize interference with maintenance access. Local public works agencies may be pressured by a public concerned with environmental values into channel maintenance practices that leave a little more vegetation. Because of federal or state laws, mitigation plantings may be required. These typically occur at a safe distance from the project channel or canal and may be located completely off the project site or even in an entirely different watershed. These landscaping requirements, mitigation plantings, or other project amenities are, at worst, threats to the design objective of smooth, unobstructed channels and unobstructed maintenance roads and, at best, public relations necessities that increase the project costs.

The field of channel hydraulics does itself a disservice by limiting itself to developing hypothetical models with the narrow design assumptions that are inherent in conventional channelization projects. The challenge awaiting the hydraulic engineering profession is to learn how to better model stream channels that can be self-sustaining in dynamic equilibrium, as opposed to constructing maintenance-intensive "stable" canals.[10] A community's flood-damage-reduction objectives can be met with projects that are modeled more after the dynamics found in nature than after the dynamics found in a controlled laboratory flume. Traditional engineering designs must continually fight the natural tendencies of channels to meander, to transfer and deposit a bed load, and to harbor plant growth. By changing our design assumptions to model our projects after dynamic, natural systems, these natural features that continually insist on recurring in channelized canals can be planned and important functional components of the design rather than expensive conflicts with the channel design.

Conventional Bank Stabilization Methods

The most prevalent form of stream-channel modification or degradation is the bank stabilization project, not only as a part of flood-control project design, but also as a widespread response to the destabilization of stream channels due to

urbanization or other land-use changes. Because the objective of traditional channelization projects is to stop the natural erosion and meandering of a stream
channel, the channel bottom and banks must be "armored" or made stationary by
lining them with rock or concrete. Grade-control structures and energy dissipaters
are also commonly found in conjunction with channelization projects to dissipate
the energy of the high-velocity flows. Paving or riprap is commonly used downstream of these structures.

Stream-bank failures can be a result of changes in the watershed or a localized
problem. As described in chapter 4, the increased runoff caused by urbanization of
a watershed tends to erode channels wider and deeper. Typically, urban structures
are situated too close to a stream channel, which adjusts to increased urban flows
and sediment loads by excessively eroding, depositing, and meandering.

Erosion is a natural process, but it can be greatly accelerated by human activities.
If structures are put into the path of an eroding stream, a conflict between the
stream and those structures is inevitable. Of course, the most sensible option is to
zone or regulate structures an adequate distance from stream and river meander
zones, just as we should zone for flood-damage protection. The Army Corps of Engineers estimated in a report to Congress in 1978 that out of 3.5 million stream bank
miles, 575,000 miles had erosion problems.[11]

Professional engineering projects are normally sponsored and designed by government agencies, which commonly use stone riprap; concrete pavement; rock
gabions; bulkheads made of steel, concrete, and aluminum; asphalt mixes; sack
revetments; and dikes, groins, and jetties to stabilize banks.[12] The design philosophy is to harden the banks to stop the natural erosion processes. Usually, all or
most of the natural vegetation is removed in order to carry out the bank construction project. Riprapping is a favored practice because simple charts designate appropriate rock size for anticipated flow velocities, and it is simple to dump rock
down the channel slope from the stream bank after the vegetation is removed.

Property owners concerned about the loss of land, erosion, and endangered
structures will dump onto the stream-bank sides any material they may have acces-
sible to divert flows from the bank. Old cars, concrete rubble, oil drums, car tires,
and gunite (sprayed concrete) are common bank-lining materials used. A not uncommon occurrence is a bank protection "chain," begun when one property owner
places bank protection works against one bank, thereby narrowing the channel
width, speeding up the flows, and deflecting an even greater erosive force against
the downstream neighbors' property. Those neighbors react with bank protection
works of their own, creating more problems for the next downstream sites, and so
on down the stream.

In fact, professional engineers get themselves locked into this cycle as well, for
they usually cannot avoid the downstream impacts that their bank stabilization projects cause, either. The recent engineering tradition of bank stabilization project design is normally associated with negative impacts to the environment. This is
unfortunate because there is no sound reason for bank stabilization and environmental quality or diversity to be mutually exclusive objectives.

The first most notable environmental impact of traditional bank stabilization projects is the dramatic aesthetic transformation of a diverse natural environment to an environment of concrete, riprap, or metal. The projects ironically tend to remove the vegetation, which has particularly well-adapted qualities for soil stabilization. The loss of riparian cover also brings on loss of wildlife habitat, water-quality degradation, and loss of instream life. Rough, uneven stream banks provide the best aquatic habitat. The loss of sediment from eroding banks contributes to a stream starved for sediment, which will usually be compensated for by erosion problems downstream. Attempts to eliminate erosion also greatly reduce the depositional forms along a creek and therefore can reduce the regeneration of riparian growth and reduce pool and riffle sequences for aquatic life.

All streams erode their banks to some extent, and the diversity of the physical conditions in a natural stream are created by undercut banks, bar formation, and channel migration. Erosion of a stream bank is balanced by deposition downstream. A natural alluvial stream erodes into areas of mature, climax, riparian vegetation and then deposits point bars downstream that are invaded by pioneer flood-tolerant species such as willows and cottonwoods that love disturbed areas. Erosion and channel migration are tied to the stream's vegetative cycle and vice versa. Stream-bank protection projects that are based on imposing channel stability as opposed to encouraging self-adjusting equilibrium reduce the rates of change in these cycles; create more uniform channel conditions, depths, and velocities; and decrease aquatic habitats.

The Waterways Experiment Station of the U.S. Army Corps of Engineers has published excellent documents summarizing the literature on the environmental impacts of bank stabilization projects and the range of practices in bank stabilization.[13] The Natural Resources Conservation Service has updated its handbooks to address the need to integrate more environmentally sensitive techniques into bank stabilization practices.[14] There is genuine interest in most engineering circles to make such projects more environmentally acceptable.[15]

Two common engineering practices frustrate the design and execution of sustainable, functioning stream-channel restoration or "stabilization." One practice is the design of conventional engineered channels intended to reduce the variables of meanders, pools, riffles, floodplains, and other components and treat revegetation as an add-on not related to the natural dynamics of the stream. The other practice is similar in that it entails localized "band-aid," or "fix-it," projects that do not pay attention to the watershed influences and stream dynamics influencing the stream reaches of concern. The task at hand, as in the design of channel modifications for flood-damage reduction, is to change the philosophical underpinnings of the bank stabilization strategy.

The Problems with Conventional Flood-Control Channel Design
The Unintended Results of Channelization Projects

A great deal has been written since the 1940s on the environmental impacts of structural flood-control measures. Much less, however, has been done on follow-up evaluations of the actual performance and costs of flood-control facilities as compared with their intended costs and design objectives. The engineering profession has operated on the assumption that once construction is completed, the major job is done, but the experience of the last fifty years has shown that the results of many channelization projects have been at cross purposes with their intentions.

Equilibrium Lost

The possible responses to channelization and the possible interactions in the stream system are varied and complex. Generalizations about channelization projects should be avoided, and each project needs to be evaluated separately. The reader should be aware of the developing knowledge about such projects and the types of problems that are associated with them. Relationships among erosion, deposition, and sediment concentration in natural stream channels with alluvial bed and bank materials are not well understood. The conventional and generally accepted assumption is that channelization increases the channel slope, which causes an increase in the velocity of the water. This then facilitates erosion of the bed and banks, increasing the sediment concentration until a new balance is achieved between the sediment load and discharges.[16]

One of the best ways to develop a sense of the performance problems as well as the environmental impacts of these projects is to read about the channelization projects documented by experts or the accounts written for the popular press. Titles such as "Channelization: Shortcut to Nowhere," "How to Kill a River by 'Improving It'," "Crisis on Our Rivers," and "The Gravediggers" convey the anguish felt by some writers observing the results of channelization projects.[17]

In 1982, the Federal Emergency Management Agency (FEMA) and the U.S. Geological Survey released a pamphlet and tape-slide presentation for the lay public called "Channel Straightening—A Potential Problem." This apparent first attempt by government to raise the issues of channelization for general public consumption introduces the basic concept of the "geomorphic equilibrium" of streams. The slide show is useful in explaining to both a lay audience and water professionals that the flowing water and sediment that a stream carries have adjusted to the environment over a long period of time, and there is often a price to pay if that equilibrium is upset. Photographs and records of conditions in the Big Spring Creek in central Montana before and after channelization show that project consequences include unplanned flooding, erosion, sedimentation, and damage to structures (see figure 5.3).[18] *Channelized Rivers* by Andrew Brookes provides an excellent literature review of the biological, physical, engineering, and institutional aspects of stream channelization and should be a part of any agency or home library.[19]

Downstream effects of channelization projects may include flooding and erosion because of the change in timing and magnitude and duration of downstream flows. Excessive erosion and sedimentation do commonly occur in these projects, and in most cases, without expensive maintenance, the new channel will return to

FIGURE 5.3. NATURE BATS LAST.

(a) Sediment filling in the lower San Lorenzo River channelization project, Santa Cruz, California. *Photo credit:* Philip Williams Associates. (b) Meandering returns to a channelized stream on the Walla Walla River, Milton-Freewater, Oregon. *Photo credit:* U.S. Army Corps of Engineers. (c) Buckling of concrete channel on channelized portion of Tecolote Canyon Creek, San Diego, California. (d) Undermining of concrete channel from reestablished vegetation after a lapse of five years in maintenance, South branch of Underwood Creek, tributary of the Menominee River, Milwaukee, Wisconsin. (e) Undercut bridge supports on a channelized stream. *Source:* U.S. Geological Survey and Federal Emergency Management Agency slide show, "Channelization, A Potential Problem." (f) In transition from a dirt-lined to a concrete-lined channel, a meandering channel carves a path through the concrete channel, Los Angeles River, California.

its original meandering course. Bank erosion problems downstream and upstream of concrete and riprapped channels are frequent. The straightened channel increases hydraulic efficiency by providing a straight and smooth conduit to pass the flows, but the increased velocity and discharge erode the channel banks downstream and may undermine the end of the concrete channel.[20] It has been observed that when such concrete channels fail, as in large-magnitude floods, results are often more disastrous than they might have been had the channel not been altered in the first place. According to Robert Curry, a geomorphologist, "Straightened channels, with their steeper gradients and higher velocities will, upon abandonment during flood, often assume a braided or meandering pattern much to the detriment of the city established along its banks."[21] Sedimentation of downstream stretches can result in loss of channel capacity and subsequent increase in frequency of flooding.[22]

While channelization projects may cause instability in the channelized reach and downstream reaches, the most dramatic adjustments can be system-wide slope changes. Straightening a meandering stream can increase the channel slope by providing a shorter channel path. (The stream does not travel as far to drop a given elevation, so the gradient increases.) The increase in slope can cause degradation of the streambed, which can progress upstream. That, in turn, can cause bank collapse and considerable bank erosion, locally enlarging a channel width by two or three times. Erosion may then work its way upstream as a series of "knickpoints," or steps in the bed. Upstream erosion supplies more sediment to the downstream areas. Eventually, because of the downstream sedimentation, the channel slope may begin to return to a less steep slope.

Clear Creek, a tributary to the South Platte River near Denver, is a good example of the impacts a channel modification project can have on its tributaries. The degradation of the main channel of the river caused by channelization undermined the bridge abutments spanning the river, which are now being replaced at great cost. At the same time, the banks of the creek entering the river are collapsing because the creek channel bottom is dropping to conform to the gradient of the river it is entering. After the main channel has lowered its gradient, the tributary forms a "waterfall" where it joins the main channel, and the waterfall continues to advance up the tributary, progressively eroding the channel bed upstream.

A good case representing a great diversity of watershed-wide disturbances over many miles due to channelization is the previously mentioned one of the Kissimmee River, which suffered loss of flood storage, wetlands, wildlife, fish, and water quality as a result of a channel-straightening project. A natural, meandering stream channel is much longer than a straightened channel. The transformation of the 100-mile-long meandering Kissimmee River to the 50-mile ditch A-38 is a good example of that. The longer, meandering channel had greater storage capacity for water than the straighter, shortened channel of the project. The associated sloughs and wetlands acted as a sponge for floodwaters before they were drained by the channelization. By rushing the flows at fast velocities instead of holding them back in the nat-ural system, the upstream areas may get better drainage and lower flood stages, but the downstream areas can be greatly impacted by increases in floodwaters.

To summarize, the effects of channelization in the straightened and upstream reaches may include: higher flow velocities, increased sediment transport, steeper channel slope, degradation of the channel and head cutting, unstable channel banks, river braiding, and degradation of the tributary channels. Downstream ef-fects can include deposition of sediments in the channel, aggradation, loss of channel capacity, and increases in flood stages. A number of laboratory and field studies have recorded the adjustment of straightened channels toward their original meandering state.[23] The responses of a channelized stream depend on the character of the bed and bank materials and sediments, their erodability, and the geologic stratification of the area the stream flows through.

Considerable regional differences can be found in the channel responses to chan-nelization, and so the public and public officials interested in these issues should become familiar with the local or regional experience. That may require gathering some experts and a camera and taking a few field trips to projects in the area so you can see for yourself what the situation is. In the meantime you should become fa-miliar with the following channelization cases so that you know what questions to ask in the event that a channelization project is proposed in your locale. This chapter ends with a list of questions to help guide you.

Channelization Cases

A frequently referenced, professionally documented case study on the effects of channelization on stream hydraulics is John Emerson's study on Blackwater River, published in 1971.[24] Channelization in the Blackwater River in Johnson County, Missouri, sixty years ago doubled the gradient, which increased the rate of erosion for the river and its tributaries. The widening, deepening, and shortening of the channel increased the velocity of the water, which caused erosion of the channel sides and increase of the gradient. The widening of the channel also caused a col-lapse of bridges. At one site, a bridge was replaced by a larger bridge in 1942, and in 1947 collapsed again. Most bridges in Johnson County had to be replaced or length-ened and have additions made to vertical supports. Erosion after channelization av-eraged almost 5 feet in depth a year. The unchannelized portion of the channel downstream began to flood frequently. Two successive generations of fenceposts were buried by over-bank deposits on the downstream floodplain—amounting to about 6 feet of deposition in fifty to sixty years. A number of public hearings con-ducted in the 1940s indicated that flooding had increased since channelization and that the effectiveness of the lower end of the channelization area was being reduced by sedimentation, which slowly progressed upstream. The channelization enabled more floodplain to be used in the upper reaches of the river but also resulted in erosion of farmland, bridge repair and replacement, and downstream flood and sedimentation damages.

A 1982 study by Robbins and Simon concluded that channel modifications on Tennessee streams caused channel downcutting, headward erosion, downstream aggradation, accelerated scour, and bank instabilities and in some cases were damaging bridges more than fifty years later.[25]

A paper prepared by Gary Griggs, a professor at the University of California at Santa Cruz, records the effects of a Corps of Engineers channelization project on the San Lorenzo River in Santa Cruz.[26] In the 1950s, serious flooding occurred on the San Lorenzo River, which Griggs attributes to heavy logging and land clearing in the San Lorenzo basin and logjams at bridges, backing flows up. Logjams and channel obstructions diverted flood flows and caused the stream to change its alignment and scour out bridges and private developments. In a 1955 storm, lives were lost, 2,830 people were displaced, and damages amounted to $8.7 million. The Corps project was built in 1959 to respond to those flood damages and featured levees at the lower stretches of the river and a channelization project that lowered the channel grade by more than 6 feet to increase the slope and capacity of the channel. In order to scour sediments from the channel, the flow velocities were designed to be extremely high: 7.9–24.7 feet per second.

As a result of the false sense of security created by the project, Santa Cruz intensively redeveloped the "former" floodplain for urban uses over a period of ten years. A 1975 survey showed that sedimentation of the channel had significantly reduced the project's capacity. The city used a bulldozer to uproot all channel vegetation in the belief that the roots were holding the sediment and preventing the high velocities from scouring. Scouring of the sediment, however, still did not occur. Because project channel maintenance is the sole responsibility of local governments, the city of Santa Cruz was left with a sediment removal bill that it could not afford—a $3 million initial removal cost and a $200,000 annual maintenance cost. Although designed to provide protection from the 100-year-recurrence-interval flood, the levees were almost overtopped in 1982 during a flood that had a recurrence interval of thirty years. This was of immediate concern because the city was legally back within the 100-year floodplain, and high premiums would have to be charged to property owners.

The effect of increasing the channel slope by one-third upset the equilibrium conditions established over thousands of years. Sea level was the ultimate base for the San Lorenzo, but due to channel excavation, high tides extended inland $2^{1}/_{2}$ miles. When the San Lorenzo River enters the ocean, the sediment load drops, and the sediment has been progressively filling in the channel behind this stream-ocean boundary, much as sediment would fill in behind a dam in a reservoir. This process of sedimentation has continued up the channel until the channel has returned to a more stable or constant slope. Periodic channel surveys have indicated that a pseudo-equilibrium has been reestablished. For a reach of the project, the new equilibrium channel has a different profile than either the original or the designed channel; the channel bottom is now above the initial designed bottom and 2.7 to 3.6 feet above the original natural channel. The U.S. Army Corps of Engineers made no mention of deposition problems in its design manual except to recommend frequent dredging. Army Corps annual maintenance costs were estimated at $25,000 as compared to the actual costs of $200,000. Almost forty years later, the city of Santa Cruz is still engaged in correcting the problems of the river. In the late 1980s the city initiated a planning process using river restoration strategies and bridge modifications as the primary methods to address flood management needs.[27]

An important case that has caught the attention of national hydraulic engineering circles is the Corte Madera channelization project located in the cities of Ross and Larkspur in Marin County north of San Francisco. The case raises serious questions for channelization projects because it brings to light vulnerabilities inherent in the basic technical assumptions used to design such projects. A channelization project on Corte Madera Creek completed in 1972 was designed to convey the "Standard Project Flood," or in this case about the one-in-200-year flood. However, in both 1982 and 1986 the channel did not perform as anticipated and flooded the surrounding community. In the 1982 flood, the channel overflowed with flows of approximately 5,000 cfs, which was equivalent to only the one-in-20-year flood flows. Flood flows were 6 feet higher than expected. The channel failure in 1986 occurred at lower flows.

Marin County hired consultants to evaluate the reasons for the project failure,[28] and recent reports by the Army Corps of Engineers essentially conclude that a significant cause was the failure of the design engineers to anticipate that the storm flows would be transporting a significant amount of sediment.[29, 30] The large quantities of suspended sediment carried by the storm flows resulted in slower than expected flow velocities. As described in chapter 4, channelization projects are frequently designed to produce supercritical flows that move large volumes of water quickly at low stages. Because the water was laden with sediment, the flows never attained a supercritical state and were actually subcritical, or much slower—and deeper. Standard hydraulic engineering practices leave out the role of sediment in flood hydraulics and assume "clear water" flows. As stream observers note, many urban streams—as well as rural ones—run muddy during storms. Because of our limited understanding of sediment transport, the hydraulic models used to design these projects frequently do not adequately represent this component of flood flows.[31, 32]

The possible explanations for the failure of the Corte Madera concrete flood-control channel were: (1) that sediment could have accumulated in the channel before the flood, increased the channel roughness, and reduced channel capacities;[33] (2) that sedimentation of the channel downstream of the project could have lowered velocities and affected upstream water levels by creating a backwater effect;[34] and (3) that the sand, gravel, and boulders up to 18 inches in diameter carried as bed load during the flood increased the roughness and reduced flow velocities.[35] The planned construction of additional channelization upstream was never completed, and the possibility was raised at one point by the Army Corps that that contributed to the problems. The experts are now reaching agreement that the most significant cause of failure among all the possibilities was assuming clear-water flow in a concrete channel during a storm.

The Unintended Results of Bank Stabilization Projects

As we have just established, when a channel is modified locally, it frequently causes changes up or downstream in spite of attempts to control the stream's response. In general, an engineer concerned with channel stabilization should not attempt to develop straight channels. Bends in channels are formed by the processes of erosion and deposition. Erosion without deposition to assist in bend formation results only in caving banks that continue to erode and widen. The principles of sediment transport and deposition should guide all our stream projects whether the objective is to better convey flood flows or to correct excessive erosion of stream banks.[36]

To impose an unnatural alignment on a stream, the standard engineering practice, as described, is to line the banks of the channel with rock or concrete. Even though banks may be protected by riprap, gabions, or other materials, an actively meandering channel can take out the materials or destroy the structures. Rock and gabions and concrete can be undercut by degrading channels. Flows can circumvent the armored banks and form new channels around the armored banks.

Concrete and riprap can be buckled and displaced by plant growth. Concrete suffers the particular disadvantage that the hydrostatic pressure of water accumulating in the soils behind the lining results in the cracking and buckling of the concrete. If a constant and expensive maintenance program is not put in place, these traditional bank protection works can quickly deteriorate. Research projects are badly needed to inventory the condition of different bank stabilization works that represent a variety of life spans to evaluate their performance, longevity, and actual maintenance costs.

An interesting study done as a master's thesis at California State University at Chico made an inventory of riprapped sites along the Sacramento River that were rocked under a federally authorized project (1958–59) referred to as the Chico Landing to Red Bluff Sacramento River Bank Protection Project.[37] The project was justified on the basis of protecting agricultural lands from eroding and reducing downstream dredging costs. The report concluded that the riprapped sites had met a diversity of fates. A number of sites had eroded behind the riprap; in some cases, the river took the riprap out; and in other cases, changes in river meander left the riprapped bends as abandoned meanders in a backwater isolated from the main river. In some cases, the riprap helped control erosion, but a common feature of those sites was erosion at the up and downstream reaches at the end of the riprap.

Finally, at some sites, the riprap had been buried by sediment by a continually adjusting river. The report established that because of the failures or limited benefits of the projects, the actual benefits in relation to costs did not meet the federal project efficiency requirements. Using figures from the federal government records on the feet of Sacramento River riprapped and the costs of those projects, the study determined that the average cost of riprapping along the Sacramento in 1970s dollars was $95 a lineal foot.

The problems associated with conventional bank stabilization public works projects are exacerbated by the problems of destabilized stream channels caused by the effects of urbanization described in the last chapter. Luckily, the field of stream management has taken a quantum leap forward with the greater understanding developed in the past few decades on the dynamics of streams described in chapter 4. It is now much more widely known that if a stream's channel width, depth, and meander are out of balance with its slope, channel bed material, and discharge, efforts to stabilize banks or reduce excessive sedimentation or erosion will ultimately be met with little success.

Recent Trends in Flood-Damage and Erosion Reduction Projects Design

A number of significant recent developments are going to lead us out of the era of conventional channelization and riprap projects and into the restoration era. One such development, which cannot be underestimated, is the commitment of top-level federal agency managers to change their agency missions. Equally important, however, are the advancements being made by the technical staffs of those agencies to develop new project design assumptions and methods.

The Army Corps has released an engineering manual, *Engineering and Design: Channel Stability Assessment for Flood Control Projects,* that calls for the integration of fluvial geomorphology and hydraulic engineering practices to improve the design assumptions and methods used in channel modification projects.[38] It is the intention of the Office of the Chief of Engineers of the Army Corps that this document be the design guide for all future channel projects. The document articulates the concept of the dynamic equilibrium of rivers. It directs the engineer to use field-derived knowledge of the many interacting variables affecting the dynamic of a particular stream, in combination with hydraulic models, to design for equilibrium, i.e., more natural conditions.

Another important development is the beginning of efforts to evaluate projects after they have been constructed and in use for a number of years in order to compare their performance to the original objectives of the projects. A candid and informative report released by the Army Corps describes the post-project-construction in-field review of both flood-control and bank stabilization projects. Through that report we learn of the vulnerabilities of the conventional practices that have been in use and the areas of stream dynamics—such as grade-control problems—in which we have the greatest knowledge gaps.[39] After flood-control projects are constructed, no one collects in-the-field measurements of the actual storm-flow velocities and stages to confirm whether the projects actually accommodate the discharges they are designed for.

Accompanying this quest for improving the science of hydraulic engineering are the efforts of hydraulics researchers and practicing engineers to further develop hydraulic models and combine the use of models to better simulate field conditions, as well as to encourage more substantive field data to be used to calibrate the models. In situations where the dynamics of the flood wave are important, or the streambed is subject to cycles of scour or deposition, or the floods cross a broad and complex floodplain, or flows vary from subcritical to supercritical reaches, the most popular model, the HEC-2, is inappropriate to use.[40] One concern that is gaining ground among flood-control engineers is that sediment transport and deposition are not typically integrated into the models used to design flood-control channels. An additional concern under more consideration by the engineering community is the assumption that channel beds and banks are stationary and do not erode or fill during large floods. Predicting scour and fill can be complex, but not including consideration for scour during flood flows can mislead results in determining channel capacities and lead to unnecessarily expensive channel or floodplain modifications.[41, 42]

Researchers involved with improving the technology used to design flood-control channel projects are calling for the identification of sediment transport issues early in the design process, and the changing of project design assumptions to better reflect realistic long-term maintenance and management needs. A call has been made by government researchers for providing more guidelines on how to incorporate vegetation into bank stabilization and flood-control channel designs to better address channel erosion control, flood conveyance, and channel equilibrium. A recognition of the connection between natural vegetation and stability of erosion control projects is being made.[43–47]

The flood-control channel design of the near future will be the "multistage" channel that re-creates the river and floodplain features described in the last chapter that are so critical for maintaining the natural functions of rivers. Flood-control and river restoration projects should begin to look the same. First, the equilibrium, "bankfull" channel, described in chapter 4, should be properly sized to create the conditions for the desired sediment transport. It is no more desirable for a "flood-control" channel than a natural stream channel to fill with sediment. A bankfull channel that is properly sized with the correct widths and depths should not experience excessive sedimentation or excessive erosion. As it is now, the wide bottom, trapezoidal, and rectangular channels have a tendency to perform as sediment trappers, often creating prohibitive maintenance bills, as in the San Lorenzo River case.[48–52]

The bankfull channel should be stabilized by a riparian corridor to help prevent

invasion of sun-loving rushes and reeds and hold the shape of the channel. The riparian corridor should be flanked by a floodplain that conveys and stores flood
flows and sediment.

The implications of this kind of channel modification design are that we should
be able to evolve to a situation in the near future where we do not make distinctions between "flood-control channels" and "river restoration projects" except that
the flood-related projects will be concerned in greater detail with modeling the influence of floodplain widths, vegetation, sediment, and sediment transport on the
ability of the stream channel to convey flood flows. Project rights-of-way or widths
will be determined by acquisition of the lands or easements necessary to accommodate the natural stream features of bankfull channels, floodplains, and riparian
habitats. Even rivers constrained by existing development can be creatively restored to attempt to create these features to the extent possible, as described in
Chapters 7 and 9.

Several flood-control projects have been designed based on this concept of modeling the project channel after nature. Figure 5.4 illustrates the Wildcat–San Pablo
Creeks flood-control project constructed by the Army Corps of Engineers in
Richmond, California, in 1986. The top cross-section illustrates a conventional
trapezoidal flood-control channel, and the bottom cross-section illustrates the multistage channel design with a bankfull channel, riparian corridor, floodplain, and
berms. This "natural-like" channel was possible in this case to fit within the same
project right-of-way (250 feet wide) as the conventionally designed project and provides protection for the same-sized flood (100-year-recurrence-interval). The creek
channels are being managed for both ecological and flood-damage-reduction
objectives.[53, 54]

Other projects designed on these principles include Trout Brook Creek in West
Hartford, Connecticut; Rapid Creek in South Dakota; and Amazon Creek in Oregon.
The latter two projects are of interest because they are attempts (by a state agency
in South Dakota and the Army Corps in Oregon) to restore channelization projects
constructed in the past while keeping flood conveyance as a design objective.[55–57]

While the nature of "channel modification" projects should be improving in the
near future based on the knowledge and experience we are gaining from these early
demonstration projects, the modification of stream channels should still be viewed
as a last resort to reduce flood damages. The most cost-effective way to manage
floodplains is to avoid the conflicts between flood-hazard areas and development to
begin with. Land-use planning and zoning, storm-water management programs
that encourage the natural absorption and release of rainwater, relocation of structures from hazardous areas, and the flood proofing of structures to prevent water
damages are all aimed at removing our structures from the river rather than removing the river from our environment.

Short flood walls built around houses or along neighborhoods and designed like
the old WPA rock walls—if done on a sensitive scale—can be a community amenity

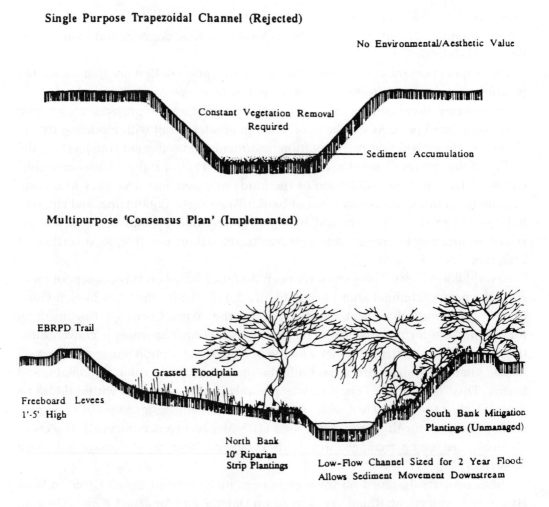

Single Purpose Trapezoidal Channel (Rejected)

No Environmental/Aesthetic Value

Constant Vegetation Removal Required

Sediment Accumulation

Multipurpose 'Consensus Plan' (Implemented)

EBRPD Trail

Grassed Floodplain

Freeboard Levees 1'-5' High

South Bank Mitigation Plantings (Unmanaged)

North Bank 10' Riparian Strip Plantings

Low-Flow Channel Sized for 2 Year Flood Allows Sediment Movement Downstream

Designs for Wildcat Creek Flood-Control Project

FIGURE 5.4. WILDCAT–SAN PABLO CREEKS CROSS-SECTION: A "TWO-STAGE" FLOOD-CONTROL CHANNEL WITH A MEANDERING BANKFULL CHANNEL AND FLOODPLAIN.
Source: Philip Williams Associates, San Francisco, California

and reduce flood damages. Levee projects usually produce fewer disruptions to streams than channel modification projects. Levees have their own controversies, however, involving how stable they are and their tendency to fail; whether it's appropriate for them to support riparian vegetation; and the possibility that they constrict floodplains upstream, thereby creating flood problems for downstream communities. Nonetheless, the channel modification project should probably be the last option on the list for resolving a flood problem unless it entails a floodplain restoration project.

The field of stream-bank restoration has undergone a veritable revolution in the 1990s. The revival of 1930s technologies using "willow wattles" and other kinds of bundles of both live and dead vegetation to add structure and strength to destabilized hillsides and stream banks is leading to the replacement of the conventional riprap projects. The publication of the "Soil Bioengineering" engineering manual by the Natural Resources Conservation Service signals the formal revival by federal agencies of the kinds of revegetation work they used to perform before the 1950s era of concrete made plants unfashionable working materials. Watershed managers are now realizing that stream-bank restoration projects must consider watershed influences on the stream corridor and that plant materials ultimately offer the greatest range of remedies likely to succeed for correcting watershed and stream-channel problems.[58] The last chapter of this book is dedicated to that topic.

Questions to Ask

Elected representatives, government officials, and agency staff reviewing flood-control project plans and citizens interested in proposed plans should ask the sponsors of flood-control and bank stabilization projects the following questions. These questions have been compiled from interviews with engineering staff in the U.S. Army Corps of Engineers, staff in the Natural Resources Conservation Service, engineers in local water agencies, floodplain management experts, hydrologists, and engineers. These experts were asked what questions they felt the public should pose to the proper officials when a flood-damage-reduction project or bank stabilization project is being proposed by a local, state, or federal agency.

If a Flood-Control Project Is Being Planned

1. Is this project being proposed to make new urban development possible, or is the purpose of it to protect existing development? If it is being proposed to make new development possible, why is the community being asked to subsidize the developer with a project? Why aren't land-use regulations in the form of floodplain zoning being used instead to avoid the inherent problems of building structures in a hazard area?

2. Who will benefit from the project, and who will be paying for it? Also, are benefits considered to be on a local, regional, or national basis? Are there other, more appropriate or less hazardous sites available for development in the same region, so that the costs and risks of floodplain development can be avoided?

3. Do we have good information on the locations, the frequency and magnitude, and the areal extent of the flood problem?

4. What information are the flood frequency estimates based on? How reliable is that information? Do you consider the flood frequency estimates to be conservative or to represent a middle range?

5. Do we know specifically what is causing the flood problem? Is it caused by new urban development? Is it caused by stream-channel constrictions from road bridges, railroad bridges, debris in the channels, culverts, or structures too close to the stream? What is being done to remove or redesign the source of the problem or to avoid more of the same problems by planning the community's future growth?

6. Have "nonstructural" alternatives such as floodproofing, elevating, and relocating structures been evaluated as serious considerations?

7. What level of flood protection is being proposed? Is the community being given choices about what it feels are acceptable levels of risks, given the costs of the proposed remedies?

8. What kind of citizen participation will there be in the project planning? Will the interested citizens be invited to meetings to be briefed on the project plans, or will the citizenry take part in the formulation of the plans?

9. What is being done to integrate the other political jurisdictions or concerns of other government agencies into the early planning process?

10. What funding opportunities does the community attract if we design a multi-objective plan?

11. How much do these projects typically cost, and what is the typical (as opposed to the projected) planning time until construction or implementation for the kind of project being proposed?

12. If some kind of modification to the stream corridor is required in order to address the problem, are all the design options being considered?

13. Are the performance limitations of project alternatives being openly discussed?

14. Is it possible to direct questions to the technical staffs in the agencies in order to obtain individual opinions on the project proposals? (Be alert to differences of opinion.)

15. Are hydraulic or hydrologic models being used to design the project? How much field data is being used to calibrate them? What are the known strengths and weaknesses of the particular models being used?

16. How were the maintenance costs derived? From the experience of local agencies, what are the average maintenance costs for a similar project in this region?

17. What are the potential public safety issues associated with this project? Is there a history of casualties associated with these kinds of projects in this region?

18. If a levee project is being proposed, where is the flood going to overtop the levees first if a greater-than-design flood occurs?

19. If a channelization project is being proposed, has the ability of the channel to transport sediment been addressed? If this is an Army Corps project, have the sediment-transport and/or hydraulics experts at the Hydraulic Engineering Center in Davis, California, or at the Waterways Experiment Station in Vicksburg, Mississippi, reviewed the project design?

20. What will be the potential effects or impacts of the project up and downstream of the project boundaries?
21. Are potential erosional and depositional features resulting from the plan specifically identified?
22. What are the strategies being proposed for erosion control, bank and bed stabilization?
23. Will soil bioengineering or other environmentally sensitive methods of bank stabilization be used in the project?
24. If channel modification is to occur, will a natural bankfull channel with riparian vegetation, meanders, and pool-riffle sequences be an integral component of the project design?

If a Bank Stabilization Project Is Being Planned

1. Whose land or what structures are being protected by the project, and who is paying for the project?
2. Can the structures in danger be moved or relocated at a lower cost than that for stabilizing the stream banks?
3. What is the cause of the "destabilization"? Is it a bridge abutment, existing bank protection, or other feature that might be modified to prevent the problem?
4. Will the stabilization works cause bank erosion on the opposite downstream bank? Will it potentially cause erosion upstream or downstream of the bank protection?
5. Will the project require removal of the native vegetation and ongoing maintenance to keep the vegetation from returning? What are the typical long-term maintenance costs for similar projects?
6. Will project maintenance require the use of herbicides?
7. Will the stabilization project reduce aquatic habitat and riparian wildlife habitat, or will it enhance those habitats?
8. Have the dynamics of the stream been studied so that potential reactions of the stream to the project have been considered? Do potential reactions include the stream forming unwanted cutoffs through meanders or change of gradient?
9. Are the project and the project's costs being compared with other potentially less costly stabilization methods?
10. Have soil bioengineering techniques (using live or dead plant materials) been evaluated as a project alternative?
11. How have similar projects on this stream or in this region performed on a long-term basis?
12. What social, historical, environmental, and economic impacts could result from this project? Will we be gaining or losing opportunities for enhancing the community's identity, aesthetics, and economic welfare as a result of this project?

NOTES

1. U.S. Army Corps of Engineers, Office of the Chief of Engineers, *Hydraulic Design of Flood Control Channels,* Engineer Manual No. 1110–2–1601 (Washington, D.C., 1970).

2. Andrew Brookes, *Channelized Rivers, Perspectives For Environmental Management* (New York: John Wiley, 1988).

3. Edward L. Thackston and Robert B. Sneed, *Review of Environmental Consequences of Waterway Design and Construction Practices As of 1979,* Technical Report E–82–4, (prepared for the Office of Chief of Engineers, U.S. Army Corps of Engineers, Washington, D.C., April 1982).

4. Luna Leopold and Thomas Dunne, *Water in Environmental Planning* (San Francisco: W. H. Freeman, 1978).

5. Harry H. Barnes, *Roughness Characteristics of Natural Channels,* U.S. Geological Survey Water-Supply Paper 1849 (Washington, D.C.: U.S. Printing Office, 1967).

6. Interagency Task Force on Floodplain Management, *A Status Report on the Nation's Floodplain Management Activity: An Interim Report* (Washington, D.C.: Federal Emergency Management Agency, April 1989).

7. Joe DeVries and Carl Franks, "HEC-2 Water Surface Profiles Users Manual" (Davis, California: Hydrologic Engineering Center, U.S. Army Corps of Engineers, September 1982).

8. R. K. Linsley, Jr., M. A. Kohler, and H. L. H. Paulhus, *Hydrology for Engineers* (New York: McGraw-Hill, 1975).

9. A. L. Prasuhn, *Fundamentals of Hydraulic Engineering* (New York: Holt, Rinehart and Winston, 1987).

10. Richard D. Hey, "River Mechanics," *Journal of the Institute of Water Engineers,* 40 (1986).

11. Thackston and Sneed, *Review of Environmental Consequences.*

12. Malcolm P. Keown, *Streambank Protection Guidelines for Landowners and Local Governments* (Vicksburg, Mississippi: U.S. Army Corps of Engineers Waterways Experiment Station, October 1983).

13. Jim E. Henderson and F. Douglas Shields, *Environmental Features for Streambank Protection Projects,* Technical Report E–84–11 (Vicksburg, Mississippi: Waterways Experiment Station, U.S. Army Corps of Engineers, 1984).

14. Soil Conservation Service, "Soil Bioengineering for Upland Slope Protection and Erosion Reduction" in *Engineering Field Handbook,* 210–EFH (Washington, D.C.: U.S. Department of Agriculture, October 1992).

15. Chester O. Martin and Hollis H. Allen, *Proceedings of the U.S. Army Corps of Engineers Riparian Zone Restoration and Management Workshop,* February 24–27, 1986 (Vicksburg, Mississippi: U.S. Waterways Experiment Station, U.S. Army Corps of Engineers, February 1988).

16. Edward A. Keller, "Channelization: Environmental, Geomorphic, and Engineering Aspects" in D. R. Coates, ed., *Proceedings of Geomorphology and Engineering* (London: George Allen and Unwin, 1976).

17. Brookes, *Channelized Rivers, Perspectives.*

18. The Federal Emergency Management Agency and U.S. Geological Survey, "Channel Straightening . . . A Potential Problem," Earth Sciences Assistance Office, Office of Earth

Sciences Applications, U.S.G.S., Mail Stop 720, National Center, Reston, Virginia 22092. Pamphlet and slide show released in 1982 by the Federal Emergency Management Agency. FEMA does not have this slide show in stock, but some government libraries may have copies.

19. Brookes, *Channelized Rivers, Perspectives*.

20. Leopold and Dunne, *Water in Environmental Planning*.

21. Robert R. Curry, "Rivers, A Geomorphic and Chemical Overview" in Ray T. Oglesby, Clarence A. Carlson, and James A. McCann, eds., *River Ecology and Man* (New York: Academic Press, 1972).

22. Arthur D. Little, Inc., "Channel Modification: An Environmental, Economic, and Financial Assessment," Report to the Council on Environmental Quality (Washington, D.C.: Executive Office of the President, 1973).

23. Keller, "Channelization: Environmental Aspects," and Brookes, *Channelized Rivers, Perspectives*.

24. John W. Emerson, "Channelization, A Case Study," *Science* 173 (July 1971).

25. Clarence H. Robbins and Andrew Simon, "Man-Induced Channel Adjustment in Tennessee Streams," U.S. Department of Interior, U.S. Geological Survey Open File Report 83–43 (Lakewood, Colorado: U.S.G.S., 1982).

26. Gary Griggs, "Flood Control and Riparian System Destruction: Lower San Lorenzo River, Santa Cruz County, California" in Richard E. Warner and Kathleen M. Hendrix, eds., *California Riparian Systems* (Berkeley: University of California Press, 1984).

27. San Lorenzo River Task Force, *San Lorenzo River Concept Plan*, prepared by Roma Design Group, Philip Williams Associates, Harvey and Stanley Associates (Santa Cruz, California: June 1987).

28. William Vandievere and Philip Williams, "Flood Analysis of the Jan. 4, 1982 Storm: Corte Madera Creek, Marin Co., California," Report by Philip Williams Associates for Marin County, June 27, 1983.

29. Ronald R. Copeland and William Thomas, "Corte Madera Creek Sedimentation Study," Hydraulics Laboratory, Department of the Army Waterways Experiment Station, Corps of Engineers (Vicksburg, Mississippi, January 1989).

30. U.S. Army Corps of Engineers, Sacramento District, "Supplemental Information Paper II, Corte Madera Creek Flood Control Project (Marin, California, October 1989).

31. Philip Williams, "Review of Corps of Engineers Sedimentation Study on Corte Madera Creek," Report to District Engineer (Marin County Flood Control District, April 27, 1989).

32. Philip B. Williams, "Rethinking Flood Control Channel Design," *Civil Engineering* (American Society of Civil Engineers) 60, no. 1 (January 1990).

33. David R. Dawdy, "Comments by David R. Dawdy on the Performance of Corte Madera Creek," December 27, 1989, prepared for the Ross Historical Society and Concerned Citizens of Ross, California.

34. U.S. Army Corps of Engineers, "Supplemental Information Paper II."

35. Vandievere and Williams, "Flood Analysis" and Williams, "Review of Corps."

36. Daryl B. Simons and Fuat Senturk, *Sediment Transport Technology* (Fort Collins, Colorado: Water Resources Publications, 1977).

37. Thomas Kraemer, *The Sacramento River, Glenn, Butte and Tehema Counties: A Study of*

Vegetation, Deposition and Erosion and a Management Proposal, Master's Thesis, California State University, Chico, 1981.

38. U.S. Army Corps of Engineers, *Engineering and Design, Channel Stability Assessment for Flood Control Projects,* Engineering Manual 1110–2–1418 (Washington, D.C.: Department of the Army, October 31, 1994).

39. Robert W. McCarley, John J. Ingram, Bobby J. Brown, and Andy Reese, *Flood-Control Channel National Inventory,* Miscellaneous Paper HL–90–10, (Vicksburg, Mississippi: Hydraulics Laboratory, Waterways Experiment Station, U.S. Army Corps of Engineers, Department of the Army, October 1990).

40. Peter Goodwin, associate professor of civil engineering at University of Idaho, Boise, interview, San Francisco, California, 1991.

41. Williams, "Rethinking Flood Control Channel Design."

42. James MacBroom, "Open Channel Design Based on Fluvial Geomorphology," *Water Forum 1981,* American Society of Civil Engineering, 1982.

43. William A. Thomas, "Example of the Stable Channel Design Approach," *Hydraulic Engineering Proceedings of the 1990 Conference,* vol. 1 (San Diego, California: American Society of Civil Engineers, July 30–August 3, 1990).

44. Ronald R. Copeland, "Stable Channel Analytical Design Method," *Hydraulic Engineering Proceedings of the 1990 Conference,* vol. 1 (San Diego, California: American Society of Civil Engineers, July 30–August 3, 1990).

45. F. Douglas Shields, Jr., and Ronald R. Copeland, "Environmental Design of Channels—Can It Be Done?" *Hydraulic Engineering Proceedings of the 1990 Conference,* vol. 1 (San Diego, California: American Society of Civil Engineers, July 30–August 3, 1990).

46. U.S. Army Corps of Engineers, "Environmental Engineering for Local Flood Control Channels," Engineering Manual 1110–2–1205 (Washington, D.C., 1989).

47. U.S. Army Corps of Engineers, "Final Report to Congress: The Streambank Erosion Control Evaluation and Demonstration Act of 1974" (Washington, D.C., 1981).

48. U.S. Army Corps of Engineers, *Engineering and Design, Channel Stability Assessment.*

49. Williams, "Rethinking Flood Conrol Channel Design."

50. MacBroom, "Open Channel Design Based on Fluvial Geomorphology."

51. U.S. Army Corps of Engineers, "Streams Above the Line: Channel Morphology and Flood Control," *Proceedings of the Corps of Engineers Workshop on Steep Streams,* Seattle, Washington, October 27–29, 1992, Miscellaneous Paper HL–94–4 (Vicksburg, Mississippi: Waterways Experiment Station, September 1994).

52. Nelson R. Nunnally and Edward Keller, *Use of Fluvial Processes to Minimize Adverse Effects of Stream Channelization,* Report No. 144, Water Resources Institute, University of North Carolina, July 1979.

53. U.S. Army Corps of Engineers and Soil Conservation Service, *Environmental Mitigation, Wildcat and San Pablo Creeks,* Office Report, Sacramento District, February 1989.

54. A. L. Riley, "Overcoming Federal Water Policies: The Wildcat–San Pablo Creeks Case," *Environment* 31, no. 10 (December 1989).

55. James MacBroom, Penelope Sharp, and Edward Hart, *River Processes in Connecticut,* prepared for Connecticut Department of Enironmental Protection by Milone and MacBroom, Inc., Cheshire, Connecticut, October 1990.

56. Steven Abt, Chester Watson, J. C. Fischenich, and Mitchell Peters, "Bank Stabilization

and Habitat Aspects of Low-Flow Channels," *Land and Water* 39 (January–February 1995).

57. City of Eugene and Lane County, *West Eugene Wetlands Plan* (Eugene, Oregon, 1992).

58. Soil Conservation Service, U.S. Department of Agriculture, "Soil Bioengineering for Upland Slope Protection and Erosion Protection," Part 650, *Engineering Field Handbook,* Chapter 18, October 1992.

CHAPTER SIX

Restoration Is Ancient History

What is a history chapter doing in a book about urban stream restoration? Both the inspiration and the concepts supporting modern-day restoration practices and the institutional barriers against them are inherited from recent history. How we are practicing urban waterway restoration at the millennium can't be separated from the historical foundations of restoration planning and field practices that originated in the 1930s. Likewise, the country's current status with restoration programs is inherited from historic, built-in institutional barriers and conflicts with restoration found in outdated government policies and programs. The historical context for professional practice in fields such as engineering, landscape architecture, resource management, and economics has both assisted and frustrated the development of the field of restoration. It is not possible to get a "handle" on the field of ecological restoration without an awareness of the history that has delivered the practice to this point.

It is important to realize that the field of restoration is not new but in fact has an ancient heritage. The field seems to appear ominously when cultures realize they are in a crisis in terms of sustaining their economy or national survival. Restoration methods such as soil bioengineering, which are considered by many to be new and untried technologies, date back to ancient use and reappeared in 1930s government manuals. Of course, cultures that lived in balance with their environments did not need to develop the concept of restoration. They provide us with models for environmental management.

The concepts we perceive as modern, such as sustainable resource management and development and adaptive management, are certainly not new in the history of the United States. Having this knowledge then confronts the student of restoration with the imperative that what is missing is the political will to practice these concepts.

Part of the contemporary context for urban stream restoration is the ideological battle between the wise-use movement and the environmental movement, a conflict that dates to the post–Civil War era. Unless the executive and legislative branches of government embrace resource management and restoration concepts appropriate to the end of the twentieth century instead of the 1800s, the field of restoration will be relegated to trying to cover for the damages caused by extractive, single-purpose resource use, rather than serving as one strategy in a package of measures to steer the economy on a sustainable course. Communities that are confused by the current water-planning concepts used by the federal system to evaluate the economics of project alternatives (known as the National Economic Development Plans) can find their philosophical basis in turn-of-the-nineteenth-century American history.

An understanding of history helps explain the paradox that without the fine traditions of civil engineering, biology, resources management, economics, and landscape architecture, we would not have a restoration profession; however, those fields are all currently in some way in conflict with this newly evolving discipline. The civil engineer who has to concrete or rock stream channels, the fisheries biologist who relies on stream-channel check dams and structures, and the landscape architect whose design objective is to use water as part of a controlled, picturesque, gardenlike landscape are manifestations of historical philosophical trends that clash with the project design objectives of the restorationist. History can tell us why that is happening. It is then up to us to acknowledge and respect the traditions of environmental engineering, biology, and design and adapt the best of their traditions so that they complement rather than conflict with the practice of restoration.

Environmental Management, Restoration, and Environmental Design: An Ancient Heritage

Those of us involved in what we promote as the newly evolving profession of environmental restoration like to think of ourselves as the vanguard, innovators and leaders of a new movement, originators of new ideas. However, conservation of resources, environmental preserves, resources management, environmental restoration, and the consideration of quality of life in human settlements are ancient history. It would be foolish to assume that water pollution, soil erosion, stream sedimentation, flooding, and loss of riparian forests have not been problems for the human race before—and given the historical record, they will probably continue to be problems well into the future. It would be improper to proceed with a discussion of restoration without recognizing that historical concepts and practices are responsible for the present development of the field of restoration.

The work of Frederick Law Olmsted in the 1860s to the late 1800s to create urban waterway greenways and the Depression era government literature produced in the 1930s to 1940s on restoration techniques provide the underpinnings for the current American urban waterway restoration movement. Those of us practicing urban stream restoration techniques are simply carrying forward a revival of 1930s and earlier traditions. Further exploration of the historical roots of environmental restoration, resources management, and design of landscapes and towns relevant to today's restoration practices takes us back to before the Roman Empire.

For those who want to involve themselves in the contemporary topic of "liveable cities," it would be instructive to become familiar with the history of landscape design as far back as 3500 B.C. in the Euphrates Valley, and Nile River Valley, where trees were planted and water channels were dug to modify the hot climate, provide aesthetic amenities, and convey religious and symbolic concepts. Water, plants, and recreations of nature continued to be integrated into landscapes, and the tradition was carried by the Persian culture to the Mediterranean cultures of North Africa,

Spain, and later Italy. Italian landscape design of the Renaissance went on to profoundly affect sixteenth- and seventeenth-century France, and France in turn influenced England. The English then promoted the idea of improving upon nature and creating "natural" features such as lakes and ponds to compose a picturesque environment that would blend visually into the existing natural system. Olmsted carried that tradition into his design of Central Park in New York City. Later, he encouraged developing communities in the United States to integrate creeks and greenbelts into the design of cities and towns, to use native plant materials in planting projects. He even tried to create interest in the idea of reclaiming western mining sites.[1]

Examples of restoration efforts and significant attempts to manage natural resources appear in history books. Tacitus, writing on the reign of Roman Emperor Tiberius, describes Tiberius trying to coordinate the management of the Tiber River. Tiberius needed to balance the needs of the various cities in the Tiber River watershed, including the city of Florentia on the Arnus River and the cities of Interamna and Reate in the Nar River watershed, in order to control the flooding of the Tiber in Rome. Proposals to divert the flows of tributary rivers away from the Tiber were eventually abandoned. Protestors of the project argued that "nature had admirably provided for human interests in having assigned to rivers their mouths, their channels, and their limits, as well as their sources. Regard, too," wrote Tacitus, "must be paid to the different religions of the allies, who had dedicated sacred rites, groves and altars to the rivers of their countries. Tiber himself would be altogether unwilling to be deprived of his neighbor streams and to flow with less glory."[2] Tiberius ended up weighing a complexity of factors including project feasibility and the cultural values of the cities potentially affected, as well as the regional economy—not just Rome's particular interests to reduce flood damages—to arrive at a decision on whether to build the project.

A reference to an ancient restoration attempt includes Hadrian's Villa. Hadrian's Villa at Tivoli, Italy, is described as having an area designed as a wooded park called the Valley of the Tempe, which was to recall a legendary forest said to have been at the foot of Mt. Olympus.[3]

Hugo Schiechtl, a pioneer in the use of contemporary soil bioengineering techniques (using plants to stabilize watershed slopes), believes that brush wattles, also called fascines (bundles of live or dead branches), have been used in stream stabilization projects for centuries. He finds it likely that the Romans used these fascines, noting that *fascine* comes from the Latin *fasciae*, meaning to bind or to bundle.[4]

In 1938 and 1939, W. C. Lowdermilk, who was then the assistant chief of the Soil Conservation Service under H. H. Bennett, chief of the service, took a world tour for the purpose of surveying the experience of "the old world" in conservation activities. This trip produced a remarkable collection of letters and photographs, which both documented a tradition of ancient attempts to restore the environment[5] and provided a sobering record of civilizations whose failures are tied to the ruin of the cultures' natural resources.[6,7]

Lowdermilk reports from his trip to Italy that as early as the twelfth century an office of magistrate alle acque was established (and was still existing in the 1930s) to manage the flash floods from the streams coming from the north and the sediment accumulation in stream channels. There was a very real danger at that time that the lagoon separating the mainland from Venice would be filled with erosional debris. This was the result of the deforestation of the headwaters of the Po River. Among his observations is an interesting comparison of the relative effectiveness of rigid concrete fences along the beach shorelines and the use of wattle plantings and plantings of rows of tamarix. The beach was stabilized under vegetative means at the low cost of five lira per lineal meter; the fences of concrete were not only much more expensive, they were also found to be ineffective. During Lowdermilk's visit in the 1930s, the Italians were putting in "an enormous amount of work . . . to establish surface drainage to reforest the slopes and to establish base levels of cutting by the construction of check dams."[8]

Lowdermilk attributes to Rome an advanced view of water management and conservation, which included the use of check dams and erosion-control basins for stream stabilization and agricultural conservation and the use of rainwater cisterns to catch storm runoff and provide water supplies. He comes to the conclusion that modern-day restoration practices originate four to five thousand years ago with the Phoenicians, who were forced to react to the wholesale removal of the forests of Cyprus and Cedars of Lebanon in the mountains. The resourceful Phoenician farmers used rock wall terraces and other means to stabilize and restore the land and drainage. We can speculate that watershed restoration and conservation techniques are probably as ancient as agriculture on all continents.

Lowdermilk observed a tradition of restoration work organized in phases in both the French and Italian Alps, where steep drainage in glacial geology produces an inherently unstable environment. The watershed stabilization work was done in phases based on monitoring the response of the environmental forces to works already put in place. Lowdermilk refers to this as the "chess game" approach, which gives us an important model for our current approaches to restoration. He states in one of his letters to Bennett, "Let me emphasize that in undertaking the control of water and erosion on a large scale, experiences thus far in Europe which we have appraised, indicate the wisdom of treating the problem as a gigantic chess game. We will learn as we proceed and revise our plans and structures on the basis of our progressive experience."[9] Today we refer to this concept as adaptive management.

References indicate that conservation activities closely related to what stream restorationists do today were occurring in the 1600s. A discourse on forests by John Eaveland in 1662, with an illustration of reforestation techniques using root cuttings, appears in a recent book, *A Forest Journey*, by John Perlin.[10] A report written in 1959 by an engineer from the Los Angeles Flood Control District concerned with evaluating channel stabilization strategies begins, "References to upstream engineering works date back to around 1600 in Europe, with special emphasis on check dam systems to minimize channel down-cutting and to stabilize side slopes coming into prominence in the middle 1800's. Reports available from French and Swiss alpine regions indicate that the number of projects which combine channel stabilization systems with reforestation efforts have been steadily increasing in those countries since this time."[11]

An author on conservation history reports that "until the middle of the 18th Century nothing new was learned about propagating fish that had not been recorded by the Chinese many centuries before Christ." In 1741 a German successfully artificially fertilized trout eggs, and two illiterate Frenchmen are credited with the rediscovery of artificial fertilization nearly a century later.[12]

Historians also point out that history contains the lesson that civilizations have failed as a result of their inability to manage or restore watersheds. The decline of Mesopotamia is attributed to agricultural practices that silted streams and canals and poisoned soils with salt from irrigation. The Babylonian civilization declined with the sedimentation of its irrigation canals. Extensive erosion turned areas of Syria into desert, and the North American city of Timgad was rife with gullies and buried under soil when discovered by French archaeologists of the early 1900s.[13-15]

A society's desire to repair the environment and to establish preserves of undamaged or natural landscapes would be a natural response to the fact that the society senses a crisis or threat to itself because of environmental destruction. Although most ancient records and writings have not survived to modern times to fully inform us on ancient environmental issues, it's easy to speculate that those cultures made attempts to reverse their environmental predicaments. For some civilizations the responses were too late or did not correct the roots of the problems. The resources required to correct problems once they are allowed to advance to a certain scale can be prohibitive. We too must grapple with the concept that there are impacts to the environment that are irreversible.

Certainly, restoration as a movement and a scientific discipline in the United States can be tied to the periods of history in which there was public concern and alarm about the nation's resources. Those periods include the post–Civil War unregulated exploitation of resources by industries; the tragedy of the "dust bowl" in the 1930s; the public revolt at freeway construction through city centers and pollution of air and rivers in the 1960s; and the concern over population growth, global warming, ozone depletion, and loss of ecosystems and biodiversity in the 1990s.

The Post–Civil War Conservation Movement

Individuals involved in restoring streams today will almost inevitably find themselves interacting with local conservation and flood-control districts and federal agencies such as the Soil Conservation Service (recently renamed the Natural Resources Conservation Service), the Army Corps of Engineers, the Bureau of Reclamation, and the Geological Survey. The current missions of these agencies were defined by the events and philosophies of the mid-1800s through the 1930s. The present represents a defining moment in history as to whether these agencies remain stalemated in what are outdated environmental management concepts or successfully progress to contemporary ecological management and restoration concepts.

With the notable exception of the U.S. Geological Survey, these federal and local agencies have been known as the purveyors of stream straightening and channelization projects, vegetation removal and channel riprapping, levee and reservoir building. These projects have been done with the objectives of stopping streambank erosion, controlling flooding, and saving water for agricultural and urban uses. These forms of "conservation" may not be what most people today think of as conservation. The missions of these "conservation agencies" are carryovers from government programs and ideas from the 1890s to the 1930s. These agencies still construct what are considered environmentally damaging "conservation projects," but people in the agencies are also developing a more environmental perspective on how to approach the ever present problems of erosion and flooding. An understanding of these agencies can't be developed without learning about the history behind them. For example, when George Bush was a candidate for president in 1988, he described himself as a "Teddy Roosevelt" conservationist. The current competing philosophies in the United States on appropriate environmental management strategies and public policy have their origins in the mid–Teddy Roosevelt era.

The essence of the conservation movement of the 1890s to the 1920s has been described as "rational planning to promote efficient development and use of all natural resources" by Samuel Hays, a conservation historian.[16] It was a scientific movement in which professionals were to determine natural resources uses and management techniques, as opposed to legislators or special interests making the determinations. The philosophy was that decision making was to be centralized rather than grassroots based or controlled by "selfish interests." The other component of the philosophy was that conservation was to foster the most efficient use of resources. This definition of conservation was in part a well-intended response to the public's reaction against corporations and political entities that had become too powerful and corrupt. The period of the late 1800s and early 1900s is referred to by American historians as the progressive era, which was typified by the spirit of the conservation movement that began then. Conservation was a popular reaction to the overbearing post–Civil War influence of private corporations on resource use and ownership.

Teddy Roosevelt and his chief of the Bureau of Forestry (the predecessor to the United States Forest Service), Gifford Pinchot, well represent one philosophy of environment management: that conservation should involve the development of natural resources and the prevention of waste, and that the resources should benefit the many and not be used for the profit of a few.

Teddy Roosevelt is probably the first organizer of a national-level conference on conservation issues. In 1908 he assembled Congress members, governors, scientists, and outdoor sports association members to convene the White House Conference on Natural Resources. The conference is credited with establishing a National Conservation Commission headed by Pinchot and with motivating the formation of conservation agencies in forty-one states. The following year Roosevelt organized an international conference, the North American Conservation Conference, which assembled representatives from Canada, Newfoundland, Mexico, and the United States to discuss how to manage natural resource questions on an international level. That conference discussed broader topics than the one the year before, which had combined the issues of public health, game preservation, and protection for nongame species. A worldwide conference was approved, but the next administration did not follow up on the conservation agenda. However, Roosevelt and Pinchot had succeeded in institutionalizing the idea of conservation.[17]

The 1908 conference focused on the scientific management of natural resources, but it did not take into account wildlife concerns or broader environmental quality issues such as the aesthetic or noneconomic values of the landscape. Shirley Allen, a conservation historian, notes that "one speaker at the conference brought up the subject of the natural scene and the importance of conserving it but was listened to, apparently, only with politeness."[18] Raising the issue of conservation was a great contribution to the nation, and calling attention to the issue also brought into view different ways of perceiving the task of resources management. While it was the Roosevelt conservation philosophy that introduced the idea of managing forests for sustained yield on a long-term basis, it was also that philosophy that rationalized the damming of Hetch-Hetchy Valley in Yosemite National Park to create a water supply for the city of San Francisco in 1914. The conflict over Hetch-Hetchy is used as the historical example that epitomizes the competing views of resource management. Opposed to the damming was John Muir, who has become an American symbol of the point of view that decisions about resources management should not be based only on economic efficiency but should also integrate aesthetic, spiritual, and other nonmonetary values that may be difficult to quantify.

That era articulated the differences between resources conservation and what later became known as environmentalism. The conservation of the late nineteenth century introduced the ideas that resource use should be centrally planned for the greater public good and that it should be multipurpose, integrating uses such as water supply, flood control, and hydroelectric energy production. It also defined resource management as a centralized decision by government scientists or technicians. This concept conflicted with the American political tradition of and need for addressing needs at the local level and grassroots participation. It gave us the efficiency standard for measuring the public value of projects that left out important noneconomic values such as the preservation of species and unique resources, environmental aesthetics, social and community-based values. When you read about National Economic Development Plans in contemporary federal water-planning documents describing the methods used to calculate the costs and benefits of water projects, you can read with the understanding that those water plans represent the Pinchot efficiency philosophy of the 1800s as opposed to the more complicated philosophy of Muir. Muir insisted that issues of resource management should go beyond a simple mathematical calculation of whether a government project's costs would be exceeded by marketplace benefits of useful water supplies or monetary benefits of reducing flood damages to structures. He argued that unique scenic, recreational, educational, and social values that were part of our national heritage were being left out of the formula.

Another important person credited with providing thinking that formed the basis of the conservation and environmental movement is George Marsh, also a figure of the post–Civil War years. His book *Man and Nature,* published in 1864, raised the issue of human impacts on the environment and introduced the thinking that those impacts were irreparably changing the balance of nature. He warned that the changes would cause serious consequences to our long-term well-being and that to compensate for the ecological damage we should protect the disturbed environments and allow ecological processes on their own to re-create a balance to restore the environment. He also suggested, however, that there are appropriate times when we should take the more difficult course of intervening in an attempt to restore the environment to a balance.

As a minister to Turkey and Italy and a traveler in the Near East, Marsh was impressed with the profound negative impacts of human beings on natural resources, and he wrote to alert Americans to the potential consequences of our destructive actions on the environment. He also advocated the restoration of forests and advised that people should learn the mechanical rules governing the balance of nature so as to live in better harmony with nature and re-create a balance where it had been disrupted.[19]

George Marsh was a man ahead of his time. It really took until the 1930s for Americans to begin to develop both the public will and the scientific knowledge to manage the environment based on the objective of encouraging a self-sustaining balance and equilibrium in the environment. Aldo Leopold's *Game Management,* published in 1933, described the relationships between game animals and the carrying capacity of their habitats. Leopold devised management strategies that would bring the wildlife in balance with the capabilities of the environment to support it. He is considered by many to be the modern pioneer in the science of environmental management and restoration. As the 1930s progressed, many water and resource management professionals began to advocate that the country needed to advance from a multi*purpose* view of resources *use* to a multi-*objective* view of resources *management*. This basis of "environmentalism" recognized that besides the construction of economically efficient water projects for water supply, energy production, and flood control, the water planners needed to implement plans and projects with broad social benefits, including: the economic well-being of a region's population; the development of a diverse economy based on improving or preserving self-sustaining commercial and recreational fisheries; tourism and recreation; ecological preservation; scenic preservation; and the saving of historic and scientific values of natural resources.

Many Americans now accept as a given the concepts of wilderness preserves, national parks, preservation of species for the sake of knowing they are there, resources management, and even the intangible values of the natural world for the human and community spirit. While our concept of conservation may be broader and more complex than that of earlier conservationists such as Teddy Roosevelt and Gifford Pinchot, those leaders did make the concept of conservation a national crusade, along with the help of citizens' associations. That crusade came at a critical time, when forests in particular were alarmingly devastated, fisheries extinct or declined, and wildlife wastefully exploited, with no national policy to moderate the rampant misuse of the resources. Historians describe the movement as a grassroots one, and important pioneering citizen organizations were formed, such as the American Forestry Association, the American Fisheries Association, and the American Ornithological Union. Ordinary, albeit public-spirited, citizens were involved and were joined by dedicated scientists, and together they accomplished a great deal. However, according to one conservation historian, "Among some congressmen, government officials, and state legislatures [conservationists] were widely regarded as a nuisance."[20] That statement could be an indicator of both the necessity for and the effectiveness of the early conservationists.

Although this Teddy Roosevelt–era concept of conservation, which heavily influenced the missions of today's resource management agencies, was an important advancement in our nation's management of resources, it does not represent the broader, prevailing views of the contemporary public. The narrow definition of conservation as associated with the concept of efficiency is out of date, and our government's agencies should not be practicing a previous century's model of resource management.

For the end of the twentieth century I would propose that we catch up with George Marsh—or even with Emperor Tiberius. This country *still* does not use multi-objective resource management as the basis for developing federal water plans and projects. Rather than basing the treatment of our waterways on an economic-efficiency objective, it would be more desirable and, ironically, more efficient to base our river projects on the Marsh idea of using nature as a model of balance. If we direct our pursuits to understanding how to re-create that balance, we will have a system that sustains us and does not constantly work against us. If our river projects to reduce flood damages or bank erosion are designed so as to come in balance with nature rather than to overcome nature, the efficiency of that change will surprise us by the economy of the project design and the reduction in long-term project maintenance. Of course, as George Marsh pointed out, we're better off not having to intervene with nature. Good urban design that avoids the conflicts between humans and rivers is the best measure. Sometimes we must intervene, and if we must, we shouldn't on the basis of a false efficiency.

American Roots of Urban Stream Restoration

The Village Improvement Societies

The phenomenon of the urban forestry movement can be equated with the groups that worked to organize neighborhoods and towns to plant street trees to improve the environment in inner cities in the 1970s and 1980s. The philosophy behind the urban forestry proponents is that communities need to foster individual involvement with the surroundings. A critical component of the quality of life in cities, therefore, is the mobilization of individuals to become involved in the planting and greening of those cities. The urban streams movement that originated in the 1980s borrowed from the urban forestry movement in that it recognizes the necessity of community involvement in responding to the task of reclaiming the urban stream as a community amenity. Without the neighborhood and town level of concern, the resource will be lost to abuse, lack of interest, vandalism, and burial. John Brinckerhoff Jackson, a historian of the American landscape, reminds us that neighborhood-level activities have their origins in the 1860s and 1870s in the innumerable village and rural improvement societies organized to beautify American towns and improve the quality of life. He attributes to B. G. Northrop, a clergyman and member of the Connecticut Board of Education, the status of "father of the town improvement movement." Jackson says, "It was he who in the [eighteen] seventies promoted the tree-planting and beautification programs that transformed the towns of the Northeast and it was also he who made Arbor Day—the creation in 1874 of Governor Norton of Nebraska—a national observance."[21] Jackson also credits the popularity in the 1860s and 1870s of the concern with quality of the landscape and life in towns to Donald Mitchell, a writer, and Horace Bushnell, a theologian who proposed celebrating the country's centennial in 1876 by planting "centennial" trees and groves. The American landscapes of lawns and rows of street trees and natural communal spaces is a tradition from that era.

By the 1870s, according to Jackson, there were no less than two hundred village improvement societies in New England alone, and the institution spread throughout the nation to the California coast.

Jackson is careful to point out the importance of the role of women in the environmental quality movement of that era. He characterizes the Rural Improvement Society as a women's organization and the 1876 centennial plantings that continued along roadsides up to the 1900s as projects of women's clubs. That example was followed after the turn of the century by men's clubs and highway departments. An important colonial American philosophy that the "pursuit of happiness" meant the participation in public affairs was kept alive by those women. In the meantime, however, the American landscape became increasingly transformed by the emerging philosophy that rather than a reflection of individual or humanist values, the landscape was a reflection of economic values.

The Sport Fishing Associations

Probably the most direct lineage of the current day's practices and organizations involved in stream restoration are the sport fishing organizations, which were formed as early as the 1800s.

Serious losses of fish resources had already occurred in this country by the 1600s.

The first closed fishing season was enacted in Massachusetts in 1652 because of the serious decline of fish populations due to the settlement of the land and the consequent damming and polluting of streams and relentless harvesting of fish. The first government fisheries agency goes back to 1856 in Massachusetts. Later, in 1865, New Hampshire and Vermont also created fishery agencies. In 1871 Congress established the U.S. Fish Commission, the forerunner of today's U.S. Fish and Wildlife Service, to investigate the cause of the depletion of the U.S. fisheries.[22]

The American Fisheries Society formed in 1870 and began publishing its *Transactions of the American Fisheries Society*, which has been published since then without interruption. It is believed to antedate all other specialized groups in natural science and conservation.

The idea of stream habitat improvement as an element of fisheries restoration can be traced to the Institute of Fisheries Research at the University of Michigan, which in the 1930s issued bulletins on methods to improve trout streams and lakes for fish.[23] At the 1935 annual meeting of the American Fisheries Society held in Tulsa, Oklahoma, the standing committees included one on foreign relations and one on "relations with federal, provincial and state governments," as well as a pollution study committee and a fish policy committee. A division of the society was also concerned with environmental protection and legislation. The *Transactions* from 1935 could be mistaken for the agenda and proceedings for a 1990 conference on the environment sponsored by an organization such as the Society for Ecological Restoration.

A paper presented at that conference reported on the progress of stream restoration projects in New York State and Iowa. In New York, using Civilian Conservation Corps crews, 46 miles of trout stream habitat were improved during the 1934 field season. Over two thousand individual pool improvements were installed consisting of log and stone dams, retaining walls, readjustment of boulders, and log and stone deflectors. The report stated that willow plantings were some of the most worthwhile projects undertaken. Downed timber and brush were used to deflect flows from eroding banks, and a number of other restoration techniques were experimented with.[24] The Iowa stream restoration projects were using a combination of brush, rock, and small-tree stream-bank deflectors to protect eroding banks. The material used was salvaged from nearby, and the practitioners noted that those deflectors, if well placed, could be more effective than more elaborate structures.[25] Important experience with stream restoration techniques can be found by the researcher who takes the time to rediscover these reports and documents.

Many attribute the origins of the modern-day citizen-based movement for fisheries and stream habitat preservation and restoration to the efforts of Izaak Walton, who lived in England between 1593 and 1683. Walton wrote the definitive work on fish and sport fishing, *The Compleat Angler*, which earned him the distinction of being considered the "patron saint" of the sports fisher. *The Compleat Angler* is reputed to be one of the most frequently reprinted books in history, competing closely with the Bible. Izaak Walton studied the behavior and habitat of fish near where he lived in the heart of the financial district of London. His proximity to the Thames River and its tributaries within 20 miles of London gave him plenty of opportunities to fish.

In the United States the Izaak Walton League was formed in 1922 by a group of fifty-four fishermen who wanted to save the Mississippi River from pollution and other threats. Sports people in England had by then set up a system of River Keepers, in which a person would "adopt" a river and watch out for any harmful practices hurting the river. The American sports fishers adopted that model, and a 1927 article by Everett Lowry in the League's magazine, *Outdoor America* (which is still published), urges members to "pick out your favorite river and divide it into convenient assignments . . . where the enemy is strongly entrenched, [so that] shock troops may be brought up from the League's state division."

Post–World War I anglers became increasingly concerned over the declining fishery resources, and by the early 1930s the Izaak Walton League of America was well organized. The League began a long tradition of sports fishers being active in the political process, public education, and stream restoration projects in order to save the sport fishing streams of the country. Until the restoration movement revival of the 1980s, the Izaak Walton League remained the pillar of interest and concern not only in remote sport fishing streams but in urban centers as well.[26] It continues that tradition today.

The idea of "catch and release" regulations (regulations mandating the release of fish caught by sports fishers) originated from Institute of Fisheries research as early as the 1950s. In 1949 the fishing tackle industry organized the Sport Fishing Institute, which coordinated nationwide fish conservation activities and funded fellowships and research grants for fish biologists at universities.[27]

The Dingell-Johnson Act in 1950 authorized a federal aid program of fish restoration and provided the needed incentive for states to start fish conservation programs. The Dingell-Johnson program was responsible for the construction of community fishing lakes and the acquisition of public access to millions of acres of fishing streams and lakes; it even conducted research on estuarine fisheries.

The sports fishers were the advocates behind federal legislation during the 1930s through the 1950s that resulted in the Fish and Wildlife Coordination Act. That act authorized river basin studies to evaluate the effects of water projects on fish and wildlife and to recommend corrective actions. The studies led to the incorporation of fish screens, fish ladders, hatcheries, and water-flow management strategies as integral parts of water development projects. The Fish and Wildlife Coordination Act is very important to environmental and restoration groups today because it enables the U.S. Fish and Wildlife Service—which in many respects acts as a federal watchdog for the environment—to participate in the water project authorization and appropriation process. The federal project sponsor is required to consult with the service but is not required to accept its recommendations. The service therefore has had to rely on public groups and other federal or state agencies to support its positions. There has been a traditional alliance between this agency and public advocates for healthy streams.

Stream Restoration: A Child of the Thirties

Works Progress Administration and Civilian Conservation Corps

The "black blizzards" of the 1930s were the tragic result of plowing the arid and semi-arid Great Plains soils for wheat and cotton crops. The replacement of prairie grasses with plowed soils and the phenomenon of cyclical droughts created the loss of topsoil in wind storms so dramatic that soil from Oklahoma ended up in the streets of New York and Washington, D.C. A single storm in 1934 is estimated to have blown away three hundred million tons of fertile soil, similar to the tonnage of soil dredged to construct the Panama Canal.[28] That natural disaster was a contributor to the economic disaster, the Great Depression of the 1930s. In response to those tragedies, Franklin D. Roosevelt involved the government in environmental restoration in a manner that has not since been duplicated. In 1934 Roosevelt appointed a National Resources Board, which completed a comprehensive, national, natural resources inventory and described remedial actions to reverse the destruction of resources. In 1936 Roosevelt convened a restoration-conservation conference that would, again, be quite familiar to the conference attender of today. Attended by hunting and fishing group members, government officials, and environmental specialists, it contained the kind of objectives contemporary conferences have: to inventory resources, identify conservation problems, and describe techniques and policies to apply to the problems. The annual North American Wildlife and Resources Conference continues to this day.[29] Following that, the Wildlife Restoration Act of 1937 gave financial assistance to states to acquire and restore habitats for wildlife including prairies and wetlands.

This was the historic debut for stream restoration and environmental restoration to be organized and funded on a substantive scale in the United States. The possibility of restoration work was directly related to and dependent on the establishment of the Works Progress Administration and the Civilian Conservation Corps, which were created both to restore the land and to provide jobs. Environmental restoration was suddenly advanced to the front of the national agenda—in part by the need to create jobs for the massive numbers of unemployed. Twenty-five percent of the population, or approximately 12–15 million people were unemployed, and the principal motivation behind the Works Progress Administration was to distribute a wage in return for labor. It succeeded at that goal admirably, for during its tenure between 1935 to 1942 the WPA dispensed $13 billion and employed an incredible 8 million people.

The mass use of hand labor produced a public landscape that probably won't be re-created on that scale.[30] The WPA enlisted unemployed people of all ages and classes and concentrated on carrying out labor-intensive work in or near urban centers. The hours of arduous handwork appear in beautiful stone retaining walls, masonry seats and details, outdoor theatres, shelters, gardens, and woodland settings in cities in a manner and to a degree that in ordinary times would be unthinkable.[31] In 1938 alone, Chicago planted 36,000 trees and 180,000 shrubs, and Philadelphia planted 170,000 trees and shrubs.[32]

The Civil Conservation Corps, a close cousin to the WPA in that it provided large numbers of people with their first remunerative employment, had a strong conservation and education mission, and its membership was considered more selective. There was a moral incentive behind the CCC beyond the WPA's economic and jobs mission, which was to "build men through the process of building in the wilderness."[33] The CCC was established by Congress in 1933, and by the time it was closed out in 1940 it had enlisted 2 1/2 million men. The enrollees were organized into companies of two hundred under army officers who operated the camps while civilian supervisors and landscape architects supervised reforestation projects, soil erosion control projects, fisheries and stream restoration projects, recreational projects, and watershed inventories. Implementation of this program was astonishingly efficient. More than fifteen hundred camps of 200 men each were established throughout the country within three months, with 300,000 men enrolled at one period.[34]

The largest number of CCC camps were located in state and national forests and parks and revolved round the idea of providing an environment that could develop human potential through a disciplined regimen, culture, education, and the teaching of technical skills. Each CCC camp had its own life, which included a newspaper, dances, and entertainment. There was a comradery, identity, spirit, and sense of purpose that influenced the care and quality of the work done.

Frederick Law Olmsted is credited with greatly influencing the landscape architects who directed the design of the CCC projects in a naturalistic style. He promoted the idea that all construction be of strong, durable materials and quality workmanship and possess a character natural to the landscape.[35] The projects are, in fact, known for their unusual durability.

It is difficult for a contemporary practitioner of stream restoration not to encounter the lasting and aesthetically pleasing work of the WPA and CCC along streams (see figure 6.1). Their use of natural materials on the site, hand-placed rock work, cuttings from plants, brush deflectors, and watershed gully repair, etc., has become the foundation of the current day's stream restoration technology. It is also no accident that the return of the government-funded conservation corps beginning in the late 1970s and early 1980s is simultaneous with the rebirth of restoration work. There are times that restoration work can involve the use of heavy equipment to reshape channel geometry or place rock, poles, or cribwalls, but a majority of stream restoration projects require only a modest-sized crew of workers who use care in the way they work and materials compatible with the stream environment. Labor- as opposed to equipment-intensive work is the norm in restoration projects.

The materials used in the construction of a project have everything to do with its character, aesthetics, and performance. The 1940s and 1950s brought in the era of concrete, and an engineer's project that was not conceived in concrete could not be

FIGURE 6.1. CIVILIAN CONSERVA-
TION CORPS AND WORKS PROGRESS
ADMINISTRATION STREAM WORK.
(a) Civilian Conservation Corps,
1938. (b) California Conservation
Corps, 1990. (c) Civilian Conserva-
tion Corps floodwall on San Luis
Obispo Creek, California (d) Works
Progress Administration rock bridge
on Wildcat Creek, California.

perceived as a serious, professionally designed project. Concrete can have unsur-
passable structural advantages for certain purposes. However, it has taken a fifty-
year period or so of observation to understand that it's not the appropriate material
for every structural problem. If we are trying to create long-term stability in natural
systems such as streams and rivers, which are dynamic systems that adjust and
change over time, then we need to use materials with the greatest capability of adjusting with those systems. The longevity of the porous, hand-placed rock work, the
wood cribwalls, and the associated revegetation are testimony to the wise selection
of materials and design of many of those 1930s projects. Even the very structural
projects of that era usually respected the aesthetics of the natural surroundings and
so retain or even add an inestimable value that the channel locked in concrete can't.
From a technical as well as an aesthetic perspective, it can be more desirable to use
plants, rocks, wood, and vegetative debris than concrete to achieve the same ends.

In hindsight it is also possible to observe that some of the WPA and CCC stream work did not need to be as structural as it was, and there are cases where it comes into conflict with restoration projects, but certainly the work of those organizations gives us a tradition to improve upon in our current day's restoration work.

The idea of the conservation corps and environmental restoration did not return until the Kennedy-Johnson era in the 1960s. In 1964 Congress enacted a law that established the important Land and Water Conservation Fund, which has funded many environmental restoration, public lands acquisition, and park development projects. In addition, the Economic Opportunity Act of 1964 established the Jobs Corps as one of the programs located in the Office of Economic Opportunity and assigned it a conservation mission resembling that of the CCC. Conservation centers were designed to provide a residential program that would help develop a corps member's social and personal skills and sense of community and provide training and educational programs. The next two decades would be characterized by a bipartisan interest in the conservation corps concept, but by the 1980s the presidential commitment to the concept waned until another renewal of executive support in the 1990s.

The Federal Watershed Management Programs of the New Deal

The New Deal under the Franklin D. Roosevelt administration inherited the previous progressive era's distrust of monopolies, advocated regulation of private enterprise in the public interest, and supported resource conservation and the small family farm. The New Deal furthered the concept of both resource and economic planning, and resources planning agencies purported to deal with "national" resources, which included human and institutional resources as well as land, water, and minerals.[36]

A national resources planning organization (which took on various names and forms) was established in the decade between 1933 and 1944 and prepared a comprehensive program of public works and river basin plans and studies, as well as coordinating and establishing priorities for the work of the Army Corps of Engineers, the Tennessee Valley Authority, and the Bureau of Reclamation. The National Resources Planning Board was authorized to consult with federal, regional, state, and local agencies in developing public works, to list them in order of their relative social importance, and to act as a clearing house and coordinator for all the levels of government. Relative social importance was measured by the criteria set out in Executive Order 8248: "the greatest good to the greatest number of people; the emergency necessities of the nation; and the social, economic and cultural advancement of the people of the United States."[37] After the abolition of the National Resources Planning Board, the executive branch never again had the same influence to either prepare overall water resources plans or evaluate the merits of plans proposed by the water project construction agencies. The creation of new water programs, policies, and projects became more controlled by congressional policy and appropriation committees with which the agencies aligned themselves. This change contributed directly to the pork barrel system of water project planning described by water historian Arthur Maass, in which congressional representatives trade political favors for gaining water projects in their districts.[38]

The National Industrial Recovery Act of 1933 and the Emergency Relief Appropriation Act of 1935 injected large sums of money into public works projects as well as work relief programs as a response to the depression. In addition to the Works Progress Administration already mentioned, the Public Works Administration (PWA) provided loans, grants, and technical assistance to state and local governments for the construction of water supplies; sewage plants; and drainage, irrigation, flood-control, and power projects. The PWA also made planning and construction grants to federal water agencies.

Beginning in 1933, the Bureau of Reclamation was made a part of the federal public works programs and began construction of drainage and irrigation projects financed by the PWA and emergency relief acts. Congress also provided that some of the bureau's projects be partially paid for by labor and supplies from the Works Progress Administration and the Civilian Conservation Corps. The cooperative projects of the Soil Conservation Service created at this time with the WPA and CCC provide the present-day model for stream restoration activities and methods. Likewise, the Forest Service Watershed Conservation projects have left us a valuable record and heritage of restoration techniques.

Soil Conservation Service

In response to the environmental catastrophe of the dust bowl, the Soil Conservation Service was established in the Department of Agriculture in 1935. The Soil Erosion Service, started in 1934, had developed forty-one soil and water conservation demonstration projects using Civilian Conservation Corps labor drawn from fifty camps. Impressed by this, Congress established the Soil Conservation Service to survey soils and soil erosion and to provide technical assistance with water and soil conservation projects to other public agencies on the national, state, and local levels. Later, the service was authorized to carry out a national program of flood control, snow surveys, and research on the relationships between weather and soil erosion.

The operative unit of the Soil Conservation Service, which continues to the present, was a decentralized district staffed by technicians with training in a variety of disciplines, including soil science, hydrology, botany, forestry, and game management. Any state legislature could enact a law authorizing the setting up of soil conservation districts where landowners could vote themselves into cooperative soil conservation programs just as you might form a school district. Since 1937, when the first districts were organized, all the states have authorized them. By the 1970s over three thousand SCS districts had been organized, embracing 96 percent of the nation's farmland. Their grassroots nature is evidenced by the more than fourteen thousand people that serve without pay on their governing bodies.[39, 40] The Soil Conservation Service has had many positive impacts over the years on the nation's streams and watersheds. It has been an advocate of managing areas to maximize wildlife habitat, reduce stream siltation from erosion, provide buffer zones along creeks, plant hedgerows and windbreaks, and carry out other erosion control projects. The modern-day stream restoration expert can see the features of these SCS programs in the landscape.

In the 1930s the Soil Conservation Service, in particular, and the U.S. Forest Service managed Civilian Conservation Corps camps. A significant amount of work was done in those camps on watershed stabilization. A review of records stored in the National Archives in Washington, D.C., show that in some camps conservation crews were taught to keep records on precipitation and collect stream-flow data. Detailed curricula were prepared by the Department of Interior for use by the SCS, Forest Service, and National Park Service on "soil erosion engineering" and "woodland" management in cooperation with experts in those agencies.[41] The country's first extensive literature on gully erosion control, revegetation, sedimentation control, and stream-channel stability was produced. The Soil Conservation Service issued an *Erosion-Control Handbook* in 1934,[42] as did the U.S. Forest Service in 1936.[43]

U.S. Forest Service

The U.S. Forest Service had a head start by the 1930s in the area of conservation because its mission for providing conservation assistance to farmers, lumbermen, and others managing their forestlands had been established early under Gifford Pinchot in the U.S. Department of Agriculture in 1898. Under Pinchot the Forest Service had directed a great deal of attention to the management and conservation of the neglected national forests, as well. The establishment of the Soil Conservation Service eclipsed the Forest Service's traditional role of assisting farm-based forestry, but the Forest Service continued its tradition (to the present) of doing considerable research on stabilizing nonagricultural lands, including urban areas, construction sites, highway slopes, and surface-mined land. Much Forest Service research has been done on stream-channel stabilization.

Particularly noteworthy publications that came out of the 1930s era and are now used as modern-day "bibles" for stream-channel restoration were written by Charles J. Kraebel of the U.S. Forest Service. Kraebel, who worked at the California Forest and Range Experiment Station in Berkeley, with the assistance of Arthur Pillsbury, wrote the *Handbook of Erosion Control in Mountain Meadows in the California Region*, released in April 1934.[45] The diagrams and methods using brush piles, rock and live vegetation, "tree plugs," brush "mattresses," check dams, and gully wattles reappear in the literature on stream-channel stabilization for the next fifty years. Kraebel's *Erosion Control on Mountain Roads: A Handbook for the California Region*, written for the Forest Service in 1935, appears to be the first publication in North America to explain the techniques of installing "contour wattling" to stabilize extremely difficult and steep road cuts.[46] *The Use of Brush Mats in Road Erosion Control* (1939) by B. Hendricks is another useful work,[47] as is the Forest Service *Fish Stream Improvement Handbook* from 1936.[48] While the titles suggest that there is a narrow application for those land stabilization techniques for meadows and roads, that is far from what has been the actual practice. During the era of concrete land stabilization, the information in those handbooks almost attained the status of a lost art, but the techniques have returned to use and are now being applied to a wide range of stream- and riverbank stability problems.

The last chapter of this book, which describes environmentally sensitive streambank restoration methods, uses some diagrams from those books. Experience with those methods in both North America and other locations in the world has improved on some of the designs in the handbooks. The basic concepts will probably endure as the restoration sciences mature, however, because many (although not all) of the methods generally recognized the dynamics of stream systems.

Tennessee Valley Authority

The Tennessee Valley Authority was created in 1933 as a New Deal agency and given remarkable authority over the entire 40,910-square-mile watershed of the Tennessee River, which includes portions of seven southeastern states. This unique government corporation is the only agency with the authority to carry out all federal functions in the development and management of water and related land resources within a geographical area. The TVA is a wholly owned government corporation in which all powers are vested in a three-member board of directors appointed by the president. Unlike the Corps of Engineers, the TVA is required to obtain approval for its budget from only one set of congressional committees, the Appropriation Committees of the House and the Senate.[49, 50]

The TVA is often described as a bold experiment in which water supply, flood control, navigation, and power development were all managed and coordinated by one planning entity. From a financial standpoint, TVA programs fall into two categories, the power program financed by rate payers and the water resources programs funded by the federal budget process. The TVA is well known for its electrical power program, which includes producing the power and distributing it as well.[51]

Gilbert White, the well-known geographer, describes in a foreword to a TVA publication the manner in which the TVA represents a landmark in the way governments can approach water resources management: "The administrative mechanism for managing a comprehensive program of water use and control under a single agency was rarely realized, and was never duplicated in the United States. Opposition from established agencies having responsibility for single sectors such as navigation or soil conservation was too powerful. But notwithstanding the resistance to fusing administrative authority in a single agency, the ideal of integrated river development was cherished in the United States and abroad."[52]

The mission of the TVA, notably, was not restricted to water resources development projects. It was recognized that the severe damages to the environment caused by development, forest clearing, and mountainside farming and the resulting devegetation, erosion, and sedimentation had to be addressed as a significant component of the TVA program. Soil conservation, forestry, and fish and wildlife enhancement programs were established.[53]

Like the Soil Conservation Service and the U.S. Forest Service, the TVA produced pamphlets and manuals on environmental restoration and accomplished stream restoration work, farm erosion-control programs, and reforestation. The 1939 *Manual for Soil Erosion Control in the Tennessee Valley* is another valuable resource for someone starting a stream restoration library.[54]

Although the TVA may stand out in many people's minds as a great dam builder, the agency has in fact represented the vanguard in addressing floodplain and stream management problems. By the early 1950s the TVA had built twenty multi-purpose dams on the main stem and tributaries of the Tennessee River. These projects greatly reduced the heights of major floods in the Tennessee and lower Ohio and Mississippi river systems, but it became apparent to the TVA that large reservoirs could be only one component of a flood-damage-reduction system. Many towns in the region still faced damaging floods from streams. In 1953 the TVA began a program in which it worked with states and local communities to establish floodplain zoning, land-use planning, flood proofing, and other nonstructural means to reduce flood damages from streams. The success of that approach provided a model for the nation and resulted in federal legislation by 1960 that authorized the Army Corps of Engineers to administer a similar nationwide program of floodplain management, which is still in place as the Floodplain Management Services Branch.[55] The TVA began as an innovation in regional, multi-objective watershed management and is generally regarded to have been one of the most successful among the large water development agencies in adjusting its mission and strategies to input by professional floodplain managers and changing public views on the environment.

NOTES

1. Frederick Law Olmsted, *Forty Years of Landscape Architecture,* ed. F. L. Olmsted, Jr., and Theofora Kimball Hubbard (New York: G. P. Putnam's Sons, 1922).
2. Tacitus, *Annals I. 75–79 on the Reign of Tiberius, First Century A.D.*
3. Michael Laurie, *An Introduction to Landscape Architecture* (New York: American Elsevier Publishing, 1975).
4. Hugo Schiechtl, *Bioengineering for Land Reclamation and Conservation* (Canada: University of Alberta Press, 1980).
5. W. C. Lowdermilk, *Tracing Land Use Across Ancient Boundaries, Letters on the Use of Land in the Old World to: H. H. Bennett, Chief, Soil Conservation Service* (Washington, D.C.: USDA Soil Conservation Service, 1940).
6. W. C. Lowdermilk, "Conquest of the Land," *Pamphlets on Erosion,* vol. 5 (Washington, D.C.: USDA Soil Conservation Service, 1941).
7. W. C. Lowdermilk, "Soil Erosion and Civilization," *Pamphlets on Soil,* vol. 5 (Washington, D.C.: USDA Soil Conservation Service, 1939).
8. Lowdermilk, *Tracing Land Use Across Ancient Boundaries.*
9. Lowdermilk, *Tracing Land Use Across Ancient Boundaries.*
10. John Perlin, *A Forest Journey* (New York: W.W. Norton, 1989).
11. William Ferrell, "Report on Debris Reduction Studies for Mountain Watersheds," Los Angeles County Flood Control District Dams and Conservation Branch, November 1959.

12. Richard H. Stroud, "Fisheries and Aquatic Resources" in Henry Clepper, ed., *Origins of American Conservation* (New York: Ronald Press, 1966).

13. William E. Sopper, "Water Conservation; Watershed Management" in Henry Clepper, ed., *Origins of American Conservation* (New York: Ronald Press, 1966).

14. Lowdermilk, "Conquest of the Land."

15. William Van Dersal and Edward Graham, *The Land Renewed: The Story of Soil Conservation* (New York: Oxford University Press, 1946).

16. Samuel P. Hays, *Conservation and the Gospel of Efficiency* (Cambridge: Harvard University Press, 1959).

17. Shirley Walter Allen, *Conserving Natural Resources* (San Francisco: McGraw-Hill, 1966).

18. Allen, *Conserving Natural Resources.*

19. John B. Jackson, *American Space, The Centennial Years 1865–1976* (New York: W. W. Norton, 1972).

20. Henry Clepper, "The Conservation Movement: Birth and Infancy" in Henry Clepper, ed., *Origins of American Conservation* (New York: Ronald Press, 1966).

21. Jackson, *American Space.*

22. Stroud, "Fisheries and Aquatic Resources."

23. Stroud, "Fisheries and Aquatic Resources."

24. John R. Greeley, "Progress of Stream Improvement in New York State," *Transactions of the American Fisheries Society*, 65th Annual Meeting, Tulsa, Oklahoma, September 9–11, 1935 (Washington, D.C.: American Fisheries Society, 1935).

25. Aitken, Iowa, "Stream Improvement Work," *Transactions of the American Fisheries Society* (see note 24).

26. Interview with Karen Firehock, director of the Save Our Streams Program of the Izaak Walton League, Arlington, Virginia, May 7, 1990; Karen Firehock, "Happy Anniversary, Save Our Streams," unpublished paper for Izaak Walton League, Spring 1989; Fred James, "Izaak Walton, His Life and Times," *Outdoor America* (Arlington, Virginia: Izaak Walton League) 55, no. 2 (Spring 1990).

27. Stroud, "Fisheries and Aquatic Resources."

28. M. M. Leighton, "Geology of Soil Drifting on the Great Plains," *Scientific Monthly* 47, p. 22–23.

29. Oliver S. Owen, *National Resource Conservation* (New York: Macmillan, 1975).

30. Phoebe Cutler, *The Public Landscape of the New Deal* (New Haven, Connecticut: Yale University Press, 1985).

31. Cutler, *The Public Landscape of the New Deal.*

32. Cutler, *The Public Landscape of the New Deal.*

33. Cutler, *The Public Landscape of the New Deal.*

34. Allen, *Conserving National Resources.*

35. Cutler, *The Public Landscape of the New Deal.*

36. Beatrice Hort Holmes, *A History of Federal Water Resources Programs 1800–1960*, Miscellaneous Publication No. 1233, Economic Research Service, U.S. Department of Agriculture (Washington D.C., June 1972).

37. Holmes, *A History of Federal Water Resources Programs.*

38. Arthur Maass, *Muddy Waters: The Army Engineers and the Nation's Rivers* (Cambridge: Harvard University Press, 1951).

39. Owen, *National Resource Conservation.*

40. Allen, *Conserving Natural Resources.*

41. Allen, *Conserving Natural Resources.*

41. U.S. Department of the Interior, Office of Education, *Emergency Conservation Work, Soil Conservation, Outlines of Instruction for Educational Advisers and Instructors in Civilian Conservation Corps Camps,* Vocational Series No. 14 (Washington, D.C.: Government Printing Office, 1935).

42. Some of the useful documents written during this period include: Quincy C. Ayres, *Recommendations for the Control and Reclamation of Gullies,* Bulletin 121, vol. 33, no. 41 (Ames, Iowa: Iowa State College, March 13, 1935); Soil Conservation Service, *Erosion Control Handbook* (Washington, D.C.: USDA, 1934); T. Buie, *Vegetative Methods of Erosion Control* (Washington, D.C.: Soil Conservation Service, USDA, 1935); *Soil and Water Conservation Handbook for the Soil Conservation Service Project and Camp Staff Members of Region Four* (Washington, D.C.: SCS, USDA, 1936).

43. U.S. Forest Service, Engineering Division, *Handbook of Erosion Control Engineering on the National Forests* (Washington, D.C., 1936).

44. Douglas Helms and Susan Flader, ed., *The History of Soil and Water Conservation* (Washington, D.C.: Agricultural History Society, 1985).

45. Charles J. Kraebel and Arthur Pillsbury, *Handbook of Erosion Control in Mountain Meadows in the California Region* (Berkeley: U.S. Forest Service, California Forest and Range Experiment Station, 1934).

46. Charles J. Kraebel, *Erosion Control on Mountain Roads, A Handbook for the California Region* (Berkeley: U.S. Forest Service, California Forest and Range Experiment Station, 1935).

47. B. Hendricks, *The Use of Brush Mats in Road Erosion Control* (Washington, D.C.: U.S. Forest Service, 1939).

48. F. A. Silcox, *Fish Stream Improvement Handbook* (Washington, D.C.: USDA Forest Service, 1936).

49. Tennessee Valley Authority, Division of Economic and Community Development, *Floodplain Management: The TVA Experience* (Knoxville, Tennessee, December 1983).

50. Holmes, *A History of Federal Water Resources Programs.*

51. Beatrice Holmes, *History of Federal Water Resources Programs and Policies, 1961–1970,* USDA Economics, Statistics, and Cooperative Service, Miscellaneous Publication No. 1379 (Washington, D.C.: U.S. Government Printing Office, 1979).

52. Gilbert F. White, Director of the National Hazards Research and Applications Information Center, University of Colorado, Boulder, Foreword to TVA, *Floodplain Management: The TVA Experience.*

53. Allen, *Conserving National Resources;* Holmes, *History of Federal Water Resources Programs and Policies.*

54. J. H. Nicholson and John E. Snyder, *Manual for Soil Erosion Control in the Tennessee Valley, Engineering Phase* (Knoxville, Tennessee: Watershed Protection Division, Department of Forestry Relations, October 15, 1939).

55. Holmes, *History of Federal Water Resources Programs.*

CHAPTER SEVEN

Managing Floodplains

The Status of Reducing National Flood Damages

Recent History

The major players involved in federally assisted flood-control projects are the Army Corps of Engineers, the Soil Conservation Service (now the Natural Resources Conservation Service), and the Tennessee Valley Authority, which act as siblings—sometimes jealous and turf oriented, sometimes borrowing each other's ideas, and sometimes collaborating. These offspring of the thirties preside over our modern-day efforts to solve floodplain management problems. These agencies offer a range of services and projects, from structural levees, dams, and channel and dredging projects to nonstructural watershed management programs, land-use planning assistance, flood-proofing, and relocation projects. They were joined in 1979 by the Federal Emergency Management Agency (FEMA), formed by Executive Order, which administers and coordinates disaster assistance and mitigation programs and the National Flood Insurance Program.

The federal policies that direct how these agencies evaluate floodplain management alternatives, federal funding opportunities, and floodplain and project planning processes drive the outcomes for many local projects and programs along the nation's rivers, streams, floodplains, and watersheds. These agencies are undergoing what appears to be a profound transition toward new policies and programs that emphasize environmental restoration and nonstructural remedies for reducing damages from floods, such as the relocation of structures out of flood-hazard areas and the restoration of floodplains and river channels. This new direction includes greater reliance on local initiatives and funding. While the political and policy momentum is in this direction, the on-the-ground reality for communities planning their floodplain programs and projects includes many of the same barriers they faced in the 1950s in regard to being able to address flood problems in an integrated, coordinated, multi-objective, and environmentally sensitive manner. Restoration still does not have equal status with other flood-damage-reduction measures in federal programs.

The community trying to address its river management and restoration goals as they relate to flood-damage problems needs to be aware of the federal agencies and programs that can affect its rivers.

The Army Corps of Engineers and National Flood Control

The Bureau of Reclamation was established by the Federal Reclamation Act of 1902 and became involved in flood control only in that it was a by-product of water-supply reservoirs. The Department of Agriculture was involved in flood control as a part of its water-flow retardation and erosion prevention programs under the act of 1936. It was the U.S. Army Corps of Engineers, however, that was the principal agency delegated with the mission to "control floods."

The flood-damage-reduction agencies have never been at peace with the issue of how to integrate the objective of reducing floods within a watershed management framework. How does the federal government set priorities for whom it is going to help with flood problems? Equally controversial is how we best respond as a nation to the never ending, spiraling costs of flood damage.

Congressional acceptance of limited federal responsibility for flood control began in 1927 following major floods on the Mississippi River. Beginning with the Flood Control Act of 1936, after more widespread flooding, the Congress accepted national responsibility for the problem of reducing flood damages, and the U.S. Army Corps of Engineers was given the responsibility for developing flood-control engineering works. The Army Corps introduced three principal methods of controlling floods: increasing the carrying capacity of channels with "channel improvement" projects; reducing flood flows with reservoirs and detention basins; and building levees, flood walls, and conduits.

Any discussion of the Army Corps needs to recognize the long and influential tradition of the Corps in the management of the nation's water resources. The Army Corps of Engineers must really be thought of as an American institution. It began as a colonial-era agency and then successfully grew and competed in the following two hundred years for expanding public works functions and large construction budgets and heavily influenced the American engineering tradition.[1]

The principal efforts of the Corps' civil works program include navigation, flood control, beach and shoreline erosion, hydroelectric power generation, and associated recreation and water-supply projects. A fact little known about the U.S. Army Corps of Engineers is that it is the first federal agency of the United States. In 1775, the day before the Battle of Bunker Hill, the Continental Congress passed a resolution establishing a chief engineer of the army, and in 1779 it formally established a Corps of Engineers. In 1802, an act of Congress formally and permanently established the Corps of Engineers and the U.S. Military Academy at West Point, New York. The Corps was stationed at West Point and ran the Military Academy. It retained responsibility for West Point even after it moved its headquarters to Washington, D.C., until 1866. The Military Academy became the first engineering school in the United States and remained the only one for over twenty years. After the Civil War, the responsibility for operating the Military Academy was transferred from the Corps to the War Department; however, the Military Academy continued to heavily emphasize engineering, and its top graduates were offered commissions in the Corps of Engineers.[2]

In 1824, Congress gave the Corps its civil works mission, which mainly involved navigation and harbor improvements. It gained its first limited flood-control responsibilities with the establishment of the Mississippi River Commission in 1879. The Corps jealously guarded its turf over navigational improvements and objected to the early-twentieth-century conservation movement, which encouraged multiple uses of water resources, for fear that an expansion of federal responsibilities could mean the loss of its water resources projects to other agencies. The Corps eventually changed its position and was eventually successful in expanding its functions to include multiple uses such as hydroelectric power generation and assuming major obligations for flood control on the lower Mississippi and Sacramento rivers. The Rivers and Harbors Act of 1927 significantly expanded the Corps' civil works, authorizing the Corps to develop comprehensive multiple-purpose plans for every major river basin in the United States. By the mid-1930s, the Corps had prepared over two hundred of those reports, which in part became the basis for the nation's big dam construction during the 1930s.

As the Corps added to its civil works mission, it gained new clients, including real estate developers, corporate farmers, and chambers of commerce. As a result of the good relationship among those prodevelopment groups and the Corps, the number of new projects increased greatly into the 1940s and 1950s.[3]

After World War II, the civil works program became a largely civilian organization, although army officers filled the agency's top management positions, as they still do. The Corps still is organized on the basis of military lines and is both hierarchical and decentralized into thirty-six district offices within eleven divisions. Military officers direct civilian staffs in both districts and divisions. The autonomy of district offices is closely adhered to, and they are responsible for all project planning, construction, and maintenance.[4]

The Army Corps workforce, given at 37,800 personnel in 1995, is undergoing reduction; 1,800 positions were eliminated through retirements and incentives packages between 1993 and 1995, and the Corps plans to reduce its workforce by 4,900 to 7,400 people by 2000. Corps divisions now have an average of 100 staffers compared with the previous 130 staffers.[5]

Conservation groups began to show concern about the environmental impacts of Corps projects on rivers after the big dam building of the 1930s. However, broad public concern regarding environmental issues developed only in the 1960s, and the image of the Corps, for many, then shifted from hero to villain. When the Army Corps found itself a principal target of environmental critics in the 1960s, it had to contend with its public credibility and a serious image problem. The changing public attitudes and federal regulations embracing broader planning objectives, not the least of which was the National Environmental Policy Act of 1969, then placed the Corps in a much more complex political and technical situation.[6] By the 1980s the federal government's reduction in domestic services resulted in a significant reduction in project construction for all federal agencies involved in any kind of water projects. The 1990s budgets in this regard make the 1980s budgets enviable.

The Soil Conservation Service and Flood Control

Until 1935, federal participation in land management, with flood control as an adjunct, had been restricted to federal lands. In 1935 Congress passed the Soil Conservation and Domestic Allotment Act, which directed the secretary of agriculture to establish a Soil Conservation Service. The SCS was authorized to conduct soil surveys, carry out erosion control measures, furnish financial aid and technical assistance to individuals and agencies, and acquire lands.[7, 8] A 1937 amendment extended authorization of the service to cover the watersheds of all waterways previously authorized to be surveyed by the Corps of Engineers. A 1938 act gave the Department of Agriculture authority to improve the watersheds of waterways on which the Army Corps had projects, but as it happened, that authority was never used during the New Deal period. The Soil Conservation Service did not get involved in construction of flood-control project structures until after World War II, when language in a 1951 USDA appropriations act permitted eleven previously authorized (in the 1944 Flood Control Act) watershed management projects to include upstream flood detention reservoirs, "channel improvements," and other structures. Public Law 566, which initiated what is known as the Small Watershed Program, is what finally put the Soil Conservation Service into the flood-control business.[9] After amendment in 1956, the program authorized the secretary of agriculture to help locals carry out flood prevention and water conservation works and construct reservoirs of a limited size (25,000 acre feet, providing no more than 5,000 acre feet were allocated to flood protection). All costs allocated to flood protection would be borne by the federal government, and loans could be made for up to $5 million to help locals meet their share of the costs for other purposes.[10] The Soil Conservation Service joined the Army Corps, the Bureau of Reclamation, and the TVA as the fourth construction agency to place projects on rivers.

The projects that could be constructed under P.L. 566 could be for the purposes of flood prevention, agricultural water management, fish and wildlife development, and municipal and industrial water supply. In 1962, recreation was added as a purpose. The federal government bore half the costs allocated to agricultural water management, wildlife, and recreation and none of the construction costs for municipal and industrial water. Because the service was authorized to pick up all the costs of flood-control projects, a high percentage of the P.L. 566 projects were allocated to flood control. The Soil Conservation Service's flood prevention works have included large gully control, protection of road banks and fill, floodwater-retarding dams, floodways, floodwater diversions, dikes and stream-channel clearing, channelization, and stream-channel enlargement.[11]

Because the mission of the Soil Conservation Service included preserving soil fertility, reducing the sedimentation of lakes and streams, and protecting the rural landscape from abuse, and because of the grassroots connections between the service and the local soil and water conservation districts, the relationships between the conservationists and that agency were very good.

A very positive expansion of the SCS's public service began to occur in the 1960s when the agency applied the knowledge from its experience in rural conservation measures to land-use planning, erosion, runoff, sedimentation, water pollution control, and the need for establishing wildlife sanctuaries and buffer zones associated with the needs of urbanization. The Army Corps and the Bureau of Reclamation by contrast had attracted a growing public attention by the end of the 1950s that became concerned with the environmental impacts of those agencies' large dams, reservoirs, and water delivery systems. As the Soil Conservation Service proceeded with its stream channelization projects in the 1950s and 1960s, however, its public support began to be strained. By 1968 state fish and game agencies and local rod and gun clubs began to raise objections to the environmental impacts of stream channelization projects. Those organizations were joined by the U.S. Bureau of Sport Fisheries and Wildlife, officials in the Department of Interior, and national conservation organizations. By 1970 stream channelization had become a subject in national magazines and a cause of environmentalists. Opponents of channel modification projects complained that the SCS had switched its focus from its biological staff and had become dominated by an engineering agenda.[12] Hearings were held by Congress on the impacts of both Army Corps of Engineers and Soil Conservation Service channelization projects, and a report on channel modifications by Arthur Little, Inc., commissioned by the Council on Environmental Quality, was released in 1973. The Soil Conservation Service had joined the U.S. Army Corps of Engineers as a target of a widening public scrutiny and dissatisfaction.[13]

Competing Turfs and Flood-Damage-Reduction Strategies

Competitions among the water resources agencies originate from the 1930s and influence the current administration of national water resources management efforts. Some observers report that an important factor hindering the establishment of regional water management authorities in the United States was the opposition of the U.S. Army Corps of Engineers and the Bureau of Reclamation, which collaborated to prevent a competitive entity from intruding on their turf. Creation of the Tennessee Valley Authority occurred only "under conditions of national economic catastrophe when a new administration had just taken office and after the issue had been agitated for a decade by a prominent senator [George Norris of Nebraska] who had a feasible plan of action already worked out." [14, 15]

The Flood Control Act of 1936 authorized both the U.S. Army Corps of Engineers and the Department of Agriculture to engage in flood-damage-reduction-projects. Jurisdiction over federal flood-control investigations and improvements on the waterways was assigned to the Corps, but investigations of watersheds and "measures for runoff, water flow retardation and soil erosion prevention" were assigned to the Department of Agriculture.[16]

The struggle between the Soil Conservation Service and the U.S. Army Corps of Engineers to win domination of their overlapping turfs in flood-control programs set the stage for Luna Leopold's and Thomas Maddock's book, *The Flood Control Controversy*, in 1954.[17] The Soil Conservation Service initiated a program of improved land management to increase the infiltration and moisture storage capacity of upland soils. The SCS began construction of numerous small earth-fill dams along headwater streams. It is generally agreed that good land management practices conserve soil resources and reduce erosion and sediment yield, but Leopold and Maddock determined that these headwater projects had only a small effect in reducing the impacts of major floods. Hoyt and Langbein also raised the issue in their 1955 book, *Floods*, that while good land management was very much needed, there was a prevailing mythology that reforestation and good land management would somehow stop the natural cycle of flooding streams.[18]

As the structural program of the SCS expanded downstream to larger drainage areas, the Corps of Engineers felt the benefits credited to their large downstream structures would be reduced. Leopold and Maddock clarified the issues associated with the upstream and downstream reservoirs. The conclusion of their analysis was that small, upstream reservoirs and large, downstream reservoirs cannot be substituted for one another in a basin-wide flood-control scheme, because the reservoirs will provide protection for different parts of a valley. Leopold and Maddock showed that only a small portion of a drainage area in an upper watershed would be protected from floods using small upstream reservoirs because of the phenomenon that only a short stretch of valley below each dam would result in being protected. A town at the downstream confluence of a large basin would not be protected from the large floods, even by many upstream reservoirs, and would not need protection from the smaller floods modified by upstream reservoirs. A downstream site could, however, be protected from a single, large impoundment immediately upstream. This large downstream reservoir, however, obviously would not provide upstream protection for anyone.

Leopold and Maddock combined their discussion of this controversy with the message that *all* forms of flood control have relative advantages and disadvantages and inherent limitations on their effectiveness. They pointed out that people commonly confuse a degree of protection with the elimination of floods. When floods occur in excess of that for which protection has been provided, damage can be greater than if there had been no protection because of development that occurred based on a false sense of security.

Leopold and Maddock advocated the use of zoning to regulate some uses in the floodplain and suggested the use of combined land-use controls and physical control works. Zoning and subdivision ordinances can be used to reserve land for flood detention reservoirs, to prevent development that contributes to the increase of runoff or stage of a flood, and to prevent the damage and loss of property caused when development is placed in the natural path of the river's floodway. They argued that these planning solutions were the most compatible with the hydrologic nature of rivers and environmental needs and values.

These two mid-1950s books, *Floods* and *The Flood Control Controversy*, were an important introduction for the interested public and floodplain professionals to the nature of the inherent limitations of structural approaches to reducing flood damages. The books helped explain some of the trade-offs involved in the selection of different strategies. By the 1960s and early 1970s, literature began to abound on the environmental impacts and expense of reservoirs, channelization projects, levees, and other structural solutions.

The return of the concept of watershed-based planning to the consciousness of federal water agencies in the 1990s has forced a replay of the 1950s controversy. While experts agree that watershed management can change the timing and peak discharges of small to moderate storm events, and that those management measures can provide substantial benefits for storm-water management, water quality, and environmental diversity, their value does not usually extend to reducing the peak discharges for the largest storms. This is based on the phenomenon that the rare largest discharges to our rivers and their floodplains occur after the watersheds have become saturated with water so that all the precipitation ends up as runoff. These rare, large events therefore defy the best watershed management practices. This situation should not detract from our efforts to manage in a watershed context, but the relationships between watershed management and the large flood discharges should be explained to the public. Each watershed should be evaluated separately for the ability of wetland restoration, reforestation, and native habitat restoration to change the frequency of low, moderate, and high discharges. It could be theoretically possible, for example, to reduce river discharges from an average of once every ten years to an average of once every twenty years. The probability of influencing the one-in-100-year river discharges with land management will be much lower than that of influencing the one-in-10-year discharges.

Cost-Benefit Analysis and Cost-Sharing Issues

The Flood Control Act of 1935 is credited with the birthing of the cost-benefit analysis used for evaluating the public worth of a water project. Section I of the act requires what is generally known as an "efficiency analysis," in which the benefits of a project should be in excess of the estimated costs. As we established in the last chapter, the philosophical roots for this idea of efficiency originate in the earlier Teddy Roosevelt progressive era, and the New Deal period developed the practices for evaluating projects that are still in use. Although the 1936 act applied specifically only to the Army Corps and the Department of Agriculture, the cost-benefit analysis was adopted by the water-planning agencies. The cost-benefit analysis did not become the *principal* basis for agency project recommendations, however, until after World War II, because of the executive branch desire to integrate regional and local planning objectives and to assign priorities on the basis of urgency. [19]

At that early date, the Water Resources Committee of the National Resources Board, which was overseeing national resources policy, became concerned that the use of this economic-efficiency ratio was not going to give adequate attention to social and general benefits as well as economic benefits. The National Resources Board identified intangible benefits that were not easy to measure in monetary terms, such as recreational benefits and saving lives in floods. In a 1941 report, the board recommended developing "standard methods of social accounting" to provide a dollar basis to evaluate those benefits.[20]

In the same 1941 report, the issue was raised of how the federal government should best share the costs of flood-control projects with local or "nonfederal entities." The report said, "As a general principle costs should be paid as far as practicable by the beneficiaries with due consideration to benefits received. To this principle there will be two qualifications . . . provision of special aid to economically distressed areas . . . and special aid to depressed social groups." The 1936 Flood Control Act limited local contributions to lands, easements, and rights-of-way for projects. Starting in 1941, local contributions were required for land costs for channelization and levee-building projects and floodways but were not required for reservoirs. The board felt that at the planning stages, equitable distribution of costs should be decided among federal, state, local, and private beneficiaries and criticized the Corps of Engineers for not assigning costs in the context of who was receiving the benefits.[21]

In the 1950s, academics and government experts continued to raise the issues of project evaluation and cost-sharing discussed by the 1941 report. The differences of perspective among the executive offices of the president, the water agencies themselves, and Congress on these two topics largely contributed to the inability of the government in the decades following to implement the recommendation of experts to improve the project evaluation and funding process. The 1990s have seen continued grappling with how to avoid pork barrel projects, which subsidize the economically advantaged, but still provide projects for legitimate public needs, particularly to those who need assistance the most.

An Integrated "Geographic" Approach to Flood Damages

"Floods are 'acts of God,' but flood losses are largely acts of man." This pronouncement in Gilbert White's 1942 Ph.D. dissertation subsequently resulted in over four decades of efforts to reform our government's practices in floodplain settlement and management. White's dissertation, *Human Adjustment to Floods*, is considered the origin of the current concept of floodplain management.[22] The geographer's dissertation admonished water resources planners that despite the flood-control facilities construction boom that he saw beginning in the 1930s, national flood damages were increasing at an alarming rate. He attributed the problem to the singular focus on the construction of flood-control structures, the false sense of security those structures created, and the resulting vulnerable development in flood-hazard areas. Missing from the national flood-damage-reduction efforts was the integration of less expensive strategies including land-use planning and regulation, flood warning systems, flood proofing, insurance, and other methods designed to accommodate rather than overpower the phenomenon of flooding. White warned against the popular view that floods are a great adversary that we need to overpower. By operating within that perspective, he warned, "the price of victory is the cost of engineering works necessary to confine the flood crest; the price of defeat is a continuing chain of flood disaster."[23]

Until that time, no one had examined the lack of analysis going into the problem of reducing flood damages—or of measuring flood damages. White's call for a "geographical approach" to viewing the problem, as opposed to depending on expensive works, has since challenged researchers, legislators, agency administrators, and citizens. White developed a framework for a geographical approach that contained four essentials. The first was that we need to "take into account all possible adjustments which might be made to the flood hazard."[24] He mentioned that there were at least eight possible adjustments, including: elevation of land and structures; watershed management practices; structures such as levees, reservoirs, and channel modifications; flood warning systems; structural adjustments to buildings, public works and utilities (now referred to as flood proofing); land-use adjustments including regulations, relocation of structures, and land acquisition; federal public relief to cushion the social impacts of floods as long as other adjustments are not adopted; and a national flood insurance program.

The second component of the geographical approach White advocated stated that "in comparing possible adjustments for a given area, the benefits and costs of each adjustment will be evaluated on a consistent basis which recognizes all costs of appropriate remedial actions, and which considers benefits in terms of the welfare of the entire community affected."[24] He warned that there are costs and benefits that can't be assigned precise monetary values, but that need to be weighed in the decision-making process nonetheless. His third component was to consider how economic, social, and environmental factors influence the options of floodplain management. The fourth component warned that different actions including public relief, insurance, and the flood protection structures tend to favor the status quo; therefore, the desirability of seeking those kinds of actions at public expense, as opposed to other adjustments at private expense, needs to be part of the policy considerations.

The Need for Information on Flood Damages

Gilbert White also revealed the information void in which floodplain management was occurring. In 1942, the only nationwide system for collecting data on flood losses had been maintained by the U.S. Weather Bureau since 1902. White was unambiguous about the status of the country's information on floods: "Because the systems for collecting data with respect to the amount and character of flood losses in the United States are incomplete, inaccurate and inconsistent, it is impossible to estimate with accuracy the full extent of such losses. While precise measurements of the flow and peak floods have been instituted with meticulous care under the guidance of the U.S. Geological Survey, the social impacts of these events have been canvassed lamely and inadequately."[25]

In *Floods,* William Hoyt and Walter Langbein were similarly distressed over the problem of inadequate information on floods. The two authors built on Gilbert White's argument for the need for a more sound adjustment to floodplains, and their book made one of the earliest attempts to estimate the national costs of flood damages and flood-control projects.

To underscore the scale of national flood damages and the kind of costs involved with the construction of projects, the authors inspected the project records and budgets of federal agencies involved in water projects. They estimated that prior to 1936, individuals, states, and local governments spent between $300 million and $500 million or more (using 1952 dollar values) on flood protection projects, and between 1936 and 1952 approximately $232 million to meet required obligations in joint projects with the Army Corps of Engineers and $54.5 million with the Department of Agriculture. They estimated a future $4–$10 billion nonfederal expense. By the time their book was written in 1955 the Tennessee Valley Authority had already spent over $178 million on flood control; the Department of Agriculture had spent $152 million; and the U.S. Army Corps of Engineers had spent $3 billion and would require $7 billion more for projects authorized by 1952. As early as 1952, the costs of projects for reducing similar levels of damage were tripling.[26]

The Federal Floodplain Programs in Transition

Passing the Golden Age of Channelization

The "golden age of channelization" from the 1940s to the 1970s resulted in completion of or plans for the so-called improvement or modification of about 34,140 miles of waterways in 1,630 projects administered by programs of the U.S. Army Corps of Engineers and Soil Conservation Service; 28,243 miles of the projects were for channel alteration and 5,897 miles for levee work. That excludes larger federal flood-control and navigation projects of the Corps and the Tennessee Valley Authority and irrigation and drainage canal projects of the Bureau of Reclamation. Of the SCS-assisted flood-control projects 100 percent involved channel alteration, and of the Corps-assisted projects 47 percent were for channel alteration work. Of those total projects, reported in 1972, some 1,001 miles of Corps projects were still in the planning stage, and 6,518 miles of SCS projects were still in the planning stage, so a total of 20,724 miles of channelization projects had been completed at that time. Arthur D. Little, Inc., in its 1973 report, estimated a total of 200,000 miles of modified waterways constructed by states, counties, and towns.[27] Frequently, a field trip to a local stream will reveal that it has been modified—straightened, widened, etc.— by farmers or landowners who jumped on their tractors and pushed dirt around in an attempt to improve matters. A 1989 government report estimated that about 25,000 miles of levees and flood walls had been built along streams on a nationwide basis, and it used figures from 1976 to upgrade the number of river miles channelized by the Soil Conservation Service to 16,971 miles.[28]

It is easy to acquire data on the number of dams built by federal agencies. However, despite some time-consuming efforts, I was not able to obtain satisfactory estimates of the numbers or miles of channelization projects constructed since the figures were provided for the government in the early to mid-1970s. The Army

Corps of Engineers and the Soil Conservation Service are the two agencies that have constructed the largest number of channel alteration projects. The Bureau of Reclamation has constructed many large irrigation and hydropower reservoir projects, which also have provided some flood-control benefits for mostly rural areas. The Tennessee Valley Authority continued to be a leader in floodplain management until its flood protection branch was abruptly closed in 1994. A comparison of the budgets for these four federal water agencies for the years 1960–1985 immediately makes the historic dominance of the Army Corps (figure 7.1) apparent. In the 1986 fiscal year, the Corps' budget accounted for 70 percent of water resources projects; the Bureau of Reclamation, 21 percent; the Soil Conservation Service, 8 percent; and the Tennessee Valley Authority, 1 percent. The Corps' outlay for flood-control activities in the 1980s remained fairly stable around $1.1 billion and accounted for about 40 percent of its water projects; Soil Conservation Service expenditures for flood control averaged about $82 million a year in the 1980s.

From the 1960s through the 1980s, the investment in water resources projects administered by the four major federal water agencies declined by about 40 percent in real terms. The Soil Conservation Service experienced the most dramatic real decrease in appropriations for its watershed program, from $249 million in 1977 to $119 million in 1983, or a 52 percent decline in five years, and a 67 percent decline by 1990. Appropriations for the TVA increased through 1980, but its budget request for 1983 was 39 percent lower than the 1977 appropriation, corrected for inflation.[29]

By the 1990s the Natural Resources Conservation Service appropriations for its watershed program stabilized at around the $100 million level, with appropriations at $116 million for 1997.[30] The Tennessee Valley Authority underwent severe budget cuts by 1994 when its floodplain management program was cut in its entirety.[31] The total Army Corps civil works budget of around $3.7 billion annually was projected to drop to about $2 billion by 1996–1997.[32] In addition to dramatic cuts in watershed floodplain programs and civil works projects, the projects-oriented agencies have a financial liability in their aging inventory of water structures. The Government Accounting Office identifies a $125 billion inventory of projects that are reaching the end of their design life. Major structures are considered to have an average age of thirty-three years, and 12 percent of the projects are now over fifty years old.[33]

Trends in Flood Damages

The latest "Federal Interagency Floodplain Management Task Force Report" states that, using figures that adjust both for population growth and inflation, the average annual damages for 1916–1950 were $902 million and for the period 1951–1985 were $2.15 billion, an increase of 132 percent. In other words, per capita flood damages were almost 2.5 times as great from 1951 through 1985 as they were from 1916 through 1950. From 1965 through 1989 there were 657 presidential disaster declarations, of which 508 (77 percent) were flood related."[34] The White House task force

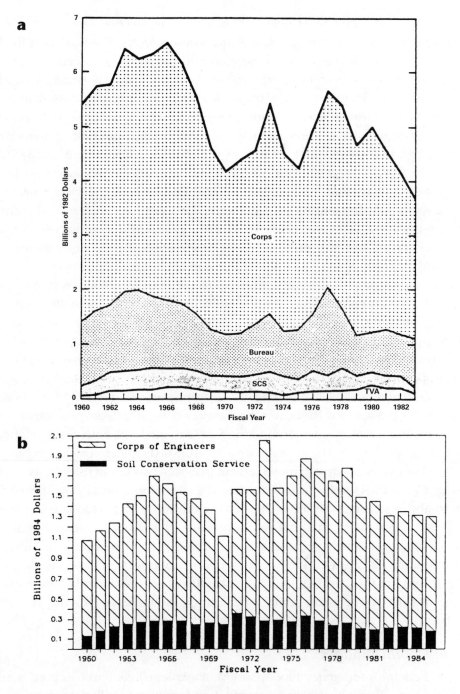

FIGURE 7.1. BUDGETS FOR FEDERAL WATER RESOURCES AGENCIES.
(a) Water resources development appropriations for the U.S Army Corps of Engineers, Bureau of Reclamation, Soil Conservation Service, and Tennessee Valley Authority. *Source:* Congressional Budget Office, 1983. (b) Comparison of Soil Conservation Service and Army Corps budgets for flood-control programs, 1960–85. *Source:* National Council on Public Works Improvement, Fragile Foundations: A Report on America's Public Works, Final Report to the President and the Congress (Washington, D.C., 1988).

created to evaluate the great Mississippi River flood of 1993 reported that during the decade ending in 1993 average annual flood damages were exceeding $3 billion. Estimates of fiscal damages from the 1993 Mississippi River flood alone were $12–16 billion.[35]

Gilbert White's prophecy has come to pass: The dependence of the federal government on expensive structural solutions in lieu of developing an integrated approach to managing floodplains has contributed to the increasing rate of flood damages and increasingly higher costs to attempt to control the damages. Serious project construction backlogs have occurred because the national budget cannot keep up with the national demand for flood damage projects. The amount of time between passage of major congressional water project authorization bills reached sixteen years during the 1970s and 1980s. Communities with dire needs to reduce flood damages have commonly faced a planning, funding, and construction ordeal of twenty to thirty years or more in order to get what the federal government has to offer for flood-damage-reduction assistance—namely, a major construction project. Many laws, executive orders, and regulations have been written that recognize the value of multi-objective flood-damage-reduction schemes that employ a diversity of structural and nonstructural measures. However, it is well known that there have been difficult barriers to implementing the policies advocating an integrated approach to floodplain management.

There are many different ways to try to quantify flood damages, and it is easy to find varying estimates in the literature by government agencies with different kinds of interests in the flood-damage field. Different sets of figures may be more representative of actual damages than others, and there are serious problems with the collection, coordination, and interpretation of the information. A 1989 interagency report discussing flood damages concluded that the dollar value of property losses continued to escalate, but much less clear is the significance of the dollar loss and loss of life relative to other factors such as the impact of losses on the overall economy.

The basic message from the government documents, however, is that there is an ongoing sequence or cycle associated with flood damages that we as a society need to break.[36] This cycle is: flooding; flood losses; disaster relief; flood-control projects attempting to modify the flood damage by storing, accelerating, blocking, or diverting floodwaters; renewed encroachment and development onto the floodplain and watershed; flooding; flood losses; and continuation of the cycle. Thus, the current data and reports support the assertion from several decades earlier that although the construction of dams, levees, and channel works have saved lives and prevented some damage, the protective works have not been able to keep pace with floodplain development rates, and in some cases, flood-control works have provided a false sense of security and encouraged additional unsound floodplain development in hazardous areas, resulting in even more damages.

A part of this flood-damage cycle has been the spiraling backlog in federally authorized flood-control projects. In 1983 and again in 1984, Congress requested that

the Government Accounting Office (GAO) report on the backlog of the nation's efforts to provide flood-control projects. The GAO reported that the average time
spent on planning and design studies before construction began on an Army Corps
flood-control project was an incredible 25.9 years.[37, 38] At about the same time, the
Congressional Budget Office estimated that the time between project evaluation
and completion of construction was between 26 and 28 years.[39] Notwithstanding efforts by Congress and the administration to deauthorize unfunded and locally un-
supported water projects, the backlog of authorized but unfunded projects has
become quite large. The GAO has not updated its evaluation of project planning
times and project backlogs. Interviews with reliable sources placed the planning-to-
implementation range for both Army Corps and Soil Conservation Services projects
at 17–20 years during the 1980s. In 1996 an Army Corps task force was formed to
recommend ways to shorten planning times, and it reported an average of 8.2 years
between planning starts and construction, although it is not clear what length of recent history this average represents. The Corps considers an ideal planning
schedule with everything going smoothly to be four years.

The Army Corps in Transition
Difficult Planning Policy Issues

In 1980, at the request of the House Committee on Science and Technology, the
National Science Foundation produced a study using a committee of experts to
develop specific program recommendations to improve national flood-damage-
reduction efforts. The National Science Foundation sent thirty-one recommendations to Congress. Its report contains a list of issues and recommendations that are
almost identical to those identified by the experts in the 1940s and 1950s for improving the evaluation and selection of flood-damage-reduction alternatives and
sharing the costs with state and local interests. Despite a history of legislation;
drafting and redrafting of regulations; reports of presidential and congressional
commissions; and executive orders responding in whole or in part to the recommendations of the early advocates of floodplain management, the federal government, with a few exceptions, has conducted the vast majority of its flood-control
project planning in the 1990s much as it did in 1945.[40]

Some of the barriers to changing the national system of flood-damage reduction
can be attributed to differences of opinion among administrations on the appropriate emphasis of the federal role in floodplain management. However, in examining the historical cycles of efforts to make changes in this area, it becomes clear
that the different branches of government ultimately made genuine attempts to
adopt and carry out many of the policies advocated by the floodplain managers. It
appears that competition over *which* branch of government was to establish the
new policy for such important aspects as planning objectives, cost-benefit calculations, and cost-sharing provisions was as responsible or even more responsible for
the inability to make changes than the issue of what kinds and extent of federal involvement in the management of floodplains are appropriate. A continuation of

such policy stalemates is disheartening to communities struggling to solve their local flood problems—but not an unlikely scenario for the future.

The Benefit-Cost Analysis

There has been an unending historical cycle of efforts by the legislative and executive branches alternately to broaden or narrow the scope of the flood-control project cost-benefit analysis. Only a few changes of significance differentiate the 1990s cost-benefit analysis for what is referred to as the National Economic Development—or the preferred "least cost"—plan from what was practiced in the 1940s. Although new missions have been authorized for the Army Corps to become involved in environmental restoration, the single-objective National Economic Development (NED) cost-benefit analysis still reigns as king, as will be described in the section on the Environmental Corps. The NED analyses are applied to public works facilities and structures to evaluate their suitability for congressional authorization and appropriation. These analyses give preference to traditional civil works projects and then accommodate restoration as a feature that can be added to the civil works projects if they are cost effective.

Most Corps projects and budgets are for civil works structures, and the concept of using environmental restoration projects instead to attain the same or similar flood-damage-reduction objectives is still not a well-defined or acknowledged concept within the Corps. Restoration is generally perceived at best to be a complementary feature of a civil works project to provide ecological benefits that have little or no practical value in storm-water and floodplain management. The traditional philosophical framework of the Corps, in which environmental benefits are considered to compete with and are trade-offs with the objectives of conventional civil works projects, prevents the Corps from perceiving that restoration projects can be constructed and planned *in lieu of* conventional structures to attain the same (and more) flood-damage-reduction objectives and benefits.

Reformers have argued that the impacts of projects to fish and wildlife, water quality, downstream flooding, and other environmental and social values should be integrated into the costs side of the NED cost-benefit analysis. Weight should be given to less tangible or quantifiable benefits such as environmental restoration to society as a whole. Economists critical of the current NED analysis have said that the efficiency analysis of a plan should be done in a manner that allows a planner to consider it in relation to all other useful purposes that are possible to achieve. These economists have also recommended that the discount rate used in calculating the cost-benefit analysis must attempt to realistically reflect the future benefits and costs society will assign to the plan. For example, what are the *real* future costs of repairing or replacing a concrete channel? What are the future benefits of a floodplain greenway for avoiding long-term flood damages and providing a local tourist industry? They have also pointed out that project evaluation policies can discriminate against low-income areas with poor housing stock.[41–45]

Only a few changes have occurred over the past fifty years of defining the most important project benefits within the narrow context of "flood-damage reduction." In 1965, benefits could be assigned to future development in a floodplain made possible by a project. The Flood Disaster Prevention Act of 1973 required that "without-project" conditions assume land-use controls are in place in a designated 100-year floodway in undeveloped areas, thereby narrowing the benefits that can be claimed for future development. The other modification in the concept of benefits was to exclude water-quality improvements as a project benefit for reservoirs because that conflicted with the Environmental Protection Agency's policy of reducing the sources of pollution as opposed to just diluting the pollution.[46]

The benefits assigned to future development of a floodplain are referred to as intensification or location benefits. These benefits are a double-edged sword for the floodplain manager. They have made it possible to economically justify some innovative restoration and floodplain evacuation projects such as the restoration of Wildcat Creek in a poverty community, and the Indian Bend Wash project in Scottsdale, Arizona, which helped create a new community for the Yaqui Indians and provide local jobs to attain "area redevelopment benefits." The other edge of the sword is that "location" benefits could also be used to justify flood-control projects in areas where, due to the nature of the hazard, the project would encourage unwise development. A potential example of this could be to justify a flood-control project for the Natomas Basin at the confluence of two large rivers near Sacramento, California, where any failure of the project would devastate the new community that would develop as a result of the project.

The 1973 provisions requiring that without-project conditions assume that land-use controls are in place in undeveloped areas has resulted in creating a bias against using nonstructural flood-damage-reduction measures in the cost-benefit analysis. Structural measures are assigned benefits because they remove the necessity to incur flood proofing or elevation costs, for example, but nonstructural measures can only produce benefits by providing protection in excess of the 100-year flood elevation.

The two most significant changes to the cost-benefit analysis from the environmental viewpoint came in the 1986 Water Resources Development Act (WRDA). The first reform calls for selecting a project with the greatest net benefits as opposed to a project with very large flood protection capabilities. This spares communities from having to base a flood protection project's design on reducing risk from the Standard Project Flood (SPF), which is catastrophic in nature and rarely expected. The SPF approximates the flood that would occur if the most severe storm considered possible to a region occurred when the ground is saturated and conditions are already favorable for watershed runoff. This basis of planning imposed large and expensive projects on communities.

In theory, a community could now find that it derives the most benefits from a small project for the most frequently occurring floods. However, the pressures of the National Flood Insurance Program usually dictate that communities and the Corps design projects to address at minimum the risks associated with the one-in-100-year flood.

The second reform came via Section 907 of the 1986 WRDA, which states that benefits attributed to a project for the purpose of environmental quality shall be deemed to be at least equal to the costs of such measures. Now adding environmental features to an NED plan does not necessarily kill a project by raising the costs side of the ratio—a common occurrence for projects planned before 1986, because environmental benefits were counted only as costs in the analysis.

Project costs continue to be narrowly defined as construction costs, with a gradual increase in discount rates being the only major change for that side of the benefit-cost ratio. Unintended social or environmental costs and impacts caused by projects, or "externalities," have not been integrated into the analysis. A significant effort was made by the Carter administration to integrate broader environmental and social objectives into the economic analysis, but the new standards were rescinded by the Reagan administration before they could begin to be implemented.[47]

The traditional cost-benefit analysis and the recent revisions to it to make environmental restoration possible have not removed the biases against the use of nonstructural flood-damage-reduction alternatives. One of the most frequently mentioned barriers to the use of nonstructural measures is the continuation of the policy to assign nonfederal land acquisition costs to the costs side of the benefit-cost ratio, making it difficult to arrive at a ratio greater than one for nonstructural projects that do not have a specific authorization for restoration as a project purpose.[48, 49]

The fact that structural measures can be assigned benefits for the costs avoided from regulating floodplains, flood proofing, or elevating structures up to the one-in-100-year flood elevation, but nonstructural measures are limited to producing benefits for protection beyond the one-in-100-year regulatory floodplain for new development in floodplains is a bias found against nonstructural measures in the cost-benefit analysis. The celebrated Army Corps Charles River natural valley storage floodplain acquisition project in Massachusetts could not have proceeded if this provision had been applied to that project. The plan was justified on the basis that the project, which uses regulation and land acquisition, avoids the development of the 100-year floodplain, thereby freeing the floodplain as a flood storage area and providing the project benefits. Another bias contained in the cost-benefit analysis against nonstructural measures is that the so-called internalized expenses such as flood insurance premiums and deductibles must be deducted from the benefits. This compares to being able to claim the total average annual damages as benefits for structural plans. Most relocation and flood-proofing projects are limited to only the most frequently flooded areas within the one-in-10-to-15-year floodplains because of the nature of the cost-benefit analysis. For the analysis to produce a feasible project, the project needs to entail structures of high value that are flooded frequently.[50–52]

As a result of the great 1993 Mississippi River flood damages, the subsequent White House task force on that flood, and a specific request from Congress in the 1996 Water Resources Development Act, the Army Corps is concerned with identifying and removing the barriers to initiating nonstructural responses to reduce national flood damages. A recent report identified the following additional issues associated with the cost-benefit analysis that need to be clarified or resolved if we are to encourage the relocation of structures or communities from hazardous flood-plains and the restoration of floodplains:[53]

- Relocations are considered "lost opportunity costs" because of the loss of income caused by the move from an old location "chosen in the market." Sometimes locations in floodplains do not represent market choices, due to ignorance of the hazards or the past practice of segregating minority populations in undesirable floodplain or wetland environments. Changes of location can be a national benefit and not a cost. Repeated flood damages can be avoided for an infinite period of time, and national benefits can be achieved as well by an upgrading of housing stock or the stimulation of the local economy by rebuilding.

- "Intensification" of existing land use, restoration of land values, and location changes in land use are considered unclaimable benefits of floodplain evacuation projects. This does not take into account the contemporary reality that numerous communities have undertaken projects to further develop existing tourist-based economies based on "river walks" and river town identities. These economies could be eclipsing the market value of older, once more established industrial economic bases. A new floodplain park or greenway has many on-site values for recreation and tourist-based industries, and a greenway can have widespread influences on the economic growth, property values, and tax base of the whole community adjacent to the floodplain.

- Calculating benefits on the basis of average annual damages avoided does not adequately take into account the regional and national benefits of avoiding for perpetuity through relocation the costs of the great catastrophic floods that can literally destroy a community.

- We can claim total avoided average annual damages as a flood-control benefit for structural projects. For structural projects it is also assumed you do not need to purchase flood insurance as part of risk avoidance. The private expenses of flood insurance premiums and deductibles are subtracted from the benefits side of the equation for nonstructural projects. The economic theory that prevents the complete accounting for damages avoided in floodplain buyouts, relocations, and restoration projects is based on the assumption that existing property values in the flood-hazard area (as compared to similar properties outside the hazard area) already take into account the costs of flood insurance and lower market prices caused by the hazardous location. This assumption includes the concept that the floodplain occupants have the full knowledge of the risks associated with the location, so that the prices of the floodplain properties are discounted. The reasoning, therefore, for not including the full flood-damage-reduction benefits in relocation projects is based on the theory that the value of the potential damages avoided is already accounted for in the lower market values of the floodplain properties. For this theory to have relevance, full knowledge of the risks must be present and then that knowledge must be translated into lower market values. The theory does not take into account the possibility that floodplain occupants may not realistically have much or any knowledge of the risks, nor does it take into account the possibility that riverfront properties may actually be more valuable in the marketplace than other comparable properties.

• Good floodplain management policy should dictate that the first benefits calculated for a flood-control project should be for those measures that help a community *avoid* or *prevent* a hazardous situation such as floodplain evacuation or restoration. The next level of benefits should be assigned to those measures that *control* damages that can't be avoided. A study of flood-control cases shows that the Army Corps cost-benefit analysis reverses this order, with the consequence of eliminating the potential benefits of the nonstructural measures from the analysis because most of the benefits are claimed by the structural measures.

• Even floodplain lands donated by public or private entities as a contribution to a flood control project show up as a federal project cost. This increases the total value of the flood-control project, thereby ironically increasing the nonfederal share of the total project costs. If the project is not specifically authorized as a restoration project, the value of these donated lands, which are considered a federal cost, can prevent a feasible cost-benefit ratio.

• Land costs as determined by the Army Corps at full market value can for a number of circumstances provide a project with inflated costs, which the nonfederal sponsor must then share. These circumstances can include assigning full market value to lands with limited market values because they are regulated as flood-hazard areas, contain toxic wastes, etc.

• When the cost-benefit analysis is calculated for a project that elevates structures or moves them to a new location, a separate cost-benefit analysis is done for each structure. This means one household may be elevated or moved, while its neighbor next door is not served in any way. Costs and benefits calculated on a structure-by-structure basis ignore the benefits inherent in moving whole neighborhoods or communities. Using an incremental structure-by-structure evaluation as opposed to a neighborhood-based evaluation can result in providing or denying federal assistance to similarly situated and deserving households and not necessarily result in saving federal expenditures.

• A lack of land-use planning for relocated structures and inattention to community needs can lead to unpopular relocation projects that split neighborhoods and leave communities with reduced property values compared to the old sites located in the hazardous areas.

• While the expertise and focus of the Army Corps are on engineering, there is no national or institutional benefit to restricting the calculated benefits of Army Corps projects to engineering ones. This restriction only puts barriers in the way of the Army Corps to establish successful collaborative projects with other federal (or nonfederal) agencies. For example, the Federal Emergency Management Agency considers it a benefit to remove structures from the floodplain to avoid potential future costs to the nation for National Flood Insurance and Disaster Assistance claims, whereas the Corps does not calculate these avoided costs as benefits.

- The average annual costs of structural projects do not take into account a realistic estimate of the repair and replacement schedules and costs of concrete channel linings, levees, and other structural components. Maintenance costs due to natural geomorphic influences on engineering channels, levees, and reservoirs are commonly underestimated. Avoiding these costs for the long term should be a part of calculating the benefits for alternative floodplain restoration projects.

- Corps project planning steps and processes frequently do not fit in well with community initiatives for floodplain planning, relocations, and restoration.

Some of the problem in implementing reform of the analysis has been the lack of explicit congressional action. The 1936 Flood Control Act did not provide an operational definition of costs and benefits, stating that projects are to be considered feasible economically if "the benefits to whomsoever they may accrue are in excess of the estimated costs" (49 STAT.1570). National economic efficiency was a popular notion in the late New Deal period, when considerable attention was given to the construction of public works projects as a way to stimulate the economy out of a depression. It is important to recognize, however, that that was not the only objective of the major water statutes. Redistribution of income to different classes of people or selected, needy locations or regions and conservation of resources were other recognized objectives.

Arthur Maass, a political scientist and expert on national water policies, attributes the fact that the executive branch has not strayed from the narrow interpretation of economic efficiency in the benefit-cost analysis principally to the successful efforts of policy makers concerned about limiting the size of federal expenditures on water projects. He opposes this method of controlling project approval and expenditures because "to control expenditures by imposing on the planning agencies criteria that confine the types of benefits that can be used in designing and evaluating projects without considering explicitly the policy implications of these criteria, can mean that a restricted budget is invested in a group of projects that does not fulfill the community's objectives as well as one or more other groups of projects might fulfill them. A procedure which, for the purposes of limiting expenditures, excludes from project design all benefits other than those related to efficiency has the result of foreclosing any real consideration of alternative objective functions."[54]

Many government officials and academics feel that the principal problem is not that many benefits may be hard to quantify, because there are ways of measuring and assigning comparison weights to different objectives. An efficient planning process would entail the development of alternative plans by the agencies using different trade-off weights in designing for different objectives. Congress could then select from the multi-objective functions. Arthur Maass, for example, cites case studies of federal interstate highway programs as a precedent for this process. He contends that the now elaborate review machinery could be dismantled and used more efficiently in the beginning of the planning process to construct the weighted design functions.

Maass identifies what he saw as the major reasons officers of the executive branch have chosen to use the narrowly defined cost-benefit analysis as the budget control technique. First, it is an indirect technique and, therefore, difficult for opponents to reach and change. Second, some policy makers believe that the only legitimate federal objective should be the increase of national income, and that redistribution of income to disadvantaged or underdeveloped regions, for example, is not an appropriate government function. In addition, there are professionals who work in the cost-benefit field who do not necessarily object to multiple-objective planning, but their own focus by virtue of being economists has been on how to perfect the efficiency objective of the cost-benefit analysis. Economists also inherently tend to give greater weight to the precision of efficiency ratios than to descriptions of other benefits. Finally, there are those executives who support a restricted definition of benefits in order to hold down the number of projects and expenditures for whom it is consistent to support or be indifferent to the inefficiency this system creates in the planning process. That is because the resultant complexity and length of this process serves as just another way to defer demands on the budget.

The Multi-Objective Plan

The many observers of flood-loss-reduction planning agree on the trends that have occurred in planning concepts and procedures. The first significant change was a shift from single-purpose toward multiple-purpose planning, which was accomplished from the turn of the century to the 1950s; by the end of the 1970s a significant advance toward multi-objective planning had been made.

In early water-planning efforts, the development of a project was based solely on its costs. The 1936 Flood Control Act, the so-called "Green Book" (a 1950 report issued by the federal Inter-Agency Committee on Water Resources), and Circular A-47 (1952), which developed policy guides for federal water agencies, then established the ground rules for the use of the efficiency or cost-benefit analysis based on the concept of national economic efficiency. National economic efficiency became the single objective by which water resource projects were planned until the 1970s. In the 1960s, President Kennedy approved a policy document referred to as Senate Document 97, which addressed the consideration of preservation and protection of natural resources and the enhancement of the "well-being of all the people" in the planning process. House Document 465 issued in 1966 recommended that national policy be carried out that integrated different alternative methods of reducing flood damages. The National Environmental Policy Act of 1969 added environmental quality as an objective to which plans had to be responsive. The River and Harbor and Flood Control Act of 1970 cited the enhancement of *regional* economic development, the well-being of the people, and national economic development as objectives of federal water projects. In 1973, the Water Resources Council issued approved Principles and Standards for the planning of projects that formally integrated multi-objective planning into the planning process and were to be applied to all federal agencies involved in water and watershed projects.

These Principles and Standards provided for National Economic Development and environmental quality (EQ) as coequal objectives for water resources planning, with social well-being and regional development included as "accounts" after the costs and benefits were figured for the NED. The chief of engineers of the Army Corps of Engineers translated these guidelines into a series of seven integrated engineering regulations, which were referred to as the "200 series." Bill Donovan, who was chief of the Flood Plain Management Services at that time and was active in the development of the 200 series, described it as a rational planning process in which aspects of water and land resources planning were *systematically* analyzed with both economic and environmental criteria.[55] The regulations emphasized the equality of the two national objectives: National Economic Development—efficiency—and Environmental Quality, which required a nonmonetary as well as a monetary consideration. The EQ objective was considered not as an "add-on" to the planning process but rather as integral to the process. The process was based on the Corps' broadened planning experiences acquired in its involvement in experiments in the 1960s in its mission to pilot wastewater studies and its urban studies program. According to one of the drafters of the new system, "The overall approach is predicated on the philosophy that plans, whatever their number, whether nonstructural or structural, should be publicly acceptable, implementable, and feasible from an economic, social and environmental standpoint."[56] The system of planning did allow the recommendation of a plan with a benefit-cost ratio below unity. The Principles and Standards were further amended in 1977, and the concept of "multiple means" was introduced formally into the Principles and Standards by the Carter administration in 1979 with the requirement that a nonstructural plan be provided as an alternative in the planning process.

The heyday for multiple-objective planning did not have time to realize many results and ended abruptly in 1980 when the Carter administration Principles and Standards were rescinded by a new administration, and the basis of planning reverted to the single objective of national economic efficiency. The Principles and Standards for designing water projects were changed to the currently used Principles and Guidelines, which removed environmental quality and social well-being as project objectives, and we returned full circle to the 1950s "Green Book" efficiency model for civil works projects.

Cost Sharing

Disagreements over cost-sharing policies for water projects and the related power struggles between Congress and the administration were blamed for the sixteen-year impasse after the 1970 Water Resources Development Act (the Army Corps water projects omnibus bill), which became the last true Army Corps construction authorization bill until the 1986 Water Resources Development Act. Before 1986, local or "nonfederal" project partners would have projects authorized at a 75–25 percent federal-nonfederal ratio. By the 1980s the Reagan administration was increasing the required nonfederal share of federal water projects to 35 percent and more, including the requirement that the once free planning documents provided by the federal government be paid for by a 50 percent charge on project feasibility reports. The 1986 Water Resources Development Act formalized these practices as policy, with the consequence that the 25 percent nonfederal share of water project costs was in most cases going to increase to 35 percent and could go as high as 50 percent. Cost sharing with the locals or states is also now beginning at the planning stages rather than the construction stages after Congress reacted to a Government Accounting Office report that 73 percent of the Corps' feasibility studies found no economically justified projects.[57] The 1996 Water Resources Development Act changed almost all the Corps programs to 65–35 percent cost sharing.

Higher costs added to the daunting planning uncertainties have hindered community participation in federally assisted projects, particularly in the context of the tax revolts and deficits of state and local government in the 1980s and 1990s, in which the competition for the local and state tax dollar for diverse social needs has been particularly intense. Although it has been argued by policy makers and administrators that the increased financial participation of locals translates into greater local involvement in determining project designs, the perspective from local project participants is that the rigid cost-benefit analysis even as reformed by the 1986 act and the rescinding of past 20–80 percent cost-sharing arrangements providing incentives for nonstructural alternatives (as provided by Section 73 of the 1974 WRDA) create effective barriers to the floodplain restoration alternatives presented in this book.

The current provisions in the NED planning guidelines do not encourage the design of environmental quality plans or nonstructural alternatives as part of the flood-control planning process. The main feature of the NED plan after 1986 is to increase substantially the nonfederal share of project costs. Accommodating the financial need of a community is left to the discretion of the assistant secretary of the army in charge of civil works. The Corps is to build the so-called least-cost NED plans that maximize net benefits, and any project enhancements beyond that that may be in a locally preferred plan are to be paid for solely by the community or nonfederal interests. This policy effectively translates into the assumption that the corps will construct channelization or levee projects for flood control, but that environmental features of some kind can be tacked on only if the community pays for them. The NED plans maintain the barriers against any model in which a different design philosophy is used to build more natural, balanced channels integrated with other environmental features.

Poverty areas, in theory, can appeal to the secretary of the army for a change in cost-sharing arrangements, but in practice that is not occurring. My own experience working in the community of North Richmond, California, with a poverty rate of 64.5 percent, confirms the difficulty of communities in arranging cost sharing for water projects based on social and economic needs and realities.[58] According to congressional staff, only one project in the country, Three Mile Creek in Mobile, Alabama, has ever been approved for a waiver of standard cost-sharing policies. That waiver ultimately required the approval of both the Office of Management and Budget as well as the Secretary of the Army.[59] The Kentucky Tug Fork (in Pike County) and Clover Fork (in Harlan County) projects received 100 percent congressionally mandated federal funding for a package of structural and nonstructural projects for this poverty Appalachian region under Section 202 of the Energy and Water Development Act of 1981. The handful of poverty areas that have been served by Army Corps projects, such as Allenvile, Arizona; Tug Fork, Pike County, and Clover Fork, Harlan County, Kentucky; and Wildcat and San Pablo creeks, Richmond, California, have occurred because of intense political pressures to develop creative cost-benefit and cost-sharing arrangements. A review of cost-sharing provisions for similar floodplain evacuation, floodplain restoration, and greenway projects shows widely varying costs incurred by local entities, with some poorer communities paying substantially more than wealthier ones for similar project "outputs." An example of this can be seen by comparing the 45–55 percent non-federal-to-federal cost sharing for the poverty community of North Richmond on Wildcat Creek, California, for a floodplain restoration project, with the 20–80 percent cost sharing for a floodplain restoration and acquisition project in middle- to upper-middle-class Littleton, Colorado.

Just as the cost-benefit analysis used by the Army Corps presents barriers to the practice of nonstructural measures such as floodplain evacuation and restoration, the cost-sharing policies for projects also present barriers to those options. The nation used to use cost-sharing policies to provide incentives for nonstructural projects, between 1974 and 1982, and the historic record shows that that was a period when such projects flourished. From 1986 to 1996 no incentives were provided for nonstructural measures, and the 1996 Water Resources Development Act took us a further step backwards by increasing the cost sharing for restoration projects. Under the 1995 Ecosystem Restoration Guidelines of the Army Corps, restoration project cost sharing was set at 25 percent nonfederal and 75 percent federal. Nonfederal cost sharing for all flood-control projects was increased by WRDA 1996 to 35 percent (Section 202), and cost sharing for "environmental protection and restoration" projects was increased to 35 percent (Section 210), as it was for "aquatic ecosystem restoration" (Section 206). The increased cost sharing for restoration and environmental projects will provide a significant incentive for communities with historic flood problems to work within their pre-1986 existing project authorizations, which have better (25–75 percent) cost-sharing arrangements and have the most barriers to selecting floodplain restoration alternatives, rather than opt for getting the authorities for restoration projects provided since 1986.

As will be discussed in greater detail in the next section, "The Environmental Corps," cost-sharing policies that require the nonfederal sponsor to be responsible for all lands, easements, and rights-of-way place one of the most onerous barriers against a floodplain acquisition-restoration or evacuation project. A local project sponsor that opts for a channelization project or a project with levees set close to a river can avoid paying costs that are likely to accrue above 25 or 35 percent.

The Water Resources Development Act of 1996 does address the ability-to-pay issue by requesting the secretary of the army to consider per capita income data for the county or counties where a project is located when arriving at a cost-share agreement. This is an improvement over past policies, but the jury is out on what reforms the secretary may propose. The policy still doesn't address the problem faced by poor communities—not infrequently inhabited by minority populations—located in well-to-do counties that do not serve those poverty areas.

In the interest of holding down Army Corps water-project expenditures, the federal government clings to the use of an outmoded cost-benefit analysis and an inequitable cost-sharing system that are biased against low-income areas and nonstructural solutions. A well-meaning national environmental lobby has advocated the federal cost-sharing policies in the belief that such policies will reduce the number of projects and thus reduce damage to the environment. Unfortunately, endorsement of such policies strikes a blow to our efforts to focus reform through the development of a planning process designed to fulfill desirable objectives. It is inconsistent and contradictory for environmental advocates to challenge the use of the cost-benefit analysis as an oversimplified means to justify the selection of projects for federal assistance but then to accept the use of too simplified cost-sharing arrangements as a critical aspect of the project justification process. Moreover, the cost-benefit analysis for national benefits and the cost-sharing system should not be the only determinants for qualifying projects for federal support. If we are going to promote a new era of planning based on watershed needs and units, then local priorities, needs, and objectives must be incorporated into the plans along with a national recognition of broader, locally generated goals for social and environmental needs.

The mood of those in the federal agencies, the administration, Congress, and public interest groups involved in reform of water policy is that reform will follow if nonfederal participants must pay more for a civil works project. Their position is that this change in cost-sharing provisions will produce more socially and environmentally acceptable projects because if the project isn't good, the public won't stand for paying for the bill. Public support for a project is ultimately assumed by the successful completion of a federal and nonfederal cost-share agreement. In fact, a review of flood-control cases can show that the signing of such an agreement by a local entity to join a federal agency in a project may reflect only how desperate a community is to get federal help for a flood problem. What the project looks like, how it ultimately performs, and the cost of maintaining it may be a source of community division, anguish, and resignation. The community involved in the design of a flood-control project is not typically given a full array of alternatives for designing and funding a solution. Until the public is informed on the diversity of options to solve its problems and is given nondiscriminatory options for funding different alternatives, how can we argue that communities are showing support for the projects by contributing money for their construction? The federal water planning system does not represent a free-market-choice system for solving flood problems because it does not offer an array of possible projects at fair prices.

Differences among locally placed environmental and community organizations and national environmental groups on policy strategies are of course linked to the different perspectives of the experiences of the organizations. National environmental and policy reform groups generally view federal involvement in flood-damage reduction as unnecessary, expensive, environmentally damaging "pork" consisting of congressional monetary favors to their districts. Locally placed environmental organizations have different perspectives enforced by their experiences as members of communities that have been suffering from repeated flood damages, often for decades.

Locally active floodplain managers and advocates of reform do witness abuses of the federal water project system. We watch as some of our fellow citizens make money off of the National Flood Insurance Program, waiting for the next flood to cash in again on their policy. We watch while federal disaster assistance is spent in the billions to repeatedly bail flood-prone areas with irresponsible land-use planning out of their emergencies. We watch as the development community is subsidized by flood-control projects to build in hazardous areas which could be avoided by sound land-use zoning.

One way to react to abuses of the system and increasing federal costs for national flood damages is to advocate removal of the federal government from floodplain management. Certainly, greater acceptance of floodplain management responsibilities by state and local entities is desirable. However, the reality of the political situation is that if a region suffers serious flood damages, federal disaster payments are not going to be withheld. Politics abhors a vacuum. If there are disasters, federal and/or state governments will have to react. We need to make a decision then. Which do we want to emphasize, the use of federal and state funds for disaster assistance or the use of such funds for the avoidance of disasters? If we choose the latter, we need to then make a commitment to design federal flood-damage-reduction programs that most fairly and rationally serve local needs.

The other difference attributable to a local perspective, which applies in many (but not all) areas (as desperate as this may sound to a beltway environmentalist), is that on the average the local environmentalist can be better off working with the more trained, sophisticated, and environmentally staffed Army Corps teams than solely with understaffed local flood-control and public works districts. The statistics in the first part of the chapter tell this story: locals account for over 200,000 miles of river channelization, while the federal agencies are responsible for somewhere under 50,000 miles of project channels. While our locally based planning models call for greater emphasis on state and local involvement in floodplain and watershed planning, we do not want to lose the concept of federal agencies being a part of our consensus team-planning approaches. Simply cutting federal involvement from the picture does not contribute to the team planning we are looking for. We do not want to return to the bad old days when "flood control" was driving a local public works bulldozer down the riverbed.

Finally, the position of many grassroots groups, which has now been embraced by most national environmental organizations, is that it is better to change the mission of the existing federal authorizations and their appropriations than lose the appropriations—for there is no such thing as adding on appropriations for new watershed restoration programs in a period of strict fiscal restraint and budget balancing. Reform of the existing programs appears to be the most realistic strategy for those of us advocating change.

Recent proposals in cost-sharing policy have surfaced in which the Army Corps' ability to share costs with nonfederal partners would be based on local initiatives to conduct floodplain zoning, organize flood-warning and flood-proofing systems, and institute other nonstructural measures and programs. The level of federal assistance could range from 25 percent to 75 percent depending on local commitments to live responsibly with the floodplain.[60] The concept of using cost-sharing formulas as incentives as opposed to barriers to federal involvement is a most encouraging development. However, the historical dragons of the Office of Management and Budget's concerns over federal spending, and ambiguities over policy reform present in environmental and other interest groups are perhaps unintentionally neutralizing this important effort at reform by advocating locking in the maximum possible federal share to 50 percent. This change will most likely undercut the movement toward reform because many or most projects coming up for congressional appropriations are part of the vast backlog of already authorized projects, which were approved for 25 percent, 35 percent, or no more than 50 percent nonfederal funding levels. The proposals for 50–50 percent cost-sharing provide no incentives for all the backlogged communities.

What should be done about the huge backlog of Army Corps projects, which could sap most of our federal dollars away from the more contemporary restoration projects now being planned? A reasonable political assumption is that congressional representatives are going to make the backlogged, already authorized projects in their districts their appropriations priorities in the years to come. It cannot be assumed that every preexisting project authorization represents a valid national or even local interest. The political nature of any authorization list must be acknowledged. Part of the backlog phenomenon must be attributed to the fact that marginal and even inappropriate projects remain in "authorization limbo" with little chance of implementation because of the political discomforts of deauthorizing projects. The Army Corps should take a page from the Natural Resources Conservation Service watershed program reform book. A good strategy is for the agency to conduct a dispassionate and objective evaluation of authorized projects and weed out the projects and project features that do not conform to present-day priorities and standards. Congressional direction could then use cost-sharing provisions to provide incentives to those communities to take greater responsibility for floodplain management in order to receive their federal assistance.

Federal water-project planning has been and will continue to be driven on the basis of the scarce federal dollar. The great irony is that a reformed system using objectives-based planning and technical designs based on concepts of geomorphology instead of solely on channel hydraulics would reduce both the federal share of costs and the total project construction bill. Objectives-based planning for civil-works restoration projects will save federal dollars because:

- different technologies, such as stream restoration strategies, can lower project costs because of lower construction and maintenance expenses;
- different labor-intensive construction and maintenance techniques may contribute to local economies just as the Works Progress Administration did in the 1930s and 1940s;
- protection measures against the smaller, more frequent floods instead of the larger, 100-year floods will reduce the cost of many projects; and
- other federal, state, and local agencies will be motivated to share their costs because the projects have more objectives.

Many nonstructural and environmentally sensitive design measures do incur higher land acquisition costs. However, these need to be balanced against the long-term costs of maintaining and eventually replacing structural engineering works, sediment removal costs, vegetation removal, and the unintended impacts of or performance problems common to the traditional project design. Fiscally responsible policy making and project design must weigh the true, long-term costs of traditionally designed projects against the costs of land acquisition. The long-term benefits of land acquisition need to be acknowledged for providing risk-free environments in perpetuity.

The current federal NED project evaluation under which the majority of civil works projects will continue to be governed (assuming the political reality that only a few new authorizations under new restoration guidelines are possible) is so narrow that only those communities with the most influential representatives will be able to circumvent the planning system through a long and costly process and get a project that meets community needs. Such a system does not stop pork-barrel projects; it only makes them more time consuming and expensive. Under the current system, wealthy communities will tend to get less-than-well-designed flood-control projects, and the poorer communities will get no projects. The bottom line is that only a planning process that recognizes the need for multi-objective planning and ensures that those objectives are met by the project under consideration for federal assistance will produce water development projects with genuine local and national benefits. Raising the costs of projects will not get us where we want to be.

The Environmental Corps

In the fall of 1989, Lieutenant General Henry J. Hatch, commander of the U.S. Army Corps of Engineers, gave a presentation at the Globescope Pacific Conference in Los Angeles, widely covered by the media, in which he explicitly established the Corps' responsibility for integrating environmental quality into its mission and priorities.

He stated that the environment "is *the* most significant engineering issue of the next decade," that "engineers must look at [their] work in a broad social and environmental context," and that "environmental engineering, in its broadest definition, must not only mitigate environmental costs of development, but must also directly attack environmental issues as a purpose for the engineering effort itself." Significantly, Hatch also embraced the idea of "sustainable" development as an ethic for guiding the Corps' work, in which projects would be based on sound, long-term economic and environmental principles.[61] The idea of renaming the Corps the Army Corps of Environmental Engineers circulated. What form will the new environmental corps take? The possibility that the Corps will move beyond the turn-of-the-century concept of "wise use" of resources to the sustainable management of resources is now before us.

New Ecological Restoration Missions

New congressional authorities are directing the Army Corps into a restoration mission. General Hatch was in part responding to a directive to the Corps in the 1986 Water Resources Development Act (Public Law 99–62) contained in Section 1135, which authorized the secretary of the army to carry out a two-year demonstration program to modify the structures and operations of Army Corps' previously constructed projects for the purpose of improving the environmental quality of the projects—i.e., to take part in environmental restoration projects. A $25 million appropriation was authorized, and the nonfederal share of the cost was set at 25 percent. The main political motivation behind Section 1135 was to enable the Corps to help the state of Florida restore meanders to the Kissimmee River. The 1990 Water Resources Development Act (Public Law 101–640) upgraded Section 1135 from a demonstration program to a program with an annual appropriation of $15 million. Sections 305, 306, and 307 of the 1990 WRDA added a significant congressional directive to the Corps to adopt an environmental mission. Section 306 of this act states, "The Secretary shall include environmental protection as one of the *primary* missions of the Corps of Engineers in planning, designing, constructing, operating and maintaining water resources projects" (emphasis added). Section 307 states: "There is established as part of the Corps of Engineers Water Resources Development Program, an interim goal of no overall net loss of the nation's remaining wetlands base, as defined by acreage and function, and a long-term goal to increase the quality and quantity of the nation's wetlands, as defined by acreage and function." It directs the secretary of the army, in consultation with the Environmental Protection Agency and the Fish and Wildlife Service, to develop a wetlands action plan to achieve a goal of no net loss. The act also contains the potential for a change in ability-to-pay policies (Section 305) by which the secretary is authorized to reduce any nonfederal cash contribution required on the basis of local, and not statewide, economic and financial data. In the 1992 Water Resources Development Act, Section 204 authorizes the Corps to integrate restoration into its dredging projects.

In late 1995, final Army Corps ecosystem restoration guidelines were issued to carry out the provisions in these congressional authorities.[62] These guidelines are applicable to *all* civil works planning authorities including flood control, dredging, and navigation. The definition of ecosystem restoration used in the guidelines represents the contemporary and sophisticated concept of restoring the structure, functions, and values of ecosystems with the goal of protecting or achieving biodiversity and managing for a whole system rather than a particular species. A watershed-based planning concept is recommended, as is the role of the Army Corps as a member of an interdisciplinary planning team. Cost-sharing arrangements for ecosystem restoration projects were made favorable and competitive to those with existing civil works authorities. Feasibility studies costs would be shared 50–50 percent, and project implementation costs would be shared 75 percent federal and 25 percent nonfederal. The usual complete nonfederal obligation for maintenance would apply. The application of these restoration guidelines seems to face an uncertain future, however, with many of the Army Corps district offices being uninformed of their existence or ill-informed on their use.

Section 206 of the 1996 WRDA authorizes "Aquatic Ecosystem Restoration and Protection Projects" that are to be "cost-effective," at 35 percent nonfederal cost sharing. Section 503 of the 1996 act authorizes "Watershed Management Restoration Development" technical assistance in planning and design at 50 percent cost sharing. The additional restoration and watershed management missions are welcome, but the higher cost-sharing requirements, particularly in comparison to pre-1986 authorizations, will probably deflate demand for these project categories.

On the issue of economic evaluations of restoration projects, the restoration guidelines state that the federal objective in water resources is to contribute to the National Economic Development, that the NED is to be selected unless the secretary of the army finds there are overriding reasons to select another plan. An overriding reason to select another plan can be that the civil works budget assigns priority to the restoration of ecosystems. These ecological restoration activities do not need to show net NED benefits and should be viewed on the basis of their nonmonetary benefits, or "outputs." Reports must show the justifications for accepting trade-offs between gained environmental outputs and losses in NED outputs. When NED benefits are forgone due to an ecosystem restoration alternative, those reduced benefits will be treated as project costs. According to the Corps guidelines, "There also may be NED benefits associated with a plan formulated for the restoration objective, such as increased flood damage reduction, which should also be appropriately documented in the NED account." The guidelines go on to state that the cost-effectiveness of the ecosystem restoration activities will be evaluated.[63]

The planning framework for the new environmental corps has been painstakingly worked out through the careful preparation of reports leading up to the release of these guidelines.[64–66] The planning framework represents giant steps forward even though restoration is still an unequal partner in how it is perceived as a benefit. As the guidelines are currently being applied by the Corps districts, the benefits of restoration remain a neutral influence at best when the NED cost-benefit analysis is made for a flood control project. The only way restoration benefits may add to the benefits side of the NED analysis is if they reduce flood damages. If restoration activities reduce flood-damage benefits, restoration benefits become a cost. Restoration benefits are prevented from becoming costs if they are deemed cost-effective. Only after the NED plan attains a cost-benefit analysis exceeding 1:1 can quantifiable benefits attained from such analyses as the monetary value of Average Annual Habitat Units be added on, just as recreation benefits can be added on incrementally after calculating the NED plan's cost-benefit ratio. Presumably, since floodplain restoration projects provide direct flood-damage-reduction benefits, we should be seeing those benefits in the NED calculations.

The good news is the barriers to restoration are falling away. The disappointment is that restoration is not actually a "primary" mission of the Corps; it is still an ancillary one and not a coequal mission. Imagine someday a policy statement that directs, "flood-damage-reduction benefits will not be considered costs if they do not conflict with the restoration objectives and benefits of dynamic equilibrium watersheds and rivers." One of the reports issued by the Army Corps leading to the adoption of their guidelines recommends:

> The Corps should assure that all policy statements, guidance and training for field operating units make it clear that a NED plan is not required to justify a federal interest in environmental restoration and that money valuation of environmental outputs is not a precondition of budget support for an environmental restoration project.[67]

The million-dollar question asked by a Corps staff member at a recent annual meeting of the Corps' Environmental Advisory Board is, "What will be the reaction of the administration's Office of Management and Budget if they get a group of projects with a cost-benefit ratio of 1:1.2 with ecological restoration benefits associated with it, and a group of projects with 1.3 or greater ratios with no restoration features? Which ones will make it into the authorization and appropriations acts?"[68]

Future Opportunities and Uncertainties

The commitment of the Corps of Engineers leadership to developing environmental restoration as a bona fide mission in the 1990s is unquestionable. The difficulties in making profound shifts in policies and planning processes and methods are still before us, however. Only patience, understanding, and open communications and minds will get us to our collectively shared goals to improve the options of government services to communities. The Corps is developing a new constituency in the environmental community as that community sees the huge potential of the Corps to carry a significant restoration mission. Personnel in the Corps say with pride that it is now the largest restoration agency in the world.

There are going to be major and minor hurdles ahead of us on this road to the new restoration mission. It is even too early to forecast what all the hurdles will be, not to mention what strategies will be used to get over them. A preview of the issues the Corps will be addressing in the future follows.

Among the greatest threats to the restoration mission is the backlog of desperate communities that have authorized flood-control projects going back as far as fifty years coming up against budget-balancing measures. How can new restoration projects with no preexisting authorizations compete in this context? The most unfortunate aspect of the new restoration mission is that the Corps is interpreting the congressional authority for restoration projects as applying to new projects or newly authorized purposes for civil works projects. Restoration measures cannot be integrated into existing authorized but as yet unconstructed projects without going through more political steps. This is particularly tragic for the many communities that could build the public coalitions necessary to getting stalled projects into the implementation phase and could more easily develop the funding packages for flood-damage-reduction projects that are team designed, multi-objective, and restoration oriented.

Instead, these communities with old authorizations are advised not to reformulate their projects to include restoration because that could forever doom their chances of receiving federal assistance. That advice is based on the current policy that states if restoration is added to a flood-control project—even if that restoration is floodplain restoration done for the purpose of increasing flood-conveyance capacities or floodplain storage—the planning must start over with a new congressional authorization. To avoid such a depressing scenario, communities are urged to keep their old authorizations and accept channelization or levee projects under the old NED planning system, with the possibility of trying to make them a bit "greener" under the constraints of the NED plans.

Two examples of this dilemma are currently being played out in Mill Creek, Cincinnati, Ohio, and Napa River, Napa, California, flood-damage-reduction projects. The Napa project's original authorization dates to the 1940s, and the Mill Creek project was authorized in 1970. Both projects have environmental opposition to their channelization features as a part of the complicating factors preventing their implementation. In another example, the city of Pacifica, California, and the San Francisco District of the Army Corps abandoned the restoration planning option for the San Pedro Creek. Luckily, they managed to maneuver restoration features into an existing Section 205 continuing authorities project begun in the early 1980s to avoid redoing their past planning documents. The Louisville Army Corps District has recommended terminating its old 1970 Mill Creek plan and reformulating a plan that is more environmentally sensitive. However, it is advising that reformulation under the new restoration guidelines be considered a last-resort option, which the local sponsor may not be able to afford for two reasons. The first is that it will be difficult to get the required authorization for the added project purpose of restoration. The second reason is that given the administration's new policy direction favoring higher percent cost-share requirements for new flood-damage-reduction projects, the local costs for a reformulated project will exceed the costs of their existing, authorized channelization project.

The Napa River project had strong local support for reformulation of a channelization project under the new ecological restoration guidelines. The preference of the local sponsor is to restore the floodplain for flood conveyance rather than to deepen and widen the river channel. Critical to support for that alternative was the 75–25 percent cost-sharing policy under the 1995 ecological restoration guidelines, which matched their cost-sharing arrangement under existing flood-control project authorizations. That option was abandoned, however, because of Washington-based warnings that a reformulation to include restoration as a project purpose would require reauthorization, which would realistically kill any future chances of a federally assisted project.

The second greatest threat to a prosperous restoration program is the ambiguous messages being conveyed already from the Office of Management and Budget. One of the Corps' top restoration project priorities, the Upper Sacramento River in California, was not accepted on the administration's project list. Restoration is being encouraged as a new mission, but when it needs support in the budget process, it may very well take a backseat to other traditional priorities.

A bright star in the Corps restoration efforts has been the overwhelming popularity of the Section 1135 restoration program. Everyone seems to want a 1135 project, and the backlog of requests is described as going from the District of Columbia to the moon and back. Despite its overwhelming popularity, this program labors under an annual $20 million limit, with each project limited to a cap of $5 million, including land values and costs. An obvious improvement would be to shift more funds into this program. Even after the cost-sharing increases made in the 1996 WRDA, the program retains its 75–25 percent costs sharing. Environmental interests would like to see the program expanded from its current limitation of addressing only environments impacted by existing constructed Corps projects. At this point, given the barriers to adding restoration features to the backlog of unconstructed but congressionally authorized projects, there is a certain irony in the fact that it is easier to restore a system after it has been damaged than to prevent the damages to begin with by allowing older authorized structural projects to use restoration methods. Presumably, Congress could eliminate this inherently expensive scenario by using the next Water Resources Development Act to clarify that restoration purposes can be addressed in all its previous authorizations.

The budgets for the two technical assistance programs for states and local entities for floodplain and land and resources management started to crash in the 1980s. The Floodplain Management Services Branch and the Section 22 Program for Planning Assistance to States fell to about $6.5 million for floodplain services and $1.5 million for the Planning Assistance to States Program. These programs were established in the 1960s to integrate land-use planning and other nonstructural options into the plans the Army Corps provides to communities for flood-damage reduction. A hopeful sign in 1997 was the president's budget increase for these programs, respectively, to $10 million and $3 million.

The restoration guidelines will be only as good as communications within the Corps on their existence and how to implement them.

A number of additional barriers to implementing restoration projects may remain in place unless some policy ambiguities and problems are addressed. The most critical issues are how to best value land costs for restoration projects and how to share their costs. Most restoration projects associated with or designed in lieu of conventional flood-control projects will involve floodplain and/or wetland restoration, which means that greater acreages of land, easements, and/or rights-of-way will be required.

Assuming that its restoration priorities are going to be centered around flood-control and dredging projects, the Corps is going to need to address its backlog of flood-control projects. Most of those projects are channelization and levee projects. A project planning assumption under the NED-based system is that all lands, easements, and rights-of-way are first a local or nonfederal responsibility. When the total project costs start to exceed 50 percent, the federal government shares the costs at a 50:50 ratio. The channelization and levee projects are perpetuated by this cost-sharing policy, which rewards them with the narrowest project rights-of-way. Most of the existing authorizations require a minimum 25 percent nonfederal contribution, while some require a 35 percent minimum contribution. It is in the interest of local sponsors to keep the land costs at a minimum so that they do not exceed these minimum percentages. This disincentive kills the options of setback levees or floodplain restoration percentages. This is a disincentive as well for communities to take on relocations of structures from the floodplain.

Communities that insist on pursuing more environmentally sensitive options are rewarded with the whole bill associated with these options. Because it is the strategy of the NED to create a "least-cost" plan, it defines the necessary rights-of-way as only those lands needed for a channelization project or a project with levees constructed as close to the channel as possible. Any lands, easements, or rights-of-way that are not necessary for the least-cost NED plan with narrow boundaries are considered the total cost of the nonfederal sponsor. Communities that have selected floodplain restoration or floodway greenways as project features operate outside Corps project boundaries or without Corps participation entirely. They must fund those acquisitions and project components through other government and private programs because it is too hard to implement such multiple-objective projects under NED Corps policies.

The other nail in the coffin of restoration alternatives is that the cost-sharing rules on land costs prohibit the assigning of credit to the local sponsor for lands, easements, and rights-of-way acquired with the assistance of other federal programs. This runs counter to the current efforts to join federal programs with overlapping objectives in cooperative ventures. Cooperative ventures can reduce counterproductive conflict of missions among agencies and provide greater value for the federal dollar spent. There seems to be increasing "give" in this area, in that the Corps is accepting community block grants, which ultimately are "passed down" federal dollars, and state-administered, post-disaster, FEMA mitigation grants, which originate from the federal government as local or "nonfederal" contributions. Funds from various Housing and Urban Development programs, National Flood Insurance mitigation grants, federal Land and Water Conservation funds, and other federal monies that pass through state governments before arriving at the local level are qualifying as nonfederal funds. This adds to the planning opportunities as well as to project planning confusion as to what constitutes a "nonfederal" contribution.

The last and final assault on restoration alternatives is that lands are valued at top market value *even if they are donated* by a local entity. When land occupies a hazardous flood zone, that should logically deflate its market value even if it requires purchasing. The full-market values show up as total project costs, thereby raising the local share of project costs even if the land has been donated. Such project costs can kill a favorable project cost-benefit ratio.

It is unclear how the new restoration guidelines will be applied to land costs. An issue that must be resolved in new congressional project authorizations as well as old is that land acquisition is an integral and critical part of most restoration projects and should be considered a restoration feature at the 65–35 percent cost-sharing ratio. Unfortunately, the 1996 Water Resources Development Act requires a 35 percent local share for construction costs and all lands, easements, and rights-of-way in the new Aquatic Ecosystem Restoration (Section 206) authority. Donated lands should be considered part of the nonfederal contribution and should not raise the total costs levied against local interests. Land contributions should be considered a national benefit because they are aiding in the storage and conveyance of floods and contributing toward long-term avoidance of future damages by removing or distancing structures from hazard zones. Land values in floodplains and wetlands should not be represented at their potential full-market values if they are to appear on the costs side of the benefit-cost ratio.

Finally, as the Corps enters flood-damage-reduction efforts from a watershed perspective, can watershed land management efforts performed by local soil and water conservation districts and watershed councils that reduce peak flows and retard timing of runoff be assigned as a nonfederal contribution to a project?

The actual social and economic benefits of restoration projects must become a part of this movement toward the environmental corps. The first glaring problem that conflicts with the Clinton administration's strong commitments to environmental justice is the systematic exclusion of most poverty areas from federal assistance with flood and floodplain problems. This exclusion occurs because the major portion of benefits of any older civil works project or newer restoration project is tied to the value of the property being protected from floods. The secretary of the army was directed under Section 305 of the 1990 Water Resources Development Act to reduce nonfederal costs of projects on the basis of the "local" financial status of communities and to take into account the ability of a community to pay. Again, because of fiscal constraints, the administration is resistant to giving some communities a better deal than others. The problem with that position is that current policies enforce systematic discrimination against poorer populations. Many such communities are located in hazardous areas because of past discriminatory housing segregation of minorities onto floodplains and wetlands. The use of county-level demographics to determine ability to pay is often not a legitimate means of determining poverty. It is not unusual for impoverished areas to be located in hazardous bottomlands adjacent to wealthy residences safely located on high grounds such as bluffs, terraces, and hills. Lower-lying flood-hazard areas are often politically neglected and disenfranchised even if they are located in or near wealthy counties.

The NED recognizes what it calls national benefits, but it doesn't recognize locally important economic and social benefits of restoration projects. For example, an unusual Army Corps stream restoration project on Wildcat Creek in a poor, minority community has made an environmental education program possible at the local school. The school is a critical community resource and focus. The ongoing work created by a stream restoration project—done in lieu of a channelization project— has provided jobs for at-risk youth. Educational opportunities, crime reduction, and jobs creation for local youth are not considered "national benefits, and so they cannot under the current system influence our choices of project alternatives.[69, 70]

The Natural Resources Conservation Service

Recent Developments in NRCS Watershed Programs

The watershed programs of the Natural Resources Conservation Service (originally the Soil Conservation Service) have their origins in the 1944 Flood Control Act, or Public Law 534, and the 1954 Flood Control Act, or Public Law 83–566, the latter of which has been the real foundation of the service's stream and watershed management activities. Public Law 566 provided broad authority to address any planning needs in a watershed. The River Basin Surveys and Investigations program continues to fund planning and technical assistance to local resource conservation districts. The other planning function of the NRCS is for specific project planning that is expected to result in a federal-local cooperative watershed project. The third major component of the contemporary NRCS watershed program budget is the "watershed and flood prevention operations" that contain project construction and implementation activities. The main mission of these programs is flood-damage reduction and watershed protection. Sediment control, stream-channel stabilization, grade stabilization, water storage, "land treatment" or soil erosion control, fish and wildlife, habitat restoration, and recreational development are all included among the project purposes. The service maintains a central office in Washington, D.C., but most of its activities are carried out in about 3,050 field offices in the fifty states and Puerto Rico. Four technical service centers provide support for engineering, watershed planning, soil mechanics laboratories, soils, biology, forestry conservation and management, and plant materials, etc. In 1990 there were a little over twelve thousand employees.[71] By 1994 the agency had reduced its number of personnel and consolidated some of its functions into six newly created regional offices. The 1994 Federal Crop Insurance Reform and Department of Agriculture Reorganization Act both streamlined and added new activities, as well as a new name, to the agency. The new Natural Resources Conservation Service had a number of resource management programs transferred to it, including the Wetland Reserve Program, Waterbank Program, Forestry Incentive Program, and Great Plains Conservation Program.

Funding for the P.L. 566 Watershed Program started out at $5 million in 1954 and over the years increased to a high point of $160 million in the early 1980s. During the Reagan administration the budgets for NRCS programs were cut with the intent of phasing out the functions of the agency. Congress annually reinstated funds to the agency, but the result was a greatly impacted budget. Most of the attention focused on the implementation of the 1985 farm bill, or the Food Security Act of 1985, P.L. 99–198, administered by the Agricultural Stabilization and Conservation Service. Often referred to as the sodbuster act, the program contains a Conservation Reserve Program administered by state and local agricultural stabilization and conservation committees. The reserve program targets the 45 million acres of farmland that are the most erodible. In exchange for entering land into the reserve, which can include valuable wetland and riparian areas, program participants receive annual rental payments, and they can receive additional payments for reestablishing vegetation on the sites. While this program will hopefully produce positive results for watershed conditions, it is unambiguously a farm-related program.[72] The Bush administration submitted budgets to continue the NRCS programs in general and its watershed programs specifically, which was a cause of relief to the NRCS employees, but that administration nonetheless enacted substantial budget cuts.[73] The Office of Management and Budget (OMB) staff advocated the deauthorization of many of the Public Law 534 and 566 projects. The Clinton administration's position on the P.L. 566 program has generally been that unless the program makes substantive progress toward being a watershed management and restoration program, the OMB is inclined to zero-out its budget.

The 1954 P.L. 566 Small Watersheds Program directed the NRCS to serve upper watershed areas with watershed management and flood-control projects. These areas were for the most part the rural areas of the country. The Army Corps received the urban parts of the watershed "turf," and so the rural character of the NRCS watershed programs has a long tradition. The organizational structure of the NRCS is based in locally formed resource, or soil conservation, districts, which now number about three thousand in the country. Inevitably, many of those resource conservation districts have become more urbanized and have had to face the watershed management problems typical of urban development. The NRCS has then adapted itself to serving those urbanized constituents. Notable examples of active NRCS urban project areas are the Chicago, Illinois, area and the Santa Clara Valley around San Jose in California. Amendments to P.L. 566 by the 1990 Food Security Act were intended to put limitations on NRCS involvement in urban areas. The act requires that no less than 20 percent of the primary project benefits of the Small Watershed Program must specifically serve rural areas. The other significant change the 1990 act made to P.L. 566 was a new 50 percent federal-local cost-sharing provision for preservation of wetlands, which occurs as part of flood-control, water-quality, and fish and wildlife projects.[72]

The service has continued the work and commitments it had already made in urban areas, and programs have been added administratively by the Clinton administration secretary of agriculture, undersecretary for natural resources and the environment, and chief of the NRCS as described in chapter 2, including the Urban Resources Partnership Program, a collaboration with the Environmental Protection Agency, the Department of Interior, and the NRCS Urban Resources technical assistance program. The provisions of these programs include assistance with urban forestry, community gardens, and urban stream restoration.

The Recent Record in Stream Modification Projects

There is a consensus opinion among observers within the Natural Resources Conservation Service, Congress, and the Office of Management and Budget, as well as among representatives of the environmental movement interviewed for this book, that the traditional channelization project represents the Soil Conservation Service of a past era.[73] The NRCS has its share of channelization projects located in older plans, many of which have languished on the inactive or deauthorized list.[74] It has been the opinion of OMB staff for some time that most of those old plans should be "retired."[75] Starting in the 1980s, stream modification plans began to take on more environmental features, and the agency culture began to abandon its channelization emphasis of the 1950s to 1970s. The 1980s were characterized more by environmentally selective and sensitive clearing and snagging performed with the objective of increasing channel capacity for floods while leaving a natural riparian environment intact. By the 1990s the service was doing more of what it refers to as "spot work," which identifies specific locations of channel constrictions or problems and treats those acres rather than doing a wholesale channel clearing project. It also was doing more "one-sided" channel modifications, in which a channel's dimensions are enlarged by disturbing only one side of the channel and retaining the meander and natural channel geometry or shape as much as possible. The 1980s saw the replacement of authorized channelization projects with plans using new design assumptions.[76]

Some attribute this shift in practice to the grassroots nature of the NRCS planning process and the growing local movement away from channelization projects. Some point out the influence the National Environmental Policy Act has had on the reform of project design objectives. Others give credit to a certain predisposition of NRCS personnel and agency culture to be more interested in environmental issues, although the agency can suffer from a certain amount of hard engineering vs. environmental schizophrenia. It is without question that the Natural Resources Conservation Service management in the Clinton administration has had a committed priority to formally change the mission of the P.L. 566 Small Watershed Program. The pressures of the White House and the Office of Management and Budget to reduce the federal deficit and avoid financially and environmentally costly projects, combined with congressional legislative initiatives to reform the objectives of the program and the commitment to reform by NRCS top management, are converging to create an overhaul of the program.

Starting in 1994, the new NRCS conducted an evaluation of all the active P.L. 566 projects, with the objective of substantially reducing their structural features and responding to the backlog of watershed projects by eliminating unnecessary or infeasible projects. As early as 1958, there were not enough funds to meet the demand for construction, and the backlog grew to slightly over $2 billion during the 1970s. By 1994 the backlog had decreased to $1.25 billion through congressional allocations to projects. Due to concerted efforts by the NRCS between 1994 and 1996, the agency administratively reduced the backlog from $1.25 billion to $811 million.

A 1996 evaluation of P.L. 566 shows that 95 percent of the program's projects were flood-control related in 1981, dropping to about 70 percent in 1994. Watershed protection projects rose from less than 10 percent to over 40 percent; erosion control projects increased from less than 10 percent to almost 40 percent. Water quality projects increased from less than 5 percent to about 15 percent. In 1996 about 50 percent of all new projects submitted under P.L. 566 consisted primarily of land treatment measures.[77]

To administratively reduce the number of projects on the backlog list, the chief of the NRCS established a committee representing the broad stakeholders in the program, including traditional agricultural interests, environmental and professional organizations, and other federal agencies, to review the backlogged projects. The objective for the review was to eliminate from watershed project plans any structures that were no longer needed, had lost local support, or could not "measure up to today's economic, environmental or social standards."[78] The review involved both Washington, D.C., and locally based NRCS teams.

The result of this backlog review was the identification of 2,732 miles of flood-control channel work and 634 dams that were unneeded or no longer justified and therefore could be eliminated. As of February 1996, two-thirds of the structural measures in the backlogged plans were officially removed, reducing the backlog by $439 million. The goal was to strike 90 percent of those measures by December 1996. Even given that worthy administrative effort, the structural backlog is such that if the remaining 320 projects were to be funded at today's levels it would take 25–30 years to complete the backlog. This is complicated by the fact that there are 186 watershed protection projects also in the implementation phase competing for the same funds.[79]

It is interesting to note that during this backlog review, the NRCS found the greatest local investment in channelization projects to be located in the southern United States. Louisiana was the most serious customer with nine hundred projects, which were reduced through this process to three hundred or fewer.[80]

A legislative initiative organized by the political action committee of the Coalition to Restore Urban Waters started in 1993 led to a P.L. 566 reform act using a bipartisan effort led by Democrat Representative Elizabeth Furse and Republican Senator Mark Hatfield, both of Oregon. The subsequent Watershed Restoration Act (H.R. 1331 and S626) authorized the program funds to be used for river, stream, and wetland restoration in both rural and urban areas and encouraged the use of soil biotechnical bank stabilization and contemporary ecological restoration methods described in this book. The legislation also established priorities for projects that employ youth service and conservation corps and benefit the most economically disadvantaged communities. Grants under the restoration option would be available for soil and water conservation districts, resource conservation districts, local governments, schools, nonprofit organizations, conservation corps, and agricultural extension service programs. The act came frustratingly close to passage as part of the 1996 Farm Bill, but the legislative effort died in the 105th Congress due to Republican party leadership opposition. The Department of Agriculture and NRCS have taken initiatives to make administrative changes in the spirit of the Watershed Restoration Act, but the legislative requirement in P.L. 566 that any project must have a minimum of 20 percent of its benefits assigned to a rural area effectively prevents the NRCS watershed program from serving urban constituents. A positive legislative gain for the NRCS to increase its involvement in floodplain management came in the 1996 Farm Bill (Federal Agriculture Improvement and Reform Act). This act gives the agency authority to purchase floodplain easements under the Emergency Watershed Protection Program to restore agricultural land to wetlands and floodplains.

The NRCS Planning Process

Compared to the Army Corps of Engineers planning processes, the Natural Resources Conservation Service is an interesting study in contrasts. The service has always had a very decentralized and grassroots-based planning process. The soil and water conservation districts and resource conservation districts that are organized on a county-wide basis are usually the local entities to originate project proposals and, as the local sponsors, have equal authority with the state NRCS offices and the federal NRCS in the project planning process. The NRCS is given an annual appropriation for its project planning and construction services, but unlike the Bureau of Reclamation and the Corps it does not get large lump-sum, long-term budget appropriations for specific projects.

The history of grassroots support for Small Watershed Program projects can be attributed to much more inclusive local involvement and influence over projects than is the case with Army Corps projects. A legally qualified local agency must apply for assistance from a designated state agency, which is usually a state soil conservation committee. In practice, projects generally have joint or multiple sponsors—rather than just one local sponsor—including one or more soil conservation district together with other groups who join as endorsers of the project to show community support. The state committee can do its own investigation and hold public hearings to determine whether there is sufficient widespread interest and agreement on the proposed project. The project requires a "high priority rating" by the state conservationist before it is eligible for federal planning assistance. State criteria require sponsors to demonstrate that the project will benefit a substantial number of people and that it is widely supported throughout the watershed.[81] Given the degree of local and state scrutiny of NRCS projects, there has been *some* built-in control over the controversial pork-barrel projects that may benefit only a few. Congressional committee staff report that they are unaware of public challenges to funded Natural Resources Conservation Service projects between 1980 and 1990.[82] Not only are decision making and setting priorities for projects regional or decentralized processes, authorization and appropriations at the congressional level are a one-step process, greatly simplifying the political process for the local entity. (The Army Corps' recent effort to delegate more decisions to districts and divisions is an effort to emulate this system, but the agency culture and size has so far been a barrier to its successful practice.)

The cost-sharing practices for Natural Resources Conservation Service projects are significantly different from those of the Army Corps for both structural and non-structural projects. The federal government provides 100 percent funding for structural measures for flood-damage reduction as long as the locals provide the water rights, land easements, and rights-of-way. However, up to one-half of the lands, easements, and rights-of-way may be funded with P.L. 534 or P.L. 566 funds if the lands are allocated to public fish and wildlife and recreational uses. An unspecified "equitable share" of costs allocated to agricultural and wildlife uses of water can be required of local sponsors. A local entity must maintain and operate any structures. Another significant feature of the NRCS cost-sharing policies is that nonstructural measures or projects that combine nonstructural with structural solutions do not suffer cost-sharing disincentives. The cost-sharing arrangements are the same for both kinds of projects, and the local share for implementation of nonstructural measures does not exceed 25 percent.[83] Proposals to increase the required local share have failed, and the farm bills have upheld those long-standing policies. Although the NRCS and the Army Corps come under the same directives of the national Principles and Guidelines for water projects and National Economic Development plans, the NRCS projects have much greater flexibility to accomplish restoration because they can recognize fish, wildlife, and recreational purposes for sharing land costs, and they may include "watershed protection benefits" in their cost-benefit analysis. Otherwise, NRCS personnel report a sense of frustration over the barriers against restoration and environmental innovations inherent in the NED analysis.

The manner in which NRCS projects have been authorized and funded has not been free of criticism. Both land management improvements and "land treatment" provided by private landowners, as well as land easements, rights-of-way, and utility relocations, have been credited toward nonfederal contributions to projects. The lack of monitoring of watershed improvements can make this component of federal-local agreements vulnerable to lack of adequate follow-through or implementation. The Government Accounting Office has raised the issue of the accountability of the current system as a result. "Land treatment" represented 55 percent of the total nonfederal share for all the approved projects up to 1979.[84] While there should be incentives for good watershed conservation practices, a simple and unintrusive system of monitoring, evaluation, and follow-up should be in place to protect government investments.

NRCS has had to respond to congressional inquiries on what the actual ecological outputs, or benefits, have been for its watershed and technical assistance programs. Congress also asked for a cost-effectiveness evaluation of program delivery from the standpoint of ecosystem impacts. The agency responded to this request in 1995 with a cost-effectiveness evaluation centered on how staff time was used to implement the program. The ecological outputs focused on watershed and water-quality models, wildlife habitat indexes, etc. While the ecological output measurements were reasonable given the time constraints of the study, the cost-effectiveness measurements were not well developed.[85] The service could consult with the Army Corps on its cost-effectiveness evaluations, which could be integrated early into the NRCS project evaluation phases, as the Corps is proposing to do for new restoration projects it hopes to implement.

The Tennessee Valley Authority: A Different Model for Floodplain Management

By the early 1960s the Tennessee Valley Authority had become more of a stream management agency than a water development agency.[86] Under the influence of James E. Goddard, an engineer now nationally recognized for his important contributions to floodplain management, the TVA started a floodplain land-use planning program as early as 1953. Historians Jamie and Dorothy Moore observed, "Turning conventional wisdom upside down, Goddard said it was possible to have flood damage mitigation without a structural project—but not possible to achieve structural mitigation without attending to non-structural elements."[87] The Community Flood Damage Mitigation Assistance Program was the result of this philosophy, and it was based on working in a partnership with locals to employ a combination of regulatory, nonstructural, and structural solutions to reduce flood damages.[88]

The TVA became the first large water development agency to integrate into its working assumptions on flood-damage-reduction programs the idea that nonstructural measures were going to have to be an important part of helping communities avoid flood damages. The nonstructural measures included a mix of strategies proposed by the experts in floodplain management in the literature of the forties and fifties. They included emergency warning systems, flood proofing, relocation of structures from hazard areas, land-use planning, and regulations to control future development in flood-prone areas. The TVA provided evaluations of alternatives, floodplain maps, and flood profile charts. The agency not only assisted in designing regulations to fit local needs but they also helped in gaining their adoption—at no cost to the community. The strategy of the TVA was to assure that the plans and regulations were the *community's* and not the TVA's. The planning was done with the full participation of citizens and officials through task forces.[89]

By the 1980s the TVA had constructed 26 miles of channelization projects. The TVA record lists ten projects. This mileage is remarkably low given the record of the tens of thousands of miles constructed by the U.S. Army Corps of Engineers and the Soil Conservation Service. Most important, the TVA thoughtfully reevaluated the use of channelization projects, and its literature points out that the effectiveness of channelization depends on continued maintenance of the channel. The agency calls attention to the problem of the ability of the projects to remain effective being dependent on controlling future upstream development, which, over a period of time, can make the design capacity of a project inadequate. In June 1980 these factors and the public sensitivity to the environmental impact of these projects resulted in the TVA adopting a new policy, which discourages the use of stream channelization projects for flood control and encourages the use of nonstructural measures to the fullest extent possible.[90]

In September 1982 the TVA entered into an agreement with the West Eight County Association of Soil Conservation Districts within the Tennessee River Watershed in the state of Tennessee, in which the TVA agreed to provide technical and financial assistance to implement environmentally sensitive *stream renovation* projects. The TVA saw stream renovation as a superior alternative to channelization and defined renovation measures as "the selective removal of silt, sand, and gravel plugs; log jams; snags; drift accumulations; brush; downed trees; and other debris within the channel along certain stream reaches to facilitate stream flow. The work [is] generally confined within the existing top of banks; and no channel straightening, deepening and widening are contemplated for area streams as a part of these activities."[91] The TVA cooperated with the pioneering of environmentally sensitive snagging and clearing projects.

The TVA became known for its leadership among the federal agencies engaged in water resources management protection and development for trying to reconcile conflicting agency missions and promote team planning approaches, and its Flood Protection Branch was a national advocate for multi-objective floodplain management.

The Flood Protection Branch and the stream renovation programs came to an abrupt end in October 1994. Long-term investments in community relationships, technical floodplain planning assistance, and land-use planning to 350 flood-prone localities was ended. The only remaining flood-risk-reduction function is the operation of reservoirs for flood purposes. Staff at the TVA that were removed from their floodplain management jobs had managed to quantify the flood-damage-reduction benefits from their community-based land-use planning programs over a series of decades.[92] Though this evaluation did not save the TVA Flood Protection Branch, it could be applied to further federal program evaluations. The tragic loss of this branch is considered by the floodplain management community to be a squandering of a solid public investment in flood-prone communities.

The Federal Emergency Management Agency

The Federal Emergency Management Agency was created by executive order in 1979 to coordinate federal disaster assistance programs, which were, at the time, spread among different federal agencies and departments. The Federal Insurance Administration and the Federal Disaster Assistance Administration were transferred from Housing and Urban Development to FEMA, giving it an important floodplain management role.[93]

The two FEMA programs of greatest interest to the local floodplain manager are the National Flood Insurance Program started in 1968 and the Hazard Mitigation Assistance Program, which was begun in 1985 and provides for state-administered grant funds for conducting mitigation projects to avoid future flood damages. The National Flood Insurance Program is present in fifty states and nearly twenty thousand communities.[94] The grant portion of the program is initiated through the development of state or community mitigation plans. The goal of the grants program is to avoid future disaster assistance and flood insurance payments.

The National Flood Insurance Program

The National Flood Insurance Program (NFIP) has been described as the centerpiece of federal efforts at flood risk reduction, and the status of national floodplain management cannot be intelligently viewed without understanding its role. In essence, insurance against flood damages is made available to communities that meet some minimum land-use planning regulations. The fact that there are now nearly twenty thousand communities participating in this program attests to its significance. It has been my experience that in some communities the staff of the public works departments know about the National Flood Insurance Program, but the industrious and often overworked citizens who volunteer their time on city planning commissions may never have been exposed to the existence of a federal program that has authority over local land uses. Because the land-use regulations of the NFIP may be the only game in town to manage development in floodplains, and because the program can have beneficial results, stream conservation activists, and environmentally conscious officials, in particular, need to develop a familiarity with this program. They also need to be aware of the very real potential limitations of this program.

The program essentially requires that, in order for a community to be eligible for flood insurance, the local government must adopt an ordinance requiring that buildings be flood proofed before they are permitted to be built in the 100-year floodplain. The "flood-proofing" standards specify that in new constructions and substantial renovations, the bottom of the lowest floor must be elevated to the level of the base flood elevation (or the elevation of the flood having a 1 percent chance of being equaled or exceeded in any given year, also called the one-in-100-year flood). Nonresidential units must be flood proofed with reinforced walls, watertight doors, and other architectural means. Mobile homes must be bolted to permanent foundations. No new construction can occur that would result in the cumulative effect of increasing the flood level by as much as a foot during the base flood. State or local laws and ordinances may have more controls on the allowable increases in flood levels.

The National Flood Insurance Program uses a specific nomenclature to guide land use in floodplains. It divides the one-in-100-year floodplain into two regulatory zones: a "floodway," which includes the stream channel, and a "floodway fringe" outside of the floodway. The floodway is the channel of a stream and its environs and this area must be kept free of most encroachment from fill and development. Farming, pasture, forestry, recreation, and open space are permitted in this zone. The area between the floodway and the boundary of the 100-year flood, or floodway fringe, is the portion of the floodplain that can be obstructed with development, but the development cannot increase the water surface elevation of the 100-year flood more than 1 foot (figure 7.2). Flood maps also delineate the one-in-100-year and one-in-500-year floodplains, and insurance is made available for those areas as well. Under the "emergency" flood insurance program, property owners in eligible communities can obtain a certain amount of insurance coverage on existing structures at federally subsidized rates, even though the studies and rate maps required for the regular program may not be completed for some time. The emergency phase coverage is limited, but after a study has produced maps of the floodway; the elevation of the base flood (BFE), or the one-in-100-year flood; and the one-in-500-year floodplain boundaries, the Flood Insurance Rate Map (FIRM) is released and higher insurance coverage is available under the regular program. The emergency program was scheduled to be phased out in 1991, but it continues with a small number of participants (204 out of 19,000 communities in 1997).

The responsibilities of the Federal Insurance Agency (FIA) in implementing the program include: identifying communities that have flood-hazard areas; providing the identified communities with flood-hazard boundary maps so they can adopt these minimal land-use and design measures to be eligible for the emergency program; publishing flood insurance rate maps so that communities can adopt more stringent land-use measures to become eligible for the regular program; and assuring enforcement of a community's approved land-use measures. The significance of the National Flood Insurance Program is that there are now national minimum standards for the development of floodplains. A 100-year floodplain has widely been accepted and tested by time and politics and the courts as a planning and regulatory standard. Hydrologic data collection and analysis for determining floodplain boundaries have been standardized by FEMA, and related technical assistance programs have been developed.[95] Most agree that the NFIP introduced an important step toward the initiation of floodplain management, but much has been written and said about its limitations and the next steps that should follow in a national program.

As described, the NFIP operates under two components: the emergency phase and the regular phase. By 1990, some 98.4 percent of communities were in the regular phase, and only 1.6 percent were in the emergency phase. Initially, it is possible for a community to become eligible under the emergency program without having to enact or implement land-use regulations. Fulfillment of the land-use measure entrance requirement is achieved by local approval of a resolution as provided in a

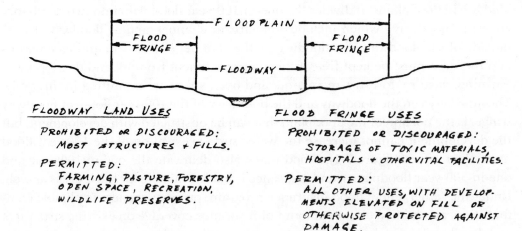

FLOODPLAIN

FLOOD FRINGE — **FLOODWAY** — **FLOOD FRINGE**

FLOODWAY LAND USES

PROHIBITED OR DISCOURAGED:
MOST STRUCTURES & FILLS.

PERMITTED:
FARMING, PASTURE, FORESTRY,
OPEN SPACE, RECREATION,
WILDLIFE PRESERVES.

FLOOD FRINGE USES

PROHIBITED OR DISCOURAGED:
STORAGE OF TOXIC MATERIALS,
HOSPITALS & OTHER VITAL FACILITIES.

PERMITTED:
ALL OTHER USES, WITH DEVELOP-
MENTS ELEVATED ON FILL OR
OTHERWISE PROTECTED AGAINST
DAMAGE.

RELATIONSHIP BETWEEN FLOODPLAIN, FLOODWAY, AND FLOOD FRINGE AREAS.

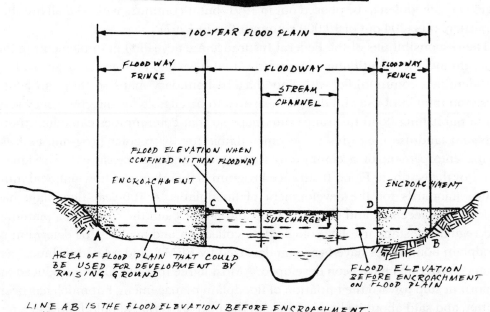

100-YEAR FLOOD PLAIN

FLOODWAY FRINGE — FLOODWAY — FLOODWAY FRINGE

STREAM CHANNEL

FLOOD ELEVATION WHEN CONFINED WITHIN FLOODWAY

ENCROACHMENT

ENCROACHMENT

SURCHARGE*

AREA OF FLOOD PLAIN THAT COULD BE USED FOR DEVELOPMENT BY RAISING GROUND

FLOOD ELEVATION BEFORE ENCROACHMENT ON FLOOD PLAIN

LINE AB IS THE FLOOD ELEVATION BEFORE ENCROACHMENT.
LINE CD IS THE FLOOD ELEVATION AFTER ENCROACHMENT.
★SURCHARGE IS NOT TO EXCEED 1.0 FOOT (FEMA REQUIREMENT) OR LESSER
AMOUNT IF SPECIFIED BY STATE.

FIGURE 7.2. THE NATIONAL FLOOD INSURANCE PROGRAM FLOODWAY AND FLOODWAY FRINGE. *Source:* Federal Emergency Management Agency, Federal Insurance Administration.

model resolution by the FIA. All that is required is for the community to substitute its name, governing body, state, etc., on the form. The major commitment made by the resolution is that the community will enact what amounts to token land-use regulations at a specified future date. The portions of the requirements oriented toward restricting *new* construction are virtually ineffective. Vague language in the regulations and the fact that flood boundary and elevation data can be acquired from any source make it possible for communities to choose information sources suitable to their intentions. Development-oriented communities have been known to select data that will not interfere with floodplain construction to avoid FIA compliance criteria. Some communities use limited data to conscientiously attempt to regulate floodplain development.[96]

Considerable success has been achieved in identifying flood-prone communities and bringing them under the emergency program and then establishing them in the regular program. Achieving status in the regular program for many communities has not occurred without pain or great effort. The challenge for the Federal Insurance Agency is to prepare, review, and approve the flood insurance rate maps to prevent delay of the enforcement of land-use control measures in hazard areas. Another challenge comes from the communities that object to being designated as flood prone and contend that they should not be required to participate in the program. Some communities have appealed the designation of specific streets or areas included in the regulated flood-hazard areas. A major long-term implementation issue has been the adequacy of federal monitoring to insure that land-use control measures are effectively adopted after a community is approved for the program.[97]

Beginning with the Carter administration and continuing with the Reagan administration, the Federal Insurance Agency has taken substantial measures to better enforce the NFIP by bringing legal action or other sanctions against communities that violate the requirements for local regulations.

The FIA has held training sessions for states to assist them in monitoring local compliance with the NFIP. FEMA, with some fanfare, suspended the city of Tarpon Springs, Florida, from the NFIP program in November 1983 because the city allowed the construction of a large number of residences at an elevation below the established flood levels.[98] FEMA's first actions in enforcement were to bring suits against communities that had received insurance claims as a result of flood damages but that the government felt had violated the FIA contract because of negligence. In so-called subrogation claims, the government has brought suit to recover flood-damage claims it has paid because of negligence by locals to adequately maintain flood-control projects. The FEMA suit against Jefferson Parish and Saint Bernards Parish near New Orleans, which attemped to recover $93 million worth of claims, was one of the first such actions of the Reagan administration Justice Department.

In 1986 new NFIP rules revising certain aspects of the flood insurance program went into practice. The most important change was formal establishment of a procedure to put a community on probation when the FIA determines that it is not adequately enforcing its floodplain ordinance. The procedures include providing written notice, issuing press releases, and assessing a $25 premium surcharge on all flood insurance policy holders. If satisfactory changes by locals do not occur, then a community on probation can be suspended from the program. By 1990, 88 NFIP policy holders had received notification of potential violations and inadequacies in compliance with the flood insurance program; 11 communities were put on probation; and 3 communities were suspended from the program. Approximately 175–200 communities a year on the average are suspended temporarily from the flood insurance program because of failures to adopt or enforce adequate floodplain regulations. A majority of the communities then respond to the problems and get back into the program.[99, 100]

The question of how much "teeth" the National Flood Insurance Program has in assuring changes in local land-use practices remains an important one, despite the measures that have been taken to improve local compliance with the program.

Other than suing to recover claims, FEMA essentially has to rely on other federal agencies for sanctions, including the Federal Housing Administration, Veterans Administration, HUD, and others that should refuse to authorize loans, grants, and subsidies in flood-zone areas not covered by NFIP insurance.

At an Army Corps of Engineers conference on nonstructural flood control, an official of the Corps questioned the adequacy of the guidelines for entering into contractual agreements with local governments for the regular program phase. A major limitation of the NFIP is that the regulations apply only to new development. The NFIP does not provide incentives for local planning, relocation, or flood proofing of existing structures. Local regulatory programs generally adopt the minimum standards of NFIP, but those standards do not require modifications to existing uses unless "substantial improvements" are made to the structures. Substantial improvements are defined as those that exceed or equal 50 percent of the market value of the structure before the structure was damaged or before the improvement started. Those provisions have not been vigorously enforced because of local political pressures and the difficulties in determining when the 50 percent threshold has been reached. Estimating the pre-flood value of a structure is often difficult. After a flood, repairs or alterations are often made incrementally without exceeding 50 percent of the structure value in any one year.[101, 102]

A few other limitations or potentially significant drawbacks of the NFIP to be aware of are the following:

- The NFIP's criteria for defining floodways does not take into account an area greater than the estimated 100-year floodplain and, therefore, can contribute to increasing flood damages by encouraging development in flood-hazard areas adjacent to that designation.
- Although the NFIP provides nondiscriminatory minimum standards, the need for more specific standards is apparent to the state and local governments.

Areas subject to high-velocity flows, flash floods, combined flooding and erosion, mud flows, etc., require specific standards related to the local realities.
Likewise, areas with different urban and rural land uses, population densities,
and planning goals require different standards.[103]

- Significant substantive weaknesses in the regulations are that they allow the
  rise of stage in rivers and floodways from new construction, and that while the
  first floor in a structure is supposed to be constructed above the 100-year flood
  stage, no freeboard is designed into the standard to accommodate the impacts
  of future development.[104]

- Each year, FEMA carries out community field monitoring studies (Community
  Assistance and Program Evaluation Reports—CAPES) to determine if communities are properly administering regulations. The studies involve visits to the
  community and do provide some monitoring and deter blatant violations. However, FEMA has done little to monitor damages to structures after flooding, and
  because of inadequate staff and funds, federal and state monitoring has been
  unsatisfactory. Most monitoring occurs at the local level and depends, in the
  main, on complaints from citizens and from random building inspections.[105]

Finally, for those of you who want to direct your community to sound floodplain
regulation and "nonstructural" remedies for flooding problems, you need to be prepared to educate the public on the advantages of combining NFIP regulations with
additional locally relevant regulations. It is best to think of the NFIP regulations as
a minimum effort upon which you can build an adequate floodplain management
program. The NFIP will not help you address the need to prevent culverting or
channelization of streams. The regulations do not necessarily encourage streamside
greenbelts or development setbacks. They do not address the need to preserve or
manage riparian habitat zones.

An unintended impact of the NFIP in some areas is that when communities
become aware of the implications of having developable land designated as an
NFIP flood-hazard area, they have a strong incentive to try to arrange for structural
solutions in order to get their land out of the federal insurance designation. Thus,
an effect of the NFIP is that it can ultimately promote demand for structural projects. Some observers have noted that the narrow width of the floodways on the
Flood Insurance Rate Maps are compatible with the Army Corps of Engineers practice of constructing channelization and levee projects with narrow boundaries. The
demands of the Flood Insurance Program, combined with federal subsidies for
some flood-control works, can, if you are not diligent in heading it off, undermine
nonstructural floodplain management.[106–108] A similar unintended result of the
NFIP is that the program facilitates development in flood fringe areas that later
may be discovered to be more hazardous than anticipated. This is related to the
issue explained in chapter 4 that due to regional land-use changes or adjustments
in flood-frequency estimates made possible by longer periods of flood records, the

elevation of the one-in-100-year flood is raised and the areal extent of the 100-year floodplain increased.

Researchers in the 1970s–80s approached the problem of evaluating the effectiveness of local floodplain management programs by surveying and conducting case studies of communities in the National Flood Insurance Program. Some recent significant studies have been done on the problem of evaluating NFIP effectiveness, and the fact that each study devises a slightly different definition of "effectiveness" attests to the difficulty of trying to measure it. The general impression these studies leave with the interested evaluator is that the National Flood Insurance Program probably does not encourage an increase of development in flood-hazard areas, but that it does not do much to decrease new development in hazard areas, either. The program's major accomplishment may be that it encourages safer structures in hazard areas, alerts potential floodplain occupants to the hazard, and makes the occupant more financially involved in taking on the risks. The NFIP represents a major accomplishment in floodplain management, but it also represents our understanding of floodplains as it existed in the past and needs to advance to respond to the land development pressures of the next century.

Recent Reforms in Flood Insurance and Disaster Assistance Programs

In 1990 a new incentives component was added to the National Flood Insurance Program, called the Community Rating System (CRS). The CRS is voluntary but provides a means for a community to reduce its flood insurance premiums by 5 percent to 45 percent by taking actions that go beyond meeting the minimum flood insurance standards. The rating system assigns credits to a community's efforts to provide public information activities on flood hazards, floodplain mapping and regulatory activities, flood-damage-reduction measures, and flood preparedness activities. These credits can then translate into insurance rate reductions. It has been suggested that a similar rating system be used as part of a federal-nonfederal cost-sharing incentives system in which high-rating communities would receive more federal assistance.

The great Mississippi River flood helped advance the concept of acquisition and relocation of properties in floodplains. President Clinton signed into law the Hazard Mitigation and Relocation Assistance Act of 1993. That act changed the federal-nonfederal cost sharing to 75–25 percent for cooperative flood-damage-avoidance, hazard mitigation grants and requires FEMA to spend 15 percent of disaster relief funds on mitigation to avoid future damages. FEMA directed an unprecedented $45 million for acquisition and relocation for Mississippi River flood recovery through the Section 404 Stanford Act Hazard Mitigation Grant Program. As of April 1994 the federal government had approved applications from sixty-one communities for acquisition or relocation of over four thousand buildings. As many as six thousand buildings are likely to be acquired or relocated.[109]

Evaluation of the national response to the 1993 Mississippi River floods raised a number of issues that were in part responded to in the National Flood Insurance Reform Act of 1994 (also known as the Reigle Community Development and Regulatory Improvement Act or P.L. 103–325). The White House report on the Mississippi River flood estimated that only 10–20 percent of insurable buildings in the flood-hazard areas were covered by the NFIP. The report estimated that the NFIP coverage of insurable buildings on a national scale was only in the range of 20–30 percent. The report also noted the continuing difficulty of enforcing the NFIP provision that substantially damaged and substantially improved buildings in flood-hazard areas meet the NFIP regulations. The ambiguities of the definition of substantial damages interfered with implementation of this component of the program. Lender compliance in requiring flood insurance at the time of building purchase and long-term maintenance of the policies were found inadequate. Adequate flood-hazard maps were also found to be a problem.[110]

The reform act of 1994 helps address these issues and should provide more incentives and sanctions to improve community compliance with the NFIP. It provides a better definition for "repetitive loss" structures. It expands insurance coverage to include the costs of compliance with local and state land-use controls, which can include flood proofing, elevation, and relocation; provides more federal assistance to locals for floodplain mapping; and increases maximum coverage amounts. It greatly bolsters enforcement by prohibiting disaster relief payments to any property that previously accepted disaster assistance on the condition of purchasing insurance but failed to do so. It prohibits waiver of the requirement to purchase flood insurance as a condition of receiving federal disaster assistance. It requires lenders to escrow flood insurance premiums and authorizes them to require purchase of flood insurance or to purchase and charge the borrower for the insurance.[111]

Communities interested in buying-out and removing or relocating properties in flood-hazard areas typically put together a fund-raising package of different federal, state, and local programs. The reform act has created a new source of funds from the insurance premiums paid into the NFIP to use for the acquisition of insured properties. In addition to the Section 404 Hazard Mitigation Grants, communities may receive federal assistance from other programs, including Department of Housing and Urban Development community development block grants, and Economic Development Administration grants. State and federal wetland restoration programs are often used to supplement those sources, particularly if one of the goals is to restore a more natural floodplain and associated wetlands.

The relatively new Hazard Mitigation Grants Program has a number of bugs to be worked out. The hazard mitigation plans that direct the priorities for the grants need to be better coordinated with federal and state disaster assistance plans and funds, which are quickly dispersed in flood emergencies. The hazard mitigation plans frequently do not have enough local participation, and the community participation in their development is not representative enough. There are reports of federal disaster assistance funds undercutting well-construed local hazard mitigation plans that focus on removing the causes of future damages such as culverts, undersized bridges, and levees too close to rivers instead of rebuilding them with disaster funds.

Technical Issues of Floodplain Management

The Chances of a Large Flood

In order to understand the probability of overbank floodplain flows and what damages may result from them, basic data on stream flows must be gathered and maps of the areal extent of potential flood flows must be made. Floodplain management requires information on the natural flows of streams, the probable increase of flows due to changes in land use, the boundaries of floodplains, the velocity and timing of flood flows, and the chance of flash floods, among other basic information. The amount of stream-flow data, weather data, and procedures used to estimate flood frequencies and make floodplain maps determines the effectiveness and the options a planner will have in designing floodplain management plans. To develop an intelligent understanding of the technical issues involved in making flood management plans, it is necessary to begin this section by briefly describing the kinds of information used by engineers and planners.

The U.S. Geological Survey, (USGS), through its Water Resources Division, investigates the occurrence, quantity, quality, distribution, and movement of both surface and groundwater throughout the United States, Puerto Rico, and several trust territories. The USGS is the principal federal water data agency and collects and disseminates about 70 percent of the water data currently used by all levels of government and private entities. A large-scale computerized system (referred to as WATSTORE) was established in 1971 to update the Survey's water data processing procedures. Files are maintained for the storage of surface-water, quality-of-water, and groundwater data measured on a daily or continuous basis and on annual peak values for stream-flow stations. The Geological Survey maintains continuous-record stream discharge gauges that record the water-surface elevations of streams.[112] The flow of a stream is expressed in cubic feet per second (or cubic meters per second in metric measurement). This measurement of the flow or rate of discharge is calculated as the cross-sectional area of the flowing water multiplied by the velocity. The next chapter describes how citizen volunteers can collect this discharge data for their own streams. Different stream discharge measurements are related to the water-surface elevations or stage (height) of the flows. Rating curves are drawn on graph paper to establish the relationship between stage heights and discharges from data collected at each gauging station where flow measurements are taken. These gauging stations then provide the raw data on which planners are ultimately dependent for developing national flood frequency information and floodplain mapping.

The frequency with which different size floods occur is central to the problem of flood management and determining the level of risk a community should plan for. However, "flood frequency" is a widely misunderstood term. Flood frequency refers to the *probability* of a flood of a certain magnitude occurring; it does not refer to a *prediction* of that flood occurring during a certain period of time. As described in chapter 4, floods, or flows that go over a stream's bank, are relatively common; most rivers, on the average, flood their banks approximately two times in three years (see figure 4.1). The occurrence of floods is studied as a probability problem, the underlying premise being that the floods occurring on a river during a specified period constitute a sample of the floods that will occur in that river's future. We assume that there is a *probability* that a flood of equal magnitude to the largest flood recorded in a forty-year period will occur during the next forty years.

One of the most practical methods for estimating flood frequency is the construction of a flood-frequency curve, which relates the sizes of floods to the frequency of their occurrence. Large, catastrophic floods generally have a low frequency, while smaller floods, such as a bankfull flow, occur much more often. To construct a flood-frequency curve, the highest discharge recorded at a stream gauge station for each year of record is tabulated and then each annual peak is assigned a recurrence interval.

The recurrence interval is simply the mean (statistical average) waiting time between occurrences of a given-sized flood. It can be used to determine the probability of an event, but it cannot be used for prediction. Prediction includes identifying the time and place of occurrence. Since stream flow cannot be predicted, flood frequency is expressed as the probability of a given discharge being equaled or exceeded in any one year. The reciprocal of the probability is the recurrence interval expressed in years. If the recurrence interval of a given-sized flood is one in fifty years, the probability of occurrence is .02 in any given year. Engineers often call this the fifty-year flood, which the unaware public confuses with a prediction that that size flood will cyclically occur once every fifty years. Since river flow is not cyclical, the fifty-year flood can occur in any year (refer to table 7.1).[113]

A wonderful anecdote came out of the public meetings held by the White House task force after the Mississippi River flood of 1993, which can be helpful to the layperson trying to understand the use of probability in describing flood frequency:

> At one of the public meetings attended by the Review Committee, a young Missouri farmer provided a correct explanation of the possibility of experiencing a 100-year flood. He described a bag of 100 marbles, with 99 clear marbles and one black marble. Every time you pull one of those marbles out, and it's black, you've got a 100-year flood. After each draw, you put all 100 marbles back in the bag and shake it up. It's possible that you could pull the black one out two or even three times in a row. To represent the uncertainty of estimating a 100-year flood, it's also possible that the bag could hold two or three black marbles.[114]

It is useful to know various aspects about a flood, such as the recurrence interval of a flood of a certain magnitude, just described; the highest instantaneous flood peak; the largest flood volume; and the longest period of flow above a certain level.

The primary methods for computing peak flows are contained in a Water Resources Council bulletin from 1981, *Guidelines for Determining Flood Flow Frequency*, Bulletin 17B. Four categories of flood-peak data recognized by that

Table 7.1. The Probability a Flood of a Certain Magnitude Will Occur

Percent chance that a certain magnitude will occur in:	Flood Magnitude					
	5-yr	10-yr	50-yr	100-yr	500-yr
One year	20%	10%	2%	1%	.29%
Five years	63%	41%	10%	5%	2%
Ten years	87%	65%	18%	10%	2%
Fifty years	99.8%	99.5%	64%	40%	9.5%
One hundred years	99.9%	99.9%	87%	63%	18%
Five hundred years	99.9%	99.9%	99.9%	99.6%	63%

Adapted from: E. M. Wilson, Engineering Hydrology (New York, Macmillan Press, 1977).

document are: systematic stream-flow records, historic data on floods, comparisons of streams with similar watersheds, and estimation of runoff from precipitation.

The system widely used to develop flood-frequency data from stream-flow and historic data is the "log-Pearson Type III." Stream-flow data from similar watersheds can be used to extrapolate values of stream flows for ungauged streams. The differences in the watersheds being compared have to be accounted for. Generally, a multivariate regression analysis is used to determine the relative importance of the different watershed variables. The estimation of runoff from precipitation uses assumptions about the hydrologic characteristics of a watershed to estimate the runoff from a real or theoretical storm. These characteristics and their interrelationships are usually mathematically modeled in a computer program. The most widely used models for a rainfall-runoff analysis of flood peaks are the U.S. Army Corps of Engineers' HEC-1 model, the Soil Conservation Service's TR-20, and for small urban watersheds the NRCS's TR-55. The U.S. Geological Survey uses the Distributive Routing Rainfall Runoff Model, or DR3M, and the Precipitation Runoff Modeling System, or PRMS.[115] The Environmental Protection Agency has developed a storm-water management model (SWMM) for urban areas where water quality is a concern.[116] The Army Corps of Engineers' HEC-1 model and HEC-2 model, which determines water-surface elevations for floods, are the most widely used because they represent a standardized methodology in which the computer programs are widely available and easy to use.

Floodplain Mapping

The planning tool that anyone who wants to regulate land to reduce hazards must have is a floodplain map. The process of floodplain mapping first involves estimating the recurrence interval of peak flows in which a planner might use a variety of methods to cross-check and adjust the results. Stream-flow data and rainfall data are the very basic information upon which all other information development depends. The amount and quality of this basic data determine the accuracy of all estimates of the frequency of floods and the areal extent of flooding.

In the absence of good stream-flow data, there are well-standardized methods for estimating the flood-frequency curve from other data. The other data might include rainfall records within the watershed or rainfall and stream-flow records in a neighboring watershed. Procedures for constructing and using hydrographs (graphs of stream discharge as a function of time) and the conversion of rainfall records to stream-flow data are followed with some variation by all of the agencies involved in flood-control work. (Hydrographs are explained in chapters 4 and 8.) The conversion of rainfall records to stream-flow data requires some extrapolation of the data and several assumptions, all of which contribute to uncertainty in the final flow-frequency estimations. Rainfall is usually measured only at one or two points in a watershed, and the actual average rainfall over the watershed must be inferred from those point measurements. In addition, only a fraction of the rainfall in the watershed becomes stream flow and what does reach the stream is delayed, the amount of delay depending on whether the water reaches the stream by surface or subsurface flows. The amount and timing of runoff is also affected by land use. Ideally, hydrologists would like to have a record of flood flows on a stream acquired from gauging stations extending back over forty or fifty years. Flood-frequency charts can then be made, but even those charts are limited in their ability to predict the peak flows associated with large recurrence intervals.

The next step of floodplain mapping is to construct a rating curve that estimates the stage of water elevation for different discharges (see figures 7.3 and 7.4). Combining the information on flood frequency and stage-discharge relationships provides the elevations of the 10-, 50-, and 100-year-recurrence-interval flows. The elevations of those flows are then superimposed on a topographic map to construct a map that estimates the areal extent of flooding that may be caused by different frequency flows. If several gauging stations exist along a river, a water-surface profile or gradient can be constructed for any flood by constructing a line representing the elevation decrease for the same recurrence-interval flow. The area of valley inundated can be projected from those profiles for different sections of stream. The most commonly used method of floodplain mapping is to use the HEC-2 model to determine the water-surface profile. The areal limits of flooding are then determined with the use of a detailed topographic map. These flood-hazard maps are generally time

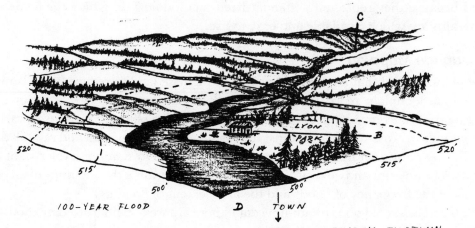

CROSS-SECTION OF FREMONT CREEK AT PARK, ILLUSTRATING FLOODPLAIN

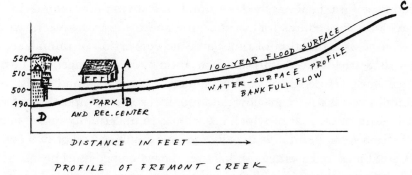

PROFILE OF FREMONT CREEK
AT BANKFULL FLOW, AND PROFILE AT FLOOD STAGES

FIGURE 7.3. FLOODPLAIN AND FLOOD PROFILE.

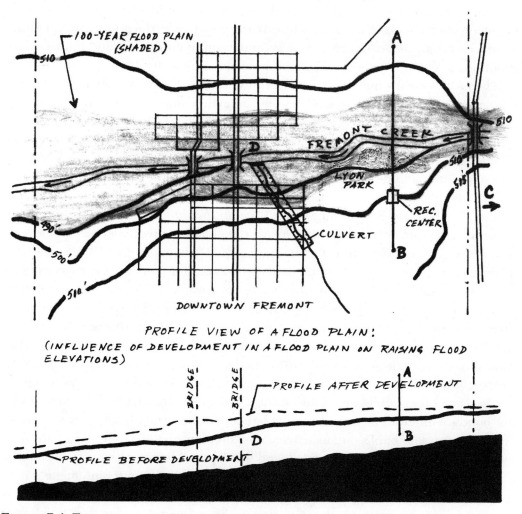

PLAN VIEW OF A FLOOD PLAIN:

—100-YEAR FLOOD PLAIN
(SHADED)

510

A

FREMONT CREEK

510

D

LYON
PARK

510

515

C

CULVERT

REC.
CENTER

B

490'

500'

510'

DOWNTOWN FREMONT

PROFILE VIEW OF A FLOOD PLAIN:
(INFLUENCE OF DEVELOPMENT IN A FLOOD PLAIN ON RAISING FLOOD
ELEVATIONS)

BRIDGE

BRIDGE

A

—PROFILE AFTER DEVELOPMENT

D

B

—PROFILE BEFORE DEVELOPMENT

FIGURE 7.4. FLOODPLAIN AND WATER-SURFACE PROFILE IN A DEVELOPED AREA.

consuming and expensive to produce, and the demand for them exceeds the ability of government agencies to produce them. However, they provide the regulatory basis for local floodplain zoning and for the federal flood insurance program. A 100-year floodplain and the one-in-100-year floodwater surface profile have been drawn in figures 7.3 and 7.4 for the hypothetical Fremont Creek watershed that appeared in chapter 1 (figure 1.1).

Priorities for Data Used in Developing Plans

Most local public works engineers define their responsibility as designing storm-water transport and storage facilities. They emphasize the size of culverts to carry storm water, usually using the rational method (discussed in chapter 4). They normally do not approach the problems of collecting and analyzing hydrologic information to manage the effects of land-use changes on the watershed. As a result, planners often cannot acquire the information they need from public works departments or project development agencies to develop planning or land management solutions to the problems caused by urbanization of a watershed.

The most typical situation is that the raw data available to the planner or project design engineer may be some basic rainfall data; there may be some stream gauging records on larger stream channels. It is common, therefore, to need to synthesize data from the size of rainstorms expected, the characteristics of the watershed, and the dimensions of the stream channel, as well as historic flood data from nearby gauging stations to develop data needed to understand the magnitude, frequency, and timing of peak flows.

Luna Leopold and Tom Dunne wrote *Water in Environmental Planning* in 1978 to respond to this problem, and they provide the planner with guidelines on the kind of information needed for watershed planning.[117] Leopold and Dunne help the planner learn to use a variety of methods for calculating peak discharges, timing of flows, and frequency of floods in order to derive reasonable estimates on the hydrologic nature of the watershed. For predicting the occurrence of floods, the damages they may produce, and how to manage the water, Leopold and Dunne delineate several features of floods that may need to be assessed by engineers and planners. The volume of storm runoff needs to be estimated for different storms in order to design storage for flood flows. It is necessary to estimate peak flood discharges to design bridges and other public works and storage measures. The elevation of flood stages for floods of different recurrences must be estimated in order to determine whether and where stream banks or constructed embankments will be overtopped, the area of valley bottom that will be flooded, and the depth of flooding that can occur. It is also useful to know velocities of flow across the valley bottom to anticipate potential damage to structures and channels. Time distribution of a storm hydrograph is necessary for determining the duration of inundation to plan for floodwater storage. Storm hydrographs can be added together to determine the effects of various tributary inputs of flow and channel characteristics on flood discharge at a downstream point. The rate of a rising flood flow also needs to be known to determine the feasibility of the use of flood-warning and evacuation systems.[118]

Acquiring and using this information necessary to a watershed management and planning approach are hampered by the project construction emphasis given to flood management by the federal government. Experts still criticize the project-building agencies for proceeding without adequate data for designing projects. The real commitment of those agencies can be to the collection of economic project-justification data at the expense of adequate environmental data. Their priorities are to develop flood-stage damage curves to justify the need for a flood-control project and then to calculate the necessary hydraulics data for designing conduits with the proper dimensions and features to convey water at certain volumes and velocities through a constructed system.[119–121] More time and resources should go into determining possible adjustments to the floodplain such as the redesign of structures. The constriction or backup of flows caused by poorly designed bridges may be the actual major cause of flood damages. Removing or relocating a few structures may solve the greatest portion of the problem. Floodplain planning, zoning, and wetland restoration may solve other problems. Local governing bodies need to request that their county, city, or town staffs collect and evaluate information on these other possible measures. The National Flood Insurance Program has this broader planning approach as its ultimate objective, and it should be the common objective for all agencies with a flood-damage-reduction mission.

Accommodating Changes in Land Use

Engineering staffs may not regularly update their data on the floodplain and the frequency of flooding used in the design of their storm-water and flood management systems. Most notably, the land-use changes associated with urbanization may be lacking. Land-use changes can quickly overwhelm the original planning assumptions that the design of projects is based on. Urbanization may increase flood peaks and volumes because of decreasing permeability within the watershed. More water runs off paved areas and runs off faster. If increasing urbanization in a watershed undergoing urban growth is not taken into account, large floods will overwhelm the storm-water and flood management systems with increasing frequency. A textbook for flood-basin planning, USGS circular 554, *Hydrology for Urban Planning*, described in chapter 4, calculates the effects of urbanization on flood flows.[122] One of the effects is the reduction in lag time between the start of a storm and the stream flood crest. The increased storm runoff caused by impervious surfaces is also calculated. Unless the models used to design and operate the flood management facilities use information derived from local planning departments on actual and projected growth, the ability to plan for water management breaks down.

An example of this problem can be seen in the flood damages on the Russian River from the February 1986 storms in Northern California which have been attributed to the planning error of failing to notice the increased urbanization in the Laguna Basin (which includes the cities of Santa Rosa, Rohnert Park, Windsor, and Sebastopol). Data show that even though the 1986 flood levels on the upper Russian River were less than those measured in a 1964 flood, the downstream stage rose at an unanticipated speed in the 1986 storm as compared to the 1964 flood crest. The rainfall levels in 1986 also were less in the Laguna Basin than in the 1964 storm. A local geologist determined that the cause of the unanticipated timing of the flood crest was due to the contribution of urbanization in part of the Russian River Basin.[123] What this case illustrates is not that adequate models are not necessarily available for good water basin planning, but that adequate data do not find their way into the models. The Federal Emergency Management Agency does not ask for analysis of projected future development. It requires only a "current condition" analysis. However, at little extra cost, a local agency can have both analyses done at the same time. It has to be aware of the need and be willing to pay for it, however.[124]

Adequacy of Stream-Flow, Watershed, and Floodplain Data for Planning

Suppose that a flood-control channel project is designed to pass a flood peak of 5,000 cubic feet per second (cfs) and provide protection for a 50-year-recurrence-interval event. Three years after the flood works are completed, a flood flow of 7,000 cfs occurs, and flood damage results. The analyst can ask, "Was the hydrologic basis in error, or did this happen to be the one-in-100-year flood?" There is no definitive way to answer that question. A not atypical situation is the story of the American River flood-control plans and efforts in California. The hydrologic record for that watershed is relatively short (about ninety years), so that significant flood events can cause major readjustments in estimates of flow frequency. In 1956 the Folsom Reservoir was built on the American River, and the original design authorization for the reservoir was based on 1949 calculations, which showed the reservoir providing protection for the 500-year-recurrence-interval flood. A flood event in 1955 altered the statistical predictions derived from the flood records, and as development increased in the downstream Sacramento metropolitan area, the engineers estimated by 1961 that the Folsom Reservoir and levee system provided protection from the 120-year flood. In 1986 a storm calculated as the 70-year-recurrence-interval flood forced the evacuation of more than seven hundred people in the area, and flows exceeded the design capacity of the channel by about 17 percent. As a result of that flood, the Army Corps replotted the flood-frequency curve for the American River and now estimates that the Folsom Reservoir and levee system provide protection against the 63-year flood occurrence. Thirty-seven years after believing it had protection from a rare, one-in-500-year storm flow, the Sacramento metropolitan area is back to the drawing boards trying to meet NFIP requirements to provide protection for the one-in-100-year flood. Such a situation does not mean that the flood-control engineers were incompetent; to the contrary, they made a reasonable statistical estimate from the available information. As time brought more information on the kinds of flows we could experience on the American River, the hydrologists drew new flood-frequency graphs to include the new data. New development in the floodplain also contributed to some of the necessity to adjust the flood protection figures.[125]

The American River case is a particularly complicated one, for it also has involved the controversies of what the best method is for estimating flood peaks, what the best operations plan should be for the regulation of flows by the existing Folsom Reservoir, and what assumptions should be used in determining the amount of flood regulation provided by upstream hydropower reservoirs.[126]

The Army Corps method of estimating peak flows, as compared with the widely used FEMA methodology, often results in more conservative (higher) estimates of flood risk on such rivers as the American River (expected probability vs. computed probability analysis). While the Army Corps system used to develop the statistical estimates of probability, which often results in higher discharge values for the one-in-100-year flood, can provide a community with greater assurances for protection, that system has been criticized for being overly cautious and costly. Inflated values for one-in-100-year floods can help an agency better attain an estimate of large damages and thereby increase its chances of attaining a good cost-benefit ratio. Such values may mislead communities about risks and place unnecessary costs on communities trying to comply with the National Flood Insurance Program.

The use of different storage and operating assumptions for existing reservoirs can also significantly reduce the probability of flood damages for an area such as Sacramento. However, the options of reoperating and redesigning existing reservoirs are not usually found in the alternatives analyses in government flood-damage-reduction studies because the agencies do not want to contend with the institutional issues involved. Not only are there difficulties in estimating the natural or unregulated flood frequencies for a changing watershed through time, we must also add in the complications, opportunities, and uncertainties involved with the operations of river systems regulated by reservoirs and the potential human or government error in those operations.

The point that must be emphasized is that uncertainty in flood-frequency estimates is a given. We have not been collecting stream-flow data for long, and, in many instances, we are extrapolating data from one watershed to make estimates on another. Conditions change in a watershed over time. The tragedy of flood-control project planning is that the engineering design documents state with no equivocation that project "A" *will* provide protection from "X" storm flows. Based on that, the cost-benefit analysis is set in a dollar amount to create a mathematical ratio. Those numbers then determine whether a project will be justified. That planning approach does not accommodate the realities of the reliability of our data and frequently does not accommodate the complexities and options of operating our water systems.

Some flood-control planners feel that the project evaluation and planning system must be kept simple because public officials are not really capable of understanding or willing to accept the complexities of probability analysis. However, as time passes, a wider public is going to be exposed to more of these American River stories. The public has not been prepared with an understanding of the difficulties of flood probability analysis; they know only that they are given absolute figures by flood officials. Given this situation, it would make for a more honest and credible planning approach to express our information more in terms of ranges. For example: "This project is designed to provide protection from a given discharge that is likely to range between a one-in-50 to a one-in-100-year frequency. (Another way to express this is that the one-in-100-year flood may range between these two different values for discharge.) However, likely future development could mean that this storm discharge may occur on the average of once in every 25 or 50 years." Costs and benefits can also be expressed in a range of values—and include a more realistic diversity of factors, as discussed previously. This approach would radically alter the planning and project evaluation process, but it has the marked advantage of being more realistic and more honest given our knowledge of how time is likely to change the variables. Our planning practices have not yet caught up to our knowledge of the complexities, but the current efforts of the Army Corps to introduce "risk and un-certainty" into their project planning evaluations is a welcome advance in that direction.

As it is now set up, the Army Corps risk analysis for flood-control projects will evaluate the data used to develop the flood-frequency estimates, conveyance, roughness, cross-sectional channel geometry, and stage-damage relationships. The performance of a levee project, for example, will be described as expected to con-tain a flood of a certain recurrence interval such as the one-in-100 year discharge with a certain reliability, such as a 90 percent reliability. Some structural and insti-tutional variables are used to help determine the levels of confidence or uncertainty associated with the flood-damage-avoidance estimates. The Federal Emergency Management Agency is involved in setting confidence level requirements under this system for establishing its flood insurance coverage. According to current policy, all projects are now subject to this analysis.

The consequences of this new analysis are that the traditional term "level of pro-tection" will no longer be used to describe project performance and a routine adding of feet to levee or channel heights above the design capacity, called free-board, will be replaced with a probabilistic description of levee or channel perfor-mance. The concept is that a balancing of economics and reliability will be made so that we are not mindlessly designing very conservative (meaning large) dams, levees, and channel projects compared to what is adequate for the community being protected. Some fear that this approach will result in the federal government as-sisting local entities to build inexpensive levees, which will be more prone to being broken (breached) or overtopped. In contrast, the restoration community has found the current conservative standard requiring the overdesign of projects to be one of the most significant barriers to the Army Corps adopting more environmentally sen-sitive and affordable floodplain and channel restoration projects. It is the hope of restoration professionals that risk and uncertainty will provide badly needed design flexibility rather than result ironically in the reinstitutionalization of rigid design standards by requiring very high reliability ratings for projects.

An important action we could take to reduce some of the uncertainty of our data on flood flows and flood frequency is to collect more stream-flow data. This is a case in which more is better. The accuracy of the base hydrologic data is directly depen-dent on the period of data sampling, and it is also dependent on the relevance of those data to the watershed being studied—and so numbers of data stations are im-portant as well.

The number of gauging stations and the number of stations with a lengthy his-torical record have a direct bearing on our ability to calculate meaningful flood-frequency estimates. What is the national record, then, for collecting stream-flow data from gauging stations?

There was a clear trend toward increasing both the number of data-gathering sta-tions and the number of stations with a long history of record keeping from 1900 until 1980, after which total numbers of gauges began to decrease. The number of stations with a long history of record keeping began to decrease in the mid-1980s, and there has been a definite trend in recent years for reducing the USGS budget for data collection. There was a net loss of 133 stream-gauging stations between 1983 and 1985, and the level of funding for the federal-state cooperative continuous stream-gauge data collection program fell to 1950 levels.[127, 128] A congressional effort in 1995 to abolish the U.S. Geological Survey was fortunately thwarted but not without significant damage to its water resources budgets.

An important factor that continues to influence the adequacy of our stream-flow database is how many stations remain that actually measure natural hydrologic conditions as opposed to flows controlled by human beings. Water *management* stations provide information only on upstream release from reservoirs. *Hydrologic* stations measuring natural phenomena protected by wilderness areas or national parks or in small undeveloped watersheds are becoming the most important providers of hydrologic data, according to Phil Cohen, chief hydrologist of the U.S. Geological Survey. The percentage of gauging stations that are hydrologic as opposed to water management is not known at this time.

A Survey of Floodplain Restoration and Management Measures

Stream Management Replaces Snagging and Clearing Projects

A common activity of local flood-control districts that consumes large portions of special assessment district budgets is the removal of vegetation from both natural stream channels and channels engineered as flood-control projects. Commonly referred to by public works engineers as "snagging and clearing," these projects remove or trim back live trees and brush and dead trees and branches located in and along stream channels and floodplains. The objective of these projects, whether located along a flood-control project or along a natural stream channel, is to remove dead snags and live vegetation to allow more high-water flows to pass through the stream channel before the channel overflows and thereby to reduce the width of floodplain flows. In many areas of the country the methods of riparian vegetation management are being improved so that flood-damage-reduction goals are being attained and the riparian and floodplain corridor is being managed in a manner that is more compatible with the environmental and aesthetic values the stream provides to the community. In some cases, old project maintenance assumptions are being changed to give environmental and aesthetic considerations more weight over reducing the stages of flood elevations. It should be noted that whether significant flood-damage-reduction benefits are attained by clearing and snagging is being reconsidered by flood-control engineers in the federal water agencies.

Local public works departments and flood-control districts have the most flexibility to balance environmental and flood-damage-reduction objectives along waterways that are not modified by federally funded projects. Residents located along such waterways should not hesitate to request local public works officials to optimize the balance between flood-control objectives and aesthetic and environmental values for snagging and clearing projects. Innovative local and natural stream-channel management programs include the Marin County, California, flood district's stream management program, in which a trained stream biologist directs a local conservation corps crew to carry out environmentally sensitive vegetation removal along the waterways to balance bank erosion prevention and avoidance of unnecessary floodwater backups or overflows. Planning the projects ahead of time with local residents is part of that program.[129] Other communities have local ordinances that guide local districts and resident riparian maintenance, management, and clearing activities.[130]

Those residents located along federally assisted flood-control project channels will find that a local project sponsor such as a flood-control district will have signed a channel maintenance agreement with the participating federal agency as a condition of federal involvement in the channel project. In that situation, you can obtain a copy of the maintenance manual to determine what agreements were made. Once you see what agreements were made, you may want to ask for a renegotiation of maintenance methods and activities between the sponsoring federal and local agencies.

Federal and local agency snagging and clearing projects historically have resulted in the destruction of a stream environment. Trees are removed from banks, and wood debris is hauled out of the stream channels in order to remove blockages to flow and increase the capacity of a channel to carry flood flows. Conventional clearing and snagging normally consists of removing all obstructions from a channel as well as a significant swath of vegetation at a specified width along its banks, using bulldozers, drag lines, and other heavy equipment. Starting in the 1970s, as a result of pressure from environmental organizations and concerned citizens, some clearing and snagging projects began using a new stream-channel management model for an environmentally sensitive way to reduce damage from frequent overbank flows.

Some removal of debris and vegetation can reduce stream-channel "roughness" or resistance to flood flows significantly, but that condition must be maintained consistently over time to provide benefits. The typical impacts of conventional snagging and clearing can be increased channel erosion and widening of channels; removal of shade from the channel and increased water temperatures; loss of a riparian buffer to trap nutrients and sediment; and reduction of food sources and habitat for fish. Loss of fish habitat can be a significant environmental consequence; one study showed 50 percent fewer catchable-sized fish in snagless sections of the Missouri River.[131]

When natural stream channels are made into flood-control channels, they have been designed for the primary engineering purpose of conveying water efficiently. They are also treated largely as an engineering work and undergo "maintenance." The prevailing attitude for both the project design and the maintenance is that engineering objectives necessarily conflict with any biological values. Because of that attitude, the flood-control channels are maintained according to a well-charted routine in which they are regularly mowed and burned or sprayed to prevent growth of vegetation.

A well-designed flood-control project will not set up this inevitable conflict between engineering and environmental objectives. Because of historical practices in channel engineering, however, in most cases we are presented with conventionally designed flood-control channels in which vegetation is assumed to be a detriment to maintaining the flood capacity of the channel. Nevertheless, there are options for addressing maintenance, despite original design assumptions.

Let us assume you have a dirt-lined trapezoidal channel that has some vegetation growth and consequently some wildlife colonize between routine maintenance activities. Flood-control projects are usually designed with some freeboard, or extra capacity, as a safety factor. The routine maintenance activities of wholesale vegetation removal frequently occur every three, five, or more years, based on an assumption that you can "let the channel go" for a certain period of time without seriously impacting its capacity. Instead of wiping out the channel environment every few years, however, doesn't it make more sense to establish how much growth the channel can actually accommodate annually and maintain it at that level? You may be able to work with state or local flood-control engineers to determine what percentage of the channel can be encroached with vegetation and help them maintain it at that level. Perhaps 20 percent of the channel can have some vegetative growth. It is more environmentally responsible, and more aesthetic for the adjacent community, than a scorched-earth policy of no vegetation. Federal projects are designed conservatively, so they often have capacities that exceed the design of the original flood-control objective in addition to the freeboard. A reasonable balancing objective would be to allow for reduction of half the free board space so that environmental objectives can also be accounted for.

The districts involved in maintenance can lower the maintenance costs as well as develop greater community support for the maintenance program if they shift from a routine maintenance program, to a prescribed maintenance program. In a prescribed program maintenance takes place only when the vegetation reaches a threshold where it actually creates a problem or until an injury level has been reached. The term injury level originates from the field of integrated pest management. It refers to taking action—for example, against insects, weeds, or rodents—when the plants or animals reach the point that they are measurably harming the system. Until that point is reached, it is wasteful—i.e., uneconomical—to act.

Prescribed management requires determining how much sediment or vegetative buildup is allowable. A monitoring system is set up to determine when actions are needed, and actions are taken in a way that is sensitive to ecological and engineering concerns. Different reaches of streams with changing conditions should be assigned different flood-control or environmental enhancement objectives based on the flood risks and the value of environmental opportunities.[132]

We now know that it is possible to design a clearing and snagging project that meets channel capacity objectives and creates more acceptable levels of disturbance to environmental resources. Such contemporary projects use an interdisciplinary team to survey the stream and design a plan that is compatible with fish and wildlife needs, good forestry management practices, and hydraulic needs. Examples of model projects include the St. Joseph and Tiffin rivers in Ohio; the Chico Creek project in North Carolina, where a lawsuit made way for that alternative over a channelization project; and the Wolf Creek project in Fayette County, Tennessee.[133] As a result of those experiences, the American Fisheries Society and Wildlife Society published a very useful guide with photographs to guide the planning of such projects. The guide provides diagrammatic and pictorial guidelines for when instream snags and debris should be left, rearranged, or removed.[134]

The guide recommends that instead of removing a swath of trees and vegetation from a stream bank, individual trees can be selected to remain to attain a predetermined density. Hardwood canopy trees are usually selected to remain over dense-growth trees such as willow and cottonwoods. Tree trunks have been observed to create less flow resistance than dense undergrowth, so the undergrowth and the lower tree branches are pruned. Further reduction in flow resistance can be obtained by pruning limbs that lie below a certain flood stage. A row of trees aligned with the flow of current offers much less resistance than perpendicular blocks of vegetation (refer to figure 7.5). Biologists are suggesting that it may be better from an environmental perspective to clear trees in the floodplains to reduce channel resistance, than to remove trees near a bankfull channel. Removal of trees near a channel has more potential for destabilizing that channel and impacting fisheries and other instream life.

Most clearing and snagging specifications call for removing leaning trees. This is probably too simplistic a criterion, because many healthy trees lean over to catch sunlight and remain that way for many years. Some suggest removal of dead or dying trees, but some of those are critical den and nesting sites. Determination of tree removal then should consider a variety of factors, including that tree's overall condition, its potential for falling, the amount of undercutting it may be causing, the potential for wind throw, etc. Some leaning trees may be topped instead of removed. Tree removal should be managed so that stumps are left to help retard bank erosion.

Some innovative clearing and snagging guidelines drawn up for the Chico Creek project included:

- Do not remove embedded logs or snags, logs parallel to the channel, or logs that do not significantly impede the flow.
- Leave small debris accumulations unless trapped on logs being removed.
- Restrict machinery and vehicle access to selected locations and along lines perpendicular to the stream.
- Cut logs or trees into small lengths by hand so that they can be dragged out by cables rather than using tractor equipment in the floodway.
- Mark all the materials to be removed before the job begins.

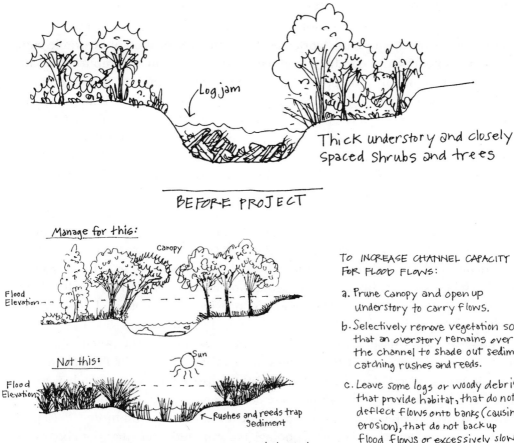

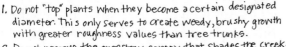

FIGURE 7.5. MANAGEMENT ALTERNATIVE TO SNAGGING AND CLEARING.

This last specification is probably the most critical. I have witnessed many well-intentioned public works and conservation crews trash a stream corridor because the directions were not clear, or because they were not well supervised or trained. A government report states that workers using only hand tools and chain saws completed an environmentally sensitive project on 80 miles of river at the average cost of $1,000 per mile.

Recent reports issued by the Army Corps of Engineers and other government researchers raise the issue of whether the benefits of snagging and clearing are worth the efforts and environmental costs. The benefits are generally restricted to reducing the frequency of overbank flows for the more frequent and smaller floods.[135–137]

Floodplain Restoration for Storage and Conveyance of Flows

The advantages of floodplain restoration are frequently overlooked in the focus of restorationists on stream-bank work and the related restoration of favorable bankfull channel widths and depths. Floodplain restoration can accomplish the same objective that channelization projects are meant to attain: the conveyance of higher volumes of water within a given area. Whether your concern for flooding relates to a small stream or a large river, reclaiming floodplains by removing structures in them, setting back or removing levees, or even excavating wider floodplains between terraces can provide substantial flood-damage-reduction benefits. Some floodplains have been filled for development purposes, and removal of that fill can re-create areas once occupied by historical floodplains.

Flood-damage-reduction benefits from floodplain restoration can come in two forms. One benefit is that a greater volume of discharge can be conveyed down a given width of corridor at lower stages. Figure 7.6 shows the excavation of a wider floodplain. Greater discharges can flow through this cross-section at lower stages if the floodplain space is increased. A second potential benefit is that the floodplain may act something like a reservoir does and provide storage of flood flows, so that greater volumes of water are "held" upstream during a flood.

The great 1993 Mississippi River flood raised the issue of the potential benefits of improving the storage of floodwaters in the Mississippi River floodplains. The popular press raised the question of whether upstream levees, which were restricting the river flows and making them deeper and higher, were increasing structural and overtopping risks to downstream levees and communities.[138] Reports written by hydrologists and geomorphologists compared river-stage data before the complex system of levees and reservoirs was built on the Mississippi with the post-project flood stages. The comparisons showed that the pre-levee stages were lower. One study estimated that the restoration of 13 million acres of floodplain wetlands could have kept the Mississippi River in its banks during the 1993 flood.[139] The theory behind this phenomenon is known, and the technology to measure the tendency of floodplains to store water is finally available with our hydraulic modeling

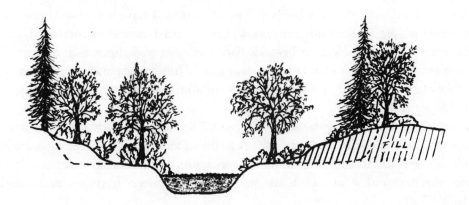

FIGURE 7.6. FLOODPLAIN RESTORATION.

capabilities, but putting this knowledge into practice in floodplain management is only in its infancy.[140] One modeling effort to determine the floodplain storage capacity of the Willamette River is being undertaken by the Portland District of the Army Corps of Engineers.[141]

The ability of a floodplain to store water is analogous to how a reservoir stores water. Reservoir storage allows the rate of outflow to be less than the rate of inflow of floodwaters to the reservoir. This buildup of water volume in the reservoir allows the water to flow out downstream at a more acceptable rate. A reach of river can be made analogous to a reservoir and its length, width, and depth calculated as storage space for floodwaters. Of course, a river that can overflow onto floodplains and into associated wetlands and sloughs has a larger storage capacity than a river channel constricted by structures such as levees, berms, and flood walls.[142]

The latest innovations in flood-control project design take into account the concept of floodplain restoration as a more environmentally sensitive and sustainable way to increase the conveyance of flood flows. Hopefully, future projects will also integrate this concept of flood storage. It should be stressed, however, that this is neither a new nor an unpracticed concept. The Army Corps of Engineers' Charles River Natural Valley Storage Project planning occurred between 1968 and 1972, and all floodplain easements and acquisitions were accomplished by 1984. The flood easements (4,860 acres) and wetlands (3,250 acres) acquired through purchase were calculated by the Corps to provide storage for 50,000 acre feet, a typical volume for a New England reservoir.

The Charles River watershed drains into the Boston, Massachusetts, area, and this storage project provided effective flood-risk reduction for that urban area for large storms in 1979 and 1982.[143] While this is the most celebrated case of a flood-storage project, other nonstructural projects—such as the Prairie du Chien, Wisconsin, relocations project; the Littleton, Colorado, floodplain park projects; and the extensive Sacramento River bypass system in California—represent well-known examples of the same concept being used at different scales.

A few flood-control projects are being designed to either protect and restore floodplains or emulate floodplain features. Hydraulic engineers are referring to these improved flood-control channel and floodplain cross-sections (or shapes) as two-stage or multistage flood-control channels, as described in chapter 5. The channel and floodplain shapes are modeled after the bankfull channel and floodplain features found in nature rather than undergoing excavation as a rectangular or trapezoidal channel. (Figures 7.6 and 7.7 illustrate floodplain restoration projects.) The restoration of the features of bankfull channels and floodplains to previously channelized streams is now beyond the conceptual stages, with plans to restore those features to the Amazon Creek channelization project near Eugene, Oregon, and the Rapid Creek, Black Hills, South Dakota, channelization restoration project. Figure 7.7 shows the design concepts for such restoration of previously channelized or culverted streams. Both restoration options can improve floodwater conveyance and may help foster channel storage.[144]

RESTORING FLOOD CONTROL CHANNELS AND CULVERTED STREAMS TO MORE NATURAL SYSTEMS:

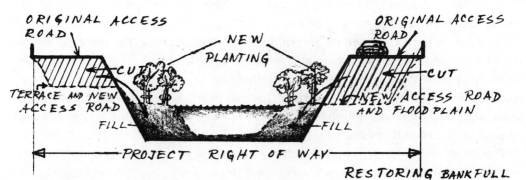

ORIGINAL ACCESS ROAD

NEW PLANTING

ORIGINAL ACCESS ROAD

CUT

CUT

TERRACE AND NEW ACCESS ROAD

NEW ACCESS ROAD AND FLOOD PLAIN

FILL

FILL

PROJECT RIGHT OF WAY

RESTORING BANKFULL CHANNEL GEOMETRY — RESTORE A TRAPEZOIDAL CHANNEL TO A MORE NATURAL CHANNEL. CUT AREAS INCREASE CROSS-SECTIONAL CHANNEL CAPACITY, ENABLING RESTORATION OF BANKFULL CHANNEL, A RIPARIAN CORRIDOR AND FLOOD PLAIN.

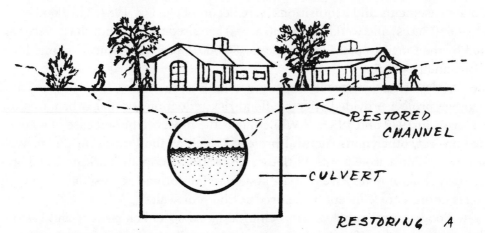

RESTORED CHANNEL

CULVERT

RESTORING A CULVERTED SECTION — USE THE NATURAL CHANNEL GEOMETRY FROM AN OLD AERIAL PHOTO OR NEARBY SECTION OF NATURAL CHANNEL. (ASSUMES RELOCATION OF STRUCTURES IN A REDEVELOPMENT PROJECT)

FIGURE 7.7. RESTORING FLOOD-CONTROL CHANNELS AND CULVERTED STREAMS TO MORE NATURAL SYSTEMS.

Flood-Damage-Reduction Measures Compatible with Local Community Character

It cannot be stressed too often that land-use planning efforts that site structures out of the way of hazardous flood zones are the most effective, long-term solutions to avoiding the costs of flood damages. Communities often opt to accept some flood risk and live with past land-use mistakes. The financial and environmental costs of projects should be balanced against "do nothing" options. If the do-nothing option is unacceptable, there are a number of options for protecting the environmental values of the waterways while reducing flood risks.

It is not uncommon to see old Victorian homes in river cities that have a long flight of steps up to the first floor. If you keep an eye out for neighborhoods where this kind of elevated architecture is common, you may locate an urban stream or one that once flowed through the area but is now underground in a culvert. Residential, commercial, and industrial architecture can easily combine design features to protect a building from floodwaters. Buildings can be placed on high foundations or sited on mounds. Walls or low levees integrated into the site plan can protect the whole building or just vulnerable entrances such as doors, windows, and outside cellar entrances. One or all of these features can be integrated into an attractive site design, and the untrained eye would probably miss the functional aspects of the architecture. A number of government documents and manuals are now available for the home and business owner and public official who wants access to flood-proofing technology.[145–155] Figure 7.8 shows floodplain encroachment, and figure 7.9 illustrates a series of design options that can be used in urban areas to reduce the conflicts between encroachments in floodplains and the protection of waterways. Stream and floodplain corridor cross-sections A thru C illustrate removing a structure from a hazardous area by relocating it, elevating it above the high-stage flood flows, and protecting it with berms or levees.

Relocating structures and even whole towns, such as in Soldiers Grove, Wisconsin, and Allenville, Arizona, may require more initial capital than other project alternatives, but they have the distinct advantage of giving people in impossibly blighted areas a new start with a significantly higher quality of life and a long-term future. This should enter into a community's equation, even if the federal water-planning cost-benefit analysis doesn't take it into consideration.

An advantage of flood walls and "ring" levees around structures is that major structural alterations to buildings are avoided, and as long as the walls or levees are not overtopped, the buildings should not come in contact with floodwaters or be exposed to hydrostatic forces. In case of overtopping or seepage, however, drain valves or discharge pipes need to be integrated into the designs. Flood walls or berms can be integrated into a residential or commercial setting as part of the local ambiance and aesthetic. If they are designed with sensitivity and integrated into gardens, trails, or city creekside parks (figure 7.10), the walls can become a valued landscape feature in the tradition of WPA-style work (also refer to figure 6.1). A downside to any flood wall, berm, or levee project is that a wall or levee failure due

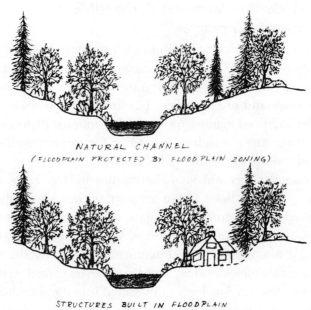

FIGURE 7.8. FLOODPLAIN ENCROACHMENT.

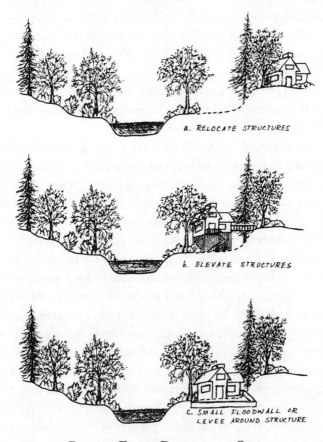

FIGURE 7.9. MEASURES TO REDUCE FLOOD DAMAGES TO STRUCTURES.

FIGURE 7.10. FLOOD WALLS AS LANDSCAPE FEATURES.

to overtopping can result in damages equal to or greater than if the structures had not been built. The resident must consider the likelihood of this occurring.

Flood walls integrated into a residential design usually provide greater flexibility and less maintenance than dirt levees, and they can be integrated into practically any type of structure. Materials for flood walls are generally more expensive than materials for levees, but flood walls may offer a less costly means of protection than elevation, for example. Attention needs to be directed to designing the gaps in the flood walls for driveways, sidewalks and doors, and other entrances. Closures can include permanently hinged doors or doors or dams designed to slide into a slot constructed in the wall and stored nearby when not in use. Whichever system is used, the closures should be secured tightly and incorporate a gasket to prevent leaking (figure 7.11). With flood walls and levees, it is desirable to provide for draining any water that collects behind them from seepage or rainwater. A check valve, which is designed to allow water to flow in only one direction, can be installed. The check valve has to be kept clear of debris, or it may jam open as the water rises.

Modification to the structures themselves is often considered a temporary or

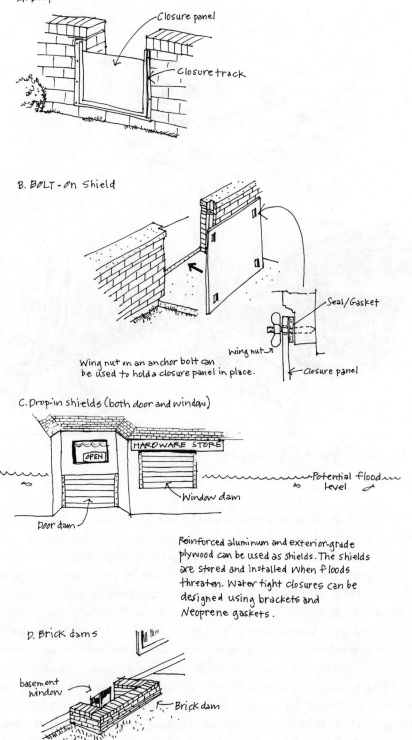

A. Drop-in Shield

Closure panel

Closure track

B. BOLT-on Shield

Seal/Gasket

Wing nut

Closure panel

Wing nut on an anchor bolt can
be used to hold a closure panel in place.

C. Drop-in shields (both door and window)

HARDWARE STORE

OPEN

Potential flood level

Window dam

Door dam

Reinforced aluminum and exterior-grade
plywood can be used as shields. The shields
are stored and installed when floods
threaten. Water tight closures can be
designed using brackets and
Neoprene gaskets.

D. Brick dams

basement
window

Brick dam

FIGURE 7.11. DOOR AND WINDOW DAMS.

ancillary measure to a more expensive channelization, levee, or dam project. This is unfortunate, because the use of inexpensive door and window dams, for example, can protect highly valued possessions in a home or business with a minimum amount of plywood and hardware. Such measures can provide low-tech and instant relief from flood damages on their own or in conjunction with other measures such as floodplain restoration projects.

Door and window dams can be constructed of aluminum or plywood, or a combination. Aluminum can buckle under heavy water pressure, so it may need additional reinforcement. Exterior-grade plywood is also commonly used, but plywood can warp if it is not stored properly. It will also need to be reinforced with some type of wood frame. Besides a drop-in dam or shield, a bolt-on shield can be designed using T-bolts, wing nuts, anchored bolts, or latching dogs. Neoprene and rubber are good materials for making closures fit snugly and watertight. These flood-proofing systems require someone to be at the location to put them in place before flooding occurs. Communities should organize a flood-warning system to use in concert with flood-proofing measures if an extensive area such as a business district uses then. The door and window dam system also assumes that the shields are stored in a place that is known and easy to access.

Some communities opt to elevate structures in place, so that the lowest floor is above selected flood levels (figure 7.12). Buildings can be raised on soil mounds, concrete foundations, or piers, posts, or columns. In general, the steps for elevating a building in place are essentially the same for all cases. A cradle of steel beams is inserted under the structure, jacks raise the beams to the desired new height, and a new elevated foundation is constructed. The structure is then lowered onto the new foundation and reconnected. Various flood characteristics of the site need to be known, such as the expected velocity and elevation of the flood flows so that the foundation can be designed and constructed to withstand the specific characteristics.

Regional or local levees or flood walls are more common than individual ring levees around a property or isolated area (figure 7.13). The levees or flood walls are typically constructed parallel to a water course for long distances to separate the flood flows from human-occupied portions of the floodplain. Levees are controversial remedies because they interfere with natural river processes, including meandering, erosion, and deposition and the related growth of riparian forests and sustenance of instream life. Levees and flood walls can artificially raise the water-surface elevation of rivers, and, depending on when they were built and the nature of the compacted fill used to construct them, they are vulnerable to breakage, as well as overtopping. Inherent in the use of flood walls and levees is the need to provide local drainage to the river through the floodplain barrier.

Flood walls can have advantages over levees in that they are constructed of stronger materials, are thinner and take up less space, and generally require less maintenance. They can be creatively constructed out of a variety of materials. Flood walls built on a large scale (over 4 feet) can have the distinct disadvantage of walling off a river from community and public access. This is a central issue in the

FIGURE 7.12. ELEVATED HOMES.

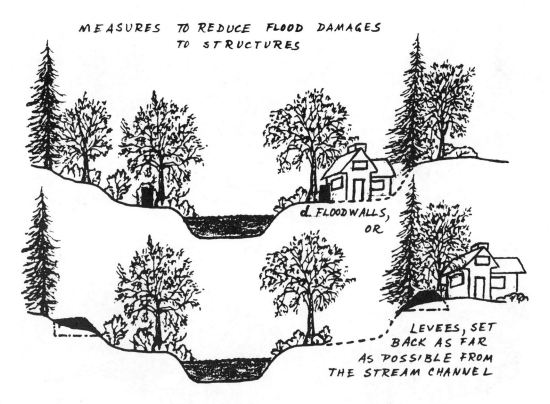

MEASURES TO REDUCE FLOOD DAMAGES TO STRUCTURES

d. FLOODWALLS, OR

LEVEES, SET BACK AS FAR AS POSSIBLE FROM THE STREAM CHANNEL

FIGURE 7.13. REGIONAL FLOOD WALLS AND LEVEES.

community opposition to a flood wall option proposed by engineers for the Los Angeles River. The Army Corps has designed and erected folding and removable flood walls in Monroe, Louisiana, and a flood wall with removable panels and steps in Waterloo, Iowa.[156]

When compared to the environmentally destructive channelization and reservoir construction projects, levees and flood walls may provide a less intrusive means to avoid flood damages. The more levees and walls are set back from a river, the more river and floodplain functions and storage are protected. Levees can provide opportunities for riparian restoration, particularly if research and changing practices continue to indicate that vegetation on levees and rock revetments is an asset to their stability rather than a liability.[157–159] Flood walls and levees can protect natural features of stream channels even with impaired floodplain functions compared to the classic straightened, rocked, and cleared stream channel associated with channelization.

Landscape Modification Measures

Floodplain restoration is one of the most desirable landscape modifications to reduce flood damages, particularly if the restoration is designed to return the dynamics of a meandering river and return the natural river pulses of inundations and

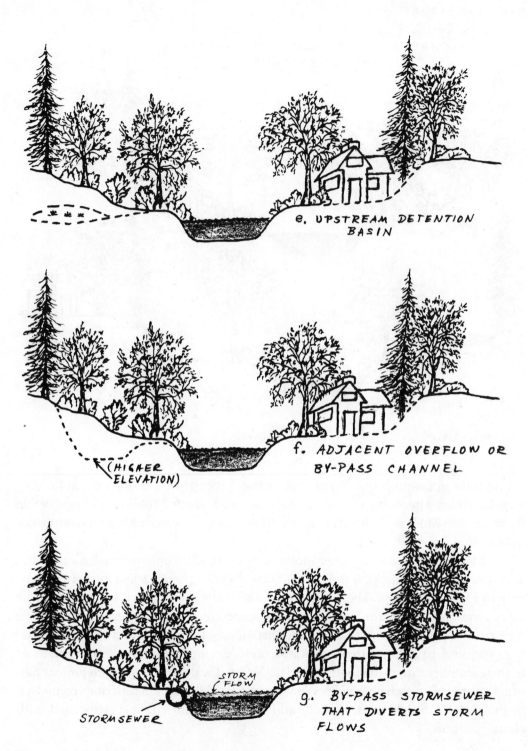

e. UPSTREAM DETENTION BASIN

f. ADJACENT OVERFLOW OR BY-PASS CHANNEL

(HIGHER ELEVATION)

g. BY-PASS STORMSEWER THAT DIVERTS STORM FLOWS

STORM FLOW

STORMSEWER

FIGURE 7.14. OVERFLOW LANDS AND FACILITIES.

sediment deposition and transport. Other landscape modifications that can provide wetland restoration benefits while protecting the integrity of a stream and river corridor are bypasses and retention and detention basins (figure 7.14). Depending on how these measures are designed, they can either have high ecological values or they can detract from the natural environment. Bypass channels, if designed incorrectly, can result in the natural waterway silting in, because of elevational differences between the two channels, or because the discharges for the natural channel are disrupted enough to play havoc with the natural channel sediment transport. If an overflow channel is designed correctly, it can provide restored riparian and wetland acreage and spare the original channel from channelization.

Detention and retention basins have historically been designed as uninspired holding basins for flood and storm waters. "Detention" refers to storage areas for storm-water flows that hold water for a relatively brief period of time, while retention basins act as small reservoirs that store water usually for future use in addition to providing a flood-control function. If a reservoir is created to emulate the features of a natural pond, lake, or bog, it can double as a project with restoration features. Likewise, a retention basin can graduate from a square, grass-lined basin to a wetland restoration project where the grading of the landscape is done so as to emulate the gradual elevation changes characteristic of natural wetland systems. Detention basins are similar in concept to floodplain restoration projects in that the objective is to change the timing of the runoff to the main channels and reduce the peaks of the discharge hydrograph.

In densely developed urban areas with little or no land available for floodplain or wetland restoration, an urban stream can be saved from the impacts of erosion and flooding due to increased runoff by diverting the excess flows into a culvert. This system retains the urban stream as a natural feature but diverts flows at least greater than the 2-year storm (flows greater than the 10-year storm would be preferred) into an adjacent pipe and then to a large river, bay, or lake. The storm flows coming out the end of the pipe can create problems wherever they land, or they can be used creatively for wetland restoration. The problems associated with culverts can plague this bypass system, but it is at least better than losing the natural creek to concrete, riprap, channelization, or other typical urban creek syndrome.

NOTES

1. Arthur Maass, *Muddy Waters: The Army Engineers and the Nation's Rivers* (Cambridge: Harvard University Press, 1951).
2. Maass, *Muddy Waters*.
3. Maass, *Muddy Waters*.
4. Jeffrey Kim Stine, *Environmental Politics and Water Resources Development: The Case of the Army Corps of Engineering During the 1970's,* Ph.D. dissertation, University of California, Santa Barbara, June 1984.
5. "Corps to Reshape Districts," *Environment and Natural Resources,* September 18, 1995.
6. Stine, *Environmental Politics*.

7. Beatrice H. Holmes, *A History of Federal Water Resources Programs, 1800–1960,* Miscellaneous publication No. 1233, Economic Research Service U.S. Department of Agriculture (Washington, D.C., June 1972).

8. William G. Hoyt, and Walter Langbein, *Floods!* (Princeton, New Jersey: Princeton University Press, 1955).

9. Holmes, *History of Federal Water Resources Programs.*

10. Holmes, *History of Federal Water Resources Programs.*

11. Beatrice H. Holmes, *History of Federal Water Resources Programs and Policies 1961–1970,* Miscellaneous publication No. 1379, Economics, Statistics, and Cooperative Service, U.S. Department of Agriculture (Washington, D.C.).

12. Holmes, *History of Federal Water Resources Programs and Policies, 1961–1970.*

13. John Wilkinson, *Report on Channel Modifications to Council on Environmental Quality,* vol. 1 & 2 (Cambridge, Massachusetts: Arthur D. Little, Inc., March 1973).

14. Frank Munger and Anne Houghton, "Politics and Organization in Water Resources Administration: A Comparative Study of Decisions," *Water Resources Research* 1, no. 3 (1965).

15. Otto Eckstein, *Water-Resources Development, The Economics of Project Evaluation* (Cambridge: Harvard University Press, 1961).

16. Holmes, *History of Federal Water Resources Programs, 1961–1970.*

17. Luna B. Leopold and Thomas Maddock, Jr., *The Flood Control Controversy* (New York: Ronald Press, 1954).

18. Hoyt and Langbein, *Floods.*

19. Holmes, *History of Federal Water Resources Programs, 1961–1970.*

20. Holmes, *History of Federal Water Resources Programs, 1961–1970.*

21. Holmes, *History of Federal Water Resources Programs, 1961–1970.*

22. Gilbert F. White, *Human Adjustment to Floods, A Geographical Approach to the Flood Problem in the United States,* Research Paper No. 29 (Chicago: University of Chicago, 1945).

23. White, *Human Adjustment to Floods.*

24. White, *Human Adjustment to Floods.*

25. White, *Human Adjustment to Floods.*

26. Hoyt and Langbein, *Floods.*

27. Wilkinson, *Report on Channel Modifications.*

28. Federal Interagency Floodplain Management Task Force, *A Status Report on the Nation's Flood Plain Management Activity: An Interim Report,* prepared by L. R. Johnston Association (Washington, D.C.: FEMA, April 1989).

29. Congress of the United States Congressional Budget Office, *Current Cost-Sharing and Financing Policies for Federal and State Water Resources Development* (Washington, D.C., July 1983).

30. David White, Public Affairs Office, Natural Resources Conservation Service, Washington, D.C., personal communication, April 1996.

31. Greg Lowe, Stream Operations Branch, Tennessee Valley Authority, Knoxville, Tennessee, personal communication, April 1996.

32. "Corps to Reshape Districts," *Environment and Natural Resources,* September 18, 1995.

33. Government Accounting Office, Natural Resources Management Issues, GAO/OCG–93–17TR, Washington, D.C., 1992.

34. Federal Interagency Floodplain Management Task Force, A Status Report.

35. Interagency Floodplain Management Review Committee, *Sharing the Challenge: Floodplain Management into the 21st Century*, for the Administration Floodplain Management Task Force (Washington, D.C., June 1994).

36. Water Resources Council, *A Unified National Program for Flood Plain Management* (Washington, D.C., September 1979).

37. U.S. General Accounting Office, Report by the Comptroller General, *Water Project Construction Backlog—A Serious Problem with No Easy Solution*, GAO/RCED–83–49 (Washington, D.C., January 26, 1983).

38. U.S. General Accounting Office, Report to the Chairman, Committee on Environmental and Public Works, U.S. Senate, *Update on Army Corps of Engineers' Planning and Designing Time for Water Resources Projects* GAO/RCED–84–16 (Washington, D.C., January 4, 1984).

39. U.S. Congressional Budget Office, *Efficient Investments in Water Resources: Issues and Options* (Washington, D.C., August 1983).

40. A. L. Riley, *Floodplain Use and Misuse* (Berkeley: University of California, 1987).

41. Otto Eckstein, *Water Research Development: The Economics of Project Evaluation* (Cambridge: Harvard University Press, 1958).

42. J. U. Krutilla and O. Eckstein, *Multiple Purpose River Development* (Baltimore, Maryland: Johns Hopkins Press, 1958).

43. J. U. Krutilla, *Efficiency Goals, Market Failure and the Substitution of Public for Private Action, the Analysis and Evaluation of Public Expenditures, the PPB System* (Washington, D.C.: U.S. Government Printing Office, 1969).

44. J. L. Knetsch, "Value Comparisons in Free Flowing Streams," *Natural Resources Journal* 11, no. 4 (1971).

45. Douglas Darcy and Howard Kunreuther, *The Economics of Natural Disasters* (New York: Free Press, 1969).

46. Bory Steinberg, *Flood Damage Prevention Services of the U.S. Army Corps of Engineers: An Evaluation of Policy Changes and Program Outcomes During 1970–1983*, Ph.D. dissertation, George Washington University, Washington, D.C. (Dissertation 84–D–2, USACE, February 1984).

47. Water Resources Council, "Manual for Procedures for Evaluation of National Economic Development Benefits and Costs in Water Resources Planning (Level C); December 14, 1979," issued as regulation 44 Federal Register 72, 892, 1979; "Manual for Evaluation of Environmental Quality Effects and Costs," December 14, 1979; issued as regulation 45 Federal Register 64, 366, 1980, Washinton, D.C.

48. Leonard A. Shabman, *Improved Formulation and Evaluation of Nonstructural Elements for Water Resources Plans in Flood Hazard Areas* (Washington, D.C.: Water Resources Council, October 1979.

49. Gerald Galloway, *Nonstructural Measures in Flood Damage Reduction Activities* (Washington, D.C.: Water Resources Council, July 1980).

50. U.S. Army Corps of Engineers, *The Development of Non-structural Alternatives, A Policy Discussion by the St. Paul District* (St. Paul, Minnesota, May 1979).

51. William Carson, *National Economic Development Benefits for Nonstructural Measures*, Hydrologic Engineering Center, U.S. Army Corps of Engineers (Davis, California: October 1980).

52. *Physical and Economic Feasibility of Non-structural Floodplain Management Measures*, Hydrologic Engineering Center, U.S. Army Corps of Engineers (Davis, California, March 1978).

53. Ann L. Riley, "Some Responses of Communities and Army Corps of Engineers Districts to Federal Planning Policies in Order to Implement Floodplain Evacuation Projects," prepared for Institute for Water Research, U.S. Army Corps of Engineers, unpublished, August 1996.

54. Arthur Maass, "Public Investment Planning in the United States: Analysis and Critique," *Public Policy, Harvard College* 18, no. 2 (Winter 1970).

55. William Donovan, former chief of the Flood Plain Management Services Branch, U.S. Army Corps of Engineers, Washington, D.C., interview, October 1985.

56. William J. Donovan, "Economic, Social and Environmental Requirements and Related Considerations in Planning for Water and Land Resources," *Proceedings, Social Scientists Conference, Social Aspects of Comprehensive Planning* (Memphis, Tennessee, September 20–24, 1976), vol. 1, 1977.

57. Hunter L. Spillan, staff assistant to the House of Representatives Subcommittee on Energy and Water Development, Washington, D.C., personal communication, May 1990.

58. Ann L. Riley, "Overcoming Federal Water Policies, The Wildcat–San Pablo Creeks Case," *Environment* 31, no. 10 (December 1989).

59. Hunter Spillan, personal communication, 1990.

60. Doug Plasencia and David Conrad, "A New Approach to Corps of Engineers Flood Control: A White Paper," Association of State Floodplain Managers and National Wildlife Federation Washington, D.C., 1995.

61. Lieutenant General Henry J. Hatch, commander, U.S. Army Corps of Engineers, "Overview for Testimony at Globescope Pacific," Globesscope Pacific Symposium, Los Angeles, November 2, 1989.

62. U.S. Army Corps of Engineers, Department of the Army, *Ecosystem Restoration in the Civil Works Program*, Water Resources Policies and Authorities, Engineering Circular No. 1105–2–210 (Washington, D.C., June 1, 1995).

63. U.S. Army Corps of Engineers, *Ecosystem Restoration*.

64. Leonard Shabman, *Environmental Activities in Corps of Engineers Water Resources Programs: Charting a New Direction*, IWR Report 93–PS–1, Water Resources Support Center, Institute for Water Resources (Fort Belvoir, Virginia, November 1993).

65. Kenneth Orth, *Cost Effectiveness Analysis for Environmental Planning: Nine Easy Steps*, IWR Report 94–PS–2, Institute for Water Resources, (Alexandria, Virginia, October 1994).

66. Timothy D. Feather, C. Russell, K. Harrington, and D. Capan, *Review of Monetary and Nonmonetary Valuation of Environmental Investments*, IWR Report 95–R–2, Institute for Water Resources, Alexandria, Virginia; and Waterways Experiment Station, Vicksburg, Mississippi, February 1995.

67. Shabman, *Environmental Activities*.

68. U.S. Army Corps of Engineers, *Environmental Advisory Bulletin: A Report of Findings for the 53rd Meeting*, Chief of Engineers Environmental Advisory Board, Headquarters Army Corps (Washington, D.C., April 11–13, 1995).

69. U.S. Army Corps of Engineers, *Environmental Advisory Bulletin*.

70. Riley, "Overcoming Federal Water Policies."

71. Committee on Appropriations, "Hearings Before the Subcommittee on Rural Develop-

ment, Agriculture and Related Agencies," House of Representatives, 101st Congress, Part 4: Agricultural Programs (Washington, D.C., 1990).

72. Bob Foster and Tim Sanders, staff assistants to the House Subcommittee on Rural Development, Agriculture and Related Agencies, Washington, D.C., personal communication, May 1990.

73. Duane E. Jenkins, staff of the Office of Management and Budget, Washington, D.C., personal communication, May 1990.

74. Thomas Wehri, assistant director for watershed operations, Watershed Project Division, Soil Conservation Service, Washington, D.C., personal communication, May 1990.

75. Jenkins, personal communication, 1990.

76. Wehri, personal communication, 1990.

77. Natural Resources Conservation Service (NRCS), *Interim Report of the Backlog Review Team: A Review of P.L. 83–566 Projects*, Watershed and Wetland Division (Washington, D.C., March 1, 1996).

78. NRCS, *Interim Report of the Backlog*, 1966.

79. NRCS, *Interim Report of the Backlog*, 1966.

80. Ed Reichart, chief of the Watersheds and Wetlands Division, Natural Resources Conservation Service, Washington, D.C., personal communication, October 1994.

81. Beatrice Hort Holmes, *History of Federal Water Resources Programs and Policies, 1961–1970*, Miscellaneous Publication Economics No. 1379, Statistics and Cooperative Service (Washington, D.C.: U.S. Department of Agriculture, 1979).

82. Foster and Sanders, personal communication, 1990.

83. Committee on Appropriations, "Hearings Before the Subcommittee on Rural Development, Agriculture and Related Agencies," 1990; Warren Lee, chief, Watersheds and Wetlands Division, National Resources Conservation Service, Washington, D.C., personal communication, October 1996.

84. Government Accounting Office, Community and Economic Development Division, *Congressional Guidance Needed on Federal Cost Share of Water Resource Projects When Project Benefits Are Not Widespread*, Report No. CED–81–12 (Washington, D.C., November 13, 1980).

85. Natural Resources Conservation Service, *Conservation Technical Assistance and Watershed Evaluation* (Washington, D.C., 1995).

86. Beatrice Hort Holmes, *History of Federal Water Resources Programs and Policies 1961–1970*, Miscellaneous Publication No. 1379, Economics, Statistics and Cooperatives Service (Washington, D.C.: U.S. Department of Agriculture, September 1979).

87. Jamie W. Moore and Dorothy P. Moore, *The Army Corps of Engineers and the Evolution of Federal Flood Plain Management Policy*, Special Publication No. 20, Institute of Behavioral Science (Boulder: University of Colorado, 1989).

88. Moore and Moore, *The Army Corps of Engineers*.

89. Tennessee Valley Authority, Division of Economic and Community Development, *Floodplain Management, the TVA Experience* (Knoxville, Tennessee, December 1983).

90. Tennessee Valley Authority, *Floodplain Management*.

91. Tennessee Valley Authority, *Floodplain Management*.

92. Greg Lowe, Stream Operations Branch, Tennessee Valley Authority, Knoxville, Tennessee, personal communication, April 1996.

93. Federal Interagency Floodplain Management Task Force, *Floodplain Management in*

the United States: An Assessment Report, prepared by L. R. Johnston Association, (Washington, D.C.: FEMA, 1992).

94. Doug Plasencia, "Testimony of, Before the Committee on Environment and Public Works, Subcommittee on Transportation and Infrastructure, U.S. Senate, for Association of State Floodplain Managers," (Washington, D.C., February 14, 1995).

95. Larry Larson, executive director of the Association of State Floodplain Managers, Department of Natural Resources, Madison, Wisconsin, "Hazards Research and Applications Workshop," University of Colorado, Boulder, July 20–23, 1986.

96. Leo Cheatham, "An Analysis of the Effectiveness of Land Use Regulations for Flood Insurance Eligibility," Division of Business Research, Mississippi State University, October 1977.

97. David H. Howell, "Urban Flood Management: Problems and Research Needs," *Journal of the Water Resources Planning and Management Division* (American Society of Civil Engineers), 103, no. WR2 (November 1977).

98. Federal Emergency Management Agency, memorandum to mayor of Tarpon Springs, July 30, 1983; and FEMA press release No. 83–108, November 4, 1983.

99. Mike Robinson, chief of the Program Policy and Compliance Division, Office of Loss Reduction, Federal Insurance Administration, Washington, D.C., personal communication, November 1990.

100. Frank Thomas, assistant administrator, Office of Loss Reduction, Federal Insurance Administration, Washington, D.C., personal communication, November 1990.

101. William Holliday, *Seminar Proceedings: Implementation of Non-Structural Measures,* U.S. Army Corps of Engineers Policy Study 83–G520 (Washington, D.C.: July 1983).

102. Jon A. Kusler, *Regulation of Flood Hazard Areas to Reduce Flood Losses,* vol. 3, Institute of Behavioral Science, Natural Hazards Research and Applications Information Center (Boulder: University of Colorado, 1982).

103. Kusler, *Regulation of Flood Hazard Areas.*

104. Larson, "Hazards Research and Applications Workshop."

105. Jon A. Kusler, "Innovation in Local Flood Plain Management: A Summary of Community Experience," prepared for the Water Resources Council, Natural Hazards Research and Applications Information Center (Boulder: University of Colorado, 1982).

106. Kusler, "Innovation in Local Flood Plain Management."

107. Raymond Burby and Steven French, "Coping with Floods: The Land Use Management Paradox," *American Planning Association Journal* (July 1981).

108. Philip Williams, "The EIR Process As a Tool for Implementing Flood Plan Management Policies," *Flood Management Conference Proceedings,* California Deptartment of Water Resources (Sacramento, California, October 24–25, 1978).

109. Interagency Floodplain Management Review Committee, *Sharing the Challenge: Floodplain Management in the 21st Century.*

110. Interagency Floodplain Management Review Committee, *Sharing the Challenge: Floodplain Management into the 21st Century.*

111. Association of State Floodplain Managers, "Summary of the Title V National Flood Insurance Reform," *News and Views* (October 1994).

112. U.S. Geological Survey, "Operation of Hydraulic Data Collection Stations by the U.S. Geological Survey in 1985," Open-File Report 85–640 (Washington, D.C., 1985).

113. Luna B. Leopold, *Water, A Primer* (San Francisco: W. H. Freeman, 1974).

114. Interagency Floodplain Management Review Committee, *Sharing the Challenge: Floodplain Management into the 21st Century.*

115. David R. Dawdy, consulting fluvial geomorphologist, San Francisco, California, personal communication, 1991.

116. Federal Interagency Floodplain Management Task Force , *A Status Report.*

117. Luna B. Leopold and Thomas Dunne, *Water in Environmental Planning* (San Francisco: W. H. Freeman, 1978.)

118. Leopold and Dunne, *Water in Environmental Planning,*

119. Gilbert White, director, Natural Hazards Research and Applications Information Center, University of Colorado, Boulder, interview, June 1985.

120. Susan K. Tubbesing, ed., *Natural Hazards Data Resources: Uses and Needs* (Boulder: University of Colorado, Institute of Behavioral Science, 1979).

121. Kenneth R. Wright, Peter Binney, and Marilyn Stokes, of Wright Water Engineers and Write-McLaughlin Engineers, Denver, "Adequacy of Data Resources for the Needs of the Consulting Engineer to Local Government" in Susan Tubbesing, ed., *Natural Hazards Data Resources: Uses and Needs,* 1979.

122. Luna Leopold, *Hydrology for Urban Planning,* U.S. Geological Survey Circular 554 (Washington, D.C., 1968).

123. Tom Richman and Eugene Boudreau, "Flood Planning: Ignorance Protects Development," *The Paper,* Monte Rio, California, May 7, 1986.

124. David R. Dawdy, consulting fluvial geomorphologist, San Francisco, California, personal communication, March 1991.

125. Bill Edgar, executive director, Sacramento Area Flood Control Agency, Sacramento, California, phone interview, November 1990; and "Draft Informational Memorandum regarding the American River Watershed Investigation," Sacramento Area Flood Control Agency, Sacramento, California, November 6, 1990.

126. National Research Council, *Flood Risk Management and the American River Basin, An Evaluation,* Water Science and Technology Board (Washington, D.C.: National Acadamy Press, 1995).

127. Charles Parrett, unpublished data on number of continuous-record gauges operated by the Water Resources Division, U.S. Geological Survey, Helena, Montana, phone interview, March 1986.

128. Bruce Parks, hydrologist, Office of Water Data Coordination, Water Resources Division, U.S. Geological Survey, Reston, Virginia, phone interview, March 1986.

129. Don Engler, creek naturalist, Public Works Department, Marin County, California, personal communication, June 1990.

130. Sacramento County, "Natural Streams Plan," *Sacramento County Natural Streams Combining Land Use Zone Ordinance,* Sacramento County Natural Streams Task Force, Department of Planning and Community Development, Sacramento, California, 1980.

131. F. Douglas Shields and Nelson R. Nunnally, "Environmental Aspects of Clearing and Snagging," *Journal of Environmental Engineering* 110, no. 1 (February 1984).

132. A. L. Riley, D. Jacobs, J. King, and S. Daar, *Vegetation Management Handbook,* Division of Planning, California Department of Water Resources, The Resources Agency (Sacramento, California, December 1982).

133. Edward L. Thackston and R. B. Sneed, *Review of Environmental Consequences of Waterway Design and Construction Practices as of 1979,* Technical Report E–82–4, U.S. Army Corps of Engineers Waterways Experiment Station (Vicksburg, Mississippi, April 1982).

134. American Fisheries Society, Wildlife Society, and International Association of Fish and Wildlife Agencies, *Stream Obstruction Removal Guidelines* (Bethesda, Maryland, 1983).

135. Institute for Water Resources, "Environmentally Sensitive Stream Modifications Workshop Report," Memorandum CEWRC–IWR 1165, U.S. Army Corps of Engineers (Fort Belvoir, Virginia, April 13, 1993).

136. F. Douglas Shields and Roger H. Smith, "Effects of Large Woody Debris Removal on Physical Characteristics of a Sand-bed River" *Aquatic Conservation: Marine and Freshwater Ecosystems* 2 (1992), pp. 145–163.

137. U.S. Army Corps of Engineers, *Channel Stability Assessment for Flood Control Projects*, Engineering Manual 1110–2–1418 (Washington, D.C., October 31, 1994).

138. D. T. Shaw, "The Shaw Report," *St. Louis Post-Dispatch*, December 28, 1993.

139. W. K. Stevens, "Restoring Wetlands Could Ease Threat of Mississippi Flood," *Science Times, New York Times*, August 8, 1995.

140. Luna B. Leopold, "Flood Hydrology and the Floodplain," *Water Resources Update*, no. 95 (Spring 1994) (Universities Council on Water Resources Southern Illinois University, Carbondale, Illinois).

141. Philip Williams Associates, *An Evaluation of Flood Management Benefits Through Floodplain Restoration on the Willamette River* (Portland, Oregon, February 1996).

142. Luna B. Leopold, "Flood Hydrology and the Floodplain."

143. National Park Service, Department of Interior, *A Casebook in Managing Rivers for Multiple Uses*, also sponsored by Association of State Wetland Managers and Associates of State Floodplain Managers (Washington, D.C., October 1991).

144. Steven R. Abt, Chester C. Watson, J. Craig Fischenich, and Mitchell R. Peters, "Bank Stabilization and Habitat Aspects of Low-Flow Channels," *Land and Water* 39 (January–February 1995).

145. "Implementation of Nonstructural Measures," Seminar Proceedings, U.S. Army Corps of Engineers, Institute for Water Resources, Policy Study 83–G520 (Fort Belvoir, Virginia, July 1983).

146. H. James Owen, "Annotations of Selected Literature on Nonstructural Floodplain Management Measures," Hydrologic Engineering Center, U.S. Army Corps of Engineers (Davis, California, March 1977).

147. "Flood Proofing Regulations," U.S. Army Corps of Engineers (Washington, D.C., June 1972).

148. "Design Manual for Retrofitting Flood-Prone Residential Structures," Federal Emergency Management Agency, FEMA 114 (Washington, D.C., September 1986).

149. "Flood Proofing Techniques, Programs and References," National Flood Proofing Committee, available from the U.S. Army Corps of Engineers, CECW–PF (Washington, D.C., 1994).

150. Shirley Bradway Laska, "Flood Proof Retrofitting: Homeowner Self-Protective Behavior," Monograph #49, Program on Environment and Behavior, Natural Hazards Research and Applications Information Center, Institute of Behavioral Science #6, University of Colorado, Boulder, 1991.

151. "Flood Proofing, How to Evaluate Your Options," National Floodproofing Committee, U.S. Army Corps of Engineers (Washington, D.C., July 1993).

152. "Flood Proofing Technology in the Tug Force Valley," National Flood proofing Committee, U.S. Army Corps of Engineers (Washington, D.C., April 1994).

153. "A Flood Proofing Success Story Along Dry Creek at Goodlettsville, Tennessee," National Flood proofing Committee, U.S. Army Corps of Engineers (Washington, D.C., September 1993).

154. "Local Floodproofing Programs," National Floodproofing Committee, U.S. Army Corps of Engineers (Washington, D.C., June 1994).

155. "Flood Proofing, How to Evaluate Your Options," National Floodproofing Committee.

156. Nelson R. Nunnally, F. Douglas Shields, Jr., and James Hynson, "Environmental Considerations for Levees and Floodwalls," *Environmental Management*, 11, no. 2 (1987).

157. Nunnally, Shields, and Hynson, "Environmental Considerations."

158. F. Douglas Shields, "Woody Vegetation and Riprap Stability Along the Sacramento River Mile, 84–5–119," *Water Resources Bulletin* 27, no. 3 (June 1991).

159. F. Douglas Shields, Jr., and Donald H. Gray, "Effects of Woody Vegetation on Sandy Levee Integrity," *Water Resources Bulletin* 28, no. 5 (October 1992).

CHAPTER EIGHT

Citizen-Supported Restoration Activities

Citizen groups have defined, promoted, practiced, redefined, and instructed others in waterway restoration. Activities related to restoration of waterways performed by citizen groups have included the monitoring of water quality and ecosystem conditions, data collection on stream flows and stages, the formation of watershed councils, the design of resource management and restoration plans, and the execution of restoration and management projects and programs. Citizen organizations contain a range of participants from novices who want to learn or contribute in some way to their community, to people with extensive professional training who are advancing the practice of and knowledge about restoration. This chapter is dedicated to the property owner next to a stream, conservation and service corps members, volunteers, citizen activists, students, scouts, fishing club members, conservation organization members, chambers of commerce members, and other "do-gooders."

Citizen volunteer monitoring of water quality; stream, river, lake, and marsh habitat; and ecological quality, hydrology, and storm flows has evolved as a mainstay of scientific data collection. The attitudes of scientists and agency personnel evolved quickly from concern that volunteer-collected data could be inaccurate to enthusiasm for this 1980s and 1990s phenomenon as a critical component of many programs. The 1994 edition of the *National Directory of Volunteer Environmental Monitoring Programs* issued by the Environmental Protection Agency lists 517 citizen organizations in 45 states plus the District of Columbia. The recent growth of citizen monitoring can be measured from the first (1988) edition of the directory, which listed 44 monitoring programs in 24 states.[1] Most such groups are involved in monitoring water quality. The Audubon Society in Minnesota has developed a citizen wetland-monitoring protocol with the EPA involving up to 35 volunteers.[2] Citizen volunteers in Pennsylvania have assisted the National Weather Service with flood forecasting, and volunteers in California have monitored flood flows and their stages to establish the capacities of creek channels to convey floodwaters in order to influence stream management practices.

Citizen monitoring cannot replace our nation's system of professionally collected water-quality, water-supply, and groundwater data, but it does add a critical complementary dimension to data collection efforts. The benefits include narrowing gaps in the data collected by government collection programs and educating a new generation of scientists through engaging students and national and local service corps members in monitoring projects. Community-based data collection programs also increase the general public's involvement in watershed management as well as our awareness of water issues and the importance of government data collection programs.

Public involvement with urban (and rural) waterways has gone beyond data collection. An era of citizen-based environmental restoration projects began in the 1980s. As chapter 6 points out, citizen-sponsored waterway restoration simply carries forward a time-honored tradition. It is no accident that the return of the civilian conservation and service corps beginning in the 1970s is coincident with the revival of projects to restore the physical features of streams, rivers, lakes, and marshes. While many projects that restore the physical configurations of streams trapped in concrete, riprap, or culverts use heavy machinery to remove soil, concrete, and rock and perform grading, most restoration projects require labor-intensive efforts to return vegetation to ecosystems. The most common waterway restoration projects can use limited or no heavy equipment. The evolving era of waterway restoration currently involves a collaboration of local, state, and nationally sponsored civilian service corps, most of which are nonprofit organizations, with nonprofit citizen environmental organizations. Frequently, a mix of government, private, and corporate or business-sector funds are used to sponsor restoration.

Citizens are providing not only the brawn but also the brains for environmental restoration projects. Citizen nonprofit organizations are leaders in the contemporary restoration movement as organizers of restoration forums, workshops, and conferences. They serve as innovators in restoration methods and provide "clearing houses" for practitioners to interact and share field and project design, implementation, and monitoring experiences. Nonprofit groups have initiated and encouraged government and university involvement in the restoration field and have vigorously advanced the practice of forming partnerships among universities, governments, businesses, consulting firms, and citizen organizations to carry out restoration initiatives. Included among the organizations that have pioneered in or significantly advanced waterway restoration strategies and practices are Ducks Unlimited, Trout Unlimited, the Nature Conservancy, the Society for Ecological Restoration, the American Fisheries Society, the Association of State Wetland Managers, the Waterfront Center, Soil and Water Conservation and Resource Conservation districts, and the member organizations of the Coalition to Restore Urban Waters, including the National Association of Service and Conservation Corps. This is not an exhaustive list, but it is representative of the breadth of the citizen-based restoration movement.

Watershed Hydrology Data for Citizens to Collect
Stream-Flow Discharges, Stage of Flows, and Hydrographs

Pam Romo was busy taking care of children and family concerns at her home in Walnut Creek in the outlying suburbs of the San Francisco Bay area when she heard that a large flood-control project was planned for parts of Tice Creek in the Walnut Creek Basin, which flows through her backyard. Concerned, she acquired the environmental impact report prepared by the county and learned that the county and the U.S. Army Corps of Engineers were planning to build an extensive bypass system that would divert flows away from the creek into a large culvert and 800 feet of channelization. Although she was aware that there were some regular flooding problems along sections of Tice Creek, the ambitious project located in a small 4.18-square-mile watershed within the Walnut Creek Basin seemed out of scale with the extent of the problem. It also appeared that downstream residents would be paying for impacts caused by upstream developers. In particular, the state-required report seemed to indicate that there was little empirical data (quantifiable information based on field observations) on the flooding problem.

Pam soon discovered that there was no gauging station to measure the stream flows on Tice Creek, and she reasoned that someone should actually measure the flows in the creek to better estimate what the situation really was. She organized the Friends of Tice Creek by knocking on the doors of neighbors and distributing surveys to the households in the watershed. She wrote a letter to the county asking good questions about the need for such a project. The intelligent questions and the existence of a citizens group held back the project planning. At that point, the county distanced itself from the project and asked the city of Walnut Creek to address the issue.

In the meantime, Pam went to a nearby university and got help from a professor and a graduate student to set up a stream gauge in her backyard. Her plan was to collect information that could be used to help design the most logical solutions to the Tice Creek flood-damage problems. They surveyed a cross-section of the creek in the Romos' backyard (figure 8.1). This information was used to make a cross-sectional diagram of a creek, shown in figure 8.2. A cross-section diagram using a large number of surveyed points can help point out the changes in channel shape between the bankfull channel and the floodplain that are difficult to see in a field observation. Their surveyed cross-section provided the exact dimensions of the bankfull channel width and depth, floodplain and terrace.

The cross-sectional survey was done with a surveying level and rod. Such a survey does not have to use expensive surveying equipment. You can stretch a measuring tape across a stream so that it is horizontal and tight. Put the zero end on the left bank facing downstream because that's the traditional practice. The measuring tape will provide the horizontal measurements for the cross-section. Note the width of the bankfull, or active, channel. Choose a nearby "permanent" reference point, or datum, that you can easily identify again; this might be a marker on a fence post, tree, bridge, or other structure. This will be an arbitrary starting elevation—which you could call 100 feet. Later, if it's desirable, this marker can be surveyed to an actually known elevation (in feet above sea level) at a U.S. Geological Survey or other official benchmark in the area. Stretch some string very tightly from the datum to a horizontal point on the opposite side of the creek. Take a stick that is measured in inches (or borrow a surveyor's rod) and at about every foot along the measuring

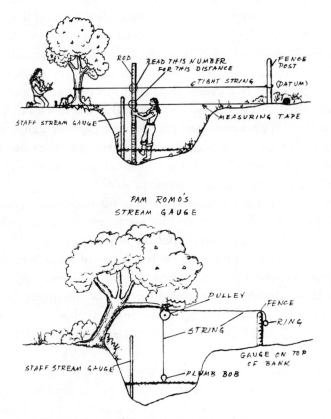

FIGURE 8.1. HOW TO TAKE STREAM DISCHARGE MEASUREMENTS.

tape, measure the vertical distance between the string and the channel bottom. Have a friend write these vertical heights down for each one-foot horizontal point. Make at least ten measurements and then compute the average depth from them.

Another useful piece of information is how high the flows are for different storms. To measure the height, or the stage, of the flows, Pam and her helpers put a gauge in the stream. The gauge was a piece of wood about 6 feet high and 6 inches wide marked off in $1/10$ths of an inch. It was put on a straight stretch of creek where the bottom was stable and nailed to a willow tree with the bottom of the gauge pushed securely into the creek bed. The gauge was near their cross-section, so they knew its elevation. They were worried that the gauge might be in a place that would catch debris going down the creek, which would make the water rise in that spot and give an inaccurate reading. Just in case something like that might happen, they decided to put together a second makeshift gauge consisting of a string weighted down by a plumb-bob that dangled from a pulley attached to a tree limb overhanging the creek. When Pam wanted to measure the elevation of the water, she would lower the plumb-bob to the surface of the water and then measure how much string was left against a post or gauge located on the bank. (See figure 8.1.)

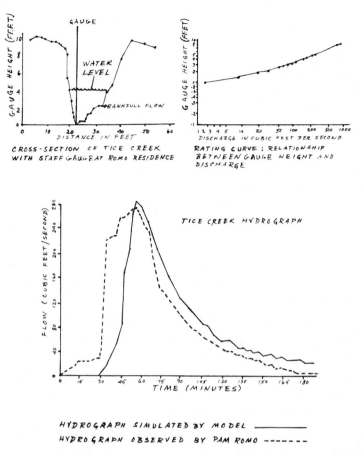

FIGURE 8.2. HOW TO PLOT A CROSS-SECTION, RATING CURVE, AND HYDROGRAPH.
Source: David R. Dawdy and Harsh Saluja, "Kinematic Wave Routing in Urban System Modeling," 1986.

"Shanghai" bright red fingernail polish made neat, easy-to-read $1/10$-inch markings for the wood gauge on the top of the stream bank.

Last, they installed in the Romo's backyard a good-quality rain gauge borrowed from the university. That winter of 1986 there were heavy rains in California. When it started to rain, Pam would go out to the rain gauge and every five minutes record how much rain had fallen and empty the gauge. Then she would run over to her staff gauge and record how high the creek was. Immediately after that she would throw an orange peel in the water at the start of the straight reach of creek and time how many seconds it took for the orange peel to reach a marker about 30 feet downstream. She would then run back to the rain gauge and start the routine over. After an hour, besides attracting the curiosity of the neighbors and the aid of several young neighborhood assistants, Pam had more hydrologic data on Tice Creek than any government agency.

By reading the elevation of the rising storm flows on the staff gauge, Pam could go back to the drawing of the cross-section and know exactly how deep and wide the water was flowing when she read the gauge. She knew the velocity at that stage by dividing the 30-foot length of creek by the number of seconds it took the orange peel to cover the 30 feet, which provided a feet-per-second velocity. The velocity times the width and depth gave her the storm-flow discharges.

Velocities are measured professionally by current meters held in the water, and the rate that they rotate is recorded. Pam's system of using a float gave a very reasonable measurement, however. It is best to take a number of velocity measurements in different parts of the channel, i.e., the sides and the middle, and average the results of five to ten measurements. Because the surface velocity is a little greater than the velocity of the deeper water, multiply the average figure by 0.8 to convert the surface velocity to a mean velocity. It is best to measure velocities in a relatively straight channel reach and try to make your measurement over a distance at least equal to the width of the stream. A longer distance is even better. Because velocities can vary from the center and sides of the creek flow, try to throw your float into different parts of the creek so that the values best represent a mean surface velocity. Pam used orange peels because they float well, they're easy to see in rainy conditions, and there was an orange tree in her backyard. You could use sticks or any other convenient, easy-to-see, buoyant items. (On large streams with difficult visibility—particularly in the pouring rain—I have found plastic, red-and-white fishing bobbers the easiest to throw with some accuracy and locate on their downstream course.) The channel length you use to measure velocities may very well be constrained to something less than the ideal because of visibility problems, or because the floats get stuck in channel debris.

After recording data from a number of storms, Pam was shown how to make a flood-frequency curve from her data. This provides a plotting of the stream-flow discharges against the probability that those discharges will reoccur (recurrence intervals) (figure 8.2). An easy-to-understand, step-by-step explanation for making your own flood-frequency graph is contained in *Water, A Primer* by Luna Leopold.[3] The math for determining the recurrence-interval values involves simple addition and division. Students and volunteers are encouraged to add two additional references to increase your understanding of basic hydrologic fieldwork: *A View of the River* by Luna Leopold[4] and *Water in Environmental Planning* by Tom Dunne and Luna Leopold.[5]

The combined readings of the rainfall and stream flows made it possible to construct a hydrograph for Tice Creek. Pam discovered that, with some consistency, the peak flow in the stream occurred about fifty minutes after the rainstorm started, and the recession limb of the hydrograph dropped off about fifteen minutes later. Using Pam Romo's rain gauge and stream-flow data, consultants hired by local developers to work with Pam concluded that all the previous estimates of the channel capacity for Tice Creek were too low, and therefore some of the flood-control designs were oversized. The previous estimate by the Contra Costa County Flood Control and Water Conservation District for channel capacity was about 600 cfs, but the safe carrying capacity for the channel was recalculated at 1,000 cfs or more based on the Romo data. The consultants were also able to derive a more accurate hydrograph, which provided a more realistic picture of the characteristics of the runoff for that watershed.[6] The consultants hired to evaluate the existing hydrologic data and flood-damage-reduction alternatives used Pam Romo's data to calibrate the U.S. Army Corps of Engineers' Rainfall-Runoff Computer Program HEC-1 and Water Surface Profile Model HEC-2 and found that Pam's data were critical in establishing confidence in the model results.[7]

The existing hydrologic data on Tice Creek had been estimated using some of the most common methods when actual stream-flow data is not available. Stream-flow data available from the much larger basin of Walnut Creek were extrapolated to estimate the peak flows of the Tice Creek watershed. This provided values that underestimated the peak flows. The rational method (see chapter 4) was used to estimate the 50-year peak flows for Tice Creek, but it is generally not recommended for drainage areas over 640 acres, and the Tice Creek watershed is over 2,600 acres. The Federal Emergency Management Agency flood insurance maps were based on regional regression equations for larger basins, but data on some historical flooding information for storms in 1955, 1958, and 1962 and the measurements Pam Romo took on Tice Creek indicated that the FEMA flood estimates were too low.[8]

Additional information derived from Pam Romo's field measurements resulted in modifying the engineers' estimates of the impacts or significance of the peak flows. Contra Costa County had a reasonable generalized unit hydrograph to estimate the peak flood. However, experts reviewing the existing data felt that the use of a generalized unit hydrograph was an outdated practice and instead used the kinematic wave option in the HEC-1 model to derive a hydrograph. The consultants used Romo's data from two storms to calibrate a hydrograph that resulted in a flatter peak than the uncalibrated models. This led to the discovery that a golf course through which the creek flowed was acting as an unofficial detention basin, which led to a recommendation by the consultants that modification to the golf course could increase detention storage of the peak flows. The consultants also calculated that the increase of peak flows that would be produced under a 1991 upper watershed development scenario would be 90 cfs at one location and 81 cfs at another location, and that therefore the upstream developers should be obligated to reduce the peaks by those amounts.[9]

Finally, Pam Romo's simple two-page survey, which had been distributed to people living in the watershed by volunteers in several homeowner's associations and the Friends of Tice Creek, brought in some important information.

The first revelation was that many of the flood-damage problems were site specific and could be solved easily and inexpensively. Solutions included modifying the design of culverts to redirect the flow from culverts, thereby eliminating serious stream-bank failure sites; replacing undersized culverts that were backing up flows onto streets; reinforcing and redesigning private bridges that were constricting flows and flooding property; removing debris jams in some sections of the creek; enlarging undersized driveway culverts and removing debris from roadside drainage ditches. It also became apparent that the changes in flood frequency experienced since the 1960s could be correlated with the increased development of the upper watershed. An additional interesting feature of the survey was the response to the question on wildlife sightings. Rare animals such as bobcat and fox, as well as trout, had been sighted, establishing this riparian corridor through a suburban and increasingly urbanized area as a valuable wildlife sanctuary.[10]

The result of this effort was that upstream developers were required to put in detention facilities to accommodate the impacts of their past and present development on the changes in the runoff patterns of the watershed. The calibrated hydrograph devised by the city's consultants was used to guide the design of the new detention facilities.

Pam Romo and the Friends of Tice Creek saved their stream from a potentially environmentally damaging project, saved their tax dollars, and illustrated the power of a little bit of information. The hydrologic information station at the Romos' is a source of fun for the Romos and the neighborhood, and the Romo family has been enjoying more fresh-squeezed orange juice as a side benefit of the orange-peel float measurement system.[11]

Flood Forecasting and High Water Marks

In some communities volunteers have been organized and trained to read stream gauges and rain gauges and phone the information in to a National Weather Service office, which, in turn, warns downstream residents that they can expect flood flows to reach them by a certain time. This can provide critical time needed by downstream residents to put flood-proofing schemes into effect or, if necessary, evacuate from a flood-hazard area.

An example of such a system is a self-help flood-forecasting warning system organized by the Susquehanna River Basin Commission, which uses volunteers to improve the National Weather Service River Forecasting System. Volunteers play a major role in the warning system and in keeping the costs low. One county organized five self-help watershed warning systems for less than $500 of county funds. The National Weather Service assisted with a field survey, inexpensive rain and stream gauges, and a forecast procedure. The result was accurate flood forecasts where none existed before.[12] Another valuable service provided by volunteers is the marking of high-water points from flood flows, which can be used by hydrologists to develop and improve the accuracy of floodplain maps.

If you or your local stream group is interested in assisting public works officials in this manner, meet with the logical city, county, or regional flood-control district or public works department and learn what watersheds have the most need for peak flow information. The agencies may have staff gauges already located at bridges or key points but lack the staff to read them. If you are going to start keeping records on your own, do not rely on your memory. To mark high-water points, put a discreet line of paint on a wall, bridge, abutment, etc., and note the date and time. Also, photograph the extent of the inundation, if possible.

Regional Averages for Bankfull Discharges

Chapter 4 established that an interested citizen or professional who wants to do stream restoration work should identify the active channel that is formed by the bankfull discharges. As explained, this is the part of the stream system most restoration work focuses on because it is where the stream channel makes most of its active adjustments and maintains and forms the in-channel aquatic ecosystem, as well. We also established in chapter 4 that any stream modifications need to meet the objective of helping the stream reach an equilibrium bankfull width and depth. Figure 4.13, developed by Leopold and Dunne, can be used to estimate regional average values for bankfull widths and depths for different drainage areas. The graph shows the average values taken from data for the San Francisco Bay area; the eastern United States; the Upper Green River, Wyoming; and the Upper Salmon River, Idaho. The authors point out that there is considerable consistency even among these widely scattered regions. They attribute the similarity of the bankfull values for drainage areas in the eastern United States and the San Francisco Bay area to similar rainfall patterns, exceeding 10 inches a year. The values from the Rocky Mountain states reflect smaller annual runoff.[13, 14]

If you are practicing restoration, you can use this graph as a guide for determining reasonable bankfull widths and depths for your stream, but it is a good idea to construct a comparable graph to most closely represent the average values for your particular region. This graph is one of my most important tools in designing the stream restoration projects I do in the San Francisco Bay area.

Those of us involved in urban stream restoration may want to use a graph of regional values to get a sense of whether the stream we want to manage or restore significantly diverges from the regional averages. If our stream of interest is significantly wider and deeper than the regional average, it may tell us that it is undergoing adjustments to urbanization. My experience working in the San Francisco Bay area with this graph is that the average values represented by slope A appear to represent an adjusted urban stream equilibrium. When I checked the files that indicate which gauging station data were used to plot this San Francisco Bay graph, I found that those gauging stations mostly represented streams in watersheds that have been influenced by urban development for a number of decades. When I use this San Francisco Bay graph, I assume it represents average values for an urbanized condition. Therefore, in this case, I don't assume the urbanized creeks I'm working on should have larger cross-sections than shown on this graph because of the impacts of urbanization unless I'm in a particularly impacted or degraded situation.

There are two commonly used ways of determining the bankfull widths and depths for a particular location on a stream. One is by using field observations, as described in chapter 4 and the other is by using stream-flow data at gauging streams, which can provide flood-frequency information. The value of the 1.5–2-year-recurrence-interval discharge generally corresponds well to the bankfull discharge. Drainage areas for a watershed can be computed off of topographic maps or can be taken from the gauging station data.[15]

A good college or university project is to develop these bankfull–dimension–drainage-area relationships for the region you are in. Go to a university or government library to find the U.S. Geological Survey Water Supply Papers. There is a

Water Resources division district office for the U.S. Geological Survey located in every state except Vermont, which can help you locate copies of the Water Supply Papers.[16, 17] Select the Water Supply Papers with the stream-gauge and flood-frequency records for the streams in your area. (There are separate volumes from each year.) Make a flood-frequency curve for the annual flood for each year there are records—try to use at least ten years of data. The flood-frequency curve shows the statistical frequency for different-sized flood discharges. Use *Water, A Primer* to get step-by-step directions for making a flood-frequency curve if you are unfamiliar with this process.[18] Read the value of the 1.5-year flood from that curve to determine the bankfull discharge for the station.

Also ask the U.S. Geological Survey for their forms (form 9–207) that show the current meter discharge measurements at the gauging stations. That information will give you the channel widths and depths measured for the discharges taken. Make graphs that relate the discharges to the widths, depths, and velocities. These graphs will resemble the graph in figure 8.2 in which the discharge is plotted against the flood stages. The stages indicate the depth of the flows. The discharges can similarly be plotted against their respective channel widths. Read the values for widths, depths, and velocities for the bankfull discharge.

In this way, determine the bankfull discharges, widths, depths, and velocities for enough gauging stations to represent the overall watershed conditions in your region. It is best if you can visit the stations and check the values you computed on paper with what you see in the field, as described in chapter 4.

You can plot drainage area vs. bankfull discharge, width, and depth once you have the bankfull values determined for each station. Use double-log (log-log) graph paper (as shown in figure 4.13) to plot that data for each station and to plot the regional relationships. A regional graph is made by plotting the drainage areas taken from the Water Supply Papers for each station on the abscissa (horizontal axis) against their corresponding values for bankfull dimensions on the ordinate (vertical axis). Fit your line so that it best represents the slope through the scatter of points. The slope of this line should not be too far off from the regional slopes in figure 4.13.

Water-Quality Monitoring and Watershed Inventories

Water-quality monitoring, which involves the collection of water samples to measure chemical, biological, and physical indicators of stream and lake health, has become a common and well-established domain of citizen volunteer organizations. Scientists are now encouraging these groups to expand their concept of monitoring to include observation of the physical condition of the watershed. One inventory done by a nonprofit organization in the San Jose, California, area mapped which stream channels were in culverts, which were above ground but concrete lined or rocked, and which still had some native plant growth. The Friends of the Los Angeles River found that it was important to establish what the potential ecological values of the concrete channelized river could be. One of their priorities became to inventory the remnant natural areas in the upper watershed for native plants, birds, and animals, so that they could present a case for downstream ecological values and call public attention to the fact that the river was once a rich ecological system running through the core of the Los Angeles metropolitan area. The Friends of Chicago River have carried out similar upstream inventories to call attention to the potential values of the downstream urbanized downtown and industrialized sections of the river.

Other citizen groups find that there is strong interest in the native and sports fisheries of the region. Organizations such as the Adopt-a-Stream Foundation in the Pacific Northwest have organized citizen watershed monitoring around the theme of bringing back the salmon. Here, water quality, the condition of the riparian woodland shading the streams, and the availability of shelter and spawning habitat for fish have become important parameters to monitor.

Water-Quality Monitoring

Background

A large body of water-quality literature has been written for the interested layperson, and so the emphasis here is to introduce readers to the concepts and help them connect with the existing resources.

The federal Clean Water Act of 1972 was amended in 1987 so that not only do industrial and commercial discharges and domestic sewage come under a permitting system, but nonpoint pollution, or pollution from urban and (nonurban) runoff, does as well. "Nonpoint" pollution, or polluted runoff, is distinguished from "point" pollution, which is traced to specific factory or treatment-plant discharge pipes. The act is enforced in each state by an agency designated by the state to enforce the standards set by the Environmental Protection Agency. It is important to find out what entity is responsible for enforcement of the act in your state and to develop a relationship with the staff in that agency. Such agencies are increasingly looking to citizen interest, awareness, and volunteer monitoring to help them enforce the water-quality standards required by the act. Water-quality monitoring has actually become a model of successful citizen-government cooperation and partnership. The Environmental Protection Agency has recognized this in recent years and has developed new programs to train and assist and fund citizen groups that do water-quality monitoring.

The following reprint of "Water Quality in Urban Creeks—How the Public Can Help Curb Pollution," written by a government water-quality official and published by the Urban Creeks Council of California, provides a good outline of the water-quality issues you should be aware of:

> Water quality in urban creeks can generally be assessed from two perspectives: is the water safe for people and does the water provide good habitat for wildlife? In terms of public health, urban creeks usually have bacterial counts which do not meet safe standards for drinking or swimming, but it should be possible to make creeks and streams free of real danger to children and others who may have incidental contact with the

water. Sources of bacterial pollution can be from human sewage, usually from unintentional cross-connections of sanitary sewage lines to storm sewers, from animal waste from birds and small mammals, and to some extent, from soil bacteria. Special problems occur in wet weather, when, in some areas, sanitary sewers back up and even overflow into streets, drain into storm sewers, and eventually into urban creeks. Even where this problem does not exist, wet weather can bring a heavy input of wastes from dogs. However, high bacterial counts during weather are no more a basis for paving over a creek than for paving over bays or lakes which have similar problems in wet weather.

In terms of wildlife habitat, urban creeks often provide the only fresh-water around during dry weather months, and many are bordered by heavy vegetation. This makes many urban creeks attractive habitat for many types of wildlife: invertebrates, frogs, birds, and small mammals.

Fish life in urban creeks is highly variable, influenced by physical barriers to migration or reaches which have been converted into covered storm sewers. The aquatic life in urban creeks is subject to discharges of pollutants into storm drains, such as waste oil. In general, the most serious incidents of pollution come from businesses rather than from home-owners. Such discharges are generally illegal, and violations of both the Federal Clean Water Act and State codes.

Detecting Pollution

People whose homes are near creeks, or who walk or hike along creeks are quite often those who can quickly spot suspect pollutants which have discharged into the stream. Examples of typical discharges are *heavy foaming*, usually from cleaning products such as soaps and detergents, *discolorations* of various kinds, odors from gasoline, solvents, or sewage, and *oily films* on the water.

Locating the source of a discharge is not always easy, but it is often possible to at least identify the storm drain input from which the pollution seems to be coming. Since most illegal discharges are intermittent, it is extremely helpful if their sources can be located while they are occurring.

Complaints are especially useful when they are specific enough to provide the appropriate state or regional agency with a good chance of identifying the responsible party. For example, a good complaint is, "Water with the smell of gasoline is coming from an 8 inch steel pipe on a hillside on the west side of ABC Creek, about 100 feet south of where First Street crosses the creek." A not-so-good complaint is, "There is an oily sheen on the water in ABC Creek in the portion of the creek just south of where First Street crosses over." A good worker complaint (usually anonymous) might be, "I work for ABC auto repair shop, located at S and 10th Streets and the foreman keeps flushing out radiators onto the parking lot where the water gets into the storm drain. I've told him this could get us in trouble and he ignores me. This happens most weekdays around 11 a.m."

Any complaint can be given anonymously if there is some reason to fear reprisals. This is very common. The best way to ensure that a government field inspector locates what you observed is to arrange to meet the inspector on the scene. The protection of urban creeks from pollution is critical to shaping the public attitudes that affect whether creeks will be saved from physical destruction. Pollution control efforts depend to a large degree on public reports rather than on agency initiative.

Recent Trends

Most citizen-based organizations concerned with streams in this country have focused their concern on the quality of the water. The volunteer monitoring programs previously mentioned have now grown to represent over 340,000 volunteers in the country.[20] In May of 1988 the EPA sponsored its first national conference on citizen volunteer monitoring, organized through its Office of Water, and it has held one every other year since then.[21]

EPA's involvement in volunteer monitoring was motivated by the passage of the Water Quality Act of 1987, which provided new responsibilities and funding for identifying and cleaning up nonpoint sources of pollution, and which established the National Estuary Program. The National Estuary Program particularly encourages public education and participation in the identification and management of pollution problems. An EPA study done in 1987 on its surface-water monitoring activities recommended the use of volunteer monitoring programs to assist states in conducting inventories. Many states that were once skeptical about using volunteer information are becoming increasingly aware of the value of these programs in collecting usable information and in developing an educated and involved constituency.[22] According to EPA publications, nationally only 37 percent of America's rivers and 46 percent of lakes are monitored by government agencies, suggesting a critical role for volunteer monitoring.

EPA is supporting these efforts with a national newsletter, as well as information and conferences. The National Estuary Program has expended funds on volunteer monitoring, and some of the funds appropriated to states under Section 106 of the Clean Water Act administered by the Office of Water Regulations and Standards are designated for volunteer monitoring programs.[23]

The citizens' movement for water-quality monitoring has spread from streams to other bodies of water. There are now EPA-assisted watchdog baykeeper and soundkeeper citizen monitoring programs in San Francisco Bay, the Hudson River, Long Island Sound, the Delaware River, the Raritan River, and Puget Sound. Volunteer monitoring is occurring on lakes, estuaries, wetlands, and coastal waters—even acid rain is being monitored.[24] The increase of government and public interest in volunteer monitoring programs appears to be coincident with increasing government responsibilities for environmental quality and decreasing budgets for federal, regional, and state pollution-monitoring programs.[25]

If you or your organization or local government is interested in organizing around water-quality issues, do not reinvent the wheel. There is a significant amount of organizing experience and educational materials available from existing organizations and grassroots-sponsored government programs that can help you get started. The Izaak Walton League's Save Our Streams project has an extensive network of nine hundred local organizations that do stream monitoring. The League has developed an impressive inventory of stream-monitoring kits, water-quality fact sheets, water-quality monitoring forms, videotapes, and booklets that are all produced with the purpose of helping citizen groups organize and carry out water-quality monitoring. Notable Save Our Stream programs include the Chesapeake Bay Regional Program and the Delaware Stream Watch, as well as state-supported programs in Ohio, Indiana, Illinois, Kentucky, Pennsylvania, West Virginia, and Wisconsin.[26]

The first state-supported program was established in Maryland. The state of Maryland's Department of Natural Resources Save Our Streams Program was started by Malcolm King, a member of the Izaak Walton League, in 1970. The government program was an interesting partnership between the Department of Natural Resources and the League, in which a steering committee of conservationists directed the activities of the program. The state supported the salary and basic operating expenses of the program, and the program manager raised funds for and had access to over four hundred volunteers to do restoration and pollution-control projects. The program has since become a completely nonprofit operation.[27] In the Northwest, the Adopt-a-Stream Foundation located in Washington has an active volunteer monitoring and stream restoration program with emphasis on restoring salmonid or anadromous fish habitat. The city of Bellevue in the Seattle area holds regularly scheduled workshops for citizens on monitoring water quality and native fish populations. In the Southeast, the North Carolina Department of Natural Resources and Community Development, located in the Division of Environmental Management, has produced impressive publications such as "A Guide to Stream Walking" and "Stream Watch Manual" through their stream-watch program started in 1983. The purpose of that program was to organize volunteers to "adopt" streams near their homes. In New England, the River Watch Network located in Vermont covers the New England states with volunteer monitoring programs and has expanded its area of involvement to Texas and border areas with Mexico.

Monitoring Methods

If you are interested in the condition of a stream, you should first find out if the stream has been monitored. Many states keep records of water quality in a central location, and your state department of environmental quality or natural resources may be able to tell you if your stream has been monitored. Be sure to ask other local citizen groups if they have been involved in monitoring.

Pollution comes from a wide variety of sources and differs depending on the land uses in a watershed. Contrary to public perceptions, the pollutants most commonly found in streams are sediments and silts from eroding stream banks, not toxic chemicals such as lead, mercury, oil, and grease. Nutrients such as nitrogen and phosphorus found in fertilizers, detergents, and sewage treatment discharges, are also more common than toxics.

Three types of stream monitoring will give you information about your stream: chemical monitoring, biological monitoring, and physical monitoring. A combination of the three types gives you the most complete picture of your stream. Budget and time constraints will most likely determine what monitoring methods you choose, but the key is to supplement data that are already available.

Physical Monitoring

There are two components to physical monitoring: a watershed survey of landscape conditions and a habitat assessment. The watershed survey needs to record land uses and the approximate percentage of the land uses in the basin. The survey should estimate the percentage of impermeable surfaces and the percentage drained by storm sewers. This is important information for watershed models that estimate storm runoff volumes and rates. The location of culverts should be noted. Agricultural and forestry practices should be noted. The type of soils and geology and vegetation communities should be determined. The condition of the upper watershed, floodplain, drainages, and major channels should be observed. Note the different demographics in the watershed. Are there different cultures or economic classes located in different parts?

This kind of survey can include a one-time background investigation and periodic field inventories. The background investigation may include town and county records of your stream, maps, photos, news stories, industrial discharge records, interviews with local residents, and soils, geology, and topographic maps. These sources should help you to understand the causes of the specific chemical and biological and physical conditions of your watershed and stream. For example, high nitrogen and phosphorus concentrations may be attributed to a number of domestic, agricultural, or industrial sources. However, if you know what the mix of land use is in your watershed, you can begin to identify the sources of the pollutants. Specific restoration techniques or management practices may then be implemented once the sources are tied to land use.

Physical monitoring should include recording characteristics of your stream at a detailed, site-specific level, including the condition of waterway banks, vegetation, channel shapes, flood discharges, habitat, and social factors associated with the site. A particularly useful observation that may have a significant role in the design of any stream channel restoration effort is the slope of the stream banks (see figure 8.3). A complete field inventory is provided beginning on page 319. The measurements you take should include information that will help you understand the flow frequencies and dynamics of stream channels and floodplains.

A habitat assessment may also be part of your physical monitoring. This involves evaluating each stream reach for macroinvertebrates habitat, channel forms,

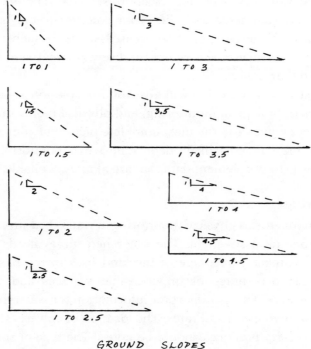

GROUND SLOPES
STREAM BANK RESTORATION HAS THE MOST OPTIONS
FOR REVEGETATION STRATEGIES AT SLOPES I TO 1.5
AND LESS. SLOPES AT 1 TO 3 TO 1 TO 4.5 (OR
LESS) ARE IDEAL. SLOPES STEEPER THAN
1 TO 1.5 OR 1 TO 2, DEPENDING ON THE SOILS, MAY
REQUIRE A MIX OF STRUCTURAL FEATURES, SUCH AS
WOOD AND ROCK WITH VEGETATION.

FIGURE 8.3. INVENTORY STREAM-BANK SLOPES.

shelter for fish, sediment deposition or scour, and riparian vegetation zone width
and condition. Habitat assessment should be set up to examine characteristics that
affect both macroinvertebrates and fish. Because aquatic environments are inherently interconnected, a healthy stream must contain good habitat for both bugs
and fish.

Chemical Monitoring

Chemical monitoring of your stream will provide you with information about pollutants that are entering it from either point sources, like factories, or nonpoint
sources, such as storm sewers. Simple chemical measurements of dissolved oxygen
levels, pH, temperature, nutrients, conductivity, turbidity, and other parameters can
be made by volunteers using simple, relatively inexpensive chemical monitoring
kits.

Chemical monitoring can help establish if state water-quality standards for designated uses are being met. Each state has set standards for chemical pollutants in
waters used for fishing, swimming, and other water-dependent activities. You can
determine if the standards have been met for the uses dedicated to your stream.

Monitoring can not only determine if water-quality standards are being violated, it can also help identify the sources of pollution. For example, because conductivity is often a symptom of industrial discharge, you may be able to link highly conductive water with a factory upstream. High chloride values may indicate pollution from septic tanks. Low dissolved oxygen usually indicates that a buildup of nutrients and algae is using up the stream's natural oxygen. Those three parameters are easy and fun to collect data on, and a number of companies sell kits for their measurement. (see "Sources of Information" at the end of this section for how to order these kits).

Ideally, chemical data should be collected weekly. It is important to keep in mind that your sample will give you an idea of the chemistry of the water only at the time the sample is taken. As temperature fluctuates throughout the day, the chemical composition of the water will change. Likewise, a factory discharge that takes place routinely at 5:00 P.M. may not be registered by a monitoring routine that takes place at noon.

The simple monitoring kits available may not detect all the pollutants in your stream. Also, because specific pollutants are not consistently present in the stream does not mean that they do not cause long-term problems. Using the above example of a factory upstream discharging at regular intervals, while the pollutant itself may be evident in the stream for only a day or two after it is discharged, stream life may be severely affected on an ongoing basis. Your monitoring may not always find the pollutant that is nevertheless having a negative effect on stream life.

Biological Monitoring

Biological monitoring using macroinvertebrates, or small insects, that live on the bottoms of streams can tell you a great deal about the health of the stream because the organisms have different tolerances to pollution, and they can be identified by lay volunteers. Biological monitoring is different from chemical monitoring in that it offers information on the impacts of pollution rather than the constituency of the water.

Macroinvertebrates are aquatic insects and crustaceans that are large enough to be seen without a microscope. They include stoneflies, caddisflies, crayfish, clams, and worms. The types and numbers of macroinvertebrates present in the stream can provide clues to the health of the stream. For example, most stoneflies are intolerant of pollution and need good oxygen levels, but the aquatic tubifex worm can withstand a great deal of pollution and can live in a stream for several days with no oxygen. A stream that supports a number and diversity of stoneflies is considered fairly healthy, while one with only tubifex worms is not.

A healthy stream has a large number of different kinds of pollution-sensitive macroinvertebrates. A polluted stream has only a few kinds of pollution-intolerant macroinvertebrates. Macroinvertebrates serve as full-time residents and monitors of the stream. The changes in the types of critters able to live in the stream will help determine if there is an ongoing pollution problem. Macroinvertebrates also can help you assess impacts from habitat disturbances. While chemical monitoring may indicate good water quality, a lack of diverse macroinvertebrate populations may tell you there is damaged habitat due to siltation of the stream, lack of adequate cover, or other structural deficiencies such as loss of pools and riffles.

Biological samples taken four times a year are usually adequate to provide an overall picture of your stream's health. By monitoring the macroinvertebrate populations in your stream before, during, and after your restoration project, you can get a sense of whether your efforts are affecting water and habitat quality.

The organizations listed at the end of this section provide training in biological water-quality monitoring involving the identification of macroinvertebrates. Their methods entail collection of macroinvertebrates using a fine-mesh net called a kick seine to trap the bottom-dwelling insects. After the bugs are collected, they are identified, and based on their types, numbers, and diversity, a water-quality rating of good to poor is assigned to the waterway.

In order to get started on any of these monitoring activities, you need to choose the parameters that you will monitor and set up a meeting with staffs from local and state government agencies to ensure that parameters and methods you choose are acceptable to them and will yield valid data.

The Links between Monitoring and Restoration

Field data should identify watershed conditions that can be associated with sediment loads, erosion, storm-water problems, nutrient loads, habitat quality, and chemical and biological constituents of water. The conditions noted should not only suggest potential restoration activities, the data should also help set priorities for those activities in order to get the biggest bang for your efforts. For example, nutrient loading may lead you to consider detention areas for parking lot storm runoff, but in fact livestock fencing around stream buffer corridors in an upper watershed grazing area may provide the greatest benefits. A bank restoration project may be considered for a site, but greater channel stabilization benefits could be derived from removing or re-installing an improperly designed upstream culvert. In any event, water and habitat quality must be linked to the physical condition present in the watershed. The following list matches on-the-ground restoration remedies with common indicators of watershed problems.

- *High temperature.* All aquatic organisms, from invisible microbes to macroinvertebrates to fish, are dependent on a certain range of temperature for their survival. If water temperatures are consistently too high, the aquatic life will be stressed and will eventually die. The most common reasons for elevated water temperatures are the release of stored water from dams and the removal of vegetation from riverbanks. The most common restoration prescription for temperature problems is the revegetation of stream channels. Dams can be removed as part of restoration projects, or in lieu of that, water trapped behind large impoundments can be released from the deeper, cooler portions of the pool.

- *Excess nutrients and chemical parameters.* While nitrogen and phosphorus are essential plant nutrients, in excess they can cause serious water-quality problems. A surplus of those nutrients can cause a dramatic increase in aquatic plant growth, sometimes altering the habitat so much that native aquatic fauna can no longer survive. The increase of instream plant growth can lower dissolved oxygen levels and increase temperature. Marsh wetland types have received significant attention for their capacity as nutrient sinks and are used with increasing frequency as the final stage of wastewater treatment. Recent research described in chapter 3 concludes that healthy riparian systems are equal to or better than marshes for removing sediment and nutrients from water. Riparian areas are better at reducing phosphorus, while marshes and other non-riparian wetlands are typically high in phosphorus and can actually contribute phosphorus to the water.

- *Degraded streamside vegetation.* Riparian vegetation can be an effective filter for nutrients in urban as well as agricultural areas. Riparian buffer zones as narrow as 20 feet make valuable contributions to water quality. This finding underscores the importance of vegetation as a part of any restoration project. The development and clearing of riparian areas not only represent a loss of the water treatment capabilities of the riparian area but may turn those damaged environments into sources of nonpoint pollution. Because such areas have served as sinks for sediment and nutrients, they can export the sediment through disturbance and erosion.

- *Sediment load imbalances.* On a national level, sediment and silt are the most common pollutants in streams. There are several problems with high sediment loads. Sediment and silts may contribute to high turbidity (a measure of the suspended solids in the water), which can raise water temperatures, reduce photosynthesis in the stream, and damage fisheries. Large sediment loads can also accumulate in stream channels, resulting in the filling of the channels and their associated wetlands. Most destabilized urban waterways are suffering from either excessive erosion or excessive deposition. The key word here is "excessive" because streams should naturally erode and transport and deposit sediments. A basic design concept behind *any* stream restoration project needs to be providing the proper shape of the stream channel, so as to transport sediment in a way that does not create a damaged landscape. Watershed treatments that either reduce excessive runoff or reduce excessive sediment transport can be critical components of a restoration plan.

- *Disruption of stream-flow timing.* Runoff entering unvegetated streams will create much more erosion than in vegetated streams. During heavy rainfalls, cement-lined channels and other channels without vegetation transport large volumes of runoff (often polluted runoff) quickly without the benefit of any biological traps or filters. Well-vegetated streams, on the other hand, trap, filter, and slowly release water over a long period of time. In areas where streams run only during the winter, revegetation may turn a rainy season stream into a perennial stream that will flow year round. Restoration of a riparian area along Mahogany Creek in Nevada increased summer stream flow by 400 percent.[28]

- *Storm-water and flood problems.* Flood management should inherently be an environmental benefit of restoration activities. Field inventories that note flooded streets, clogged culverts, and structures in flood-hazard areas should prescribe restoration measures including culvert replacements, and removal, storm-water catchment areas, structure relocations, and floodplain restoration.

- *Degraded wildlife habitat.* Watershed and stream restoration projects should return to the environment the physical "structure" needed to support aquatic and terrestrial wildlife. Floodplains should support riparian woodlands. Stream channels should contain the forms critical to instream life, including meanders, pools, riffles, and woody debris. Backwaters, sloughs, prairies, and marshes that were historic features should be returned to the landscape.

While most citizens understand the value of making inventories of environmental conditions before taking action, the monitoring of conditions after projects are completed occurs less often than it should. The traditional culture of public works projects has been to install projects—dams, weirs, retaining walls, channelization projects, grade-control structures, culverts, etc.—and the installation is considered the end of the project. Because restoration (as well as placement of public works projects) deals with changing, dynamic, natural systems, we must necessarily return to fine tune and adjust our restoration work. We must also record what went well or badly with our work so we have a learning mechanism as part of our trade.

Field Inventories

The field checklist provided here is intended to help anyone interested in pursuing stream restoration projects to organize a plan for rectifying a stream's problems. The list is designed to remind restorationists to consider the diversity of adjustments that may be appropriate to integrate into a management and restoration scheme. Ideally, this kind of inventory should be done by a team, which can include landscape architects, environmental planners, erosion control specialists, engineers, geomorphologists, hydrologists, and plant ecologists. It should be conducted before a restoration project is proposed or designed to make sure you are not missing something that should be noticed. The citizen group that uses this checklist will be a great asset in articulating the stream's problems and needs to government officials, consultants, and other groups you are working with. This field inventory can provide guidance for post-project monitoring as well as pre-project planning.

Post-project monitoring should focus on changes in the watershed; improvement of instream conditions; growth and diversification of vegetation; changes in channel erosion and sedimentation; and changes in water-quality indicators. Increases in bird and wildlife sightings and fisheries can provide the ultimate measurement of ecological recovery. Be sure to take before and after project photographs.

Field Checklist for Identifying Waterway Management Needs

Land Management Issues

Urban Development

- Storm sewers discharging into the stream. (Also note the culvert's angle of entrance into the stream in relation to the stream flow.)
- Impermeable surfaces. (Does the runoff flow into the gutter and storm drains?)
- Are there structural controls on stream meander migration? Are structures too close to the stream banks?
- Culverting up or downstream.
- Polluted runoff.
- Diversions for water supplies.
- More flows in the dry seasons because of landscape irrigation runoff.
- Less flows in the dry seasons because of water diversions or groundwater pumping.
- Sediment from construction. (Note the general size of sediment and where it comes from.)
- Industrial discharges.
- Channelization.
- Channelization maintenance with use of mowing, burning, or spraying.
- Are there gullies in the upper portion of the watershed undergoing headward erosion?
- Is the stream located in a greenbelt, park, or isolated area or is it close to development?
- Are mowing and vegetation clearing occurring close to the stream channel?

Other Land Uses

- Forestry practices and woodland uses including:
  - clear-cutting
  - stream corridor buffer zones
  - selective cutting
- Agricultural practices and land uses including:
  - crops
  - grazing (Can animals get into the streamside vegetation and channel? Is native vegetation significantly degraded? Are the soils compacted from overgrazing? Look for changes in runoff patterns, erosion, and/or sediment deposition.)
  - pesticide use
  - windbreaks, conservation plantings, or wildlife preserves
  - farm ponds
  - upstream detention basins or retention reservoirs

Watershed Influences

- What is the drainage area discharging into your restoration project site?
- What percentage of the watershed area is drained by conventional storm sewers? What percentage is in impervious surfaces?
- Is there sheet, rill, or gully erosion in the slopes of the watershed? (See glossary for definitions.)
- Are storm sewers or irrigation systems diverting water out of the watershed?
- Is the topography of the stream valley steep, moderate, or low gradient?
- Are the soils and geology of stable types or erodible? Bedrock, clays, silt, sands?
- What percentage of the watershed is in native vegetation?
- In cold regions, does ice action on drainages affect erosion or vegetation?
- Are there existing gully-control measures, instream weirs, bank stabilization projects or failed projects?
- Are floodplain conditions natural and unobstructed, or are levees, berms, or other structures located in the floodplain?

Factors Adjacent to or in the Stream Channel

Vegetation

- Are there bare banks with no vegetation, or is streamside vegetation protecting the banks from erosion?
- Is there a lack of ground cover or undergrowth?
- Is there a full canopy of riparian vegetation? Is the channel exposed to sun, or is it shaded?
- Is there a narrow or wide strip of riparian vegetation?
- Is there a good habitat for wildlife, or is the vegetation near the creek sparse?
- Are there rushes or reeds in the low-flow channel?
- Is the channel choked with growth? Or is it well shaded and clear?
- Is the channel vegetated with grass or more natural riparian shrubs and trees (in the Midwest, for example, with prairie species)?
- Are exotic non-native species contributing to a lack of riparian undergrowth or soil stability, or harming the natural biological diversity of the site?
- Are there standing or downed trees that may block the flow in the channel enough to cause flood problems during high flows?
- Is some streamside vegetation or debris diverting flows against banks and causing harmful erosion?
- Are rain gutters from buildings eroding stream banks?

Water Quality

- Are any of the following indicators of good water quality present?
  - many forms of bottom-dwelling (benthic) insects (mayflies, stoneflies, caddisflies)
  - snails and crayfish present, but not abundant
  - a few, or no rooted aquatic plants
  - no floating dark green algae
  - clear water

- sand, gravel, or cobble bottom, no mud
- Are any of the following indicators of water pollution present?
    - exposure to sun; warm water
    - large growth of aquatic plants attached to the bottom
    - no fish, snails, or crayfish
    - cloudy or murky water
    - foamy water
    - oily or discolored water
    - muddy bottom

Physical Characteristics of the Stream Channel

- Are any of the following channel constrictions causing erosion or backup of flows?
    - bridges
    - culverts, undersized culverts, or culverts installed at the wrong gradient
    - debris in channel (e.g., woody vegetation, shopping carts, urban dumping)
    - "homemade" bank protection works (e.g., car bodies, tires, oil drums, etc.)
- Are any of the following signs of unstable stream banks or bed present?
    - bed erosion (degrading); exposed bridge pilings, undercut storm culverts, undercut banks, perched (elevated) tributaries
    - bed filling (aggrading), sediment deposits covering the bed, buried culverts, reduced bridge clearances
    - erosion of banks and channel widening, bank line scalloped and irregular
    - stream straightened and re-creating a meandering pattern
    - slumping or collapsing banks
    - toe of the stream bank slope eroding out or down
- Are any of the following signs of stable stream banks or bed present?
    - banks sloped and not vertical; vegetation extending to toe of the bank
    - trees growing on the banks
    - sediment located in point bars; bars partially stabilized with vegetation
- What is the slope of the stream bank's vertical height/horizontal distance (e.g., 1:1 slope, 2:1 slope, 3:1 slope, or greater)? Are the slopes steep (1:1 slope) or gradual (3:1)? (Refer to figure 8.3.)

Channel Geometry and Profile

- What is the width and depth of the bankfull channel for the reaches you are interested in restoring?
- What is the bankfull width and depth of a nearby stable section of channel with a similar gradient, drainage area, and streambed sediment size?
- Is the gradient of the channel steep, moderate, or low?
- What is the velocity of the flows at bankfull stage, and what is the bankfull discharge in cubic feet per second?
- Are there sudden changes in the grade of the bed (headcuts or knickpoints) where the streambed is eroding or degrading in an upstream direction?

- Are there controls on the channel profile such as dams, weirs, bedrock falls, culverts, beaver dams, ponds?
- What is the average grain size of the bed sediment deposits and bars?
- What is the gradient of the channel, and how does it differ from the slope of the stream valley where it is located?
- Is the channel confined with a small or indiscernable floodplain or is the channel unconfined with a wide floodplain?

Flood Flow Information

- Does your area have a flood hazards map?
- Are you in a National Flood Insurance Program area?
- Are there records of overbank flows or flood elevations from:
  - nearby residents
  - U.S. Geological Survey records
  - newspapers
  - photographs
  - county or local public works departments?
- Are there recent high-water marks?
- What are the flood-flow discharges on your stream in cubic feet per second?
- What are the stages or elevation of those discharges?
- Have there been debris accumulations?
- What does the stream hydrography look like? Is the stream "flashy" (a short time elapses between the middle of the rainstorm and the peak of the flood flows)?

Social Environment

- Are adults or children using the stream for passive or active recreation? (Is there bank erosion caused by children?)
- Do people fish there, or is there a potential for fishing?
- Is there public access to the stream, or is it mostly surrounded by private land?
- Is there an organization in the vicinity that may have an interest in the stream, such as a neighborhood association, sport fishing group, environmental group, or chamber of commerce?
- Is there an obvious local perception that the stream is a community value or a nuisance?
- Does there appear to be potential for developing a park, open space, or trails?
- Is there potential for new development into which the stream could be integrated in a sensitive manner?
- Have you identified a local population being impacted by damages from floods or erosion?

Sources of Information for Water-Quality Monitoring and Field Inventories

Manuals, Pamphlets, and Guides

The U.S. Environmental Protection Agency is an excellent source for information on water quality and stream monitoring. There are two EPA offices to contact: Office of Community and Intergovernmental Relations, 401 M Street SW, Washington, DC 20460; and Volunteer Water Monitoring, Office of Marine and Estuarine Protection, 401 M Street SW (WH–556–F), Washington, DC 20460.

U.S. EPA has a wide variety of material available on how to set up a water-quality monitoring program. *Environmental Education Materials for Teachers and Young People* (grades K–12) lists education materials available on environmental issues, including workbooks, lesson plans, films, and computer software. *The National Directory of Citizen Volunteer Environmental Monitoring Programs,* 4th edition (EPA 503/9–90–004, Office of Water, January 1994), lists organizations and gives contacts, phone numbers, and a description of activities.

Volunteer Water Monitoring: A Guide for State Managers (EPA, 400/4–90–10, Office of Water, August 1990).

The Monitor's Handbook, LaMotte Company, P.O. Box 329, Chestertown, MD 21620, (800) 344–3100.

An Introduction to Water Quality Monitoring Using Volunteers: A Handbook for Coordinators, 2nd edition (1993) Alliance for the Chesapeake Bay, Baltimore, MD, (410) 377–6270.

Save Our Streams Volunteer Trainer's Handbook, Karen Firehock (1994) Izaak Walton League, Gaithersburg, MD.

Water-Quality Monitoring Kits

LaMotte Chemical Products, Inc., sells chemical test kits for the field and lab. For more information, write to: P.O. Box 329, Chestertown, MD 21602, or call (800) 344–3100.

VWR Scientific is a supplier of scientific instruments and chemicals. For more information, write to: P.O. Box 2643, Irving, TX 75061, or call (800) 527–1576.

Thomas Scientific is a supplier of scientific instruments and chemicals. For more information, call the main office at (609) 467–2000.

Millipore Corporation specializes in bacterial testing. For more information, call (800) 225–1380.

HACH Company is a supplier of chemical test kits for the field and lab. For more information, write to: P.O. Box 389, Loveland, CO 80539, or call (800) 525–5940.

Fisher Scientific is a supplier of scientific instruments and chemicals. For more information, write to: 711 Forbes Avenue, Pittsburgh, PA 15219, or call (800) 225–4040.

Assistance from the Coalition to Restore Urban Waters

These offices can assist with volunteer citizen monitoring.

Lake Ponchartrain Basin Foundation
3838 N. Causeway Boulevard, Suite 2070
Metairie, LA 70002
(504) 836–2215

New York–New Jersey Baykeeper
American Littoral Society
Sandy Hook
Highlands, NJ 07732
(908) 291–0176

Missouri Stream Team
P.O. Box 180
Jefferson City, MO 65102
(573) 751–4115, X 596

River Watch Network
153 State Street
Montpelier, VT 05602
(802) 223–3840

Izaak Walton League
Save Our Streams
707 Conservation Lane
Gaithersburg, MD 20878–2983
(800) BUG–IWLA

Urban Streams Council
729 S.E. 33rd Street
Portland, OR 97219
(503) 239–4065

Adopt-a-Stream Foundation
Box 5558
Everett, WA 98206
(206) 388–3559

Friends of the Chicago River
407 S. Dearborn Avenue, Suite 1580
Chicago, IL 60605
(312) 939–0490

Urban Creeks Council of California
1250 Addison Street, Suite 107
Berkeley, CA 94702
(510) 540–6669

Georgia Adopt-a-Stream
Environmental Protection Division
7 Martin Luther King Drive SW, Suite 643
Atlanta, GA 30334
(404) 656–4988

Watershed and Stream Management for Property Owners

Engineers in local or regional flood-control districts or public works departments often despair when they try to address urban stream problems because it appears that local property owners have conspired against them. It seems as though the property owners lie awake at night devising ways to create erosion and flood hazards in their backyard creeks. Public works personnel and local officials alike dread the thought of interacting with property owners over these issues because there are often latent hostilities and frustrations in the populace over stream problems. This has been one of the prime motivations in putting creeks out of sight and out of mind in culverts or in concrete behind chain-link fences.

Some local public works and planning agencies have come to realize that this social-political dynamic is a losing situation for all the interests involved. The first way to change this dynamic is to hold or attend neighborhood meetings and distribute literature to property owners explaining how they can take constructive action to help solve urban stream problems. Santa Cruz County in California prepared a *Stream Care* guide for streamside property owners to encourage responsible practices and offered county assistance in removing undesirable debris from streams. The pamphlet provides a county phone number that will connect the homeowner with a no-charge stream debris management service.[29] In some localities, such as Bellevue, Washington, a major focus of urban watershed management programs is to enlist the citizenry in correcting urban watershed problems. The Bellevue Stream Team Program has produced a plethora of stream and watershed pamphlets for city residents and businesses.[30] In the Midwest, the Northeastern Illinois Planning Commission has published excellent urban stream and wetland management publications,[31] and in the Southeast, the Georgia Soil and Water Conservation Commission has produced a notable document for property owners on stream-corridor erosion solutions.[32] The Georgia Conservancy has a videotape that is particularly appropriate for club or living-room meetings on community-based watershed management measures.[33] Nonprofit citizen groups are increasingly being solicited by government programs to do public outreach, education, and corrective projects. The following guidelines for urban stream management are useful for the public works engineer as well as for the property owners:

1. *Remove culverts where possible and avoid installing new ones.* Culverting can create as many problems as it seems to solve. In most situations, for reasons of economic efficiency culverts are designed to carry at the maximum, the one-in-10- or one-in-25-year flood. They guarantee a backup for flood flows and flooding of streets, structures, neighborhoods, and business districts during larger storms. Culverts can burst under too much hydraulic pressure, particularly if debris becomes trapped in them. The closed pipes contract the space the water moves through and thereby increase pressures and velocities coming out the end of the pipe, which frequently causes erosion problems downstream. Culverts commonly become blocked with debris or sediment, another way to create backwaters and flooding upstream of the pipe. It is not unusual to see erosional damage in stream channels upstream of culverts. That is because storm flows back up behind the culverts and saturate the stream banks; when the water finally draws down, the saturated stream banks, weakened by their water content, collapse. Culverts put in at the wrong grade are guaranteed to cause sedimentation or erosional problems.

   A public works administrator for a California city proclaimed that "out of

88 [received] calls for flooding and water problems in the 1995 floods, 86 were for culverts and two were for open creeks." It is much easier to locate and remove an obstruction in an open channel than it is to locate and correct a problem in a culvert. Such practical storm management considerations have led storm-water districts and public works departments, particularly those in older urban areas, to remove culverts.

Another incentive for daylighting creeks is to improve the aesthetics and environment of a neighborhood or a business district. The restoration project provides a "there there"— or a beautification project, a park where a derelict piece of land once stood.

2. *Replace culverts with bridges or fords.* Where stream crossings are necessary, bridges generally reduce the number of problems culverts create. Bridges do need to be designed, however, with adequate clearance for flood flows, and bridge abutments need to be designed so that they minimize the catchment of debris and deflection of flows against banks. Another option may be the use of fords, or roads that cross small streams at the stream grade and, during high water, allow the stream to flow over the road. These are more appropriate in suburban and semirural to rural areas (figure 8.4).

3. *Plan a neighborhood-coordinated response to erosion problems.* When property owners put in retaining walls, riprap, oil drums, and car bodies to stop their land from eroding, they only create problems downstream. Meet with property owners and tell them to put their money into a more effective solution: a coordinated bank stabilization plan.

4. *Leave streamside vegetation to protect property from erosion.*

5. *Set structures back from the stream* so that natural stream channel meandering and overbank flows do not endanger structures.

6. *Control livestock from access to stream corridors; fence stream corridors.* The central focus of many stream restoration projects has been the fencing of stream corridors from livestock. While fencing projects are usually associated with rural areas, many urban watersheds include lands set aside for water-supply storage, parks, grazing, or farming in the upper reaches. Land management practices have a profound effect on the quality of resources downstream in urbanized areas. Fencing livestock from creeks and river channels often offers satisfying, big-bang-for-the-bucks results.

In many areas, livestock are grazed along rivers and streams and use those resources as a source of water, food, and shelter. However, uncontrolled livestock can have a variety of detrimental effects on streams, rivers, and wetlands. Manure contributes excess nutrients to waterways and can also contribute harmful bacteria. Cattle can disturb a stream's natural equilibrium by trampling the streambeds, often resulting in an overwidened channel. Streamside vegetation is frequently obliterated, leaving banks bare and waterways unshaded.

Cattle can also compact bank soil, reducing the habitat for native vegetation (figure 8.4).

Fencing can have immediate benefits to your own property as well as to the property of downstream residents. Stream-bank caving and subsequent headward gullying can remove large quantities of soil and endanger pastures, roads, and other structures on your land. Downhill drainage or culverts won't be so inclined to fill with sediment. Water quality on your property will improve. Work with surrounding landowners to agree on the boundaries of buffer zones around creeks, streams, and rivers and fence livestock out. Landowners and leasers may be concerned about seeking alternative sources of water and shade.

FIGURE 8.4. STREAM-CHANNEL MANAGEMENT STRATEGIES.
(a) Fencing riparian areas to protect from livestock. (Note that the left side of the fence is an unprotected area and the right side is protected.) (b) A concrete ford used to create a roadway over a creek in lieu of a culvert. (c) Neighborhood stream cleanup projects can easily increase channel capacities by two to three times after the debris is removed.

Some fencing plans rotate access areas to waterways, giving the waterways a chance to recover from livestock access between rotations. Others provide cattle with water and shade in areas adjacent to stream corridors. Access to water can be provided by catching upslope spring water in tubs, pumping water to troughs, or fencing for limited access to streams.

7. *Repair gullies.* Gully restoration has its early roots in 1930s Soil Conservation Service erosion control projects on farmlands. These days, gullies are common in both urban and rural environments. They show up in backyards and parks and next to roadbeds, highways, and parking lots. Because gully repair is particularly appropriate for property owners, civilian conservation corps, and conservation organizations to carry out, the methods are described in chapter 9.

8. *Remove unwanted debris.* A major portion of stream problems can be corrected by removing garbage, junk, and dumped waste from stream channels. Debris can deflect stream flows, causing significant bank erosion. It may pollute the water; it definitely destroys the aesthetic values of urban waterways; and it can back up flows, causing flooding. Neighborhood stream cleanup projects are likely the most cost-effective flood-damage-reduction and water-quality control projects a local organization can invest in.

9. *Minimize or eliminate the use of flashboard dams, weirs, and check dams to create pools.* Homeowners (and park managers) love to create ornamental pools and swimming holes in their yards by putting in small dams. They love to create the sound of splashing water with weirs and dams. They generally don't equate the subsequent destabilized meander and erosion problems adjacent to, upstream of or downstream of the dam with their actions. The dams catch sediment and usually lessen the upstream gradient. The stream may compensate by scouring wider banks. It is common to see streams erode around the structures and very common to see downstream erosion. These structures may also interfere with fish passage and seasonal migrations. Rocks placed in creeks become weirs, grade-control structures, and flow deflectors. Unless a person has a clear grasp of stream dynamics, the seemingly harmless intention of providing aesthetic amenities to a stream channel can backfire and cause significant physical problems.

10. *Don't introduce wild or domestic animals to the riparian corridor* without carefully considering your stream management objectives. Beaver have been introduced to some watersheds as part of a stream restoration strategy, for example. If the restoration objective is to create wetlands and higher groundwater tables, beaver dams can be useful. If your restoration objective is to check the erosion of an overly wide channel, then the last thing you want is to have beaver around.

Sometimes goats will be brought into a riparian corridor to control blackberries or other invasive plants. Goats don't know a blackberry from an oak, however, so desirable species need to be protected behind wire cages.

Corrals with domestic animals, such as horses, should be located so that the waste from the corral does not run into the stream.

11. *Site septic tanks so that they will not contribute to stream pollution.*

12. *Do not dump wastes into streams!*

The Return of the Civilian Conservation Corps

A Critical Restoration Workforce

The Civilian Conservation Corps of the 1930s laid much of the groundwork for the contemporary urban stream restoration movement. Chapter 6 describes how the availability of an inexpensive and dependable labor force, a conservation ethic, and land conservation publications from that era provided the framework and inspiration for much of the urban stream restoration movement originating in the western United States in the 1980s and 1990s.

The return of the conservation corps occurred at the state and local levels in the 1970s–1990s. This has added some critical components to citizen-initiated and community-based restoration. The first is that the state and local corps have expanded the possibility of people finding entry-level work in the conservation and restoration fields in the communities where they live. Local and state corps in particular have created a number of important links between community and restoration work. Many contemporary state and local youth corps draw their workforces from urban low-income and blighted areas and offer a combination of work and education to these youth, who in turn accomplish work benefiting the communities they live in. Corps are serving as training grounds for restoration professionals because of the opportunities they offer to engage in on-the-ground work and to develop supervisory and design skills.

Corps provide an important complement to citizen volunteer-based restoration projects. Volunteers associated with sport fishing, hunting, environmental groups, community service, neighborhood associations, watershed councils, etc., have taken on an important role in sponsoring and carrying out a variety of restoration projects. This kind of participation can be critical in a practical sense for the long-term community participation needed to keep projects politically supported, maintained, irrigated, and protected from vandalism. There are, however, inherent concerns and limitations sometimes associated with community organizations that corps are not as vulnerable to.

Conservation and service corps have their own insurance for liability, accidents, workers compensation, etc. Often small nonprofit groups and community organizations that organize volunteers do not carry liability insurance, or it is difficult for them to acquire adequate insurance for restoration work. Conservation corps also enjoy the advantage of including people with supervisory, construction, and conservation work experience. The corps come outfitted with uniforms for outdoor work, safety gear, equipment, and tools. A corps labor force can provide a more predictable number of workers for a longer specified period of time than can strictly citizen volunteer forces. Much of the restoration work described in this book requires a predictabile and consistent workforce for a week to a month of full-time labor using a full-size crew of ten.

The projects in which I have been able to use citizen volunteers in combination with a locally based conservation corps have been the most rewarding experiences. Usually, the presence of conservation corps labor has ultimately made the project feasible. My usual assumption is that volunteers will accomplish a portion of the work and may make the project installation go in quicker. Most of the time (there *are* exceptions) I don't assume they are the workforce responsible for the job.

The Status of the Conservation Corps

Five state or local conservation corps with year-round or just summer youth employment existed in 1981. By 1994, there were 120 local and state youth conservation and service corps located in thirty-eight states and the District of Columbia and involving more than twenty-six thousand participants. The state and local corps are coordinated by the nonprofit National Association of Service and Conservation Corps (NASCC), which was formed in 1985 to serve as an informational clearinghouse and provide technical assistance with management, funding, and program development. Located in Washington, D.C., NASCC can help you locate your nearest local or state conservation corps. In addition to NASCC, the states of California, New York, New Jersey, and Wisconsin have state-level associations to provide networks among the state and local corps located within each state.

Federally supported service, youth, and conservation corps have been subject to an intermittent and unstable history of support. For that reason, state and local corps have provided the most consistent community presence. Local and state corps have diversified their funding sources and have made more secure and stable futures by avoiding the inconsistent history of federal support. They also have the advantage of being firmly rooted in the communities and regions where they are located so that there is a sense of continuity and investment in the localities where they work.

Federal support for the conservation corps can be graphed as a plunging and rising line since the New Deal Civilian Conservation Corps. The federal programs have tended to focus on employment for disadvantaged youth. The emphasis of the current federally supported Clinton administration Americorps is to provide youth with an experience of national service and to assist with payment of college loans. The political vulnerability of the Americorps reflects the history of federal corps.

The close of the New Deal Era and the Second World War saw the end of the Civilian Conservation Corps, but the concept reappeared in President Kennedy's Economic Opportunity Act of 1964, which established a Jobs Corps by which young people were located in Jobs Corps Civilian Conservation Centers. Most of the conservation centers were located in urban areas, and the program was one of many designed at that time to break the cycle of poverty for poor and minority youth and to stress the training of vocational skills.

In 1972 a pilot program was authorized by the Youth Conservation Act to employ youth between the ages of fifteen and nineteen for conservation work for the purpose of "developing, preserving or maintaining the lands and waters of the United States." This was a summer program in which school-age youth were employed for no more than ninety days a year. About 35 percent of its members were assigned to the Department of Interior, 30 percent to the Forest Service, and 30 percent to state programs funded by federal grants. By 1974 the pilot program was authorized as a permanent one.[34, 35]

In 1977 the Carter administration expanded federal support for the conservation corps concept by establishing a Young Adult Conservation Corps, which provided year-round conservation work for youth between the ages of sixteen and twenty-three who were out of school.[36] That program was terminated by the Reagan administration and the appropriation for the Youth Conservation Corps was discontinued. During the Bush administration, Congress required the U.S. Fish and Wildlife Service, the U.S. Forest Service, and the U.S. National Park Service to keep the Youth Conservation Corps Program alive by having each agency set aside $1 million from their regular operations funds to administer at least a low level of activity.[37]

The Job Training Partnership Act of 1982 breathed new life into the 1960s Job Corps by making it a Department of Labor program to continue the mission of making disadvantaged youth employable. Vocational training in auto repair and construction trades was the focus of that program. Through the 1980s and early 1990s the struggling Youth Conservation Corps was the only remnant of federal agency participation in youth conservation work and training. At that program's height some thirty-two thousand young people were employed under an appropriation of $60 million, but that fell to three thousand corps members under a $3 million appropriation in the Reagan-Bush era.[38]

In 1990, the National Community Service Act (Public Law 101–610) took the tack of providing competitive federal grants to states to expand full-time or summer youth conservation corps at the state or local level. The Clinton administration's 1993 National and Community Service Trust Act (P.L. 103–82) eclipsed that act and created an ambitious new federal program of national service. The main feature of P.L. 103–82 that affects the waterway restoration and existing conservation corps community is the national service funds available from either the Washington-based Corporation for National and Community Service or the state-based commissions. The act has established Americorps, which includes a continuation of the thirty-year-old, VISTA program started by President Kennedy to provide community organizing for low-income areas. Americorps also includes the National Civilian Community Corps (NCCC), which is a residential national service program for eighteen to twenty-four year olds on regional campuses located on closed or downsized military bases. The campuses are located in Aberdeen, Maryland; Charleston, South

Carolina; Denver, Colorado; and San Diego, California. The act also established a Public Lands Corps within the departments of Interior and Agriculture.

The political volatility of the federally supported corps continues with efforts of the Environmental Protection Agency and the Natural Resources Conservation Service to sponsor environmental programs with the NCCC in 1996. While NCCC and Americorps still exist, congressional efforts to discontinue those programs continue, and the EPA and NRCS programs were short-lived.

The long-term fate of urban waterway restoration will be tied in part to the stability and growth of conservation corps. Because of that, conservation corps remain a key partner in the urban waterway community of citizen organizations. The National Association of Service and Conservation Corps distributed urban waterway restoration training manuals to its member organizations in 1996.[39] Because the NASCC and its local and state conservation corps are more economically and politically sustaining, they represent the most stable workforce for the future growth of stream restoration.

NOTES

1. Environmental Protection Agency, *National Directory of Volunteer Environmental Monitoring Programs,* 4th edition, EPA 841–B–94–001, Office of Water (Washington, D.C., January 1994).

2. Wetlands Watch Program, Program Coordinator Cheryl Miller, National Audubon Society, 26 East Exchange Street, #207, St. Paul, Minnesota.

3. Luna B. Leopold, *Water, A Primer* (San Francisco: W. H. Freeman, 1974).

4. Luna Leopold, *A View of the River* (Cambridge: Harvard University Press: 1994).

5. Thomas Dunne and Luna Leopold, *Water in Environmental Planning* (San Francisco: W. H. Freeman, 1978).

6. Questa Engineering Corporation, *Drainage and Flood Study for the Tice Creek Watershed,* submitted to the City of Walnut Creek (Point Richmond, California, 1986).

7. David R. Dawdy and Harsh Saluja, *Kinematic Wave Routing in Urban System Modeling* (San Francisco: Questa Engineering, 1986).

8. Questa Engineering, *Drainage and Flood Study for Tice Creek.*

9. Dawdy and Saluja, *Kinematic Wave Routing;* and Questa Engineering, *Drainage and Flood Study for Tice Creek.*

10. G. Scott Morris and Pamela A. Romo, *Tice Creek Flood Damage Survey Questionnaire Evaluation,* Walnut Creek, California, September 30, 1986.

11. Pam Romo, founder of Friends of Tice Creek, Walnut Creek, California, personal communication, 1989.

12. Stewart K. Wright, "Self-Help Flood Damage Reduction in the Susquehanna River Basin," *Evaluating the Effectiveness of Floodplain Management Techniques and Community Programs,* Seminar Proceedings, Special Publication 10, by the Tennessee Valley Authority in cooperation with the Federal Interagency Floodplain Management Task Force, May 1984.

13. Dunne and Leopold, *Water in Environmental Planning.*

14. Leopold, *A View of the River.*

15. Dunne and Leopold, *Water in Environmental Planning.*

16. Contact the Hydrologic Information Unit, U.S. Geological Survey, 419 National Center, Reston, Virginia 22092, 707–648–6817, to locate the nearest Water Resources Division district office and find out about other information sources.

17. "Guide to Obtaining U.S.G.S. Information," U.S. Geological Survey Circular 900 (Washington, D.C.: U.S. Government Printing Office, 1989).

18. Leopold, *Water, A Primer.*

19. Larry Kolb, of the San Francisco Regional Water Quality Control Board, *Creek Currents,* vol. 4, no. 3 (fall 1989) (Berkeley, California, Urban Creeks Council).

20. Environmental Protection Agency, *National Directory of Citizen Volunteer Environmental Monitoring Programs,* 4th edition.

21. Environmental Protection Agency, *Citizen Volunteers in Environmental Monitorings, Summary, Proceedings of the 2nd National Workshop* (New Orleans, Louisiana, December 1989).

22. Environmental Protection Agency (EPA), *Volunteer Water Monitoring: A Guide for State Managers,* EPA 440/4–9–010, Office of Water (Washington, D.C., August 1990).

23. Thomas Armitage, Office of Marine and Estuarine Protection, Environmental Protection Agency, Washington, D.C., personal communication, December 1990.

24. EPA, *Volunteer Water Monitoring.*

25. *The Volunteer Monitor,* the National Newsletter of Volunteer Water Quality Monitoring, vol. 2, no. 1 (1990).

26. Karen Firehock, director, Save Our Streams Program, Izaak Walton League, Arlington, Virginia, personal communication, May 1990.

27. Richard Klein, program director, Save Our Streams Program, Maryland Department of Natural Resources, Baltimore, Maryland, personal communication, 1990.

28. Environmental Protection Agency, *Upper Grande Ronde River Temperature Modeling Projects,* prepared by Tetra Tech Inc., EPA Assessment and Watershed Protection Division, and Oregon Department of Environmental Quality (Washington, D.C.: Office of Water, 1994).

29. Santa Cruz Planning Department, *Stream Care: A Guide for Streamside Property Owners* (Santa Cruz, California, circa 1989).

30. City of Bellevue, Stream Team Program, Storm and Surface Water Utility, 301 116th Avenue S.E., Bellevue, Washington.

31. Northeastern Illinois Planning Commission, *Streams and Wetlands: A Resource Worth Preserving* (Chicago, fall 1987).

32. Georgia Soil and Water Conservation Commission, Metro Atlanta Association of Conservation Districts, USDA Soil Conservation Service, Georgia Environmental Protection Division, *Guidelines for Streambank Restoration* (Atlanta, 1994).

33. Georgia Conservancy, "Stream of Conscience: Natural Solutions for Clean Water," videotape, 15 minutes, Atlanta, Georgia, 1993.

34. Grover M. Barham, chief, Division of Youth Activities, National Park Service, and Francis Gipson, Office of Youth Activities, National Park Service, Washington, D.C., interview, May 1990.

35. Youth Conservation Corps Act of 1970, as amended by Public Law 93–408, September 3, 1974.

36. Youth Employment and Demonstration Projects Act of 1977, Public Law 95–93, August 1977.

37. Barham and Gipson, interview.

38. National Association of Service and Conservation Corps, *Conservation and Service Corps Profiles* (Washington, D.C., August 1989 and Spring 1991).

39. A. L. Riley and Moira McDonald, *Urban Waterways Restoration Training Manual for Youth and Conservation Corps,* a project of the U.S. Environmental Protection Agency and USDA Natural Resources Conservation Service, National Association of Service and Conservation Corps (Washington, D.C., 1996).

CHAPTER NINE

A Survey of Urban Watershed and Stream Restoration Methods

Restoration Responses to Common Culprits of Watershed Imbalances

E. W. Lane's scale of watershed variables (in figure 4.5) can be tipped off balance by changes in sediment types and amounts, flow discharges, and slopes of the channel. The common culprits causing the imbalances are removal of native vegetation, increase in erosion from development, increase and concentration of storm runoff into storm-water culverts, and modification of stream channels involving widening, straightening, or filling. Citizen response to these common problems with the positive solutions of watershed fencing, planting, culvert removal, storm-water management, gully repair, and erosion control are also increasingly common.

Revegetation

The replacement of natural environments such as prairies, savannah woodlands, grasslands, chaparral, woodlands, marshes, and bogs with human-created environments has had a profound effect on the movement of water through watersheds. As described in chapter 4, the replacement landscape commonly changes the hydrology of the watershed in both the quantity and the timing of discharges. Revegetation projects from planting and burning prairies (even in urban residential neighborhoods) to planting trees have become a popular citizen volunteer activity.[1] Tree planting projects have historically been a staple of conservation corps and citizen volunteer activity. Some of those projects in the past were misguided attempts at "conservation" in which it was assumed that any tree planting was going to be beneficial. Some of those projects created a new set of problems, however, because exotic or nonindigenous species have invaded natural environments and crowded out the native species that were well adapted to and grew in balance with other plants. Well-intentioned non-native plantings can actually change watershed conditions for the worse. In some midwestern environments, wooded waterways have replaced open prairie wetlands, and tree removal has been necessary for the restoration of the landscape.

Revegetation projects can sometimes be best accomplished by planting nothing.

The best revegetation project from the standpoint of ecological diversity, and the most economical, may be the project that simply creates the conditions needed for native vegetation to "reinvade" a site. Fencing livestock from riparian corridors in order for native riparian species to recover is a good example. The systematic weeding of exotics in small acreages to allow reseeding and regrowth of nearby natives in the weeded zones, as being practiced by citizen volunteers in Australia, is another example.[2]

Plant Stock

Most people's experience with planting involves planting seeds in a garden or buying containers of plants at nurseries and planting them in a yard. Seeding can be a very good way to get a quick cover of grasses, wildflowers, or annual plants, and the seed is inexpensive compared to the amount of ground cover attained. Container stock is at the other end of the expense scale. Shrubs and trees can be purchased in one-, five-, ten-, fifteen-gallon, and even larger containers and pots. The cost goes up significantly as the size increases. Traditional landscaping projects designed and installed by landscape architects or other design professionals usually use container stock along with some form of sprinkler, bubbler, or drip irrigation system.

Restoration projects use some of the same plant stocks and irrigation systems as landscapers, but the objectives of a landscaping project and a restoration project are usually quite different. A landscaping project is organized around carrying out a program on a site centered around some desired human uses or activities. A restoration project is attempting to re-create, emulate, or achieve some semblance of an indigenous plant and animal ecosystem. For this reason, the plant species, the planting stock, and the planting methods often differ for restoration projects.

Usually, revegetation of a waterway begins with pioneer species that easily root from cuttings or start from seed. A quick cover, extensive rooting, and substantial plant structure are needed to stabilize slopes and reduce stream scour and runoff erosion. In riparian environments, pioneer plants that provide those functions are willow, cottonwood, and alder, with dogwood following close behind. Once established, these plants can create the environment required for a succession of other riparian species, including such species as maples, ash, sycamores, buckeyes, and oaks. The different successions that take place are particular to different environments and different parts of the country. Some practitioners plant a whole succession at once on a site. For example, they may use cuttings of willows and dogwoods and then plant from containers maples and oaks, which do not grow from cuttings and represent a more mature tree canopy and riparian system. Restorationists may combine all the different kinds of plant stock on one restoration site.

The other major types of plant stock are tubes, liners, and bareroot plants (figure 9.1). Some native-plant nurseries make container stock available in narrow tall pots to encourage deep rooting and discourage the pot-bound condition of roots circled around in the pot. Tubes are a small variation of this concept; many young plants

FIGURE 9.1. PLANTING STOCK. LEFT TO RIGHT: LINERS, 5-GALLON DEEP CONTAINERS, TUBES, 1-GALLON CONTAINER.

with good long roots can be easily carried out into the field in cases of tubes. Liners are usually plastic six-packs of small rooted plants. Bareroot seedlings or larger trees can be bought in quantity at lower prices than tube or container stock.

The larger bareroot trees have their roots wrapped in burl-wrap. Bareroot seedlings come packed in bundles with their roots wrapped in a moist absorbent material and plastic or wrapping paper to keep the moisture in. Two of the advantages of bareroot stock are that you can transport many trees to the field, and they are easy to plant. One disadvantage is storage needs. The packing material around the roots can easily dry out if you are not vigilant. Too much moisture can produce mold problems for the plants.

Reliance on container stock has fallen out of favor with restorationists for a number of reasons in addition to expense. First, container stock tends to take a long time to acclimate to its new surroundings and grows more slowly than other plant stocks. The smaller tube plants, bareroot plants, cuttings, and seeds can outgrow larger container plants because their roots are forced to immediately adapt to their new environment. In contrast, the roots in container stock may temporarily confine their growth to the nursery soil from the pot, stunting the plants growth potential. It is well known among practitioners that 1-gallon stock can arrive at the same as or a greater height and size than 5-, 10-, or 15-gallon stock planted at the same time. The smaller plant stocks are not invulnerable, however. It is critical to plant them at the right season so that they get the rainfall and other weather conditions they need to become established. Smaller stock can also be more vulnerable to pest, animal, and human damages. In contrast to container stock, cuttings do not have roots, therefore large quantities usually have to be planted to assure that you will have a high enough survival rate.

The site, project objectives, and plant stock availability will all determine what plant stock you use. If your restoration site is located in a very public area, in a high-vandalism neighborhood, or on school grounds, larger plants seem more likely to survive. Larger trees and shrubs also have a higher rate of survival in the face of dog, child, and other kinds of urban abuses.

Planting Methods

Small plant stock from bareroot seedlings or tubes can quickly adapt to their new environments and attain fast growth rates in good conditions. Small plants are more vulnerable to pest damage, grazing animals, and human traffic—particularly children. You may want to use larger container stock to avoid these disadvantages and to more quickly change the microclimate or environment of the site if you are doing successional plantings of a number of species. Some species may survive much better assisted by some shade of larger container stock or aggressively growing cuttings.

Bareroot and tube seedlings can be quickly and easily planted using a mattocks, pick, tire iron, or construction bar. Shove the bar or pick into the ground to make a hole, pull it out, and drop the seedling in. Hold the plant so the roots dangle down, straight into the hole. Fill the hole around the roots by pushing the dirt back into the hole. Tamp down the soil so that there are no air pockets around the roots.

Container stock is heavier to handle and to transport into the field. Trees in containers 15 gallons or larger usually require two people to handle. To plant a container tree, first dig a hole twice as large as the plant's container. To remove the tree from the container, work a shovel around the perimeter of the root ball to loosen it. Knock the bottom of the container with a shovel, if necessary, while holding the tree and container at an angle to force the root ball out of the bottom of the container. Shake the tree out of the container rather than pulling it out by the stem. This will reduce the damage to the tree and roots. When the tree is planted, fill the loose soil back into the hole so that all the roots are covered but the crown of the plant (where the roots meet the stem) is left above ground.

Most riparian trees are not delicate and can tolerate the removal of some of the container soil from their roots. Prune off circling or kinked roots. If you remove a lot of root mass, however, you will need to prune the tree after planting. Removing some of the potted soil and breaking up the root mass of the tree some helps the tree to adapt more quickly to its new environment. Otherwise, the tree roots will tend to stay in a root ball form in the rich nursery soil rather than grow out into the ground. Tamp the dirt in the hole as you plant to avoid air pockets.

One common mistake made in tree planting is to plant with tangled or circling roots, which can destabilize or even strangle the tree. For many species of trees, burying the crown below the ground will cause the stem to root. Riparian species are usually more resistant to this problem, however, because of the sediment-laden environment many of them live in. Roots left above ground will dry out and die. Refer to figure 9.2 for illustration of common planting errors.

The seasonal planting times selected can make a major difference in plant survival. Because bareroot and container trees and shrubs have roots, there is greater flexibility on the timing of planting projects than when cutting stock is used. Cutting stock is the most vulnerable to transplant shock and is best used when the plants are dormant, in the fall and winter months, to reduce that shock. Bareroot trees are next in vulnerability to transplant shock, and container trees have the greatest advantage of surviving the shock of planting. Bareroot plant stock is made available by nurseries in winter and early spring, and so spring plantings are typical for this stock. In the dry climates of the West, it is best to plant container stocks in the fall to facilitate root growth in the cooler, wetter winter season. In the northern portions of the country and the Midwest, with cold winters and frozen ground, planting of containers is better done after ground thaw in the spring to allow the plant to become established before the next winter. In the wet and mild southern states, it is

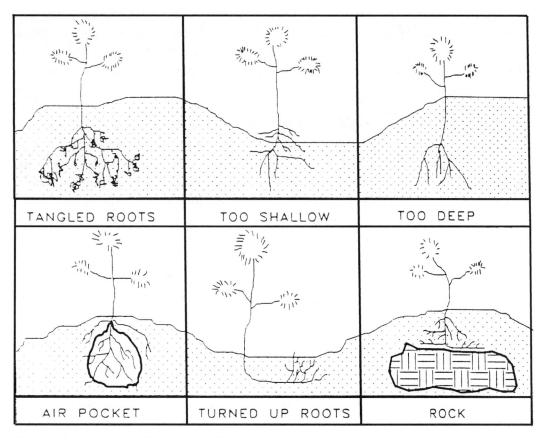

FIGURE 9.2. COMMON MISTAKES IN TREE PLANTING. *Source:* California Department of Fish and Game.

best to plant from fall to early spring before the flood season of the spring and summer.

In the southern states, as in the west, fall plantings are the most successful. The South can have hot and droughty conditions from June to September, but the October-to-December conditions of warm soils and moisture are good for root growth. Plantings of cuttings in the South and West are best timed for the fall and early winter months, whenever the plants first become dormant. Experience appears to show that although the plants' top growth is dormant, the cuttings in these mild climates are growing roots and becoming established below ground, so that when they begin to leaf in the spring, the plant has a good head start. Most Midwest and northern restoration projects begin in the spring after ground thaw.

Restoration plantings don't normally use fertilizers, although a ground mulch can help many species survive more easily. We assume if we have matched the native species correctly to its environment and conditions, it will adapt well to its new surroundings.

Container trees and shrubs are usually a substantial economic investment. To protect our investment, we have found it worthwhile to add screens to prevent animal damage and cages to reduce damages from people to plants we install in urban restoration projects. We have lost many trees to rats gnawing on tree bark and unthoughtful humans physically damaging the trees. Figure 9.3 illustrates our urban tree-protecting cages. For any and all planting projects, don't forget to water immediately after you have planted. The only exception may be if you are installing the project in the rain.

Storm-Water Management and Wetland Creation

A new development in the 1990s has been the national concern for polluted runoff from streets, parking lots, highways, roof drains, and other paved areas. The Clean Water Act calls for the adoption of Best Management Practices by local entities to reduce polluted runoff. Because the trees and vegetation that grow along waterways and in wetland environments can absorb nutrients and other pollutants, local governments are encouraging the creation of wetland environments to capture and treat urban runoff before it returns to the creeks, rivers, and lakes. The projects involve diverting or capturing runoff into low-lying areas, pockets, or basins. Wetland species native to the area and compatible with the site moisture and inundation conditions should be planted. The planting of riparian buffer zones along waterways can deliver similar water-quality benefits. In these cases, the water is "treated" as it runs its normal course past tree and plant roots. In some cases, wetlands, both marsh and riparian environments, are being developed to accept water from sewage treatment plants, as a final component of the water treatment process.

As a result of the intensified efforts of local and regional agencies to adopt "best management practices," storm-water management manuals have proliferated within the last two decades (chapter 4's endnotes include a few notable manuals). Management practices are typically grouped into five main categories: control increases in runoff and increase storm-water infiltration; control erosion and sed-

FIGURE 9.3. URBAN TREE CAGES.

imentation; protect drainages and stream channels; minimize sources of pollution from sewage and wastewater; and control storm runoff pollution.[3] These practices are broken down in greater detail in the following lists.

To Control Increases in Runoff and Increase Storm-Water Infiltration

- Disconnect drainpipes from roofs.
- Drain to landscaping and into Dutch or French drains.
- Use porous paving.
- Remove concrete surfaces and plant in their place.
- Construct seepage basins, detention and retention ponds.
- Create overflow wetlands.
- Use parking lots as temporary runoff storage.
- Integrate rainwater cisterns into architecture.

To Control Erosion and Sedimentation

- Zone development away from steep slopes and high-hazard erosion areas.
- Modify grading and construction practices to maximize natural landscapes and minimize cuts and fills.
- Modify road building and parking lot design practices.

- Construct sediment filters and traps.
- Carry out revegetation, seeding, and mulching projects.
- Carry out upper watershed erosion control projects.

To Protect Drainages and Channels

- Protect riparian vegetation with ordinances and setback development requirements.
- Restore balanced channel dynamics and vegetation.

To Control Storm-Water Runoff Pollution

- Control debris entry into storm-water systems.
- Provide for easy and environmentally acceptable disposal for motor vehicle oils, antifreeze, etc.
- Sweep roadways, clear catch basins.
- Create vegetative buffer zones along waterways.

To Minimize Sources of Pollution from Sewage and Wastewater

- Conserve water, including reusing gray water.
- Use composting, earth-based, or chemical toilets.
- Use appropriate technology for on-site treatment of residential wastes.

Stopping Gullies, the Watershed Killers
What Makes a Gully

Gullies are commonly associated with rural pastures and croplands, but you might be surprised how frequently they occur in the urban landscape, in backyards, in city and regional parks, and along urban drainages. Figure 9.4 shows a human-devouring gully in a park in San Diego caused by the concentration of rainfall into trenches created by dirt bikes on the slopes of Tecolote Canyon. The rain runs down the trenches and scours a deep V-shaped channel where the slope reaches the bottom of the canyon. The deep trough that occurs as a result progressively deepens and moves upslope, causing the canyon-like effect in the photo. This upslope movement of erosion is called headward erosion. When I saw this gully, it was moving up the slope at a fast clip of 4–6 feet a year and, in concert with others like it, was causing serious erosion problems. As a matter of fact, the canyon erosion was being blamed for the filling of Mission Bay, into which Tecolote Creek flows. It's a good policy to act fast when you find an active headward-eroding gully, because often as they become larger, they can be remarkably destructive, enlarge at alarming rates, and be difficult to stop. Put a stake in the ground a good distance off to the side of the head of the gully and note the date on the stake. Check back at regular intervals to determine how fast the head of the gully is progressing uphill. Make quickly eroding gullies your priority for attention—particularly if they threaten a road or structure. Some gullies will stabilize on their own or may advance slowly. A gully could erode down to a hardpan soil or bedrock, for example, and leave banks close

FIGURE 9.4. HEADWARD GULLY,
TECOLOTE CANYON, SAN DIEGO,
CALIFORNIA.

to their stable angle of repose. In such a case the gully stabilizes and does not experience much further erosion.

There are two major classes of gully. I call one class the downhill-runoff gully and the other the uphill-erosion gully. The major distinction between the two is the source of the gullying: concentrated runoff from an uphill location, or a disturbed slope located downhill or downstream of the gully. (Refer to figures 9.5 and 9.6.) The Tecolote Canyon gully just described is an example of a downhill-runoff gully caused by the concentration of runoff from an upslope location, which starts an erosive channel that widens and deepens as more water collects on its way downhill. It later becomes an upward-erosion gully when the deep V-shaped gully at the bottom of the hill starts to progress uphill. The upward-erosion, or headward-erosion, gully is caused by a disturbance in the grade of a streambed or slope that starts downstream or downslope and moves upstream or upslope. A very common example of headward erosion is caused when streams or drainages are put into a culvert to go under a road. Often the culvert is laid in the ground deeper than the original bed or grade of the drainage, and that deepening of the streambed grade creates a waterfall effect that progressively erodes the channel bed in an upstream direction.

You must first determine whether your gully is the downhill-runoff type or the

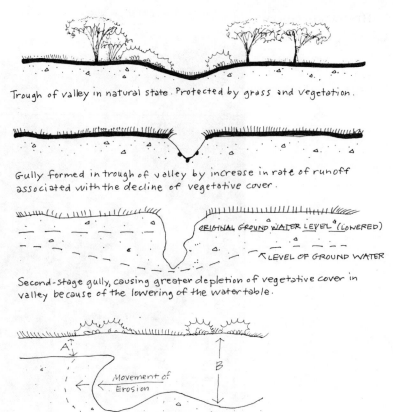

Trough of valley in natural state. Protected by grass and vegetation.

Gully formed in trough of valley by increase in rate of runoff associated with the decline of vegetative cover.

ORIGINAL GROUND WATER LEVEL (LOWERED)

↖ LEVEL OF GROUND WATER

Second-stage gully, causing greater depletion of vegetative cover in valley because of the lowering of the watertable.

A↕

B↕

←Movement of Erosion

Gully depth "A" increases to depth "B" as the gully erosion moves up slope.

FIGURE 9.5. THE SUCCESSIVE STAGES IN THE FORMATION OF A GULLY FROM AN INCREASE IN DOWNHILL RUNOFF.

uphill-erosion type, or if it contains both types like the Tecolote Canyon example. You need to do this in order to address the causes of the problem. The uphill erosion caused by a change in grade is usually the most difficult to address. As described in chapter 4, streams will adjust their grade to their base level. If that base level is changed, the equilibrium of the channel will be significantly disturbed. Removing a culvert, restoring the original stream grade, and constructing a bridge for a stream crossing are the optimum solutions to culvert problems. The optimum is not always possible, however, and you may want to use a ford crossing at the grade of the streambed instead of a culvert, or replace the existing culvert with a correctly sized one at the right grade and slope. (Refer to "Solving Problems with Channel Grades and Culverts" in the next section.)

Sometimes a change in stream or hillside grade occurs because of something localized, such as someone digging a swimming hole in a creek or putting a small dam or culvert in a channel. Other times, a long stretch of creek cuts a deeper channel because urbanization has increased the flows in the creek or a channelization pro-

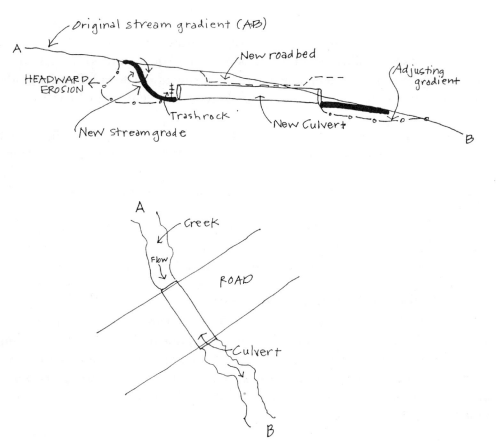

FIGURE 9.6 HEADWARD, OR UPHILL, EROSION CAUSED BY A CHANGE IN STREAMBED GRADE.

ject has caused the creek to deepen and widen. A tributary entering a stream or a river undergoing deepening will cut a deeper mouth to enter the larger, deepened waterway. The tributary will in turn deepen its channel progressively upstream to readjust its slope to its deeper mouth. A chain reaction occurs when the grade of a stream channel is lowered, the influence of that change sometimes reaching into the highest portions of the hillsides of the watershed. A bedscarp, or change of grade in the bottom of the channel, will move progressively upstream, and you will often see a small waterfall where that change in grade is located. The smaller drainages in the upper portions of the watershed that feed into the downcutting tributaries will in turn erode down to enter the tributaries. Sometimes those upper watershed gullies adjusting to grade or base-level changes are referred to as continuous gullies.

It is critical at this point to distinguish between an instream grade adjustment and an upper watershed drainage system where gullies occur. The uppermost watershed drainages are usually dry and act as collectors and conveyers of water only when it is raining. For a majority of situations, the only location appropriate to construct a check dam is in the smaller, upper watershed drainages, which carry rainfall to the downhill stream channels only intermittently. It is not recommended that you construct check dams, dams, or weirs of any kind in stream channels or major drainages. Restrict the use of the gully repair strategies presented here to upper, steeper watershed gullies draining 25 acres (0.04 square miles) or less. If your problem is a channel gradient adjustment occurring in the downhill lower gradient drainages and stream channels, refer to "Solving Problems with Channel Grades and Culverts."

It was a frequent practice in the 1930s for conservation corps to build sediment storage check dams. However, experience reveals that the sediment catchment in such projects is of too little volume to provide worthwhile benefit. Worse, the dams caught sediment in stable drainages and destabilized them by diverting flows around the filled-in drainages. If a watershed has an erosion problem and is contributing to a stream-channel sedimentation problem, the remedies should emphasize fencing of livestock from waterways, regulated construction methods, catchment of runoff on development sites, and revegetation projects.

How to Restore Gully-Damaged Drainages

To restore drainages damaged by gullies first determine whether the gully was caused by a lowered drainage or slope grade or by downhill runoff. Be observant of the factors influencing the watershed. It never ceases to amaze how something as unobtrusive as a trail or path can cause a serious gully by concentrating rain in one location. Use the following checklist when you go into the field to help you determine the source of the problem:

Downhill Runoff

Rain runoff is being concentrated by:
- individual culverts
- rain spouts from buildings
- road drainage ditches or culverts
- sidewalks, trails, paths, driveways, patios, or other compacted or paved surfaces
- dirt-bike (bicycle or motorcycle) trails
- off-road vehicles damaging the landscape
- vegetation removal, including tree removal, or displacement of native vegetation with landscaping that does not address runoff and erosion needs
- grazing that removes vegetation cover, compacts soils, and damages streambeds and streamside vegetation
- wide-scale use of culverts and storm drains that prevent water from soaking into wetlands, detention areas, and tree-lined waterways.

Uphill Erosion

- The main stream channel or its major tributaries have been channelized, and the upstream gradients are adjusting as a result.
- Culverts have lowered the grade of the streambed.
- Deepening of the drainages has occurred to convey flows under roads, bridges, railroads, and other structures.

- Streams have been buried underground for long reaches to enable development on top of them.
- Natural geologic forces are lifting the landscape, and the creeks and rivers are adjusting by eroding downward. (Climatic change may also be causing channel incision.)

If you have an uphill-erosion problem, then your first restoration projects are going to be located at the lower end of the watershed, and you are going to work progressively uphill to treat your gully problems. You will need to address the source of your problem, or your work will be in vain. If wide-scale watershed adjustments are occurring because of large-scale channelization or culverting projects, you should consider the option of not trying to attempt a restoration project, because the stream channels will need to deepen and/or widen to adjust to the new watershed conditions. The best way to decide on a practical action is to confer with a local expert from a college or government agency, such as the Natural Resources Conservation Service, who is a hydrologist or geomorphologist. You will need advice from someone who understands the bigger picture of watershed adjustments as well as the localized influences. The best situation is to have that person join you on a site visit.

My experience is that approximately eight out of ten problem situations can be traced to badly sized or installed culverts. Because of the amount of disruption culverts cause in landscape stability and the relative economy in correcting the problem, culvert-removal projects are usually beneficial and cost-effective. Once you have corrected the culvert problem (or other source of the problem), move up the drainage to the first change in grade, or headcut, and restore that first. Be sure to look for minor sub-headcuts advancing upslope inside the more major headcuts. If you repair a major upslope headcut without tending to downslope adjustments, a minor downslope headcut can move upslope and undermine your repair work upslope.

While this book will provide you with the steps for constructing a simple, permeable, brush pile check dam, not all gullies require check dams. Check dams should be strategically placed in the lower part of the gully network so as to help stabilize the base level of the main gully and other smaller drainages and gullies feeding into it from above. Gullies in which the bed or banks are being invaded with vegetation can be helped along with the planting of willow or cottonwood posts to speed the revegetation process. Gullies can erode to bedrock or acquire an armoring of large loose rock. These too should probably just be treated with plantings.[4, 5]

A gully that is perched up in a hillside and is caused by downhill runoff is sometimes referred to as a discontinuous gully. You will find a culvert, roadway, driveway, or some other feature feeding water to it. The first step in a restoration project for that common situation is to divert the drainage flow to more stable areas in the landscape; break up the drainage and divert it into smaller sub-drainages; and/or reduce the erosive force of the runoff with revegetation projects using the soil bioengineering methods described in this chapter.

Redistributing the runoff can be as simple as using a pick and shovel to dig water bars, which are new drainages directing runoff into heavily vegetated areas. Sometimes a more complicated regrading plan requires a back hoe or front loader. This can be the simplest or most problem-ridden aspect of your restoration project because a real hazard in redirecting runoff is the re-creation of a gully in a different spot.

Project Steps to Repair a Gully

Once you have located the source of your problem and have established your restoration priorities, you may decide that it is necessary to construct a gully check structure to stop a destructive gully. There are two classes of gully check dams: permeable, or porous, and impermeable, or nonporous. The impermeable act as small solid dams and are made of wood boards, logs, rock, compact earth, or concrete. The permeable dam allows more water movement through the structure in a manner reminiscent of a beaver dam. These porous dams are constructed of brush piles, vegetative cuttings from native riparian plants, hay bales, loose rock, and gabions (rock-filled wire cages).

Constructing a successful check dam is harder than you may think. It is very easy to construct a failure. The checks are built to slow the runoff and to collect the sediment the runoff is transporting so that it drops off behind the check. This raises the gradient of the gully and helps smooth out the slope. Refer to figures 9.7 and 9.8 on the construction steps. It is best to use check dams in a series of three or more so that they can act in concert to establish a new slope. The elevation of the toe of the uphill check dam should establish the elevation for the top of the spillway of the downhill check, as shown in figure 9.9. If the downhill check dam is placed at too low an elevation, the gully can still move upward and undercut the upper check dam.

Our experience indicates that impermeable check dams are more vulnerable to failures than porous ones. One of the most common failures of a check dam is caused by the dam filling with sediment. The gradient is flattened, and then subsequent runoff will meander around the sides of the dam. This results in the dam blowing out or being knocked down by the overflows. Nonporous dams, made of wood, for example, must be designed with spillways large enough to direct the flows over the dam so the water doesn't overflow around the sides and take the dam out. Before designing your check dam, confer with your state Natural Resource Conservation Service office for help on designing the proper-sized spillway (figure 9.10). The ends of the dams need to be tied back into the sides of the gully by at least 3 feet. Rock energy dissipaters should be placed at the foot of all check dams. Omitting that feature can result in the water spilling over the dam, eroding away the foot of the dam, and causing the structure to collapse. Finally, make sure your check dams are constructed perpendicular to the flow, and be careful not to place a dam just uphill of a meander. A misplaced dam can direct flows into a gully bank and create more erosion and instability. To avoid blow-outs, undercut dams, and the construc-

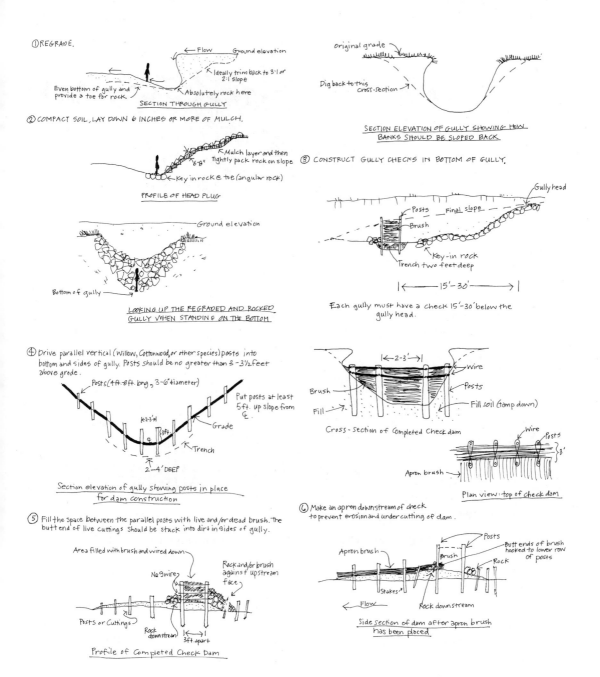

① REGRADE.

← Flow   Ground elevation

Even bottom of gully and provide a toe for rock.

Ideally trim back to 3:1 or 2:1 slope

Absolutely rock here

SECTION THROUGH GULLY

② COMPACT SOIL, LAY DOWN 6 INCHES OR MORE OF MULCH.

Mulch layer and then tightly pack rock on slope

6"-8"

Key in rock @ toe (angular rock)

PROFILE OF HEAD PLUG

Ground elevation

Bottom of gully

LOOKING UP THE REGRADED AND ROCKED GULLY WHEN STANDING ON THE BOTTOM

original grade

Dig back to this cross-section

SECTION ELEVATION OF GULLY SHOWING HOW BANKS SHOULD BE SLOPED BACK

③ CONSTRUCT GULLY CHECKS IN BOTTOM OF GULLY.

Gully head

Posts   Final slope

Brush

Key-in rock

Trench two feet deep

|← 15'-30' →|

Each gully must have a check 15'-30' below the gully head.

④ Drive parallel vertical (Willow, Cottonwood, or other species) posts into bottom and sides of gully. Posts should be no greater than 3 - 3½ feet above grade.

Posts (4ft.-8ft. long, 3-6" diameter)

Put posts at least 5 ft. up slope from ℄.

|← 2-3' →|

3 ft.

Grade

Trench

2-4' DEEP

Section elevation of gully showing posts in place for dam construction

⑤ Fill the space between the parallel posts with live and/or dead brush. The butt end of live cuttings should be stuck into dirt in sides of gully.

Area filled with brush and wired down

No. 9 wire

Rock and/or brush against upstream face

Posts or Cuttings

Rock downstream

|← →| 3 ft. apart

Profile of Completed Check Dam

|← 2-3' →| Wire

Brush   Posts

Fill   Fill soil (Tamp down)

Cross-Section of Completed Check dam

Wire   Posts

3'

Apron brush

Plan view: top of check dam

⑥ Make an apron downstream of check to prevent erosion and undercutting of dam.

Apron brush   Posts

Butt ends of brush hooked to lower row of posts

Brush

Rock

Stakes   Rock downstream

← Flow

Side section of dam after apron brush has been placed

FIGURE 9.7. PROJECT STEPS TO REPAIR A GULLY.

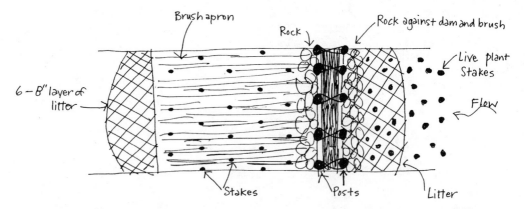

FIGURE 9.8. PLAN OF A COMPLETED CHECK DAM.

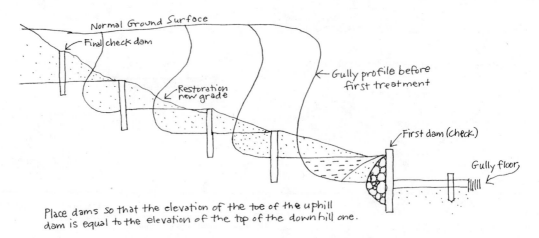

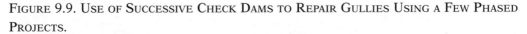

FIGURE 9.9. USE OF SUCCESSIVE CHECK DAMS TO REPAIR GULLIES USING A FEW PHASED PROJECTS.

tion of inappropriate, large-sized dams, it is recommended that you build check dams no greater than 3 feet high.[6]

We restrict our check-dam constructing activities to porous dams. Porous check dams allow more water and sediment to shift through them and therefore are generally less vulnerable to blow-outs. They are usually easier and less expensive to construct. Serious leaks and structural failures are often easier to fix with adjustments you can make after they are tested by the first rains. If they do fail, you have usually lost less time and money than if you constructed a nonpermeable dam. The purpose of these check dams is to use inexpensive, easily available, and temporary materials to stabilize small-to-medium gullies so that the ultimate protection is provided by the establishment of new plant cover. The check provides enough temporary stability to the landscape for planted cuttings to get a start to help bind the soil, collect sediment, and stabilize the grade.

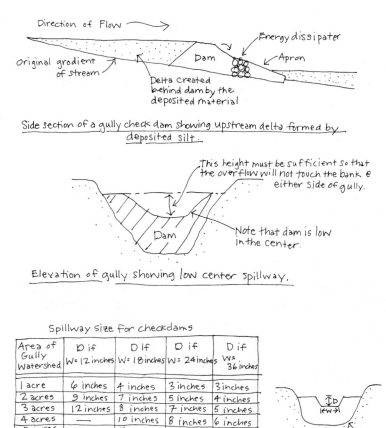

FIGURE 9.10 BASIC DESIGN FEATURES OF AN IMPERMEABLE OR NONPOROUS CHECK DAM.

The permeable check dam described here is one we recommend from a large assortment of possible check dam designs. It comes from a 1935 document published by Iowa State College for the Emergency Conservation Work program of the Civilian Conservation Corps.[7] This publication caught our attention because it was the culmination of monitoring and record keeping on the performance of twenty-five thousand check dams of various designs installed on Iowa farms in the early 1930s and was prepared for conservation corps workers. It is referred to as the double-post-row, crosswise-brush type of check dam and is recorded as being suitable for medium and large gullies as well as small ones. The object of this type of check dam is not to induce filling of sediment behind a dam but to prevent further erosion and cutting and to establish an environment that supports revegetation of the gully. Because the main materials involved are live and dead brush, its practicality covers wide geographic areas, urban and rural. This Iowa Engineering Experiment Station publication states, "Judging from field performance under conservation camp conditions, the double post row dam is the most dependable of the brush types by a good margin." A field inspection after an intense rain of 4 inches showed that 250 check dams, the majority of which were double-post-row dams, were functioning well, with problems reported in only five of them.

Figure 9.11 shows the installation of double-post-row dams constructed by two different crews of East Bay Municipal Utility District rangers in Calaveras County in Northern California in the heavy rainfall year of 1995.

The first step in the Calaveras County project was to fence cattle from the site. Livestock grazing is incompatible with gully repair. The next step was to pull back the vertical headcut of the upper portion of the gully to an angle that prevents the widening of the gully caused by chunks of earth breaking off in vertical columns. After shaping the headcut, we compacted the soil with a gas-driven compactor and with the back sides of shovels, rakes, and other hand tools. We then put down a layer of mulch 6 inches or deeper. These treatments help prevent the loosening and piping, or movement, of soil up through the rock layer you will put in place on top of the mulch. To stop the headward movement in any gully, no matter the source of its creation, the portion of the gully that is cutting headward needs to be rocked. The rock should be angular—not round river rock—and should be arranged by hand after it's dumped in place so that the rocks lock into each other. You should be able to walk on the rock without it rolling around under your feet. Lay the rock by first keying it in to a ditch dug about 1–2 feet below the grade of the gully. This anchors your rock work and keeps the whole rocked slope from slipping downhill. If you have enough rock, the optimum design is to rock all the way up to the top of the gully to the original ground elevation.

To construct the double-post, brush check dam, select a site 15–30 feet downhill of the gully head. Dig a trench across the gully 2–3 feet deep and 3 feet wide. Cut willow or poplar posts 4–8 feet long and 3–6 inches in diameter. Place two parallel rows of posts 3 feet apart in the trench across the gully and run them at least 5 feet up the gully sides. Fill in the trench, compacting the soil around the posts. The posts should stand no more than 3-½ feet above grade. The average height of these check dams in the CCC publication was 2 feet. Fill the space between the posts with dead and/or live brush. A good design is to alternate a layer of live brush in between some dead layers. The live poles or brush need to have their butt ends shoved into the gully sides so they can take root and grow. Using No. 9 thickness wire, wire the brush down tightly to the posts after each new layer is placed between them.

At the same time you are placing brush perpendicular to or across the width of the gully to make the brush dam, you should also be laying down some brush on the downstream end of the check dam that can serve as an apron (figure 9.7). Catch the stem ends of the brush in your check dam and point the brushy part of the plants downstream. This brush will act as a below-dam energy dissipater to catch flows going over and through the dam.

The final step in the project is the most important. After the rock is placed and the dam and apron are constructed, you need to install live stakes and poles in the entire project area. Refer to the sections "Installing Cuttings" and "Poles, the Riprap Substitute." Tamp 1-inch-diameter or thicker cuttings that are 2 feet long into the

FIGURE 9.11. INSTALLATION
OF A DOUBLE-POST ROW DAM
AT CALAVERAS COUNTY,
CALIFORNIA.

soil between the rock and on the gully sides. Move the rock around if you need to, to accommodate the cuttings. Stake the entire bottom of the gully and apron. Stake up the gully sides until you run out of time or plant material.

The double-post, brush check dams shown in figure 9.11 were constructed and staked in approximately three hours using an average of six field workers. The crews had access to a front loader–backhoe tractor and a professional operator, which greatly reduces the time required to regrade the gully. Each gully repair required about two one-ton trucks of gathered plant material. About two one-ton pickup trucks of rock were used. Fence construction and redistribution of runoff required time in addition to that.

The key to success is to remember that the physical construction work is being done to establish the site conditions to make plant growth possible. If you are installing the project in the dry season in a western climate, the last step is to bring in a water truck and thoroughly water the project. If the project is installed while it's raining, or in wet soils, the watering can be left out. If you are having a dry year and there is little soil moisture to support plant growth, then you will probably need to water routinely (once a week, every two weeks, or once a month, depending on the climate).

We are encouraging the use of post or pole cuttings on these sites as the main strategy for revegetation. Frequently, gullied landscapes are characterized by lowered ground water tables caused by the degraded drainages. Post or pole cuttings 3 inches or greater in diameter and 4–10 feet long can survive longer in drier sites and have the advantage of being driven deeper and closer to groundwater.

Common Errors Made in Check Dam Construction:

1. Check dams are put too low in the watershed and are blown out.
2. The spillways are left out of impermeable check dam designs. Spillways are not required in porous check dams. (Refer to figure 9.10.)
3. Not enough effort is made to revegetate the site with live posts, cuttings, or seed after the check dams are constructed.
4. The site is too dry to support the growth of vegetation, and supplemental irrigation isn't supplied.
5. The planting is timed before a hot, dry season rather than a wet season.
6. The rock is not angular and is not packed tightly enough so runoff pipes the soil through it. The rock is not keyed in to a ditch.
7. The ends of the dam are not adequately keyed in to the sides of the gully.
8. The dams are too high (over 3-½ feet) and the water spilling over, through, and around them undercuts the structure.
9. The energy dissipater and apron are not added to the toe of the dam.
10. The dams are set at angles perpendicular to the banks instead of to the flow and therefore divert flows to the sides of the gully.
11. The projects are not monitored after the first couple of substantial rainstorms to detect problem areas where gully flows are eroding around dams or undercutting them. Usually, some adjustments in rock or brush placement are needed.

Stream-Channel Restoration

Traditional stream- and river-channel "restoration projects" consisted of improving river channels for navigation by removing river snags and natural debris to allow barge and boat passage. Later, the concept of adding "instream" structures such as logs and creek bank deflectors for creating better fish habitat was developed. Stream-bank restoration then evolved as an offshoot of soil conservation programs. All of those eras contributed to our knowledge base of rivers and streams, but the contemporary restorationist realizes that those restoration activities were usually done without the advantage of understanding stream dynamics.

"River training" projects were carried out on a large scale using dikes, groins, spurs, and booms to narrow rivers and affect their meanders. Those training projects were generally done to narrow and deepen river channels to aid navigation, as opposed to restoring natural river functions. The structures, made of fill, rock, boulders, gabions, concrete, logs, and other materials, are mounds that jut out from riverbanks into the channels. They force rivers to drop sediment behind the protrusions and force deeper flows around these jetties. A similar concept has been used on a much smaller scale in streams by fish biologists in order to re-create meanders.

These smaller-scale fish habitat structures have been referred to as deflectors. Streams and creeks were turned into grassed channels, and check dams were placed in stream channels to flatten grades and catch sedimentation and/or create pools.

Today we know that restoration is a complicated science, in which the objective of an ecological restoration project is to restore at least some of the natural structure, dynamics, and diversity of a historical ecosystem. Many bank stabilization or fish habitat enhancement projects have failed because they were planned without knowledge of how the environment would react to them. Unanticipated environmental damage has been caused as a result of many projects. Bank stabilization, erosion control, fish, and instream habitat enhancement will be the rewards of good watershed management practices and the careful design of stream-channel restoration based on the principles described in chapter 4. The use of a check dam, groin, boulders, logs, grasses, or trees does not a restoration project make if the principles are not applied to the materials.

Restoring the Balance in Stream Dynamics

The field of stream and river restoration took a quantum leap with the greater understanding developed in the past few decades on the dynamics of streams. Rather than approaching a stream project as a stream-bank repair or flood-control project, we instead diagnose the cause of the watershed imbalance and prescribe a remedy to return the balance.[8-10] Most likely, the two most common symptoms of channel instability a stream manager will observe in urban areas are the degrading or incised channel, which is identified by bed erosion, including headcutting of the streambed; and the aggrading channel, which is typified by a stream without pool and riffle sequences and a shallow, wide streambed with a silty bottom.

The degrading or incised stream channel in figure 4.9b has eroded 10 feet downward in just three years. The bottom of the creek used to be level with the storm-water pipe entering the creek. The channel incision in this case was caused by an increase in stream flows from urban runoff being directed into the stream channel.[11] Other activities that can cause channel degradation include the cutting off of stream meanders, or straightening, as mentioned previously, and the removal of streamside vegetation or woody debris so that they no longer help the stream channel resist the erosive force of the flows. Sometimes large decreases in sediment input into streams, usually caused by an upstream dam, can cause channel degradation downstream because the erosive power of the water is increased.

Stream degradation generally refers to a lowering of the streambed elevation over a long period of time and represents a stream system in which the slope, discharge, and velocity are such that more sediment is transported than is supplied to the system. An entrenched channel usually refers to the condition in which a stream has eroded the channel bed in relatively short order and the stream channel no longer sends frequent flows to its floodplain. The entrenched channel becomes confined by these vertical banks and continues to erode vertically. These vertical banks can become vulnerable to collapse and erosion. Incised channels usually refer to those that are eroding at an accelerated rate and are eroding vertically and horizontally. The confined flood flows of entrenched and incised channels can be dramatically erosive, as the photo in figure 4.9b shows. An incised channel can be difficult to restore. Revegetation projects are usually the most effective for helping the channel reach a new equilibrium.

Aggrading channels generally begin to erode wider banks. Aggrading channels represent a condition in which the stream does not have sufficient flow velocities or slope to transport the sediment load entering the stream system. Accelerated aggradation can occur when a channelization project upstream has degraded the upstream area and increased the sediment loads being carried to the downstream areas. Aggradation can also occur because the construction of a housing development has caused a great deal of sediment to wash off the construction site into the creek. Anything that disturbs the land and creates erosion, such as timber harvesting, mining, construction, etc., can cause aggradation of stream channels by contributing an excess sediment load to the system. The aggradation shown on the tributary to the Issaquah Creek in Washington (figure 4.9c) was caused by upstream residential development. Culverts delivered fast-flowing runoff from the development to the stream. The erosive power of the runoff caused a debris flow of water and sand, gravel and cobbles. The stream dropped its load at the bridge in the photo where two undersized culverts are located, now buried under the bridge. The culverts slowed the velocity of the flood flows, and the stream dropped its load behind them and progressively filled the channel upstream with its load.[12]

Overly wide and laterally unstable channels can be restored to an equilibrium condition by returning the channel to a lower width-depth ratio. A width-depth ratio that would foster an equilibrium condition can be arrived at by determining what the ratio was before the stream was destabilized or by comparing the site with other similar channel types composed of similar sediment. A corrected width-depth ratio can help produce the stream power needed to transport the stream's sediment load.[13] Lateral instability can be corrected with bank erosion controls such as brush piles and tree revetments, root wads, or other vegetative means, which narrow the channel, trap sediment, and help new vegetation get established.

The shape of a channel that will provide greater equilibrium among the interactions of the sediment load, the slope, and the discharges of the stream can be designed by emulating streams in relative balance that have similar watershed sizes, discharges and, slopes and are composed of similar soils and land forms. Stream geomorphologist Dave Rosgen has advanced the methodology for helping determine an equilibrium shape for streams by estimating the ranges of values of width-depth ratios for different classifications of streams in various landscape types.[14] This was described in greater detail in chapter 4.

Solving Problems with Channel Grades and Culverts
Channel Grades
Culverts, channel straightening, and removal of meanders are among the greatest culprits for creating imbalances in the slopes of stream channels. In-channel grade-

control structures such as concrete weirs, dams, drop structures, sills, chutes, and flumes are often used to stop the slope imbalances caused by those problem features.

The concept of a graded stream described in chapter 4 should guide your approach to grade-control problems in streams. A stream in equilibrium is described as a graded stream in which the slope is delicately adjusted to provide just the velocity needed to transport the sediment load being supplied from the watershed. Streams degrade or aggrade and change their shapes, sizes, and meanders to adjust to changes in the watershed. The first questions you need to ask when you see what looks like a stream's effort to adjust its slope are, What is causing the adjustment? Can you address the problem by planting the channel to encourage soil stability and allow the widening and deepening that must proceed to adjust to urbanization? Will upstream water catchment projects put stream discharges in better balance with sediment loads? Are structures such as culverts or bridge abutments creating the grade problem?

Once you have addressed the options for watershed management measures, you can consider in-channel modifications to help promote the channel's return to a state of dynamic or quasi-equilibrium. A popular and conventional way to respond to abrupt changes in stream gradient has been to construct grade stabilizers or drop structures intended to stop the movement of bedscarps or to flatten gradients. Grade stabilizers are used to form an artificial control point to stop grade adjustments from traveling upstream and include weirs, chutes, and flumes. In channels with sudden changes in grade of 2 or more feet, a drop structure is constructed to handle the erosive force of the resulting waterfall. Such structures typically have an armored or concrete plunge pool, and many have concrete posts that serve as energy dissipaters.

Civil engineers as well as fisheries habitat restorationists are learning that instream structures may result in unintended channel adjustments. A recent study issued by the Army Corps of Engineers in which flood- and erosion-control projects were inspected reported that "the unknowns in the proper design of grade control structures far outweigh the knowns."[15] High- and low-gradient stream channels generally present the most problems for stabilization with conventional weirs or dams or placement of instream habitat structures. Habitat-creating, "instream" structures, including low-stage check dams, channel constrictors, and deflectors, can catch gravels; create pools, riffles, and meanders; and affect grades. The structures may help re-create a stream's balance and therefore restore habitat for fish if the stream, for example, is too wide and too straight for its gradient. However, the use of these structures does not compose a restoration project if they are not matched correctly with the environment they are put in.[16, 17]

Constricted stream flows can take the structures out. In some cases, stream channels may meander around structures. Stream channels in low-gradient landscapes tend to be depositional areas, and efforts to create pools there can be futile. Typically, streams decrease in gradient as they go downstream; the frequency and length of riffles and rapids also decrease; and the distinctions among pools, runs, and riffles naturally should become less apparent. Within high-gradient streams, some reaches have particularly steep slopes, forming shallow turbulent riffles, rapids, or, in extreme cases, waterfalls. High-gradient streams (over 3 percent slope) with confined channels have a high probability of taking out structures. Increasing the habitat values in some high-gradient streams, which often have bedrock or boulder surfaces, can have significant limitations because the channels lack spawning gravels.

Evaluations of check dams, weirs, and other grade control structures commonly confront the well-intentioned designer with a "blown out" stream channel, complete with eroded banks, buckling dams, and pieces of weirs strewn about the landscape. The stream often takes a new course around the structures. The usual explanation is that by flattening the slope with dams, the channel increases its sinuosity and changes its course to form a longer channel.

The goal of restoring the grade or slope of a streambed should be to bring the slope of the channel in balance with the valley slope and the sinuosity of the stream. The channel sinuosity is the stream's adjustment of its slope to the valley slope. The channel slope is less steep than the valley slope (except for braided channels on steep alluvial fans) because it is meandering along the same valley distance using a longer path—like a curvy road coming down a mountain slope. The sinuosity is equal to the valley slope divided by the channel slope. The channel slope is equal to the valley slope divided by the sinuosity and the valley slope is equal to the channel slope × sinuosity. Figure 9.12 illustrates the removal of failing concrete weirs on Wildcat Creek. After the weirs were removed, a restoration channel slope was designed by dividing the valley slope by the proper sinuosity. The slope was attained by dividing up the creek bed into gradual drops with steps and pools.

Culverts

All engineering works, including culverts, are designed to fail at some point. The Achilles's heel of storm-water culverts extends beyond the false economy of designing them for very low flows, however. Their chronic installation mistakes may cause the most widespread problems. Stream channels can be destabilized for extensive distances by culverts if the stream-channel gradients are disrupted. If culverts are put in at an angle that deviates from the stream's equilibrium slope, they will create depositional and erosional reaches up and downstream of the culverts.

Storm-water culverts can act as mini-dams, create depositional areas that fill channels, cause headcutting, or create downstream erosion from the concentration of flows. Frequently, the upstream effects of culverts are more profound than the downstream impacts because they result in the stream having to make adjustments to grade along a significant distance.

Culverts often result in headward erosion or degrading of the slope upstream and creating an aggraded, steeper slope downstream (refer to figure 9.13). Erosion typically occurs immediately downstream of a culvert, but channel adjustments

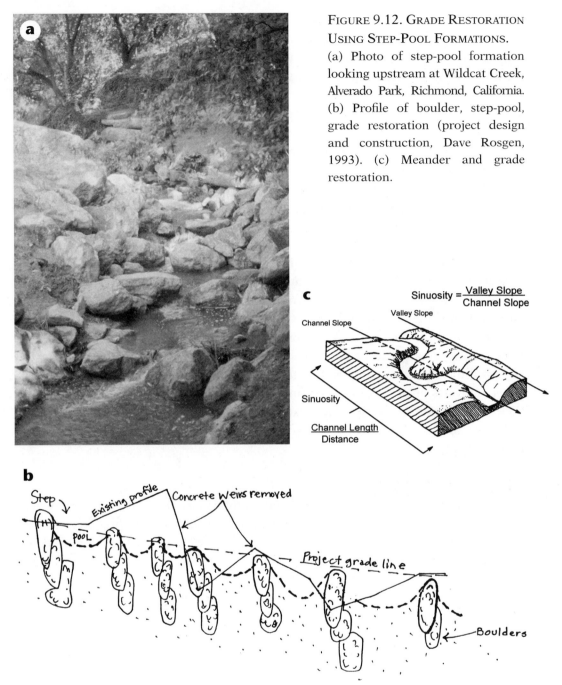

FIGURE 9.12. GRADE RESTORATION USING STEP-POOL FORMATIONS.
(a) Photo of step-pool formation looking upstream at Wildcat Creek, Alverado Park, Richmond, California. (b) Profile of boulder, step-pool, grade restoration (project design and construction, Dave Rosgen, 1993). (c) Meander and grade restoration.

downstream of the erosion zone can include deposition. Sometimes culverts will create sedimentation zones upstream of a culvert because they become clogged or sediment fills in behind a culvert that is too high on the upstream end. Channel bed erosion occurs for some distance downstream of the culvert in such cases because discharges are increased in relation to the sediment transport.

Upstream impacts of culverts can include the culvert acting as a dam in storms, flooding the areas behind it, and raising the water profile for floods behind it. They may cause deposition and subsequent channel filling behind the culvert. They can create headward erosion up into the watershed if they are installed too low in the ground. They are frequently blamed for blocking fish passage.

A well-known geomorphologist, Thomas Maddock, Jr., states that "because of the enormous numbers of highway culverts in the U.S., their combined impact on stream morphology is probably greater than any other of man's activities."[18]

Culvert-removal projects are being done to correct these problems. They are occurring as well in order to re-create riparian reaches as a strategy to increase a waterway's water quality by restoring the biological and physical functions of the natural system. Culvert removal has resulted in the return of reaches of City Creek in Salt Lake City, Utah; Woonsquatucket River in Providence, Rhode Island; Napa Creek in downtown Napa, California; Strawberry, Blackberry, and Codornices creeks in Berkeley, California; Baxter Creek in El Cerrito, California; and Jolly Green Giant Creek in Arcata, California. Other culvert-removal projects are under design in Washington, Minnesota, Texas, and Oregon to restore business areas and neighborhoods. In some restoration projects culverts are replaced with the ground-level crossings called fords or with bridges. Both those alternatives can impact stream dimensions and slopes, but the impacts can be much less than culverts. Where culverts must remain, realignment with stream meanders, readjustment of their slopes, and the use of culvert extenders on the up and downstream ends can reduce localized destabilization caused by excessive erosion and deposition (refer to figure 9.13).

Restoring Stream Banks

Faced with a stream-bank erosion problem, public works officials' and landowners' first instincts are usually to drop rock or riprap in eroded areas. This can cause several problems. First, because the cause of the erosion has not been removed, the problem continues. Second, the riprap is usually a blight on the landscape. Government resources agencies are increasingly opposing its use because the rock can eliminate critical fish resting and hiding areas available in more natural stream banks. Finally, the rock typically causes more erosion up and downstream and on the stream bank opposite where it is placed.

Any hard objects placed on stream banks can perpetuate erosion problems. Stream currents are deflected off rocks, concrete rubble, and other objects and create eddying that erodes the stream banks up and downstream of the objects. The hard objects can also deflect currents to the opposite bank, causing that bank to be undercut. To avoid these complications, restoration strategies are based on returning plant cover to stream banks because of the superior ability of plants to hold soil, protect banks, and create a stabilizing influence on the stream. Extremely difficult sites may require structural components such as jacks, lunkers, dirt-filled gabions, rock work, and cribwalls to rebuild a stream bank and offer temporary

1. Culverts Too High or Too Low

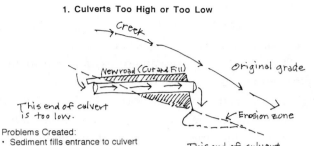

Problems Created:
- Sediment fills entrance to culvert
- Storm water flows over the road top
- Headward erosion from grade change

Problems Created:
- Plunge pool forms under culvert which can erode up hill and undercut stream bank and road
- Down stream erosion caused by faster velocities and grade changes

Remedies:
- Place culvert at similar grade as the original creek bed before putting in road fill
- Use a bridge crossing over creek
- Use an at-grade crossing or ford
- Put culvert extender on downstream or upstream ends of culvert to help compensate for grade changes
- Use rock energy dissipaters and plant cuttings in stream reach where culvert flows reenter stream

2. Culvert Too Small or Unmaintained

CULVERT EXTENDER

Problems:
- Storm flows back up and create upstream drainage problems
- Sediment and debris dropout in front of culvert blocking movement of storm flows
- Stormwater flows overtop of culvert
- Culvert breaks, buckles and "blows-out" in worse case

Remedies
- Use state road engineering culvert sizing specifications and expand to an even larger size if you can afford it. Consider combining two culverts.
- Schedule a regular maintenance program
- Replace culverts with bridges or fords

3. Stream Meander Changes or Culvert Alignment is Wrong

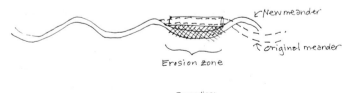

Problems:
- Stream erodes around culvert
- Erosive action displaces and moves culvert

Remedies:
- Realign culvert, replace with bridge or ford

FIGURE 9.13. COMMON PROBLEMS WITH CULVERTS.

stability while plants become established. Other stream-bank restoration methods based solely on live and dead plant materials in designed systems can address a majority of stream-bank restoration needs.

There are four major categories of stream-bank revegetation methods. One category emphasizes the use of dead brush, trees, or tree stumps to create channel deposition or sediment transport in desired places; the second category stresses the use of small cuttings or large poles cut from riparian trees to immediately emulate and reintroduce the structure riparian plants provide to streams; the third uses different systems or arrangements of dead and live cuttings to add structural strength to stream banks while replanting them; and the fourth uses significant structures in difficult urban situations in order to make stream-bank revegetation possible. All categories share the common trait, as restoration methods, of providing the conditions necessary to revegetate the riparian corridor along the stream.

Brush Deflectors, Tree Revetments, and Rootwads

Instead of rushing out to your bank erosion site with rock, run out to it with some dead tree branches or even a dead tree. George Palmiter reintroduced the concept in the 1980s of using brush piles staked to stream banks to reduce erosion. He devised a stream-channel inventory system that includes identifying snags that back up flood flows or deflect flows onto banks, causing harmful erosion. His stream-channel inventory produces a plan in which some snags are removed and at other sites, snags or downed trees are cabled to an eroding bank to help restore it to a vegetated environment. The cabled brush slows the velocities against the eroding bank and can create a protected environment in which plant growth can be reestablished (figure 9.14).[19]

The tree revetments bank restoration method is based on the same concept as the Palmiter brush piles. This method is being used widely and increasingly perfected by the Missouri Department of Conservation in Jefferson City.[20, 21] Whole trees are cabled against tree banks (figure 9.15), strung in a line along a bank erosion zone. Although the Missouri tree revetment program doesn't describe the integration of live plantings into the tree revetments, that is a recommended addition. The branches of the dead trees will slow velocities on the outside stream-channel bends and catch sediment and debris, making the site conducive to volunteer vegetative growth. Most disturbed sites will greatly benefit by the addition of live cuttings driven through the brush piles into the soil of the stream banks. The revetments will provide immediate protection and aid the establishment of live riparian growth. These live plants then take root, eventually stabilizing the bank and eliminating the need for the dead branches and trees.

Both of these systems are sadly underused. The plant materials are inexpensive (amounting to the cost of collection), the installation is simple, and, according to the Missouri Department of Conservation, the success rates are good—particularly for tree revetments. Experiment with these techniques as a substitute for riprap in your area.

FIGURE 9.14. PALMITER BRUSH DEFLECTOR.
Lindo Creek, Chico, California.

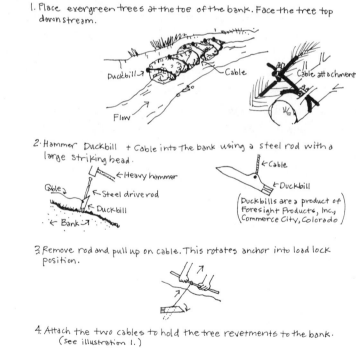

TREE REVETMENTS

1. Place evergreen trees at the toe of the bank. Face the tree top downstream.

Duckbill   Cable   Cable attachment

Flow

2. Hammer Duckbill + Cable into the bank using a steel rod with a large striking head.

Heavy hammer   Cable
Cable   Steel drive rod   Duckbill
Duckbill   (Duckbills are a product of
Bank   Foresight Products, Inc.,
      Commerce City, Colorado)

3. Remove rod and pull up on cable. This rotates anchor into load lock position.

4. Attach the two cables to hold the tree revetments to the bank.
(see illustration 1.)

5. Place a second row of trees on top of the bottom row.

For more information, contact: The Missouri Department of Conservation
P.O. Box 180
Jefferson City, Mo. 65102-0180

FIGURE 9.15. INSTALLING TREE REVETMENTS.

The combined use of rootwads and vortex rocks (see glossary) to return stream-channel equilibrium is a practice being refined by Dave Rosgen (see figure 9.16). Because they are usually the central structural features of his restoration projects, rootwads and vortex rocks serve as a signature for his work. Rootwads are tree trunks that are uprooted with their roots attached. Rosgen uses systematically placed rootwads to fortify stream banks and hold his desired equilibrium channel shape and meander. Vortex rocks may also do double duty as part of the step-pool formations described earlier. At the Blackberry Creek channel re-creation project in Berkeley, California, we used vortex rocks placed at the meander crossovers to both help direct the meanders and dissipate energy with small gradient drops.

Rosgen uses rootwads because of their unique ability to emulate the naturally occurring functions of riparian tree roots, which not only hold stream banks in place, but also create a channel current eddying that serves to keep sediment suspended and transported along the watercourse. His vortex rocks placed across stream channels concentrate the stream flows toward the center of the channel, where they can then be directed toward the outside bends and help desired meanders form. The rocks not only contribute to the stream dynamics needed to transport sediment, they also create downstream scour zones for fish and invertebrate habitat.

The use of "instream structures" such as rocks, logs, tree roots, etc., has a long history in fisheries habitat restoration practices. As discussed in the earlier section "Channel Grades," structures must be placed in rivers with knowledge of the type of stream channel you are working with and a good geomorphological analysis of what the consequences of the structures will be on channel equilibrium.

Installing Brush Piles and Tree Revetments

Tree revetments and Palmiter brush piles work under the same principle: that of slowing erosive velocities at outside bends of streams. Because tree revetments appear to be a more successful approach at this time than brush piles, we recommend the use of trees. Brush piles and tree revetments are installed essentially using the same principles. (Refer to figures 9.14, 9.17 and 9.18.)

Brush piles are the most low tech and simple to use. They are particularly well suited for small streams in backyards where an urban property owner (or renter) wants to retard an erosion problem with minimum costs. Drive fence posts or—much better if you can get them—live willow posts (see next section) in parallel rows along the stream bank about 4 feet apart. Place the dead brush, cuttings, or plant material against the slope of the stream bank in between the rows of poles. Wire the brush down against the stream bank by stringing the wire in a criss-cross fashion between the posts. After completing the wiring, hammer the posts down a little farther into the ground. This helps tighten the wiring. Figure 9.18 illustrates this brush and live post revetment. Figure 9.17 shows a slightly different system in which brush piles are bundled together and then wired to fence posts driven into the bank. In some projects I combine these methods to fit the brush and live plantings

FIGURE 9.16. CHANNEL RESTORATION WITH ROOTWADS AND VORTEX ROCKS.
Installation of rootwads on Wildcat Creek at Alverado Park, Richmond, California (Dave Rosgen, 1993).

to the site conditions. Plant live stakes through the brush piles into the soil to maximize the effectiveness of the project.

Tree revetments are installed using the following steps:

1. The trees used for the bank protection revetment should be first laid out next to a stable reach of bank downstream of your problem area. This can be accomplished by tying into an overhanging tree root. The stable point prevents water

PALMITER BRUSH PILES:

Materials: Dead trees, brush, wood debris, wire, fence posts, live stokes

Installation steps:

1. Grade back undercut slope

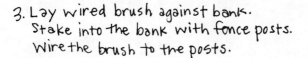

2. Bundle brush with wire

3. Lay wired brush against bank. Stake into the bank with fence posts. Wire the brush to the posts.

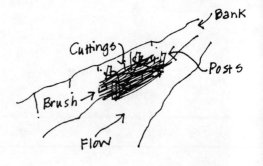

4. Drive cuttings into the brush piles.

For more information and a slide-tape show contact:
The Institute of Environmental Sciences
Miami University
Oxford, Ohio

FIGURE 9.17. INSTALLING BRUSH PILES.

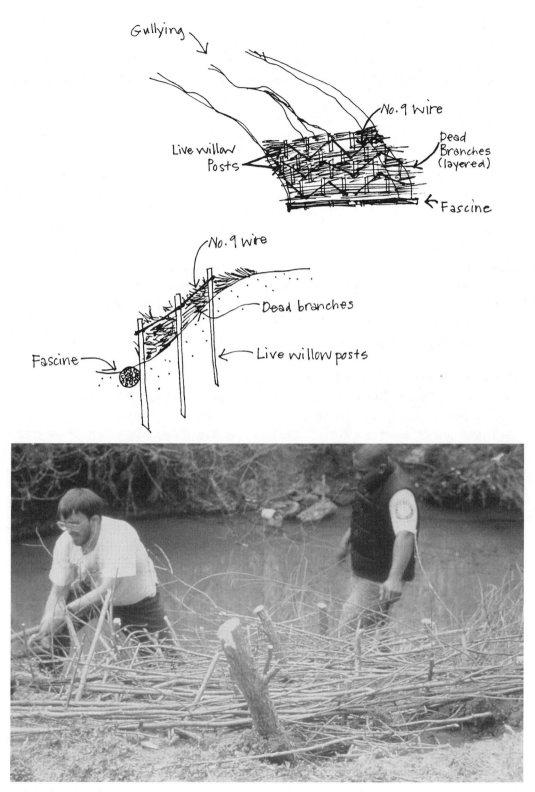

Gullying

No. 9 wire

Dead
Branches
(layered)

Live willow
Posts

Fascine

No. 9 wire

Dead branches

Fascine

Live willow posts

FIGURE 9.18. INSTALLING BRUSH AND LIVE POST REVETMENTS.
Installation on Proctor Creek, Atlanta, Georgia.

from cutting behind the trees and causing a structural failure. (Refer to figure 9.15.)

2. Cut or collect enough dead or live trees to make a double row (or more) at the base of each eroded bank (15–30 trees per 100 feet of bank will be necessary, depending on their length). If a tree is not branched at its base, drill holes 1 foot up the trunk of the tree large enough to accommodate the cable. Trees should be in reasonably fresh condition when installed. It is best if there is little or no loss of suppleness from drying, but realistically you will need to work with what trees are available for you.

3. Beginning on the most downstream portion of the eroded bank, place the first row of trees at the toe of the bank (where the bank meets the creek bottom) with the butts pointing upstream. Placing the first row of trees above the toe could result in undercutting of the revetment and eventual failure.

4. Anchor trees to the bank with arrowhead or duckbill anchors (figure 9.19) using $\frac{3}{16}$-inch cable. These anchors can be driven easily with a post pounder to a depth of 4 to 5 feet. Alternatively, you can use 5-$\frac{1}{2}$-foot metal fence posts with holes as an anchor. Attach the cable through a hole in the bottom of the post using cable clamps or crimps. Then drive the cable and post into the side of the bank.

5. Once the anchors are driven and set into the bank, cable can be strung through the hole drilled in the butt of each tree, wrapped, and fastened with either cable clamps or crimps. There should be no slack in fastening cables.

6. Trees must be snug to the toe of the bank once installed. Movement of the trees during high flow could result in structural failure.

7. Trees should be overlapped so that no significant gaps exist between trees. Likewise, there should not be any significant gaps between trees and stream bank. Each tree should overlap the preceding tree by approximately 30 percent of its length and be cabled or wired to it tightly to create a continuous structural unit.

8. Place the second row above the first row of trees in the same manner.

9. Plant live cuttings through the revetment into the stream-bank soil.

Once the tree revetment is complete, a regular inspection schedule should be maintained to avoid structural loss. After the first storm, look at the revetment to identify weak cables or wires and locate areas where flows may be trying to undercut the revetment. The corrective work after the first storm flows is as much part of the project as the initial installation. Re-anchoring loosened trees in problem areas can usually be done with minimal cost and effort. Inspection should be subsequently conducted seasonally and after every major flow event.

Practitioners of this method find that evergreen trees perform better than broadleaf trees in catching sediment and providing bank protection. They prefer just-cut live trees over dead ones, if they are available. They also emphasize the importance of installation with tight rather than slack cables. Loose cables can allow the revetments to be buffeted by high flood flows, which can cause damage to

FIGURE 9.19. DUCKBILL ANCHOR FOR SECURING TREE REVETMENTS OR BRUSH PILES. Cobbs Creek, Meadowdale Park, DeKalb County, Georgia.

stream banks. The tree revetments perform most effectively if live cuttings are driven through them into stream banks, hastening the revegetation process.

Installing Cuttings

Cuttings taken from riparian species of plants that root and grow when they are stuck in the soil serve as the foundation of stream restoration practice. Many people can equate the experience of using cuttings to taking stems from a house plant like a geranium and sticking them in pots of dirt, where, if watered, they will root and form new plants. Soil bioengineering systems use bundles and layers of live cuttings from plants to reestablish plant communities. There are several advantages to these systems. First, the plant material is essentially free except for the costs of collecting and transporting. Second, the systems provide immediate structure and stability to a slope even before rooting and growing. Finally, once plants have rooted and sprouted, the ability of such systems to bind soil and provide strength to slopes is well evidenced by many successful stabilization projects.

Description

Willows are the most common species for these systems because of the abundance of many species of willows in stream, river, and lake environments all over the country. Willow species are real survivors under even difficult conditions, and you can usually find them in quantity. There are many other species, both sun and shade loving, that can also be used. Cottonwood and dogwood species are commonly among them.

There are a variety of ways to collect, prepare, and install plant materials in soil-bioengineering systems. Cuttings, taken from branches of bushes and trees, are sometimes referred to in restoration literature as live stakes. These cuttings are literally used like stakes to hold layers of vegetation in the ground, but they provide an additional benefit to your project because they will root and grow. Cuttings may be 1–3 inches in diameter and 1½–3 feet long. Pole plantings are taken from larger plant material and may be 3–6 inches in diameter and 4–10 feet long (figure 9.20). These are obviously harder to get into the ground, but they offer significant structural benefits in protecting stream-bank toes and helping revegetate a site. Their use was started in recent years in the Southwest, where dry soils and extreme heat make it difficult for plants to survive. The large poles survive better than the smaller cuttings because they have a greater capacity to store water and energy until they develop root systems. The length of the pole also helps it tap ground water located in deeper underground aquifers. Pole plantings have now caught on around the country, and I hope that you will try using them because of their versatility.[22–24]

Collection

Small restoration projects using cuttings and poles for 100–200 feet of stream bank require at least four to five large truck loads (¾-ton truck or larger) of plant material. This quantity underscores the importance of finding an appropriate, local site for plant material. The simplest way to locate such a site is to ask local naturalists or native plant experts. Ideally, you should identify and record the location of the desired species while they are in leaf from spring to fall. Once the plants drop their leaves in dormancy, identifying some of the species you want to use becomes much more difficult.

The easiest way to collect and transport cutting and pole stock to the restoration site is to remove large branches from trees and shrubs and place them in the truck. If it's a hot, windy day or you have far to travel, tie a tarp over the plant materials to keep them from drying out and dying before you reach the project site. Once at the site, stick the butt ends of the vegetation into the creek to keep them wet. If there is no creek water to use for temporary storage, prepare the plant materials (see "Preparation" below) and put them in buckets of water after arriving at your site. Otherwise, prepare the material for planting just before you want to plant it.

Preparation

Preparation of the cuttings should involve cutting the fatter stems near the base of main branches of shrubs or trees rather than using the new growth tips, which are thinner and more vulnerable to damages. Cut pieces from the stems at least 18 inches to about 3 feet long and 1–3 inches thick for cuttings, 4–10 feet long and 3–6 inches thick for poles.

The butt end of the cutting is the end that is planted. It should be pointed when you make the cutting for two reasons. The point identifies the butt end, so you don't accidentally plant the cutting upside down in the ground, and it makes it easier to drive the cutting into the soil. Use sharp tools to make the cuttings so you don't

FIGURE 9.20. CUTTINGS AND POLES.
(a) Willow pole being installed by a Minnesota Conservation Corps member on Minnehaha Creek. (b) Dormant cuttings are planted on Blackberry Creek's slopes (fascines are sprouting near channel) in California. (c) Same view of Blackberry Creek, California, six months later.

mangle them with loppers or pruners and thereby make them vulnerable to moisture loss and other problems.

Installation

In soft or wet soils, cuttings can be gently tamped into the ground with a mallet.
Soils that are dry or compacted are harder and slower to work with. It is often necessary to prepare a hole for installing a cutting in that case. Prepare a hole for a cutting in dry soil by driving a piece of rebar into the ground and pulling it out. Gently
tamp the cutting into the hole created by the rebar and avoid stripping the bark.
Roots start from points in the inner bark so loosening of the bark from the wood destroys the root-sprouting ability of the cutting. Be careful not to damage or split the
cutting when hammering it in because that significantly hurts its survival capabilities. The deeper the cutting is set, the better. A good goal is to bury four-fifths of it
below ground. Shallow planting results in too few roots below ground, too many
leaf shoots above ground, and early death to the cutting because the scanty roots
cannot supply water and nutrients rapidly enough for the greater mass of foliage.
Wooden or sand- or shot-filled mauls can be used instead of metal hammer heads to
reduce damage to the plant material.

Figure 9.21 shows the use of cuttings to revegetate stream banks or slopes.
"Joint" planting refers to planting cuttings through riprapped slopes. Planting cuttings can be difficult work if the site has been graded, compacted, and rocked with
large stone. In that situation larger and longer pole cuttings may be easier to install
and more successful than shorter cuttings. The revegetation strategy shown in
figure 9.21 is easy to teach a neighborhood, or individual property owners, and
needs only a limited amount of plant material.

Poles, the Riprap Substitute

Large "cuttings" of branches or trunks of riparian species as large as tree-planting
stakes are the underused workhorses of restoration. The planting of large poles
adds more structure to the toe of a slope than a rock does. First, the pole is anchored
3–5 feet or more under the streambed. Even before it is rooted, substantial catastrophic discharges and velocities would be required to move it. If a number of
poles are placed close together as in a picket fence, they offer a substantial toe-of-
slope wood structure. They grow into instant trees with all the structural advantages of roots and shading to help a plant succession begin on the site.

Willows and cottonwoods are particularly good species to use for poles. Cut 3–6-
inch-diameter trees and branches into average lengths of 6–8 feet with a chain saw
and remove all the lateral branches. Sharpen the bottom end to a point to ease
planting. Planting poles in soft, moist soil is easier than planting them in hard, dry
soil, but even good site conditions have challenges because of how deep you need to
plant poles. At least half of the pole should be driven into the soil. Make a hole first
as illustrated in figure 9.22, using a construction stake, which is a steel rod with a
point on the end. This process works best with a team of two working together. One

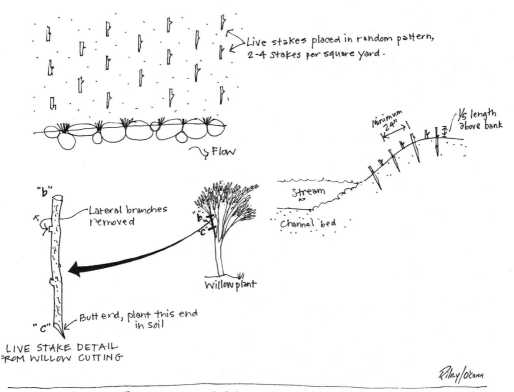

Live stakes placed in random pattern, 2-4 stakes per square yard.

Flow

Minimum 24"

⅕ length above bank

Stream

Channel bed

"b"

Lateral branches removed

Willow plant

Butt end, plant this end in soil

"c"

LIVE STAKE DETAIL FROM WILLOW CUTTING

Riley/O'conn

INSTALLATION OF LIVE STAKES SHOWN WITH AN OPTIONAL ROCK TOE KEY

FIGURE 9.21. INSTALLING LIVE CUTTINGS.

person holds the stake, and the other hammers it in. The stake holder needs to wiggle the stake after every few blows of the hammer to make it possible to remove the stake after it has made the hole. After the hole is as deep as you can get it, remove the stake and place the live post in it. Put a 2 × 4-inch board on top of the live post to hammer it in. The board makes it easier to hammer the pole in and protects the pole from splitting. After hammering the pole in as far as you can, saw off the top few damaged inches.

The Illinois State Water Survey uses an excavator with a steel ram to mechanically make planting holes. If you have the budget to use heavy equipment, that can speed up your project, but our experience is that conservation corps labor usually installs posts efficiently and quickly. We have found that the use of a jackhammer or power auger can speed the making of good planting holes. The real advantage of mechanically made holes is that they can usually be driven deeper than manually made holes.

Poles should be set deep enough to maintain contact with the water table but not so deep that they are completely submerged for long periods of time. Long periods of submergence will kill them. Some project designs use poles installed in the stream channel to help slow and deflect flows away from a stream bank, but in those

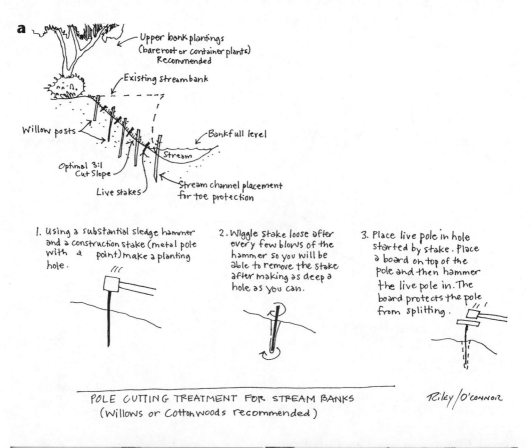

a — Upper bank plantings (bare root or container plants) Recommended

— Existing streambank

Willow posts

— Bankfull level

Stream

Optimal 3:1 Cut Slope

Live stakes

Stream channel placement for toe protection

1. Using a substantial sledge hammer and a construction stake (metal pole with a point) make a planting hole.

2. Wiggle stake loose after every few blows of the hammer so you will be able to remove the stake after making as deep a hole as you can.

3. Place live pole in hole started by stake. Place a board on top of the pole and then hammer the live pole in. The board protects the pole from splitting.

POLE CUTTING TREATMENT FOR STREAM BANKS
(Willows or Cottonwoods recommended)

Riley/O'Connor

b

c

FIGURE 9.22 POLE TREATMENT FOR STREAM BANKS (WILLOWS OR COTTONWOODS RECOMMENDED).

(a) Hand installation [refer to part (a) of figure 9.20]. (b) Installation of 10-foot poles using an excavator and steel ram in Court Creek Watershed, Illinois. *Photo credit:* Illinois Water Survey. (c) Later view of same stream-bank restoration showing growth from poles. *Photo credit:* Illinois Water Survey.

cases, even if the poles die from prolonged submergence, they still serve that useful structural role.

Biotechnical Slope Stabilization

The terms being used to describe plant-based systems for stream-bank and slope restoration are *soil biotechnical slope stabilization* and *soil bioengineering.* As chapter 6 discusses, in many cases, the systems have ancient origins, going back to Sumarian and Roman civilizations. The strategies come to us today via 1930s government manuals on erosion control. Robbin Sotir, of Robbin Sotir Associates in Marietta, Georgia, can largely be credited for the recent wide exposure and reintroduction of these methods. Other firms also are now incorporating the use of these methods, increasing the availability of the technology. The Natural Resources Conservation Service is promoting the use of soil bioengineering in its engineering field handbook for slope protection and erosion control and the Army Corps of Engineers has released its first report on soil bioengineering.[25–28]

Soil bioengineering systems are composed of live and sometimes dead plant materials that are bundled or arranged in a way that provides both an immediate structural component to hold a stream bank and living plant materials, which ultimately provides long-term slope protection. A soil bioengineering system the layperson may be familiar with is a wattle, which is called a fascine by soil bioengineers so it is not confused with live bush fences also called wattles.

A *fascine* is a cigar-shaped bundle of cuttings planted in trenches on the contour of a slope (figure 9.23) to provide structural strength to the slope and help break the movement of runoff downslope as it enters the stream.

Brush layering is an appropriate system to use for revegetation of fill or a newly constructed slope. Cuttings are layered on terraces perpendicular to the slope so that they will root into the bank or hillside. The live brush is then covered with soil so that only the growing tips protrude from the slope, helping to reduce the velocity and stress of flows against stream banks (figure 9.24).

Brush matting shows up in many old erosion control documents. The growing ends of the plant material are stuck in soil, and the plants are held flat against the slope by wire. The plants take root while the mat helps prevent soil erosion and adds a protective layer across the surface of a bank or slope (figure 9.25).

Branch packing has been widely used to repair gullies or other eroding surfaces in projects on farms and in parks. In situations where runoff from roads or other surfaces is creating gullies or slope caving, the disturbance can be packed with layers of live and dead branches to fill the gully, slow runoff, and start plant growth (figure 9.26).

Geotextile fabrics are sometimes used in conjunction with these soil bioengineering systems (figure 9.27). These fabrics are woven netting made out of either synthetic or natural fibers, and they can be stapled into soils to help protect them from erosion. The oldest and most well-known fabric is jute netting, which can help reduce erosion from rain and runoff in upper slope and watershed areas but has

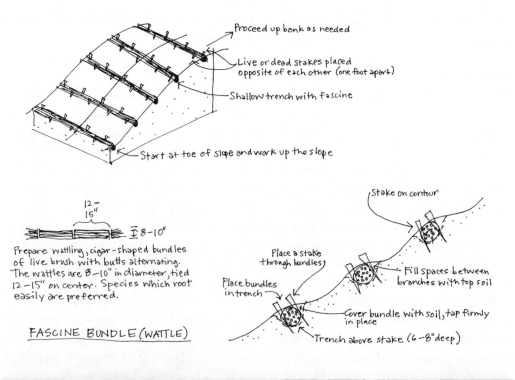

Proceed up bank as needed

Live or dead stakes placed opposite of each other (one foot apart)

Shallow trench with fascine

Start at toe of slope and work up the slope

12-15"

$\overline{\text{I}}$ 8-10"

Prepare wattling, cigar-shaped bundles of live brush with butts alternating. The wattles are 8-10" in diameter, tied 12-15" on center. Species which root easily are preferred.

FASCINE BUNDLE (WATTLE)

Stake on contour

Place a stake through bundles

Place bundles in trench

Fill spaces between branches with top soil

Cover bundle with soil, tap firmly in place

Trench above stake (6-8" deep)

FIGURE 9.23. INSTALLATION OF FASCINES.
Refer to part (b) of figure 9.20 for photo of fascine growth.

limitations for use near stream channels because it does not function well in heavy water flows.

Synthetic fiber blankets have the disadvantage of not being biodegradable. A variety of natural fiber, erosion-control fabrics made from cotton, jute, sisal, and coir are now on the market. Coir fabrics are popular for use in waterways because they have high tensile strengths, are resistant to rot, and withstand high stream flows and velocities.[29, 30]

To repeat earlier advice, I suggest that you get help from experts who have field experience with these strategies because it is difficult to learn everything you need to know from a book or training manual.

Also, a common misconception about these plant systems is that they are limited in use because they are successful only in sunny, open stream-channel environments. In fact many shade adapted riparian species that occur in abundance can be used in these systems. Examples of such plants are dogwood (*Cornus* species), ninebark (*Physocarpus* species), berries (of the *Rubus* species), snowberry (*Symphoricarpos albus*), some species of viburnum, and elderberry (*Sambucus* species).

Fascines

Fascines are bundles of cuttings 3 feet or longer and about 8–10 inches wide. They should be planted above the elevation of the base or low flows in stream channels so that they do not die from being under water too long. The fascines are laid end to end on the contour of a slope. They protrude from the slope a few inches and that way provide a terrace that helps break up and protect the slope. The stabilization project should start at the bottom and work up the slope.

Fascines are one of the most shallow soil bioengineering systems decribed here in that the bundles are buried only a few inches below the grade of the slope. Some practitioners like to use fascines to secure, revegetate, or rebuild the bankfull channel bank. I have found, however, that fascines are very vulnerable in this active channel zone because they are not deeply imbedded and can be washed out if they have not had much time for plant growth to become well established. For this reason I restrict their use in the area of the active channel to small creeks draining watersheds under half a square mile. Their most appropriate use is for intercepting and slowing rainfall runoff down terrace slopes.

Use the following steps to install fascines, as illustrated in figure 9.23:

1. Some workers should prepare the cuttings and make the fascines while others are preparing the slope for planting by digging the trenches.
2. To make a fascine bundle, mix cuttings from a few riparian species to increase the chances that at least one species will adapt well to the site. Willows and cottonwoods, for example, won't do well if they are located too high on a dry slope with little moisture. To make the bundle, alternate butts and growing tips. When the bundle is about 10–12 inches thick, tie it together tightly with a string every 15 inches or so. It should squeeze down to an 8–10-inch bundle.

3. To prepare the slope for fascine rows, use a hand-held level to stake a level contour at the base of the hill. This is best accomplished with two people. One person holds the level and instructs the second where to place stakes on the contour every 3–4 feet. After the contour is staked, dig a 12-inch-wide and 6-inch-deep trench directly above the stakes.

4. Line the trench with fascines by coupling the ends of the fascines together. Stake them where they join to hold them together.

5. This step is the most important to do correctly. Sift and tamp soil down into the fascine with a shovel, filling it with as much dirt as possible. You want to maximize dirt-plant contact. Walk up and down the trench, packing dirt into the fascine as the finishing touch.

6. Add stakes through the bundle at the top of the trench. If you can, cross the stakes over the bundle to help hold it in.

7. Install more fascine rows in the same manner. On 2:1 slopes, space the rows 3–4 feet apart. On 3:1 slopes, space the rows no more than 6–8 feet apart.

8. If you are on a dry slope at a high elevation or in a dry western or southwestern environment, complete the project by watering the fascines with a water tank truck or other available means.

9. Figure 9.23 shows that wood stakes are used to hold the fascines into the slope. Ideally, the fascine stakes are made of 2-foot-long, 2 × 4-inch boards cut on a diagonal so that the top of the stake is flat and the bottom is a point. If it is going to be difficult to make stakes from 2 × 4s, it may be more practical to purchase bundles of 2–3-foot-long, pointed wood construction stakes from a construction-hardware retailer. Live cuttings can also be driven through the fascines both to aid in holding them in place and to help revegetate the site.

Brush Layering

Brush layering is also installed on a contour and has the advantage that it can be used to stabilize new-fill slopes. It can be combined with fascines or other systems. Rather than adding fill to reslope a bank or terrace, we recommend using the parent soil from the bank to reconstruct the slope (refer to figure 9.24). Because brush layering uses long lengths of plant material installed deeply into the slopes, I frequently use this system in combination with pole cuttings in the active bankfull channel zone. To understand what brush layering looks like, picture a lasagne in which the noodles are the plant material layered between the sauce and meat, representing the soil. The steps to installation are as follows:

1. Start the project at the bottom of the slope and work uphill.

2. Using an excavator or shovel, trench a bench or terrace on contour about 3 feet back into the hill slope. The trench should be angled downward.

3. While the trenching is being done, some workers should prepare cuttings that are approximately 4 feet long, or about a foot longer than the depth of your bench. As with fascines, you may want to try a mix of plant species.

4. Push the butt ends of the cuttings into the soil at the back of the bench. Build a

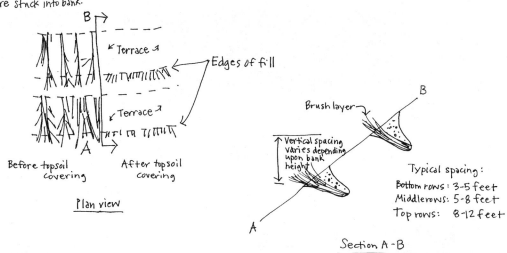

Plant cuttings laid on top of
excavated terrace. Butt ends
are stuck into bank.

B →

← Terrace ↗

Edges of fill

← Terrace ↗

A →

Before topsoil
covering

After topsoil
covering

Plan view

Brush layer

B

Vertical spacing
varies depending
upon bank
height

A

Typical spacing:
Bottom rows: 3-5 feet
Middle rows: 5-8 feet
Top rows: 8-12 feet

Section A-B

RILEY/O'CONNOR

FIGURE 9.24. INSTALLATION OF BRUSH LAYERING.
Lindo Channel, Chico, California. *Photo credit:* Streaminders, Chico, California.

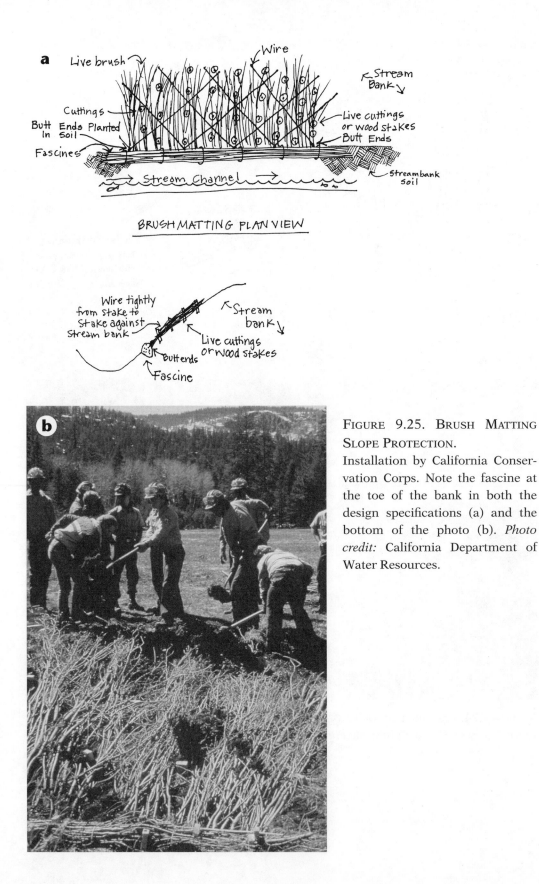

a

Live brush

Wire

Cuttings

Butt Ends Planted
In Soil

Fascines

Stream
Bank

Live cuttings
or wood stakes

Butt Ends

Streambank
Soil

Stream Channel

BRUSH MATTING PLAN VIEW

Wire tightly
from stake to
stake against
stream bank

Stream
bank

Live cuttings
or wood stakes

Butt ends

Fascine

b

FIGURE 9.25. BRUSH MATTING
SLOPE PROTECTION.
Installation by California Conservation Corps. Note the fascine at
the toe of the bank in both the
design specifications (a) and the
bottom of the photo (b). *Photo
credit:* California Department of
Water Resources.

brush layer about a foot thick. Place the cuttings in layers in a criss-cross fashion on the bench.

5. Backfill the soil onto the bench and tamp it down with your feet and shovels. Each lower bench can be back-filled using soil from the trench being dug uphill. Leave about a foot of the growing tips of the cuttings extending from the slope.
6. Continue to trench benches uphill about every 4 feet on 2:1 slopes.
7. Water the project if you are on dry slopes in a dry climate.

Brush Matting

We generally restrict the use of brush matting on stream banks to filling in between brush layering, fascines, or pole plantings. Much of the system is shallow in that it is just tied against the ground surface. It's a good system for providing complete coverage on a bank or terrace, filling in unplanted spaces not covered by the other soil bioengineering systems. Brush matting is installed using the following steps: (Refer to figure 9.25.)

1. Prepare cuttings about 6 feet long or more.
2. Start the project above the base flow of the stream bank. Dig a trench parallel to the slope. Push the butt ends of the cuttings into the soil in the trench. Bend the cuttings over the slope so that they lie smoothly against it.
3. Drive live and/or dead stakes into the slope in a checkerboard pattern so that the stakes are about 18 inches apart. Also drive stakes into the trench between the butt ends of the cuttings.
4. Wire the branches down onto the slope as tightly as you can by stringing the wire in a criss-cross fashion to the stakes. Use small U-shaped fence nails hammered into the sides of the stakes to attach the wire. Hammering the nails on top of the stakes has a tendency to split them. The wire can be awkward to work with, and it can snap and break. We recommend experimenting with a coil fiber string that is now available. Regular string will break down too quickly in cold, wet, and icy weather.
5. After stringing the wire to the stakes, hammer the stakes into the ground to tighten the matting against the slope. Cover this mattress with a thin layer of soil.
6. Backfill and compact the trench where the butt ends are planted.
7. If planted in dry soil, or dry Western climates, water in the project.

Branch Packing

Branch packing is installed using the following steps to repair small gullies and slumps in slopes: (Refer to figure 9.26 for installation directions.)

1. Drive dead stakes or, better, live poles into the bottom of the project area. Set them 2–3 feet apart. Drive more rows of poles up the slope of the gully or slump every 2–4 feet, depending on the size of the gully.
2. Lay live cuttings between the vertical stakes on the bottom of the gully similar

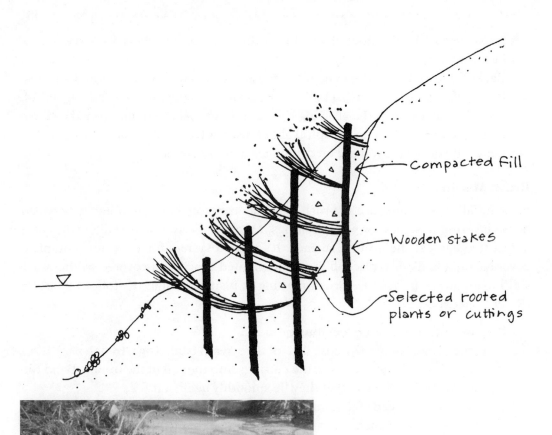

Compacted fill

Wooden stakes

Selected rooted
plants or cuttings

FIGURE 9.26. BRANCH PACKING
SMALL GULLIES AND SLUMPS.
Installation of branch packing at
Cobbs Creek, Georgia. *Photo credit:*
A. L. Riley. *Illustration credit:*
Robbin B. Sotir and Associates,
Georgia Soil and Water. Marietta,
Georgia.

FIGURE 9.27. GEOTEXTILE EROSION CONTROL FABRICS AS COMPONENTS OF SOIL BIOENGI-
NEERING SYSTEMS.
The fabric is laid parallel to the direction of flow. The lowest fabric type is made of coconut
fiber, which withstands high velocities and the changing dynamics in the bankfull channel
zone. The upper layer is straw fabric. (Brush layering is installed between the two fabrics.)

    to the way you would install a brush-layering project. The cuttings should stick
    out of the slope 6–12 inches.

3. Fill in dirt on top of the brush layers and compact it. Work up the gully this way
    until you have reconstructed the slope.

4. A variation on this design is to add dead vegetation across the hill slope between
    the poles to help break the fall of runoff down the slope and allow more slope
    stability so seed and other unplanted volunteer growth can take root. (Refer to
    figure 9.18.)

5. Water any live cuttings and poles if planting on a dry slope or in a dry western
    climate.

Restoration for Particularly Difficult Urban Situations

In urban settings the restorationist will be confronted with spaces that are too
narrow for a creek to pass through them with the proper floodplain, meander, and
channel widths. The first goal of any creek restoration design is to try all possibilities of restoring the channel width and depth, stream channel length, and meander
shape that may best help the creek attain a low-maintenance equilibrium. When
all possibilities of attaining the desired bankfull channel dimensions, meanders,
and floodplain have been exhausted, the designer then considers how best to

compromise the creek's natural dynamics. Of course, the best design compromises the natural creek dynamics to a minimum.

The compromise the restorationist often faces is having to use "armor," as opposed to restoring stream banks to a natural state. Hardening stream banks with rock, gabions, and cribwalls can be done in aesthetic and sensitive ways, however. When enhancing or restoring some of the values to an urban creek, it is easy to get into a clash of conflicting values over what is possible and desirable for the creek. Sometimes professionals or members of the public who do not have exposure to the aesthetic and environmental potentials of a highly urbanized creek will view any enhancements or restoration as futile. The urban creek restorationist, however, appreciates the values of a creek even with its compromised functions or features. Some of the most celebrated and appreciated urban creeks and rivers are lined with WPA rock (for example, the San Antonio River), have compromised riparian vegetation, and are straighter than they should be. The downside is that these streams and rivers are not sustainable and self-renewing environments but require human intervention over time to rebuild walls, replace footings of structures, etc. The upside is that the stream or river is in place as a community presence and amenity.

The ultimate need in these compromised situations is to know what combinations of structural and revegetation solutions are options for maximizing environmental values. The objective should always be to revegetate the waterway. Conventional structural practices such as containing creeks in culverts, concrete walls, or gabion baskets should be relegated to the obsolete. There *are* environmental and practical alternatives to conventional engineering practices. We need to progress from the assumption that a compromised urbanized waterway is a lost cause to the understanding that with creative efforts it can be celebrated as an enhanced environment. Finally, we all need to guard against the "overdesigned" project. A project using too conservative an assumption regarding the ability of vegetation, soil bioengineering, and other environmentally sensitive solutions to hold streambanks is not a well-designed project.

Materials that conventionally have been used to destroy the aesthetic and environmental values of urban waterways, such as gabions, rocks, and cribwalls, can be used in new ways as tools of restoration. Gabions made up of wire baskets filled with rock and log cribwalls are familiar to many structural engineers as common building materials for everything from highways to railroad embankments and rivers. Those structures are now being used in different ways as components of restoration and enhancement projects. Even though such structures are not known for their environmental values, designed and used correctly, they can become instruments of restoration. Used incorrectly, they can remain destabilizing and harmful to the environment.

Jacks

Added to the tool chest of potential structures besides rock, gabions, and cribwalls are A-jacks and lunkers. Large steel jacks that look something like the jacks a child plays with have been used historically as bank-rebuilding structures for moderately sized rivers. They appear in Army Corps of Engineers literature on bank restoration options. In recent years, they have been manufactured in different sizes, opening up the possibility of using them for smaller stream restoration projects as well as for larger lakeshore and riverbank projects. These jacks can be easily maneuvered and set in place by conservation crews to stabilize the toes of waterway banks. The jacks' ability to grab soil and to interlock adds to their capacity to provide shoreline or bank toe stability, which exceeds the capacity of quarry stone of similar weight. These jacks are relatively easy to handle, are versatile and can be arranged to fit various site conditions, and are environmentally unobtrusive.[31, 32] For these reasons, we consider jacks to be a restoration tool that may see wider use in the future (figure 9.28).

Lunkers

Lunkers are also enjoying wider application in conjunction with their promotion by the Illinois Water Survey.[33, 34] They are boxy structures made of boards and rebar and are often helpful in bank stabilization projects that emphasize improvement of fish habitat. The lunker is placed into an excavated bank, covered with soil, and planted with vegetation. Underneath the bank, the open box creates a cool, deep pool that can provide protection for fish (figure 9.29).

Gabions

Gabions and rock are probably the most commonly overused and misused materials in waterway projects. Gabions are wire cages filled with rock and placed on the water side of stream banks to protect the area from erosion. They are popular because they provide an inexpensive building material that is easy to purchase, transport, and handle. They are often incorrectly installed, however, and, as a result, are frequently blown out of stream banks and scattered downstream. They also have a tendency to be unsightly. However, if they are used sparingly as structures to support revegetation in difficult situations, they can be considered a restoration alternative. The correct use of gabions as a restoration tool involves the proper excavation of the stream bank, the filling of the cages with both rock and soil, and the covering of the gabions with soil and plants.

Gabions are overused because they are inexpensive, are easy to transport and install, and provide a structural fix to a problem. Almost all gabion projects could be replaced with the soil bioengineering methods described above. The only times we have used gabions have been to substitute them for concrete retaining walls in situations where structures inappropriately sited too close to a waterway needed protection. The advantage of a gabion over a concrete wall is that it is a flexible and porous structure and can be planted.

One of the disadvantages of using gabions in urban situations if they are not covered completely with soil and planted is that youngsters like to pick the rocks out of the cages and throw them around as good sport. Also, the wire of the cages is

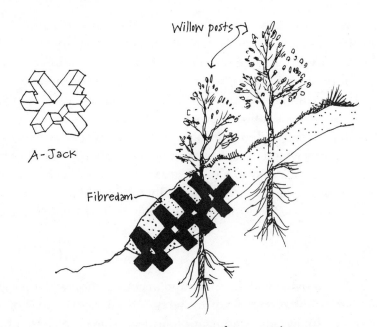

Willow posts

A-Jack

Fibredam

A-jacks are interlocking concrete jacks (40 pounds) that are more stable than riprap during high intensity storms. Dense root systems of Willow, Dogwood and other species will intertwine throughout the A-jack rows, creating greater stability.

Illinois State Water Survey Division,
Illinois Department of Energy and Natural Resources

A-JACK DESIGN AND INSTALLATION

FIGURE 9.28. A-JACKS, INTERLOCKING STABILIZERS FOR TOES OF SLOPES. Two sections form an A-jack.

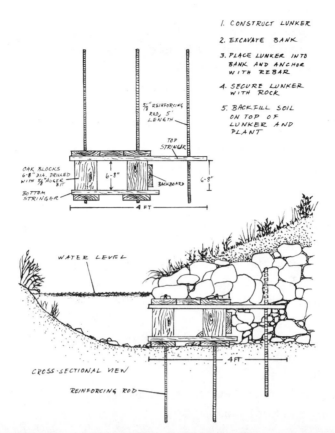

INSTALLATION OF LUNKERS

1. CONSTRUCT LUNKER

2. EXCAVATE BANK

3. PLACE LUNKER INTO BANK AND ANCHOR WITH REBAR

4. SECURE LUNKER WITH ROCK

5. BACKFILL SOIL ON TOP OF LUNKER AND PLANT

5/8" REINFORCING ROD, 5' LENGTH

TOP STRINGER

OAK BLOCKS 6-8" DIA, DRILLED WITH 5/8" AUGER BIT

BACKBOARD

BOTTOM STRINGER

6-8"

6-8"

4 FT

WATER LEVEL

CROSS-SECTIONAL VIEW

REINFORCING ROD

4 FT

FIGURE 9.29. LUNKERS REBUILD BANKS FOR FISH HABITAT.
Lunker assembly. *Photo credit:* Illinois Water Survey.

vulnerable to decay, particularly in the salt air of coastal cities. And the wire can be cut and vandalized.

These practical problems with gabions in urban settings joined with our objective to restore ecological systems with our projects should relegate the gabion to a rarely used status to revegetate a site. When we do use one, we turn it into a planting medium filled with soil and use it as a structural component to rebuild a slope. After that it should be buried and planted on. A good gabion is an invisible gabion. Follow these steps in using gabions, which are illustrated in figure 9.30.

1. Determine the correct width and depth dimensions for the bankfull channel. Once those are determined, excavate the stream bank being restored so that the gabions fit into the bank without protruding into the bankfull channel.
2. To fill the gabion, start with a layer of rock in the bottom of the cage. Fill the spaces between the rock with soil. Continue these rock-and-soil layers until the gabion basket is filled.
3. When adding soil to the gabion, you should lay cuttings in the soil so that the growing tips stick out the holes of the basket. Also, you can line the inside of the basket with filter fabric if the potential piping of soil on the outside face is an issue.
4. After constructing the gabion in this manner, backfill soil over the top of it so that you can no longer see the basket. You may want to use some brush layering in the backfill.
5. Plant the top of the new slope with cuttings and/or container or tube stock.
6. Water the project after installation.

If the gabion is installed so that it protrudes into your bankfull channel, you may create erosion problems at best or blow the gabion out at worst.

Rock Work

Rocks can be dumped on a stream bank like trash, or they can be carefully hand-crafted into aesthetic WPA-style walls that can support vegetation. While such walls are very structural, they too have a role in restoration. We refer to this as rock work, as opposed to riprap. In highly urbanized situations where houses, businesses, and other structures have been crowded next to stream corridors, the meander and movement of the stream are frequently constricted to the point that any natural erosion can quickly threaten a structure. In such constricted situations, a hand-laid rock wall can be built to provide a stable bank.

These rock work projects are in some ways a symbol of the 1930s. They were overused then, as they were installed in many situations that did not involve a conflict between eroding banks and structures. In many instances, they were probably make-work projects. The modern-day urban stream restoration movement, however, is making use of this alternative for difficult sites with vertical banks and minimum setbacks for structures. Concrete rubble can be used in place of rock and still look just like a rock wall. The spaces between the rocks or rubble pieces can be

GABIONS

How to use correctly for Restoration Projects

1. Transport in collapsed form

2. Construct into boxes, wiring diaphragms into the centers to add to their structural strength.

Top
Diaphrag
Edge

3. Correctly position the Gabions into the EXCAVATED stream bank.

Existing
Wrong way

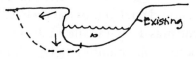
Existing
Right way
Correct excavation →

A. Excavate bank back and below stream bed

Existing

B. Place gabions in slope using steps (the wire boxes)

4. After placing the gabion wire boxes, fill them with soil and rock. To fill the gabion, put a layer of rock on the bottom, then fill the spaces with soil. Put another layer of rock on the soil and then fill soil in around this layer of rock. Continue this rock-soil sandwich until the basket is full. Wire the top down.
SOIL
ROCK
SOIL
ROCK

5. Place dirt on top of gabions

6. Plant on top of gabions with grasses, shrubs and trees

FIGURE 9.30. GABIONS AS RESTORATION STRUCTURES.

planted with cuttings as the wall is constructed. A beautiful, green-growing rock wall can be an aesthetic streamside amenity in an urban setting. It beats sheet metal or concrete any day.

Rock work is distinguished from riprapping in that it entails the careful and artful placement of work by hand along a stream channel. Refer to figure 9.31 for construction steps for a WPA-style rock wall.

1. Determine the bankfull width and depth dimensions of the channel. Excavate the stream banks back 2 feet greater than the bankfull width. Excavate the channel bed at the toe of the bankfull channel below grade about 2-½ to 3 feet. (Larger streams or rivers may require deeper installations.)

2. Starting at the trench at the toe of the slope, lay rock or concrete rubble to start your wall below the grade of the bed of the stream. This will toe-in the project and help stabilize the wall even if the creek is degrading from the impacts of urbanization.

3. When the wall height reaches above the base flows of a perennially flowing stream, add cuttings to the project. Push the butt ends of the cuttings into the stream bank as far as you can. The cuttings need at least 2 feet of soil to root in. Carefully place the rock or rubble on and next to the cuttings so you don't damage them. The cuttings should stick out of the rock wall by 6 inches.

4. To facilitate anchoring the cuttings deep into the bank as you construct the wall, hammer rebar into the bank to create planting holes. Tamp the cuttings gently into the holes.

5. Water the structure when the project is completed.

Log Cribwalls

Cribwalls are another holdover from the 1930s WPA projects (figure 9.32). They have also been widely used on freeways, in mines, and as multipurpose retaining structures. Urban stream restoration groups often use donated logs from utilities or public works tree-removal projects. The stream banks are excavated and rebuilt with a log-cabin–like structure. The structure is filled with dirt, rock, and cuttings so it can support vegetation. Like gabions and rock, this restoration alternative should be reserved for the particularly difficult projects in urban settings that require a substantial structural solution. Consider a wood cribwall as a replacement for a concrete retaining wall.

In one of our inner-city project sites, the cribwall does double duty stabilizing banks and providing safer access to the creek for children than the existing steep banks. Because they are made of logs, they also are an aesthetic addition to an urbanized area or park. As a soil bioengineering alternative, they provide a structure for the reestablishment of plant growth. The most common question asked about cribwalls is How long do they last? This is dependent on the type of wood of the logs and the severity of the climate. Wood cribbing in rainy Northern California has been observed to hold up for over a hundred years. Wood cribwalls that are well vegetated should be considered "temporary" structures in which vegetation provides

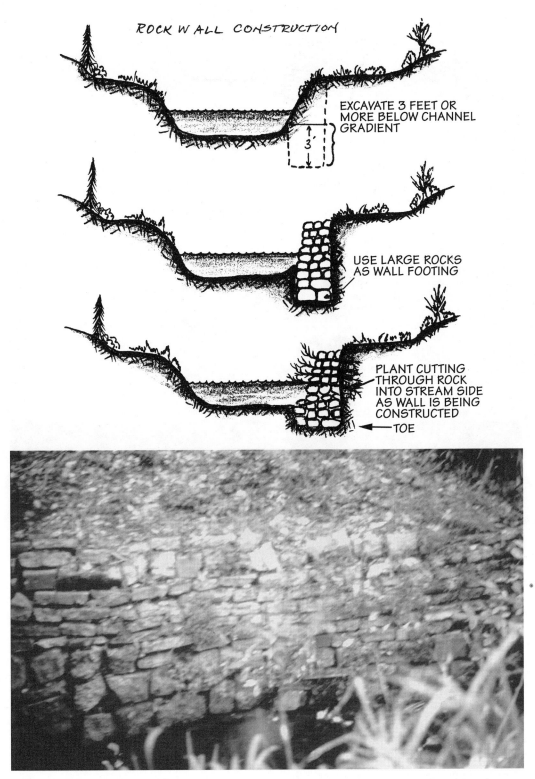

ROCK WALL CONSTRUCTION

EXCAVATE 3 FEET OR MORE BELOW CHANNEL GRADIENT

3'

USE LARGE ROCKS AS WALL FOOTING

PLANT CUTTING THROUGH ROCK INTO STREAM SIDE AS WALL IS BEING CONSTRUCTED

TOE

FIGURE 9.31 ROCK WALL CONSTRUCTION.
Construction of planted rubble wall, Glen Echo Creek, Oakland, California.

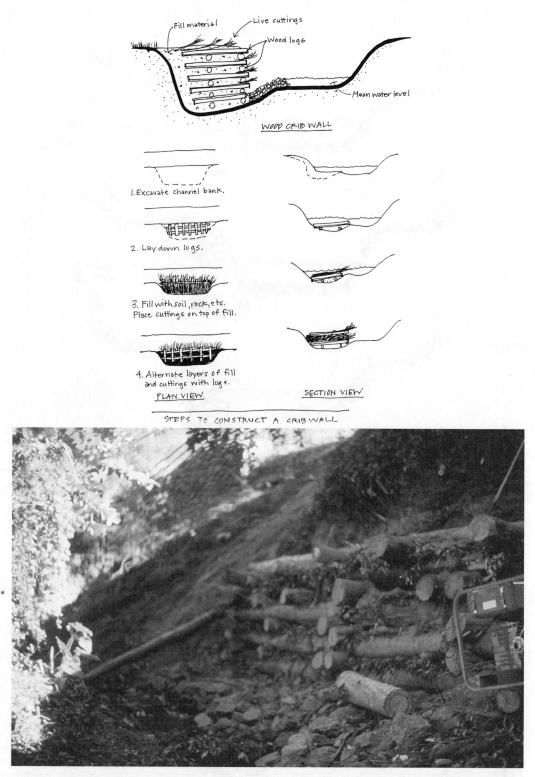

Fill material — Live cuttings

Wood logs

Mean water level

WOOD CRIB WALL

1. Excavate channel bank.

2. Lay down logs.

3. Fill with soil, rock, etc. Place cuttings on top of fill.

4. Alternate layers of fill and cuttings with logs.

PLAN VIEW

SECTION VIEW

STEPS TO CONSTRUCT A CRIBWALL

FIGURE 9.32. CRIBWALL CONSTRUCTION.
Construction of cribwall, Courtland Creek, Oakland, California.

the permanent or long-term solution to the bank restoration. Follow the steps listed below (and illustrated in figure 9.32) to construct a wood cribwall:

1. Determine the bankfull width and depth of the channel. Excavate as much as 10 feet back into the slope from the bankfull channel. Grade the excavation at a slight angle back into the slope so that the logs in the cribwall facing the waterway will point upward. Also, excavate below the grade of the streambed by 2½–3 feet or more to toe-in the project.
2. Lay logs in the excavated area in a log-cabin fashion.
3. Fill the log structure with rock and soil. Place cuttings on the soil and cover with a layer of soil before starting the next series of logs.
4. Water the structure when the project is completed.

The Steps to Designing a Restoration Project for a Degraded Urban Waterway

The following section synthesizes the information this book has presented on restoration, so that if you have successfully absorbed the information this book has presented so far, you will be able to understand these project design steps. These are the steps we use at the Waterways Restoration Institute for daylighting a creek from a culvert and completely re-creating a stream. We also follow these steps to reshape stream channels and meanders that have been substantially impacted by straightening, widening, or armoring with concrete. This design process assumes the worst case: that all the basic components of a stream system—the bankfull channel, floodplain, riparian vegetation, and terrace—require re-creation. The design steps are as follows:

- Determine if your watershed is:
  (a) fully urbanized; (b) undergoing a new phase of urbanization, continuing from past development; or (c) in the beginning stages of urbanization. Use this information in the next steps to determine if it is necessary to design a larger floodplain into your project to absorb the consequences of future channel widening and deepening. For channels expected to undergo more future adjustments, soil bioengineering systems will need to be installed deeper than what I've been recommending below the stream bottom grade and the width of the riparian corridor restoration increased, so that even with some future stream adjustments, a protective buffer of vegetation will remain. Refer to chapter 4 if you need to review the impacts of urbanization on stream channels.

- Develop regional averages for the bankfull widths, depths, and discharges of streams for different-sized drainage areas using stream cross-sections that represent an "urban equilibrium." If they are available for your region, use existing graphs such as the one in figure 4.13 to begin. Select gauge data that represents urban streams in the subregions or physiographic setting in which you are working that have a similar average annual rainfall. Remember, many of these gauge stations don't represent natural conditions but may give you a good idea of the average conditions for urban streams in your region.

• Survey cross-sections of stream channels, floodplains, and terraces that appear to be in urban equilibrium and use them as "reference" sections to guide restoration of the project site. These reference sites should have similar slopes, soils, bank materials, and channel bed materials as well as drain the same drainage area.

• Interview the neighborhood residents on their recollections of stream widths, depths, and meanders, flood stages, and instream life.

• Acquire whatever historical photographs are available for the channel. Sometimes neighborhood residents have good photographs. Otherwise, aerial photography available from the U.S. Geological Survey or other agencies can at minimum help you determine historical meanders and channel alignment and may provide information on channel widths.

• Select a restoration bankfull width and depth based on combining your observations from the above steps.

• Use a variety of methods to cross-check the values you choose for bankfull width, depth, and discharge. Use a rating curve of discharges versus stages to estimate a bankfull discharge for your field-selected bankfull channel depth. If the period of record of streamflow measurements is limited, acquire U.S. Geological Survey data on mean annual flows and use regional ratios of the relationships between mean annual flows and bankfull flows to estimate the latter. Effective discharges (equivalent to dominant or bankfull discharges) can be estimated using flow duration curves and sediment rating curves. It may be desirable to estimate the stream power or average stream bed shear stress for selected flows to assess the ability of the channel to transport sediment and to avoid excessive erosion. These analyses are beyond the scope of this book and should be done by a trained hydrologist, fluvial geomorphologist, or geologist.

• Using your selected value for bankfull width, use the following equations to estimate the channel meander length and amplitude or breadth of the meander:
  - Average meander length = 11 × width of bankfull channel (between 10 and 14 channel widths)
  - Average meander amplitude = 2.7 × width of bankfull channel
  - The radius of curvature is approximately ⅕ of the meander length and averages 2.3 × the bankfull channel width.

• Using these average values for channel shapes, draw a calculated restoration design meander to scale for use in the restoration project and site design drawings.

- Make observations of stream cross-sections at similar drainage areas with similar slopes, soils, and geology to determine whether and to what extent floodplains are part of the regional landscape features. Floodplains are highly variable and can't be associated with bankfull channel dimensions. The width of the floodplains for a restoration project can be varied with the generalization that the more floodplain you can design into the project, the better.

- Add any floodplain restoration features to your restoration cross-section. Even in regions where floodplains are naturally very subtle or small features of the natural landscape, it can be beneficial to include some floodplain into your restoration cross-section. This provides adjustment room for a bankfull channel that may continue to widen because of ongoing or future land-use changes.

- Transfer the drawing of the calculated bankfull channel restoration meander including the floodplain required to accommodate the channel width and its meander amplitude onto transparent paper and place it over your site map. The features of urban development—utilities, streets, etc.—may overlap on your meandering channel and floodplain. First consider the options for relocating these structures as a part of the process of drafting redevelopment plans and site designs for the project area. Desirable slopes for channel banks and terrace banks range from 1:1 to 1:3 depending on project right-of-way options and need for public access. Natural channel banks range from 1:1 to 1:2 slopes. For purposes of facilitating public access to the stream and preventing bank erosion from children trampling the steeper banks, sections of the banks can be graded 1:3 or greater. This grading back of banks is most compatible on the point bar side or inside bends of meanders, where it can serve to extend the floodplain. If it is necessary to restrict the restoration corridor project right-of-way, it is better to save space by making the banks steeper and not narrowing the room needed for the meander amplitude.

- Vary the meander shape to fit the site conditions and add to or subtract from the floodplain area depending on the site constraints and opportunities. Run a string along the length of the calculated channel drawn above to measure the number of feet of meandering channel. The string should follow where the thalweg, or deepest part of the channel, flows (see figure 1.4). (For example, using a map scale of 1 inch = 20 feet, if the string measurement is 10 inches, the channel meander is 200 feet.) Divide the channel meander by the straight distance the meander travels. This gives you the meander sinuosity. If in this case the straight distance is 100 feet, the meander sinuosity is 200 ÷ 100, or 2. Run the 10 inches of string along your site map and fit the channel meander in and around site obstructions, always fitting the length of the string into 100 horizontal feet on the plan—or within the meander distance. (This is your design meander, as shown in figure 9.33.) If you can't meander the string into the site plan within the correct meander length, that means your stream channel is too short and therefore may not be in the desired equilibrium. In figure 9.33 the

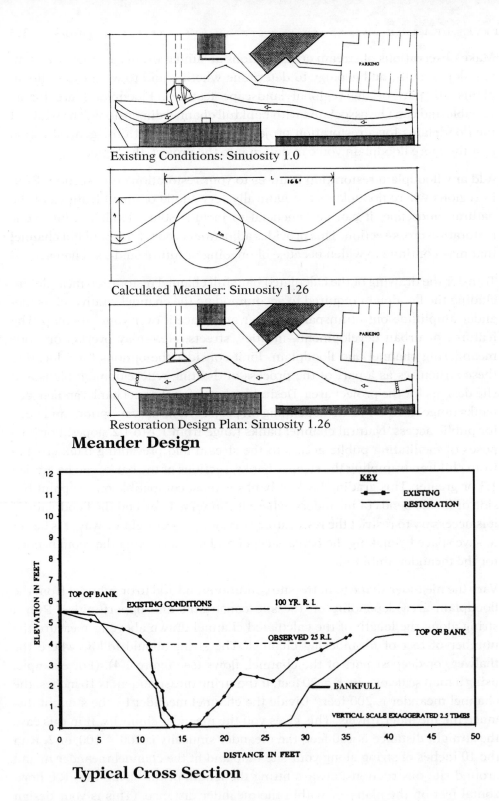

Existing Conditions: Sinuosity 1.0

Calculated Meander: Sinuosity 1.26

Restoration Design Plan: Sinuosity 1.26

Meander Design

Typical Cross Section

FIGURE 9.33. A RESTORATION DESIGN PLAN.
Codornices Creek at Fifth Street, Berkeley, California. *Source:* Waterways Restoration Institute.

calculated meander length for a 16-foot-wide bankfull channel was 166 feet. The channel meanders 210 feet within this distance (a sinuosity of 1.26). Within a 166-foot distance, the pre-project (existing conditions) channel meanders for 175 feet (a sinuosity of 1.0). For the same 166-foot reach on the restoration channel, the channel meanders 210 feet to equal the calculated meander distance. The shape of the meander was selected to follow the meander that was evolving on its own in the constrained site with a radius of curvature of 20 feet as opposed to the calculated 35 feet. The widened and lengthened restoration channel has contributed to the more stable stream banks.

- Survey the valley slope and channel slope with a level. Cross-check your value for channel sinuosity calculated above by correctly matching sinuosity, channel slope, and valley slope. Sinuosity = valley slope ÷ channel slope. Channel slope = valley slope ÷ sinuosity.

- In the event that it is absolutely impossible to avoid the stream channel being too short, and/or the change of grade is substantial between the up and downstream boundaries of the project, the energy of the stream channel will probably need to be dissipated with some step-pool or vortex rocks. The steps should be designed with rock and break up the channel slope into small increments of elevation change. Do not design deep plunge pools that can undercut the step structures and start headward erosion up the channel slope. The "steps" should be located at the channel crossover points, and the pools should help form the outside bends of the meander.

- If the excavation of a new or restored floodplain is a part of the restoration project, the floodplain elevation should be designed to be equal to (or possibly higher than in difficult urban situations) the top of the bankfull channel. For some urban stream and river restoration projects, the main objective may be to restore the floodplain portion of the river system in order to restore riverine wetlands, meander belts, and wildlife habitat and provide for floodwater storage. In some cases, this may entail removing levees, berms, or flood walls to allow flooding. In other cases, it may be necessary to excavate portions of the floodplain that have been filled.

- Floodplain restoration designs needs to take into account the historical relationship between the floodplain and the bankfull channel. If a restoration objective is to reestablish the structure and functions of a floodplain, it is advisable to acquire historical data from interviews, records, reports, maps, photos, etc., on flood discharges and landscape features to understand the historic relationships between the active channel and floodplain. Because of the impact of land-use changes, the channel may be deeply incised and/or the floodplain elevation may be much higher than the channel because of accelerated deposition. Any floodplain restoration can ideally reconnect a floodplain to its current

FIGURE 9.34. STREAM RESTORATION IN A RESIDENTIAL SETTING: JOHNSON CREEK, PORT-
LAND, OREGON, AT THE PHILPOTT RESIDENCE.
(a) Before restoration: A failed concrete retaining wall and stream bank. *Photo credit:* Dennis
O'Connor. (b) Removal of concrete wall and regrading of bank for brush layering installation.
Photo credit: Dennis O'Connor. (c) Toe of bank secured with coir geotextile wraps around
soil, brush layering, poles, and cuttings. Container plants are planted on the upper slope. (d)
One year after installation. (e) Top-of-bank landscaping integrated into residential setting.
Credits: The project was sponsored by the Urban Streams Council of the Wetlands Conser-
vancy, Portland, and the city of Portland, Oregon. Project design and installation by Dennis
O'Connor, Todd Moses, and Esther Lev.

active channel, which may mean designing the floodplain lower than its historic elevation. The entrenchment of active channels can occur because of natural influences as well as land use changes. Natural channels may not have discernible floodplains, so it is not a requirement of a restoration project to excavate a floodplain into the landscape.

- Estimate the discharges for the larger flood flows above the one-in-1.5-year flood. This can be done using flood-frequency data, watershed rational-method models, or more sophisticated models. For the frequent situation that little data exists on observed stream flows for bankfull discharges or greater, calibrate or cross-check your results by taking measurements of stream velocities and stages for a few storms as described in chapter 8.

- Estimate the flood stages for the one-in-10-year, one-in-25-year, one-in-50-year or greater discharges on the design cross-section. Use field observations whenever possible.

- Note the velocities associated with the discharge estimates for the different-size storms. If they range above 6 feet per second, you may want to create or enlarge floodplain areas to help absorb the impact of the flows. Intensive soil bioengineering may be required on terrace slopes for erosion control.

- If there is a reservoir regulating flow releases to your stream, one of your project design considerations may be to bring in experts to develop a plan for reoperating the reservoir. It may be advantageous to reduce reservoir releases during large floods for greater flood-damage-reduction benefits and to increase releases during the more frequent, smaller floods to return some of the floodplain functions and diversity.

- Use a variety of tools to assist your restoration design, including watershed and landscape processes models, hydraulic models, and stream classification by channel types. Rosgen's stream classification (figure 4.16) can provide a framework for determining if your design values for ratio of bankfull width to depth, entrenchment ratio, and sinuosity are reasonable for the type of stream you are restoring.

Figure 9.34 provides a sequence of photographs to show what a restoration project looks like before, during, and after installation. It illustrates a failed stream bank in a residential setting involving the removal of a failed concrete wall, the restoration of the bank with brush layering, fascines, and coir fabric. A conventional landscaping for a residential yard was installed on top of the bank.

FIGURE 9.35 (*facing page*) STREAM RESTORATION IN AN URBAN PARK SETTING: BLACK-BERRY CREEK, BERKELEY, CALIFORNIA, AT THOUSAND OAKS ELEMENTARY SCHOOL.
(a) Before restoration: A hard surface playground. (b) Excavation of culvert. *Photo credit:* Gary Mason. (c) Restoration channel after the first storms, three months after restoration. Note formation of point bars, the vortex rocks in the foreground, and sprouting fascines and cuttings along the channel. The bank slopes are secured with cuttings and geotextile fabric. (d) Photo of same location as in part (c) taken one year later. (e) Blackberry Creek Park at the school, two years after installation. Also refer to book cover for restoration of Baxter Creek at Poincett Park, El Cerrito, California.
Credits: The project was sponsored by Urban Creeks Council of California, Parent Teachers Association of Berkeley, Berkeley Unified School District, the city of Berkeley, and the California Department of Water Resources. Project design and installation by Urban Creeks Council of California, Wolfe-Mason Associates, and Waterways Restoration Institute.

Design Considerations for Daylighting Projects

Daylighting projects use the same design steps just described. One difference is that more emphasis is often placed on the importance of historical data to determine where the channel should be located and what type of channel used to exist in the location. The costs for soil excavation, transport, and dumping at a new location will be the determining factor as to whether the project will be affordable. The best possible scenario is to find another use for the soil as near as possible. One of our most cost-effective daylighting projects used the excavated soil to help develop a nearby community garden. Demolition and removal of the old culvert must be provided for as well. Finally, a civil engineer must determine whether breaking open a culvert in the middle of an underground stormwater system will impact the ability of the flows to continue to move through the downstream culvert under the proper pressure. Head loss equations based on the length, size, roughness, and slope of the downstream culvert must be calculated. Head loss can be compensated for in the restoration project by designing the downstream reentry of the creek into the culvert so that the water backs up to a prescribed depth to re-create the water pressure. Finally, headwalls for supporting the cut culverts must be designed and budgeted in construction costs.

Figure 9.35 illustrates a stream daylighting project in an elementary schoolyard that serves as both an urban neighborhood park and a school playground. The new stream was graded and the channel shaped and secured with willow and dogwood posts, brush layering, fascines, coir and straw fabrics, and vortex rocks.

NOTES

1. William R. Jordan, III, ed., *Restoration and Management Notes* 13, no. 1 (Summer 1995).
2. Joan Bradley, *Bringing Back the Bush: The Bradley Method of Bush Regeneration* (Chicago, Illinois: Lansdowne Press, 1988).

3. J. Toby Tourbier and Richard Westmacott, *Water Resources Protection Technology: A Handbook of Measures to Protect Water Resources in Land Development* (Washington, D.C.: Urban Land Institute, 1981).

4. Burchard H. Heede, "Analysis and Guidelines for Watershed Rehabilitation" in Robert N. Coats, ed., *Proceedings, Symposium on Watershed Rehabilitation in Redwood National Park and Other Coastal Areas* (Humbolt County, California: Center for Natural Resources Studies, JMI Inc., and National Park Service, August 1981).

5. Burchard H. Heede, "Designing for Dynamic Equilibrium in Streams," *Water Resources Bulletin* (American Water Resources Association) 22, no. 3, (June 1986).

6. Liza Prunuske, *Ground Work: A Handbook for Erosion Control* (Marin County, California: Marin County Resource Conservation District, 1987).

7. Quincy Ayres, *Recommendations for the Control and Reclamation of Gullies,* Bulletin 121, Iowa Engineering Experiment Station, Iowa State College, Ames, Iowa, vol. 33, no. 41, March 13, 1935.

8. U.S. Army Corps of Engineers, *Channel Stability Assessment for Flood Control Projects,* Engineering Manual 1110–2–1418 (Washington, D.C., October 1994).

9. Philip B. Williams, "Rethinking Flood-Control Channel Design," *Civil Engineering* (American Society of Civil Engineers) 60, no. 1 (January 1990).

10. Nelson R. Nunnally and Edward Keller, *Use of Fluvial Processes to Minimize Adverse Effects of Stream Channelization* (Raleigh: Water Resources Research Institute, University of North Carolina, July 1979).

11. Bob Fuerstenberg, hydrologist, Surface Water Management Division, King County, Washington, personal communication, 1990.

12. Fuerstenberg, personal communication.

13. David L. Rosgen, "A Classification of Natural Rivers," *Catena* (Amsterdam, Netherlands) 22 (1994) p. 169–199.

14. Rosgen, "A Classification of Natural Rivers."

15. Robert W. McCarley, John J. Ingram, Bobby J. Brown, and Andrew J. Reese, *Flood Control Channel National Inventory,* Miscellaneous paper HL–90–10, Flood-Control Channel Research Program, U.S. Army Corps of Engineers Waterways Experiment Station (Vicksburg, Mississippi, October 1990).

16. Dave Rosgen and Brenda L. Fittante, "Fish Habitat Structures, A Selection Guide Using Stream Classification," *The Restoration of Midwestern Stream Habitat,* symposium proceedings of 52nd Midwest Fish and Wildlife Conference, Minneapolis, Minnesota, American Fisheries Society, December 4–5, 1990.

17. Gary Flosi and Forrest L. Reynolds, *California Salmonid Stream Habitat Restoration Manual* (Sacramento: California Department of Fish and Game, Resources Agency, August 1991).

18. Thomas Maddock, Jr., "A Primer on Floodplain Dynamics," *Journal of Soil and Water Conservation* (March–April 1976), p. 44–59.

19. C. Neil Herbkersman, *A Guide to the George Palmiter River Restoration Techniques* for Institute of Water Resources, U.S. Army Corps of Engineers, Fort Belvoir, Virginia, by the Institute of Environmental Sciences, Miami University, Oxford, Ohio (undated, circa 1985).

20. Missouri Department of Conservation, "Stream Restoration Specifications, Tree Revetments" (Jefferson City, Missouri, January 1991).

21. Missouri Department of Conservation, "Tree Revetments for Streambank Stabilization" (Jefferson City, Missouri, 1991).

22. Donald Roseboom, W. White, and R. Sauers, *Streambank and Habitat Strategies along Illinois River Tributaries*, Governor's Conference on the Management of the Illinois River, State of Illinois, (1991), p. 112–122.

23. Don Roseboom, "Willow Posts Add Depth to Stream Bank Stabilization," *International Erosion Control Association News* (January–February 1995).

24. Illinois State Water Survey, "The Willow-Post Method for Stream Bank Stabilization," miscellaneous publication 130 (Peoria, Illinois, May 1992).

25. Charles Kraebel and Arthur Pillsbury, *Handbook of Erosion Control in Mountain Meadows*, U.S. Department of Agriculture, Forest Service, California Forest and Range Experiment Station (Berkeley, California, 1934).

26. Hugo Schiechtl, *Bioengineering for Land Reclamation and Conservation* (Lincoln: University of Nebraska Press, 1980).

27. Donald H. Gray and Andrew T. Leiser, *Biotechnical Slope Protection and Erosion Control* (New York: Van Nostrand Reinhold, 1982); and Donald H. Gray and Robbin B. Sotir, *Biotechnical and Soil Bioengineering Slope Stabilization, Practical Guide for Erosion Control* (New York: John Wiley and Sons, 1996).

28. Soil Conservation Service (now NRCS), U.S. Department of Agriculture, *Soil Bioengineering for Upland Slope Protection and Erosion Protection*, Part 650, Engineering Field Handbook, Chapter 18 (Washington, D.C., October 1992); and Hollis H. Allen and James R. Leech, Waterways Experiment Station, U.S. Army Corps of Engineers, *Bioengineering for Streambank Erosion Control, Report 1, Guidelines*, Technical Report EC-97-8 (Vicksburg, Mississippi, April 1997).

29. Robbin B. Sotir and Associates, *1991 North American Coir Geotextile Seminars*, published in Cooperation with the United Nations Trade Center and Coir Board of India, September 1991.

30. Department of Civil and Environmental Engineering and Continuing Engineering Education, University of Michigan, *Proceedings, Workshop on Biotechnical Stabilization*, sponsored by Geotechnical of Geo-Environmental Systems, National Science Foundation, August 21–23, 1991, Ann Arbor, Michigan.

31. Don Roseboom, "Waukegan River Restoration in Urban Parks," *Land and Water* 38 (September–October 1994), p. 33–36.

32. William G. McDougal and Frank S. Atkinson, *A-Jacks Armor Units* (Corvallis, Oregon: Oregon State University and Erosion Control Technologies Corporation, 1994).

33. Don Roseboom, *Case Studies on Biotechnical Stream Bank Protection* (Peoria, Illinois: Illinois State Water Survey, 1994).

34. Don Roseboom, *Case Studies*.

Glossary of Terms

Abrasion Removal of stream-bank soil as a result of sediment-laden water, ice, or debris rubbing against the bank.

Aggrade The raising of a stream-channel bed with time due to the deposition of sediment that was eroded and transported from the upstream watershed or the channel.

Armoring Formation of a layer of rocks on the surface of a streambed that resists erosion by water flows. The rocks can be naturally occurring, caused by the scour of smaller particles from high discharges, or placed by humans to stop channel erosion.

Bankfull channel The stream channel that is formed by the dominant discharge, also referred to as the active channel, which meanders across the floodplain as it forms pools, riffles, and point bars.

Bankfull discharge Refer to "Dominant discharge."

Bar A sand or gravel deposit found on the bed of a stream that is often exposed during low-water periods.

Base flow The flow that a perennially flowing stream reduces to during the dry season. It is supported by ground-water seepage into the channel.

Base level The elevation to which a stream-channel profile has developed.

Bed The bottom of a channel.

Bed load Sediment particles up to rock, which slide and roll along the bottom of the streambed.

Bedscarp or nick point An abrupt change of grade in the bottom of a stream channel that moves progressively upstream; the change in grade forms a waterfall. Also, the location where a streambed is actively eroding downward to a new base level.

Bed slope The inclination of the channel bottom.

Butt end The bottom end of a cutting taken from a riparian plant that will root if planted in soil (it is opposite the budding tip's end of the cutting).

Caving The collapse of a stream bank by undercutting due to wearing away of the toe or an erodible soil layer above the toe.

Channel-forming discharge See "Dominant discharge."

Check dam A structure placed bank to bank downhill from a headcut on a hillslope to help revegetate a gully.

Cut bank The outside bank of a bend, often eroding opposite a point bar.

Cut off A channel cut across the neck of a bend.

Daylight In the restoration field, a verb that denotes the excavation and restoration of a stream channel from an underground culvert, covering, or pipe.

Deadman A log, block of concrete, rebar, or other object buried in a stream bank that is used to tie in a revetment with cable or chain.

Degrade The lowering of a stream-channel bed with time due to the erosion and transport of bed materials or the blockage of sediment sources.

Dike (groin, spur, jetty, deflector, boom) A structure designed: (1) to reduce water velocity as stream flow passes through the dike so that sediment deposition occurs instead of erosion (permeable dike), or (2) to deflect erosive currents away from the stream bank (impermeable dike).

Discharge The volume of water passing through a channel during a given time, usually measured in cubic feet per second.

Discount rate An interest rate that takes into account the future value of dollars currently being expended. In the case of water project discount rates, the interest is figured on an annual basis for a reasonable life of the project. The discount rate recognizes the value of the potential opportunities lost into the future by tying funds up into a water project that could go to other uses. Both the interest rate selected and the length of time it is applied can greatly affect the calculated costs for a project.

Dominant discharge The channel-forming discharge responsible for the active channel that over a period of time carries the most sediment. The discharge, in terms of flood frequency, usually has a return period or recurrence interval of 1.5 to 2 years in natural channels. This represents a flow condition where the stream flow completely fills the stream channel up to the top of the bank before overflowing onto the floodplain. It is also referred to as the *effective discharge*.

Eddy current A circular water movement that develops when the main flow becomes separated from the bank. The eddy current may then be set up between the main flow and the bank.

Energy dissipater An apron of rocks, logs, concrete baffles, or other materials that slows down water flowing through a culvert or ditch, or over a dam, and thereby reduces its erosive force.

Evapotranspiration The process by which plants take in water through their roots and then give it off through the leaves as a by-product of respiration.

Failure Collapse or slippage of a large mass of bank material into a stream.

Fill material Soil that is placed at a specified location to bring the ground surface up to a desired elevation or angle of slope.

Filter fabric A polypropylene textile used to keep soil separate from water. Comes in many different forms and is used for constructing roads, lining ponds, and in many erosion control projects.

FIRM map Flood insurance rate map used to establish the insurance rates for structures under the National Flood Insurance Program.

Floodplain The land adjacent to a channel at the elevation of the bankfull discharge, which is inundated on the average of about 2 out of 3 years. The floor of stream valleys, which can be inundated by small to very large floods. The one-in-100-year floodplain has a probability of .01 chance per year of being covered with water.

Flood stage An elevation for the water level at high flows.

Floodway A regulatory floodplain under the National Flood Insurance Program that includes the channel and that portion of the adjacent floodplain that is required to pass flood flows (normally the one-in-100-year flood) without increasing the water surface elevation more than a designated height (1 foot in most areas).

Ford An at-grade stream crossing that uses the bottom of the channel in lieu of a bridged or culverted crossing.

Grade-control structure A weir, dam, sill, drop structure, or other structure used to control erosion in stream channels with steep grades or where the slope has been destabilized.

Greenbelt Strip of natural vegetation growing parallel to a stream that provides wildlife habitat and an erosion and flood buffer zone. This strip of vegetation also retards rainfall runoff down the bank slope and provides a root system that binds soil particles together.

Ground-water flow Water that moves through the subsurface soil and rocks.

Ground-water table The depth below the surface of the ground where the soil is saturated (the open spaces between the individual soil particles are filled with water).

Headcut A break in slope at the top of a gully or section of gully that forms a "waterfall," which in turn causes the underlying soil to erode and the gully to expand uphill.

Headcutting The action of a bedscarp or headward erosion of a locally steep channel or gully.

Hungry water Clear water minus its expected suspended sediment, usually released from an impoundment that has excess energy, which erodes sediment from the downstream channel.

Impermeable material A material that has properties preventing movement of water through it. Nonporous.

Incised channel A stream that has degraded and cut its bed into the valley bottom. Indicates accelerated and often destructive erosion.

Infiltration That portion of rainfall or surface runoff that moves downward into the subsurface rock and soil.

Keyway, key The notch excavated into the side of a gully or stream to anchor a check dam or other structure.

Lifts Layers of loose soil. Used to specify how much loose soil should be laid down at a time before it must be compacted or wrapped in geotextile fabrics.

Longitudinal profile A graphic presentation of elevation vs. distance; in channel hydraulics it is a plot of water surface elevation against upstream to downstream distance.

Meander A sinuous channel form in flatter river grades formed by the erosion on one side of the channel (pools) and deposition on the other (point bars).

Mulch A substance placed over the soil surface to inhibit weed growth, conserve moisture, and in some cases, prevent heat loss. Examples include straw, wood chips, and leaves.

Nick point The point at which a stream is actively eroding the streambed to a new base level.

Noncohesive soil Soil particles that have no natural resistance to being pulled apart at their point of contact, for example, silt, sand, and gravel.

Overbank flow Water flow over the top of the bankfull channel onto the floodplain.

Perennial grass A grass that lives for more than one growing season. All visible leaves die back each year, but the roots send out new growth in the spring. Perennial grass roots are typically deeper than those of annual grasses.

Piping The process by which water forces an opening around or through a supposedly sealed structure, such as a check dam or levee. As water flows through, the opening usually grows larger and the water carries away sediment or levee material.

Point bar A bank on the inside of a meander bend that has built up due to sediment deposition opposite a pool.

Pool A location in an active stream channel, usually located on the outside bends of meanders, where the water is deepest and has reduced current velocities.

Rapid drawdown Lowering the elevation of water against a bank faster than the bank can drain, leaving a pressure imbalance that may cause the bank to fail.

Rational method or formula A simple technique for estimating peak discharge rates based on average rainfall intensity (i), the drainage area (A), and a coefficient based on watershed characteristics (C). The discharge in cubic feet per second is derived from the following formula: $Q = CiA$. The rational method is commonly applied to areas as large as 5 square miles but is preferably used for drainage areas under a half square mile. The 2-, 5-, 10-, 25-, and 50-year flood recurrence discharges can be estimated with this formula.

Reach A section of a stream's length.

Rebar Steel rod used primarily for reinforcing concrete. It has a variety of uses in restoration work, including planting of cuttings in hard ground.

Revetment A facing of stone, bags, blocks, pavement, etc., used to protect a bank against erosion.

Riffle A shallow rapids, usually located at the crossover in a meander of the active channel.

Rill erosion Removal of soil particles from a bank slope by surface runoff moving through relatively small channels. The water collecting from these small channels may then concentrate into a larger channel downhill to form the start of a gully.

Riparian Referring to the riverside or riverine environment next to the stream channel, e.g., riparian, or streamside, vegetation.

Riprap Heavy stones used to protect soil from the action of fast-moving water.

Rootwad A tree stump with roots that is strategically placed in a stream bank as part of rebuilding or restoring the bank. The stump may be dead wood or live and capable of sprouting and rooting.

Roughness A term used by hydraulic engineers and hydrologists designating a measurement or estimate of the resistance that streambed materials, vegetation, and other physical components contribute to the flow of water in the stream channel and floodplain. It is commonly measured as the Manning's roughness coefficient.

Scour The erosive action of flowing water in streams that removes and carries away material from the bed and banks.

Sediment Soil particles that have been transported from their natural location by wind or water action.

Sediment deposition The accumulation of soil particles on the channel bed and banks.

Sediment load The soil particles transported through a channel by stream flow.

Seepage Groundwater emerging on the face of a stream bank.

Setback Denotes the positioning of a levee or structure in relationship to a stream bank. A setback levee is placed a substantial distance from a stream to allow it to meander without consequences to the levee and to accommodate a floodplain that can store and convey flood flows. A setback regulation of a certain number of feet can be a requirement for the placement of urban buildings away from a stream-channel bank.

Shear Force parallel to a surface as opposed to directly on the surface. An example of shear would be the tractive force that removes particles from a stream bank as flow moves over the surface of the slope; a floating log that directly strikes the bank would not be a shear force.

Sheet erosion The removal by surface runoff of a fairly uniform layer of soil from a bank slope from *sheet flow* or runoff that flows over the ground surface as a thin, even layer not concentrated in a channel.

Sloughing (or sloughing off) Movement of a mass of soil down a bank into the channel (also called slumping). Sloughing is similar to a landslide.

Soil bioengineering Also referred to as biotechnical slope protection. Involves the use of live and dead woody cuttings and poles or posts collected from native plants to revegetate watershed slopes and stream banks. The cuttings, posts, and vegetative systems composed of bundles, layers, and mats of the cuttings and posts provide structure, drains, and vegetative cover to repair eroding and slumping slopes.

Spillway The place at the top of a dam or check dam over which water flows.

Stream bank The side slopes of an active channel between which the streamflow is normally confined.

Stream-bank erosion Removal of soil particles from a bank slope primarily due to water action. Climatic conditions, ice and debris, chemical reactions, and changes in land and stream use may also lead to bank erosion.

Stream-bank protection works Structure placed on or near a distressed stream bank to control bank erosion or prevent failure.

Streambed See "Bed."

Stream power Directly related to the sediment transport rates of a stream and measured as the loss of potential energy per unit length of stream channel. It refers to the ability of a stream to do work.

Surface runoff The portion of rainfall that moves over the ground toward a lower elevation and does not infiltrate the soil.

Suspended load Finer-grained particles carried in suspension by stream flows in the water column.

Swale Small depressions, natural or humanmade, that carry water only after a rainfall.

Terrace An abandoned floodplain that is located at a higher elevation than the current active floodplain.

Texture Refers to relative proportions of clay, silt, and sand in soil.

Toe The break in slope at the foot of a stream bank where the bank meets the bed.

Top of bank The break in slope between the bank and the surrounding terrain.

Tractive force The drag on a stream bank caused by passing water, which tends to pull soil particles along with the stream flow.

Trash rack A barrier placed at the upstream end of a culvert to trap debris but allow water to flow through.

Unravel To lose material from the edges of a revetment.

Urban equilibrium This term is used to describe a channel that has changed from its natural or original shape but has finished adjusting to the urban influences affecting it so that it is relatively stable in its planform and meander and has achieved a new balance in its bankfull width and depth, so that it is neither excessively eroding nor depositing and has healthy riparian growth.

Velocity (of water in a stream) The distance that water can travel in a given direction during a period of time. Usually expressed in feet per second.

Vortex rocks Rocks placed in a streambed to help direct flows for the formation of meanders and creation of riffles and pools. The rocks are so named for their ability to contribute to sediment transport through the channel.

Watershed An area confined by topographic divides that drains a given stream or river.

Wave attack Impact of waves on a stream bank.

Weathering Physical disintegration or chemical decomposition of rock due to wind, rain, heat, freezing, thawing, etc.

Weephole Opening left in a revetment, bulkhead, or wall to allow ground-water drainage.

Weir A barrier placed in a channel to divert fish or water.

Index

About the Author

Ann L. Riley has seventeen years of experience in government at the federal, state, and local levels. She is a cofounder of the Urban Creeks Council of California and of the national organization, the Coalition to Restore Urban Waters. As executive director of the Waterways Restoration Institute, she is engaged in the design and installation of stream restoration projects and the evaluation of national water policy for the National Research Council, the Institute for Water Resources, and various national and state task forces.